AND SCENERY IN BRITAIN

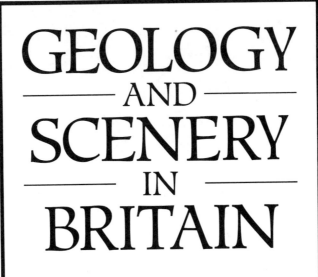

GEOLOGY
— AND —
SCENERY
— IN —
BRITAIN

JOHN WHITTOW

CHAPMAN & HALL

University and Professional Division

London · Glasgow · New York · Tokyo · Melbourne · Madras

Published by Chapman & Hall, 2–6 Boundary Row, London SE1 8HN

Chapman & Hall, 2-6 Boundary Row, London SE1 8HN, UK

Blackie Academic & Professional, Wester Cleddens Road, Bishopbriggs, Glasgow G64 2NZ, UK

Chapman & Hall, 29 West 35th Street, New York NY10001, USA

Chapman & Hall Japan, Thomson Publishing Japan, Hirakawacho Nemoto Building, 6F, 1-7-11 Hirakawa-cho, Chiyoda-ku, Tokyo 102, Japan

Chapman & Hall Australia, Thomas Nelson Australia, 102 Dodds Street, South Melbourne, Victoria 3205, Australia

Chapman & Hall India, R. Seshadri, 32 Second Main Road, CIT East, Madras 600 035, India

First edition 1992

© 1992 John Whittow

Typeset in 10/12 Times by Colset Pte Ltd, Singapore
Printed in Great Britain at the University Press, Cambridge

ISBN 0 412 44380 5

A catalogue record for this book is available from the British Library

Library of Congress Cataloging-in-Publication data

Whittow, J.B.
  Geology and scenery in Britain/John Whittow.
    p.   cm.
  Includes bibliographical references and index.
  ISBN 0-412-44380-5
  1. Geology — Great Britain. 2. Landforms — Great Britain.
I. Title.
QE261.W458 1992
554.1 — dc20
                                              92-7646
                                                 CIP

Contents

Acknowledgements

The publishers wish to thank the following for permission to use their photographs: Cambridge University Committee for Aerial Photography for Figs 3.2, 8.9, 12.3, 12.11, 14.2, 14.6, 15.1 and 17.4; Aerofilms Ltd for Figs 5.3, 5.5, 7.7, 7.8, 8.4 and 10.8; the British Geological Survey for Figs 4.3 and 4.4; the Royal Commission on the Ancient and Historical Monuments of Scotland for Figs 11.2 and 12.6; Mr John Dewar for Figs 12.9 and 14.10; Dr D. Ratcliffe for Fig 14.3; Mr A. Holland for Figs 2.3, 2.6 and 4.2; Dr B.J. Knapp for Figs 6.4, 9.4 and 9.5; Mr J.S. Haggas for Fig. 10.6a; Dr K. Simpkins for Fig. 7.3; Professor B. Goodall for Fig. 13.4; Dr A. Stroud for Figs 16.11, 16.13, 17.3, 17.8, 17.9, 18.3, 18.5 and 18.6. The author supplied the remainder of the photographs.

Figures 10.1, 10.2, 11.5, 12.1, 12.2, 12.4, 12.8, 13.3, 14.4, 14.9, 15.2, 15.3, 15.8, 16.1, 16.2, 16.4, 17.1, 18.2 and 18.4 are based on material prepared by the British Geological Survey, by kind permission of the Director: Crown Copyright. Fig. 2.5 was kindly supplied by Mr A. McCrostie; Fig. 10.6b is by Mr C. Odling-Smee.

Figures 12.7, 17.1 and 17.2 are based on diagrams in *The Geology of Scotland*, edited by G.Y. Craig (1st edn) and appear by permission of the publishers Oliver and Boyd. Figure 14.1 is based on material published in *The Structure of the British Isles*, by J.G.C. Anderson and T.R. Owen, and is reproduced by permission of Pergamon Press Ltd. Figure 11.3 is reproduced from *Edinburgh Geology* (1st edn) by permission of the Edinburgh Geological Society. Acknowledgement is gratefully given to Professor C. Embleton; Professor D.L. Linton; Professor E.H. Brown; Professor S.H. Beaver; Professor A. Straw; Professor K.M. Clayton; Professor T.N. George; J.L. Roberts; J.W. Perkins; C.C. Fagg; Professor J. Rose; J.B. Sissons; and S.I. Tomkieff, on whose work Figs 2.9, 3.1, 3.10, 7.1a, 7.4, 8.6, 8.7, 10.3, 10.7, 12.4, 12.7, 12.10, 13.2, 14.5, 14.7, 15.5, 17.1 and 17.2 are partly based.

The author is pleased to acknowledge with gratitude the assistance of Chris Holland who typed the manuscript and of Heather Browning, Sheila Dance and Judith Fox who drew the figures. Thanks are also due to Erika Meller who assisted with the photography and printed the majority of the photographs. Last, but not least, I would like to thank my wife, Diane, who gave endless assistance with data collection and compilation of the index.

Preface

It has been several years since the trilogy of Penguin books on the geology and scenery of the British Isles, written largely by the present author, went out of print. Since those three books appeared there have been considerable advances in both geological and geomorphological knowledge, especially in relation to events in the Tertiary and the Quaternary. Much more is known about offshore geology, especially in connection with North Sea oil exploration, and many geological structures have been reinterpreted on the British mainland. Many of these new interpretations are included, for example, in the third edition of *Geology of Scotland* (Edited by G. Y. Craig, 1991), which was published just as *Geology and Scenery in Britain* went to press. Some long-held ideas on such disparate issues as Wealden sedimentation, tor formation, and the evolution of the River Thames have been questioned and alternative hypotheses introduced. Considerably more is now known about Quaternary events in Britain leading to the rejection of such formerly established 'sacred cows' as the Wolstonian type-site in England and the Perth Readvance in Scotland. Many of the ideas on drainage and landform evolution in South-East England, proposed by Wooldridge and Linton, have been recently revised. It is now recognized that Cainozoic earth movements, *epeirogenesis* and faulting were considerably greater than formerly realized and that Britain's neotectonic history is, therefore, much more dynamic, as expressed by the magnitude of some recent earthquakes. Consequently, it has been thought necessary not only to revise but also to rewrite much of the material previously contained in *Geology and Scenery in England and Wales* and in *Geology and Scenery in Scotland*. The two earlier publications were designed to appeal to students beginning at universities, polytechnics and colleges of further education. But *Geology and Scenery in Britain* is also designed to appeal to upper sixth-formers and interested laymen who are just awakening to the diversity of British scenery and are seeking explanations of its genesis.

I have not attempted to write a textbook of geological principles or a geological history of Britain, which would be quite impossible within the context of this book. Thus, the opening chapter is intended merely to give an extremely concise account of the main processes involved in the moulding of British rocks and landforms into the present-day scenery. In each of the chapters there are numerous references to an extensive bibliography which relates both to the 'classic' and to the more modern books and articles on the relevant regions. Should the reader so desire, much more detailed information can be found in the *Memoirs of the Geological Survey*, none of which have been listed in the bibliographies but which can be found on most university library shelves. Instead, reference has been made to the more concise and more easily accessible Guides published by the Geologists' Association, the Quaternary Research Association and the Geographical Association. Of greatest value, however, for those seeking more detailed information are the nineteen *Handbooks of British Regional Geology*, produced by officers of the British Geological Survey. It will be seen that some of the bibliographic references in the present volume are geographical rather than geological – landscape also reflects the cultural evolution of society, especially in terms of the built environment. It has been claimed, in fact, that 'landscape is an index of civilization'.

Attempts have been made to explain some of the more technical terms when they first appear in the text, but the reader is advised to refer to good reference dictionaries in order to clarify definitions. *The Penguin Dictionary of Physical Geography* and *The Penguin Dictionary of Geology* are two books which would be of particular help.

J.B. Whittow

The shaping of Britain   1

It has often been remarked that 'Britain is a world by itself', a statement reflecting the fact that its scenery embodies, at a very small scale, almost all the rock types and landscape features found in countries of considerably greater extent. Its mountains are not of great height nor its rivers of great length, but it is impossible to travel for many kilometres without crossing a geological boundary, and it is this irregular juxtaposition of contrasting rocks that gives British scenery its remarkable variety. The apparent jumble of symbols and colours in two of the maps produced by the British Geological Survey, depicting the geology and the structures of Great Britain, can be disentangled to reveal a chronological framework which illustrates that in general the older, more complex and harder rocks and structures occur in the West and North, while the younger, less deformed and less resistant rocks and structures are confined largely to the East and South. This broad division is what distinguishes upland from lowland Britain, each division having its own distinctive groups of landform and landscape patterns. Thus, nothing could be more contrasting, for example, than the smooth rolling and relatively undeformed chalk downlands of southern England when compared with the rugged, heavily faulted and glacier-gouged volcanic rock peaks of western Scotland and Snowdonia (Fig. 1.1). Such differences of course, reflect not only the

Figure 1.1 The glacial trough of Nant Gwynant with Snowdon beyond, carved in the rugged terrain of Ordovician volcanic rocks.

geology but also the fact that the southernmost tract of England was never over-ridden by Pleistocene ice sheets, whereas the greater part of northern Britain's scenery has been considerably modified by the Pleistocene Ice Age, as will be shown below. The geology map also illustrates that rocks can be classified into three broad groups according to their mode of formation: sedimentary, igneous and metamorphic. It is these so-called *solid* rocks that create the geological foundation of the British landscape, though in places this 'skeleton' is shrouded by a 'skin' of materials deposited only in the last million years or so by relatively modern rivers, ice sheets and ocean waves. Such sediments have been termed *superficial deposits* or *drift* by the British Geological Survey.

Before examining the regional differences of landscape, outlined in the following chapters, it will be necessary for the reader to grasp certain essentials which underpin any volume of this type. First, one needs to understand the broad principles of rock formation and the way that rocks are then, over lengthy periods of time, affected by the tectonic forces of folding, faulting and crustal uplift: such mechanisms and events are concerned with internal or *endogenetic* factors (Anderson and Owen, 1980; Holmes, 1992). Second, one has to comprehend how external or *exogenetic* factors have played their part in shaping Britain's natural scenery. These latter studies, encompassed under the science of *geomorphology*, have demonstrated how the changing climates of Cainozoic times have governed both the rates and the intensities of weathering and erosion and therefore how the landforms have been modelled by the various agencies of water, wind and ice (Goudie, 1990; Stephens, 1990). Such fluvial, marine, aeolian and frost processes are, of course, constantly at work today, though the glaciers have long since disappeared. Third, one requires some knowledge of soil genesis, or *pedology*, to explain the great variety of British soils and the way they have evolved by the slow weathering of both solid and drift to create the diverse patterns of soil distribution (Avery, 1990). However, if it is to be further understood how the mantle of natural vegetation has slowly clothed the British countryside since the end of the Ice Age (Tansley, 1949) then it will be necessary to know the ways in which mankind has impacted on this fragile veneer (Vincent, 1990). Over several millenniums the various British immigrants have not only completely changed the face of the countryside by the introduction of various agricultural and silvicultural practices but also slowly created a built environment which, at least in its formative days, was strongly dependent on the geological and geographical resources of the British terrain. Water power, coal, various metals, timber and building stone have all been exploited to greater or lesser degrees and a knowledge of their spatial distribution allows one to add the final information necessary to understand how Britain's scenic heritage has envolved (Hoskins, 1973). It is now possible to draw together the disparate threads of geology, geomorphology, pedology, biogeography and historical geography to explain how the delicate tapestry of British scenery has been fashioned.

Rocks and structures

The most common rocks in Britain are the sedimentaries which geologists have separated into two divisions: first, the 'transported sediments' which have been carried various distances before being deposited; and second, those sediments which have accumulated largely *in situ*, partly as dead plant and animal remains and partly as chemical precipitates, before becoming transformed into solid rocks by chemical processes and compaction.

The transported sediments are generated by the slow weathering of existing rocks which break down into a variety of particle sizes, ranging in magnitude from the boulder to the tiniest mineral grain. These unconsolidated materials move first by gravity, descending the hill slopes by a process termed *solifluction*, before entering the stream networks that characterize all but desert environments (in which wind is the main transporting agent). Stream currents hasten the movement by rolling the larger pebbles along the river bed, bouncing the gravel and carrying the fine-grained silts and muds in suspension. Not surprisingly the battering suffered in the river channel smoothes out the pebble's angularities and reduces its size. Wherever the river enters an ocean or lake its current slackens and most of its burden is dumped. The bulkiest materials are abandoned first, nearest to the shoreline where they may in due course be converted into conglomerates; the coarse sand grains are carried farther out where they will become converted to *arenaceous* rocks, while the smallest and lightest particles are carried into deeper water before being transformed into clays, mudstones, siltstones and shales. Such are the mechanisms by which the majority of sedimentary rocks are formed, being laid down layer upon layer, each bed being separated from its neighbour by a *bedding plane*. The beds of rock, or *strata*, are interrupted by vertical cracks known as *joints*, thereby creating a kind of latticework within the solid rock. In sedimentary rocks the joints result from shrinkage when the sediment dries out, but it is these lines of weakness that are exploited by weathering and erosion when the strata are eventually uplifted to create land surfaces. It will be shown how joints can also be formed in igneous and metamorphic rocks (for different reasons). In folded rocks, anticlines are generally eroded more easily because their joints are open. Conversely, *synclinal* joints are more tightly compressed, assisting many downfolds to resist erosion and project as high land (see p. 345).

Sandstones are some of the commonest sedimentary rocks, all comprising myriads of colourless or white quartz grains but differing in their range of colours and textures. The white or pale-coloured sandstones are virtually free from the iron mineral haematite, but the majority are stained by iron oxide to create every shade of pink, red, orange and brown. Sandstones can also be differentiated according to their grain size and shape. The very coarse and pebbly sandstones create some of Britain's most obdurate landforms but are of little use as a building stone. Because of its tough, angular quartz grains, however, the pale arenaceous rock known as Millstone Grit has magnificent grinding properties. Conversely, the finer and more uniformly grained sandstones, often bonded by a natural cement of calcite, are highly prized by the stonemason who terms them *freestones* because of the ease with which they can be worked. The finest of these are the sandstones created from windblown desert sands whose grains are rounded rather than angular. The finer-grained sediments, with higher proportions of clay minerals, are known as *argillaceous* rocks, although many of these sedimentaries often contain significant amounts of calcareous and/or carbonaceous materials. If the rock has no decayed carbonaceous matter it is significantly lighter in colour and if the proportions of clay and lime are roughly equal it is termed a *marlstone* (or *cementstone*), which not only weathers into a productive soil but has also been utilized in its crushed state for both agricultural and industrial purposes.

Despite millions of years of compaction on the ocean floor, clays, shales and mudstones remain soft enough to be worn down relatively rapidly to form plains and vales once they have been uplifted from beneath the ocean. Only where they are toughened by interbedded sandstones, as in central Wales and southern Scotland, have the argillaceous rocks made anything more than a minor contribution to the British uplands. Significantly, Britain's major coalfields, containing seams of dark-coloured, highly carbonaceous material derived from decayed plant remains, are normally found in lowland areas where the coal-bearing rocks have survived only because they have been downfaulted or deformed into synclinal (basin) structures by earth movements.

Of the non-transported sedimentary rocks only the limestones have had any significant influence on landforms and building materials, and it will be seen how both the chalklands and the Jurassic stonebelt of England exhibit quite distinctive hill landscapes amid the lowland plains. Furthermore, the limestones of Carboniferous age are massive enough to have played an important role in the building of such well-known upland landscapes as those of the Pennines, the Mendips and limited parts of North and South Wales, although limestones are relatively scarce elsewhere in Wales, the Lake District and the Scottish Highlands where the soils have been derived from mainly 'acidic' rocks. Limestones differ fundamentally from sandstones and shales because, instead of being made up of rock particles, they are composed almost entirely of shells and skeletons of marine organisms. The purest and whitest limestone of all is the calcareous mud known as the *Chalk*, whose genesis is described on page 58. Not surprisingly, the soils derived from the calcareous rocks now support a flourishing vegetation rich in calcium-loving flora (*calcicoles*).

If most sedimentary rocks are formed beneath the oceans then all the crystalline or igneous rocks, by contrast, are spawned in the bowels of the earth (hence their name, for igneous means 'fire-formed') and therefore they are derived directly or indirectly from the molten magma which seethes beneath the crust and occasionally bursts out at the surface from a volcanic vent or crack. Today Britain has no active volcanoes, although volcanic rocks make up some 20 per cent of its present land surface, reflecting the prolonged spells of *extrusive* vulcanicity which have occurred periodically throughout geological time but especially in association with the three major mountain-building episodes of Caledonian, Hercynian and Alpine times (see below). Not all igneous rocks are of volcanic origin, however, for some of the molten material never broke through the crust but cooled more slowly at depth to form such rocks as granites. Because they remained in the underworld such deep-seated rocks have been termed *plutonic* or *intrusive* rocks.

Volcanic rocks were initially extruded as molten lava or as billowing clouds of ash, pumice and cinder, or simply as rock fragments shattered by the explosion. It is difficult to think of parts of Britain being swamped by lava flows like those of modern Iceland, but many of the plateaux of the Inner Hebrides and those overlooking Glasgow are built from layer upon layer of dark-coloured basalt whose tiny crystalline structure indicates the rapidity of its surface cooling. Not all lavas have such a high proportion of dark-coloured iron minerals, however, and where there is a high proportion of silica minerals, as in the Lake District or Snowdonia, the lavas can be yellowish or pinkish, as in the rhyolites. The plutonic rocks, because they cooled more slowly at depth, have larger, coarser crystals. Granites are almost invariably light-coloured because they are composed essentially of quartz crystals together with two other minerals known as *mica* and *feldspar*. Granite's overall colouring, in fact, varies between red, pink and grey, depending on the type of feldspar present. Because of the different chemical compositions contained within other plutonic rocks, however, some of them, such as gabbro, are extremely dark in colour. Dolerite is another common dark-coloured igneous rock, whose crystals are smaller than those of the gabbros but larger than the crystals of the extrusive lavas, suggesting that dolerite must have cooled and solidified near the surface but without actually breaking through. When molten rock attempts to make its way to the surface other than through a volcanic vent it will penetrate lines of weakness in the crustal rocks. Where it squeezes along bedding planes it solidifies into a sheet of igneous rock termed a *sill* which, once uncovered by erosion, often forms a distinctive rock step on the hillside. Alternatively, the molten lava rises to the surface by means of a vertical crack in the crust, ultimately solidifying to form a *dyke*. Other types of igneous intrusion, such as *laccoliths*, will be described in the various regional chapters, especially those relating to Scotland. Igneous rocks develop sets of joints which vary in character according to the rock type. Some volcanic rock joints are vertical but in lava flows the jointing patterns always develop perpendicularly to the cooling surface of the flow which in some cases may be inclined at an angle. A different type of jointing can be found in plutonic rocks where the patterns may be curvilinear and allow rocks to shed concentric layers by the process known as *exfoliation* as pressure is slowly released when the surface rock becomes exposed. Thus, in granite domes there is a tendency for the landforms to be gently rounded except where they are characterized by tor formation (see p. 34).

The third major group of rocks is termed *metamorphic* because it refers to those sedimentary and igneous rocks that have been severely altered by the effects of intense pressure and/or heat. The simplest type of metamorphic change occurs when the lowest layers of sedimentary rocks become subject to increasing pressure from overlying strata. Moreover, since rock temperature increases with depth within the crust, new minerals will form to replace the existing ones (a process known as *recrystallization*), thereby creating a whole new rock type. In a sandstone, for instance, the quartz grains are squeezed so closely together that they become virtually 'fused' into a metamorphic quartzite, an extremely hard white rock conspicuous in some of Scotland's shapliest peaks. Limestones, too, are so compacted that their shelly structure is obliterated and a marble is formed. Whenever clays, mudstones and shales are subjected to these types of pressure their particles are flattened and their minerals realigned. Continued pressure from tectonic folding may create a totally new structure termed *slaty cleavage* and the rock transformed into a slate. Slates split most easily along these newly imposed lines of weakness which cut indiscriminately across former bedding planes. Other metamorphic changes occur due to contact with magmatic bodies within the earth's crust. Thus, when molten magma is intruded into sedimentary strata not only are the latter deformed but also those nearest to the intrusive material are altered by the effects of heat and chemical fluids. Around all plutonic *batholiths* and other large buried igneous structures the surrounding rocks have been baked into metamorphic *aureoles*, many of which are associated with valuable mineral lodes due to the chemical changes involved. Most metamorphism occurs during periods of mountain-building, at times when continents collide, vulcanicity

CAINOZOIC	QUATERNARY	HOLOCENE	Post-glacial. Flandrian.
		PLEISTOCENE	The Ice Age.
	TERTIARY	PLIOCENE MIOCENE OLIGOCENE EOCENE PALAEOCENE	S.E. England submerged in parts. Major drainage initiated. A widespread uplift. Alpine folding and faulting. Sediments of south coast of England. Sands and clays deposited in south-east. Igneous activity and vulcanicity in north-west Scotland.
MESOZOIC	CRETACEOUS	CHALK GREENSANDS GAULT WEALDEN	Marine deposits in a sea covering much of England and Scotland. Freshwater deposits in south-east England.
	JURASSIC	OOLITES etc. LIAS	Marine deposits of limestone and clay. They have survived largely in central England and Inner Hebrides.
	TRIAS — NEW RED SANDSTONE	KEUPER BUNTER	Formed mostly in inland lakes. Some desert sandstones found largely in English Midlands and southern Scotland.
PALAEOZOIC	PERMIAN — NEW RED SANDSTONE	MAGNESIAN LIMESTONE	A period of mountain-building and rock-folding - Hercynian or Armorican.
	CARBONI-FEROUS	COAL MEASURES MILLSTONE GRIT 'MOUNTAIN' LIMESTONE	Deposits mostly in shallow water. Vulcanicity in central Scotland. Limestones formed in a sea covering much of England and parts of central Scotland. Granite formation in south-west England.
	DEVONIAN AND OLD RED SANDSTONE		Marine deposits in Devon and Cornwall, red beds in fresh water in Hereford and South Wales. Widespread deposits in eastern Scotland.
	SILURIAN		A period of mountain-building and rock-folding - Caledonian. Widespread granite formation in Scotland.
	ORDOVICIAN		The rocks of Wales, the Lake District and the Southern
	CAMBRIAN		Uplands were formed, mostly as marine deposits. In

This line represents a time at least 600 million years ago.

	PRE-CAMBRIAN OR ARCHAEAN	DALRADIAN MOINIAN TORRIDONIAN LEWISIAN	This epoch may have lasted for at least 3,000 million years and included the Laxfordian and Scourian mountain-building episodes. During this time the old rocks of Anglesey, Shropshire, Charnwood, the Malverns and much of north-west Scotland were formed.

Figure 1.2 Geological succession in Britain.

increases, deep rock-melting accelerates and rocks are crumpled, crushed and torn apart by crustal deformation.

Figure 1.2 shows the chronological order of rock formation in Britain, with the time dimension going from bottom to top. The four eras of the left-hand column have been subdivided into a number of geological periods, the relationships of which were initially worked out by careful studies of fossil assemblages contained within the sedimentary rocks. Although the complete British succession is shown in Fig. 1.2, it cannot be said that all the formations are present in every region: Scotland lacks many of the Mesozoic and Cainozoic strata, while few of the Precambrian and Lower Palaeozoic formations are represented in England. In general, it may be said that the farther north and west one progresses the older the rocks become. But the chronological progression from south-east to north-west is not a simple one, for in places it is possible to pass from younger to older rocks and then back to younger ones again. Indeed, in places there are major gaps in the stratigraphic record, illustrating either that the rocks of a particular age were never laid down or, more probably, that the strata were deposited but were later destroyed by erosion before further rock layers were formed on the eroded surface. Such a gap or hiatus in the record is known as an *unconformity*. A further complication to the normal law of superposition – oldest rocks at the bottom and newest at the top – is found in northern Scotland, for here severe over-folding and thrust-faulting has turned the succession upside down.

The latter example is an extreme case of tectonic upheaval during the time of enormous crustal stresses engendered by episodes of mountain building. These *orogenies*, as they are termed, have affected the British crustal rocks on several occasions as continents have collided, leading to the crumpling and foreshortening of many kilometres of the crust (Owen, 1976). The folded rock structures and associated vulcanicity of the two oldest Precambrian mountain-building episodes, the Scourian and Laxfordian (Fig. 1.2) can only be seen to any extent in north-west Scotland. The Caledonian orogeny of Lower Palaeozoic times, however, has left the most widespread imprint on the rocks of Britain and its structures dominate the landforms and geological trend lines in most of upland Britain, including much of Scotland, the Lake District and most of Wales. In these regions the 'grain' of the relief, including river valleys, escarpments and mountain ranges, shows a preferred alignment from south-west to north-east because it is governed by the dominant Caledonian fold axes and fault lines. At the close of Carboniferous times a further mountain-building episode, with pressures this time from a more southerly direction, caused the Hercynian fold-mountain ranges to impose new east–west alignments on all the Precambrian and Palaeozoic rocks of southern Britain. The folds and faults are most marked south of the so-called Hercynian Front in South Wales (although they are buried by younger rocks in South-East England), but the Hercynian structures can also be seen as far north as the Midland Valley of Scotland. This orogeny was of particular significance because it folded all the carbonaceous rocks of Upper Carboniferous age, thereby creating the British coal basins. The final tectonic upheaval occurred in the Cainozoic era, when the Alpine orogeny folded the strata of Mesozoic and Palaeogene age which occur largely in southern England. Nevertheless, the stresses from this orogeny also caused widespread faulting and vulcanicity in western Scotland, ultimately creating some of Britain's most spectacular landforms. Both the Caledonian and Hercynian orogenies also had their associated volcanic episodes, the legacies of

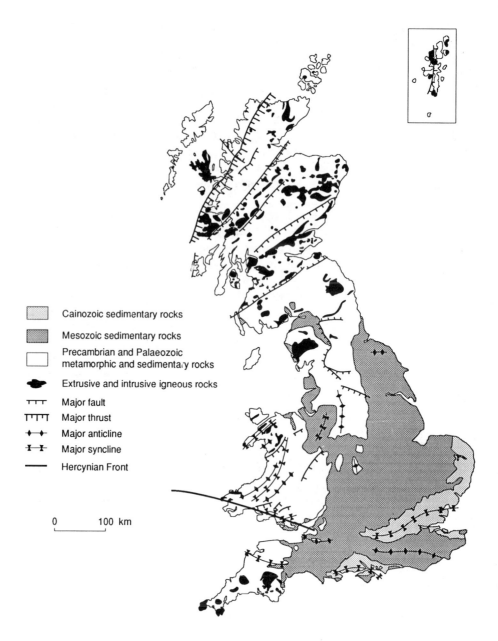

Cainozoic sedimentary rocks

Mesozoic sedimentary rocks

Precambrian and Palaeozoic metamorphic and sedimentary rocks

Extrusive and intrusive igneous rocks

⊤⊤⊤ Major fault

⊤⊤⊤⊤ Major thrust

←●─●→ Major anticline

⊢─⊣ Major syncline

── Hercynian Front

0   100 km

Figure 1.3 Generalized geology and structure of Britain.

which can now be seen in the denuded plugs, lavas, thick beds of *pyroclastic* ('fire-broken') materials, sills and dykes, to say nothing of the unroofed plutonic batholiths. It will be shown how both the extrusive and intrusive igneous rocks play considerably increasing roles in landform genesis as one travels from south to north, i.e. from younger to older rocks (Fig. 1.3.).

After the turmoil of mountain-building had ceased some 15 million years ago and the enveloping oceans had withdrawn from Britain's landmass when it was tectonically uplifted in response to *isostatic* readjustment because of the widening Atlantic Ocean, Britain must have presented a scene quite different from that of today. Judging from the fossil record the climate was subtropical and an unbroken swathe of lush vegetation would have stretched across into the continent, since the Straits of Dover did not appear until the Late Pleistocene. The uplands of Scotland, northern England and Wales would have been relatively modest in height and as yet unsullied by the vagaries of the Pleistocene Ice Age. But because most of the high land lay in the west the Cainozoic drainage pattern was characterized by mainly east-flowing rivers which were already carrying their sandy and muddy sediments to the swampy bays and estuaries of a slowly expanding North Sea. This water body occupies the site of a gradually deepening *geosyncline*, a downsag in the crust due to the increasing weight of Mesozoic and Cainozoic sediments in which the North Sea oil and gas reserves were later to accumulate. Such crustal deepening has had to be counteracted *isostatically* by tectonic uplift farther west in the upland zone of Britain. Pulsatory crustal uplift over many millions of years, therefore, has not only caused the British mainland to tilt downwards from west to east but has also led to increased fault movement in the West in order to accommodate some of the movement. It is not by chance that Britain's oldest rocks occur in the farthest west of Scotland and that its newest sediments fringe East Anglia. Because Britain's Atlantic tract has experienced the greatest amount of uplift it has also suffered the greatest erosion of rock strata and therefore the maximum downwearing of its relief. As a corollary, much of the denuded material, having been transported eastwards by rivers, has helped fill the subsiding North Sea downwarp of which East Anglia and the London Basin form part of the perimeter. For similar reasons the British coastline exhibits a dichotomy between the rugged, cliffed and highly indented solid rock coastlines facing the Atlantic and the smoother, low-lying, drift-fashioned shorelines of the North Sea (Steers, 1964; 1973). Running water has not only helped lower the general level of the uplands but also played a leading role in the fashioning of the lowlands. Weathering and erosion have been just as significant on the gently inclined rock strata of the English lowlands as they have on the contorted rocks of the mountainlands. Consequently, the exposed escarpments of the chalk downs and the Cotswold limestone ridge, for example, have slowly receded as they have been undermined by *spring-sapping* (see p. 64), *landslips* (see p. 45) and solifluction. As these harder sedimentary scarps have retreated so they have exposed the underlying clays to the erosive processes and it is along these tracts of relatively weaker rocks that the major rivers have carved out their courses as they became adjusted to the structural grain. Since the drainage adjusts itself to the alignment or *strike* of the strata, these particular water courses are termed *strike streams* or *subsequents* (see p. 18). From such selective stream development scarp-and-vale landscapes have been created – the type of scenery which typifies much of southeastern England. Scarplands (or *cuestas*) of this type are less extensive in the upland zone, where the escarpments are more likely to mark the eroded edges of lava flows or the faulted phenomena known as *fault-line scarps* (see p. 276).

The junction between hard and soft rocks is usually marked by an escarpment or sudden fall of ground, but this is not invariably the case and in many instances precise geological boundaries in Britain have been blurred or buried. There are two reasons for this imprecision. First, weathering and erosion smooth out rocky angularities on the slopes, thereby creating gentler hillsides which contribute to the generally rolling character of the British scene, where gentle curves far outweigh the vertical and horizontal lines that one would expect to find only in a countryside devoid of solifluction and water erosion. Second, the Pleistocene Ice Age has completely remodelled the majority of British landforms, dumping countless tonnes of glacial and fluvioglacial sediment across much of the terrain to create most of Britain's ubiquitous *drifts*. When one adds the other superficial materials, such as riverborne and marine alluvium and the windblown sands, most of which have accumulated in post-glacial times (the *Flandrian*) it is remarkable that any solid rock is exposed at the surface at all, except along the coastline and on the mountain summits.

As the climate of western Europe deteriorated some 2 million years ago, the Atlantic winds, which previously had supplied the rain, now brought heavy snowfall to Britain's uplands as the Pleistocene Ice Age slowly became established. Drifting snow, blown off the mountain summits by the prevailing south-westerlies, settled in the north-east-facing hollows where, protected from sporadic sunshine, it gradually hardened into glacier ice. Glaciers carved out their mountain *cirques* (called *cwms* in Wales and *coires* or *corries* in Scotland) while the dome-like summits became fretted by sharp cliffs which, encroaching on the smooth ridges, chiselled their crests into sharp *arêtes*. As the glaciers grew in size they moved downhill to fill the valleys previously carved out by rivers. Moving ice by itself is incapable of erosion but once it incorporates frost-shattered material it is capable of large-scale but selective abrasion of the underlying topography. Thus, the upland ice caps severely remodelled the upland zone, creating vertical cliffs, U-shaped valleys, fjords and the ice-smoothed rock knolls termed *roches moutonées* where none had previously existed. Pre-glacial watersheds became ice-breached, old river patterns dismembered and new valley lakes spawned in the overdeepened glacial troughs. Most of the ancient pre-glacial soils were also swept away and, together with the glacial boulder clay, or *till*, the glaciofluvial sands and gravels, became dumped somewhat indiscriminately in the lowland (Ehlers *et al.*, 1991). The ice sheets and their meltwaters also modified the pre-glacial landsurface by breaching escarpments, lowering ridges, creating *meltwater channels* and fashioning the drift into smooth whalebacked hills, known as *drumlins*, in addition to creating other glacial drift landforms termed *kettle holes*, *eskers, kames* and *moraines*. Kettle holes are created when blocks of ice buried in the glacial drift finally melt as the climate ameliorates; eskers are narrow ridges of sand and gravel probably formed in a former stream tunnel beneath or within an ice sheet; kames are steep-sided conical hills of glacioflavial materials, created from crevasse fallings in ice sheets; moraines comprise heterogeneous mixtures of ice-dumped material and can be found in sheets or as linear forms. The extent of the various ice sheets is shown in Fig. 1.4, from which it will be seen how southern England was never overidden although it endured a severe *periglacial* or 'frost' climate when the ground was frozen solid by *permafrost* similar to that of Arctic Canada today (Bowen *et al.*, 1986).

As the Ice Age waned, Britain's earliest Palaeolithic settlers appeared, eking out a living on the tundra-like landscape and using primitive stone artefacts fashioned from either chalk flints or hard igneous rocks. While they remained hunters and gatherers, the earliest settlers must have coped more easily with the bare stony uplands and the coastal headlands, for, in the ameliorating climate of the Flandrian, impenetrable forests and marshes had colonized the lowland vales and plains of the south and east. By the time Neolithic farmers brought their domesticated livestock and more sophisticated agrarian economy to Britain, however, the

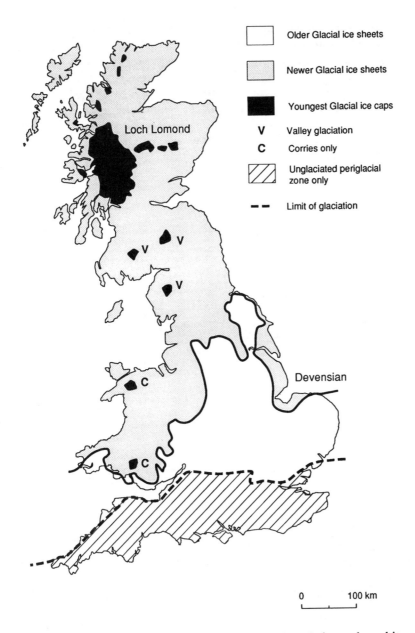

Older Glacial ice sheets

Newer Glacial ice sheets

Youngest Glacial ice caps

V Valley glaciation

C Corries only

Unglaciated periglacial zone only

– – Limit of glaciation

Loch Lomond

V V

V

C

Devensian

C

0   100 km

Figure 1.4 Glacial limits during the Pleistocene Ice Age in Britain.

bare, stony uplands would have been largely unsuited to their needs and it was to the rolling grassy chalklands and limestone ridges of south-eastern England that they turned to make their permanent settlements, although they faced constant problems of permanent water supply. Thus they built Britain's first real villages on the pale, treeless chalky hills and traded their carefully worked flints and wares along the bare ridgeways, high above the thickly forested lowlands. Rudimentary metalworking during the so-called Bronze and Iron Ages of the Flandrian allowed some clearing of the lowland forests, but it was not until the advent of Saxon times that the more durable metal tools and the heavy plough witnessed a gradual reclamation of the marshy valleys and the forested clay vales. Henceforward, the settlements tended to abandon the hilltops and move downhill, with many towns of Roman, Saxon or Norman derivation being located strategically at river-bridging points or at scarp-foot springlines, not only to obviate the problems of water supply but also to utilize the waterpower for Britain's early industries. Not until the Industrial Revolution did this close geographical link between natural resources and human settlement begin to break down. None the less, the heritage of these former subtle associations between people and landscape has survived in the vernacular architecture of Britain's countryside, especially where local stone was utilized (Penoyre and Penoyre, 1978). Even then the relocation of eighteenth- and nineteeth-century manufacturing industry was usually governed by the presence of Carboniferous coal, iron ore, fireclay and brick clay. The ancient metal industries, once dependent on rural water power and charcoal from the local forests, also became rapidly relocated, helping swell the growth of

Figure 1.5 The prairie-type landscapes of East Anglia where arable farming has led to the loss of many hedgerows.

Britain's major industrial cities on or near the coalfields. Both the English and the Scottish Midlands are so dominated by relatively modern industrial urbanization, formerly related to geological mineral wealth, that it is impossible to describe their landscapes without reference to this remarkably rapid transformation.

The burgeoning population of modern Britain has made considerable inroads into the natural scenery of this tiny island and it is not only the built environment which is the culprit, although an area the size of Berkshire, Buckinghamshire, Bedfordshire and Oxfordshire has disappeared beneath bricks and concrete since 1949. New farming methods have, since 1939, also led to the loss of 95 per cent of England's lowland grass cover, 50 per cent of England's fenland and almost 50 per cent of its ancient lowland woods (Rackham, 1986). Moreover, in the first forty years after the Second World War no less than 175,000 kilometres of hedgerow have been destroyed particularly in East Anglia (Fig. 1.5). Never before has the British countryside witnessed such a rapid change as it has in the latter half of the twentieth century (Mercer and Puttnam, 1988).

Bibliography

Anderson, J.G.C. and Owen, T.R. (1980) *The Structure of the British Isles* (2nd edn). Pergamon. 251 pp.

Avery, B.W. (1990) *Soils of the British Isles*. CAB International. 463 pp.

Bowen, D.Q., Rose, J., McCabe, A.M. and Sutherland, D.G. (1986) Correlation of Quaternary glaciations in England, Ireland, Scotland and Wales. *Quat. Sci. Reviews*, **5**, 299–340.

Ehlers, J., Gibbard, P.L. and Rose, J. (eds) (1991) *Glacial Deposits in Great Britain and Ireland*. Balkema. 589 pp.

Goudie, A.S. (1990) *The Landforms of England and Wales*. Blackwell. 394 pp.

Holmes, A. (1992) *Principles of Physical Geology*. Chapman and Hall.

Hoskins, W.G. (1973) *The Making of the English Landscape*. Hodder & Stoughton. 240 pp.

Mercer, D. and Puttnam, D. (1988) *Rural England: Our Countryside at the Crossroads*. Queen Anne Press. 240 pp.

Owen, T.R. (1976) *The Geological Evolution of the British Isles*. Pergamon. 167 pp.

Penoyre, J. and Penoyre, J. (1978) *Houses in the Landscape: A Regional Study of Vernacular Building Styles in England and Wales*. Faber. 175 pp.

Rackham, O. (1986) *The History of the Countryside*. Dent. 445 pp.

Steers, J.A. (1964) *The Coastline of England and Wales* (2nd edn). Cambridge University Press. 750 pp.

Steers, J.A. (1973) *The Coastline of Scotland*. Cambridge University Press. 335 pp.

Stephens, N. (1990) *Natural Landscapes of Britain from the Air*. Cambridge University Press. 288 pp.

Tansley, A.G. (1949) *The British Islands and Their Vegetation* (2 vols). Cambridge University Press. 930 pp.

Vincent, P. (1990) *The Biogeography of the British Isles: An Introduction*. Routledge. 315 pp.

It is somewhat difficult to select a starting-point from which to commence a journey through the varied landscapes of Britain, but where better than Bristol, sometimes called the birthplace of geology, to introduce the reader to the fascinating story of Britain's geology and scenery? Bristol stands at a geological crossroads, for here the scarped landscapes of lowland Britain give way to the old, hard rock terrains of the upland zone (Savage, 1977). To the west lie the gnarled and rugged countrysides of Wales and the West Country, whose scenery comprises not only the contorted bones of Britain's ancient geological skeleton but also the vestiges of Britain's once ubiquitous Celtic culture whose imprint still dominates many of these western landscapes (Shorter *et al.*, 1969). Eastwards, beyond the Cotswold scarp, the scenery could not be more contrasting: smooth vistas of flat-topped hills and broad clay vales characterize the English lowlands, where the heritage of Anglo-Saxon and Norman cultures survives beneath the veneer of modern farming and urban growth. Stretching from the Bristol Channel to the North Sea, these gentle lowlands have been fashioned from the newer, less crumpled sedimentary rocks which, throughout much of southern and eastern England, clothe the ancient strata of Britain's primeval framework. In much the same way, the Bristol district marks the transition between the boundless corn-fields of eastern England and the irregular mosaic of meadow, moor and crag that enhances the western scene.

The Bristol region and the River Avon

William Smith, widely regarded as the father of English geology, determined the fundamental succession of rock strata while living on the outskirts of Bristol in the late eighteenth century. Little wonder that this was where Smith first recognized the major principles of stratigraphy, for the Bristol region is a microcosm of England's geology and scenery (Kellaway and Welch, 1948; Walker, 1972). With the exception of the Ordovician and the Permian, it has exposures of every main group of sedimentary rocks dating from the Cambrian and Silurian rocks at Tortworth (Curtis, 1968; 1972) to the Upper Jurassic strata of the Cotswolds.

Dundry Hill (233 m), whose northern slopes are now lapped by the city suburbs, is the area's best viewpoint for those wishing to understand the landscape. The honey-coloured freestones of Dundry's church and village reflect the presence of the Upper Jurassic limestone that caps this detached fragment of the neighbouring Cotswold Hills. However, no matter where they occur in Britain the Lias clays (which here underlie the limestone) have generally proved to be a poor foundation for the overlying rocks, and the slopes of Dundry Hill, being no exception, are therefore scarred by landslips. Many of these occurred during the Ice Age when ice sheets stood only a few miles away to the north and when frost-heaving in the Lias clays caused the overlying rocks to crack and founder in the process known as *gullying* and *cambering*. Even in more recent times, whenever heavy rainfall lubricates the clays, slipping has periodically taken place in this region, as the builders of Georgian Bath discovered to their cost (see p. 110).

Looking north from Dundry Hill (Fig. 2.1) one can identify where the level-topped hills of grey Carboniferous Limestone are trenched at Clifton by the Avon gorge. To the west, the wooded hills between Portishead and Clevedon are truncated by sea cliffs composed of Old Red Sandstone marls and conglomerates (Reynolds and Greenly, 1924) though Weston-super-Mare is flanked by a ridge of Carboniferous Limestone. Away to the east, however, it is a younger limestone that flanks the deep Avon valley at Bath, and this is the same golden oolitic stone of Jurassic age which caps Dundry Hill. No matter in which direction one looks, the ridges and hills appear to be flat-topped while the rivers can be seen to be flowing alternately in broad vales and then in narrow gorges, passing indiscriminately from newer (softer) to older (harder) rocks and back again. Although an explanation of the anomalous course of the Avon will be given below, a glance at Fig. 2.1 illustrates how these older and newer rocks have been denuded into two contrasting scenic types. The older group comprises strata as old as the Cambrian and Silurian but mainly of Old Red Sandstone and Carboniferous age, all intensely folded and faulted by a mountain-building episode which had already terminated before the transgressing Mesozoic seas advanced and completely buried this ancient landsurface with thousands of metres of their sedimentary deposits. In contrast, this blanket of younger rocks, including New Red Sandstones, Jurassic clays and limestones, has been only gently folded and tilted and it is these almost

Figure 2.1 Structure of the Bristol region, looking south-east.

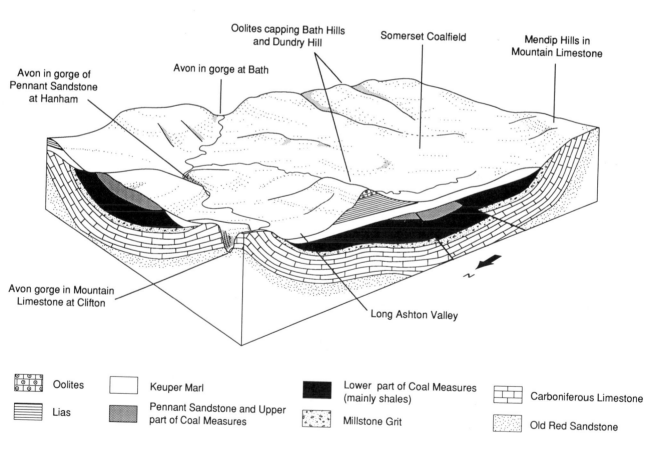

Oolites capping Bath Hills and Dundry Hill

Somerset Coalfield

Mendip Hills in Mountain Limestone

Avon in gorge of Pennant Sandstone at Hanham

Avon in gorge at Bath

Avon gorge in Mountain Limestone at Clifton

Long Ashton Valley

Oolites

Lias

Keuper Marl

Pennant Sandstone and Upper part of Coal Measures

Lower part of Coal Measures (mainly shales)

Millstone Grit

Carboniferous Limestone

Old Red Sandstone

horizontal strata that have been fashioned into the flat clay vales and the relatively unbroken crestlines of the neighbouring Cotswolds limestone hills. Continuing erosion has ultimately removed many layers of these covering rocks, wearing back the Cotswold escarpment to reveal the older contorted rocks but leaving behind such unconsumed relics as Dundry Hill as lonely outliers perched on the formerly buried land surface. Stripped of its younger covering rocks, the exhumed ancient land surface around Bristol reveals the long-buried structures. Narrow ridges and isolated hills mark the east–west folds that continue westwards beneath the Bristol Channel and through the South Wales coalfield before terminating in the concertina crumples of Pembrokeshire's distant sea cliffs. Such corrugated structures are the mere stumps of a once mighty mountain chain that, during the so-called Hercynian orogeny, folded all existing strata, including the British Coal Measures, especially those of South Wales and those around Bristol, some 300 million years ago (Isaac *et al.*, 1982). When traced eastwards, however, these strongly folded structures disappear abruptly beneath the shroud of overlying limestone, sandstone, chalk and clay that mantles south-eastern England.

Parts of the Bristol and Somerset coalfield have remained buried by remnants of this younger cover so that to the south of the city layers of red Triassic marl and blue-brown Lias clay hide the actual coal seams (Moore and Trueman, 1937). Only to the north and east of Bristol have the Coal Measures been exposed at the surface (Moore and Trueman, 1939), yet the scenery has little of the grime and dereliction normally associated with coalfields. Even during maximum production the buried part of the coalfield near Radstock remained a pleasant rural area and now that all the West Country collieries are closed the Avon countryside has lost much of its heavy industrial veneer. Today only the industrial archaeologists explore its overgrown canals, aqueducts and dismantled railways that once served this important relic of Britain's Industrial Revolution. Among the Coal Measures strata thick beds of sandstone, the Pennant Sandstone, occur, identical in character to that which plays so important a part in the scenery of the South Wales coalfield. Unlike the Pennant Sandstone of South Wales, however, (where the plateaux have been uplifted to more than 300 m) the sandstones around Bristol form only low hills through which the River Avon has carved a gorge at Hanham (See Fig. 2.1). Wherever this dark grey-red sandstone outcrops it has been used extensively as a building stone, bringing a sombre hue to the eastern suburbs of Bristol, such as Hanham and Fishponds, and to the northern rural villages of Frampton Cotterell, Iron Acton, Winterbourne and Coalpit Heath. The most distinctive rock in the Bristol area, however, is the dove-grey Carboniferous Limestone which is trenched by the Avon at Clifton.

It has been seen how the rivers of the Bristol district appear to pass indiscriminately from soft rocks on to hard rocks and back again. It may be asked, for example, why the Avon does not follow an 'easy' route through the valley at Long Ashton rather than continue to carve its way through the hard limestone by means of the spectacular gorge at Clifton. And the latter gorge is only one of several which punctuate the otherwise gentle passage of the Avon *en route* to the sea.

The explanation lies in the fact that the Bristol Avon is really two rivers, the first a youthful headstream flowing unhindered on the younger, more uniform and relatively undisturbed rocks which form the Cotswolds, the second a mature river which explores the complex intricacies of a primeval land surface now stripped of its covering rocks, as described above (Frey, 1975). At the start of its journey high on the Cotswolds near Tetbury, the Avon heads off eastwards down the gentle dip of the oolitic limestone, indeed its direction is consequent upon this eastward tilt of the rocks and all rivers of this type have therefore been designated as *consequent* streams. Some authors have claimed that the Avon headwaters once flowed into the Thames, but this claim must remain speculative. Once the river reaches the softer clays near Malmesbury, it swings southwestwards, lazily following the line of the Oxford Clay vale all the way to Melksham. Indeed, the Avon helped widen this broad vale as its meandering waters subsequently took advantage of the grain or 'strike' of the more easily eroded rocks, hence this part of its course is known as a 'subsequent' reach. The remainder of its course is less easily explained, for it seems to defy the laws of stream formation. Below Melksham the Avon turns abruptly westwards and commences a circuitous but scenically spectacular route back through the harder Jurassic limestones of the Cotswolds (Fig. 6.1). Its tree-lined gorges at Bradford on Avon and Bath have been cut by a vigorous, down-cutting river now heading rapidly towards the Severn estuary. After emerging from the Cotswold gorges the Avon crosses the wide alluvial plain beyond Keynsham prior to entering the Hanham gorge (Fig. 2.1). Less beautiful than the Clifton gorge, because it is entrenched into the darker rocks of the Pennant Sandstone, the Hanham gorge is nevertheless thickly wooded and is quite attractive near Conham, where the Avon swings through a deeply carved meander before entering the urban sprawl of Bristol. It is this section of its course that is the most anomalous for the river bears little relation to the underlying rock structures in marked contrast to the simple accordance with structure exhibited by its headwaters. One needs to understand the evolution of another major British river, the Severn, in order to clarify the history of the Avon itself. The sudden change of direction at Melksham probably occurred several million years ago as an indirect result of the growing dominance of the Severn in western England. Helped by the gradual deepening of the Bristol Channel, in part due to faulting, the Severn's tributaries began to cut deeply back into the Cotswold escarpment and to capture the headwaters of the east-flowing rivers. Following its capture the Avon thus inherited a quicker route to the sea, henceforth using its surplus energy to cut down into the Mesozoic cover rocks. As periods of crustal uplift renewed its vigour it became so firmly entrenched that it managed to maintain its new westward course even when the Mesozoic rocks were stripped away and its drainage became superimposed on to the old hard rocks at Hanham and Clifton. Some recent writers have rejected the view that the Bristol gorges were created slowly by rivers being painstakingly lowered from a former cover of younger rocks long since destroyed. Instead, they believe that the defiles were cut rapidly by streams operating beneath or at the fringes of a melting ice sheet a mere million years ago. It was the presence of such an ice sheet, they claim, that diverted the Avon southwards to cut the Long Ashton gap. If this is so, one wonders why the Avon later abandoned the 'easy' southern route and by chance discovered the newly formed gorge.

The Mendip Hills

Looking out from Dundry Hill, the southern skyline can be seen to have been formed from a flat-topped upland, some 300 metres in height, whose scenery resembles that of the Derbyshire Peak District. Although considerably smaller in scale, the Mendips have the same carboniferous limestone plateaux embroidered with green fields and sporadic moor all seamed with grey stone walls (Atthill, 1976). Most of the attractive scenery occurs around the margins where the steep slopes are furrowed by dry stream courses and honeycombed by lengthy cave systems from which hillfoot streams emerge. The remarkable limestone features, termed *karst*, can be seen on an even grander scale in the Pennines (see Chapter 10). Because of its mineralization the Mendip countryside has been periodically scarred, like the Pennines, by lead and zinc mining. Though metal mining has now ceased, some Mendip villages are constantly disturbed by limestone quarry blasting and the passage of heavy vehicles. Yet away from the quarries and the tourist towns and villages, which are located at each of the hillfoot springs, the short-turfed limestone hills retain a feeling of solitude.

Striding away through the Somerset marshes, a line of smaller limestone hills, geologically part of Mendip, leads westwards through Wavering Down, Leadon Hill, Sandford Hill and Bonwell Hill to the coastal peninsula of Brean Down and out to the island of Steep Holm. Their rocks were bent by the same folding episode which crumpled the Mendip limestones and contorted and fractured the strata of the Bristol coalfield. A few million years after this mountain-building episode had terminated, hot tropical climates began to prevail in southern Britain; at this time the Mendip Hills must have stood high above the desert basins where Triassic red marls were slowly accumulating. Sporadic storm erosion of the Mendip summits would have brought ephemeral torrents of limestone pebbles down their wadis while screes of riven limestone blocks would have accumulated slowly on their slopes. The eventual cementing of all this detritus as an apron around the limestone massif produced the so-called dolomitic conglomerate that now forms a hillfoot bench on which the settlements stand (Welch, 1929). The same intense erosion would also have uncovered the older rocks buried in the cores of the limestone upfolds so that today the four highest summits are built not from limestone but from Old Red Sandstone that now projects above the limestone surface owing to its greater resistance (Figure 2.2) (Welch, 1933). On the sandstone's more acid soils Black Down (325 m), North Hill, Penn Hill and Beacon Hill carry a cover of dark moorland whose tiny streams soon disappear underground once they cross on to the tracts of porous limestone (Ford and Stanton, 1968). These same streams reappear, greatly swollen in volume, at each of the hillfoot settlements that ring the massif, especially at the aptly named cathedral city of Wells. If these settlements have no water-supply problems, the same cannot be said of such villages as Priddy and Charterhouse on the dry limestone uplands, where they were sited to exploit the veins of lead ore. Since primitive lead weights have been discovered at the excavated site of the prehistoric Iron Age Glastonbury lake village the Romans were obviously not the first to exploit the local mineral wealth. Today, only disturbed ground marks the former hilltop workings, though a lonely Roman road marches across the deserted summits above Mendip's combes and gorges. Yet half a million years ago, long before the Roman invasion, these bare hills were occupied by some of Britain's earliest settlers. The worked flints associated with rhinoceros bones, found at Westbury-sub-Mendip, suggest that the caves were once inhabited by Palaeolithic hunters, while the heaths around Priddy and Chewton Mendip are dotted with much later Bronze Age burial mounds.

Earlier writers believe that the deeply cut gorges at Cheddar, Ebbor and

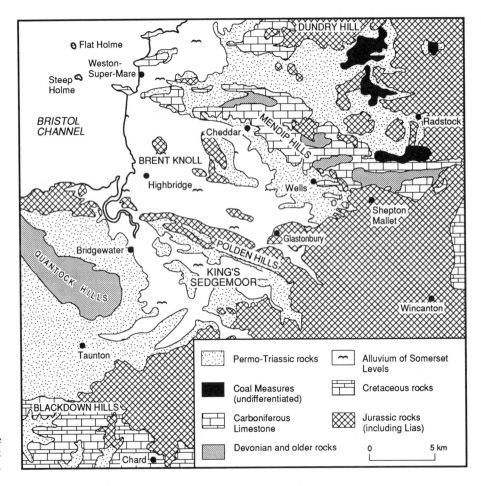

Figure 2.2 Geology of the Mendips and the Somerset Levels region.

Burrington Combe were created by the roof collapse of underground streams following the joint patterns of the massive limestone (Smith, 1975). More recent authors, however, claim that roof collapse on this massive scale was unlikely and that surface streams must have carved the valley network on the plateau top before chemical erosion had opened up the limestone joints by solutional processes; indeed, the interlocking spurs of the original river are still apparent at Cheddar. These modern ideas also depend on a much later period of overdeepening of the surface valleys during the Ice Age when the Mendip limestone and its ground water would have been frozen solid by permafrost similar to that of modern Arctic Canada. Thus, some modern writers see the Mendip gorges as relatively recent arrivals on the scene just as others have disputed the traditional geological antiquity of the River Avon gorges. Whatever their age, the precipices, pinnacles and clefts of the Cheddar Gorge produce Mendip's most dramatic scenery (Fig. 2.3). It is interesting to note that because the gorge runs east–west and the strata dip steeply southwards the south-facing cliffs of the gorge are formed from the sloping bedding planes; conversely, the north-facing cliffs, steepened by rockfalls, often stand vertically and remain deep in shadow.

Somerset's wide green marshlands, laced with ditches (rhynes) and, save for the pollarded willows, almost bereft of trees, stretch from the Mendips to the sea (see Fig. 2.2). Underlain by easily eroded red Keuper Marls and Lias clays these western fens have been built up by interbedded layers of alluvium, peat and marine clay. The low line of the Polden Hills divides the northern Vale of Avalon from the southern basin of Sedgemoor, although other ridges and 'islands' provide valuable flood-free sites for the scatter of marshland villages (Hawkins, 1954). While Burtle, Meare, Wedmore and the Westonzoyland ridge stand only a few metres above the flat water meadows, the steep hills of Brent Knoll and Glastonbury seem to tower above the marshy latticework of waterways and willow-fringed roads.

The origin of these waterlogged lowlands has caused much speculation, for although their post-glacial chronology is well documented, including the construction of the Sweet Track 6000 years ago (Europe's oldest man-made footpath), little was known of their history during the Ice Age. It has now been shown, however, that the shelly sands of the Burtle Beds, which create low ridges in the marshland, were formed as tidal shoals during a high interglacial sea level between two major British ice advances. Furthermore, it is now known that one early ice

Figure 2.3 The Cheddar Gorge, Mendip, showing the vertical north-facing cliffs and the dip of the limestone strata on the opposite slopes.

advance, perhaps of Anglian age, having moved down the floor of the Irish Sea basin, impinged on the north Devon coast thereby impounding the entire drainage of the Severn estuary that lay outside the glacial limits. A large pro-glacial lake may have formed over the Somerset plain, possibly overflowing through a gap at Chard before escaping to the English Channel via the River Axe (Stephens, 1970). The remnants of this speculative lake may have been the forerunners of the Somerset Levels, although there is firmer evidence of their subsequent history. Following a marine incursion some 8000 years ago, reed swamps are known to have grown on the resulting mantle of silty clay. As the decaying vegetation accumulated into layers of fen peat a woodland cover became established on the peaty islands which had begun to build up as acid raised bogs (mosses) above the water levels. During the last millennium BC increased precipitation must have led to further river flooding and renewed fen formation before a final marine transgression in Romano-British times deposited the coastal clay belt, 8 kilometres wide (Kidson, 1971). Henceforth, this sediment, standing 6 metres above the levels, was not only to act as a barrier to the seaward flow of landward flood water but also would offer a flood-free location for the early coastal settlements; now it serves as a 'causeway' for road, rail and motorway.

From earliest times the peaty clays have provided the hay meadows and summer pastures for farms located on the higher ground but the constant drainage improvements since medieval times have gradually alleviated the flood risk and therefore increased the length of the grazing season (Williams, 1970). On the raised ridges and 'islands' the lighter soils have always been cultivated; cider apple orchards still vie with corn and root crops for the best land but the once widespread withy (willow) beds which fringed the marshes are rapidly disappearing and with them the traditional basket makers. Likewise, the rare combination of bog and fen plants on some of the raised mosses between Shapwick and Westhay is suffering from the major inroads of commercial peat cutting.

Devon and Cornwall

To the west of the shingle spits of Bridgewater Bay (Kidson, 1960) the peaty marshes of the Somerset Levels are suddenly replaced by the red marl country of Devon and Somerset which rolls southwards to the Black Down Hills and wraps right around the isolated mass of the Quantocks. Although the scenic transition is not as dramatic as that of the Scottish Highland Line (see Chapter 15) or that exhibited along the Welsh border (see Chapter 7) the Quantocks mark one of Britain's most important geological boundaries; they stand on the so-called Tees–Exe line that divides highland from lowland Britain. Here the bright New Red Sandstone of the English lowlands is left behind; from hereon westwards the dull brown and grey markedly folded Palaeozoic rocks, bolstered by massive granite domes, build the remainder of the South-West peninsula, the most topographically subdued element of highland Britain (Dearman, 1970; Henricks, 1959). Despite the complexity of the geological structures the general impression is one of smoothness; of far-spreading coastal platforms rising gradually to isolated rolling uplands whose summits exhibit a marked uniformity of levels. This can be explained by the fact that ancient surfaces carved flat by the sea have been periodically uplifted and slowly denuded and dissected by weathering and erosion.

Furthermore, since the ancient rocks have been stripped of their cloying mantle of heavy red-brown Mesozoic clays their gaunt ribs tend to show through the stony soils so that Devon and Cornwall have more widespread moorlands and patches of bare rock than any of the other counties in southern England. It is these wind-swept western hills and rugged coasts that appeal especially to visitors from the English lowlands, where manicured farmlands prevail and wilderness is scarcely seen. Yet the journeys of these visitors through the West Country are made difficult because of the deeply dissected nature of the landscape. The rolling hills and smooth plateaux are frequently scored by narrow, steep-sided river valleys the lower reaches of which have been drowned by the sea. The contrast between the open moorland and the deeply cut wooded valley is the quintessence of Devon and Cornwall's scenic charm. In *Westward Ho!* Charles Kingsley captures their unique appeal when he notes how the valleys are

> like no other English scenery. Each has its upright walls, inland of rich oakwood, nearer the sea of dark green furze, then of smooth turf, then of weird black cliffs which range out right and left into the deep sea, in castles, spires and wings of jagged iron-stone.

Devon and Cornwall have been carved in part from an enormous downfold that strikes from east to west, a structure known as a *synclinorium* because the major syncline is puckered with innumerable smaller folds (Durrance and Laming, n.d.; Edmonds *et al.*, 1985). These minor structures are admirably displayed in the sea cliffs of west Devon and Cornwall where Atlantic waves have sliced a section right across the major downfold. The broad central area of the synclinorium is occupied almost entirely by the dark shales of the Culm series of Carboniferous age (Dearman and Butcher, 1959) giving to large tracts of North Cornwall and Central Devon a general uniformity of badly drained soil and undulating land-form that together produce a relatively undistinguished and featureless interior, except where the thickly wooded incised valleys of the Taw and Torridge wend northwards to the sea.

The Taw and Torridge river courses are quite anomalous for, with the exception of Cornwall's River Camel, the remainder of the region's drainage flows southwards. It is generally agreed that the preponderance of south-flowing rivers can be explained by a prolonged crustal uplift along the northern shoulder of the South-West peninsula, an elevation that explains the height of Exmoor and also its sudden descent to the sea along its partly faulted northern shores. But while the Fal, Fowey, Tamar, Teign and Exe rise only a short distance from the Atlantic coast and have managed to retain their original south-flowing courses, the Camel, Torridge and Taw have all been captured by vigorous north-flowing streams cutting back on the steeper north-facing slopes (Wooldridge, 1954). It is now possible to explain the tortuous routes of these latter rivers: the headwaters of the Camel rise just north of Bodmin Moor and initially flow south as if to join the Fowey before swinging north-westwards to Padstow; the Torridge, like the Tamar, rises near Hartland Point and first flows southwards, as if to debouch at Plymouth, but instead swings north to Barnstaple Bay; similarly, many of the Taw's right-bank tributaries rise on Exmoor, flow southwards alongside some of the Exe's headstreams (Kidson, 1962), before swinging north to Barnstaple. The remarkable vigour of the north-flowing 'pirate' streams will be better understood when the steep-sided massif of Exmoor is examined in more detail.

To reach the spectacular scenery of the north Devon coast many visitors have first to pass through the rich agricultural lands of the Vale of Taunton Deane. Here the deep red loamy soils once supported the great estates of ecclesiastic manors but today the picture is a colourful patchwork of smaller farmsteads. On the heavier clay soils dairying is still widespread but on the lighter, better-drained soils fringing the steep-sided Quantocks, livestock farming predominates, with the rolling summits themselves still being used for summer grazing as they have been for centuries. Although somewhat higher than the Mendips the Quantocks (384 m) are only half their area and lack the latter's spectacular gorges because, instead of Carboniferous Limestone, the Quantocks are formed from mainly arenaceous rocks (Webby, 1965b). Geologically, they are a scaled-down version of the much bulkier massif of Exmoor and its adjacent Brendon Hills (Webby, 1965a). Their threefold division of coarse sandstones and conglomerates (Hangman Grits) in the north, slates and thin limestones (Ilfracombe Beds) in the centre and glossy purple-grey slates (Morton Slates) in the south, is an almost exact replica of Exmoor itself. The Quantocks' vegetation also resembles that of Exmoor. Patches of heather moor survive, especially on the thinner soils of the grits, while remnants of a formerly widespread semi-natural oak/ash woodland, the 'murmurous woods' described by Wordsworth, clothe the sheltered valleys and combes. However, both the Quantocks and Exmoor are now suffering from the encroachment of widespread conifer plantations along their eastern margins.

The wildest tracts of Exmoor survive only on the highest summits and, like the beautiful wooded valleys of the northern coastlands, cannot be fully appreciated until one has skirted the isolated sandstone hills between Minehead and Porlock, of which Selworthy Beacon (308 m) is the most notable. At first the red marly Somerset lowland appears reluctant to give way to the bulky massif of Exmoor, so the low coastal cliffs between Watchet and Minehead exhibit fine exposures of almost horizontal Lias clays and limestones and particularly of Keuper Marls (Thomas, 1940). These same red, grey and green marls reappear in the sheltered Vale of Porlock, a downfaulted basin between the headlands of Devonian sandstones. The Porlock area exhibits extensive hillside and valley woodlands and Horner woods contains one of Britain's largest continuous survivals of sessile oak forest. But immediately one embarks on the notorious Porlock Hill, where the road suddenly rises some 300 metres above the shore, the famous Exmoor landscape rapidly unfolds as the wooded Holnicote Estate is left behind.

Because the upland has never been overridden by ice sheets, the soils beneath the Exmoor heaths are deeper and potentially more fertile than on most British moorlands. Thus, modern Exmoor has something of a clinical, cared-for appearance, unlike the stark wilderness of Dartmoor. Prior to the nineteenth century Exmoor's plateaux were covered with unbroken tracts of heather, gorse and bracken, like those that still exist above 300 metres on Dunkery Beacon (519 m), Winsford Hill and Withypool Hill. Reclamation of the moorland fringes was achieved rapidly once the impervious iron pan beneath the boggy peat was broken up to allow surface water to drain away through the somewhat porous Devonian rocks. Once the newly drained sandy soils had been liberally dressed with lime to counteract their acidity, the plateaux were divided up into fields enclosed with stone-faced earth walls, and sometimes planted with beech trees. Nevertheless, the level treeless skylines of central Exmoor do not generate dramatic landscapes – the scenic attraction is reserved for its deeply carved valleys and its coastline. The older south-draining valleys, which feed into the River Exe, have been eroded largely in less resistant slates and are therefore broader and more cultivated than their northern counterparts, formed on the tough gritstone rocks. Both in the southern valleys and on the uplands the commonest settlements are likely to be slate-roofed farmsteads and hamlets tucked away in the hollows. Because Exmoor's more youthful north-flowing rivers have had insufficient time to adjust their valley profiles to the precipitous coastal slopes, they descend headlong in a flurry of waterfalls and rapids through narrow tree-lined gorges cut in the resistant Hangman Grits. The way in which a sudden surge of energy in such a steeply flowing stream system can rapidly transform an age-old landscape was graphically illustrated one fateful August night in 1952. A 24-hour cloudburst, during which 9 inches of rain fell on the sodden moorland, caused the East and West Lyn rivers to rampage through their gorges and tear house-sized boulders and mature trees from their banks (Kidson, 1953). This remarkable debris load not only virtually obliterated central Lynmouth but also brought about a permanent change in the river course. The shortage of flat sheltered settlement sites on this coast has meant that Lynmouth, like Porlock and Combe Martin, has had to be squeezed into the narrow rocky coastal inlets, shielded from the prevailing winds. Because thick mossy woodlands rarely flourish right down to the shore except where they occupy leeward coasts, the floral richness of Exmoor's verdant coastline is unique in Britain. Here one finds oak coppice on the well-drained soils of the steeper slopes, oak mixed with birch on the drier slopes, and hazel in the damper parts. On the valley bottoms, however, ash, alder and wych-elm flourish among the oaks at places like Watersmeet.

Between the wooded bays some striking rocky cliffs and headlands mark the outcrop of the harder rocks, but because the trend or strike of the strata is not quite parallel with the coastline alternate beds of resistant grit and more friable slate meet the shore at an oblique angle (Evans, 1922). Such gritstone headlands as the Great and Little Hangman have, therefore, withstood wave attack better than the neighbouring slates of the intervening coves (Keene, 1986). One of the most remarkable of the coastal landforms, however, is found at the Valley of the Rocks near Lynmouth, where a line of castellated gritstone pinnacles separates a streamless valley from the sea (Fig. 2.4). Opinion is divided between those who believe the valley to be a product of river capture, since truncated by marine

Figure 2.4 The Valley of the Rocks, Exmoor, carved in Old Red Sandstone grits.

erosion, and those who claim that it was produced by an ephemeral glacial melt-water stream running parallel to the southern limit of a former northern ice sheet banked up against the bulwark of Exmoor (Dalzell and Durrance, 1980).

The western coasts of Devon and Cornwall

Around Ilfracombe the irregular coastal landforms are due partly to faulting, partly to the highly disturbed bedding and partly to the finely textured cleavage of the silvery-grey slates (Shearman, 1967). These, together with the thin fossi-liferous limestones, have been intricately fashioned by the sea into a ragged cliff line and a reef-girt shoreline (Arber, 1974). At Bull Point the coast swings round to a north–south alignment and exposes the western ends of the Exmoor fold axes to the relentless bludgeoning of the Atlantic waves. With the sole exception of the southern shore of Barnstaple Bay, the remainder of this western coastline cuts at right angles across the grain of the South-West peninsula, which means that waves have eroded differentially along the hard and soft rock bands to produce a fretted coast of headlands and bays.

The low promontory of Morte Point, carved from glossy slates, protects the sandy beaches of Woolacombe where erosion has picked out the softer purple, brown and greenish sandstones to fashion a lengthy west-facing bay. Because the steeply inclined slabs of the succeeding red and yellow sandstones are somewhat harder they project as 60 metre cliffs at Baggy Point which in turn shelter the smaller bay at Croyde. It is in this area that several glacially transported erratics have been found (Kidson and Wood, 1974; Stephens, 1970). At Saunton, however, this alternating coastline of bays and headlands is replaced by a 5 kilometre stretch of dunes. Achieving heights of 30 metres, the dune system of Braunton Burrows is one of the most impressive in Britain. Constantly supplied by sand blown onshore from the tidal beaches of Saunton Sands, the most active dune ridges along the shore rise inland to the higher, older dunes. Between them are marshy hollows ('slacks') where rushes and willows flourish (Willis et al., 1959).

Seaward of the drowned and silted estuaries of Barnstaple Bay and its once bustling ports of Barnstaple, Bideford, Instow and Appledore, the smaller dune system of Northam Burrows matches that of Braunton across the bay. Unlike the latter system, however, it has built up behind the Westward Ho! shingle ridge.

Barnstaple Bay and the coast as far south as Boscastle has been cut into rocks of Carboniferous age known as the Culm Measures (Prentice, 1960). At first, the short north-facing coastline runs parallel with the strike of the rocks to produce scenery not unlike that of the Exmoor coast, albeit at a less elevated and more subdued scale. Here the picture postcard village of Clovelly clings to its steep wooded slope. Lying isolated several kilometres offshore, to the west of Hartland Point, is the lonely Lundy Island, a cliff-girt plateau carved from granite. This is not a granite as old as Dartmoor, however, but a Tertiary granite emplaced a mere 50 million years ago (Dollar, 1942). At Hartland Point the coastal alignment reverts to one which slices right through the ends of the tightly compressed anticlinal and synclinal axes (Fig. 2.5). The highly contorted rocks exposed along the shore contributed to Steers' (1948) conclusion that Hartland Point has the finest coastal scenery in England and Wales, for 'the combination of first-rate cliffs, interesting physiographical features, good inland views, and a large assort-ment of flowers on the cliff tops makes the Hartland district pre-eminent'. Because the regional watershed lies near to the northern coast the short, north-flowing streams have had little time to broaden their valleys. Thus their courses are deeply incised into the solid rocks in the form of narrow gorges. Where marine erosion has 'short-circuited' the middle section of the stream valleys, spectacular coastal waterfalls occur; that at Speke's Mill descending almost 50 m vertically. Furthermore, marine erosion has also cut across the north-flowing Milford Water to leave parts of its former valley high and dry above the shore. From Hartland Point to Boscastle's High Cliff (222 m) and Tintagel's romantic ruins perched on a splintery stack, the rocky coastline rarely descends below the 60 metre contour (Wilson, 1952).

Cornwall's lengthy (430 km) coastline exhibits almost every type of rock, ranging from intrusive granites and serpentines, through extrusive volcanics, metamorphic slates and schists to sedimentary sandstones, siltstones and limestones (Balchin, 1983). Because of their different degrees of resistance this rock miscellany has created some of England's finest coastal scenery (Arber, 1949; Owen, 1934). Under the unceasing attack of marine erosion the weaker strata have been excavated into an assortment of bays, clefts and caves, while the harder rock ribs have been whittled into a bewildering array of arches, blowholes, stacks, reefs and islands. Despite their highly folded and faulted structures the cliffs are usually flat-topped because most have been cut into uplifted platforms fashioned by higher sea levels of Plio-Pleistocene age. Bare rock is rarely seen in the intervening bays or in the deeply cut river valleys because of their infillings of a stony rubble

Figure 2.5 Coastal scenery near Hartland Point, North Devon, showing marine erosion of a steeply folded anticline in Upper Carboniferous shales and sandstones.

known as 'head'. This mixture of clayey material and angular frost-shattered stones was formed during the Ice Age, when Devon and Cornwall, together with the rest of unglaciated southern England, endured a severe periglacial climate. The effects of the alternate phases of freezing and thawing are best seen on the hilltops of the granite outcrops whose tors are surrounded by aprons of shattered rock fragments known as *clitter*. This rubbly head has sludged slowly down the gentle slopes, thereby creating the region's characteristic smooth profiles and filling the valleys with superficial material into which the post-glacial streams have quickly incised their channels.

It was once thought that Pleistocene glaciers never reached South West England but it has recently been shown that ice sheets moved down the dry floor of the Irish Sea basin as far as the Isles of Scilly (Mitchell and Orme, 1967; Scourse, 1986). Deposits on St Martin's in the Scillies, at Trebetherick Point in Cornwall and at Fremington and Croyde in Barnstaple Bay have been identified as glacial till, while giant erratic boulders have been recorded at Croyde and Saunton in north Devon and at Porth Leven in Cornwall. Their means of emplacement remains controversial: were they carried in the ice sheets or merely by floating icebergs? A further controversy surrounds the age of the sandy clays at St Erth in the depression mid-way between St Ives Bay and Mounts Bay. A century ago some geologists thought the deposits were of Miocene or Pliocene age, but today a Pleistocene (possibly glacial) age is favoured (Mitchell, 1965).

Both the Scillies and Penwith, the westernmost toe of Cornwall, have been carved from granite, a coarsely crystalline rock whose name is synonymous with hardness and durability (Hall, 1974). Because of its toughness granite forms virtually all the hill masses of Cornwall and south Devon where it has been fashioned into smooth-shouldered heather-clad uplands. Despite its strength the granite's joint patterns have allowed rain water to penetrate and help rot the rock until the sounder masses become isolated from each other as tors, surrounded by depths of rotted material known locally as 'growan'. Wherever the sea has invaded this weathered landform it has rapidly removed the growan and left the bare rock upstanding as joint-controlled cliffs, turretted sea stacks and tor-crowned reefs; the word 'tor' is derived from the Celtic *twr*, meaning tower (Balchin, 1983).

The low heathery ridge of Penwith, between St Ives and Land's End, and almost surrounded by sea, remains the most Celtic part of England. Its profusion of prehistoric stone monuments mimics the naturally monolithic tors and their rocking stones ('logans'), while its standing stones ('menhirs'), its stone circles, carved crosses and cyclopean burial chambers ('quoits') litter the hilltops. Below them, perched on ledges beneath the grey cliffs or tucked into tiny coves, the ruined tin mines and sturdy fishing quays testify to an almost forgotten way of life on this rockbound coast, found today only in the pictures of the nineteenth-century Newlyn school of artists. The coastal footpaths lead past the working villages of St Just and Pendeen which illustrate how the silvery-grey granite was used to construct the miners' cottages, churches, farms and gnarled stone 'hedges' (Pyatt, 1971). The grey coastal cliffs, however, are emblazoned with yellow lichen, sea pink and thrift, interrupted by coves of dazzling white sand where the disintegrating granite has broken down into crystals of sparkling quartz and spangled mica. Where the rock joints are closely spaced, shingle-charged waves have ground out narrow clefts ('zawns'), while the intervening buttresses have survived as pinnacled headlands wherever the joints are more widely spaced (Fig. 2.6). Land's

Figure 2.6 The granite coastline at Land's End, Cornwall.

End itself displays every type of this finely tooled cliff scenery that so resembles architectural forms (Robson, 1949). The Isles of Scilly represent the final phase of granitic landform denudation by marine agencies; their scores of islands are little more than a scatter of half-submerged tors sometimes linked by tombolos of shingle or patches of head (Osman, 1928).

The southern coasts of Cornwall and Devon

Between Penzance and Torquay almost the entire coast has been sculptured from severely folded and faulted rocks of Devonian age although they differ in character from those of north Devon because the former were laid down in deeper water farther from a coastline (Dearman, 1969). Thus the south-coast sediments are finer-grained and lack the massive gritstones of the Exmoor coast. Instead they contain many beds of metamorphic slates ('killas'), layers of volcanics and intrusive dolerites and, above all, some sandstones and thick beds of limestone. Except in Mount's Bay, where granite forms Trewayras Head and the distinctive St Michael's Mount, granite fails to reach the southern coastline, though an interesting assemblage of Precambrian rocks builds the Lizard and the area around Start Point. In addition to the lithological contrasts between the north-west and the south coasts the scenery, too, is different. While the north- and west-facing coasts are generally high, bold and rocky the southern shores are less elevated, less rugged and are characterized by deep wooded inlets, termed *rias*, that carry the sea far into the heart of the region. Of these drowned river estuaries the most notable are at Helford River, Carrick Roads, Fowey, Plymouth Sound and the Hamoaze, Salcombe and Dartmouth.

Near to Porth Leven, on the eastern shore of Mount's Bay, a freshwater lake, Loe Pool, 2 kilometres in length, is separated from the sea by a shingle beach composed almost entirely of flints. Since Beer in east Devon is the nearest outcrop of the Chalk it is difficult to explain the origin of this flinty shingle bar. Modern opinion has rejected the idea of two opposing coastal spits slowly meeting to close off the mouth of the River Cober in favour of an alternative theory based on our modern knowledge of the Channel's sea-floor geology. It is now thought that an offshore bar formed on an exposure of the Chalk when sea level stood some 100 metres lower during a cold period of the Ice Age and that, as the sea rose in postglacial times, the bar was driven gradually onshore to become trapped in Mount's Bay. This hypothesis has also been used to explain the origin of the beaches at Slapton (p. 31) and at Chesil (p. 45).

Britain's southernmost promontory, the Lizard, exhibits an unusual countryside developed upon a patch of some of its oldest rocks. A great mass of black, red and green serpentine is the dominant rock; this and a later gabbro have been intruded into a bedrock of mica and hornblende schists. This ancient block is separated from the much younger Devonian rocks to the north by a zone of highly crushed material in which jumbled slices of Cambrian, Ordovician and Silurian sediments occur. The whole complex represents a time when the Hercynian mountain-building episode drove the Lizard mass northwards along low-angle thrust-faults, thereby overriding, shearing and smashing into a breccia every rock series that stood in the path of this monstrous lithological bulldozer (Scrivenor, 1949). Today, the thin soils developed on the serpentine create a barren landscape of treeless heaths at Goonhilly and Predannack Downs, contrasting markedly with the more fertile farmed soils developed on the schists and gabbro, for long celebrated as producing Cornwall's best grain harvest. Yet the unimproved gabbro country of Crousa Downs, where myriads of boulders still litter the surface, illustrates the laborious cost of land reclamation. In the colourful coastal settlements of Mullion, Kynance and Coverack, known to countless tourists, many of the older buildings are constructed from roughly hewn blocks of serpentine. But while this greenish-red rock may produce dramatic coastal scenery it is badly jointed and cannot compete with granite as a building material. Thus, some of the Lizard churches are built of light grey granite.

The Lizard's Helford River, with its moss-laden oakwoods, is the westernmost of the rias that make such a notable contribution to the scenery of the South-West peninsula. They were formed during the Ice Age when world sea level fell by 100–150 metres, causing rivers deeply to incise their existing valleys and extend their estuaries across large tracts of newly exposed sea floor (Heyworth and Kidson, 1982). As sea level rose again, following the melting of the ice sheets, the so-called Flandrian transgression gradually drowned the newly established coastal woodlands of the coastal plains to create Britain's 'submerged forests', the stumps of which are exposed at low tide, at places like Mount's Bay. More importantly, the inundation flooded the incised river valleys so that the former meanders are now deepwater tidal creeks where large ocean-going vessels can lie safely at anchor. Subsequent silting has tended to infill parts of the rias, especially in eastern Devon where the larger river catchments supply greater quantities of

sediments than do their Cornish counterparts. Consequently, a contrast can be
seen between the deepwater rias to the west of Torquay and the partly silted rias
of the Teign, Exe and Otter whose mouths are half enclosed by shingle or sand
spits. The deeper inlets have not only functioned as valuable anchorages since time
immemorial, especially at Plymouth and Falmouth, but have also encouraged
market gardening to flourish by allowing the Gulf Stream's warming influence to
permeate far into the peninsula. Nevertheless, the sinuous waterways have also
hindered freedom of movement across country, with ferries only gradually being
replaced by bridges along this coastline of inordinate length. Yet the sheltered
creeks, with their hanging woods of oak, beech and sycamore enclosing picturesque villages, retain their considerable scenic appeal.

Between the drowned estuaries lengthy stretches of rocky coastline culminate in
some dramatic headlands, though in general the sea cliffs are not as high as those
along the northern and western coasts. They have all been carved from a wide
variety of killas, limestones and sandstones, except for the craggy tract between
Bolt Tail and Start Point where resistant schists stand out as sharply defined
cliffs and headlands (Dineley, 1961). The highly folded killas between Falmouth
and Plymouth have produced a shoreline of intricate detail. Their variously
coloured rocks are themselves enhanced by the clifftop flowers and other plant
life that clings to every niche provided by the highly weathered cleavage of the
slates.

The southernmost peninsula of Devon, known as the South Hams, comprises
an east–west tract of less resistant red and grey Devonian shales and slates
(Meadfoot Beds) flanked to the north by a narrow belt of Dartmouth slates and
to the south by an elevated platform of schists. Wherever the waves have attacked
the Dartmouth slates small blunt-nosed headlands occur, while in the 130 metres
high schistose coastal platform, deeply notched by the Salcombe ria, the local
streams plunge through deep combes before reaching the jagged coast. Start Bay
has a much smoother coastline because of the long flinty shingle spit that has
closed off the irregular shoreline and the freshwater lagoon of Slapton Ley from
the open sea (Mottershead, 1986). It was probably formed in a similar way to that
of the Loe Bar (p. 30) when an offshore bar was driven onshore some 6000 years
ago by a rising post-glacial sea level. At the southern end of Start Bay the old
village of Hallsands was built on a 4 metre Upper Pleistocene raised beach platform once protected by the shingle beach noted above. To provide concrete
aggregate for the extension of Plymouth dockyard in 1897, 650,000 tons of shingle
were removed by dredging, based on an assurance from 'experts' that further
shingle would accumulate naturally in due course. Since the beach is of great
antiquity, however, no new shingle was forthcoming and, deprived of its shield,
Hallsands was destroyed by a great storm in 1917.

It is interesting to speculate whether some of the Hallsands shingle helped
construct any of the streets and buildings in Plymouth itself, thereby obliterating
large sections of a well-preserved Middle Pleistocene raised beach that forms the
famous Hoe some 30 metres above the shore. The same wave-cut surface, devoid
of its beach material, can still be seen truncating the folded Devonian rocks at
Mount Batten (Fyson, 1962; Hobson, 1978). Though this naval dockyard is now
part of Plymouth's built-up area, Mount Batten must have been an island towards
the close of the Ice Age, judging by the 8 metre raised beach platform (of last
interglacial age) fringing Plymouth Hoe. It was these high Pleistocene sea levels,

together with those Pliocene age, that cut the extensive coastal platforms which make such a major contribution to the scenery of the South-West.

Like the deep estuary of Plymouth Sound, the narrower opening of the River Dart is yet another illustration of the remarkable way in which sea level in Britain must have fluctuated during the last million years. Unlike Plymouth Sound, however, the drowned valley of the Dart was not selected as the site of a major city. Instead, picturesque Dartmouth, clinging to its sheltered slope, such pretty riverside villages as Dittisham nestling in its tree-bowered creek, and the climbing lanes of ancient Totnes, at the Dart's lowest bridging-point, can, in combination, be seen to make significant contributions to Devon's scenic heritage. Between Totnes and Dittisham the Dart cuts through outcrops of dark volcanic lavas and other igneous rocks of Devonian age. Although the east–west tracts of softer sedimentary rocks have been eroded into gentler slopes by the tributary streams, the igneous rocks invariably form bold wooded crags round which the Dart is forced to weave its meandering course.

The popular tourist resort of Torquay has expanded northwards across its rugged hard rock headland to incorporate Babbacombe and Oddicombe, and southwards on to the less resistant New Red Sandstone of the smoother Tor Bay coast to link up with Paignton and almost reach the fishing port of Brixham perched on the limestone point of Berry Head (Perkins, 1971). The complexity of Torquay's geological make-up is reflected in the variety of its landforms and in its unusual contrasts of colour: rocks vary from bright red, through black, to greyish white; hidden coves sport beaches of yellow sand; jutting headlands are clothed in frothy green woods or emerald swards; while overall, the darker mantle of pine trees is stitched with pastel-toned Victorian villas and hotels. Torquay's promontory is criss-crossed with faults and has been invaded by igneous intrusions. Its highly folded Devonian limestones, slates and sandstones have, therefore, been brought up sharply against patches of virtually flat-bedded New Red Sandstone and dark exposures of dolerite (Fig. 2.7).

One of the best viewpoints from which to view this pot-pourri is the summit of Petit Tor near Oddicombe. Its hill has been partly quarried because Petit Tor's pinkish-grey limestone is capable of being highly polished and is greatly prized as an ornamental 'marble', though it is not a true metamorphic marble in the strictest sense. The view to the south shows how Oddicombe Bay has been fashioned from a patch of New Red Sandstone lowered by parallel faults between the two projecting limestone masses of Petit Tor itself and the larger one at Ways Hill. The limestone cliffs of Anstey's Cove contrast with the dark silhouette of nearby Black Head whose dolerite sill has resisted wave attack more successfully than the beds of slate which surround it. Farther south and west the steeply folded limestones of Hope's Nose and Daddy Hole Plain have been planed across by former sea levels to create platforms some 60 metres above the modern shore where waves now surge through the newly cut arch of London Bridge (Mottershead *et al.*, 1987). The view westwards from Petit Tor illustrates how a higher 90 metre platform has been dissected into separate limestone knolls of Lummaton Hill, Windmill Hill and Dainton Hill by the deeply incised River Fleet. Though the well-jointed Devonian limestone is hard enough to create steep bluffs and bold coastal headlands it is, like Carboniferous Limestone, extremely soluble when attacked by rain water. Thus, as in the Mountain Limestone country of the Pennines (Chapter 10), passages have been carved through the Torquay limestone by former under-

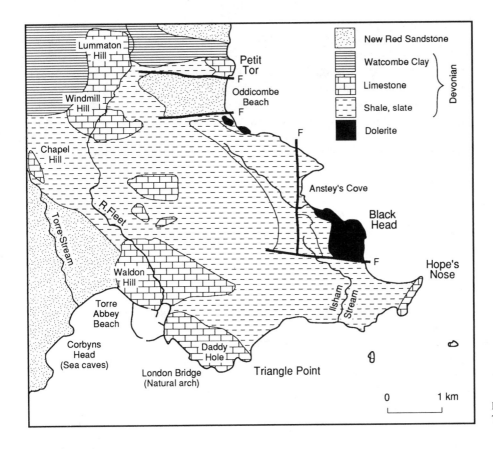

Figure 2.7 Geology of the Torbay area.

ground streams. The most famous cave is that of Kent's Cavern where nineteenth-century excavations proved that Palaeolithic cave dwellers hunted animals now long extinct in Britain: mammoth, cave bear, woolly rhinoceros, sabre-toothed tiger and Irish elk, to name but a few.

The granite moorlands

The last of South-West England's landscapes to be considered are among its grandest and wildest. These are the granite lands of Devon and Cornwall, where the crystalline rocks are grey in colour and coarsely grained in texture because the great molten mass (batholith) cooled slowly as it solidified at great depths in the earth's crust. Though the enormous subterranean granite batholith stretches from Dartmoor to the Scillies it has been exposed at the surface only in a handful of places as the overlying cover rocks have been stripped slowly from the domes by weathering and erosion (Brammall and Harwood, 1932; Dearman, 1962). Most of the sedimentary rocks into which the molten mass was intruded have been changed by the intense heat and pressure into narrow encircling zones of metamorphosed rocks known as *aureoles* (Perkins, 1972). Since the granite is more resistant than these surrounding rocks it projects above them as smooth-shouldered hills: granite landscapes, when viewed from afar, are gently swelling and only rarely do they verge on the spectacular. Because igneous rocks have neither the bedding planes nor the true jointing of sedimentary rocks, granite offers relatively few chinks for

---

the elements to exploit. Nevertheless, there are sufficient pseudo-joints (horizontal and vertical shrinkage cracks) to undermine the strength of even this most durable of rocks. Once the smooth domes become pitted by weathering, small surface pools of water help accelerate the rotting until bosses of granite become isolated from each other and surrounded by aprons of sandy gravel. On the larger granite domes, where vertical 'joints' are few and far between, the rock breaks down by a process termed *exfoliation*, in which thick curvilinear sheets of granite are shed periodically from the dome, like an onion being peeled of its outer skin. In due course these sheets disintegrate into a scatter of granite blocks (clitter) that gradually slide down to the shallow valley floors. These are the so-called *moorstones* used by primitive man to build his megalithic structures and also the rudimentary enclosures and field walls that pattern the granite moors.

Many of the bald-headed granite hills have been sculptured into tors, the architectural character of which led our ancestors to see them as the works of legendary giants (Fig. 2.8). Some geologists believe that these castellated rocks towers were formed deep beneath a tropical land surface during Tertiary times when warm percolating rainfall rotted the bedrock to depths of 20 metres. The latticework of 'joints' allowed the ground water to etch out rough blocky outlines in the buried granite. Meanwhile, atmospheric processes were wearing away the cover rocks until, several million years later, the buried tor began to emerge at the surface (Linton, 1955). The final episode saw frost, wind and rain add the finishing touches to the turreted rocks (Fig. 2.9). An alternative view disputes the theory of

Figure 2.8 Dartmoor tors, showing weathering of granite.

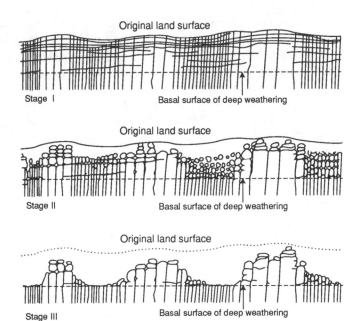

Original land surface

Stage I   Basal surface of deep weathering

Original land surface

Stage II   Basal surface of deep weathering

Original land surface

Stage III   Basal surface of deep weathering

Figure 2.9 Evolution of tors (after D.L. Linton).

ground-water rotting during tropical periods prior to the Pleistocene, replacing it with a suggestion that the angular tors were created by severe Ice Age frost-weathering of all well-jointed rock masses exposed at the surface, whether they are unbedded granite or bedded sandstone (Palmer and Neilson, 1962). It is true that though tors are most commonly seen in granite landscapes they are also found in other non-granitic but well-jointed rocks, such as those which form the gritstone scarps of the Pennines.

Dartmoor is not only the largest granite massif south of the Scottish Highlands but its highest summit, High Willhays (621 m) is the southernmost bastion of upland Britain (Brunsden *et al.*, 1964). Its misty moorland, rising dramatically above the fertile Devon farmlands, is little more than a heathery wilderness of bracken and wind-flattened grass where bright green miry hollows alternate with gently swelling tor-crowned hills. Its slowly running streams emerge from the tussocky black peat hags, before tumbling over bleached granitic rocks in the fairly broad open valleys of the high moors. As the radiating headwaters of such rivers as the Dart, Teign, Tavy and Plym reach the perimeter of the dome, however, they possess enough energy to cut deep lonely defiles in whose shelter oakwoods flourish. The road from Tavistock to Ashburton, for example criss-crosses the Dart gorges at Dartmeet, New Bridge and Holne Bridge.

Dartmoor, like the neighbouring Cornish moorlands, was not always uninhabited (Gill, 1970; Harvey and St Leger-Gordon, 1953). During the Bronze Age (1800–500 BC) some of Britain's earliest farmers constructed their primitive villages and enclosures ('pounds') on the lower, less boggy tracts of the southern part of the moor. Grimspound, for example, has a massive blocky retaining wall enclosing the ruins of twenty-four hut circles. By the Iron Age (fourth century BC), as the climate slowly deteriorated, the high moors became virtually abandoned and the large hill forts were constructed only on the peripheral foothills. Henceforward, until late Norman times, when Dartmoor became the major source of Europe's tin, the central massif remained a deserted wilderness. Nevertheless, in medieval times two or three centuries of tin-mining brought a brief prosperity to Dartmoor's perimeter settlements of Tavistock, Ashburton, Plympton and Chagford, the so-called stannary towns where tin was assayed (Hoskins, 1964). It also saw the building of the substantial granite church towers in the tiny moorland villages, with that at Widecombe-in-the-Moor being the most notable. The tiny surviving patches of primeval woodland, such as Wistman's Wood, suggest that Dartmoor may once have carried a thicker tree cover, though Forestry Commission plantations are now encroaching from the valleys on to the open moorland. Centuries of grazing by domestic animals have contributed largely to Dartmoor's treeless vistas where today nothing breaks the stillness save the croak of ravens and the bleat of mist-dampened sheep.

All the remainder of the granite bosses in South-West England occur in Cornwall, the largest of which are (from east to west) Bodmin Moor, St Austell, Carn Menellis and Penwith. All produce landscapes similar to that of Dartmoor but because of their lower elevation and their smaller bulk their moorlands are nowhere near as extensive. Moreover, that of Penwith is cliffed by the ocean in the Land's End peninsula, as described above.

Bodmin Moor is the wildest and least tamed. Betjeman described its Cheesewring Tor (381 m) as a group of 'gigantic nodding mushrooms' and spoke of the way in which 'unfenced roads wind between granite boulders and isolated cottages, with patches of treacherous marsh between'. Both the Cheesewring and Rough Tor have been disfigured by stone quarrying, with the carefully dressed blocks from the De Lank quarry being chosen to rebuild the Eddystone lighthouse. As on Dartmoor, tin-miners have also left their mark on the Cornish granite lands, especially on Carn Menellis and Penwith. During the cooling of the granite, veins and lodes of tin, copper and lead extended out into the surrounding killas and these have been worked sporadically since pre-Roman times. The alluvial or stream tin, washed down the valleys after weathering of exposed veins, was the first to be worked out, so that many of the valley floors have been disfigured by water-filled hollows and heaps of spoil left behind by the tin-streamers. Only the deeper tin lodes are now being worked, mainly around the granite village of St Just near Land's End. But the legacy of earlier mining is found on most of the granite masses, largely in the form of derelict engine houses with their gaunt ruined chimney stacks.

Another mineral, china clay, produced during the cooling and crystallization of the granite, has also been considerably exploited, especially around St Austell. China clay is formed by the chemical alteration of the granitic mineral feldspar into a snow-white clay known as kaolin. The close relationship between the parallel fissures of china clay and the tin veins suggests that both were formed by chemically charged vapours during the cooling phase of the molten mass, rather than by simple weathering of solid granite. Today, the Hensbarrow district has a unique landscape, its deep white clay pits, some now filled by turquoise water, hedged around with gleaming white pyramids of waste quartz sand.

Bibliography

Arber, M.A. (1949) Cliff profiles of Devon and Cornwall. *Geog. J.*, **114**, 191–7.
Arber, M.A. (1974) The cliffs of North Devon. *Proc. Geol. Assoc.*, **84**, 147–58.

Atthill, R. (ed.) (1976) *Mendip: A New Study*. David & Charles. 287 pp.

Balchin, W.G.V. (1983) *The Cornish Landscape*. Hodder & Stoughton. 234 pp.

Brammall, A. and Harwood, H.F. (1932) The Dartmoor Granites. *Quart. J. Geol. Soc.*, **88**, 171–237.

Brunsden, D., Kidson, C., Orme, A.R. and Waters, R.S. (1964) The denudation chronology of parts of south-western England. *Field Studies*, **2**, 115–32.

Curtis, M.L.K. (1968) The Tremadoc rocks of the Tortworth Inlier, Gloucestershire. *Proc. Geol. Assoc.*, **79**, 349–62.

Curtis, M.L.K. (1972) The Silurian rocks of the Tortworth Inlier, Gloucestershire. *Proc. Geol. Assoc.*, **83**, 1–36.

Dalzell, D. and Durrance, E.M. (1980) The evolution of the Valley of the Rocks, North Devon. *Trans. Inst. Br. Geogr.* (NS), **5**, 66–79.

Dearman, W.R. (1962) *Dartmoor*. Guide No. 33. Geol. Assoc.

Dearman, W.R. (1969) An outline of the structural geology of Cornwall. *Proc. Geol. Soc.*, **1654**, 33–39.

Dearman, W.R. (1970) Some aspects of the tectonic evolution of South-West England. *Proc. Geol. Assoc.*, **81**, 483–92.

Dearman, W.R. and Butcher, N.E. (1959) The geology of the Devonian and Carboniferous rocks of the north-west border of the Dartmoor granite. *Proc. Geol. Assoc.*, **70**, 51–92.

Dineley, D.L. (1961) The Devonian system in south Devonshire. *Field Studies*, **1**, 121–40.

Dollar, A.T.J. (1942) The Lundy complex: its petrology and tectonics. *Quart. J. Geol. Soc.*, **97**, 39–77.

Durrance, E.M. and Laming, D.J.C. (eds) *The Geology of Devon*. University of Exeter, 346 pp.

Edmonds, E.A., McKeown, M.C. and Williams, M. (1985) *South West England* (4th edn). British Regional Geology. HMSO. 138 pp.

Evans, J.W. (1922) The geological structure of the country around Combe Martin, north Devon. *Proc. Geol. Assoc.*, **33**, 201–28.

Ford, D.C. and Stanton, W.I. (1968) The geomorphology of the south-central Mendip Hills. *Proc. Geol. Assoc.*, **79**, 401–27.

Frey, A. (1975) River patterns in the Bristol District, in R. Peel, M. Chisholm and P. Haggett (eds), *Processes in Physical and Human Geography*. Heinemann. 148–65.

Fyson, W.K. (1962) Tectonic structures in the Devonian rocks near Plymouth, Devon. *Geol. Mag.*, **99**, 208–26.

Gill, C. (ed.) (1970) *Dartmoor: A New Study*. David & Charles. 314 pp.

Hall, A. (1974) *West Cornwall*. Guide no. 19. Geol. Assoc.

Harvey, L.A. and St Leger-Gordon, D. (1953) *Dartmoor*. Collins. 273 pp.

Hawkins, D. (1954) *Sedgemoor and Avalon*. Robert Hale. 181 pp.

Henricks, E.M.L. (1959) A summary of the present views on the structure of Devon and Cornwall. *Geol. Mag.*, **96**, 253–7.

Heyworth, A. and Kidson, C. (1982) Sea-level changes in southwest England and Wales. *Proc. Geol. Assoc.*, **93**, 91–112.

Hobson, D.M. (1978) *The Plymouth Area*. Guide no. 38. Geol. Assoc.

Hoskins, W.G. (1964) *Devon*. Collins. 600 pp.

Isaac, K.P., Turner, P.J. and Stewart, I.J. (1982) The evolution of the Hercynides of central South West England. *J. Geol. Soc.*, **139**, 521–31.

Keene, P. (1986) *Classic Landforms of the North Devon Coast*. Guide No. 6. Geographical Association, Sheffield.

Kellaway, G.A. and Welch, F.B.A. (1948) *Bristol and Gloucester District*. (2nd edn). British Regional Geology. HMSO. 91 pp.

Kidson, C. (1953) The Exmoor Storm and the Lynmouth Floods. *Geography*, **38**, 1–9.

Kidson, C. (1960) The shingle complexes of Bridgewater Bay. *Trans. Inst. Brit. Geogr.*, **28**, 75–87.

Kidson, C. (1962) The denudation chronology of the Middle Exe. *Trans. Inst. Brit. Geogr.*, **31**, 43–66.

Kidson, C. (1971) The Quaternary history of the coasts of South-West England, with special reference to the Bristol Channel coast, in K.J. Gregory and W.L.D. Ravenhill (eds), *Exeter Essays in Geography*. University of Exeter. 1–22.

Kidson, C. and Wood, T. R. (1974) The Pleistocene stratigraphy of Barnstaple Bay. *Proc. Geol. Assoc.*, **85**, 223–37.

Linton, D. L. (1955) The problem of tors. *Geog. J.*, **121**, 470–87.

Mitchell, G. F. (1965) The St. Erth Beds: An alternative explanation. *Proc. Geol. Assoc.*, **76**, 345–66.

Mitchell, G. F. and Orme, A. R. (1967) The Pleistocene deposits of the Isles of Scilly. *Quart. J. Geol. Soc.*, **123**, 59–92.

Moore, L. R. and Trueman, A. E. (1937) The Coal Measures of Bristol and Somerset. *Quart. J. Geol. Soc.*, **93**, 195–240.

Moore, L. R. and Trueman, A. E. (1939) The structure of the Bristol and Somerset coalfield. *Proc. Geol. Assoc.*, **50**, 46–67.

Mottershead, D. N. (1986) *Classic Landforms of the South Devon Coast*. Guide No. 5: Geographical Association, Sheffield.

Mottershead, D. N., Gilbertson, D. D. and Keen, D. H. (1987) The raised beaches and shore platforms of Tor Bay: a re-evaluation. *Proc. Geol. Assoc.*, **98**, 241–57.

Osman, C. W. (1928) The granites of the Scilly Isles and their relation to the Dartmoor granites. *Quart. J. Geol. Soc.*, **84**, 258–92.

Owen, D. E. (1934) The Carboniferous rocks of the north Cornish coast and their structures. *Proc. Geol. Assoc.*, **45**, 451–71.

Palmer, J. and Neilson, R. A. (1962) The origin of granite tors on Dartmoor. *Proc. Yorks. Geol. Soc.*, **33**, 315–40.

Perkins, J. W. (1971) *Geology Explained in South and East Devon*. David & Charles. 11–102.

Perkins, J. W. (1972) *Geology explained in Dartmoor and the Tamar valley*. David & Charles.

Prentice, J. E. (1960) The stratigraphy of the Upper Carboniferous rocks of the Bideford region, north Devon. *Quart. J. Geol. Soc.*, **116**, 397–408.

Pyatt, E. C. (1971) *Coastal Paths of the South West*. David & Charles.

Reynolds, S. H. and Greenly, E. (1924) The geological structure of the Clevedon-Portishead area. *Quart. J. Geol. Soc.*, **80**, 447–67.

Robson, J. (1949) Geology of the Land's End peninsula. *Trans. Roy. Geol. Soc. Cornwall*, **17**, 427–54.

Savage, R. J. G. (1977) *Geological Excursions in the Bristol District*. University of Bristol.

Scourse, J. (1986) *The Isles of Scilly*. Field Guide. Quat. Res. Assoc.

Scrivenor, J. B. (1949) The Lizard-Start problem. *Geol. Mag.*, **86**, 377–86.

Shearman, D. J. (1967) On Tertiary fault-movements in North Devonshire. *Proc. Geol. Assoc.*, **78**, 555–66.

Shorter, A. H., Ravenhill, W. L. D. and Gregory, K. J. (1969) *Southwest England*. Nelson. 340 pp.

Smith, D. I. (1975) The geomorphology of Mendip – the sculpting of the landscape, in D. I. Smith and D. P. Drew (eds), *Limestones and Caves of Mendip*. David & Charles. 89–132.

Steers, J. A. (1948) *The Coastline of England and Wales*. (1st edn). Cambridge University Press. 644 pp.

Stephens, N. (1970) The West Country and Southern Ireland, in C. A. Lewis, *The Glaciations of Wales and Adjoining Regions*. Longman. 267–314.

Thomas, A. N. (1940) The Triassic rocks of north west Somerset. *Proc. Geol. Assoc.*, **51**, 1–43.

Walker, F. (1972) *The Bristol Region*. Nelson. 409 pp.

Webby, B. D. (1965a) The stratigraphy and structure of the Devonian rocks in the Brendon Hills, west Somerset. *Proc. Geol. Assoc.*, **76**, 39–60.

Webby, B. D. (1965b) The stratigraphy and structure of the Devonian rocks in the Quantock Hills, west Somerset. *Proc. Geol. Assoc.*, **76**, 321–44.

Welch, F. B. A. (1929) The geological structure of the central Mendips. *Quart. J. Geol. Soc.*, **86**, 45–76.

Welch, F. B. A. (1933) The geological structure of the eastern Mendips. *Quart. J. Geol. Soc.*, **89**, 14–52.

Williams, M. (1970) *The Draining of the Somerset Levels*. Cambridge University Press. 287 pp.

Willis, A. J., Folkes, B. F., Hope-Simpson, J. F. and Yemm, E. W. (1959) The vegetation of Braunton Burrows. *J. Ecol.*, **47**, 1–24, 249–88.

Wilson, G. (1952) The influence of rock structures on coastline and cliff development around Tintagel, north Cornwall. *Proc. Geol. Assoc.*, **63**, 20–48.

Wooldridge, S. W. (1954) The physique of the South West. *Geography*, **39**, 231–42.

The south coast and the chalklands

3

It may reasonably be asked why the south coast is treated in the same chapter as the chalklands. By way of explanation it will be shown how the Chalk makes a major contribution to the coastal landforms of southern England from Beer Head to the Cliffs of Dover. Many people are familiar with the sort of chalk scenery exemplified by Lulworth Cove, the Needles, Beachy Head and its neighbouring Seven Sisters, while to some, dazzling white sea cliffs are virtually synonymous with southern England's scenic heritage.

The Chalk is not, of course, the only rock to be exposed along the lengthy Channel coast, for older rocks contribute to the landforms of south Devon, Dorset and Kent, while younger rocks contribute to the shorelines of Hampshire and the Isle of Wight. Although all these rocks are of widely differing ages they are all of sedimentary origin and none is older than the New Red Sandstones (Permian and Trias) of east Devon whence the next stage of our journey commences. The ruggedness associated with the older Palaeozoic sedimentaries and the tough igneous and metamorphic rocks of the South-West peninsula is missing from the landforms of southern and eastern England where bare rock is scarcely seen except at the coast itself. Yet, despite the contrasting lithologies, textures and colours of the various Mesozoic and Tertiary sandstones, limestones and clays in South-East England, their landforms have been given something of an affinity by virtue of the fact that they have all been affected by folding during Britain's newest mountain-building episode (the Alpine, which climaxed 40–50 million years ago). Many of the tighter folds have been picked out by marine erosion to create the spectacular coastal features of Dorset, while the gentler folds are responsible for the more subdued swellings of Sussex and Kent. Nevertheless, because the phases of sedimentation in the Mesozoic and Tertiary southern seas followed a fairly ordered progression, uninterrupted by the Tertiary volcanic episodes which dominated north-western Britain, the resulting strata have been fashioned into repetitive suites of similar landforms characterized both by their symmetry and their linearity. Straight and seemingly endless clay vales are paralleled by lengthy cuestas of sandstone or limestone, where isolated hills are the exception rather than the rule. These extensive ridges introduce the only semblance of hill country into the otherwise flat terrain of lowland England, even though the topography described in this chapter and the next never exceeds the 300 metre contour. Southern and eastern England, therefore, is a gently 'corrugated' land of scarp and vale etched out by trellis-shaped drainage patterns. Only where marine erosion has attacked the edges of this gently folded but relatively ordered landscape are the harder rocks of the ridges terminated abruptly by precipitous coastal headlands. The less resistant clay vales, by contrast, have allowed the sea to penetrate far inland, as in Poole Harbour and Southampton Water, for example. For the purposes of this chapter only the coastline between Torbay and Selsey Bill will be examined. The stretch of coast from Selsey Bill to the Straits of Dover will be described in Chapter 4.

South-east Devon

Once the mist-shrouded bastions of Dartmoor and the rugged bays and headlands of Torbay and the South Hams have been left behind, the east Devon countryside takes on a much gentler countenance, though no less attractive for all that. East Devon is manifestly part of lowland Britain, for east of Dartmoor the rocks are not only younger but are also less durable than their Palaeozoic counterparts farther west. This is also 'Red Devon' since soils derived from the New Red Sandstone mantle almost the entire terrain save the highest of its gently swelling hills. Even these eminences have been carved largely from a russet-coloured sandstone, although this is not the New Red Sandstone but the Upper Greensand of Cretaceous age. As a reminder of the former widespread covering of younger rocks that once extended far into the West Country some of these greensand hills are themselves capped with layers of chalk that have long been isolated by denudation from the main outcrop of the Chalk farther east. Only the Black Down Hills and some of the Lyme Bay coastal headlands have retained their chalk capping, although the remarkably thick layers of flinty gravel on the Haldon Hills, south of Exeter, suggest that the chalk (and Eocene(?)) cover once stretched at least as far as Dartmoor (Hamblin, 1973). In this particular case, however, prolonged Tertiary weathering has dissolved the Chalk but left behind the telltale flints.

Below the flat-topped forested skyline of the Haldon Hills another remarkable geological survival can be found at Bovey Travey (Edwards, 1976). Here, in a narrow basin aligned along the seismically active Sticklepath Fault, a thick succession of Oligocene clays and sands overlies layers of flinty gravel and greensands similar to those of the neighbouring Haldon Hills. Subsidence along the fault line allowed a lake to form some 30 million years ago into which layers of very plastic white and brown clays were deposited, rich in kaolinite derived from Dartmoor's weathered granite. Unsullied by quartz sand and mica, these so-called *ball clays* provide the basis of a local pottery industry though much of the clay is exported to Italy and to the Potteries of North Staffordshire. The same rivers that once brought the weathered materials from Dartmoor and filtered out the coarser quartz and mica minerals also washed trunks of sequoia trees and various exotic plant remains down into 'Lake Bovey' where they became petrified into lignite beds.

Nowhere exemplifies the vivid richness of 'Red Devon' better than the ramparts of brightly coloured sandstone sea cliffs between Dawlish and Teignmouth. Although lacking the stature of the North Devon cliffs or the ruggedness of their Cornish counterparts, these New Red Sandstone cliffs blaze like an Arizonan sunset. Their sedimentary rocks, of Permian and Triassic age, are in fact a product of ancient desert environments for they accumulated in arid basins bounded by mountains of Devonian and Carboniferous rocks. Many millions of years ago, occasional flash floods, similar to those that once carried debris down the Mendip slopes (p. 19), brought fragments of Carboniferous Culm rocks from the 'roof' that must still have covered the Dartmoor granite. Simultaneously, Devonian quartzite and limestone detritus would also have been washed down from the western mountains to the dry basin floor. Once they became cemented these fragmental rock materials were converted into thick beds of Permo-Triassic 'concrete' known as *breccia*, and wherever these breccias outcrop between Dawlish and Exeter they form steep-sided ridges often heavily forested. Many visitors make their first aquaintance with the terracotta seacliffs from the train at Dawlish, for here the railway runs along the shoreline. The rock faces illustrate how the strata are nothing more than gigantic fossil desert sand dunes heaped up by south-easterly winds some 200 million years ago. Today's prevailing westerlies have fashioned a modern counterpart in the array of coastal dunes of Dawlish Warren. In previous centuries a double line of dunes, the Outer and Inner Warrens, were separated by a tidal creek, but twentieth-century wave erosion and tidal scour have combined to destroy the spit on which the Outer Warren stood; today only the narrow Inner Warren protects the Exe estuary from the Channel.

The broad Exe estuary extends inland for more than 10 kilometres but unlike the deepwater rias farther west that of the Exe is brim-full with muddy sediments brought down to sea level from the largest river catchment in the West Country. The gently rolling hills which flank this placid inlet have been moulded from different types of New Red Sandstone rocks. Everywhere their bright red soils bring a rosy glow to the already rich tapestry of hedged fields, ancient copses, thatched cottages and sandstone church towers in the nestling villages. The pretty settlement of Topsham, founded by the Romans at the head of the estuary, pre-dates the attractive cathedral city of Exeter itself which, like most of the east Devon towns, has a warmth of colour largely attributable to the frequent use of New Red Sandstone in the buildings. Moreover, the nearby exposures of Permian volcanic rocks are also of reddish hue (represented by the darker blocks in the city walls) and it was upon such an igneous bluff that Exeter's aptly named Rougemont Castle was raised (Tidmarsh, 1932). Furthermore, most of the modern city has been built from local bricks fired not only from red Permian clays but also from the red-stained Culm shales which form the city's northern ridge.

The sandstone hills and seacliffs around Exmouth give way eastwards to a narrow outcrop of the Budleigh Salterton Pebble Beds, the lowest member of the Trias. These massive conglomerates, composed of well-rounded, purple-coloured quartzites, were deposited by east-flowing Triassic rivers, then cemented into almost horizontal beds of sandy shingle, before subsequently being eroded into a ridge which now extends northwards to the Exeter–Sidmouth road. Like beds of similar age that form Cannock Chase in Staffordshire (see p. 142) which are equally porous, their sandy and gravelly soils are of little use for agriculture, so that their outcrop is now clothed with heathland and conifer plantations. Most of the scenic interest, however, is provided by the coastal cliffs, for here ocean waves have exposed the Pebble Beds near Budleigh's promenade. It is modern wind-scouring that has created the spectacular honeycomb weathering of the rock face but it was the wind action of Triassic deserts that faceted and polished the stones of the black pebble layer below the sandstone; wherever they have a triangular appearance such stones are termed *dreikanters* (that is, three-cornered), a sure indication of arid weathering.

Lyme Bay and the Dorset coast

From any of the coastal hills around the attractive resort of Sidmouth the great sweeping curve of Lyme Bay can be seen stretching away to its eastern termination at Portland Bill. Except for the Chalk outliers which form headlands at Beer and Seaton (Smith, 1961; 1965), this is a smooth coastline devoid of major headlands and deeply etched bays because marine erosion continues to cut relentlessly land-wards into rock strata with lithologies so similar in resistance to wave attack that they have been worn back at almost uniform rates. Furthermore, since the bedding of the sedimentary rocks is almost horizontal the landforms of east Devon and west Dorset alike are characterized by wide tablelands deeply dissected by small, south-flowing rivers, all abruptly terminated by the scimitar curve of the coastline (House, 1989). With the major exception of Chesil Beach, therefore, Lyme Bay has lengthy stretches of sea cliffs broken at rare intervals by narrow river valleys which provide the only access to the shore and the only sites for the few coastal settlements. The cliffs themselves vary in character, standing high and steep where the rocks are strong and well jointed but collapsing into jumbled landslips where the hard rocks are underlain by unstable clays (Arber, 1940).

This unspoiled tract of the Channel coast was one of the first places to be explored by the early geologists and they have described the many classic sections of its highly fossiliferous Jurassic and Cretaceous strata. Apart from its ammonite fossils, the coast is also known for the great variety of colours displayed by its flat-lying or gently tilted rock strata. The various stages in the evolution of these sedimentary rocks are explained in Fig. 3.1. In ascending age one can distinguish the vivid Red Marls of the Keuper (Trias); the black shales; the white and blue limestones of the Lias (Lower Jurassic); the yellow sands, clays and shelly lime-stones of the Middle Jurassic; the grey, green and yellow beds of the Gault Clay

Figure 3.1 Stratigraphic evolution of East Devon (after J.W. Perkins).

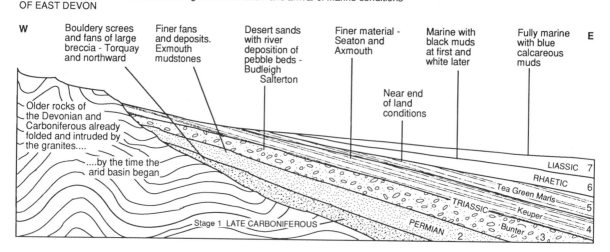

and Upper Greensand (Cretaceous); and finally, the youngest rocks of all, the dazzling white layers of the Chalk (Cretaceous). It is the interbedding of these clays, sands and limestones that has given rise to one of the most characteristic of Lyme Bay's landforms, that of its coastal landslips. While surface water can percolate through the porous limestones and sandstones it cannot pass through the thick impermeable layers of clay. Thus the overlying sandy layers are slowly washed away, thereby removing their support from the uppermost strata. Brunsden and Goudie (1981) have described several types of mass movement, including falls, slides and flows. Great tabular masses have collapsed, or slid towards the sea, carrying fields, roads and occasionally buildings down to the shore. Because some of the slipping is rotational the rock layers tilt backwards as they slide, slowly adding to the jumbled mosaic of undercliffs and chasms, especially at such nineteenth-century landslip sites as Whitlands, Dowlands and Bindon (west of Lyme Regis) and at Stonebarrow (east of Charmouth). Between these two coastal towns the Black Ven undercliffs are composed of spectacular semi-liquid mudflows rather than the blocky landslips described above. During lengthy periods of rainfall the Black Ven Marls (Lower Lias) degenerate into mudflows that move at noticeable speeds, carrying vegetation and other debris down towards the terminal lobes which project across the beach and into the sea (Fig. 3.2). Because iron pyrites are present in the Jurassic rocks the landslips occasionally cause spontaneous combustion, giving rise to reports (Arber, 1973) that Lyme Regis has its own smoking volcano!

East of Charmouth the gentle rise and fall of the dissected Dorset tablelands marks the gradual transition from the closed and tightly knit countryside of Red Devon to the open, voluptuous curves of the Wessex downlands (Taylor, 1970). Along the coastline the severed edges of the flat-bedded strata build such yellow-topped eminences as Golden Cap and Thorncombe Beacon, where tiny outliers of Upper Greensand sit upon horizontal Jurassic rocks. The few coastal inlets are marked by such settlements as Seatown and West Bay (Bridport Harbour) before the sea cliffs dwindle away eastwards near to Burton Bradstock (Ager and Smith, 1965). Not only does West Bay mark the beginning of the coastal exposures of Dorset's famous oolitic limestones (see pp. 107–8) but it is also the starting point of one of Britain's most spectacular shingle beaches, the remarkable Chesil Beach. Running for 29 kilometres in a smoothly graded arc, the shingle ridge first hugs the shore, then encloses a long brackish lagoon known as the Fleet, before striking across the open sea to link the Isle of Portland with the mainland. As it is traced eastwards both its height and width increase until at Chesilton it is 14 metres high and 183 metres wide. Its flinty pebbles (derived primarily from the Chalk but probably reworked in Eocene and later times) also show a uniform increase in size from west to east, grading up from pea size at West Bay to long diameter of 40 millimetres at Chesilton (Carr and Blackley, 1973). Because of its regular grading it is claimed that local fishermen, fog-bound or benighted, can make a landfall and tell precisely where they are. There are many theories to explain the beach's symmetrical line and its uniform change of pebble size but the most acceptable is that which explains it as a fossil barrier beach formed by the post-glacial rise of sea level since when no new material has been added or subtracted. Pebbles move along the beach in both directions, but because of the prevailing westerlies and therefore the dominant longshore drift, the main movement is eastwards, thereby explaining the increasing dimensions in that direction. The Portland cliffs not only

Figure 3.2 Black Ven
landslip, Dorset. Upper
Greensand (Cretaceous) rocks
have slumped seawards on an
unstable mass of underlying
Liassic shales and clays (Black
Ven Marls).

act as a gigantic groyne but add some local cherts and limestones to the shingle
at the eastern end (Fig. 3.3). A similar pebble beach linking Portland to Weymouth
is composed almost entirely of limestone shingle. The Isle of Portland, described
by Hardy as 'a Peninsula carved by Time out of a single stone', is a treeless, barren
place, pockmarked with quarries as a testimony to the quality of its sparkling
white limestone (Portland Stone), chosen by Wren to rebuild some of London's
most historic edifices after the Great Fire of 1666. The highly prized beds of freestone (2 metres thick and known as the Whitbed and the Basebed) are overlain by
the less valuable shelly limestone (the Roach) which, because of its uneven texture
and shell casts, is unsuitable for carving. Nevertheless, the Roach's unyielding
stone has helped build the sturdy harbour walls at Portsmouth and Portland naval
bases in addition to the well-known Cobb at Lyme Regis. Portland Bill itself is one
of Britain's best examples of a raised beach dating from the last (Ipswichian)
interglacial some 120 000 years ago.

The Isle of Portland is the gently dipping southern limb of an anticline the arch
of which has been eroded to reveal the core of older Jurassic rocks (House, 1961).
The least resistant of these, the Oxford Clay, has been worn down into a low vale
now occupied by Weymouth and partly submerged beneath Weymouth Bay

(Brookfield, 1978). Such easily eroded clays parallel the coast as far as Osmington Mills where, earlier this century, the dark, crumbly, shaly cliffs were the scene of one of Britain's greatest mudflows. A supersaturated mass of Gault Clay burst through a narrow band of harder Jurassic rocks and poured like a lava flow down to the seashore. East of here, however, the coastal scenery takes on the grandeur imposed by tougher strata, especially by those of the omnipresent Chalk whose undulating surface contours reach the coast at several places in the so-called Isle of Purbeck, a geological if not a topographical island. The same Alpine folding which threw up the Weymouth anticline also folded the Jurassic and Cretaceous rocks of Purbeck and nowhere are these outer ripples of the Alpine storm better displayed than on this attractive stretch of the Channel coast. The northern limit of the 'isle' is the chalk ridge running from the great coastal precipice of White Nothe in the west to Old Harry Rocks in the east (see Fig. 3.4). The ridge of almost vertically dipping chalk strata is known as a hog's back, in which dipslope and scarp face are of comparable steepness (see p. 75); in places the neighbouring Jurassic beds have also been upended by the ancient paroxysm to create a wonderful array of coastal landforms (Phillips, 1964). Figure 3.4 illustrates how the more resistant Portland and Purbeck limestones form an almost horizontal plateau to the south of Swanage Bay. It also shows how their northern extremities have been bent vertically downwards by the folding before disappearing beneath the

Figure 3.3 Chesil Beach, Dorset, looking westwards from the cliffs of the Isle of Portland.

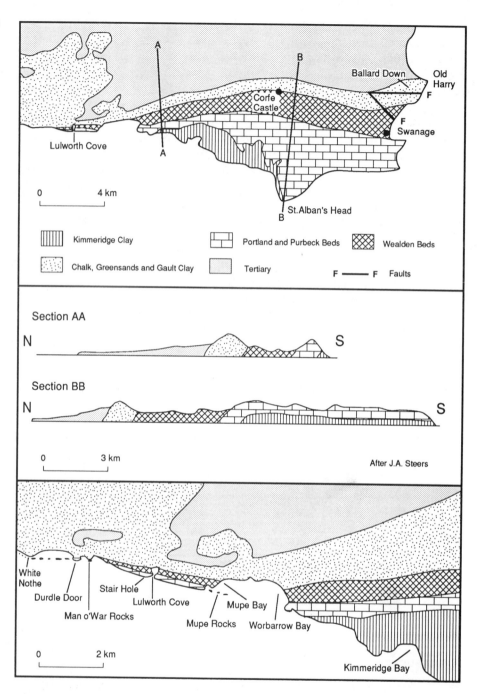

Figure 3.4 Geology of the Dorset coast at the Isle of Purbeck.

Wealden Clay vale in which Swanage is located. As these fold structures are traced westwards through Worbarrow Bay and Lulworth Cove, the horizontal Purbeck plateau element disappears and only the narrow vertical limestone element survives (often referred to as the 'barrier'). Even this decreases in width until its outcrop is finally pinched out near Durdle Door.

Below the 150 metre bastion of White Nothe, where grassy downlands tower above beating waves, the hard chalk of Bat's Head has been penetrated to form the arch of Bat's Hole. Nearby, the westernmost tiny remnant of the Portland Stone 'barrier' appears seaward of the chalk downs, whittled away to leave only the Cow and Calf sea stacks. Beyond the dazzling chalk cliff of Swyre Head there are many examples of the way in which waves have breached the 'barrier' and made short work of the Wealden sands and clays in its rear. Nowhere is this more clearly illustrated than behind the 'barrier' of Man o' War Rocks and, more notably, next to Durdle Door's marine arch. Where the Portland/Purbeck 'barrier' establishes itself onshore in St Oswald's Bay its outcrop widens until Stair Hole is reached. Here, in this much photographed Alpine crumple, the sea has only just breached the 'barrier' and is beginning to attack the less resistant rocks (Fig. 3.5). A more advanced stage of breaching has occurred at Lulworth where the gap is wider and the penetration deeper; waves have already scooped out the Wealden Beds to create the curving symmetry of the Cove itself and are now picking at the base of the chalk cliff. To the east, Mupe Bay and Worbarrow Bay are two larger versions of Lulworth Cove that have coalesced to form one wider bay, with the stacks of Mupe Rocks continuing the line of the limestone 'barrier'. The entire coastal stretch between Worbarrow Tout and St Aldhelm's Head is composed of almost horizontal beds of alternating dark shales and thin limestones known as the Kimmeridge Clays. Where the smooth limestones extend seawards from the foot of the low vertical cliffs they form the flat slabs of the Kimmeridge Ledges. Despite

Figure 3.5 Stair Hole, Lulworth Cove, Dorset. Folding of Alpine age in rocks of Portland and Purbeck (Upper Jurassic) age.

their name these are not true clay cliffs, although there are some signs of slipping and undercliff formation. The tougher Portland and Purbeck beds stand more than a kilometre inland where their plateau edge forms an encircling escarpment.

The south-eastern corner of Purbeck's coastal plateau is built chiefly from gently inclined limestones descending southwards to form the cliffs between St Aldhelm's Head and Durlston Head. Down at sea level the chert beds of the Portland formation build the flat, wave-washed slabs of Dancing Ledge, while the overlying Purbeck Limestone of the plateau top has been disfigured by centuries of sporadic quarrying. This tough, almost black, freshwater limestone of Wealden age, characterized by a jumbled fossil assemblage of freshwater snails, is much sought after for its ability to take a good polish. Resembling metamorphic marble in its appearance, the dark Purbeck stone has been extensively employed in the interior decoration of churches throughout southern Britain. Other less fossiliferous and less valuable Purbeck limestones help build the grey stone villages of the Isle, but because of the thin stony soils and lack of access to the sea on this rockbound coast, Purbeck has neither a flourishing agricultural nor a fishing economy. It remains, therefore, a relatively unpeopled wilderness known mainly to soldiers exercising on its deserted hills or to tourists tramping its coastal path. Since Purbeck's eastern coast is cut across the strike of the rocks rather than running parallel with it, the scenery changes from a linear shoreline to a corrugated one of hard rock headlands alternating with bays carved from the less resistant beds. North of the quarries of Tilly Whim Caves the resistant Upper Purbeck limestones project as Peveril Point while, more impressively, the eastern end of Purbeck's chalk spine is sharply truncated by the sea at Handfast Point. The faulted and upended chalk strata have been spectacularly worn by waves into the cave of Parson's Barn and the partly tumbled sea stacks of Old Harry and his Wife. The sliver of chalk known as the Foreland also became detached from the mainland at the turn of the century and clearly demonstrates the stages of sea stack formation. Between the two hard rock series described above the tract of country occupied by the less resistant Wealden sands and clays has been denuded into a vale in which the holiday resort of Swanage has developed in the sheltered eastern bay.

Dorset is Thomas Hardy country and every landscape is redolent with memories of the great regional novelist (Benfield, 1950). This is particularly true of the remaining stretches of the Dorset Heaths ('Egdon Heath') which flourish on the podsols of the Tertiary clays, sands and gravels between Bournemouth and Dorchester ('Casterbridge'), a foretaste of the scenery of the extensive Hampshire Basin. The same tectonic episode that crumpled the Dorset coastal rocks also affected the deeper underlying strata, creating fold structures in which oil has accumulated beneath southern England. Thus, the solitude of the Wessex heaths, captured so graphically by Hardy, has now been broken by the paraphernalia of Britain's largest onshore oilfield at Wytch Farm to the south of Poole Harbour. Though screened by conifers, the oilfield development contrasts starkly with the unspoiled tracts of heather and gorse, the thickly wooded islands of Poole Harbour and with the far-spreading marshlands along the Frome valley, guarded by the old Saxon town of Wareham with its causewayed approach. The drowned river estuary of the Frome, which flows along the axis of the synclinal basin, is part of a formerly extensive east-flowing drainage system (known as the 'Solent River') to be described below (p. 51). Today, Poole Harbour's drowned landscape illustrates how its sandy knolls have been converted into islands while the dales and dingles of the former river valley have been transformed into an intricate coastline as sea level gradually rose in post-glacial times. The water body itself is sheltered from the open sea by the opposing sandspits of Sandbanks and South Haven peninsula, each having grown by longshore drift in opposite directions but which have been kept apart at the narrow entrance by tidal scour. Though the Sandbanks spit has now been built over, the southern peninsula of Studland has retained most of its earlier heathland character and its rare fauna. Behind the curving sandy beach of Studland Bay a series of dune ridges has slowly enclosed a once-tidal lagoon known as the Little Sea. Projecting above the wilderness of Studland Heath two massive rocks, the Agglestone and the Puckstone, provide good viewpoints of the area. They were formed from remnants of cemented Eocene sands, similar in character to the sarsens of the chalklands (see p. 60), and were not, as local legend proclaims, thrown by a giant from the Isle of Wight in an attempt to demolish Corfe Castle! The latter stronghold, however, is certainly in a ruinous state, perched on its steep isolated hill above the grey stone village of Corfe and sited to protect the narrow gap in Purbeck's chalk ridge. This water gap was formed by a major north-flowing tributary to the erstwhile 'Solent River' (p. 52).

The Hampshire Basin and the Isle of Wight

Several writers have described the Hampshire Basin as resembling a partly flooded London Basin, and in so far as both contain great thicknesses of Britain's youngest solid rocks (those of Tertiary age) this is partly true. But there the resemblance ends, for not only is the Hampshire Basin much deeper, containing Tertiary rocks some 3000 metres thick, but the Hampshire rocks have also been more severely folded than their London counterparts. Moreover, Hampshire and the Isle of Wight possess significant exposures of Oligocene beds, missing from the London Basin (Melville and Freshney, 1982). A final contrast is provided by the character and extent of the sediments in the two basins: while the Hampshire Basin has few exposures of London Clay but vast tracts of sandier Barton and Bracklesham Beds, the London Basin's ubiquitous heavy claylands have less extensive drier patches of sandy and gravelly beds (locally represented, as shown in Chapter 4, by the Reading and Thanet Beds, Blackheath and Woolwich Series and the Bagshot Sands). Such geological contrasts, not surprisingly, have given rise to very different soil and vegetation patterns in the two basins; rarely are the forested and heathery landscapes of Hampshire replicated in London's hinterland.

Chalk downlands provide an upturned rim of hill country around the perimeter of Hampshire's low-lying expanse of Tertiary clays and sands. Although these northern and western perimeter downlands remain virtually unbroken in the great arc of Chalk that extends from Purbeck through Cranbourne Chase, Salisbury and Winchester to Bognor Regis, the same cannot be said of the southern rim of the basin. Here the sea has breached the tightly folded chalk ridge between Old Harry Rocks and the Needles and again between Bognor Regis and the eastern tip of the Isle of Wight. What was once a major east-flowing river (the 'Solent River'), rising on the Dartmoor granite and debouching somewhere near to the present Selsey Bill into shallow Palaeogene seas, has had its ancient valley subsequently inundated by a more modern marine incursion (the Flandrian) (Everard, 1954).

Today, Poole Harbour, Bournemouth Bay, the Solent and Spithead mark the line of the former trunk stream, with Southampton Water now occupying one of its main left-bank tributary valleys (Fig. 3.6) (Hodson and West, 1972). From this reconstruction it is possible to explain the otherwise anomalous north-flowing drainage patterns of both the Isle of Purbeck and the Isle of Wight, all of whose streams break through the main chalk ridge in deep gorge-like valleys, simply because they were once right-bank tributaries of a long-dismembered river system.

The earth movements of Tertiary times not only folded the sedimentary rocks of southern England but also led to protracted periods of uplift related to the opening of the Atlantic Ocean. Such spasmodic episodes meant that the history of deposition in the Hampshire Basin (and also in the London Basin) is a constantly changing record of marine, deltaic, estuarine and fluviatile environments in response to the fluctuating coastline as the base level changed. Periods of uplift saw the sea retreat and fluviatile (freshwater) beds predominate; conversely, during times of crustal sinking the seas would have advanced inland, thereby laying down varying thicknesses of fine-grained marine sediment. Such episodic deposition has ultimately created interdigitating wedges of contrasting sedimentary rocks (Fig. 3.7). In the Hampshire Basin this means that fluviatile and deltaic deposits (the coarser, sandier strata), having been brought by western rivers, are more common in the west, while marine deposits (the finer clay beds) predominate farther east, nearer to the open seas of the time (Curry, 1965). An examination of the coastal cliffs between Poole Harbour and Southampton Water shows how the rocks reflect these changing palaeoenvironments (Curry and Wisden, 1958).

Figure 3.6 Evolution of the 'Solent River'

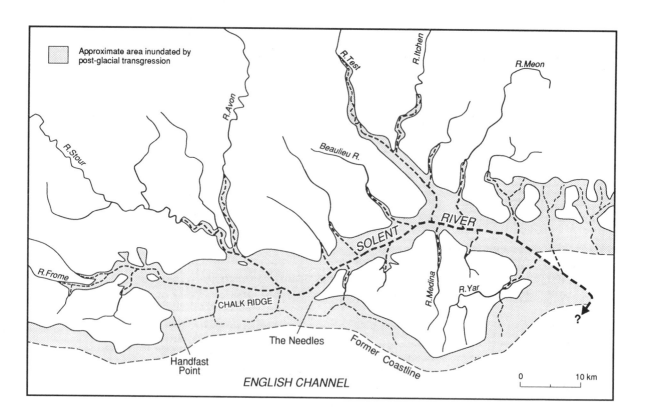

HAMPSHIRE BASIN

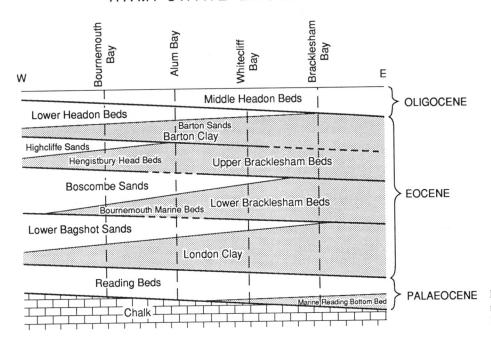

Figure 3.7 Stratigraphic relationship of the Hampshire Basin sediments.

First, in the west, the pebbly deltaic Bagshot Sands of Canford Cliffs (with some pebbles having been derived from Dartmoor) are replaced at Bournemouth by a mixed assemblage of part marine, part freshwater Bournemouth Marine Beds and Boscombe Sands (Lower Bracklesham), then by the marine Hengistbury Head Beds (Upper Bracklesham) which outcrop farther east (Curry *et al.*, 1977), and finally, to the east of Christchurch, by the mainly marine Barton Beds (Clays and Sands) (Curry *et al.*, 1977). As one approaches Milford-on-Sea all these gently dipping strata pass beneath even younger Oligocene rocks that exemplify both fresh and brackish water palaeoenvironments. The latter strata, termed the Bembridge Limestone and Marl and the Headon Beds, occur in the northern half of the Isle of Wight and in the southern area of the New Forest where the Tertiary strata achieve their greatest thickness near the southern edges of the Hampshire Basin.

Such geological contrasts explain the different character of the soils and vegetation in the Wessex region; why heathlands occur between Poole and Wimborne (Bury, 1933), why pines flourish on the sandy coastal cliffs and why oak and hazel thrive on the damper Oligocene and Eocene clays of the New Forest and in the Forest of Bere where London Clay predominates to the north of Portsmouth. Of the original broadleaf woodland only a small proportion now survives in the New Forest but its economic value has never recovered from the centuries of felling when its oaks were required for shipbuilding at such places as Lymington and Bucklers Hard on the Beaulieu River. Despite its new plantations about one-third of the New Forest is little more than a tangle of scrubby heath, where wild ponies graze the sward between bracken-infested clumps of gorse and broom (Copley *et al.*, 1966). It has changed little since Cobbett denigrated it: 'a poorer spot than this New Forest, there is not in all England'. The sandy, gravelly and boggy tracts of the New Forest have always been of little agricultural value so that farming settlements are sparse away from the coast. Those that do exist occupy ancient clearings in the forest probably dating back to the time when William I brought the area under Forest Law to provide the Crown with facilities for hunting; two-thirds of the Forest remains Crown land today. Not far from this wilderness lies the bustling port of Southampton and its multi-tidal estuary at the junction of the Itchen and Test rivers (Monkhouse, 1964).

To the east of Southampton Water the simple structure of the Hamsphire Basin has been complicated by a major anticline that has thrown up a ridge of chalk between the coast and the Tertiary clays in the downfold of the Chichester-Romsey syncline (Martin, 1938). The chalk ridge of Portsdown (Fig. 3.8), just over a kilometre wide, rises steeply above the drowned sections of the coastal plain where the sea has bitten deeply into the soft London Clay tract west of Bognor Regis to create the sheltered anchorages of Portsmouth, Langstone and Chichester harbours (Venables, 1962). These are places of tidal channels among reed-fringed mudflats, of wide horizons and deserted backwaters – all except Portsmouth with its clamourous dockyard. The inundation that flooded these inlets must also have been the one that isolated the Isle of Wight, flooded the 'Solent River' and invaded the lower reaches of the Test and Itchen estuaries to create the deep-water channel that serves Southampton. Other south-flowing (left-bank) tributaries of the ancient 'Solent River', such as the Beaulieu, Avon and Stour, have not been drowned to the same degree, while the rivers which formerly occupied the Bournemouth chines have had most of their lower courses destroyed by the rapidly receding cliffline of Bournemouth Bay. Waves were cutting back these sandy cliffs at about 1 metre per year until recent cliff-foot protective measures have succeeded in checking the retreat, just before Hengistbury Head becomes an island. In recent centuries many of the coastal irregularities created by the post-glacial marine transgression (Flandrian) have been smoothed out by the predominantly eastward drift of beach material. Small shingle spits have built up not only on the Hampshire coast at the mouth of the Beaulieu River, at Calshot (Hurst Castle Spit) and east of Selsey Bill at Pagham Harbour, which is backed by a raised beach dating from the Ipswichian Interglacial (Hodgson, 1964) (see Figure 5.1), but also at Yarmouth and Newtown Bay on the Isle of Wight.

The landscapes of the Isle of Wight 'for the most part are meddows and good downs'. So wrote Celia Fiennes in the late seventeenth century and little has changed in the intervening years (Vesey-Fitzgerald, 1949). The small enclosed fields and copses have survived both on the Oligocene clays of the north and on the Lower Greensand and Wealden Beds farther south, while the central chalk ridge and the high chalk plateau above Ventnor still support broad stretches of sheep-grazed downland. The lozenge-shaped island is neatly divided into two contrasting areas by the narrow hogsback ridge of chalk which runs from the sea stacks of the Needles eastwards to the majestic Culver Cliff. In most places on this central ridge the entire 460 metre thickness of the Chalk is represented by an outcrop no more than 800 metres wide because of the near-verticality of its beds (Fig. 3.8). Only near the middle of the island, to the west of Carisbrooke, does the central chalk exposure broaden to a width of almost 5 kilometres because here the dip is gentler. It is also here, at Brightstone Downs, that the central ridge achieves its highest elevation (213 m) and exhibits a deeply dissected network of dry valleys (see p. 59). Westwards the ridge narrows towards Freshwater as its beds again

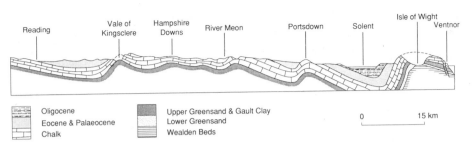

Oligocene
Eocene & Palaeocene
Chalk

Upper Greensand & Gault Clay
Lower Greensand
Wealden Beds

0   15 km

Figure 3.8 Geological section of the Hampshire chalk and the Isle of Wight.

become almost vertical; the upended strata have been carved by waves into a precipice at Tennyson Down and into the spectacular pinnacles of the Needles (Fig. 3.9). From this splendid viewpoint it is manifestly clear that the island's backbone is a continuation of the chalk ridge of Purbeck, itself sharply truncated at Old Harry Rocks. Moreover, one can more fully appreciate the extent to which the waves have exploited the softer Tertiary rocks of Bournemouth Bay once this chalk ridge, in effect the southern watershed of the 'Solent River' basin, had been breached (see Fig. 3.6).

The oldest of the Tertiary rocks of the Hampshire Basin lie immediately to the north of the Isle of Wight's chalk spine and have, therefore, been caught up in the major Alpine fold of the Purbeck–Wight structural axis. Thus, these beds have also been upended and at two well-known sections on the island's west and east coasts, at Alum Bay and Whitecliff Bay, respectively, the geological succession is exposed in two classic coastal sections (Curry *et al*., 1966). That at Alum Bay, next to the Needles, is the best known, particularly for the way in which the brillliant colours of the various sands and clays contrast with the dazzling chalk cliffs. Here

Figure 3.9 The marine-eroded stacks of the Needles, Isle of Wight, carved from beds of upended chalk. Alum Bay is on the left of the photograph.

the entire Lower Tertiary succession of Reading Beds, London Clay, Bagshot Sands, Bracklesham Beds and Barton Clay has been stood on end and squeezed into a length of a mere 500 metres of sea cliff along this southern perimeter of the Hampshire Basin. It is worth noting, at this juncture, that because the Alpine folding is more severe along its southern rather than its northern margins the Hampshire Basin is markedly asymmetrical, causing its steepest dips and thickest Tertiary succession to occur beneath the Isle of Wight (See Fig. 3.8). It will be shown in Chapter 4 how the London Basin has a similar asymmetrical structure for the same reasons.

A visitor to either Alum Bay or Whitecliff Bay cannot fail to notice that as the brightly coloured sand and clay layers are traced northwards the strata are bent back from the vertical to the horizontal. At Alum Bay the uppermost of the flat-lying beds are the blue-green sands and clays of the Headon Beds while at Whitecliff Bay the horizontal capping is of multi-coloured Bembridge Marls. A persistent layer within this Oligocene succession of the northern coast is the thin Bembridge Limestone, hard enough to create prominent coastal ledges at Hamstead, Gurnard Bay and Thorness Bay. Its main contribution in earlier centuries, however, was as a building stone. Quarried mainly at Quarr near East Cowes this shelly limestone (likened, in its durability, to the Caen Stone of Normandy) was used extensively in medieval times, not only on the island but also in the construction of Chichester and Winchester cathedrals. Most of the more recent housing in the island has been of brick as the Oligocene rocks contain some valuable brick clays. The same fairly uniform clays have been fashioned by the elements into the rather featureless scenery of the northern part of the island. The heavy clay soils support mainly parkland and permanent grassland though there are numerous copses and woodlands, of which Parkhurst Forest is the most extensive. Here, too, are the island's ports, sited on the sheltered harbours facing the mainland; the exposed cliff-girt southern coast, by contrast, is almost devoid of urban settlement, except around Ventnor.

The southern half of the island is altogether more varied both in its geology and its topography, partly due to the reappearance of the Chalk near the southernmost coastline. The villages of this attractive countryside are also more appealing and have remained relatively unspoiled by excessive new development. Godshill and Brightstone, with their thatched limestone cottages, vie with each other for the title of the prettiest village but both nestle in the central vale among the patchwork of arable fields distinguished by their reddish-brown soils. This fertile lowland has been carved from the less resistant Wealden Beds, Gault Clay and both the Greensands (Fig. 3.8). Its subdued contours are abruptly terminated in the north by the hogsback chalk ridge and are sheltered from the south by the north-facing scarp of the southern chalk downs which, at St Boniface Down, create the highest point of the island (235 m). The breached anticlinal structure of this central vale is often compared to that of the Weald (see Chapter 4) although it has much steeper dipping strata on its northern fringes and gentler dips along its southern margins than the true Weald. Both ends of the vale are open to the sea; its western cliffs are scarred by landslips in the unstable Atherfield Clay (Lower Greensand) while Sandown Bay in the east has yellowish-green exposures of Wealden Clays near Culver Cliff and bright red Sandrock and Carstone cliffs of Lower Greensand at Shanklin. Farther south, between Bonchurch and St Catherine's Point, the presence of the Gault Clay has resulted in a coastline of jumbled landslides and undercliffs not unlike those of Lyme Bay (p. 45) (Barber, 1987). Because of the gentle southerly dip there is a continuing tendency for the overlying Chalk and Upper Greensand to slide seawards across the Gault, causing constant damage to roads and property. Yet the collapsed undercliff around Ventnor, with its subtropical vegetation and mild climate, is regarded by many as Britain's answer to the Côte d'Azur.

A final word is needed to explain the island's anomalous drainage pattern. All the main rivers rise not far from the southern coast and flow northwards by means of deep gaps in the central chalk ridge before emptying into the Solent or Spithead. The north-flowing drainage pattern is, therefore, an ancient one, related to the early Tertiary 'Solent River' (see Fig. 3.6) and has survived the uplift and folding of the Alpine orogeny by maintaining a rate of downcutting that has kept pace with the tectonic uplift of the fold axes across its direction of flow. Such a phenomenon is termed *antecedent drainage* (Hutchinson, 1982) and further examples will be described in Chapter 4. The main consequent river direction in the Isle of Wight was established on the dominantly northerly dip of the island's rocks and clearly pre-dates the erosion of the central vale. Moreover, both the Western Yar and the Eastern Yar must once have risen some distance to the south of the present coastline. Marine erosion, therefore, must have destroyed large areas of land to the south of the island's southern shore after these rivers had carved their present valleys, for both have lost their headwaters. Only a slight rise of sea level would be needed to flood right through the Western Yar valley, while it is manifest that the Eastern Yar has also been severely truncated near Sandown. Only the Medina, rising on the southern chalk hills, appears not to have suffered in this respect. Because of its long north-flowing elements the island's drainage pattern is very asymmetrical (like that in Devon) for the island's watershed lies very close to the south coast. The short south-flowing streams, rising in the high chalk hills, drop steeply to the shoreline and because of their steep gradients have succeeded in cutting deep ravines known as chines. At Shanklin the waters cascade almost 100 metres down a thickly wooded gorge while at Blackgang the ravine has been cut through black shales below the Sandrock and Carstone.

The chalklands

Except at the coasts the chalklands rarely exhibit exposures of bare rock, yet they retain a very special place in Britain's scenic heritage. It has been suggested that there is nothing so quintessentially English as a downland speckled with grazing sheep, possibly because it unlocks feelings of a long-lost rural domesticity based on mutton and wool. For centuries writers have been inspired by the unploughed elemental simplicity of turf-covered downs with their wide open skies and limitless views (Whitlock, 1955). They rarely thought of chalkland scenery as being romantic or picturesque yet wrote of the downs with homespun affection, where rustic simplicity and solitude added to the pleasures of the view. In the seventeenth century John Aubrey found 'the turf is of a good shorte sweet grasse, good for the sheep, and delightful to the eye', while even the over-critical Cobbett was delighted with the Itchen valley at Winchester, whose countryside he found 'very beautifully disposed'. Wherever the pale chalk soils are barely covered by a springy turf the unwooded downlands exhibit a spaciousness, a sense of lightness and a delicacy of colouring rarely encountered in other British landscapes. Eighteenth-century 'improvers' discovered that in many of the chalklands the slopes were so gentle that they found it necessary to plant clumps of beech trees on some hilltops, simply to diversify the scene. Chanctonbury Rings, on the South Downs, is one of the best-known examples (Brandon, 1974).

Today, with changes in agricultural practices, many of the sheep have gone, replaced by hedgeless prairies of corn, but in becoming some of Britain's foremost granaries they have lost the ethos which once made the grassy downlands unique. Traditionally, most authors have accepted the view that the chalk grasslands were a product of Neolithic settlers' forest clearance. Recent research, however, suggests that chalk grassland has persisted since the end of the Ice Age even through the forest periods of the Pre-Boreal and the Boreal. Nowadays, it is only in winter when the plough has turned the soil, brought up the broken flints and exposed the naked chalk on lean-soiled hillslopes that the downlands recapture something of their former scenic glory. Nevertheless, all these are idealized visions, typical only of those areas where the Chalk has little or no superficial cover, notably Salisbury Plain and parts of the South Downs. Elsewhere, when thick layers of plateau gravels or clay-with-flints mantle the surface, as in the Chilterns, the chalklands exhibit very different patterns of vegetation and land use. Landscapes are also rather different in eastern England where they carry a thick covering of glacial material.

The Chalk is not only the whitest and purest of the limestones but also the softest and most porous. The Upper Cretaceous seas must once have covered most of Britain, with a coastline somewhere near the Outer Hebrides. Thus, far removed from the source of coarse sandy materials, the chalk sediments of England accumulated in clear waters in the form of thick, almost horizontal sheets of calcium carbonate derived from finely broken marine shells. Although appearing to be uniform in character the Chalk possesses three relatively hard beds, all of which are tough enough to have been used as building stone. This is one of the reasons why the Chalk is capable of forming steep slopes (Small, 1961), but one might be forgiven for enquiring why such a relatively soft rock is able to build hill country rising to 300 metres in elevation. The answer lies largely in its porosity, for any rainfall sinks rapidly through the strata and leaves virtually no water available to aid river erosion at the surface. Unlike the massively bedded mountain limestones of the Mendips or the north Pennines, however, the Chalk lacks extensive networks of underground stream passages and instead exhibits the properties of an enormous sponge. All the percolating ground water either passes in the direction of any outflow, such as a spring or, alternatively, accumulates in the fissures and pores of the rock layers until it forms a gigantic underground reservoir held on an impermeable base of underlying clays. Such a reservoir is termed an *aquifer*, the uppermost level of which (the water table) rises and falls in accordance with the seasonal precipitation on the land surface. Owing to the time taken for ground water to pass through the 'pores' of the Chalk there is usually a time-lag between periods of heavy rainfall and rises in the height of the water table. These fluctuations will obviously have important effects on stream flow and therefore on the presence or absence of permanent settlement on the dry downlands. In most years the bulk of Britain's precipitation falls in winter, causing the hidden water table to rise until in places it reaches the deeper valley floors of the chalklands. These are the localities where seasonal streams, known as 'bournes', flow at the surface, giving rise to the widespread occurrence of the name Winterbourne. Conversely, when the water table falls during the drier summers, the ephemeral bourne flow ceases and the downland villages must rely once more on deep wells for their water supply. Bourne flows and most chalk rivers are characterized by crystal clear waters, a measure of the dearth of clay sediments available to be transported by the downland streams.

Despite the generally waterless nature of the downlands, they are patterned by a remarkably integrated network of valleys, none of which seems ever to be occupied by surface streams, not even by bournes. These are the anomalous dry valleys of the Chalk, phenomena which add a further dimension to the billowing hills and fluted hollows of the downs. Although some major permanent rivers, such as the Thames and those of the Weald, rise on older rocks before crossing the surface outcrop of the Chalk, it has long been difficult to explain the origin of the dry valley network (Sparks and Lewis, 1957). One ingenious explanation is based on a theory of scarp recession, as illustrated in Fig. 3.10. As the scarp is cut back the adjoining vale is simultaneously lowered, causing an associated fall in the height of the springline at the junction of the Chalk with its underlying impervious beds; this in turn depresses the water table and leaves the valleys dry. Alternative explanations depend on changes of climate. The first necessitates a considerably higher rainfall which meant a permanently high water table and perennial rivers, possibly during the more tropical climates that prevailed in Britain several million years ago. The most popular view, however, suggests that the dry valley network was initiated during the Pleistocene Ice Age when the subterranean water of the Chalk's 'sponge' was permanently frozen into so-called permafrost, similar to that of modern Arctic Canada. When the water from seasonal snowmelt was unable to soak down into the rocks it would have been forced to flow across the surface where its streams would have channelled the Chalk. Enormous spreads of hilltop flint gravels were washed down the resulting valleys where they mixed with finer materials that had been sludged, by solifluction, down the hill slopes under this so-called periglacial climate. Fans of these deposits, known as *coombe rock*, can be identified at many scarp-foot sites, at valley mouths and in coastal sea cliffs, such as that at Black Rock, Brighton, where ocean waves have cross-sectioned a dry valley, uncovered a 'fossil' cliff and exposed a buried raised beach probably of last interglacial age similar to that at Selsey (see p. 54).

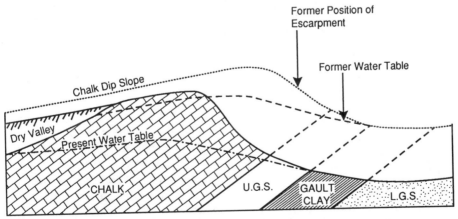

Figure 3.10 Hypothesis explaining the evolution of dry valleys in the chalklands (after C.C. Fagg).

Though at the time of its deposition the Chalk was laid down in almost level sheets of great extent, these have been caught up to a greater or lesser degree by the Alpine folding which affected southern Britain. Furthermore, tectonic uplift occurred simultaneously with this late period of mountain-building as a type of crustal compensation associated with the opening of the Atlantic. One major result has been the gradual tilting of Britain: the north and west have been uplifted and the North Sea basin has gradually subsided. This not only caused the chalk cover to be eroded from the uplands, where it now survives only in a few areas of western Scotland (see Chapter 16) but also led to the gradual wearing back of the chalklands until the main chalk escarpment now stands well back from the British uplands. Its alignment closely follows that of the other English scarplands, roughly from north-east to south-west, and reflects the regional dip of lowland Britain in a direction to the east and south-east. It can now be understood why Britain's major rivers still flow from west to east, because they followed the general tilt of the strata.

The folding of the chalklands had already begun before the Tertiary rocks of the London and Hampshire Basins were laid down, for it is known that a great deal of erosion had already taken place on the gently tilted chalk surface before the Palaeocene and Eocene rocks were deposited unconformably upon them. It was from this eroded surface, still buried over wide areas by layers of Reading, Thanet, Blackheath and Woolwich Beds, that most of the southern chalklands have been carved. In many places this partly buried chalk surface (the so-called sub-Palaeocene surface) can be seen emerging from beneath the overlying Tertiary sands and clays (Jones, 1980). Eroded remnants of the latter sediments still survive as outliers that form tiny hillocks high up on the stripped surface of the downlands, serving not only as a reminder of the former extent of the Palaeocene and Eocene cover rocks but also as settlement sites where artificial ponds can be retained on the clays. Under the tropical climates that prevailed in Britain at the time of their formation some of these residual sands and gravels became cemented by silica into a concrete-like crust across the downland summits (Summerfield and Goudie, 1980). This hard capping, similar to the 'duricrusts' of tropical Africa, was not broken up until frost action and river erosion, during the permafrost climate of the Ice Age, saw the tough siliceous sandstone layer disintegrate into a scattering of boulders termed *sarsens* (derived from 'saracen', meaning a dark stranger). The equally hard cemented gravel layers have also weathered into similar boulders known as Pudding Stones. Solifluction has carried most of these scattered blocks down the slopes and along the valley floors where they can still be seen as 'boulder trains' at places such as Clatford Bottom, Wiltshire (Small *et al.*, 1970) (Fig. 3.11). In a countryside lacking good building stone many sarsens (locally termed 'greywethers' because of their resemblance to sheep) have been cleared from the fields to be incorporated in buildings as cornerstones and lintels. More importantly, they were used by prehistoric man to construct his ritualistic structures at Stonehenge and Avebury whose monolithic stone circles give landmarks of a different character to those of the gentle chalk scenery. But of far greater significance than the sarsens was another hard material associated with the Chalk – a black or brown, glassy-textured stone known as *flint*. Flint has exercised more influence on early human history than almost any other stone in Europe, so it is important to know something of its character and its origin (Shepherd, 1972).

Flints occur as pillow-like nodules or as thin layers arranged along the Chalk's bedding planes and because of their remarkable hardness will survive long after the Chalk itself has been weathered away. When the residual flints become mixed with early Tertiary clays on the stripped Palaeocene land surface they form a stony superficial covering known as 'clay-with-flints', and wherever this 'clay cap' occurs it creates areas of damp heavy soils amongst the generally free-draining chalklands (Hodgson *et al.*, 1967). Flints are composed entirely of silica derived from the skeletons of sponges which lived in the Chalk seas and which were once disseminated as small particles throughout the mass of chalk. The silica became concentrated into layers only when the Chalk was uplifted above sea level. Once prehistoric man had discovered the art of flaking and chipping (knapping) flint into a great variety of sharp-edged tools and weapons he was able to make substantial advances in his technology that led in due course to the first agricultural revolution of Neolithic times. So valuable were the flints that they were intensively mined from underground chambers on the South Downs of Sussex and at Grimes Graves in Norfolk. From there they were taken along ancient tracks or ridgeways on the grassy chalk ridges, high above the impenetrable forests of the clay vales, to meet the needs of the early downland settlers. Some of these early farmers worked the thin pallid soils of Salisbury Plain which, because of its central location, became the focus of Britain's earliest organized society. From this node of the Wessex chalklands, chalk ridges extend to the coasts of Dorset, Norfolk, Kent and Sussex. Because the North and South Downs are both structurally and

Figure 3.11 Sarsen-filled dry valley in the chalklands. Clatford Bottom, Marlborough Downs.

geographically linked with the Weald and the London Basin they will be examined in Chapter 4.

The Wessex chalk

Salisbury Plain, with its rolling hills and deep valleys, is undoubtedly the cradle of British civilization. Its wide, empty, undulating downland is today a vast grave-yard of prehistoric chieftains, a mosaic of ancient fields and a jigsaw of primitive village remnants. Farther north on the Marlborough Downs the burial chambers of Silbury Hill and the West Kennet long-barrow exemplify the prodigious labour requirements of those times. Many centuries later, when primitive man had dis-covered how his bronze and iron tools could more easily clear the scrub and forest of the lower valleys and vales, the waterless hill country became gradually aban-doned. In their turn, later invaders, known as the West Saxons, who gave their name to Wessex, were able to carve out their farmsteads on the valley floors. They settled mainly at crossing-points on the few perennial rivers that traversed the chalklands, as the Wiltshire names of Britford, Codford, Wilsford and Woodford clearly testify. While keeping their sheep on the grassy downlands, the Saxons built their homes on gravel terraces in the sheltered valleys, and grazed their cattle on the lush water meadows that flank the bournes and larger permanent rivers. Here, too, were the earliest water mills, grinding corn grown in tiny plots on the well-drained valley sides, a far cry from the primitive stone hand querns of the earlier Neolithic farmers. Because of water-supply problems the dessicated chalk hills and plateaux, once they were abandoned, were never to be settled again; henceforth they were to be left in calm serenity.

The Wessex chalklands have been gently folded into a number of east–west folds (Fig. 3.8), though in most cases these have little surface expression except where some of the Hampshire tributary streams have become adjusted to structure (Green, 1974). Only where stronger anticlinal structures affect the strata along the Hampshire–Berkshire border are the Wessex chalklands thrown up into relatively high hills and steeper scarps. Here, to the south of Newbury, lie Walbury Hill (297 m), the highest point of the chalklands, and the imposing north-facing scarp overlooking the Greensand exposure in the denuded anticlinal vale of Kingsclere (Fig. 3.8). The Vale of Pewsey marks the western continuation of the Kingsclere anticlinal axis but its upfold has been denuded into a broader trough surrounded by infacing chalk escarpments. It is not a true river valley but a structural lowland denuded to such an extent that the Upper Greensand has been widely exposed. Its undulating floor interjects a tongue of subdued terrain for some 30 kilometres into the heart of the rolling Wessex downland country, a corridor that was to be followed to great advantage by the Kennet and Avon canal and by the main London railway link to the West Country. The entire drainage pattern of the Vale of Pewsey has been captured by the Salisbury Avon which cuts through the southern chalk scarp at Upavon, one of the few major water gaps across the main outcrop of the central chalklands. A similar anticlinal structural vale, the Vale of Wardour, has been entrenched into the Wessex chalk farther south and this, too, has had its drainage captured by Salisbury's piratical Avon. Here, however, the depth of erosion has proceeded further than in the Vale of Pewsey, revealing not only the lower Cretaceous rocks but also Jurassic clays and limestones at the core of the denuded anticline. Their contrastingly coloured soils have brought a touch of West Country scenery far into the pallid chalklands in much the same way as the picturesque town of Shaftesbury, perched on its greensand hill, has introduced an exotic stone townscape into the ubiquitous flint and brick of the downland hamlets.

From Salisbury a belt of chalk, 20 kilometres in width, extends south-westwards into Dorset before being terminated by the coastal cliffs at Lulworth. The Dorset chalk country, much of it known as Cranborne Chase, is as littered with antiquities as that of Salisbury Plain. Its great west-facing escarpment, overlooking the fertile Blackmoor Vale, culminates in the striking mass of Eggardon Hill (252 m) crowned by an imposing Iron Age hillfort. The steepness of the Eggardon escarpment is due partly to the outcrop of a thick (8 m) layer of tough sandstone, termed the Eggardon Grit, at the base of the Chalk (Kennedy, 1970). Maiden Castle, near to Dorchester, is an even more impressive fortress, its 2.5 kilometres of ramparts enclosing Britain's largest prehistoric earthwork; it remained a settled site from 3000 BC until it was sacked by the Romans in AD 43. From time immemorial the Wessex chalklands have been decorated by hill figures cut in the springy turf to reveal the bare chalk, one of the most notable being that of the 55 metre Cerne Abbas giant, to the north of Dorchester (Benfield, 1950). Here, too, are some of Dorset's prettiest villages, with a collection of eight different Winterbournes strung out along a stream of that name near to Blandford Forum. Some of their cottages are built of brick, some of stone and others of chalk pug (pulverized chalk mixed with water and mud) and many are thatched. Most hamlets are found in the narrow secluded valleys, leaving the deserted chalk hills to the prehistoric burial mounds and the ridgeway tracks. During the Middle Ages the Dorset churches and towns were often built from the profits accrued by the downland sheep farmers, but today many of the flocks have disappeared and the open grassland has been decimated by the plough. Of England's 1.3 million hectares of chalkland only 44 000 hectares have not been ploughed; ironically, the majority of the true downland survivals are to be found in the military training areas of Salisbury Plain.

Fewer tracts of natural grassland have survived on the Berkshire Downs except on the scarp itself and on the steep sides of the dry valleys. Here, the lonely hills and combes, now lightly grazed only by hares and rabbits, are bedecked each summer with a profusion of colourful lime-loving wild flowers amid the fescue grasses. Juniper and hawthorn scrub also flourish on the steeper slopes, though the stands of beech which crown the hill crests have been artificially planted. One of Britain's oldest 'green' roads, the Ridgeway, some 4500 years old, follows the highest part of the chalk cuesta and overlooks the damp clay soils of the Vale of White Horse that stretches from Swindon to Wallingford. For the most part this scarp-foot vale has been carved from the Gault Clay but a distinct shelf created by hard beds in the Lower Chalk not only forms a double escarpment but also serves as a site for scarp-foot springline settlements just above the waterlogged vale (Wood, 1968). The double escarpment is best seen north-west of Marlborough where the highest step of Hackpen Hill is formed from the so-called Chalk Rock, a hard band between the Upper and Middle Chalk, and the lower bench at Clyffe Pypar by the Melbourn Rock of the Middle Chalk. A third hard band, known as the Totternhoe Stone (Lower Chalk) is seen better in the Chilterns where its grittier rock was once quarried as a building stone. Because blocks of chalk are not very resistant to weathering, however, they have been used only sparingly for external building purposes, except at Ashdown House on the Berkshire Downs and in Uffington village. Chalk survives longest when based on brick (or sarsen) and is protected by broad eaves of thatch or tile as at the scarp-foot village of Blewbury. To the west of this pretty village, near Harwell, a tract of orchards flourishes on the lighter soils provided by the narrow outcrop of Upper Greensand where it emerges from beneath the Chalk.

Uffington Castle, an Iron Age hillfort, occupies the crest of White Horse Hill (260 m) one of the best viewpoints of the Berkshire Downs. A short distance along the Ridgeway are two of the most interesting antiquities of this breezy downland. The first is the gigantic chalk-cut hillside figure of the White Horse itself, thought to have been fashioned in the first century AD. The other is the Neolithic chambered long barrow of Wayland's Smithy, constructed from massive sarsens in 3500 BC. Below them the escarpment falls steeply away into the sheer-sided combe known as the Manger, romantically associated with the White Horse. Its origin is, of course, considerably older than the hill carving for this short dry valley was almost certainly formed by prolonged spring-sapping of the escarpment by water emanating from summer snow melt during the Ice Age. In addition, the Manger's steep slopes are scarred by a series of deeply cut parallel furrows some 120 metres from top to bottom and some 45 metres apart. These chute-like features, which give a washboard character to the scarp face, are also found farther west at Kingstone Combes, and have been explained as Pleistocene avalanche tracks formed at a time when the Berkshire Downs were mantled by thick perennial snow drifts (Patterson, 1977). Today, the lower slopes of the Berkshire Downs scarp near the Goring Gap have a scatter of erratic stones brought from Wales by outwash from a very early ice advance into the area. Such fragmentary Pleistocene drifts also cap the isolated hills around Oxford but a thick boulder clay has been discovered on the valley floor at Sugworth to the south-west of the city (Shotton *et al.*, 1980). It was once suggested that meltwaters from this ancient ice sheet were responsible for carving the deep breach through the chalk escarpment at Goring, but it is now known that the Thames was already following the Goring Gap route long before this glacial advance. Of much greater significance to the scenery, however, is the thicker mantle of clay-with-flints that occurs on the south-eastern fringes of the Berkshire Downs and this widespread cover is repeated in the neighbouring Chilterns. The heavy soils generated by this clay cap lie on the stripped sub-Palaeocene surface (p. 60) which cuts across the chalk uplands and carries several surviving outliers of Reading Beds and London Clay, survivals which demonstrate how these Tertiary clays once extended further westwards into the London Basin beyond Hungerford. Thick woodlands of beech and oak now flourish on these heavier soils, introducing an element into the chalklands quite alien to their normal landscapes.

The Chilterns and the eastern chalklands

Because of the sporadic cover of Tertiary clays and sands and the widespread presence of the clay-with-flints it is difficult to believe that the Chilterns cuesta is a major chalk ridge delimiting the northern edge of the London Basin (Coppock, 1962). Only along the escarpment itself, at places such as Christmas Common (near the M40 breach) and on Dunstable Downs (254 m) does true downland scenery prevail. Nevertheless, the Chilterns, like other chalklands, are deeply dissected by an integrated network of dry valleys some of which have valley sides of contrasting gradient, termed *assymmetric slopes* (French, 1972), due to microclimatic differences under periglacial conditions. Such valleys introduce small tracts of farmland into the heavily wooded hills but in almost every case the valley floors are streamless, though they carry thick layers of chalky mud, termed *coombe rock*, sludged down the slopes by Pleistocene solifluction. The presence of a few tiny bournes means that the Chiltern valleys have a number of scattered flint and brick villages while the hilltop settlements, in scattered woodland clearings, once depended entirely for their water supply on deep wells bored into the chalk aquifers. The only large towns of the Chilterns, at High Wycombe, Wendover, Tring and Luton, are all associated with anomalous dry gaps in the chalk cuesta, through-valleys which now serve as routes for main roads, railways and a canal between London and the Midlands. It is difficult to explain these waterless gaps except as the legacy of former left-bank tributaries of an early Thames at a time when the water table in the Chalk stood much higher. It has been suggested that these earlier left-bank tributaries must have risen, like that of the Upper Thames today, much farther to the north of the chalk scarp. The claylands across which they formerly flowed, notably those created by the Gault Clay, have subsequently been lowered at a faster rate than the chalk cuesta itself so that today the rivers of the Vale of Aylesbury take the scarp-foot drainage away via the River Thame south-westwards along the geological strike to join the Thames at the ancient Roman town of Dorchester. Nearby lies the Wallingford Fan Gravel, a Pleistocene solifluction/fluvial terrace complex (Horton *et al.*, 1981). Such river incision must have captured the formerly south-eastward flowing dipslope tributaries, leaving the Chiltern wind gaps high and dry and the Wallingford Fan Gravel perched anomalously along the foot of the Chilterns scarp.

Beechwoods clothe most of the high chalk hills and occur as hangers on the higher slopes of most dry valleys among which glades of bluebells and many varieties of orchid abound; tiny muntjac deer are commonly seen in the woodlands while Stonor Park near Henley boasts an ancient herd of fallow deer. For centuries the beechwoods supported traditional woodworking industries although the independent craftsmen, known as bodgers, have recently disappeared, finally replaced by the centralized furniture factories at High Wycombe (Reed, 1979). The few former woodland villages, with their flint churches and pretty cottages of rose-red brick and flint have now been expanded to serve as commuter settlements for London. It appears that throughout post-glacial times the Chilterns have carried a fairly dense woodland cover on their ubiquitous 'clay cap' and this may explain why the line of the Ridgeway, having followed the open grassland of the Berkshire Downs from Avebury to the Goring Gap, suddenly leaves the crest of the escarpment and selects a route below the north face of the Chilterns cuesta. Here it is known as the Icknield Way, stretching from the Thames crossing at Goring all the way to Norfolk. In fact there are two Icknield Ways: the upper one follows a narrow shelf created by the hard rock bands of the Lower Chalk whose fertile soils support excellent yields of grain from a prairie-like landscape; the lower route keeps along the springline below the Chalk and links the scarpfoot villages, including that of Marsworth, where a recently discovered organic deposit (about 180 000 years old) at Pitstone chalk quarry has been recognized as evidence of a formerly unknown British interglacial (Green *et al.*, 1984) (see Fig. 5.1). In Bedfordshire a broad exposure of Lower Greensand projects from beneath the Chalk and stands above the Gault Clay to produce a belt of sandy, hilly country, covered in woodland and parkland around Woburn and on the Brickhills in neighbouring Buckinghamshire (Owen, 1972). Around Ampthill, by contrast, an area of market gardening occurs on the gentler greensand hills.

As the chalk ridge is traced north-eastwards through Hertfordshire (Munby, 1977) its crestline becomes progressively lower because beyond Luton it was over-ridden by former ice sheets. From Letchworth onwards, therefore, the escarpment is quite subdued, never rising above the 100 metre contour; only the Gog Magog Hills near Cambridge and the Newmarket downs remind one of the Chalk's presence beneath the glacial cover. In this tract of Cambridgeshire most hedgerows have disappeared, to be replaced by almost endless vistas of cornlands. The spring-line village churches, such as that at Guilden Morden, comprise a strange mixture of local flints, chalk stone and sandstone erratics from the Chalky Boulder Clay (see p. 97). Even though the East Anglian chalk is some 50 kilometres broad it makes virtually no impact on the scenery except to contribute to the highly fertile Chalky Boulder Clay. Such a mixture of chalk and clay ensures that its soils drain reasonably well in wet weather yet retain moisture during dry spells. Little wonder that the Chalky Boulder Clay of eastern England has been utilized to produce the bulk of Britain's main arable crops, especially cereals, but in consequence these eastern landscapes have also been transformed into veritable prairies, virtually devoid of hedgerows and trees. In places, however, this characteristic scenery is interrupted where the cover of glacial outwash sands and gravels is so overwhelming that the soils are incapable of sustaining anything more than heathland. In the Breckland, for example, on a low sandy plain overlying the Chalk the Forestry Commission has planted one of Britain's largest conifer forests on the poor soils around Thetford (Fig. 3.12). In one of the heath-covered forest clearings is the site where Neolithic man discovered a bountiful supply of flints in the thinly covered Chalk. Thereafter, the shallow mines of Grimes Graves were to become one of the leading British producers of prehistoric flint artefacts which were traded over lengthy distances, especially along the Icknield Way–Ridgeway track.

Near the flint mines several fine examples of so-called patterned ground can also be seen on the heathland. During the cold conditions of the Ice Age, when ice sheets stood not far away, periglacial processes would have led to a sorting of the Breckland soils by differential freezing and thawing, thereby creating polygonal patterns that elongate into stripes where slopes steepen. Vegetation emphasizes the patterns, heather picking out the thicker sands while grass favours the intervening places where chalky soil has been uncovered. The Breckland forests also contain other features possibly formed during the later phases of the Pleistocene. Near to East Wretham several shallow ponds (meres) occupy hollows in the boulder clay which buries the chalk. It is suggested that under permafrost conditions ground water in the chalk would have frozen into discrete ice lenses the expansion of which must have caused the surface to bulge into mounds known as *pingos*. After thawing, the ground surface would then have collapsed to create circular depressions. Similar features also occur on the western edge of the chalklands at Walton Heath near King's Lynn (Sparks *et al.*, 1972). An alternative explanation for the Breckland phenomena is that they are post-glacial solution hollows whose formation was aided by acid ground water from the sandy soils and the heathland vegetation. Although the chalk scarp is a weak feature in Norfolk it is scored with relatively steep-sided valleys. But the gently rolling country around Castle Acre, sometimes termed 'High Norfolk', never reaches 100 metres in elevation and is never true downland. Only where rivers have incised deeply through the calcareous boulder clay is the Chalk exposed, except at Hunstanton in north Norfolk where a vertical sea cliff of white chalk contrasts with the underlying layers of red chalk and carstone.

To the north of the Wash the gently dipping Chalk of the Lincolnshire Wolds creates a narrow rectangular plateau ranging from 120 to 170 metres in height (Bower and Farmery, 1910). The northern tract of these lonely downlands boasts a steep western escarpment fronting the Ancholme and Witham river valleys which together form Lincolnshire's central vale. Because the Chalk seas transgressed on to a partly worn-down dome of Jurassic rocks it is noteworthy that the Wolds' western edge overlaps progressively older rocks as the Chalk strata are traced northwards (Kent and Gaunt, 1980). Consequently, as the Lower Cretaceous rocks thin out and disappear in the northern Wolds the Chalk rests unconformably on the Kimmeridge Clay of Upper Jurassic age. In north Lincolnshire, therefore, the scarp-foot vale of the Ancholme follows the outcrop of the Oxford Clay (Upper Jurassic), whereas the scenically similar clay vales of Aylesbury and White Horse have been carved from the younger Gault Clay (Cretaceous) because in these cases there is no unconformity in the geological

Figure 3.12 Forestry Commission plantation on the gravelly and sandy heathland of the Breckland.

succession. The southern Wolds, in contrast to the northern Wolds, are underlain by a thick succession of rocks of Lower Greensand and Speeton Clay age (Lower Cretaceous) whose strata have been extensively exposed by the deeply incised river systems some of which are flanked by dry meltwater channels surviving from the Ice Ace (Straw, 1961). Over wide areas around Horncastle to the west of the chalk scarp, the Spilsby Sandstone, of disputed age, is a scarp-former in its own right, though its sandy soils are less fertile than those of the Chalk.

The grassy downland landscapes of the Lincolnshire Wolds are closely comparable with those of Wiltshire: the same deeply incised dry valleys, beech-clothed slopes, sheep-grazed turf and far-spreading cornfields; even the deserted wartime airfields on the flat-topped Wolds match the military enclosures of Salisbury Plain. It was the empty chalk landscapes of Lincolnshire, devoid of the Chilterns' 'clay cap' or the ubiquitous boulder clay of East Anglia, that inspired Tennyson to write of the 'calm and deep peace of this high Wold'. The place names recall the Danish settlement of the ninth century, with the suffix 'by' indicating a village and 'thorpe' a farm belonging to a village. The highest Wolds are now deserted except for a few farmsteads strung out along the prehistoric crest-line trackway of the Bluestone Heath Road (Bygot, 1952). Settlements are tucked away in hidden valleys or located at the scarp-foot springline, including the town of Caistor founded by the Romans below the western scarp. Where the Chalk descends gently eastwards it becomes progressively masked by glacial deposits until, below its eastern bluffs around Louth, the countryside becomes little more than a coastal marshland.

Across the Humber estuary the low boulder clay coastlands are continued in Holderness where the Chalk is so deeply buried that it plays no part in fashioning the scenery. Because the straight coastline between Bridlington and the ever-changing spit of Spurn Head (De Boer, 1964) is composed only of poorly consolidated glacial drift material, marine erosion is cutting back the low cliffs at the rate of some 2 metres per year. Records show, in fact, that throughout the centuries several Holderness villages have been destroyed by cliff recession which will slow down only when the eastern edge of the Yorkshire Wolds is reached. The Holderness glacial deposits are now regarded as the type-site for a late cold phase of the Devensian (Dimlington Stadial) (see Fig. 5.1) and its plains are corrugated by curving moraines marking the various retreat phases of this last major ice sheet in southern Britain (Catt and Penny, 1966). It was along one of these moraine fronts that a former meltwater stream flowed southwards to the Humber; this was to become the River Hull and the location for the major fishing port of Kingston upon Hull (Bisat *et al.*, 1962). The western edge of the Yorkshire Wolds illustrates the way in which the overlap of the Chalk, first noted in the Lincolnshire Wolds (see p. 67) is such that the west-facing scarp now overlooks the New Red Sandstone of the Vale of York, being separated from the Keuper only by a thin ribbon of Lower Lias Clay. The remarkable attenuation of the underlying Jurassic rocks is due essentially to the influence of the Market Weighton axis (Jeans, 1968) described on p. 107. The eastern edge of the Yorkshire Wolds, where the Chalk disappears beneath glacial drift, is marked by a line of urban settlements of which Driffield and Beverley are the largest. The Wolds themselves achieve their highest elevations (240 m) along the north-western scarp (Lewin, 1969) which, beyond Acklam, swings suddenly eastwards to overshadow the broad Vale of Pickering. At the foot of this bold north-facing escarpment is a narrow shelf of Speeton Clay whose impervious shales serve as a site for a line of scarp-foot hamlets, raised above the marshy vale and located along the springline beneath the Chalk. At Saxton Brow and Snevver Scar the scarp is trenched by two dry channels formed when meltwater streams from the Vale of Pickering ice lobe ran around the glacier margin. Landscapes of the Yorkshire Wolds, like their Lincolnshire counterparts, have suffered considerable losses of chalk grassland during the post-war expansion of arable farming. Today, the higher Wolds are deserted except for the substantial farmsteads set in hollow squares of screening trees amid the endless barley fields. Lower down, among the wheat crops, the few red brick villages nestle in the deeply cut dry valleys (Allison, 1976). The drift-capped promontory of Flamborough Head marks the termination of the chalklands in northern England. Because its pore spaces have been filled with a secondary calcite the Flamborough chalk is substantially harder than that of southern England (Wright and Wright, 1942). Nevertheless, its joints have been exploited by the waves to isolate the Green Stacks and cause a cave roof collapse at the impressive Pigeon Hole.

Bibliography

Ager, D.V. and Smith, W.E. (1965) *The Coast of South Devon and Dorset between Branscombe and Burton Bradstock*. Guide No. 23. Geol. Assoc.

Allison, K.J. (1976). *The East Riding of Yorkshire Landscape*. Hodder & Stoughton. 272 pp.

Arber, M.A. (1940) The coastal landslips of south-east Devon. *Proc. Geol. Assoc.*, **51**, 257–71.

Arber, M.A. (1973) Landslips near Lyme Regis. *Proc. Geol. Assoc.*, **84**, 121–34.

Barber, K. (ed.) (1987) *Wessex and the Isle of Wight*. Field Guide. Quat. Res. Assoc.

Benfield, E. (1950) *Dorset*. Hale. 232 pp.

Bisat, W.S., Penny, L.F. and Neale, J.W. (1962) *Geology around University Towns: Hull*, Guide No. 11. Geol. Assoc.

Bower, C.R. and Farmery, J.R. (1910) The zones of the Lower Chalk of Lincolnshire. *Proc. Geol. Assoc.*, **21**, 333–59.

Brandon, C. (1974) *The Sussex Landscape*. Hodder & Stoughton. 288 pp.

Brookfield, M.E. (1978) The lithostratigraphy of the Upper Oxfordian and Lower Kimmeridgian beds of South Dorset, England. *Proc. Geol. Assoc.*, **89**, 1–32.

Brunsden, D. and Goudie, A.S. (1981) *Classic Landforms of Dorset*. Landscape Guide No. 1. Geogr. Assoc.

Bygot, J. (1952) *Lincolnshire*. Hale. 281 pp.

Bury, H. (1933) The Plateau gravels of the Bournemouth Area. *Proc. Geol. Assoc.*, **44**, 314–35.

Carr, A.P. and Blackley, M.W. (1973) Investigations bearing on the age and development of Chesil Beach, Dorset. *Trans. Inst. Br. Geogr.*, **58**, 98–111.

Catt, J.A. and Penny, L.F. (1966) The Pleistocene deposits of Holderness, east Yorkshire. *Proc. Yorks. Geol. Soc.*, **35**, 375–420.

Copley, G.H., Edlin, H.L., Hook, O. and Venning, F.E.W. (1966) *The New Forest*. Phoenix. 201 pp.

Coppock, J.T. (1962) *The Chilterns*. British Landscapes through Maps, no. 4. Geogr. Assoc.

Curry, D. (1965) The Palaeogene beds of South East England. *Proc. Geol. Assoc.*, **76**, 151–73.

Curry, D. and Wisden, D.E. (1958) Geology of some British coastal areas: *The Southampton District including Barton and Bracklesham*. Guide no. 14. Geol. Assoc.

Curry, D., Middlemiss, F.A. and Wright, C.W. (1966) *The Isle of Wight*. Guide No. 25. Geol. Assoc.

Curry, D., King, C. and Stinton, P.C. (1977) The Bracklesham Beds of Bracklesham Bay and Selsey, Sussex. *Proc. Geol. Assoc.*, **88**, 243–54.

De Boer, G. (1964) Spurn Head, its history and evolution. *Trans. Inst. Br. Geogr.*, **34**, 71–89.

Edwards, R.A. (1976) Tertiary sediments and structure of the Bovey Basin, South Devon. *Proc. Geol. Assoc.*, **87**, 1–26.

Everard, C.E. (1954) The Solent River: a geomorphological study. *Trans. Inst. Br. Geogr.*, **20**, 41–58.

French, H.M. (1972) Asymmetrical slope development in the Chiltern Hills. *Biuletin Peryglacjalny*, **22**, 149–56.

Green, C.P. (1974) The summit surface of the Wessex Chalk. *Inst. of Br. Geogr. Special Publication*, **7**, 127–38.

Green, C.P., Coope, G.R., Curran, A.P. *et al.* (1984) Evidence of two temperate episodes in late Pleistocene deposits at Marsworth, UK. *Nature*, **309**, 778–81.

Hamblin, R.J.O. (1973) The Haldon Gravels of South Devon. *Proc. Geol. Assoc.*, **84**, 459–76.

Hodgson, J.M. (1964) The low-level marine sands and gravels of the West Sussex coastal plain. *Proc. Geol. Assoc.*, **75**, 547–62.

Hodgson, J.M., Catt, J.A. and Weir, A.H. (1967) The origin and development of clay-with-flints and associated soil horizons on the South Downs. *J. Soil Sci.*, **18**, 85–102.

Hodson, F. and West, I.M. (1972) Holocene deposits of Fawley, Hampshire and the development of Southampton Water. *Proc. Geol. Assoc.*, **83**, 421–42.

Horton, A., Worssam, B.C. and Whittow, J.B. (1981) The Wallingford Fan Gravel. *Phil. Trans. Roy. Soc.* B., **293**, 215–55.

House, M.R. (1961) Structure of the Weymouth Anticline. *Proc. Geol. Assoc.*, **72**, 221–38.

House, M.R. (1989) *Geology of the Dorset Coast*. Guide no. 22. Geol. Assoc.

Hutchinson, H.N. (1982) Is the drainage of the Isle of Wight antecedent? *Trans. Inst. Brit. Geog.* (NS), **7**, 217–26.

Jeans, C.V. (1968) The Market Weighton structure: tectonics, sedimentation and diagenesis during the Cretaceous. *Proc. Yorks. Geol. Soc.*, **39**, 409–44.

Jones, D.K.C. (ed.) (1980) *The Shaping of Southern England*. Academic Press. 274 pp.

Kennedy, W.J. (1970) A correlation of the uppermost Albian and the Cenomanian of south west England. *Proc. Geol. Assoc.*, **81**, 613–78.

Kent, P. and Gaunt, G.D. (1980) *Eastern England from the Tees to the Wash* (2nd edn). British Regional Geology. HMSO. 155 pp.

Lewin, J. (1969) *The Yorkshire Wolds: A Study in Geomorphology*. Occasional Paper no. 11. University of Hull. 89 pp.

Martin, E.C. (1938). The Littlehampton and Portsdown Chalk inliers and their relation to the raised beaches of West Sussex. *Proc. Geol. Assoc.*, **49**, 198–212.

Melville, R.V. and Freshney, F.C. (1982). *The Hampshire Basin and Adjoining Areas* (4th edn). British Regional Geology. HMSO. 146 pp.

Monkhouse, F.J. (ed.) (1964) *A Survey of Southampton and Its Region*. Southampton University Press. 349 pp.

Munby, L.M. (1977) *The Hertfordshire Landscape*. Hodder & Stoughton. 269 pp.

Owen, H.G. (1972) The Gault and its junction with the Woburn Sands in the Leighton Buzzard area, Bedfordshire and Buckinghamshire. *Proc. Geol. Assoc.*, **83**, 257–313.

Patterson, K. (1977) Scarp-face dry valleys near Wantage, Oxfordshire. *Trans. Inst. Br. Geogr.* (NS), **2**, 192–204.

Phillips, W.J. (1964) The structures in the Jurassic and Cretaceous rocks on the Dorset coast between White Nothe and Mupe Bay. *Proc. Geol. Assoc.*, **75**, 373–406.

Reed, M. (1979) *The Buckinghamshire Landscape*. Hodder & Stoughton. 288 pp.

Shepherd, W. (1972) *Flint. Its Origin, Properties and Uses*. Faber.

Shotton, F.W., Goudie, A.S., Briggs, D.J. and Osmaston, H.A. (1980) Cromerian Interglacial deposits at Sugworth near Oxford, England, and their relation to the Plateau Drift of the Cotswolds and the terrace sequence of the Upper Thames. *Phil. Trans. Roy. Soc. B*, **289**, 55–86.

Small, R.J. (1961) The morphology of Chalk escarpments: a critical review. *Trans. Inst. Br. Geogr.*, **29**, 71–90.

Small, R.J., Clark, M.J. and Lewin, J. (1970) A periglacial rock-stream at Clatford Bottom, Marlborough Downs, Wiltshire. *Proc. Geol. Assoc.*, **81**, 87–98.

Smith, W.E. (1961) The Cenomanian deposits of south east Devonshire: The Cenomanian Limestone and contiguous deposits south west of Beer, Devonshire. *Proc. Geol. Assoc.*, **72**, 91–134.

Smith, W.E. (1965) The Cenomanian deposits of south east Devonshire: The Cenomanian Limestone east of Seaton. *Proc. Geol. Assoc.*, **76**, 121–36.

Sparks, B.W. and Lewis, W.V. (1957) Escarpment dry valleys near Pegsdon, Hertfordshire. *Proc. Geol. Assoc.*, **68**, 26–38.

Sparks, B.W., Williams, R.B.G and Bell, F.G. (1972) Presumed ground-ice depressions in East Anglia. *Proc. Roy. Soc. Lond. A*, **327**, 329–43.

Straw, A. (1961) Drifts, meltwater channels and ice margins in the Lincolnshire Wolds. *Trans. Inst. Br. Geogr.*, **29**, 115–28.

Summerfield, M.A. and Goudie, A.S. (1980) The sarsens of southern England: their palaeoenvironmental interpretation with reference to other silcretes, in D.K.C. Jones (ed.), *The Shaping of Southern England*. Academic Press. 71–100.

Taylor, C. (1970) *Dorset*. Hodder and Stoughton. 215 pp.

Tidmarsh, W.G. (1932) Permian lavas of Devon. *Quart. J. Geol. Soc.*, **138**, 712–73.

Venables, E.N. (1962) The London Clay of Bognor Regis. *Proc. Geol. Assoc.*, **73**, 245–72.

Vesey-Fitzgerald, B. (1949) *Hampshire and the Isle of Wight*. Hale. 434 pp.

Whitlock, R. (1955) *Salisbury Plain*. Hale. 271 pp.

Wood, P.D. (1968) *The Oxford and Newbury Area*. British Landscapes through Maps no. 11. Geogr. Association.

Wright, C.W. and Curry, D. (1958) *The Isle of Wight*. Guide no. 25. Geol. Assoc.

Wright, C.W. and Wright, E.V. (1942) The Chalk of the Yorkshire Wolds. *Proc. Geol. Assoc.*, **53**, 112–27.

The Weald and the London Basin

4

The landforms of South-East England are dominated not only by the worn-down structural dome of the Weald but also by the adjoining downfold of the London Basin. Both regions are rimmed by narrow ridges of chalk: the chalk strata which form the Chilterns descend beneath the Tertiary sedimentaries of the London Basin only to reappear farther south as the sharp cuesta of the North Downs; the latter scarp looks across the Weald to match the north-facing chalk scarp of the South Downs some 50 kilometres away. These inward-facing escarpments demonstrate that the original Wealden arch was once roofed by the Chalk whose central portions have been removed by denudation to reveal older rocks underneath (Fig. 4.1). Only in the south-eastern sector, between Eastbourne and Folkestone, has the encircling rim of chalk been destroyed by marine erosion, leaving an almost continuous chalk ridge, 290 kilometres long, surrounding a concentric succession of Lower Cretaceous rocks whose strata become progressively *older* as they pass inwards to the centre (Kirkaldy, 1958; Lake, 1975). In contrast to the Weald's geological succession, the rocks of the London Basin become *younger* as they are traced inwards towards the centre of the downfold. In this respect they match the sedimentary record of the Hampshire Basin (Chapter 3) although the

Figure 4.1 Structure of the Weald, looking westwards.

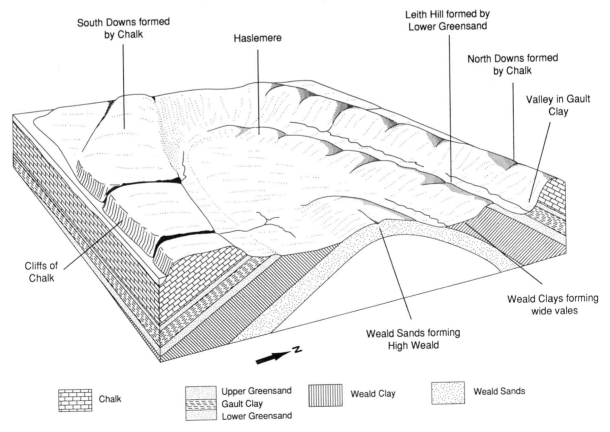

London Basin has no rocks of Oligocene age (Curry, 1965). It further resembles the Hampshire Basin because of the asymmetry of each of their structures, both having the steeper limb of the downfold along their southern margins which means that the thickest of the Tertiary sediments survive to the south of the basin's geographic centre. The tough sandstones of the central Weald are not represented in the London Basin, which means that the latter's clays, gravels and sands rarely give rise to any high ground. Furthermore, because of its more southerly location the Weald has many more examples of Alpine folding than the London Basin, but this is partly explained by the underlying presence of the bastion of the London Platform of ancient Palaeozoic rocks, occurring at no great depth beneath the capital's newer sedimentary cover rocks and giving them a degree of its own rigidity and immobility.

There are few parts of Britain that can match South-East England's diversity of parallel rock formations with their rapid transitions of landforms, soils, vegetation and land use (Mason 1979). Little wonder that the region has become a classic area in which to study the linear patterns of scarp-and-vale landscapes (Jones, 1980). Take but one example of this transition that takes place on the journey from Windsor to Horsham. The well-known oaks of Windsor Great Park flourish on the stiff London Clay but give way south of Ascot and Egham to tracts of pine and birch on the broad outcrop of the Bagshot Sands. The narrow chalk ridge of the North Downs (Robinson, 1986) is capped in most places with clay-with-flints which in turn support coppiced hazel, oak and hornbeam; without this 'clay cap' the Chalk generally carries only occasional stands of beech. On the Weald's heathlands of the Lower Greensand one sees the reappearance of pine and birch while the Weald Clay vale is distinguished by its belt of oak forest. Finally, the sandy soils of the Hastings Beds at the centre of the Weald carry a natural cover of birch and pine, though many exotic conifers have also been introduced.

The metropolis has dominated South-East England for centuries but now the city has expanded out of its basin as its suburbs have crept beyond the surrounding rim of chalk. In earlier centuries the high chalk ridge presented a barrier to expansion but by infiltrating the dry valleys and river gaps London has virtually linked up with some of the towns and villages of both the Weald and the Chilterns, notwithstanding London's Green Belt. The M25 orbital motorway has merely accelerated the expansion, leading one to speculate on what will happen to the Kentish countryside now that the Channel Tunnel is completed. This relatively unspoilt rural corner of England was beloved by Kipling, who praised the Weald for its 'wooded, dim, blue goodness'. Along with others, he also recognized its natural divisions as the Downs, the Weald and the Marsh.

The North and South Downs

Where the North Downs terminate in the East Kent peninsula they also produce the widest chalk exposure in the South-East. Their abrupt truncation at the Straits of Dover is represented by the high sea cliffs of the South Foreland, while the equally precipitous North Foreland between Ramsgate and Margate has been carved from an isolated upfold of the Chalk known as the Thanet anticline (Coleman and Luckhurst, 1967). The 'island' thus produced was once cut off from the 'mainland' by the Wantsum Channel, itself aligned along the axis of the

Wantsum syncline. Gradual silting and the building of the northern sea wall between Birchington and Reculver in 1808 terminated the navigation and 'tied' Thanet to the Kentish shore. In Roman times, however, the strategic Wantsum waterway had been navigable and guarded by forts at Reculver and Richborough, though for centuries its largest port proved to be Sandwich until that, too, declined (Robinson and Cloet, 1953). The Wantsum marshes which once supported sheep now carry fields of corn and vegetables, while the treeless Thanet landscape is also given over largely to cereals, the quality of their yields being enhanced by the added fertility of a cover of brickearth, a type of wind-carried *loess* winnowed from the Pleistocene moraines deposited much farther north during the closing stages of the Ice Age (Burrin, 1981).

Other superficial deposits overlying the Chalk have also played important roles in the diversification of Kentish downland farming. This is exemplified wherever the clay-with-flints mantle the higher parts of the North Downs, for they are either thickly forested, like the Chilterns, or support prolific orchards of apples, pears, cherries and plums in the so-called Garden of England. This is true mainly of the downland tract between the Stour and Medway rivers (Dewey *et al.*, 1925), where the orchards cling to the slopes and ridges of the dry valleys above the notorious frost hollows of the valley bottoms where the hardier hop gardens occur. Where the downs become wider, east of the Stour valley, the plateaux are too exposed for fruit growing and instead one finds Lyminge Forest, astride the 'clay cap'. Inland from Deal this rustic scene is interrupted by the anomalous development of the Kent coalfield whose seams are entirely concealed beneath a Mesozoic cover (Burr, 1909). Opened in 1913, the Carboniferous strata of the coalfield are a reminder that to the north of the belt of Wealden folding the Palaeozoic floor of the London Platform lies not far below the surface of north Kent (Stubblefield, 1954).

To the west of the Medway the northernmost ripples of the Alpine storm bring the Chalk up into the southern edge of the London Basin around Erith along a few minor anticlines, similar to the Thanet upfold. As the North Downs continue westwards they reach their highest elevations (260 m) where the London suburbs of Banstead and Caterham extend almost to the lip of the steep south-facing escarpment (Gossling, 1929). Here is Box Hill (226 m) with its patches of ancient grassland surviving on the scarp face (Fig. 4.2) amid mature beechwoods, yew and box. A little farther west along the crestline is the curious Netley Heath whose acid soils result from the sandy ridge-top deposits claimed by some to be the remnants of beaches left behind by a high Early Pleistocene sea level (see p. 83) (John and Fisher, 1984). Between Guildford and Farnham the chalk exposure narrows to become the well-known Hog's Back whose airy ridge can be explained by the almost vertical dip of the Chalk accentuated by a fault along its southern margin. Thus, the sharply defined ridge has equally steep slopes on either flank rather than the more convential cuesta landform of steep escarpment and gentler dipslope (Lake and Shephard-Thorne, 1985).

About one-fifth of the villages of the Weald occur along the scarp-foot spring-line below the Chalk, with the Guilford escarpment offering a classic example of this relationship between geology and settlement. Albury, Shere and Gomshall, with their watermills, watercress beds and half-timbered houses, all located along the Tillingbourne, are among Surrey's most picturesque villages. Moreover, one of Britain's oldest and most historic tracks, the Pilgrim's Way dating from at least the Iron Age, also follows the scarp-foot of the North Downs. On the northern flanks, where the chalk dipslope disappears beneath the younger clays and sands of the London Basin, the northern margin of the downs is also followed from London to Canterbury by another ancient routeway, the Roman Watling Street, now the Dover Road (A2). Both these ancient routes are now paralleled by their twentieth-century counterparts, the M25/M20 scarp-foot motorways, and by the M2 between Rochester and Canterbury. Wherever the long escarpment of the North Downs is breached by north-flowing rivers their gaps have become the site of at least one town: Canterbury on the Stour, Chatham and Rochester on the Medway, Dorking and Leatherhead on the Mole, and Guildford on the Wey. Only the beautiful Darent valley at Shoreham, immortalized in the paintings of Samuel Palmer, has managed to retain its rural charm.

From Farnham southwards to Petersfield the edge of the Chalk swings round in a great arc transverse to the several lines of east–west folding, not only terminating the gentle westerly pitch of the Wealden dome but also linking up the North and South Downs (see Fig. 4.1). Away from the influence of the Hog's Back fold the Chalk outcrop immediately expands into the Hampshire Downs whose steep east-facing scarp is built from the Middle and Upper Chalk. Around Alton the Lower Chalk exposure is some 3 kilometres wide but beyond it, from Binsted to Hawkley, it is the Upper Greensand that creates a bold escarpment of its own (unique in the Weald) and which rises to 170 metres near Selborne. Gilbert

Figure 4.2 Ancient chalk grassland surviving on the North Downs at Box Hill, Surrey.

White's *Natural History of Selborne* has brought fame to this tiny village hidden at the foot of the chalk scarp. Some of its magnificent beech woods, especially those on the steep Greensand slopes overlooking the Oakhanger stream, have been designated a Site of Special Scientific Interest, an act the significance of which can be more fully appreciated when it is realized that no less than 25 per cent of the broadleaf woodlands of the east Hampshire Downs have been lost to arable farming since the Second World War. The 'clay cap' is particularly well developed on the east Hampshire chalklands, explaining the density of their former forest cover. The eastern tracts of the South Downs, by contrast, are virtually free of clay-with-flints or Pleistocene beach deposits, except at Beachy Head. Thus of all the chalk exposures in South-East England it is parts of the South Downs, with their sheep-grazed turf and summit coppices, that approach most closely the idealized chalk landscapes once commonplace in earlier centuries but rarely found today. The bare chalklands are particularly striking to the east of Arundel in contrast to the Downs' western end which has retained sufficient of its 'clay cap' to support extensive chestnut and beechwoods, especially in the Queen Elizabeth Forest Park near Petersfield and high up the dipslope behind Goodwood where there are remnants of a 30 metre raised beach, possibly of Hoxnian age (Fowler, 1932).

At Butser Hill the downland escarpment swings eastwards to turn its bold front northwards towards the Weald. As in most chalk areas, the dry valleys are the most notable of the South Downs' landforms, varying in character from shallow depressions through broad winding troughs to deeply cut ravines, such as the Devil's Dyke at Poynings. Most valleys, however, are not sufficiently incised to reach the water table even in winter so that, with the exception of the Winterbourne at Lewes and the Lavant near Chichester, there are few bourne flows (Williams and Robinson, 1983). Only four south-flowing perennial rivers cut through the South Downs but, unlike their North Downs' counterparts, their gaps have rarely been utilized as sites of major towns: Arundel, on the Arun, and Lewes and Newhaven, on the Ouse, are the largest.

As on the majority of chalklands, settlements occur primarily in the dry valleys or at the scarp foot. Yet the tree-mantled earthworks of Chanctonbury Ring and the turf-covered ramparts of Cissbury Ring testify to the density of population that must have been supported during prehistoric times on these fertile but arid soils (Brandon, 1974). Typical downland turf is a product not only of the thin chalky soils but also of centuries of sheep grazing particularly by the popular Southdown breed. Much of the South Downs sheepwalk has been converted to arable in the last 70 years and of a total area of 100 000 hectares only 2600 hectares of grassland now survive, compared with a mere 800 hectares on the North Downs. In the absence of modern grazing a hawthorn/dogwood scrub has invaded the open sward. Estimates by the Nature Conservancy Council show that about 25 per cent of the South Downs grassland has disappeared since 1966.

At their eastern limit the South Downs end abruptly in the vertical cliffs of the Seven Sisters and Beachy Head, often said to be Britain's most majestic chalk cliffs (Gaster, 1929). The sea is encroaching at a rate of about 1 metre per year, causing spectacular rockfalls that are facilitated by the gentle seaward dip of the strata. Coastal recession at the Seven Sisters, for example, has truncated the courses of seven dry valleys and their intervening ridges to produce this well-known coastal switchback (Castledean, 1982). Between Cuckmere Haven and Beachy Head the lack of an undercliff testifies to the efficiency of marine erosion in clearing the great masses of fallen chalk debris; the frequency of the falls maintains both the verticality and the dazzling whiteness of the cliffs (Mortimore, 1986).

The Weald

The forested appearance of the Weald induced the Romans to call it *Sylva Anderida*, which the Saxons amended to *Andredsweald*, the 'wild' inhospitable woodland of later topographers. Despite extensive deforestation in subsequent centuries, mainly for shipbuilding and charcoal-smelting, much of the forest survives today, notwithstanding the loss of millions of trees in a devastating storm in 1987. The lithological differences, however, create concentric scarp-and-vale landforms which provide significant vegetational and scenic contrasts within the region (Gallois and Edmunds, 1965; Gibbons, 1981). The central sandstone core of the Hastings Beds is known as the High Weald to distinguish it from the surrounding belt of Weald Clay that makes up the Low Weald. Outside this broad flat trench of claylands the next rampart is the conspicuous Lower Greensand cuesta (Hayward, 1932) which in turn is separated from the encircling chalk escarpment by a relatively narrow vale, known in Surrey as the Vale of Holmesdale, carved from the less resistant Gault Clay and upper Greensand (Fig. 4.1) (Owen, 1975).

Stratigraphically below the Lower Greensand the rock succession known as the Wealden is virtually unrepresented elsewhere in Britain because its sediments were once thought to have been deposited in a large freshwater lake that extended only over South-East England. Its northern shore was the low Palaeozoic upland of the London Platform, from which most of its sediments were derived, but to the south the lake extended as far as the Paris Basin. During the 18 million years of its existence no less than 880 metres of non-marine sediments were laid down in rhythmic cycles (cyclothems) representing alternating phases of deltaic and lacustrine sedimentation. A more modern interpretation of the genesis of the Wealden rocks suggests, however, that the sandy beds are not deltaic or lacustrine but were deposited by braided rivers wandering across a vast floodplain, while the clays represent mudbanks formed when periodic uplift ceased, when erosion slowed and the rivers carried little or no sand (Allen, 1958). Whichever of the hypotheses is correct, it is manifest that three cyclothems have been recognized, each consisting of basal silts and sands with the latter increasing upwards to become harder current-bedded sandstones, occasionally capped by thin pebble beds. Thus the Wealden sequence is represented by:

Around Hastings the unstable and often slumped Fairlight Clay (shales, clays with lignites) is exposed in the sea cliffs, where small waterfalls tumble from the hanging Glens, although the main sea cliffs between Hastings and Bexhill have been carved largely from the pale yellow Ashdown Sands. Hastings Castle itself stands on a bluff of similar sandstones but the local Martello Towers, built in 1805, have already been washed away by marine encroachment. Succeeding the Ashdown Beds, the Wadhurst Clay (almost a misnomer because of its shales, shelly limestones, calcareous sandstones and ironstones) occurs in irregular patches wherever river erosion has cut through the Tunbridge Wells Sands of the High Weald between Hastings and Horsham. These clay lowlands are said to have once supported England's finest oaks, though the Wadhurst Clay's major contribution to local resources has been that of its ironstone, the basis of the Weald's formerly renowned iron industry that peaked in the sixteenth and seventeenth centuries (Sweeting, 1944). Shallow ponds between East Grinstead and Wadhurst mark the sites of the former extraction pits but the High Weald also offered two other essentials for early iron-working, namely timber for charcoal smelting and water to drive the forge hammers; indeed, the narrow steep-sided valleys of the Forest Ridges could easily be dammed to create 'hammer ponds' to drive the water wheels. The last forge, at Ashburnham, closed in 1830, unable to compete with the coke-smelted iron increasingly produced on the British coalfields during the Industrial Revolution, even though the Wealden ore has a much higher iron content than other British ores (Worssam, 1964). Further reminders of this once flourishing industry are seen in some of the place names of the High Weald. The Tunbridge Wells Sands have weathered into a broken upland of partly forested heathlands which flourish on their acid sandy soils. Although their lowest beds of soft sands and siltstones offer only moderate resistance to erosion, these are overlain by the massively bedded Ardingly Sandstone which has weathered into 15 metre high vertical crags on the valley sides (Robinson and Williams, 1976). Rock pillars have also been produced, such as the Toad Rock at Rusthall Common and the Great-upon-Little rock at West Hoathly. Some of the precipitous cliff faces on the valley sides are pierced by caves and widened by joints, known as *gulls*, that form both chimneys and passageways. All these forms, unique in South-East England, are best displayed at High Rocks and Harrison's Rocks near Tunbridge Wells and are thought to have been initiated by Pleistocene frost action (Shephard-Thorne, 1975).

So far as vegetation is concerned the free-draining acid soils of the High Weald are often given over to native birch and pine, though large exotic conifer plantations have also appeared during the present century. Not surprisingly, the historically forested nature of the area is represented by the frequent number of place names referring to woodland: the suffix *-ly* or *-leigh* (as in Hoathly and Ardingly) means a 'forest clearing'; *-den* (as in Tenterden and Smarden) implies a 'wooded vale', while *-hurst* (as in Crowhurst and Penshurst) refers to a 'copse on a hill' (Wooldridge and Goldring, 1953). In a region where wood was plentiful, timber-framed houses are found, some dating from before 1500, though unlike those of the Welsh Borders they have not been painted black and white (see Chapter 7). Weatherboarding is also characteristic of some Wealden houses and certain church spires are roofed with silver-grey wooden tiles. Much more common, however, are the rose-red local tiles, with the Weald having more tile-hung houses than any other region in Britain. Stone cottages are relatively rare, reflecting the dearth of easily worked freestones, although one of the best, the Ashdown Sandstone, was used at Bodiam Castle and Wakehurst Place in Sussex and at Penshurst Place in Kent. The most typical building stones of the Weald have long been the coarse sandy limestone (ragstone) of the Kentish Rag (Lower Greensand) together with the sandstones of Reigate Stone (Upper Greensand), Bargate Stone and Carstone (both Lower Greensand).

Surrounding the High Weald hill country the broad, horseshoe-shaped corridor of the Low Weald is relatively featureless because the easily denuded Weald Clay (Bird, 1963), like the older Oxford Clay, produces heavy waterlogged soils characterized by stands of oak, permanent grass and, in the north eastern sector, fruit orchards. Before it was efficiently drained the marshy terrain of the clay vale meant that early main roads skirted the edges of the Low Weald wherever possible. Its surrounding countryside, therefore, has a tortuous network of lanes many of which have been lowered by 2–3 metres below the adjacent fields by the constant wear and tear of wheeled traffic. The parallel but narrower belt of the Gault Clay vale is flanked by the whitish-yellow rocks of the Lower Greensand and the greenish-grey outcrops of Upper Greensand, whose soils and landforms introduce a very distinctive element into the Wealden scene. At the base of the Lower Greensand the chocolate-brown Atherfield Clay is invariably marked by a spring-line but it is the overlying Hythe Beds that make the most striking contribution to the scenery, for they generally stand out as a major cuesta. Nevertheless, there are marked facies changes within the Hythe Beds as they are traced around the Weald. In the western Weald, for example, they occur as soft sandstones with interbedded chert bands (not unlike flints in their appearance), while in Kent they contain the tough Kentish Rag and the soft sands, known as 'hassock', whose loamy soils are particularly favourable to the growth of hops. The Sandgate Beds also vary in composition, with the silts of Kent being replaced by limestones, sandstones and fuller's earth in West Sussex and Surrey. Finally, the uppermost strata of the Lower Greensand, the Folkestone Beds, are essentially hard, iron-rich sandstones. The highest summit of South-East England, Leith Hill (294 m) is built not from the Chalk, as one might expect, but from the Hythe Beds because of their protective capping of virtually indestructible chert layers. These have certainly helped maintain the eminence of Leith Hill, upon which oak, birch and Scots Pine have long flourished. Towards Guildford, however, the cherts are not so evident and the bold crests of St Martha's Hill and the Devil's Jumps survive mainly because of their cap of hard ferruginous Carstone that overlies the Folkestone Beds (Robinson and Williams, 1984). Nearby is the attractive heath-covered upland around Hindhead where the Portsmouth Road (A3) provides spectacular views eastwards across the Weald (Fig. 4.3) as it climbs over Gibbet Hill (272 m). Here, the striking trough of the Devil's Punchbowl has been fashioned by spring-sapping where the Hythe Beds rest on impervious Atherfield Clay (Knowles and Middlemiss, 1958). Some of the poorest soils of the South-East are found on the Hythe Beds and Folkestone Beds although around Hindhead the stands of Scots Pine and the larch plantations make for dramatic scenery amid the wilderness of sandy heaths. It is these same sandstone formations, moreover, that provide the main water supply for the western Weald as, sealed by the Atherfield and Weald Clays below and by the Gault Clay above, these Lower Greensand beds retain water in a perfect aquifer (Humphries, 1964). South of Haslemere, the Hythe Beds rise again to form the prominent scarps of Blackdown and Bexley Hill, both facing inwards across the Vale of Fernhurst itself carved from the Weald Clay, together providing a good example of anticlinal breaching. Each scarp foot is marked by a number of landslips, still active in wet weather, where Hythe Beds have collapsed above the unstable Atherfield Clay. As it is finally traced into East Sussex and back into Kent the Lower Greensand tapers out until, between Lewes and Eastbourne, its scarp completely disappears. South of Maidstone, near the village of Loose, however, the Hythe Beds give rise to such karstic features as disappearing streams and swallow holes where the strata consist of 'Kentish Rag'.

The Gault Clay everywhere produces a corridor of cultivated land between the heavily forested Greensands. Even though they are regularly wet the soils of the Vale of Holmesdale differ from those of the Weald Clay vale in so far as they crack more easily as they dry out each summer, thereby assisting cultivation. Moreover, since they occur beneath the chalk escarpment these Gault Clay soils are constantly enriched by calcareous material brought down by solifluction and landslips from above. The Upper Greensand creates only a narrow shelf along the face of the North Downs but at Selborne it blossoms into an escarpment in its own right. Here, in Woolmer Forest, Gilbert White noted how the trees may 'grow large, but are what workmen call shakey, and so brittle as often to fall to pieces when sawing'. So far as scenery is concerned the Gault Clay's most remarkable contribution can be viewed at Folkestone Warren where its unstable nature has caused the overlying Chalk to collapse into gigantic landslips (Osman, 1917). The weight of the toe of each successive slip initially counterbalanced the outward thrust of the slipped masses along the glide-planes within the Gault, but as the sea constantly

Figure 4.3 The vale of the Wealden Clay looking east from the Hythe Beds (Lower Greensand) escarpment near Hindhead. The escarpment continues to Leith Hill in the far distance.

removed these temporary baulks so the landslips became periodically reactivated (Fig. 4.4). Following the disastrous 1915 slip, which destroyed the Dover–Folkestone railway, modern engineering structures appear finally to have overcome the problem. At Dover the treacherous Gault Clay is well below sea level, allowing the famous chalk cliffs to present a bold seaward face across the Channel. It is in the Chalk Marl of the Lower Chalk that the Channel Tunnel has been excavated.

A few kilometres to the west of Folkestone and Hythe the Channel coast descends to the low coastal plain where the Vale of Kent, occupying the broad Weald Clay outcrop, runs out to sea. Here, the lonely windswept landscape of Romney Marsh dominates the coastal scene (Cunliffe, 1980). Wherever medieval sheep farming once featured as a dominant English land use it appears that 'wool churches' abound, founded from the wealth of the early wool merchants. This Kentish marsh is no exception and 'wherever you go in Romney Marsh, you are seldom out of sight of a church', as John Piper discovered. Although not the grandest, the little church of Fairfield, isolated among the sheep-grazed sward, epitomizes the flat, deserted marshland. The dikes and ditches of this waterlogged country cause the lanes to bend incessantly as they link such villages as Burmarsh, Newchurch, and Ivychurch with Old Romney which was once a port but is now well inland (Eddison and Green, 1988). The alluvial tracts of this coastal marsh

Figure 4.4 Folkestone Warren, Kent, with cliffs of Middle and Lower Chalk overlooking the slipped and fallen masses of Chalk and Gault Clay. Note the sea defences.

have been deposited by the streams and rivers which meandered slowly seawards across the former saltings (Ferry and Waters, 1985) that accumulated behind the great natural shingle breakwater of Dungeness, the largest accumulation of beach pebbles in Britain. Its successive shingle ridges have grown slowly eastwards, by the process known as *longshore drift*, so that the Ness itself has also migrated eastwards, necessitating the relocation of the lighthouse several times (Lewis, 1932). The shingle spits grew across the mouth of a wide bay that once stretched from Winchelsea to Hythe and whose former coastline is now marked by a line of low inland cliffs. The bay probably came into existence with the drowning of the lower Rother valley, itself formed along the easily eroded belt of Weald Clay. The Rother once reached the sea at New Romney but now breaks through the shingle at Rye several kilometres to the west of the exposed foreland (Greensmith and Gutmanis, 1990). The relative isolation of Dungeness and the copious supply of water for cooling led to its being chosen as the site for two nuclear power stations on this windswept point. Of much earlier date are the ancient ports of Winchelsea, Rye and Appledore, located on the old abondoned sea cliff. They also stand alongside the Royal Military Canal which, with the Martello Towers and Second World War pillboxes, were built at various times to frustrate threatened invasions from across the Channel. Other notable engineering structures are the numerous sea walls, such as that at Dymchurch built on the foundations of a medieval wall, that now protect Romney Marsh from catastrophic flooding. Near Eastbourne, but on a much smaller scale, the Pevensey Levels bear a close resemblance to Romney Marsh, though lacking the impressive shingle banks of Dungeness. The Pevensey marshes, too, have silted up behind the coastal spit of Langney Point, leaving the Roman and Norman fortress of Pevensey Castle well inland. The former bay was carved where the Weald Clay of the Vale of Sussex meets the coast.

A final word is necessary on the remarkable drainage pattern exhibited by the Weald where rivers have played a major part in the fashioning of one of the best-known denuded dome landscapes in Britain. In his *Principles of Geology* (1833) the eminent geologist Charles Lyell argued that the chalk scarps of the Weald could only have been cut by sea waves. Other nineteenth-century geologists believed that the river gaps of the North and South Downs were either glacial troughs or had been carved along fault lines. It was J. B. Jukes in 1862, fresh from his work in southern Ireland, who wondered

> whether the lateral river-valleys that now escape through ravines traversing the ruined walls of Chalk that surround the Weald may not be the expression of the former river-valleys that began to run down the slopes of the Chalk from the then-dominant ridge that first appeared as dry land during or after the Eocene period?

Thus the initial concept of superimposed drainage from a cover of strata since destroyed became established for more than a century. In the mid-twentieth century Wooldridge and Linton (1955) accepted that the rivers were superimposed (but in a different way) for they believed that the Wealden dome became an island when South-East England was partly submerged by a rise of sea level in Plio-Pleistocene times, leaving beach deposits at various elevations up to 180 metres on the surrounding chalklands, like those described at Beachy Head (p. 77) and at Netley Heath (p. 75). This so-called *Calabrian transgression*, which also deposited the ferruginous Red Crag sediments of East Anglia and the London Basin (see p. 94), was thought by Wooldridge and Linton to have cut a platform of marine abrasion across both the Chalk and later rocks not only on the Chilterns dipslope but also all round the 'Wealden Island'. These writers considered that the Weald's discordant drainage (where rivers that are adjusted to the Central Wealden structures suddenly break out to north and south through the high chalk rim) could be explained by superimposition from this smooth Calabrian bench. They argued that as sea level fell, the rivers running down this sloping surface cut down through the Chalk and older rocks, displaying no regard for the east–west folds within the main Wealden anticlinorium. Not only have these superimposition hypotheses been recently challenged but doubts have also been raised about the validity of a Calabrian transgression outside the London Basin. It is now thought unlikely that the Plio-Pleistocene inundation would have been sufficiently long to allow the fashioning of a wide marine platform that would have totally erased the former drainage lines. Instead, an alternative hypothesis of antecedent drainage, first proposed in 1910, has been resurrected (Jones, 1980), in which the well-adjusted rivers of the Central Weald and the discordant rivers of the chalkland perimeter can satisfactorily be explained as described below. When the Wealden dome first appeared in the early Tertiary, the small north- and south-flowing rivers that ran down its flanks would ultimately have become closely adjusted to the east–west structures of the Central Weald, especially along the easily eroded clay belts. As they flowed further away from the central axis of the dome, however, the rivers would have become large enough to keep pace with the repeated uplift of the Weald, and their downcutting energy would have been constantly renewed as they were periodically uplifted and rejuvenated. This must, therefore, have enabled them to maintain their north- or south-flowing courses across the developing secondary folds of the chalk downlands. So great was the advantageous entrenching power of these rivers that several river captures have ensued, particularly where their tributaries have cut back rapidly along the clay vales. For example, the Wey has beheaded the Blackwater, taking its Hampshire headwaters from above Alton along the Gault Clay vale to Guildford. This has produced a marked 'elbow of capture' near Farnham and left the lower Blackwater as a 'misfit' stream in its broad valley. Similarly, in Kent the Medway has captured some of the headwaters of the Stour and Darent in the Vale of Kent.

The London Basin

The landscape of this large triangular lowland has few of the topographic or scenic attractions that make the neighbouring chalklands and the Weald so distinctive. Its hills are modest, its estuarine coast is largely industrialized, its heathlands often urbanized and many of its older towns are built from the ubiquitous yellow bricks derived from the London Clay. Only its rivers bring a measure of relief from this scenic monotony, especially where the Thames cuts deeply into the Chalk between Henley and Maidenhead or where the Blackwater and Crouch empty into the breezy North Sea through the lonely Essex marshes where a slowly rising sea level is nibbling away at the convoluted coastline (Devoy, 1982). Here one can find landscapes to compare favourably with any in lowland Britain. In any study of the region's landscapes two persistent themes occur: the sequential evolution of the Thames and the inexorable growth of London.

It has already been explained how the structure of the London Basin is asymmetrical, with the central axis lying nearer to its southern rather than its northern margins (Pitcher *et al.*, 1958). Such asymmetry has had an important influence on the alignment of the Thames, for throughout the Quaternary the river has attempted to move farther and farther south down the gentler northern limb of the downfold in order to reach the central axis of the trough, a process known as *uniclinal shifting*. In its lower reaches the Thames has moved so far south that it is now impinging on the Chalk of the North Downs near Erith. The Middle Thames, however, does not leave the Chilterns Chalk until Windsor, where it finally establishes its course on the broad plain of London Clay. The asymmetry has further affected the London Basin in so far as it has caused an irregular outcrop of the Lower Tertiary rocks (Sherlock, 1960). This is particularly true of the Reading Beds, for the gentler dip of the basin's northern limb has maintained a relatively wide outcrop between Newbury and Uxbridge, together with numerous outliers left isolated by erosion on the Chiltern Hills. By contrast, the sharp upturn of the rocks along the southern margin of the London Basin has determined that the Reading Beds appear only as an inconsequential ribbon squeezed between the London Clay and the hog's-back of the North Downs chalk. Thus in the 100 kilometre tract between Epsom in Surrey and Highclere in Berkshire the Reading Beds exposure is never more than 500 metres in width (Fig. 4.5a).

The Reading Beds, however, are not the oldest of the Tertiary rocks in the London Basin for the Thanet Sands were the first of the Palaeocene rocks to be laid down as the transgressing seas flooded into the downfold of the Chalk (Figure 4.5b), but only as far west as a line drawn from Colchester to Guildford. Characteristically, the Thanet Sands overlie a basal layer of large, green-coated horned flints, termed the Bullhead Bed. This horizon of unworn flints, lying on the eroded surface of the Chalk, is thought to represent the buried clay-with-flints on their still-to be-exhumed sub-Palaeocene surface. The succeeding sediments demonstrate how the marine Woolwich Beds give way westwards to the estuarine Reading Beds (Ellison, 1983) as shown in Fig. 4.5b. The flat-topped bluffs of Bromley, Sidcup and Woolwich have been carved from the shelly sands of the Woolwich Beds but farther west the sands and mottled clays of the Reading Beds have been less built over. In rural Berkshire (Anderson, 1974) these sands produce quite fertile soils on which a few vineyards have been established, while round the towns the clays were once intensively exploited to produce the blue, red and yellow bricks which create the harlequin façades of the older parts of Slough, Reading and Newbury. Because natural building stones are absent from the basin's Tertiary rocks many older churches on the western outskirts of London include local 'rubble' in their structures (Robinson and Worssam, 1989). Those at Aldenham, Radlett, Edgware and Stanmore, for example, have incorporated Hertfordshire Puddingstone (see p. 60); those at Ruislip, Pinner and Harrow have used a dark ferricrete (Reading Beds sands cemented by iron); farther south, at places such as Harlington church and Harmondsworth Tithe Barn, the Pleistocene terrace gravel ferricretes are conspicuous in the fabric, for they have been naturally bonded, by percolation of iron-rich ground water, into massive blocks of semi-angular 'gravel-stone'. Today, however, modern buildings require countless tons of unconsolidated gravel and sand for their concrete skeletons and only the floodplain and lower terrace gravels of the Kennet and Thames can meet the incessant demand in the booming South-East. The brick pits of the London Basin, therefore, have been largely abandoned to be replaced by a rash of gravel pits, many of them water-filled where they have reached below the water table. Around Reading and Colnbrook, for example, the river floodplains now resemble a miniature Broadland, though these water bodies are also heavily used by recreationists. Near Staines other large lakes are also artificial but these represent the reservoirs for London's water supply. Nevertheless, much of the capital's drinking water is derived from the Thames which itself is constantly recharged from the chalklands' aquifer which underlies the basin.

By far the most extensive of the Tertiary sediments is that of the London Clay (Fig. 4.5) which is not only the thickest of the formations but also stretches from

(a)

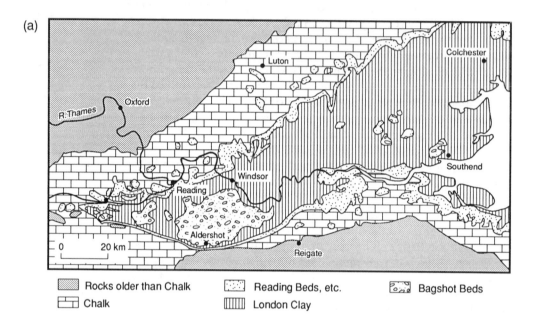

Rocks older than Chalk   Reading Beds, etc.   Bagshot Beds
Chalk   London Clay

(b)

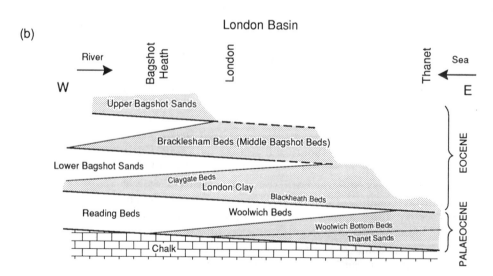

Herne Bay in Kent west to Newbury and thence north-east (under the Pleistocene cover) to Yarmouth in Norfolk. The clay has proved yielding enough to allow the excavation of London's Underground railway system but firm enough to provide a sturdy foundation for its City skyscrapers. Typically, it is a dark, bluish-grey clay that in rural areas gives rise to heavy waterlogged soils occupied largely by permanent grassland throughout the Thames Valley and the southern tracts of Essex (that is, south of the freer-draining Chalky Boulder Clay loams) (Clayton, 1957). These clay plains were once thickly wooded, though few oak woods survive, save in Epping or Windsor Forests. Yet London placenames, such as St John's Wood, Wormwood Scrubs and Enfield Chase, testify to a former forest cover. The clay plain is broken by a few isolated hills in southern Essex (for example, the Rayleigh Hills) and in north London (Highgate and Hampstead Heath) wherever patches of Bagshot Beds cap the London Clay (Wooldridge and Hutchings, 1957). Such outliers suggest that these gravelly strata must once have been more widespread in the central basin, linking up with the main Bagshot Beds outcrop around Camberley. Here, at the junction of Berkshire, Hampshire and Surrey, a rolling heathland is characterized by bleached, podzolized soils supporting little more than birch, pine and gorse. The sterile soils offer virtually no agricultural potential and have been given over, therefore, to a network of sprawling urban centres (Woking, Chertsey, Ascot, Crowthorne and Fleet) or to military establishments at places such as Pirbright, Aldershot and Farnborough (with Greenham Common as a western outlier near Newbury). It is paradoxical, when one examines the location of airfields in the London Basin, that the largest, Heathrow, occupies some of the finest agricultural land in the South-East, for it stands on spreads of well-drained fertile brickearths similar to those described in Kent (p. 75).

The evolution of the Thames

The oldest member of the Thames drainage system within the London Basin is the Kennet which, from its source near Avebury, flows due east to join the Thames at Reading. It was spawned some 65 million years ago at the same time as the 'Solent River' (p. 51) and helped supply sediments to the Reading Beds. In Pliocene times (60 million years later) a left-bank tributary of this ancient river is thought to have cut back through the Chalk and captured the entire catchment of the Upper Thames which lay outside the London Basin. From the point of capture at the Goring Gap the greatly enlarged river then flowed north-eastwards along the northern margin of the London Basin past the sites of present day St Albans and Stevenage before debouching in the Blackwater estuary of Essex (Bridgland, 1988). It is thought that this peripheral route was initiated soon after the withdrawal of the Calabrian Sea from the London Basin in the early Pleistocene (see p. 94). Although the Quaternary environments and chronology of the Upper Thames have only recently been reconstructed (Briggs and Gilbertson, 1980), the Quaternary history of the Lower Thames was first pieced together more than fifty years ago by Wooldridge (1938) who explained the sequential fashioning of the well-preserved river terraces in relation to the fluctuating sea level and the various ice advances. He believed that the river was twice diverted southwards, first from the Vale of St Albans and then from the Finchley Depression, by an ice sheet which deposited the Chalky Boulder Clay (now thought to be of Anglian age). Recent research (Baker and Jones, 1980; Green and McGregor, 1980) supports the earlier diversion but not the later one, by demonstrating that the Finchley Depression was once the valley of a northward-extended Mole–Wey river system when it was a major right-bank tributary of the early Thames during its northernmost course to the Blackwater estuary. Such an interpretation implies not only that this Weald river system crossed a London Basin brim-full with Tertiary sediments but also that this was the only mechanism by which the Lower Greensand cherts could have reached the older and higher gravels of this early Thames (Gibbard, 1985). It was the lower terrace gravels, however, that were to yield the hominoid fossil remains and the artefacts of Britain's earliest residents, at a time when the Thames had moved south. Some of the best finds have been made at Swanscombe in North Kent and in the Winter Hill Terrace to the north of Reading (Wymer, 1968).

Long before humans appeared the highest of the Thames terraces (the so-called Gravel Trains) had been formed at a time when northern ice sheets impinged on the Cotswolds, for these gravelly terraces are full of Bunter quartzite pebbles glacially transported from the Midlands Trias before being channelled by meltwater streams across the Cotswolds and thence through the Chalk via the Goring Gap into the London Basin (Hey, 1965). These purplish pebbles became mixed with the local flints to form a great swathe of terrace gravel (now standing 70 metres above the modern river) that extends laterally along the Chilterns dipslope from Goring through Henley and Beaconsfield to Watford and St Albans (Gibbard, 1989). Wherever patches of this terrace have survived dissection by chalk dry-valleys they support open heaths and commons among the Chiltern beechwoods. As the course of the Thames moved southwards due partly to uniclinal shifting and partly to glacial diversion, it gradually abandoned the higher terraces (Rose, 1983). One of the last to be abandoned was that known as the Winter Hill terrace which, at an elevation of 55 metres above present river, has left a partly loess-filled empty channel just to the north of Reading and Caversham (Shephard-Thorne and Wymer, 1977). However, the great loop of the river between Henley and Maidenhead appears to have become so deeply entrenched in the Chalk that any southward shift of its course is now impossible (see Fig. 4.5a) The most picturesque reach of the Thames lies between Goring and Cliveden, where pretty flint-built villages fringe the river and climbing beechwoods clothe the steep valley sides at Mapledurham, Wargrave, Henley and Marlow (Fig. 4.6). Nearby, Windsor Castle stands on an isolated knob of solid chalk that protrudes through the plain of London Clay. Once having escaped the embrace of the Chalk the meandering river henceforth only occasionally encounters solid rocks that border its floodplain. Gravesend and Greenwich grew up at such rare sites but generally the Lower Thames floodplain is so wide that marshes are much more common. Thus early settlers had to travel far upstream to find a crossing; it was on either flank of London's original ford that Bronze Age farmers settled at Cornhill and on the South Bank, two millennia before the Romans founded Londinium at the then tidal limit near modern London Bridge (Nunn, 1983). Here on two gravel-capped mounds the forerunner of modern London was laid out on the north bank near the Tower. Nearby, other gravel 'islands' stood above the marshes and their names, Chelsea, Battersea and Putney, indicate how the city had begun to expand by Saxon times, for the Saxon suffix -*ea* or -*ey* indicates an island (cf. *eyot*), although Thorney is now known as Westminster. These low terrace fragments were formed when a falling Pleistocene sea level rejuvenated the river, causing it

Figure 4.6 Riverside scenery where the Thames is cut into the Chilterns chalk near Mapledurham. Reading is sited on the Tertiary clays and Pleistocene gravel terraces in the distance.

to cut down into its former floodplains. The successive incisions have left a staircase of terraces up which the metropolis has gradually climbed (Smailes, 1964). Most of the older city development, but also Heathrow Airport, occupies the so-called Taplow terrace formed during the last interglacial (Ipswichian) and now standing some 9–12 metres above the river. The next highest terrace, on which Clapham Common and Pentonville stand, occurs about 30 metres above the modern river and is termed the Boyn Hill terrace. The latter, plus the Taplow and Winter Hill terraces, are all named from the Maidenhead area where they are clearly developed. Elsewhere in the basin the terrace chronology has been subdivided and new names introduced by later scholars, but for the purposes of the present volume only the most conspicuous of the terraces have been described.

Bibliography

Allen, P. (1958) *Geology of the Central Weald: The Hastings Beds*. Guide no. 24. Geol. Assoc.

Anderson, J. R. L. (1974) *The Upper Thames*. Eyre Methuen. 301 pp.

Baker, C. A. and Jones, D. K. C. (1980) Glaciation of the London Basin and its influence on the drainage pattern: a review and appraisal in D. K. C. Jones (ed.), *The Shaping of Southern England*. Academic Press. 131–75.

Bird, E. C. F. (1963) Denudation of the Weald Clay Vale in West Kent. *Proc. Geol. Assoc.*, **74**, 445–56.

Brandon, P. (1974) *The Sussex Landscape*. Hodder & Stoughton. 288 pp.

Bridgland, D. R. (1988) The Pleistocene fluvial stratigraphy and palaeogeography of Essex. *Proc. Geol. Assoc.*, **99**, 291–314.

Briggs, D. J. and Gilbertson, D. D. (1980) Quaternary processes and environments in the Upper Thames basin. *Trans. Inst. Brit. Geog.* (NS), **5**, 53–65.

Burr, M. (1909) The South Eastern Coalfield: its discovery and development. *Science Progress*, **3**, 379–409.

Burrin, P. J. (1981) Loess in the Weald. *Proc. Geol. Assoc*, **92**, 87–92.

Castledean, R. (1982) *Classic Landforms of the Sussex Coast*. Landscape Guide no. 2. Geogr. Assoc.

Clayton, K. M. (1957) Some aspects of the glacial deposits of Essex. *Proc. Geol. Assoc.*, **68**, 1–21.

Coleman, A. and Luckhurst, C. T. (1967) *East Kent*. British Landscapes through Maps no. 10. Geogr. Assoc.

Cunliffe, B. W. (1980) The evolution of Romney Marsh: a preliminary statement, in F. H. Thompson (ed.) *Archaeology and Coastal Change*. Soc. of Antiquaries. 37–55.

Curry, D. (1965) The Palaeogene Beds of South East England. *Proc. Geol. Assoc.*, **76**, 151–74.

Devoy, R. J. (1982) Analysis of the geological evidence for Holocene sea-level movements in southeast England. *Proc. Geol. Assoc.*, **93**, 65–90.

Dewey, H., Wooldridge, S. W., Cornes, H. W. and Brown, E. E. S. (1925) Geology of the Canterbury District. *Proc. Geol. Assoc.*, **36**, 257–84.

Eddison, J. and Green, C. (eds) (1988) *Romney Marsh: Evolution, Occupation, Reclamation*. Oxbow. 208pp.

Ellison, R. A. (1983) Facies distribution in the Woolwich and Reading Beds of the London Basin, England. *Proc. Geol. Assoc.*, **94**, 311–20.

Ferry, B and Waters, S. (1985) *Dungeness: Ecology and Conservation*. Nature Conservancy Council. 144 pp.

Fowler, J. (1932) One hundred foot raised beach between Arundel and Chichester, Sussex. *Quart. J. Geol. Soc.*, **88**, 84–99.

Gallois, R. W. and Edmunds, F. H. (1965) *The Wealden District* (4th edn). British Regional Geology. HMSO. 101 pp.

Gaster, C. T. A. (1929) Chalk zones in the neighbourhood of Shoreham, Brighton and Newhaven. *Proc. Geol. Assoc.*, **40**, 328–40.

Gibbard, P. L. (1985) *The Pleistocene History of the Middle Thames Valley*. Cambridge University Press. 155 pp.

Gibbard, P. L. (1989) The geomorphology of a part of the Middle Thames forty years on: a reappraisal of the work of F. Kenneth Hare. *Proc. Geol. Assoc.*, **100**, 481–504.

Gibbons, W. (1981) *The Weald*. Unwin. 116 pp.

Gossling, F. (1929) The geology of the country around Reigate. *Proc. Geol. Assoc.*, **40**, 197–259.

Green, C. P. and McGregor, D. F. M. (1980) Quaternary evolution of the River Thames, in D. K. C. Jones (ed), *The Shaping of Southern Britain*. Academic Press. 177–202.

Greensmith, J. T. and Gutmanis, I. C. (1990) Aspects of the Late Holocene history of the Dungeness area, Kent. *Proc. Geol. Assoc.*, **101**, 225–38.

Hayward, H. A. (1932) The Geology of the Lower Greensand in the Dorking–Leith Hill District. *Proc. Geol. Assoc.*, **43**, 1–31.

Hey, R. W. (1965) Highly quartzose Pebble Gravels in the London Basin. *Proc. Geol. Assoc.*, **76**, 403–20.

Humphries, D. W. (1964) The stratigraphy of the Lower Greensand of the South West Weald. *Proc. Geol. Assoc.*, **75**, 39–60.

John, D. T. and Fisher, P. F. (1984) The stratigraphical and geomorphological significance of the Red Crag fossils at Netley Heath, Surrey: a review and re-appraisal. *Proc. Geol. Assoc.*, **95**, 235–48.

Jones, D. K. C. (1980) *The Shaping of Southern England*. Academic Press.

Kirkaldy, J. F. (1958) *Geology of the Weald*. Guide no. 29. Geol. Assoc.

Knowles, L. and Middlemiss, F. A. (1958) The Lower Greensand in the Hindhead area of Surrey and Hampshire. *Proc. Geol. Assoc.*, **69**, 205–38.

Lake, R. D. (1975) The structure of the Weald – a review. *Proc. Geol. Assoc.*, **86**, 549–58.

Lake, R. D. and Shephard-Thorne, E. R. (1985) The stratigraphy and geological structure of the Hog's Back, Surrey and adjoining areas. *Proc. Geol. Assoc.*, **96**, 7–22.

Lewis, W. V. (1932) The formation of Dungeness Foreland. *Geog. J.*, **30**, 309–24.

Mason, O. (1979) *South-East England*. John Bartholomew and Sons. 217 pp.

Mortimore, R. N. (1986) Stratigraphy of the Upper Cretaceous White Chalk of Sussex. *Proc. Geol. Assoc.*, **97**, 97–140.

Nunn, P. D. (1983) The development of the River Thames in London during the Flandrian. *Trans. Inst. Brit. Geogr.* (NS), **8**, 187–213.

Osman, C. W. (1917) The landslips of Folkestone Warren and the thickness of the Lower Chalk and Gault near Dover. *Proc. Geol. Assoc.*, **28**, 59–82.

Owen, H. G. (1975) The stratigraphy of the Gault and Upper Greensand of the Weald. *Proc. Geol. Assoc.*, **86**, 475–98.

Pitcher, W. S., Peake, N. B., Carreck, J. N. *et al.* (1958) *The London Region*. Guide no. 30. Geol. Assoc.

Robinson, A. H. W. and Cloet, R. L. (1953) Coastal evolution in Sandwich Bay. *Proc. Geol. Assoc.*, **64**, 69–82.

Robinson, D. A. and Williams, R. B. G. (1976) Aspects of the geomorphology of the sandstone cliffs of the Central Weald. *Proc. Geol. Assoc.*, **87**, 93–9.

Robinson, D. A. and Williams, R. B. G. (1984) *Classic Landforms of the Weald*. Guide no. 4. Geogr. Assoc.

Robinson, E. and Worssam, B. C. (1989) The geology of some Middlesex churches. *Proc. Geol. Assoc.*, **100**, 595–603.

Robinson, N. D. (1986) Lithostratigraphy of the Chalk Group of the North Downs, southeast England. *Proc. Geol. Assoc.*, **97**, 141–70.

Rose, J. (1983) *The Diversion of the Thames*. Quaternary Research Association.

Shephard-Thorne, E. R. (1975) The Quaternary of the Weald – a review. *Proc. Geol. Assoc.*, **86**, 537–47.

Shephard-Thorne, E. R. and Wymer, J. J. (eds) (1977) *South East England and the North and East Thames Valley*. INQUA Guidebook for Excursion A4.

Sherlock, R. L. (1960) *London and the Thames Valley* (3rd edn). HMSO. 62 pp.

Smailes, A. E. (1964) The site, growth and changing face of London, in R. Clayton, *The Geography of Greater London*. G. Philip. 1–52.

Stubblefield, C. J. (1954) The Kent Coalfield, in A. E. Trueman (ed.), *The Coalfields of Great Britain*. Arnold. 154–166.

Sweeting, G. S. (1944) Wealden iron ore and the history of its industry. *Proc. Geol. Assoc.*, **55**, 1–20.

Williams, R. B. G. and Robinson, D. A. (1983) The landforms of Sussex, in The Geography Editorial Commitee, Sussex, *Environment, Landscape and Society*. Alan Sutton. 33–49.

Wooldridge, S. W. (1938) The Glaciation of the London Basin and the evolution of the Lower Thames drainage system. *Quart. J. Geol. Soc.*, **94**, 627–67.

Wooldridge, S. W. and Goldring, F. (1953) *The Weald*. Collins. 276 pp.

Wooldridge, S. W. and Hutchings, G. E. (1957) *London's Countryside*. Methuen. 223 pp.

Wooldridge, S. W. and Linton, D. L. (1955) *Structure, Surface and Drainage in South East England* (2nd edn). G. Philip. 176 pp.

Worssam, B. C. (1964) Iron Ore workings in the Weald Clay of the western Weald. *Proc. Geol. Assoc.*, **75**, 529–46.

Wymer, J. J. (1968) *Lower Palaeolithic Archaeology in Britain: as represented by the Thames Valley*. John Baker.

East Anglia and the Fens

5

Two of the flattest areas of lowland Britain share certain physiographic similarities which distinguish them from most other parts: first, they contain some of Britain's most extensive alluvial stretches, including some tracts below sea level, and second, they are composed of Britain's youngest sedimentary deposits (Chatwin, 1961). A third feature that is also distinctive, though not readily apparent in the landscape, is the status of East Anglia as the type-site for many of Britain's early Quaternary sediments. The general lack of elevation in this broad swathe of eastern England can be explained in part by the fact that it has only recently been raised above sea level and in part by the fact that its location along the flank of the North Sea basin means that its surface is constantly subsiding as Britain tilts from west to east (Shennan, 1982). The local crustal sinking is now being exacerbated by a global rise in sea level caused by polar ice cap melting due to the 'greenhouse effect'. Some experts predict that by the year 2100 not only will such shingle headlands as Dungeness and Orford Ness be submerged by a sea level 1 metre higher than at present but that large tracts of the Thames estuary, the East Anglian Broads and the Fens will also be inundated. Although this eastern region is an area of low relief it is by no means a plain, for it will be shown how the elevation varies between the Cromer Ridge (92 m) and the Fens (−2.75 m). Moreover, the superficial deposits brought by the ice sheets have not only given East Anglia its characteristic undulating countryside and fertile soils but their unconsolidated nature has encouraged the rivers to excavate some surprisingly deep valleys, especially on the northern flanks of the Cromer Ridge and in the Gipping valley of Suffolk which has been cut down through the drift into the underlying Chalk (Allen, 1984). In general, however, East Anglian landscapes are characterized by reed-fringed marshes and lazy rivers, unspoiled villages set amid rich cornlands, low, sandy and shingly coasts backed by broad marine vistas – the type of scenery that has inspired some of Britain's greatest landscape artists, including Gainsborough, Constable and those of the Norwich School.

Apart from the Chalk the underlying Mesozoic rocks play virtually no part in the modern scenery though the Fenlands occupy a broad lowland trough associated with the wide outcrop of Jurassic clays. Equally, the eastern coastlands are little influenced by the drift-covered Reading Beds and London Clay except to emphasize the region's generally low relief. Even the Chalk, whose contribution to the scenery has already been noted in Chapter 3, gives only a slight enhancement to the relief of western Norfolk and Suffolk; the distinctive colour and texture of the Chalky Boulder Clay has been its major contribution to the regional features. Nevertheless, East Anglia's main foundation remains the gently sloping surface of the buried Chalk which, throughout Tertiary times, controlled the easterly flow of such rivers as the Great Ouse as they emptied into the deepening North Sea. It was only after the close of the Tertiary era, some 2.3 million years ago, that the sea began to withdraw from England's eastern fringes but not before it had left behind a complex series of shelly, muddy and sandy rocks known collectively as the Crags.

East Anglia during the Quaternary

The soft, crumbly rocks of the Crags make very little contribution to the scenery because they consist of friable shelly sands and clays that have had little time to become consolidated since they were laid down in Plio-Pleistocene times (Ovey and Pitcher, 1948). Thus, they have been easily eroded by weather, rivers and the sea. But, of much greater significance, their fossils illustrate how the relatively temperate climatic conditions of pre-glacial times (Pliocene to Mid-Pleistocene) degenerated through several oscillations of temperature into the severe glacial and periglacial conditions of the Ice Age (later Pleistocene) (Fig. 5.1) (Gibbard and Zalasiewicz, 1988). The Crags can be subdivided into three broad groups: the Coralline Crag Formation (Pliocene) exposed as a low coastal ridge behind Orford Ness in Suffolk (Bristow, 1983); the Red Crag Formation and overlying Norwich Crag Formation that together form the bulk of the Crag deposits as they extend from North Essex to north Norfolk; and finally, the Cromer Forest Bed Formation, exposed only on the north Norfolk coast. All these strata are older than the Anglian glaciation (Perrin *et al.*, 1979), the drifts of which bury them by varying degrees, the same glacial advance that penetrated the northern fringes of the London Basin and helped divert the Thames (see Chapter 4).

Geologists have recently declared that the base of the Pleistocene should be dated as 2.3 million years old and in doing so have left the iron-stained sands of the Red Crag Formation squarely across the Tertiary–Quaternary boundary (Dixon, 1979). The best exposures of these beds, which contain the first British remains of true horses and elephants, are to be seen in the overgrown crumbling sea cliffs at Felixstowe, Harwich and Walton, although the greatly dissected Red Crag outcrop has been traced as a 12 metre thick sheet ascending westwards into Hertfordshire. Near Rothamsted, at a height of 131 metres on the Chilterns, its westernmost outlier occurs, suggesting to some experts a tiny survival of a former Calabrian 180 metre sea level in the London Basin (see p. 87) but to others simply a measure of the amount of post-depositional tilting of East Anglia in response to the subsidence of the North Sea basin.

The so-called Norwich Crag Formation is less homogeneous than that of the Red Crag and is only sporadically exposed at the surface. One of its components, the dark grey Chillesford Clay, occurring near Aldeburgh, was once thought to be the channel-filling of an ancestral Thames but is now believed to be an ancient tidal flat deposited during one of the early warm stages of the Pleistocene (Bramertonian) (Funnell *et al.*, 1979). Another part of the Norwich Crag Formation, represented by a bluish marine silt exposed along the Suffolk coast at Covehithe and Easton Bavents (Funnell and West, 1962), has now become the type-facies for one of the colder Pleistocene stages (Baventian), as shown in Fig. 5.1. The rapidly eroding coastal cliffs regularly reveal new sections and different Pleistocene sediments, so that geologists are constantly revising the stratigraphy and relative ages of the strata. Considerable advances have been made, for example, in the interpretation of the Cromer Forest Bed Formation since it was first described by Clement Reid in 1882 and which has been taken as the horizon (Cromerian) which separates the truly 'solid' rocks of the Early Pleistocene from the overlying glacial drifts of Middle and Upper Pleistocene age (Boulton *el al.*, 1984). It is best seen beneath the crumbling boulder clay cliffs of north Norfolk between Cromer and Sheringham (Fig. 5.2), though it extends as far east as

	Stages	Climate	Type Locality	Formations, boundaries, sediments, dates	
HOLOCENE	FLANDRIAN	Temperate		< 10,000 (years before present)	
UPPER PLEISTOCENE	DEVENSIAN	Glacial with cool interstadial interludes	Four Ashes, Staffordshire	LATE. Loch Lomond Stadial (10,000 - 11,500) Windermere Interstadial (11,500 - 13,000) Dimlington Stadial (13,000 - 26,000) MIDDLE. (26,000 - 50,000) Includes Upton Warren Interstadial Complex EARLY. (Pre-50,000) Includes Chelford Interstadial (C.100,000)	
UPPER PLEISTOCENE	IPSWICHIAN	Temperate Interglacial	Bobbitshole, Ipswich, Suffolk	Ipswichian lake muds (C.125,000) Max. sea level C.8 m	
UPPER PLEISTOCENE	'WOLSTONIAN' COMPLEX	'Wolstonian' ? Glacial with temperate interglacial	Glacial site to be established ⎯⎯⎯ Marsworth, Bucks	Included Marsworth Interglacial (C.180,000)	
MIDDLE PLEISTOCENE	HOXNIAN	Temperate Interglacial	Hoxne, Suffolk	Hoxnian lake muds, Nar Valley clays Sea level 20 - 30 m	
MIDDLE PLEISTOCENE	ANGLIAN	Glacial	Corton, Suffolk	Lowestoft Till Corton Sands Cromer Till	
MIDDLE PLEISTOCENE	CROMERIAN	Temperate	West Runton, Norfolk	CROMER FOREST BED FORMATION	Estuarine sands, silts, freshwater peat
LOWER PLEISTOCENE	BEESTONIAN	Cold	Beeston, Norfolk	CROMER FOREST BED FORMATION	Gravels, sands, silts, ⋀⋀⋀ Beestonian split by major unconformity = 1 million years long
LOWER PLEISTOCENE	PASTONIAN	Temperate	Paston, Norfolk	CROMER FOREST BED FORMATION	Estuarine silts, freshwater peat
LOWER PLEISTOCENE	PRE-PASTONIAN	Cold	Beeston, Norfolk	CROMER FOREST BED FORMATION	Gravels, sands, silts
LOWER PLEISTOCENE	BAVENTIAN	Cold	Easton Bavents, Suffolk	NORWICH CRAG FORMATION	Marine silt
LOWER PLEISTOCENE	BRAMERTONIAN	Cold	Bramerton, Norfolk	NORWICH CRAG FORMATION	Marine shelly sand
LOWER PLEISTOCENE	ANTIAN	Temperate	Ludham borehole Norfolk	NORWICH CRAG FORMATION	Marine silt 2 million years ago
LOWER PLEISTOCENE	THURNIAN	Cold	Ludham borehole Norfolk	RED CRAG FORMATION	Marine silt
LOWER PLEISTOCENE	LUDHAMIAN	Temperate	Ludham borehole Norfolk	RED CRAG FORMATION	Marine shelly sand
LOWER PLEISTOCENE	PRE-LUDHAMIAN	Cool Temperate	Stradbroke borehole Norfolk	RED CRAG FORMATION	Red Crag deposits
PLIOCENE	WALTONIAN		Walton-on-Naze, Essex	RED CRAG FORMATION / CORALINE CRAG FORMATION	BASE OF PLEISTOCENE 2.3 million yrs. Lowest part of Red Crag
PLIOCENE		Warm Temperate	Suffolk	CORALINE CRAG FORMATION	Pre-Pleistocene Crags

Figure 5.1 The Quaternary succession in Britain.

Bacton, the modern terminal for North Sea gas. The importance of the Forest Bed's complex series of organic clays, sands and peats, lies in the way they illustrate a virtually unbroken but far from steady transition from the temperate pre-glacial into the cold of glacial times (Fig. 5.1). It shows, moreover, how progressively developing forests of birch, pine, oak, elm and hazel grew sporadically on the eroded surface of the Crags before being overwhelmed by encroaching ice sheets (West, 1980). The first ice sheets to reach East Anglia can be dated to the Middle Pleistocene, approximately at the same time as the Winter Hill terrace of the Thames was being formed (see p. 88). It is known, however, that even earlier ice sheets must have existed in North Wales and the Welsh Borderland because erratic pebbles from these areas occur in some of the Early Pleistocene deposits of East Anglia (Funnell and West, 1962; Hey, 1976). The Mid-Pleistocene ice advances have been termed the Anglian and, notwithstanding the importance of the earlier Plio-Pleistocene water-laid sediments, it has been the glacial drifts that have made the greatest impact on East Anglia for the glaciers completely remodelled the landscape. The combined ice sheets from northern Britain and the North Sea bulldozed across the relatively soft rocks of Norfolk, buckling and overturning the older Pleistocene beds and tearing away great rafts of solid chalk before dumping them among the so-called Contorted Drifts. These comprise Britain's most spectacular example of glaciotectonics and are best seen in the sea cliffs near Cromer. The same Anglian ice sheets also impounded an enormous

Figure 5.2 The crumbling boulder-clay cliffs at Cromer, Norfolk, where the Cromer Forest Bed is regularly exposed at beach level as the fallen debris is removed by the sea.

proglacial lake in the southern part of the North Sea basin, a lake whose eventual overflow was to breach the Franco-Wealden ridge and create the Straits of Dover, thereby finally isolating Britain from the Continent.

The ice sheets of Anglian age (Hart and Pegler, 1990) were an admixture of first, North Sea glaciers, advancing from the north-east and spreading the so-called Cromer Till across Norfolk, and second, of British inland ice pushing southwards into the London Basin and moving into Suffolk from the north-west to deposit the Chalky Boulder Clay of the Lowestoft Till (Rose *et al.*, 1976). The highest land of East Anglia, the 14 kilometre long Cromer Ridge (92 m) of north Norfolk, is in fact a gigantic 'push moraine' composed of sands and gravels and created by the second advance of the Anglian ice (Sparks and West, 1964). When viewed from the north the ridge's steep wooded slopes form an impressive feature behind the low-lying coast, while its widespread cover of bracken and gorse contrasts markedly with the cultivated fields of the surrounding lowlands. The glacial out-wash streams that ran from the ice front down the southern slopes of the ridge were the forerunners of the modern Bure and Yare rivers which today meander through the Broads. They give a good illustration of the relative youthfulness of the East Anglian drainage pattern when compared, for example, with the great antiquity of the rivers of the Weald and the London Basin. Before the final glacial advances (Devensian) impinged on East Anglia there were to be at least three periods of climatic amelioration within the later phases of the Ice Age. The oldest one (the Hoxnian Interglacial) takes its name from the Hoxne brick pit in Suffolk (West, 1956), though Marks Tey in Essex is another site (Turner, 1970), when it is believed that the sea level was some 20–30 metres higher than present. To date the East Anglian equivalent of the Marsworth Interglacial (see p. 65) has not been discovered, but the last of the Pleistocene interglacials (the Ipswichian) is also named from East Anglia although in this case the sea rose no higer than 8 metres above the present level. The final ice sheet, the Devensian, hardly influenced the scenery of East Anglia because it failed to reach the Cromer Ridge, unlike the region farther to the north-west where the ice front had a profound effect on the area now known as the Fens.

Fenland

This vast embayment of flatland surrounding the Wash is not only England's largest example of continuous alluvium but is also one of its most prosperous farming areas (Doody and Barnett, 1987). Not unlike a Dutch polder in appearance (Fig. 5.3), Fenland today is a geometric tapestry with an orderliness and an artificiality that belie its former primitive character as a sodden, marshy and virtually trackless wilderness (Bloom, 1953). Very little of the original marshland now survives except at a few carefully preserved sites such as Woodwalton Fen and Wicken Fen whose undrained peat stands 2 metres higher than the other peatlands. Yet, some 40 000 years ago a vast ice-impounded lake (Lake Fenland) extended as far inland as the sites of Cambridge, Peterborough and Sleaford. The lake, some 30 metres higher than the modern land surface, occupied a basin already carved out of the yielding Jurassic clays (the Oxford, Ampthill and Kimmeridge Clays) by the combined action of the Ouse, Nene, Witham and Welland rivers. It must have been the forerunners of these Fenland rivers that made the mighty breach in the Chalk escarpment now occupied by the Wash. It has been suggested that Lake Fenland found an outlet along the valleys of the Little Ouse and Waveney rivers and thence to Lowestoft (Fig. 5.4). As the Devensian ice sheet retreated a shallow arm of the sea invaded Fenland, whose rivers then continued to dump great thicknesses of silt in their marshy estuaries, aided no doubt by the roots of salt-marsh vegetation, in the same way that the modern saltings of the Wash and the north Norfolk coast act as silt traps. Meanwhile, farther inland the post-glacial (Flandrian) alder and hazel woodlands that once flourished on the lime-rich reed-swamp soils, were gradually decaying to produce thick layers of peat (Godwin, 1968). The post-glacial succession of Fenland estuarine silts, marine clays and peats is very complex and delicately related to small changes in the relative position of land and sea (Shennan, 1982). But the difference between the inland peat fen and the coastal silt fen bordering the Wash has been fundamental in the history of drainage and the growth of settlement and farming. This simple division is broken only where 'islands' of older rocks, as at Ely and Boston, or glacial sands and tills, as at March, provided dry settlement sites some 20–30 metres above the marshes (Taylor, 1973). Such former islands can now be distinguished by their Anglo-Saxon *-ey* or *-ea* suffix in the place names of Ramsey, Whittlesey and Shippea; Ely (Eel Island) is a corrupted form. Elsewhere, the isolated older brick-built farms and their connecting roads have

Figure 5.3 The Fenlands near Southery, Norfolk, where the Great Ouse River is embanked between raised levees that stand above the polder-like fields of the reclaimed marshes. The tonal differences in some of the fields are evidence of former drainage channels.

been forced to cling to the slightly raised silt banks, known as *levees*, that formed along the meandering river channels during times of flood (Parker and Pye, 1976). Today such banks (roddons) stand ever higher as the reclaimed peats continue to shrink, dry out and blow away. At Holme Fen, near Peterborough, some 4 metres of peat have been lost since the cast-iron Holme Post was buried in the fen in 1848 (Hutchinson, 1980) and calculations show that by AD 2050 only 48 km^2 of the original 920 km^2 of Fenland will remain in their original state.

The Romans made the first attempts to drain the Fens but climatic deterioration during Anglo-Saxon times saw the Fens abandoned to become a deserted frontier region between East Anglia and Mercia, contributing to the former's isolation. Such isolation is dramatically illustrated by a remarkable Anglo-Saxon 'in-depth' defence system near Cambridge. Here, the Devil's Ditch, the Fleam Ditch and two others were constructed as defensive earthworks across the narrow chalk corridor that separated the impassable Fenland of the west (Mercia) from the

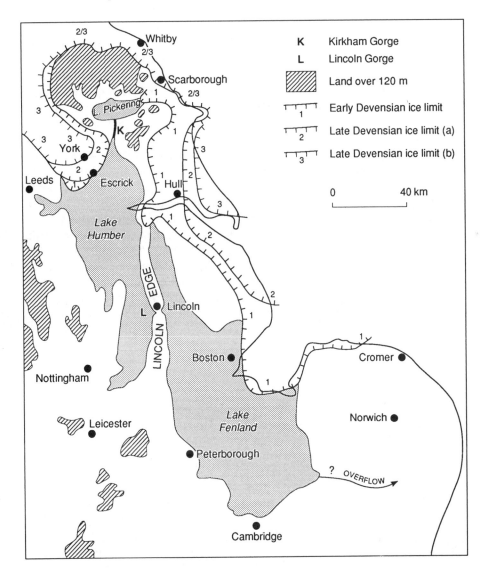

Figure 5.4 Possible extent of proglacial lakes in the Fens and the Humber region during the Devensian ice advance.

thickly wooded boulder clay tracts of East Anglia. Many old Fenland villages are aligned along the old Saxon 'shore' of the Wash (among them Moulton, Waplode and Holbeach in the south, and Wrangle, Leverton and Freiston in the west). Since Saxon times some 32 000 hectares of saltmarsh have been reclaimed and 'Domesday Book' records confirm that the silt fens and islands had become inhabited by Norman times although the peat fens remained unsettled (Darby, 1971). By the thirteenth and fourteenth centuries this dichotomy was further emphasized when such magnificent ecclesiastic structures as Ely Cathedral and Boston and Holbeach churches were built in the silt fens.

The first really successful reclamation of the peat fens began only in the seventeenth century when Vermuyden and other Dutch engineers were brought from the Netherlands by James I and financed in part by the Duke of Bedford, hence the Bedford Levels and the Bedford Rivers (Darby, 1968). Today, the artificial parallel channels of the Old and New Bedford Rivers enclose the Hundred Foot Washes that act as a winter flood-water storage receptacle for the Fens. Because of its seasonal inundation, however, this washland can only be used for summer grazing rather than arable farming. Paradoxically, the lush grassland cover has therefore protected the peat from shrinkage and erosion and the washland is now treasured as a nature reserve inhabited by many important wading birds. Such washlands are the last of the 'foul and flabby quagmires' described by the historian Camden in 1586, for elsewhere the peat fen land use has changed over the centuries from extensive sheep grazing to intensive horticulture in which crops of fruit, vegetables, potatoes and bulbs are grown. Cultivation at this level has only been achieved by 350 years of complex drainage systems, aided at first by windmills and horse mills which were then later replaced by electric pumps and by the straightening and canalizing of the rivers. Trees and hedgerows are virtually redundant in such an agricultural system but the drying of the peaty soil, unprotected from the wind, has led to many stories of wind erosion and the gradual loss of the famous Black Fens. Consequently, large tracts of peat have completely disappeared through windblow and shrinkage, uncovering poor-quality clays that cannot support such prosperous horticulture. Will the farmers eventually suffer the same fate as the fishermen and wildfowlers whose disappearance marked the demise of the natural reed-fringed meres and marshes of the original Fens? A rising sea level during the twenty-first century will certainly put the Fenlands' orchards, nurseries, market gardens and canning factories at risk.

Suffolk and Norfolk

It has already been noted how the solid geology of East Anglia has played only a minor role in the fashioning of its scenery, and thus one must look at the distribution of the superficial deposits, of glacial sands and clays and of post-glacial alluvium, peat and blown sand, in order to explain the various cultural landscapes of Suffolk and Norfolk. As in Fenland, it is these superficial deposits that have affected the soil formation and therefore the patterns of farming and settlement.

Although in southern Essex sand layers intervene in the thick layers of London Clay, where they are sometimes known as the Claygate Beds (Bristow *et al.*, 1980), of greater significance on the border of Essex and Suffolk is the way in which the boulder clays have mixed with the underlying London Clay to produce characteristically heavy unyielding soils that were once thickly forested. Today many of these broadleaf forests have been cleared to be replaced, particularly in the Sandlings of east Suffolk, by occasional patches of conifer plantations among the arable and the hayfields, and in general the mixed farming land of Essex spills over into Suffolk. In the eighteenth century John Kirby, in his *Suffolk Traveller*, noted how the county could be divided into the Sandlands (Sandlings), the Woodlands and the Fielding (Scarfe, 1972). The Sandlings lie to the east of the A12 highway and are seen most frequently between Ipswich and Southwold. Their light podzolic soils, derived from a cover of glacial sands above the Crags, support widespread heaths and commons which, because of their open, well-drained nature, were once the location of important prehistoric and post-Iron Age settlements. The Woodlands is the old name for the central two-thirds of Suffolk stretching between Haverhill and Beccles. Here is the Chalky Boulder Clay country whose fertile medium to heavy loams once supported the oakwoods on which Suffolk's half-timbered houses and shipbuilding industry formerly depended. Unprotected by forest law, these woods were cleared over the centuries, so allowing the loams to reach their true potential as valuable cornlands. This central tract of the Suffolk landscape was that most frequently painted by Constable. Its brick-built moated farmsteads, such as Moat Hall at Parham, were constructed partly for defence but also to retain valuable water in the moat when the chalky boulder clays dried out each summer. The right-angled farmstead boundaries have had a striking influence on the road patterns which twist and turn in an attempt to join up the scattered hamlets, often called Greens or Tyes, that mark the sites of common grazing lands. Suffolk's wooden windmills, once used for corn-grinding in a region where rivers were too sluggish to drive the wheels, have almost disappeared (Addison, 1950). The last of Kirby's divisions, the Fielding, comprises the western part of Suffolk between Bury St Edmunds and Mildenhall, whence it continues into Norfolk. It coincides exactly with the drift-covered chalklands and so contains the open vistas of Newmarket Downs and the forested wilderness of Breckland, as described in Chapter 3. It may have acquired its name from the long persistence of its open fields which, unlike those farther east, remained unenclosed until the late eighteenth century; significantly, it is this tract that has once again reverted to open countryside as modern farmers have grubbed up hedgerows to enlarge the size of their cornfields.

The dichotomy of the landscapes of eastern and western Suffolk is repeated in Norfolk where such contrasts have been admirably described by W. G. Hoskins (1957):

> In the east and centre of the county we find a close network of narrow, winding lanes, wandering from hamlet to hamlet and farm to farm, churches standing alone, isolated houses dotted all over the map . . . a closely packed map with hardly a straight line or an empty space in it. The west of the county is entirely different . . . far fewer lanes and byways, more villages, straighter roads, large empty spaces between the villages, the whole landscape or map more 'open' altogether.

In short, a tightly woven eastern landscape that has grown up piecemeal over centuries, and a western one on the chalklands whose broader scale was largely planned in more recent times. The Breckland, for example, had remained virtually untamed until the Forestry Commission plantings of the present century, but it was the northern parts of Norfolk that were to see the most dramatic scenic changes wrought by Coke of Holkham in the late eighteenth century. Northern Norfolk contains not only the gravelly Cromer Ridge but also vast spreads of sandy outwash from both the Anglian and Devensian ice advances (West and Whiteman, 1986). Despite the presence of some fertile loams in association with the Norwich Brickearths, most of the area is covered by light, sandy soils that are often podzolized and decalcified. By digging down into the underlying calcareous boulder clay, however, Coke and his followers were able to spread these marls over the acidic topsoil; even today the former marl pits can be seen in almost every field. The subsequent introduction of the famous Norfolk four-course rotation on to these so-called 'good sands' brought nothing less than an agricultural revolution to East Anglia (Dymond, 1985). Its poor sheepwalks and open heaths, described by Arthur Young as 'rabbit and rye country', were converted within decades into a landscape where 'abundant crops of wheat and barley cover the entire district'. Many of the large farms and the newer stately homes, which stand today amid prosperous cornfields (Shotton, 1961), were built from the ensuing wealth accumulated by the landowners (Wallace and Oakley, 1951).

In earlier centuries, Norfolk, which was England's most populous county in Norman times, had once shared with Suffolk the previous wealth that had accrued from medieval sheepfarming. Although the numbers of sheep have declined their heritage survives in the form of spectacular wool churches, much more resplendent than those of Romney Marsh (p. 82). Their tall towers rise majestically above the chequerboard of corn and copse, many of them built from flint, the only local building material in an area almost devoid of hard rock strata. Because of the dearth of suitable stone for corner blocks no less than 170 East Anglian churches exhibit flint-built round towers, the majority of them in Norfolk. Two of the most impressive are of Anglo-Saxon age and stand above the Waveney marshes at Haddiscoe. Of the square-towered flint churches two of the most interesting were built from medieval woollen industry endowments: that at Kersey (Suffolk) overlooks a picturesque group of timber-framed, red-roofed cottages whose textile workers once made the cloth known as kerseymere; the other is at Worstead (Norfolk), a village that gave its name to the renowned worsted cloth and whose attractive square of thatched and pantiled houses is dominated by its fourteenth-century church.

East Anglia's comparative isolation hindered the transport of good building stone even from places such as Barnack (Cambridgeshire) (see p. 118) except for the most important edifices. Flint remained, therefore, the most common building material and nowhere else in Britain has it been so extensively worked for this purpose. Various techniques of ornamentation, known as flushwork and chequerwork, have been used, involving the blend of knapped flint and freestone. Excellent examples of each can be seen, respectively, at Long Melford church (Suffolk) and at Norwich Guildhall, though many of the region's larger churches exhibit attractive flintwork. In other cases untrimmed flint nodules set in mortar are more characteristic, especially in the humbler cottages. This is particularly true near the coast, where rounded beach pebbles combined with brick give charm to such Norfolk villages as Trimingham, Weybourne and Kelling. A variation on this theme occurs in Suffolk and coastal Essex, where hard nodules of calcareous clay, known as *septaria*, have been used instead of flint, particularly by the Normans, to construct the redoubtable keep at Orford Castle and also at Colchester Castle.

Erwarton and Harkstead churches, between the Orwell and Stour rivers, are other examples of the use of septarian nodules. The only East Anglian limestone hard enough to have been utilized for building purposes is the shelly Coralline Crag of coastal Suffolk, especially at Aldeburgh and Orford and in the church towers of Chillesford and Wantisden. Nevertheless, in the interior of East Anglia, the commonest building materials have remained timber and brick, as shown by the superbly preserved villages of Lavenham, Long Melford, Finchingfield and Thaxted. The last two examples are in Essex and it is noteworthy how, as one passes south on to these formerly forested claylands, timber buildings become more prominent, culminating in the remarkable Anglo-Saxon wooden church at Greensted. By contrast, in the northern part of East Anglia, Norwich is a walled city built largely from imported limestone because of its great medieval importance (Bailey, 1971). Yet, in 1698 Celia Fiennes noted how its 36 churches 'are built all of flints well headed or cut which makes them look blackish and shineing'. The Normans built their formidable castle on the ridge end between the Wensum and Yare although Norwich's magnificent cathedral was sited by the River Wensum to facilitate the transport of Caen stone from France.

The Broads and the coast

Between Norwich and the sea the rivers Bure, Yare and Waveney meander lazily through marshy meadowlands before merging imperceptibly into wider stretches of shallow water known as the Broads (Ellis, 1965). These reed-fringed water bodies, unique in Britain, are known to millions of holiday-makers for their beauty and their recreational facilities. Originally they were thought to have been formed by the natural silting-up of the estuarine reaches of the rivers but it has now been shown that they are simply flooded medieval peat diggings, the peat having accumulated during swampy conditions analogous to those of Fenland (Lambert *et al.*, 1970). Research has further shown that the Broads are not simply widenings of the main river channels but are connected to them only by narrow links (Fig. 5.5). Baulks and strips of peat remain in the beds of the Broads, notably along parish boundaries, indicative of their artificial genesis. Both archaeological and documentary evidence suggests that in the eleventh to thirteenth centuries peat digging flourished at a time of relatively low sea level but that renewed crustal tilting and/or the continued rise of the Flandrian sea gradually flooded the areas stripped of peat. The recent designation of the Broads National Park is a formal recognition of the scenic beauty of this remarkable region, although the management authority is aware of the threats associated with its intense human use. For example, the considerable nutrient enrichment, resulting from sewage effluent and the run-off from excessive use of fertilizers spread on Norfolk's flourishing cornlands, has led to eutrophication and a catastrophic diminution of aquatic flora and fauna. Yet the neighbouring Halvergate Marsh, inland from Great Yarmouth, once threatened with draining and ploughing, has survived as a traditional sheep- and cattle-grazing wetland following a lengthy controversy between conservationists and landowners.

East Anglia's coastline is one of immense variety, combining stretches affected by severe erosion with tracts where deposition is clearly manifest. West of Weybourne the north Norfolk coast is characterized by salt-marshes that flank an ancient cliffline and which themselves are protected by deserted spits of sand and shingle, notably at Scolt Head Island (Steers, 1934) and Blakeney Point (Hardy, 1964). North-east Norfolk also has a lengthy tract of unstable boulder clay cliffs near Cromer that provide copious supplies of eroded material for beach formation elsewhere. South of Happisburgh a narrow line of dunes denies the sea access to the low-lying plains of Broadland, not always successfully, as testified by the breaches at Horsey in 1938 and Palling in 1953. From Yarmouth past Lowestoft and as far as Orford Ness the river estuaries have all been deflected southwards by the growth of substantial shingle spits. That at Orford is the most spectacular (Carr and Baker, 1968) but those on which Lowestoft and Yarmouth were located have been severely altered by artificial changes to their respective spits. That at Yarmouth, for instance, was cut through at various dates to assist navigation, with its present river mouth being finally established in the sixteenth century. The growth of these gigantic spits and barriers implies a plentiful supply of beach material not all of which has come from the Cromer cliffs. It has been suggested that much of the flinty shingle could have been swept up from the North Sea floor by a rising Flandrian sea level, a hypothesis based on processes similar to those which allegedly built both the south Devon beaches and that at Chesil (see Chapters 2 and 3). Pebbles can only be moved by waves, whereas sand and mud

Figure 5.5 The Norfolk Broads, with the River Bure seen winding between Hoverton Broad, beyond, and Salthouse Broad in the foreground.

can be held in suspension while they are transported by tidal currents. The accumulation of beach material against the groynes is conclusive proof that from Sheringham eastwards and southwards the net coastal movement is also in these directions. Since Blakeney Point and Scolt Head Island are growing westwards, however, it was formerly believed that from Sheringham to Hunstanton beach material moved to the west. Some experts now think that these formations are built mainly of sand brought from the west by wind, waves and currents and shaped by wave action; the shingle is thought to be merely a superficial cover moving to and fro with the waves. The lonely salt marshes landward of the spits provide suitable habitats for a great variety of birds, as do the sandy, partly flooded 'nesses' farther south at Winterton, Benacre and Thorpness.

A final word must be added on the coastal settlements many of which add to East Anglia's scenic charm. The attractive old pantiled towns of Orford, Aldeburgh, Southwold and Wells are well-known tourist attractions but it is the villages such as Cley and Blakeney crouched by their saltings, or Shingle Street with its quaint fishermen's cottages, that really epitomize the windswept openness of East Anglia's coast.

Bibliography

Addison, W.W. (1950) *Suffolk*. Hale. 312 pp.

Allen, P. (1984) *Field Guide to the Gipping and Waveney Valleys*. Quat. Res. Assoc.

Bailey, P. (1971) *The Norwich Area*. British Landscapes through Maps no. 14. Geogr. Assoc.

Bloom, A.H.V. (1953) *The Fens*. Hale. 325 pp.

Boulton, G.S., Cox, F.C., Hart, J. and Thornton, M.H. (1984) The glacial geology of Norfolk. *Bull. Geol. Soc. Norfolk,* **34**, 103–22.

Bristow, C.R. (1983) The stratigraphy and structure of the Crag of mid-Suffolk, England. *Proc. Geol. Assoc.,* **94**, 1–12.

Bristow, C.R., Ellison, R.A. and Wood, C.J. (1980) The Claygate Beds of Essex. *Proc. Geol. Assoc.,* **91**, 261–78.

Carr, A.P. and Baker, R.E. (1968) Orford, Suffolk: evidence for the evolution of the area during the Quaternary. *Trans. Inst. Br. Geogr.,* **45**, 107–23.

Chatwin, C.P. (1961) *East Anglia and Adjoining Regions* (4th edn). British Regional Geology. HMSO. 100 pp.

Darby, H.C. (1968) *The Draining of the Fens* (2nd edn). Cambridge University Press. 314 pp.

Darby, H.C. (1971) *The Domesday Geography of Eastern England*. Cambridge University Press.

Dixon, R.G. (1979) Sedimentary facies in the Red Crag (Lower Pleistocene), East Anglia. *Proc. Geol. Assoc.,* **90**, 97–116.

Doody, P. and Barnett, B. (eds) (1987) *The Wash and its Environment*. Nature Conservancy Council. 208 pp.

Dymond, D. (1985) *The Norfolk Landscape*. Hodder & Stoughton. 279 pp.

Ellis, E.A. (1965) *The Broads*. Collins.

Funnell, B.M. and West, R.G. (1962) The Early Pleistocene of Easton Bavents, Suffolk. *Quart. J. Geol. Soc.,* **118**, 125–41.

Funnell, B.M., Norton, P.E.P. and West, R.G. (1979) The crag at Bramerton near Norwich, Norfolk. *Phil. Trans. Roy. Soc Lond. B,* **118**, 125–41.

Gibbard, P.L. and Zalasiewicz, J.A. (1988) *Pliocene–Middle Pleistocene of East Anglia*. Field Guide. Quat. Res. Assoc.

Godwin, H. (1968) *Fenland: Its Ancient Past and Uncertain Future*. Cambridge University Press. 196 pp.

Hardy, J. R. (1964) The movement of beach material and wave action near Blakeney Point, Norfolk. *Trans. Inst. Br. Geogr.*, **34**, 53–69.

Hart, J. K. and Pegler, S. M. (1990) Further evidence for the timing of the Middle Pleistocence glaciation in Britain. *Proc. Geol. Assoc.*, **101**, 187–96.

Hey, R. W. (1976) Provenance of far-travelled pebbles in the pre-Anglian Pleistocene of East Anglia. *Proc. Geol. Assoc.*, **87**, 69–82.

Hoskins, W. G. (1957) *The Making of the English Landscape*. Hodder and Stoughton.

Hutchinson, J. N. (1980) The record of peat wastage in the East Anglian fenlands at Holme Post, 1848–1978 AD. *J. Ecol.*, **68**, 229–49.

Lambert, J. M., Jennings, J. N., Smith, C. T. *et al.* (1970) *The Making of the Broads: A Reconsideration of Their Origin in the Light of New Evidence*. Roy. Geogr. Soc. Res. Ser.

Ovey, C. D. and Pitcher, W. S. (1948) Observations on the geology of East Suffolk. *Proc. Geol. Assoc.*, **59**, 23–34.

Parker, A. K. and Pye, D. (1976) *The Fenland*. David and Charles. 240 pp.

Perrin, R. M. S., Rose J., and Davies, H. (1979) The distribution, variation and origin of pre-Devensian tills in eastern England. *Phil. Trans. Roy. Soc. Lond. B*, **287**, 535–70.

Rose, J., Allen, P. and Hey, R. W. (1976) Middle Pleistocene stratigraphy in southern East Anglia. *Nature*, **263**, 492–4.

Scarfe, N. (1972) *The Suffolk Landscape*. Hodder and Stoughton. 256 pp.

Shennan, I. (1982) Interpretation of Flandrian sea-level data from the Fenland, England. *Proc. Geol. Assoc*, **93**, 1, 53–63.

Shotton, F. E. (1961) Agriculture, in F. Briers, *Norwich and its Region*. British Assoc. 156–84.

Sparks, B. W. and West, R. G. (1964) The drift landforms around Holt, Norfolk. *Trans. Inst. Br. Geogr.*, **35**, 27–35.

——(1934) *Scolt Head Island*. Heffer. 234 pp.

Taylor, C. (1973) *The Cambridgeshire Landscape*. Hodder and Stoughton. 286 pp.

Turner, C. (1970) The Middle Pleistocene deposits at Marks Tey, Essex. *Phil. Trans. Roy. Soc. Lond. B*, **257**, 373–440.

Wallace, D. and Oakley, R. P. (1951) *Norfolk*. Hale. 282 pp.

West, R. E. (1956) The Quaternary deposits at Hoxne, Suffolk. *Phil. Trans. Roy. Soc. Lond. B*, **239**, 265–356.

West, R. G. (1980) Pleistocene forest history in East Anglia. *New Phytol.*, **85**, 571–622.

West, R. G. and Whiteman, C. (1986) *Nar Valley and North Norfolk*. Field Guide. Quat. Res. Assoc.

The English stone belt 6

Running in the shape of an ogee curve diagonally across the English lowlands from Dorset to Yorkshire, a narrow belt of Jurassic limestones separates the chalklands from the red clays and sandstones of the West Country and the Midlands. This line of calcareous hills projects a tract of tranquil, unspoiled countryside through the heart of England. It is the consistent use of the local building stone that has given the stone belt its continuity and visual harmony, in which 'villages resemble extended outcrops of the local quarry' and where J.B. Priestley found the stone walls 'still faintly warm and luminous as if they knew the trick of keeping the lost sunlight of centuries glimmering about them'.

In reality the stone belt is composed not simply of a variety of limestones but also includes interbedded clays, calcareous sandstones and marlstones that vary in colour, texture, thickness and porosity, although it is the golden oolitic limestone that contributes most to the scenic charm (Arkell, 1933). This mellow stone has a slightly grainy feel, not because it is made up, like many limestones, of broken shells and corals, but because it was formed from millions of tightly cemented limey pellets known as *ooliths*, owing to their resemblance to fish roe ('oolith' meaning literally 'stone egg'). Like the fine-grained sandstones, these oolites (as they are commonly known) are much sought-after freestones, popular as much for their even texture and ease of working as for their wonderful durability when used in many British cathedrals and other important buildings (North, 1930). The colours of the Jurassic limestones range from the glittering white of Portland (see p. 46), through the buff and biscuit-coloured Bath stone to the honeyed gold of the Cotswolds and the gingery ochres of the south and east Midland marlstones. Each subtle tone is related to the varying amounts of iron oxide present in the rock; in fact the Northampton and Lincoln marlstones are so rich in iron that they are termed 'ironstones' and their ores were once smelted in the steelworks at Corby and Scunthorpe (Whitehead *et al.*, 1952). It is becoming clear, therefore, that the rocks, though of similar age, vary in character as they are traced from south to north, all because their depositional history was affected by shallow submarine ridges (or thresholds) that caused distinct lithological differences from region to region. Four separate basins have been recognized, with the Jurassic rocks of Dorset and Somerset being divided from those which build the Cotswolds by an axis continuing eastwards from that of the Mendips (p. 18). In turn, the Cotswold strata (Ager *et al.*, 1973) are separated from those of Northamptonshire by an axis extending south-eastwards beneath the Vale of Moreton to Oxford, with the facies change manifesting itself in the different landscapes found on either side of the River Cherwell. The northernmost threshold, known to geologists as the Market Weighton axis, occurs some 15 kilometres north of the Humber and marks the tract where the Jurassic rocks of the east Midlands thin out so much that they have been overlapped by the younger Chalk of the Yorkshire Wolds (see p. 68). To the north, the North York Moors have been carved from a basin of Jurassic rocks quite different from those so far described, for instead of limestones the moorlands are capped by thick layers of yellowish grey calcareous sandstones. Because the conditions of deposition varied so much from basin to basin it is impossible, therefore, to identify a consistent scarp-forming horizon among the Jurassic rocks. Thus, in Dorset the hard Portland and Purbeck limestones (Upper Jurassic) create only local crests and cliffs, as described in Chapter 3. By contrast, it is the Middle Lias Marlstone (Lower Jurassic) which is the dominant scarp-former in Somerset, Northamptonshire and south Lincolnshire, while the highest and most striking escarpment of the stone belt is that of the Cotswolds, carved largely from the Inferior Oolite (Middle Jurassic) (Black, 1934). Lying apart from the true Cotswolds a younger (Upper Jurassic) limestone, termed the Corallian, creates a much smaller cuesta between Faringdon and Oxford (Fig. 6.1). Moreover, it has to be realized that the hard rock bands described above are separated by beds of clay and of poorly consolidated sands and that these have been picked out by denudation wherever rivers have cut down through the hard rock cappings. Consequently many of the stone-belt valleys are quite deeply incised into the table-like ridges and plateaux formed from the tougher limestones and marlstones. Except where they have been deformed by Alpine folding along the south coast, all these Jurassic strata, like those of the chalklands, lie in gently tilted sheets which pass imperceptibly eastwards or south-eastwards until they descend beneath the less resistant strata from which the broad clay vales of the English lowlands have been carved. Two major vales flank the stone belt: that to the east (which separates

Figure 6.1 Map of the Cotswolds, showing structure and drainage.

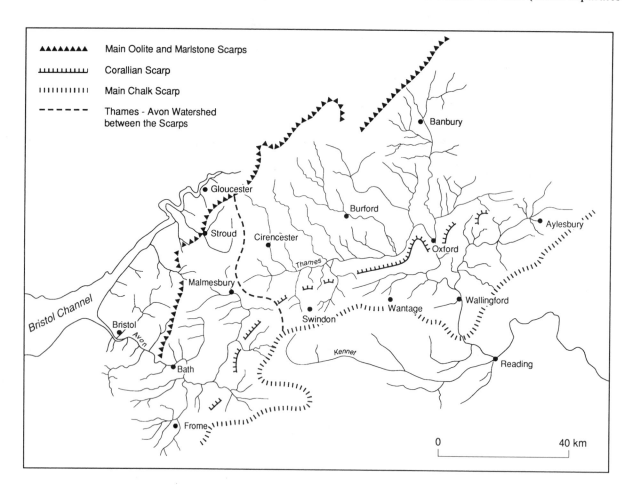

it from the chalklands) has been fashioned from younger rocks (Oxford and Kimmeridge clays of Jurassic age and Gault Clay of Cretaceous age), while that to the west (stretching from Somerset to Teeside) represents a combination of Lower Lias clays (Lower Jurassic) and the even older Keuper Marls (Triassic) which floor much of the Midlands.

The southern stone belt and the Cotswolds

It is only when they reach the Somerset border that the Dorset oolites and marl-stones manage to disentangle themselves from the geological puzzle caused by a combination of the Alpine folding along the Channel coast and the greatly over-lapping western outliers of the Chalk. Thus the landscapes of central Dorset com-prise a complex of hill and vale, breezy downland and valley woodland, whose scattered stone-built villages occupy a 'rustic world where life is uncomplicated by modernity' (Taylor, 1970). Yet from this apparent geological confusion of west and central Dorset a distinctive pattern of clay vale and limestone scarp begins to emerge once the Ham Hill limestone makes its presence felt around Crewkerne. Here such low hills as Hamdon Hill (from which the freestone takes its name) are capped by a slightly oolitic layer of shelly, ferruginous limestone of Upper Liassic age. Though not as durable as the true oolites, the golden brown Ham Hill stone has been quarried almost continuously since Saxon times, producing, in the words of Clifton-Taylor (1972), 'one of England's most seductive stones, and places such as Crewkerne, Ilminster, Martock and Montacute owe it an unending debt'. Not only was it employed locally in such relatively modest buildings as the Norman church of Stoke-sub-Hamdon, but it was also taken further afield for the more ambitious Bishop's Palace at Sherborne.

Further north, where the stone belt's minor ridge almost encloses the western end of the Vale of Wardour (Kellaway and Wilson, 1941), it is picked out by a con-centration of east Somerset villages that stand in stark contrast to the neighbour-ing Blackmoor Vale whose damper floor of Oxford Clay carries practically none. Similarly, at the eastern end of the Vale of Wardour, though not strictly part of the stone belt, there are very few settlements on the poorly drained Kimmeridge Clay, though its tiny patch of Portland stone bears a cluster of villages. One of these, Chilmark, once boasted a quarry whence the excellent stone was carried to build Salisbury Cathedral and Wilton House. Of equal renown is the buff-coloured Doulting stone once taken from an oolite quarry on the scarp slope near Shepton Mallet. It can best be seen in Glastonbury Abbey or at Wells Cathedral, although it also contributes to the attractive fourteenth-century tithe barns of the area. Around Frome the stone belt intrudes a tract of fertile farmland, with its distinctive brownish soils, between the grey limestone moorlands of Mendip and the pale chalky pastures of Salisbury Plain. Were it not for the stone-built villages it would be difficult to distinguish the extent of the Jurassic rocks in the tract between the Mendips and the River Avon. Except where they cap such conspi-cuous outliers as Dundry Hill (see p. 15) and Bathampton Down, neither oolites nor marlstones have succeeded in creating distinctive escarpments. At Bath, how-ever, the scenery begins to change, for this is where the Cotswolds begin.

In the 80 kilometres between Bath and Chipping Campden the stone belt pro-duces some of its most memorable scenery and it was on the Cotswold scarplands that Clifton-Taylor (1972) believed that 'vernacular building in stone flowered as nowhere else in Britain'. Rivers have carved the thick beds of oolite and marlstone into broad flat-topped ridges and deep winding valleys whose fast-flowing escarpment streams were able to provide both power and a means of cleansing for the woollen industry, many of whose stone-built mills now stand empty in the Golden Valley around Stroud. The name Cotswolds, derived from Saxon, means 'hills of the sheepfolds' and it was wool industry profits that helped build the spectacular churches and manor houses, mainly in the seventeenth century. Yet long before the wool industry began to flourish in the Middle Ages or even before the Saxons had built their tiny church at Bradford on Avon the Romans had found that the Avon gorge offered other attractions. Their settlement of Aqua Sulis was sited where a crustal fissure slices deeply enough into the limestones to tap the boiling mineral waters of a buried igneous mass. From such antique beginnings the classical city of Bath has evolved, climbing up the wooded slopes in a series of elegant Georgian terraces and crescents. The eighteenth-century masons made good use of the excellent golden oolite from a dozen local quarries all of which are now closed save that of Monks Park near Corsham which, paradoxically, produces one of the poorest-quality Bath stones. But not even the better-quality Bath stone had the durability exhibited by its Portland counterpart. In addition, the Georgian builders of Bath were faced with problems caused by the steep terrain of the Avon gorge, for here the hard oolitic strata are underlain by softer beds of fuller's earth that have been unable to bear their heavy burden. Several of Bath's slopes, therefore, are marked by landslips and some of its urban crescents terminate abruptly when they reach unstable ground. In a city cramped for extra development space it is a fair assumption that almost every open space on a hill slope coincides with a landslip scar, such as those at Beechen Cliff and at Hedgemead.

From Bath northwards the gently tilted cuesta of the Cotswolds becomes more pronounced, especially if one follows the A46 along the crestline of the escarpment. Although this route may offer spectacular views, it misses out such picturesque villages as Castle Coombe, nestling on the dipslope, or such interesting scarp-face settlements as Wotton-under-Edge. Nevertheless, it is impossible to miss the constantly recurring themes of the true Cotswold landscape: a chequerboard of russet ploughland and verdant woods; sheep-grazed pastures fragrant with thyme and stitched with drystone walls; clear streams with venerable stone bridges; mellow villages with homely mills and towering churches; drifts of cow parsley and elderflower along the roadside verges (Brill, 1964).

The edge of the Cotswolds scarp provides many good viewpoints, none more impressive than Frocester Hill near Stroud, (230 m), Birdlip Hill (280 m) overlooking Gloucester (Fig. 6.2), or Cleeve Hill (317 m) above Cheltenham. It was from these very viewpoints that the earliest English geologists, impressed by the differences in elevation between the crestline and the Severn Vale, began to work out the principles of rock hardness and the ways in which weather and streams wear away the softer clays more rapidly than the limestones, thereby producing vales and escarpments. They also observed that much of the rain falling on the limestone sinks underground, scarcely affecting the limestone surface, only to reappear in the form of springs at the junction between the limestones and their underlying clays. This could either be at the scarp foot or far away down the dipslope, but in either case, because the flow of water carries some clay continuously downhill, there is a constant tendency for the limestone to be undermined and the slope to be steepened. From these early observations it has become possible to explain how escarpments are slowly worn black, leaving behind detached portions of the original scarp as outliers, like those of Dundry Hill (p. 15) and Bredon Hill (293 m) between Tewksbury and Evesham. The smaller outliers, of Alderton Hill and Woolstone Hill, since they lie nearer to the Cotswold scarp around Winchcombe, have clearly become detached from the scarp at a later date than that of the great mass of Bredon. As on the scarp itself, the instability of the underlying clays has induced numerous landslips on the slopes of these outliers, especially on their steep north-western faces. Here a very hummocky terrain of mudflow lobes and old slumped blocks completely obliterates the solid geology of the footslope area. Good examples of modern mudflows may be seen at Woollashill on Bredon's northern slope, while disturbance of medieval ridge and furrow patterns and of more recent enclosures has allowed older landslips to be dated. One of the largest of the Cotswold landslips can be seen on the western slope of Cleeve Hill above Prestbury, where immense back-tilted blocks of Inferior Oolite have slid down the face from which they are now detached by deep troughs aligned along the plane of slippage (Dreghorn, 1968). Other landslips caused by the unstable Upper Lias Clay have helped erode the face of Leckhampton Hill and Charlton Kings Common above Cheltenham. It has been shown that landslide distribution on the main escarpment relates closely to the lateral changes in geology. Instability is greatest wherever the more stable Cotteswold Sands give way to the incompetent Midford Sands, or wherever the

Figure 6.2 The Cotswold scarp at Birdlip Hill, Gloucestershire, looking northwards over the Severn Valley. The Inferior Oolite is seen exposed above Upper and Middle Oolitic strata which underlie the lower slopes.

Fuller's Earth Clay occurs, especially between Stroud and Bath (Ackermann and Cave, 1967). Less spectacular slips have also occurred in the dipslope area wherever stream incision has exposed the Upper Lias Clay between Upper Slaughter and Bourton-on-the-Water.

It must not be thought that the Cotswolds escarpment always displays a completely straight alignment like that to the north of Banbury or the stretch down which the M4 descends near Chipping Sodbury. Near Gloucester and Cheltenham, for example, the scarp front is fretted and irregular, especially in such coombe-like embayments as Witcombe and Winchcombe, both flanked by high jutting promontories of oolite, most markedly at Cleeve Hill itself (Naish, 1978). It has been suggested that these coombes have not only been etched out by spring-sapping at the foot of the limestone but have also been assisted by weaknesses caused wherever northwest-trending faults cross the face of the scarp. The scarp edge between Dursley and Stroud is similarly fretted and it is here in the long, deeply cut valleys that the Cotswolds wool trade was originally centred, based on the vigorous northwest-flowing streams that descend the escarpment through the hanging woods of beech and ash. In contrast to these fast-flowing escarpment streams, whose waters swell the extensive Severn catchment, many of those that rise on the dipslope of the Cotswolds descend with gentler gradients to join the Thames drainage system; except, of course, for those which contribute to the headwaters of the Bristol Avon, as described in Chapter 2.

The majority of the backslope streams flow south-eastwards in response to the direction of dip of the Jurassic rocks (Fig. 6.1). In general, they occupy wide, flat-bottomed valleys which themselves exhibit large meanders probably inherited from a period when the rivers flowed at a higher level across layers of younger Jurassic clays that formerly mantled the now exposed oolites. The present-day rivers are relatively small in relation to the scale of the ancient valleys in which they flow, a fact which has led to speculations of river capture or climatic change. Such streams are termed 'misfits' because they are obviously no longer capable of cutting the large valleys they now occupy. An explanation may be sought in the very different permafrost climatic conditions which prevailed hereabouts during the Ice Age for, as in the chalklands, the ground water within the Cotswolds limestones would then have been permanently frozen, causing the snowmelt streams to run only across the land surface rather than descending to subterranean levels. But as in the chalklands, the disappearance of the permafrost in late-glacial times would have seen many of the Cotswolds valley systems abandoned as the drainage went underground. It is mainly the tributary valleys that have become dry and where they meet the trunk valleys they 'hang' some 6–10 metres above the main valley floors. This is because only the main consequent streams are fed from perennial springs, allowing them to continue to incise their beds, even though their own flow, robbed of snowmelt, has decreased sufficiently to change them into misfits. Even today, in years of low rainfall, some of the trunk streams tend to dry up, most notably the stretch of the River Leach above Eastleach Turville, because their surface flow is insufficient to offset the percolation loss into the well-jointed limestones. Such intermittent streams, reminiscent of chalkland bournes, are typical of most limestone landscapes, although other karstic features are rare in the Cotswolds.

The deeply cut valleys introduce the main diversity into the rolling scenery of the Cotswold hills, for they are not only followed by belts of woodland but are also the locations of most of the towns and villages, with notable exceptions such as Stow-on-the-Wold and Minchinhampton. In these relatively dry limestone uplands water supply was of paramount importance in the location of settlements, so that many villages have been sited along springlines. Most of the Cotswolds dipslope springs occur either at the junction of the Great Oolite with the under-lying Fuller's Earth Clay or where the Inferior Oolite caps the Upper Lias Clay (Arkell and Donovan, 1952). Villages such as Bibury, the Duntisbournes and Northleach are sited along the former junction, while it is the latter springline which explains the locations of such settlements as Upper Slaughter, Chipping Campden, Blockley and Bourton-on-the-Hill. The larger Cotswold towns, how-ever, have been built lower down the slopes, usually where ancient routes cross the main valleys (Hadfield and Hadfield, 1973). Cirencester, Bourton-on-the-Water, Stow-on-the-Wold and Moreton-in-Marsh are all located along the Roman road of the Foss Way though, paradoxically, the once important Akeman Street bet-ween Cirencester and Bicester is now only a minor route and carries no such settlements. The Cotswolds Jurassic Way, equivalent to the chalklands Ridgeway, though a major route along the dry crestline during the Bronze and Iron Ages, thereafter became little more than a green trackway as clearance of the valley woodlands allowed most settlements to move away from the hilltops. Neverthe-less, its effect can still be seen on parish boundaries and its former route is lined with antiquities (Finberg, 1975). Though never as populated as the Chalk during prehistoric times, possibly due to the absence of rocks sufficiently hard (like flint) to make tools, the Cotswolds can boast their own impressive earthworks and standing stones at Belas Knap, Hetty Pegler's Tump and the Rollright Stones. Furthermore, there is also a large concentration of Iron Age hill forts, partic-ularly along the Cotswold scarp edge at places like Cleeve Hill (Beckinsale and Beckinsale, 1980).

Today's Cotswolds towns are still market centres, spaced at distances based on the days of horse rather than motor transport, and with their streets wide enough to serve as marketplaces. Many of their larger houses are built from well-dressed oolitic stone, with chimneys and windows of fine masonry, but the smaller build-ings are often of limestone or marlstone rubble extracted from local quarries, though once again the chimneys and windows exhibit better-quality stonework. Almost all Cotswolds towns and villages are attractive but some are outstandingly beautiful (Finberg, 1977). An aesthetic progression from west to east would start with the elegant town of Painswick with its yew-shaded churchyard, then Bibury with its antique waterside row of cottages. Some have cathedral-like 'wool' churches and perfectly preserved medieval streets of grey-gold houses: Northleach, Burford, Broadway and Chipping Campden are the best known; Bourton-on-the-Water, where the Windrush glides beneath tiny eighteenth-century stone bridges, is one of the most perfectly contrived. But some of the lesser-known, more reticient villages, taking advantage of every fold and hollow in the hills, give, perhaps, an even greater feeling of the true Cotswolds way of life: Snowshill, high up on the scarp edge; the Barringtons, nestling by the Windrush; or scarp-foot Stanton, built entirely of mellow Cotswold stone (Lewis, 1974).

The majority of the traditional Cotswolds buildings are roofed with slivers of hard flaggy limestone known as 'slate' (Fig. 6.3), though the rock was formed quite differently from the true slates of Wales. The chief source of supply was the small village of Stonesfield, near Woodstock (hence the term Stonesfield Slates) though the quarries have long since been closed. The honey-brown flagstones, known locally as 'pendle', were hewn from underground galleries and strewn on the surface to enable winter frosts to split the rock into thin sheets ready for dressing into suitable sizes for roofing. The grading of the finished slates, with the smallest at the roof ridge and the largest at the eaves, produces a satisfying perspective and gives a harmonious colour combination with the mellow stone walling, especially where yellow lichens speckle the rooftops. South of a line from Cirencester to Burford other flaggy limestones, coarser than the Stonesfield Slates, have also been used for roofing and occasionally, as at Filkins, for vertical stone fences. Many of these slabs come from another Jurassic limestone, known as the Forest Marble (Sumbler, 1984), a term derived from the ancient Wychwood Forest whose remnants bestride the Evenlode valley. This ancient royal game forest dates back to Saxon times, though its former extent of 42 000 hectares was greatly reduced by grazing rights acquired by peripheral parishes during the twelfth and thirteenth centuries (Darby and Terrett, 1971). Today only a 570 hectare woodland at Cornbury Park remains as a testimony of this once extensive forest, for the rural landscape of the Cotswolds has long since been given over to farmland.

Broad differences in land use can still largely be accounted for according to the geological outcrops. The Forest Marble (Middle Jurassic) remains relatively well wooded between Burford and Woodstock, though Cogges Wood, near Witney,

Figure 6.3 Lower Slaughter, a Cotswold village constructed from oolitic building stone and roofed with Stonesfield Slates.

and Burleigh Wood, near Bladon, are rooted in Oxford Clay soils. The Great and Inferior Oolite landscapes, by contrast, are heavily cultivated for corn, though once they were major sheepwalks patterned with drystone walls (Emery, 1974). William Cobbett, in his *Rural Rides* of 1830, graphically describes the rich brown Cotswolds soils as a 'stone brash', for where they are ploughed they are liberally sprinkled with weathered flakes of stone. One of the Middle Jurassic limestones, lying just above the Forest Marble, is actually known as the 'Cornbrash' (Douglas and Arkell, 1928), a coarse, unevenly bedded crumbly stone which may grow good corn but is an indifferent building material despite its widespread use in towns and villages from Malmesbury (Wilts.) eastwards through Fairford (Glos.), Witney and Woodstock (Oxon.) to Bicester and Buckingham (Bucks.). A similar coarse but tougher stone, termed the 'Coral Rag', outcropping just below the Kimmeridge Clay, is part of the so-called Corallian series of the Upper Jurassic. It is hard enough to stand up as a low cuesta, between Faringdon and Oxford, whose height is sufficient to divide the Oxford Clay Vale from the Vale of White Horse (McKerrow, 1958). Wytham Hill, Cumnor Hill and Boars Hill, to the west of Oxford, owe their survival to their layers of Coral Rag, although the latter is also capped by an outlier of Lower Greensand (Cretaceous) (Arkell, 1947b). Large-scale landslips occur on the Corallian escarpment, initiated by springs occurring where the limestone perches on the Oxford Clay, but the same springline also accounts for a line of villages in the dissected hill country immediately to the east of Oxford. No less than eight such settlements can be traced in an arc from Iffley through Beckley, around the brooding Otmoor depression and across the M40 motorway to Waterperry. In Buckinghamshire the neighbouring isolated hills at Brill, Waddesdon and Quainton, however, are not an expression of the Corallian but of rare and isolated outcrops of the Portland and Purbeck limestones, last seen in Wessex. Brill Common is pitted with ancient quarries and yet the famous white limestones are missing from the hilltop village buildings which are almost entirely of brick. The Corallian scarp reaches one of its highest points in the conspicuous Headington Hill, which overlooks Oxford from the east (Arkell, 1942). Its scarred hill slopes testify to the way in which both the shelly Coral Rag limestone, full of reef corals, and the interbedded oolitic Wheatley Limestone were extensively used to construct seventeenth- and eighteenth-century Oxford, often with disastrous results. Within a few decades the poorer-quality Headington Stone began to flake, bringing a premature senility to many Oxford buildings and leading to centuries of costly restoration (Arkell, 1947a). Much of the replacement freestone has come from the Great Oolite quarry at Taynton near Burford, a source of good-quality oolite since Saxon times. Its rich golden stone was used in Oxford's Christ Church and Merton College in the twelfth to fourteenth centuries and later at Blenheim Palace, Woodstock.

Oxford itself (Martin and Steel, 1954), a Saxon foundation, was located on the so-called Summertown–Radley river terrace at a height of 4 metres above the marshy confluence of the Thames and Cherwell where these rivers are fashioning broad valleys across the damp Oxford Clay. The Upper Thames and its other main tributaries, the Evenlode and Windrush, are flanked by a staircase of oolitic gravel terraces formed during the Pleistocene when the rivers were more capable of denuding the Cotswolds than they are today. The highest terrace, the Hanborough Terrace, possibly dating from the Anglian glacial (Briggs and Gilbertson, 1973), is composed in part of Triassic pebbles derived from a veneer of glacial material termed the Northern Drift which must have been introduced from the north-west by an early ice sheet that had crossed the Midlands. The Moreton-in-Marsh lowland, however, is floored with flint-bearing glacial sands and tills which suggests that at a later stage a lobe of Chalky Boulder Clay ice from the East Midlands reached the northern edge of the Cotswolds where its meltwaters poured flinty outwash gravels down the valleys of the Cherwell and through the Evenlode gorge to help construct the Wolvercote terrace which stands mid-way in height between the Hanborough Terrace and the Summertown–Radley Terrace. The much older Northern Drift (Hey, 1986), which caps the hills to the west of Oxford, is too weathered and dissected to determine whether it was deposited during a single glacial advance, but its soliflucted material overlies the buried channel at Sugworth (see p. 64) whose infill has been dated as Cromerian in age.

The central stone belt

The River Evenlode is said to mark the eastern limits of the Cotswolds, and it is true that the golden grey church towers of Gloucestershire and Oxfordshire give way to the creamy brown spires of north Buckinghamshire and Northamptonshire once one progresses east of Chipping Norton and Banbury. Wright (1985) believes that although in these latter counties 'stone villages abound, with angles and corners and textures so very nearly Cotswold, the valley settings, wooded hillsides and wind washed western wolds have been left behind and the landscape has lost its secret places'. Although a belt of oolitic freestones continues north-eastwards as far as Lincolnshire, from north Oxfordshire onwards it is the ferruginous Marlstone, of Liassic age, that becomes the most dominant rock of the stone belt. This rich brown ironstone is older than the renowned Cotswold oolites but its ability to withstand denudation has left its outcrop as a conspicuous shelf along the foot of the Oxfordshire escarpment until near Banbury the Marlstone assumes the role of the chief escarpment former, especially in the steep face of Edge Hill (215 m). The settlements of north Oxfordshire display the Marlstone's ochreous colours to great advantage, with the attractive villages of Deddington, Adderbury, Mollington, Warmington and Horley all exhibiting a few substantial houses of regularly coursed Marlstone, although most of their humbler dwellings are built from irregular rubble, protected only at the corners with dressed freestone. Near the last of these villages is the recently abandoned Hornton quarry, whose distinctive greenish grey stone has been sought in modern times by such famous sculptors as Henry Moore. Further eastwards, especially in Northamptonshire, builders have intermixed the dark ironstones with the lighter-coloured oolites, giving the villages a busy polychrome character.

In general, the Marlstone soils bring to the central stone belt a landscape of mixed farms whose quickthorn hedges have replaced the drystone field-walls so characteristic of the Cotswolds. The wide expanse of Cornbrash, as in the Cotswolds, also supports excellent crops of barley and here the patchwork of well-maintained hedged fields with their fringing ash trees gives a sense of uniformity to this landscape of relatively unbroken horizons (Stean, 1974). In Northamptonshire shelter belts are few, perhaps because its elevations are lower, but coverts and spinneys, intended as cover for game, are more numerous than in the Cotswolds. Yet the once extensive Rockingham Forest near Corby (Peterken,

1976), thriving on the till-mantled oolites, has suffered the fate of Oxfordshire's Wychwood, for most of it has disappeared since the mid-nineteenth century.

The change of scenic character between Oxfordshire and Northamptonshire is due partly to the changing nature of the Jurassic strata, for the Great and Inferior Oolites virtually disappear as they are traced across the Moreton axis from the Cotswold basin of deposition to that of the Midlands (Thompson, 1924), as described at the beginning of this chapter. The temporary decline of the Inferior Oolite (the major scarp former both in the Cotswolds and in Lincolnshire) is of particular significance because it is replaced by the thin sandstones of the Northampton Sand and the relatively soft rocks of the so-called Lower Estuarine Series. Additionally, the very low angle of dip in the Northamptonshire Jurassic strata means that the high cuesta of the Cotswolds is here replaced by a low tableland of sandstone- or limestone-capped plateaux dissected by valleys that have cut down deeply into the underlying Liassic clays (Hollingworth and Taylor, 1946). Thus a geological map of the region is extremely complex because the clay-floored valley networks wind tortuously through the entire Northamptonshire uplands whose hills achieve only half the elevation reached by the true Cotswolds. This general lowering of the terrain in the central stone belt can partly be explained by the fact that the same Anglian ice advance which failed to override the main Cotswolds scarp did manage to cross the whole of the Jurassic country to the east of the River Cherwell. Such a decline in the height of the stone belt is analogous with the lowering of the Chalk escarpment as it is traced into the heavily glaciated tract of East Anglia.

East of the Cherwell the character of the urban settlements also changes, especially between Northampton and Kettering, for here the closely spaced towns and villages show signs of rapid modern development owing to their location mid-way between London and the industrial Midlands. Yet only a few miles from the industrialized town of Northampton the stone-belt villages of Blixworth and Earls Barton can boast the two most perfectly preserved Saxon churches in England. Where the River Nene and its tributaries have dissected the Northamptonshire tablelands several breaches have been made through the main escarpment, one of which, the Watford Gap, has been utilized as a routeway since time immemorial. First came the Roman road Watling Street (now the A5), to be followed in later centuries by the Grand Union Canal, the Euston–Glasgow railway and the M1 motorway. Such ease of access has also allowed a rash of bricks and tiles to invade the traditional stone-built villages of the region. Not surprisingly, the flanking clay belts, especially that of the Oxford Clay, have been readily exploited for brick-making, their brickfield chimneys being particularly prominent at Steeple Claydon (Bucks.), at Bletchley and around Bedford and Peterborough. The Jurassic ironstone strata, too, have been quarried for their ore, though the once flourishing iron and steel industry of Corby ceased in 1979. It ores were mined from the so-called Northampton Sand, a ferruginous bed lying beneath pale-coloured sandstones and the Lower Lincolnshire Limestone, all of Inferior Oolite age (Hollingworth and Taylor, 1951). The ironstone of Corby has an iron content of 28–34 per cent, higher than that of the Marlstone (20–24 per cent) of Lower Lias age that was once extensively mined near to Banbury. Still flourishing, however, is the iron and steel industry of Scunthorpe in north Lincolnshire, which is based on local ores that have a similar iron content (20–24 per cent) to that of the Marlstone. Here the gently dipping Frodingham Ironstone (also of Lower Lias age), is still massively exploited in opencast quarries. The ironstone bed, some 10 metres thick, ranges in character from mudstone to oolite and is noted for its giant ammonite fossils (Sylvester-Bradley and Ford, 1968).

To the west of Corby, where the wide Marlstone shelf has been trenched by the River Welland, the ancient town of Market Harborough stands at the point where the Northampton–Leicester road descends from the true stone belt to cross the river. Northwards again, past the stone-built town of Uppingham, another attractive market centre, Oakham, nestles in the Vale of Catmose, itself carved by the Welland's tributaries from a broad expanse of Upper Lias Clay. Between Oakham and Grantham the Inferior Oolite (here known as the Lincolnshire Limestone) reappears in sufficient thickness (33 m) to form another west-facing escarpment that runs parallel with that of the Marlstone (Ashton, 1980). Though not strictly a town of the stone belt, Melton Mowbray, down on the damp clays of the Lower Lias, lies in a wide amphitheatre created by a great arc-like ridge of Marlstone (Hoskins, 1957). The old town has many dignified stone buildings and is generally regarded as the headquarters of English fox-hunting, for the Quorn, Cottesmore and Belvoir hunts flourish in the 'manicured' farming landscape of coppice and hedgerow. The Vale of Belvoir, overlooked by Belvoir Castle, is also cradled by the high Marlstone scarp which, like the parallel oolitic limestone scarp, suddenly swings into an east–west alignment along the southern margin of the Vale. This curious change in the strike of the Lower Jurassic rocks on the Leicestershire–Lincolnshire border is due to the presence of a rare east–west fold of early Alpine age that interrupts the north–south grain of the scarplands hereabouts.

Typically, the Marlstone weathers into chestnut-brown soils and its richly coloured fields contrast markedly with the paler-toned farmlands of the oolitic tracts farther east. Quarries in the oolitic rocks have provided materials for such mellow old towns as Stamford, with its neighbouring stately home of Burghley House, all fashioned from freestones equal to those of the Cotswolds. Clifton-Taylor believed that 'if the Cotswolds contain more fine domestic buildings, great and small, to the square mile than any other part of England, the region of which Stamford is the centre certainly ranks next'. Thanks to river transport, the region's superb freestones (all from the Lincolnshire Limestone) have travelled far beyond the stone belt itself. The five most famous quarries, at Ancaster, Weldon, Ketton, Clipsham and Barnack, have been worked since the Middle Ages and are still in production. Barnack and Ketton stones have been used extensively in the Cambridge colleges (Purcell, 1967), while the former has also contributed to Ely Cathedral, Bury St Edmunds Abbey and the Norman structures of Norwich and Rochester. Ancaster Stone, because it is quarried farther north, between Grantham and Sleaford, has been used to construct many Lincolnshire churches in addition to some of those in eastern Nottinghamshire. Although Clipsham stone was used at Windsor Castle in the fourteenth century, it had to wait until much later before its merits were more widely recognized. It is the hardest of the Lincolnshire Limestone beds and now rivals Portland stone in popularity. Another famous quarry in the central stone belt is that at Collyweston, whose 'slates' are the eastern counterparts of the Cotswolds Stonesfield Slates. If Oxford is crowned with Stonesfield then Cambridge wears a diadem of Collyweston. Clifton-Taylor (1972) prefers both the tone and the texture of the former, while conceding that Collyweston Slates, because their flaggy limestone beds split naturally into lighter and thinner sheets, produce a roof less heavy and therefore easier to lay. Owing to these important properties Collyweston roofs can be angled at somewhat steeper gradients (up to 55°) than their Stonesfield counterparts.

The Lincolnshire stone belt

To the north of Stamford the Jurassic strata continue to exhibit the low-angle dip which characterizes the central stone belt. Thus, until Sleaford is reached their rocks create a dissected tableland known as the Kesteven plateau, heavily mantled with glacial drift. From Sleaford to the Humber, however, the angle of dip increases and the hard rock outcrop narrows accordingly (Linton, 1954). The slender ridge of Lincoln Edge spears its way northwards across the clay plains of eastern England, its cuesta of Lincolnshire Limestone (Inferior Oolite) providing virtually the only high ground between the Pennines and the Lincolnshire Wolds (Ashton, 1980). Between Lincoln and the Humber the steep escarpment face is termed the Lincoln Cliff, rarely exceeding 70 metres in height, while its gentle dipslope, the Lincoln Heath, declines to the Ancholme and Lower Witham low-lands, themselves carved from a wide tract of Oxford and Kimmeridge Clays (Evans, 1952). The open, treeless farmland of the modern Heath, still followed by the Roman Ermine Street, flourishes despite its thin, dry and hungry soils. Yet its large farms have been productive only since the mid-nineteenth-century reclamation of the Heath which was formerly known for its rabbit warrens and its agricultural poverty. Because of its drystone walls and its network of dry valleys, some authors have described the 7 kilometre Lincoln Edge as a microcosm of the Cotswolds, although it lacks the latter's enchanting villages. Indeed, most of the larger settlements on the Heath are today associated with military airfields. Nevertheless, the western face of the Lincoln Cliff is characterized by a string of ancient scarp-foot villages, located at approximately 2 kilometre intervals along the springline, itself marking the junction between the overlying Lincolnshire Limestone and the Upper Lias Clay. The cultural landscape also reflects the geology in other ways, for not only the parish boundaries but also the minor road and field patterns have been laid out at right angles to the north–south grain of the country. In this way each scarp-foot village has retained not only a proportion of the moist hay meadows on the Lias Clay of the western vale, most of whose place names include the term 'Low Fields', but also an equal proportion of the higher and drier heathland, where the term 'Heath' is included in virtually every place name.

Three important gaps break the Lincoln Edge (Straw, 1970): in the south the dry Ancaster gap was once occupied by an east-flowing Trent, most recently during the Hoxnian interglacial, and very much later became the site of a Roman settlement where Ermine Street descends from the high crestline to cross the breach. Lincoln itself, with its prominent cathedral and ancient stone houses, also stands athwart a breach in the ridge (See Fig. 5.4), but the Lincoln Gorge, formed by an ancient river long before the Ice Age, is now occupied by an artificially straightened Witham river. The northernmost gap, in Humberside, is created by the Humber estuary. The later history of the Lincoln Gorge is closely linked with the final stages of the Ice Age in eastern England for when the northern ice sheets were draped along the North Sea coast in Late Devensian times, during the so-called Dimlington Stadial (28 000 to 13 000 years ago), large ice-impounded lakes are thought to have been formed on either flank of the Lincoln Edge – 'Lake Fenland' to the east and 'Lake Humber' to the west (Fig. 5.4) though they may not have been synchronous at all stages (Straw and Clayton, 1979). When the ice front blocked both the Humber and the Wash the lakes stood at a height of 30 metres and may have been linked through the Lincoln Gorge. As the ice retreated and the Wash became unblocked 'Lake Fenland' disappeared but a lower 'Lake Humber' (15 m) persisted, using the Lincoln Gorge as its overflow. As this lake level slowly declined, the River Trent (at its Beeston Terrace stage) still unable to reach its Humber outlet, was forced to follow the Lincoln Gorge and debouch into the Wash. Ultimately, when the Devensian ice had retreated from the Humber mouth, the Trent finally returned to its northward course along the strike vale already carved out along the junction of the Trias and the Jurassic.

The North York Moors

North of the Humber, for a distance of some 40 kilometres, the stone belt completely disappears as the Chalk overlaps virtually all of the narrow exposure of the Jurassic rocks (see p. 68), except where they form a narrow bench at the foot of the Yorkshire Wolds south of Pocklington. The attenuation of the Jurassic exposure, from a width of 100 kilometres between Leicestershire and the Fens to a mere 100 metres on north Humberside, is entirely the result of the buried Market Weighton axis (described on p. 107) which separates the central England basin of Jurassic sediments from that of Cleveland and North Yorkshire (Kent and Gaunt, 1980). The different character of the rocks in the latter basin is best seen in the North York Moors, which comprise a thick succession of calcareous grits and yellow-grey sandstones of similar age to the oolites which build the Cotswolds. The northern moorlands, however, are devoid of the Cotswold cornfields and dry-stone walls, and instead their high tablelands are swathed with heather. Only their stone-built towns and villages remind us that this is the northern termination of the stone belt. The 60 metre capping of moorland sandstone overlies great thicknesses of shales, limestones and grits, known as the Deltaic Series, that were periodically laid down in a vast delta some 170 million years ago. This enormous fan of sandy and muddy sediments once grew progressively into the gulf of a tropical sea cut off from the clearer ocean waters in which the oolitic limestones were being deposited farther south. Because many of its ever shifting rivers channels (depositing the deltaic sands) were tidal they became infilled with mud banks on which transient swamp forests lived and died. In this way the russet-coloured sandstones became interbedded with blue-grey shales (the muds) whose thin organic layers were later to be compressed into narrow coal seams or thin bands of a hard black stone known as *jet*.

Where the rocks of Middle Jurassic age (part of the Deltaic Series) emerge from beneath the north-western chalk scarp of the Yorkshire Wolds they follow the parallel outcrops of the Corallian rocks (Upper Jurassic) to create the double cuesta of the Howardian Hills whose 100–150 metre crestline separates the flat alluvial Vale of Pickering from the equally featureless Vale of York. Because the strike of the Howardian Hills' strata is from north-west to south-east their escarpments face south-westwards across the Vale of York. Swinging right across this fertile vale two arcuate moraines represent the Devensian ice limits in this area (see

Fig. 5.4) (Gaunt, 1976). The slightly older Escrick Moraine succeeded in diverting the River Wharfe at Wetherby, while the York moraine provided a firm foundation for the renowned cathedral city (Palmer, 1966). The line of the Howardian Hills is breached in two places, by the deep gorge of the River Derwent south of Malton and by the broader moraine-filled and fault-guided trench between Coxwold and Gilling that divides the well-wooded Howardian Hills from the relatively treeless stretches of the substantially higher moorland plateaux. Just west of the Derwent gorge, the stately home of Castle Howard was built mainly from a locally quarried buff-coloured sandstone, the stratigraphic equivalent of the renowned Aislaby Sandstone (see below). Surprisingly, the excellent oolite from the nearby Hovingham quarry was scarcely used in its construction, though the dove-grey Hovingham rubblestone (from above the oolitic freestone) is found in Hovingham's Anglo-Saxon church and is regularly specified for modern building in the North York Moors National Park.

The highest parts of the Moors occur in the northern two-thirds, stretching from Glaisdale Moor in the east through Westerdale and Urra Moors to Bilsdale Moor in the west, all of which exceed the 400 metre contour. Their prominence is due largely to the highly resistant fluviatile Moor Grit, though the north-facing scarp of the Cleveland Hills has been carved from the older sandstones of the Lower Deltaic Series. The equally prominent western escarpment (399 m), known as the Hambledon Hills, is lithologically different, however, for it is capped by a 100 metre layer of tough marine Calcareous Grits of Corallian age, not true grits but fine-grained calcareous sandstones (Wright, 1972). These younger grits, with their interbedded limestones, build the striking scarp of Whitestone Cliff and Roulston Scar (whose white horse hill-carving is reminiscent of the Wessex chalklands), before they swing eastwards to form the southern third of the Moors and finally run out to sea at Scarborough. These Corallian rocks dip gently southwards to pass beneath the less resistant Kimmeridge Clays of the Vale of Pickering, but before they disappear the well-jointed gritstones have been weathered into wierdly shaped tors, the Bridestones, located some 10 kilometres north-east of Pickering. As these gritstone beds are traced northwards they terminate in a heavily fretted but distinct north-facing escarpment of their own, running from east to west across the centre of the Moors, with the scarp owing its steepness in part to the constant spring-sapping which occurs in the underlying Oxford Clay. So gentle is the dip of the Corallian strata that the southern Moors have been termed the Tabular Hills; their flat-topped summits have been sliced into numerous north-pointing promontories by the steep-sided valleys of the southern dales (Wilson, 1949). Here some of the south-flowing rivers have cut down so deeply that they have exposed the Lias shales on their valley floors. The smaller north-flowing streams occupy shorter dales and are all tributaries of the River Esk which follows a deeply incised route to the sea at Whitby. Farther north, at a lower level, several smaller moorland outliers diversify the scenery around the ancient market town of Guisborough; Roseberry Topping is the most conspicuous, with its scarped summit (320 m) being formed from a hard gritstone cap. Here, too, along the northern slopes of the Cleveland Hills, the Middle Lias ironstone is of sufficient quality (30 per cent purity) to have justified extensive exploitation in former years. Once the basis of an extensive iron and steel industry, the local ore ceased to be worked after 1964, and some 20 years later the large steelworks at Skinningrove was closed.

The moorland dales are remarkably deep and gorge-like, their slopes rising up in a few places to walls of bare yellow sandstone. In most cases, however, the hard rock bands protrude as valley-side shelves down whose stepped profile tributary streams tumble in waterfalls, such as Nelly Ayre Foss, before disappearing into the valley woodlands. Recent research has shown that in prehistoric times the moors were forested (Atherden, 1976) but the only significant modern survivals of the natural broadleaf woods are found in the southern dales, particularly that of Ryedale where the beautiful sandstone ruins of Rievaulx Abbey adorn the valley floor. The extensive conifer plantations of Danby, Broxa and Wykeham Forests, which blanket the eastern tracts of the Tabular Hills, have been planted because in those parts the so-called Calcareous Grit is not calcareous at all but gives a sandy acid soil most unsuitable for farming on the moorland fringes. By contrast, such northern valleys as Westerdale, Danby Dale and Glaisdale are extensively farmed and largely given over to livestock-rearing, although here the woodlands are more sparse except along the river courses. The most striking valley of all, however, is the sinuous line of Newton Dale that slices through the eastern moorlands from Goathland to Pickering, thereby providing a route for the Moors' only railway. Not only it is more canyon-like than the other dales but for much of its length this 150 metre trench is virtually streamless, posing a question as to its formation. It was originally thought that the gorge was rapidly torn out when an ice-impounded lake in Eskdale overflowed southwards. Because of the lack of strandlines and other evidence, however, current opinion favours a less spectacular explanation (Gregory, 1965). Although the Devensian ice sheets are known to have wrapped around the ice-free North York Moors the escaping meltwaters along the ice sheet's southern flanks would have been forced to lower the col at the head of the Goathland valley in order to find an exit southwards, thereafter excavating the deep valley of Newton Dale. It seems clear that Newton Dale's present stream is a misfit, totally incapable of carving out a gorge of such magnitude. The huge volume of glacial meltwater that once surged down Newton Dale would have been capable of eroding an enormous amount of bedrock and it was this, together with the fluvio-glacial outwash from the waning ice sheet, that built the large gravel delta on which the town of Pickering now stands.

The delta was built out into a pro-glacial lake, termed 'Lake Pickering', impounded in the western end of the Vale by a lobe of ice driving in from the coast (Ellis, 1987). This was part of the same Late Devensian ice advance (28 000–13 000 years ago), known as the Dimlington Stadial from its type-site in Holderness, that also closed off the Humber estuary to create glacial 'Lake Humber' (Fig. 5.4). The smaller delta-like feature that occurs ar West Ayton, near Scarborough, is in fact a kame terrace laid down by glacial meltwaters that carved out the channel of the Forge Valley before coursing along the northern edge of the Pickering Vale ice lobe. Farther east another meltwater valley, parallel to that of the Forge Valley, is now followed by both main road and railway into Scarborough and was probably formed as a marginal channel around the retreating lobe of Pickering ice. The Vale of Pickering itself owes its initial form to the downfaulted exposure of Kimmeridge Clay which separates the Chalk of the Yorkshire Wolds from the Jurassic rocks of the North York Moors. In Pleistocene times the enveloping ice sheets (see Fig. 5.4) prevented the ponded meltwaters of glacial 'Lake Pickering' from draining eastwards to the sea or westwards through the Coxwold–Gilling gap to the Vale of York. Having risen to a level of 70 metres, therefore, the lake overflowed and tore out a deep spillway southwards through the lowest col of the Howardian Hills, now known as the Kirkham Gorge. Having stabilized at a level of 45 metres during Late Pleistocene times the lake then shrank slowly away as its main source of supply disappeared. Nevertheless, a shrunken lake persisted into post-glacial times and at Star Carr there is evidence that Late Palaeolithic hunters and Early Mesolithic fishermen dwelt on its shores some 9500 years ago (Clark, 1954). But since then the peats and lacustrine clays have been artificially drained and the canalized River Derwent now flows westwards through the Vale to its exit at the Kirkham Gorge. It appears that its pre-glacial course would have been considerably shorter, flowing eastwards from the Moors to the sea via the Scalby gap now occupied merely by the Sea Cut, a tiny drainage stream. The centre of the Vale of Pickering is still poorly drained, its dampness exemplified by the frequent use of 'carr' and 'ing' in the place names. Though sheep and cattle graze its central water meadows, the Vale is fringed with arable fields both on the gravelly terraces of its northern flanks and on the chalky downwash overlying the Speeton Clay shelf below the Wolds escarpment (see p. 68).

The earliest settlers would have discovered that, in contrast to the marshy floor of the Vale of Pickering, the sandy soils of the lightly forested hilltops of the North York Moors were relatively easy to work. Thus, by the end of the Bronze Age most of the upland trees had been felled, leaving the Romans to find a bleak tableland of desolate heather moors (Atherden, 1976). The legionaries used the local grit-stones to construct the first moorland roads, while in later centuries the additional packhorse routes were picked out by stone crosses used as route markers across the misty uplands. It was the Vikings, however, who left their mark on the place names, for the moorland hills are still known as 'brows', the streams as 'becks', the coastal headlands as 'nabs' and the intervening bays as 'wykes'. Apart from a few ancient villages tucked into the moorland dales, most of the settlement clings to this deeply indented and attractive coastline, though the roads keep to the hilltops because of the steeply walled valley gradients.

Where the moorlands are abruptly truncated by the sea, the different degrees of resistance to weathering and erosion exhibited by the Jurassic shales and sand-stones have given the coastline great diversity both in height and in shape (Agar, 1960). In general, the highest headlands are built from layer upon layer of sand-stones, limestones and shales, while the clefts and wykes have been carved mainly where clays and mudstones predominate (Hemingway *et al.*, 1963). The broader bays, such as Runswick Bay and Robin Hood's Bay, are plugged with glacial drift so that their curved rims are fringed with solid rocks only at their extremities. Where the streams have cut narrow ravines down to the rocky shore they often provide the only means of access to the interior from this rockbound coast. The picturesque village of Staithes, for example, clings to the walls of Roxby Beck but its foreshore is an excellent location not only to view the curved reefs exposed at low tide but also to work out the geological structure of a wave-eroded anticline. Not far away is the spectacular Boulby Cliff, at 191 metres the highest of England's vertical sea cliffs (Fig. 6.4), but it is Whitby, nestling below the river estuary cliffs of the Esk, that rates as one of England's most memorable fishing ports (Daysh, 1958). This ancient town has managed to preserve its medieval identity of mellow sandstone buildings topped with scarlet pantile roofs and it is the yellowish grey Aislaby Sandstone from a neighbouring quarry that gives Whitby the unmistak-able air of a stone-belt town. Scarborough, too, has a striking setting around the

Figure 6.4 Boulby Cliff, where the alternating Jurassic shales and sandstones of the North Yorkshire Moors are cliffed by the sea.

castle on its sandstone promontory, a defensive site dating back to pre-Roman days (King, 1965). Between the two towns the coastal cliffs near Ravenscar have been disfigured by generations of quarrymen mining alum from the shales for use in the tanning and dyeing industries. At Ravenscar itself an almost complete succession of Upper Lias and Middle Jurassic rocks builds the highly unstable sea cliffs. Below the 30 metre limestone capping of the Scarborough Beds the yellow and grey shales of the Deltaic Series overlie thin beds of coal below which the Alum Shales are exposed between rockfalls at the cliff foot. Farther north, near Robin Hood's Bay, the same succession (without the Scarborough Beds) occurs higher up the cliff face because of faulting and here, too, just below the old alum mines the Jet Rock outcrops near the cliff top, giving the region the basis of a once thriving local industry, the carving of jet jewellery and ornaments.

Bibliography

Ackermann, K. J. and Cave, R. (1967) Superficial deposits and structures in the Stroud district, Gloucestershire. *Proc. Geol. Assoc.*, **78**, 567–86.

Agar, R. (1960) Post-glacial erosion of the North Yorkshire coast from the Tees estuary to Ravenscar. *Proc. Yorks. Geol. Soc.*, **32**, 409–27.

Ager, D. V., Donovan, D. T., Kennedy, W. J. *et al.* (1973) *The Cotswold Hills*. Guide No. 36. Geol. Assoc.

Arkell, W. J. (1933). *The Jurassic System in Great Britain*. Clarendon Press. 681 pp.

Arkell, W. J. (1942) Stratigraphy and structures East of Oxford. *Quart. J. Geol. Soc.*, **98**, 187–204.

Arkell, W. J. (1947a) *Oxford Stone*. Faber. 185 pp.

Arkell, W. J. (1947b) *The Geology of Oxford*. Clarendon Press. 267 pp.

Arkell, W. J. and Donovan, D. T. (1952) The fuller's earth of the Cotswolds, and its relation to the Great Oolite. *Quart. J. Geol. Soc.*, **107**. 227–53.

Ashton, M. (1980) The stratigraphy of the Lincolnshire Limestone (Bajocian) in Lincolnshire and Rutland (Leicestershire). *Proc. Geol. Assoc.*, **91**, 203–24.

Atherden, M. A. (1976) The impact of late prehistoric cultures on the vegetation of the North York Moors. *Trans. Inst. Br. Geogr.* (NS) **1**, 284–300.

Beckinsale, R and Beckinsale, M. (1980) *The English Heartland*. Duckworth. 434 pp.

Black, M. (1934) The Middle Jurassic rocks. *Proc. Geol. Assoc.*, **45**, 261–74.

Briggs, D. J. and Gilbertson, D. D. (1973) The age of the Hanborough Terrace of the River Evenlode, Oxfordshire. *Proc. Geol. Assoc.*, **84**, 155–74.

Brill, E. (1964) *Portrait of the Cotswolds*. Hale.

Clark, J. G. D. (1954) *Excavations at Star Carr*. Cambridge University Press.

Clifton-Taylor, A. (1972) *The Pattern of English Building*. Faber. 466 pp.

Darby, H. C. and Terrett, I. C. (eds) (1971) *The Domesday Geography of Midland England*. Cambridge University Press.

Daysh, G. H. J. (ed.) (1958) *A Survey of Whitby and Surrounding Area*. Shakespeare Head Press.

Douglas, J. A. and Arkell, W. J. (1928) The stratigraphical distribution of the Cornbrash. I. The south-western area. *Quart. J. Geol. Soc.*, **84**, 117–78.

Dreghorn, W. (1967) *Geology Explained in the Severn Vale and Cotswolds*. David and Charles.

Ellis, S. (1987) *East Yorkshire*. Field Guide. Quat. Res. Assoc.

Emery, F. (1974) *The Oxfordshire Landscape*. Hodder & Stoughton. 240 pp.

Evans, W. D. (1952) The Jurassic rocks of the Lincoln district. *Proc. Geol. Assoc.*, **63**, 316–35.

Finberg, H. P. R. (1975) *The Gloucestershire Landscape*. Hodder & Stoughton. 141 pp.

Finberg, J. (1977) *The Cotswolds*. Eyre Methuen. 141 pp.

Gaunt, G. D. (1976) The Devensian maximum ice limit in the Vale of York. *Proc. Yorks. Geol. Soc.*, **40**, 631–7.

Gregory, K. J. (1965) Proglacial Lake Eskdale after sixty years. *Trans. Inst. Br. Geogr.*, **36**, 149–62.

Hadfield, C. and Hadfield, A. M. (eds) (1973) *The Cotswolds: A New Study*. David and Charles. 322 pp.

Hemingway, J. E., Wilson, V. and Wright, C. W. (1963) *Geology of the Yorkshire Coast*. Guide no. 34. Geol. Assoc.

Hey, R. W. (1986) A re-examination of the Northern Drift of Oxfordshire. *Proc. Geol. Assoc.*, **97**, 291–301.

Hollingworth, S. E. and Taylor, J. H. (1946) An outline of the geology of Kettering district. *Proc. Geol. Assoc.*, **57**, 204–33.

Hollingworth, S. E. and Taylor, J. H. (1951) *The Mesozioc Ironstones of England: the*

Northampton Sand Ironstones: Stratigraphy, Structure and Reserves. Mem. Geol. Survey, GB. 211 pp.

Hoskins, W.G. (1957) *Leicestershire: The History of the Landscape.* Hodder and Stoughton. 138 pp.

Kellaway, G.A. and Wilson, V. (1941) An outline of the geology of Yeovil, Sherborne and Sparkford Vale. *Proc. Geol. Assoc.*, **52**, 131–74.

Kent, P. and Gaunt, G.D. (1980) *Eastern England from the Tees to the Wash* (2nd edn). Br. Reg. Geol. HMSO. 155 pp.

King, C.A.M. (1965) *The Scarborough District.* British Landscapes through Maps no. 7. Geog. Assoc.

Lewis, J.R. (1974) *Cotswold Villages.* Hale.

Linton, D.L. (1954) The landforms of Lincolnshire. *Geography*, **39**, 67–78.

Martin, A.F. and Steel, R.W. (eds) (1954) *The Oxford Region: A Scientific and Historical Survey.* Oxford University Press. 202 pp.

McKerrow, W.S. (1958) *The Oxford District.* Guide no. 3. Geol. Assoc.

Naish, M. (1978) *Cheltenham and Cirencester.* British Landscapes through Maps no. 18. Geog. Assoc.

North, F.J. (1930) *Limestones: Their Origins, Distribution and Uses.* Murby.

Palmer, J. (1966) Landforms, drainage and settlement in the Vale of York, in S.R. Eyre and G.R. Jones (eds) *Geography as Human Ecology.* 91–121.

Peterken, G.F. (1976) Long-term changes in the woodlands of Rockingham Forest and other areas. *J. Ecol.*, **64**, 123–46.

Purcell, D. (1967) *Cambridge Stone.* Faber.

Stean, J. (1974) *The Northamptonshire Landscape.* Hodder and Stoughton. 320 pp.

Straw, A. (1970) Wind-gaps and water gaps in eastern England. *East Midland Geographer*, **5**, 99–106.

Straw, A. and Clayton, K.M. (1979) *Eastern and Central England.* Methuen. 247 pp.

Sumbler, M.G. (1984) The stratigraphy of the Bathonian White Limestone and Forest Marble Formations of Oxfordshire. *Proc. Geol. Assoc.*, **95**, 51–64.

Sylvester-Bradley, P.C. and Ford, T.D. (eds) (1968) *The Geology of the East Midlands.* Leicester University Press. 400 pp.

Taylor, C. (1970) *Dorset.* Hodder and Stoughton. 215 pp.

Thompson, B. (1924) The Inferior Oolite sequence in Northamptonshire and northern Oxfordshire. *Quart. J. Geol. Soc.*, **80**, 430–62.

Whitehead, T.H., Anderson, W., Wilson, V. and Wray, D.A. (1952) *The Mesozoic Ironstones of England: The Liassic Ironstones.* Mem. Geol. Survey, GB. 211 pp.

Wilson, V. (1949) The Lower Corallian rocks of the Yorkshire coast and the Hackness Hills (North York Moors). *Proc. Geol. Assoc.*, **60**, 235–71.

Wright, G. (1985) *The Stone Villages of Britain.* David & Charles.

Wright, J.K. (1972) The stratigraphy of the Yorkshire Corallian. *Proc. Geol. Assoc.*, **79**, 363–99.

The English Midlands and the Welsh borders

7

Known variously as Middle England or the Heart of England, the region which spans this central tract is the transition zone between upland Britain and the scarp-and-vale landscapes of the southern and eastern lowlands. Its landforms reflect this gradual change for they combine scarplands, vales, basins and plains with much higher elevations (above 400 m), especially where the region impinges on the Welsh massif and on the Pennines. Its geology also mirrors the gradual change from the younger, gently tilted sedimentary strata of the south and east as they give way westwards and northwards to the older Palaeozoic rocks whose beds have been bent and fractured by earlier mountain-building periods to produce the gnarled and rugged landscapes of Wales and northern England. Moreover, almost the entire central region of England has been overrun, at various times, by ice sheets which have left their unmistakable imprint on the scenery of those parts (Keen, 1989).

Middle England is demarcated on almost all sides by striking physiographic features. In the south and east its lowlands terminate abruptly at the Jurassic escarpment of the stone belt described in Chapter 6. In the north the topographic break is not so marked but the transition from the Trent lowlands to the southern hills of the Peak District in Derbyshire and North Staffordshire is no less real. The western boundary of the Midlands is less clear-cut in terms of terrain because the Welsh Marcher country is itself a complex of bold hills and hidden valleys. Yet the Anglo-Saxons of the kingdom of Mercia had a remarkably clear idea of where their western boundary should be drawn and for most of its length Offa's Dike not only delimits the edge of the Welsh uplands but in its central parts is still followed by the English–Welsh border (Millward and Robinson, 1978). Thus, the Midlands region almost coincides with the ancient Mercian kingdom and includes most of Staffordshire, parts of Derbyshire, all of Nottinghamshire, Leicestershire and Warwickshire, the lowland part of Gloucestershire, and the whole of Worcestershire, the West Midlands and Cheshire. To these must be added the Welsh Marcher counties of Shropshire, Hereford and part of Monmouth (now in Gwent).

These central counties of England contain landscapes quite different from those of southern and eastern England. The lighter soils of the chalklands and the stone belt are here replaced by heavier red clays, much more difficult to drain and cultivate. It was not until after the clearance of the Mercian oakwoods in Anglo-Saxon times and the introduction of the heavy plough that these tenacious red soils were to be worked for the first time. Today, the medieval ridge-and-furrow patterns of those early open fields can still be seen in parts of the Midlands because their corrugations were soon to become 'fossilized' under greensward and never subsequently to be ploughed (Harrison et al., 1965). Instead, the large expanses of permanent grassland have long supported substantial populations of sheep, dairy and beef cattle. Thus, although the English Midlands cannot boast the endless vistas of cornfields that characterize south-eastern England, mixed farming is widespread, with arable on the patches of lighter soils. However,

Hereford and Worcestershire, on some of the most fertile of the Midlands soils, have horticultural landscapes to match those of the Kentish orchards. Nevertheless, one of the most striking contrasts in the cultural scenery of the two regions is found in the vernacular architecture, for, with a few notable exceptions, the homesteads of the Midlands are rarely built from stone. Instead, the ubiquitous oakwoods have long provided the basis of the characteristic half-timbering which typifies many of the older towns and villages in the Heart of England.

In so far as it spans the main water-parting between the North Sea and the Irish Sea, Midland England includes some of Britain's largest rivers: the Trent, the Severn and the lower reaches of the Wye and Dee (Linton, 1957). For the most part, therefore, this chapter will be dealing with the broad valleys of these large river catchments, though the West Midlands, Charnwood, the Potteries and especially the Welsh borderland also contain some quite distinctive hills and scarps. Indeed, one of the greatest impacts on the Midland scene has resulted from the disposition of the mineral-bearing Palaeozoic rocks that protrude like 'islands' from a 'sea' of red clays and sandstones. In fact, these older, harder patches of rock represent the underlying basement from which the younger softer 'cover' rocks have been stripped away to reveal the coal and metal ore-bearing strata of these so-called 'horsts' or uplifted blocks. Most important of these older rocks are the Carboniferous Coal Measures, whose intermittent outcrops in most of the Midland counties have ensured that the Heart of England also became the cradle of the Industrial Revolution. But while the coalfields may have dominated the economic and social history of the Midlands since the eighteenth century, thereby stamping an indelible imprint on their cultural landscape, it is the younger reddish rocks, of Permo-Triassic age, that give a coherence to the scenery of the region. It is time, therefore, to explain the genesis of these later sedimentaries, known collectively as the New Red Sandstone.

As the spasms of the Hercynian mountain-building episode slackened, at the close of the Carboniferous period, Britain had been transformed into a terrain of rugged and often fault-bounded Palaeozoic massifs divided by deep basins ready to receive the detritus soon to be worn from the newly uplifted mountain lands (Kent, 1949). Moreover, these new uplands had already begun to influence the climatic regime and it will be shown how the increasingly arid climate had an important effect on the character of the newly created Permo-Triassic sediments (Sherlock, 1947). Desert dunes began to form around the margins of an invading arm of a tropical sea in which layers of marine sandstones and limestones were deposited. The earliest were formed as Permian limestones and sandstones in a basin to the east of the newly uplifted Pennines. In Cheshire and the rest of the Midlands, however, the freshly downwarped basins were slowly being infilled, not by marine sediments but by layer upon layer of continental deposits in which the oldest Bunter Sandstones became buried first by Keuper Sandstones and finally by thick beds of Keuper Marl. Marls are calcareous clays laid down in ephemeral lakes on the floors of large desert basins known as *playas*, and it is the salty deposits of similar Triassic lakes that now form the basis of Cheshire's salt industry. As its name suggests, however, the New Red Sandstone is characterized by bright red sandstones, often displaying excellent dune-bedding structures (see p. 43) that represent the wind-blown deposits of the ancient desert basins (Wills, 1950). Additionally, lying at the base of the Bunter sandstones, there are distinctive layers of much coarser rocks: first, the rounded conglomerates of the Pebble

Beds, created by sporadic torrential stream action in the desert wadis, and second, the angular breccias which are nothing more than the cemented screes that once formed at the foot of the steeper slopes. Because all these various New Red Sandstone rocks exhibit contrasting degrees of resistance to weathering and erosion, they have given rise to important differences in the detailed modelling of the present land surface. In general, the Keuper Marls and Bunter Sandstones underlie low-lying ground, while the harder Magnesian Limestones (Permian), Keuper Sandstones and Bunter Pebble Beds stand out as hills and escarpments. Nevertheless, apart from Cannock Chase (Bunter Pebble Beds), most of the highest hills of the Midlands and Welsh borders have been carved not from New Red Sandstone but from the older Palaeozoic rocks. The Hercynian earth movements, though reduced in magnitude, continued to affect the region into Permo-Triassic times, pushing up the coalfield blocks along their bounding faults to form *horsts*, thereby causing the intervening basins to deepen even further. Although the Permo-Triassic sediments formerly buried the central parts of this block-mountain landscape they have been removed by erosion from the coalfield horsts of Shropshire, Worcestershire, Staffordshire and Warwickshire (Mitchell, 1954) as well as f.om the Precambrian horst of Charnwood. Elsewhere these characteristically red-coloured rocks completely blanket the ancient basement whose surface had already been deformed by the Hercynian earth movements. The southermost corner of the Midlands tapers out into a funnel-shaped lowland, known as the Vales of Evesham, Gloucester, Berkeley and Worcester, where the River Severn drains to the Bristol Channel.

The South Midland vales

As the Severn estuary broadens into the Bristol Channel its alluvial floodplain becomes fringed with salt marshes (Allen and Rae, 1988). Today they provide nesting sites for countless wading birds and other wildfowl, particularly at the sanctuary of Slimbridge. This narrow Vale of Berkeley, squeezed between the bold Cotswold scarp and the widening Severn estuary, is merely an appendage of Midland England. Although its red-brown soils, its extensive herds of dairy cattle and its brick-built villages are characteristic of the Midlands, it also combines features that characterize both the Gloucestershire Cotswolds and the Forest of Dean. Thus, its southern flanks boast drystone walls while the abundance of hedgerow trees reflects the neighbouring woodlands of the Forest of Dean. Reflecting the central Midland's technological achievements, Gloucestershire boasts the Severn Bridge and Berkeley's now defunct nuclear power station. Yet the great Cotswold stone tower of Gloucester Cathedral not only dominates the Vale but reminds one of the timeless nature of the nearby stone-belt structures, buildings that will survive the age of steel and concrete.

The narrow ribbon of Keuper Marl, which links the Midland New Red Sandstone with that of Avon and Somerset (see Chapter 2), is almost obliterated in the Vale of Gloucester by a cover of Lias Clay, the lowest member of the Jurassic succession (Dreghorn, 1967). The strata are clearly seen from the Severn Bridge at Aust Cliff where a dolomitic conglomerate underlies the red and green Keuper Marls (Trias) which in turn are overlain by black shales (Rhaetic) and thin blue Liassic limestones (Jurassic). Throughout the vale the greyish blue Lias clays also contain thin beds of White Lias and Blue Lias limestones, all of which dip gently south-eastwards to pass beneath the high Cotswold escarpment, but whose north-western expression is a low scarped ridge that rises some 50 metres above the Severn and Avon valley floors. The lower Severn and Avon valleys follow approximately the line where the red Triassic clay soils of the north and west meet the heavier blue-grey Liassic soils that rise gently to the Cotswolds scarp foot where their colour changes to a dirty yellow. Such soil-colour differences reflect the contrasting amount of iron compounds in the Triassic and Liassic rocks, yet when their clays are fired in the local brickworks both yield red-coloured bricks. Not surprisingly, the latter have been extensively used in the numerous half-timbered dwellings, though the golden Cotswold freestones are near enough to have been utilized in most of the vale's church towers, most notably at Pershore and Evesham. The city of Gloucester, founded by the Romans on an alluvial terrace above the Severn floodplain, is now a thriving commercial and industrial city, but its stone-built town walls are virtually obliterated. By contrast, the scarp-foot town of Cheltenham has retained much of its early Bath stone character. Its attractive Regency architecture and wide boulevards reflect the date of its development, late enough to be influenced by formal town planning. In this respect it is very different from the haphazard but picturesque medieval street pattern of Tewksbury, whose closely packed brick and timber houses and incomparable Norman abbey are squeezed between the confluence of the Avon and Severn rivers. The horticultural activity of the Vale of Evesham, though centred on Evesham itself, stretches from Tewksbury to Stratford, right across the undulating tract of the Lower Lias whose clays, limestones and shales have weathered into the fertile clay loams known as the Evesham Soil Association. It is now renowned for its orchards and its hectares of glasshouses where 'a continuing green, of leeks, cabbages, asparagus, currant bushes, gooseberries, and now maybe a vineyard of two, is powdered in spring with a froth of blossoms' (Keates, 1979).

To the south of Stratford-upon-Avon the scarp-foot zone below the Cotswold bastions of Ilmington Down and Edge Hill is known as the Feldon, its Liassic clays and limestones underlying this north-eastern extension of the Vale of Evesham. Once as heavily forested as the Forest of Arden, the Feldon's heavy soils remained virtually uncleared until the Iron Age. But when the Romans built their great road, the Foss Way, obliquely across the Midlands following the crest of the Lower Lias scarp, the new route henceforth drew settlement into this deserted zone, especially where scarp-foot springs emerged (Harley, 1964). The Feldon also exhibits excellent examples of the medieval ridge-and-furrow field pattern which, before field drains were invented, was essential to remove water from the heavy Midland clay soils. Its survival in the landscape has been explained because

> not only was it costly to cross-plough the ridges and level them, but the results were discouraging, for much of the infertile sub-soil was brought to the surface . . . The farmer therefore let well alone, the old ridges were put down to grass (Hoskins, 1957).

The last of the south Midland vales, the Vale of Worcester, is somewhat different from those already described for, instead of being overshadowed by the Cotswold scarp, the red Triassic plain of Worcester is abruptly terminated by the Malvern Hills, of Precambrian age, and by a line of hills further north built from the Silurian limestones of the Welsh border country. Attaining thicknesses of 450 metres, the Keuper rocks of Worcestershire contain rock salt and brine deposits, known since the Iron Age but worked extensively by the Romans at Droitwich from which salt roads radiate, one of the best known being the saltway from Alcester to Stratford. At Upton Warren, near Droitwich, a complex layer of organic silts in the valley of the Salwarpe tributary of the River Severn has been dated by radiocarbon means as having been deposited during a temporary warm phase in the middle of the Devensian cold period of the Ice Age, now known as the Upton Warren Interstadial (about 40 000 years ago) (Coope *et al.*, 1961). Both Welsh and English ice sheets advanced into Worcestershire but left very little boulder clay; instead, their contribution to the scenery of the Lower Severn Valley is exemplified by a remarkable suite of river terraces, comparable with those of the Thames, carved out by both Severn and Avon from the broad expanses of glaciofluvial outwash from the wasting ice sheets (Beckinsale and Richardson, 1964). This staircase of gravel terraces (Tomlinson, 1925), which gives central Worcestershire such fertile farming, is best seen between Bridgnorth and Tewkesbury on the Severn and upstream on the Avon as far as Stratford. The Bushley Green terrace, at 40 metres above the flood plain, is the highest and oldest, believed to have been formed during the draining of Lake Harrison (see p. 136), while the succeeding Kidderminster (33–24 m) and the older of the Main terraces (20–9 m) have been placed in the Ipswichian interglacial (see Fig. 5.1). The extensive Worcester terrace (8–3 m), on which the city is located, together with the younger of the Main terraces, are both thought to be of Devensian age (Stephens, 1970). Interestingly, both of the latter can be traced upstream through the Ironbridge gorge and into the Shropshire lowlands, while the Kidderminster and Upper Main terraces both terminate upstream at the lower end of the gorge. From this it has been deduced that the famous chasm at Ironbridge could not have existed before the Devensian and that it was this ice advance which diverted the Upper Severn away from the Dee to follow its present course through the gorge southwards to the Bristol Channel. The advance of Devensian ice into the Cheshire–Shropshire lowlands is known to have caused ponding of the drainage to form two pro-glacial lakes in Shropshire, at Newport and Buildwas (Wills, 1924). Despite claims by earlier writers that these later amalgamated into 'Lake Lapworth', the overflow from which is reputed to have carved out the Ironbridge gorge, more recent opinion favours a different mode of formation (Hamblin, 1986). It is now suggested that the gorge was formed as an ice-marginal channel and that 'Lake Lapworth' existed not as a single lake but as a number of smaller water bodies (Worsley, 1975).

Today, the Severn flows rapidly through Ironbridge and its unique 'fossil' urban landscape that has survived almost intact from the Industrial Revolution (Trinder, 1973); it glides round the romantically sited town of Bridgnorth, perched on its red sandstone cliffs, and down through the riverside patchwork of grazing lands on their step-like terraces; quickening its pace through the sandstone gorges clothed by the Forest of Wyre around Bewdley, it finally emerges into the softer contours around Worcester, whose pink sandstone cathedral was once surrounded by a town of half-timbered houses, now sadly depeleted (Adlam, 1974).

The Heart of England

The nucleus of the true English Midlands is the large triangular region enclosed by the valleys of the Severn, Trent, Soar and Avon (Hains and Horton, 1969). In general its scenery is muted, largely because most of its low hills are undistinguished and its vales and basins mostly broad and featureless. Moreover, the heartland has been partly overwhelmed by such sprawling red-brick industrial cities as Stoke-on-Trent, Derby, Nottingham, Leicester, Coventry and especially the West Midlands conurbation of Birmingham and the Black Country. Not surprisingly, most of these cities are located on or close to the Midlands coalfields (Trueman, 1954) which spring up like dark industrial 'oases' amid the rural 'desert' of red-marls and sandstones. It is the large remaining tracts of Midland countryside, however, that recall the yeoman England whose scenery must have helped inspire Shakespeare long before the scars of the Industrial Revolution appeared. These broad expanses of farmland are developed mainly on the damp Keuper Marls whose outcrop also coincides fairly closely with the wide valleys of the Avon, the Lower Severn, the Soar and the Trent.

Some authors, when writing of the Heart of England, think primarily of Warwickshire, whose wooded landscapes are squeezed between the Cotswolds and the industrial nucleus around Birmingham. The visitor is constantly aware of the ubiquitous red clay soils, the leafy hedgerows and the bright-red sandstone castles, churches and manors, but Warwickshire's scenery exhibits a marked contrast between the Avon Valley and the central Keuper Marl lowlands, on the one hand, and the Birmingham and Coventry plateaux on the other. That the former, predominantly rural, tract coincides with the broad swathe of Triassic and Liassic clays and that the latter represent the denuded stumps of the coalfield hill country, is essentially a geological explanation that becomes more apparent when one examines the degree of industrial development of the two divisions. The south Midlands coalfields, blanketed with patches of Pre-Devensian tills and glacial gravels (Pickering, 1957), are now largely covered by the West Midlands conurbation, Nuneaton and Coventry, respectively, while the relatively drift-free rural landscapes farther south boast such historic, unspoiled towns as Kenilworth, Warwick and Stratford-on-Avon with their half-timbering and sandstone buildings, notable among which are the castles of Warwick and Kenilworth. The Anglo-Saxon town of Warwick was built on a small knoll of Lower Keuper Sandstone in a meander of the River Avon. Stratford, by contrast, arose where a Roman road crossed the Avon. The Avon's river terraces, cleared of their riparian forest by Celtic settlers, became a zone of cultural fusion between Anglian people from the east and Saxon tribes (the Hwicce) moving from the south.

One area of Warwickshire woodland that survived longer than most was the Forest of Arden that thrived for thousands of years on the heavy Keuper Marls which here occupy a synclinal sag between the higher plateaux of the East Warwickshire and the South Staffordshire coalfield horsts. The trough is drained to the north by the Cole, Blythe and Tame, and southwards by the Alne, a tributary of the Avon, but while the northern streams flow sluggishly across marshy floodplains, the Alne tributaries are swift-flowing and are enclosed in deep, steep-sided valleys cut into the Arden Sandstone (Matley, 1912). The dense Arden oak-woods remained virtually untouched until Anglo-Saxon and early Norman times when hamlets were located in small forest clearings, as illustrated by the -*ley*,

-*worth* and -*field* suffix among the equally common place names that incorporate -*hurst* and -*wood* (for example, Haseley, Lapworth, Nuthurst and Earlswood) (Darby and Terrett, 1971). No doubt the 'magpie' architecture of the region reflects the continuing availability of oak for the timbering, especially well seen at Henley-in-Arden, laid out as a planned borough in 1185. The English elm was once so prolific in Arden that it was termed the 'Warwickshire Weed', but owing to the onset of a fatal disease in the 1970s it has virtually disappeared from the whole of Britain.

In complete contrast to the damp, leafy glades and carefully managed farmlands of the Keuper Marl country are the eminences of the fault-bounded plateaux of the central Midlands, referred to by geologists as the Midland horsts of East Warwickshire, South Staffordshire and Charnwood (Leicestershire). In east Warwickshire the bounding faults, with throws of 200–300 metres, have brought the surrounding Keuper Marls abruptly against the upstanding block of Coal Measures, Cambrian shales and quartzites, and Precambrian igneous rocks that together represent the ancient massif of stripped 'basement' which stretches some 40 kilometres from Tamworth in the north to Kenilworth in the south. The coal-bearing strata (Middle Coal Measures) are exposed only as a thin ribbon around the northern tip of the horst between Tamworth and Atherstone and along the eastern fringe near Nuneaton, where they have been worked since medieval times. Mining has now ceased on these eastern margins, leaving such forlorn colliery villages as Bedworth, Griff and Baddesley, all built from bricks baked from the neighbouring outcrop of the Etruria Marls. Though the marl pits and brickworks are now defunct, roadstone quarries have survived in the tough Cambrian quartzite exposure near Nuneaton. Elsewhere, the coal-bearing rocks descend westwards beneath the Keele Sandstone beds (Upper Carboniferous) that create the rolling countryside between Coventry, Meriden and Kenilworth. Deep shafts have recently been sunk to reach the valuable seams to the west of Coventry and this buried coalfield will soon be expanded beneath the historic city's outskirts and southwards towards Kenilworth.

The South Staffordshire horst, some 25 kilometres to the west, is similar in shape and size to that of East Warwickshire but differs from it both in the complexity of its geology and in its cultural landscape. Whereas the East Warwickshire plateau has retained much open countryside, that of South Staffordshire (now the West Midlands) coincides almost exactly with the so-called Black Country between Wolverhampton and Birmingham (Garrett *et al.*, 1958). Such industrialization is hardly surprising when one considers that the exposed coalfield here is almost 20 kilometres wide and stretches some 35 kilometres between Cannock and Stourbridge. Therefore, its coal and iron provided the basis for one of Britain's earliest and largest industrial regions. In addition to being more sharply folded and faulted than those of the East Warwickshire horst, the Palaeozoic rocks of South Staffordshire also exhibit more contrasting rock types: inliers of Wenlock Limestone (Silurian) at Walsall, Sedgeley, Dudley and Wren's Nest; intrusive dolerites in the Etruria Marls at Smethwick, Dudley and Wolverhampton; and finally, Cambrian quartzites and Precambrian volcanics in the Lickey Hills southwest of Birmingham. Unlike those of the East Warwickshire horst, however, the bounding faults here are rarely conspicuous because they are overlapped by the Triassic cover rocks almost everywhere except along the horst's western margin between Wolverhampton and the Clent Hills, and in the east near Brownhills.

Partly for this reason and partly because of the dense urban cover, it is virtually impossible in some areas to be aware of geological or even topographical contrasts as one crosses from the Triassic rocks to those of the coalfield horst. Nevertheless, the presence of the older, harder rocks and the fact that this region stands on a major water-parting between the Severn and Trent, means that there is a handful of substantial elevations. At Clent the hills of Upper Carboniferous breccias rise dramatically to 316 metres, raised some 150 metres above the Keuper sandstone on the downthrown western side of the boundary fault. The Lickey Hills reach 291 metres and the Smethwick dolerites achieve 267 metres. The Silurian (Wenlock) limestone exposures (Butler, 1939) have everywhere produced steep-sided hills on one of which Dudley Castle was founded soon after the Norman Conquest when very little settlement existed on the surrounding plateau. An early iron industry grew up at Dudley, Walsall and Wednesbury, based on Coal Measures ironstone and on charcoal from the surrounding woodlands. Yet because of medieval Birmingham's nodality, at the junction of Roman roads with the Midland salt-ways, this became the centre from which rudimentary iron goods were marketed from the sixteenth century (Wise, 1950). Some two centuries later, because of its heartland situation, Birmingham also became the focus of the Midlands canals, despite the difficulties of surmounting its plateau edge with lengthy flights of locks (Hadfield, 1966). The scene was now set for the remarkable transformation soon to be created by the Industrial Revolution, when local coal and iron-stone, Dudley limestone for flux, Coal Measures fireclay for furnace linings and excellent Triassic moulding sand for casting, were all in sufficient abundance to make the West Midlands one of the first major 'workshops of the world' during the eighteenth and nineteenth centuries (Johnson and Wise, 1950). Today Birmingham and the Black Country constitute Britain's second largest city, entwined within a network of motorways. In most places the latter are untroubled by steep terrain, though the M6 has to climb through a col between the substantially wooded Clent and Lickey Hills. These hills comprise two of the few undeveloped areas of the conurbation, other than that where the dry sandy soils of the Bunter Sandstone give a substantial area of open heath and woodland at Sutton Park, overlooked from the west by the landmark of Barr Beacon (Bunter Pebble Beds). By contrast, on the Keuper Sandstone outcrop, which rings the conurbation, the soils have neither the heaviness of the marls nor the dryness of the Bunter. Their fertility gave rise to early settlements at Bromsgrove, Sutton Coldfield and Lichfield where the red and purple Keuper Sandstone has been widely utilized in the older buildings, though the stonework of Lichfield's magnificent thirteenth-century cathedral was so badly chosen that it has needed constant repair.

Before leaving the Heart of England, attention must be given to the evolution of the drainage pattern of this region. One modern writer has asserted that long before the Anglian glaciation the English Midlands drainage may have had links with the Thames. At a later stage, it is further claimed that, prior to the deposition of the Lowestoft Till (see p. 97), a large 'Midland River' flowed through a gap in the Jurassic scarp near Melton Mowbray (Rice, 1991) before continuing in a circuitous route eastwards across what is now Fenland and joining the so-called 'Ingham River' in Suffolk and flowing to the North Sea (Bridgland and Lewis, 1991) (Fig. 7.1a). Rather less speculatively, it is also thought that the Warwickshire Avon formerly flowed north eastwards to join the Trent, once following the line of the present River Soar along the Lias Clay vale. During the reputed

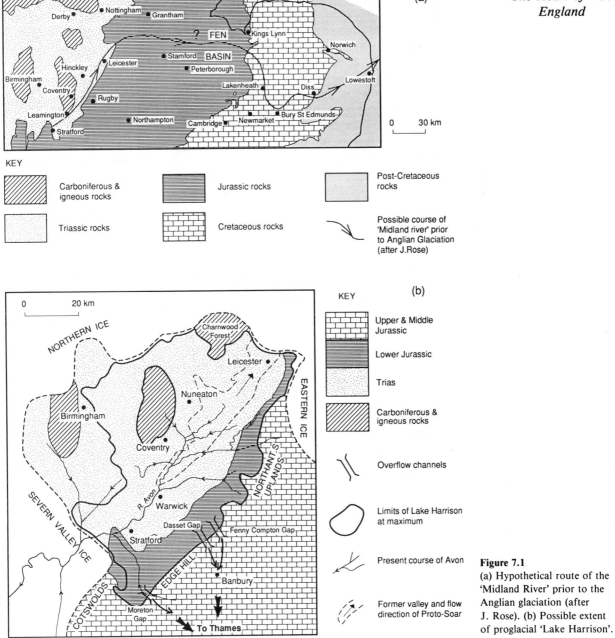

KEY

	Carboniferous & igneous rocks			Jurassic rocks			Post-Cretaceous rocks
	Triassic rocks			Cretaceous rocks			Possible course of 'Midland river' prior to Anglian Glaciation (after J.Rose)

KEY (b)

Upper & Middle Jurassic

Lower Jurassic

Trias

Carboniferous & igneous rocks

Overflow channels

Limits of Lake Harrison at maximum

Present course of Avon

Former valley and flow direction of Proto-Soar

Figure 7.1
(a) Hypothetical route of the 'Midland River' prior to the Anglian glaciation (after J. Rose). (b) Possible extent of proglacial 'Lake Harrison'.

'Wolstonian' stage of the Ice Age, however, ice sheets advanced south-westwards up this early Avon/Soar valley, blocked the river exit and are thought by some to have ponded up a massive pro-glacial lake in the South Midlands (Harwood, 1988). Known as 'Lake Harrison', the water body must originally have overflowed south-westwards into the Bristol Channel until this outlet, too, was blocked by ice advances down the Severn Valley. As the lake level rose to a height of 125 metres, it finally reached gaps in the high Jurassic escarpment at Fenny Compton, Dasset and Moreton-in-Marsh, thereby spilling its waters southwards into the Thames system (Bishop, 1958). At its maximum dimensions Lake Harrison is thought to have stretched for some 90 km between Leicester and Stratford (Fig. 7.1b) but the subsequent decay of the ice barrier in the Severn Valley allowed the lake waters to drain away in that direction, thereby initiating rapid backcutting by the newly born River Avon in a course now flowing south-westwards. By the time the retreat of the eastern ice near Loughborough had allowed the River Soar to re-establish itself, the water-parting on the 80 metre thickness of lake sediments had been shifted north-eastwards by the Avon's backcutting to its present position in Leicestershire. Thus the Avon is a relatively modern river, spawned by meltwaters from the retreating eastern ice sheets which also left deposits of outwash gravel (the Dunsmore Gravel) over wide expanses of the South Midlands, particularly well illustrated at Dunsmore Heath to the west of Rugby (Shotton, 1977). The Coventry, Rugby and Leamington area has long been regarded as the type-area for the so-called 'Wolstonian' glacial stage of the Pleistocene (Shotton, 1953; 1983), separating the Hoxnian and Ipswichian interglacial stages (see Fig. 5.1), but it has recently been claimed that the Pleistocene sediments at Wolston itself are much older, probably dating from the Anglian glaciation (Rose, 1987). Despite this disagreement in age there is no dispute over the existence of a cold period at that time, for major river-terrace gravels full of cold fauna of that age occur both in the Thames Valley and in the East Anglian river-valleys. What is needed, therefore, is for a new type-site to be discovered in the Midlands to replace that at Wolston – until then the term 'Wolstonian' will have to be retained, despite its unsatisfactory nature.

Charnwood and the East Midlands

Between the Stone belt and the Pennines the East Midlands (Marshall, 1948; Sylvester-Bradley and Ford, 1968) contains a wide variety of Palaeozoic and Mesozoic sedimentaries and even a few Precambrian rocks. In Leicestershire the exposed coalfield around Ashby de la Zouch stretches some 16 kilometres from the Trent Valley near Burton eastwards to the red brick industrial town of Coalville. Unlike the other south Midlands coalfields, that of Leicestershire has, in addition to the Coal Measures, small exposures of Millstone Grit and Carboniferous Limestone. These Carboniferous rocks, together with the much older rocks of Charnwood, comprise another of the horsts which give variety to the Midlands' geology. The easternmost of the Midland horsts is not only smaller and more complex than the others but its bounding faults are everywhere still buried beneath the red Triassic blanket. Extensive remnants of this cover of New Red Sandstone survive above the Coal Measures around Ashby de la Zouch and more widely where the partly buried Precambrian hills of Charnwood rise above the extensive sheet of Keuper Marls (Figure 7.2) (Watts, 1947). From Bardon Hill (278 m), Charnwood's highest point, it is possible to view most of this remarkable, partly exhumed sub-Triassic landscape where the red beds are being slowly stripped away to reveal 'sudden sharp and jagged outcrops pushing through the reddish soil, and high wooded ridges with long grey splintery walls of rock rising along their crests' (Miller, 1953). In the once buried primeval complex of Precambrian lavas, volcanic ashes, grits and slates, ancient rivers had carved out valleys along the north-west to south-east strike of the rocks, a direction referred to as the Charnian 'grain' (Bennett *et al.*, 1928). Modern streams (some 170 million years later) now flow along some reaches of these ancient valleys but in parts of their courses they cross on to ridges of the old, harder rocks to create deep picturesque gorges, such as the Ingleberry gorge on the Shorncliffe Brook and the Bradgate Park gorge near Newtown Linford. Such a pattern provides an excellent example of superimposed drainage, initiated when the older basement rocks were completely buried (Watts, 1903). Where the streams have cut down into the Triassic-filled valleys of the buried landscape they have been able to re-excavate quite rapidly in the former desert wadis (see p. 129) and produce broad valleys in the red marls. Where they have been superimposed on to the Precambrian rocks, however, their rate of downcutting and valley widening is severely restricted, thus producing the narrow gorges. Several of the Charnwood summits are capped by tors, possibly prepared by deep tropical weathering in Tertiary times but finally stripped by frost action during the Pleistocene Ice Age.

The ancient re-excavated trenches of Charnwood have long been used as routeways, like the old road from Shepshed up the Shortcliffe Valley and down Lingdale to Swithland and that along the Blackbrook Valley. Today, however, the more advanced technology of the road builders has enabled the M1 motorway to

Figure 7.2 Structure of Charnwood Forest, looking northwards.

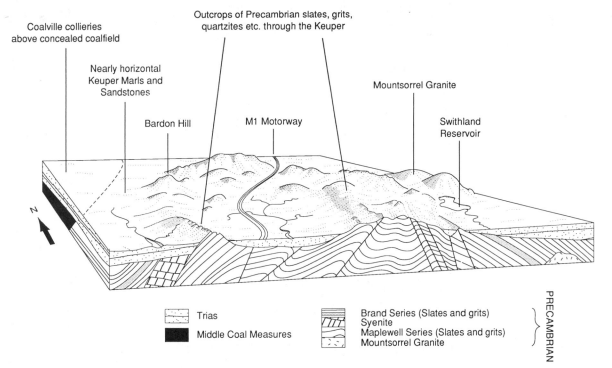

Coalville collieries above concealed coalfield

Nearly horizontal Keuper Marls and Sandstones

Outcrops of Precambrian slates, grits, quartzites etc. through the Keuper

Mountsorrel Granite

Bardon Hill

M1 Motorway

Swithland Reservoir

N

Trias

Middle Coal Measures

Brand Series (Slates and grits)
Syenite
Maplewell Series (Slates and grits)
Mountsorrel Granite

PRECAMBRIAN

sweep through Charnwood with little regard for geology or topography. No doubt some of the aggregates needed in its construction came from the nearby quarries of the partly buried granites of Groby and Mountsorrel (intruded into the Charnian rocks) (Taylor, 1934), or from the Carboniferous Limestone quarry carved into the isolated mound at Breedon on the Hill. The forlorn, water-filled quarries of Swithland, once worked by the Romans, were Midland England's only source of roofing slates until they were closed in 1887, due to competition from cheap Welsh slate. Nevertheless, Swithland slates can still be seen in many of Charnwood's drystone field walls and also as tombstones in several graveyards in both Leicester and Loughborough.

A great deal of the county of Leicestershire is drained by the River Soar, the course of which is almost coincident with the boundary between the Lias and the Trias (Straw and Clayton, 1979). West of the Jurassic marlstone escarpment, however, the Soar basin is thickly infilled with glacial drift which almost masks the underlying rocks (Rice, 1968). Not surprisingly, therefore, the heavy clay soils of the boulder clay are given over largely to permanent grass, famous for its livestock-fattening qualities, especially along the alluvial valley of the Soar itself. Westwards towards Charnwood stretch the undulating plains of the drift-covered Keuper Marl (Douglas, 1981), so typical of the Red Midlands. These waterlogged, forested claylands were quite inhospitable to early settlement prior to Saxon times and thereafter the villages were invariably sited some 10–15 metres above the ill-drained clays on knolls of glacial sands and gravels that also provided excellent water supplies: Houghton on the Hill is one such village, and in a landscape of few vertical features the spired village churches are a notable addition to the scene. Hoskins (1957) describes how Leicestershire's landscape is spattered with large brick villages and solid brick towns, though locally made bricks were not universally used until the late seventeenth century, often for houses to accommodate the growing number of textile and hosiery workers. This new wave of industry brought renewed wealth to the historic city of Leicester whose medieval grandeur had faded over the centuries: in 1654 John Evelyn wrote of the 'old and ragged City of Leicester, large and pleasantly seated, but despicably built' (Pye, 1972). The parallel growth of such towns as Loughborough and Hinckley also owed much to the bourgeoning hosiery industry during the nineteenth century, a time when the redbrick mining towns of Coalville, Woodville and Swadlingcote also sprang up on the partly buried Leicestershire coalfield. Fringing the exposed Coal Measures (Spink, 1965) a narrow rim of Keuper Sandstone provides useful water supplies and the same rocks create a low ridge between the coalfield and the banks of the Trent at Castle Donington.

Just as Warwickshire is thought to typify the scenery of the South Midlands, so Nottinghamshire is said to epitomize the East Midlands (Edwards, 1966). Though lacking spectacular landforms and high elevations, Nottinghamshire has quite distinctive landscapes each related to north–south outcrops of contrasting rock types. From the denuded arch of the Pennines, with its skirt of Coal Measures, the cover rocks of New Red Sandstone dip very gently eastwards before disappearing beneath the Lias Clay and the younger Jurassics of Lincolnshire. Surprisingly, in view of the contrasting limestones, sandstones and marls of the New Red Sandstone, each with their own distinctive scenery, the lithological changes are not accompanied by a regular scarp-and-vale landscape, largely because of the rarity of clay beds between the more resistant strata (Sherlock,

1947). Commencing in the west, a transect across the area would demonstrate that the coalfield is succeeded by the lowest member of the New Red Sandstone, somewhat paradoxically represented by the Magnesian Limestone (Permian), which is neither red nor a sandstone, but which produces one of the few prominent west-facing scarps. Thereafter the succession (Wills, 1970) can best be shown in tabular form:

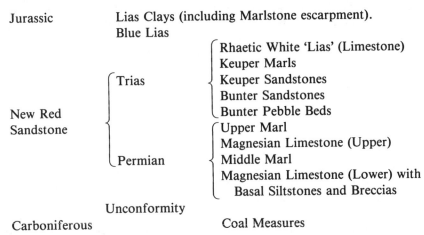

Jurassic — Lias Clays (including Marlstone escarpment). Blue Lias

New Red Sandstone:

Trias:
- Rhaetic White 'Lias' (Limestone)
- Keuper Marls
- Keuper Sandstones
- Bunter Sandstones
- Bunter Pebble Beds

Permian:
- Upper Marl
- Magnesian Limestone (Upper)
- Middle Marl
- Magnesian Limestone (Lower) with Basal Siltstones and Breccias

Unconformity

Carboniferous — Coal Measures

The exposed coalfield, which stretches into eastern Derbyshire (Spink, 1965) and is also the southern limit of the Yorkshire coalfield (Edwards, 1954), has scenery quite different from that of the broad red corridor which bestrides the Trent. The Erewash valley, for example, the setting for D. H. Hawrence's best-known novels, is now somewhat forlorn for, like many of the older colliery villages between Ilkeston and Chesterfield, its settlements no longer have associated mines. Activity has moved eastwards into the New Red Sandstone country where the coalfield is concealed beneath the cover rocks, and where pits have mushroomed in relatively unspoiled countryside, bringing with them such new mining settlements as Calveton, Blidworth and Bilsthorpe among the remants of Sherwood Forest. It was during the drilling of boreholes to ascertain the structure of the buried coalfield that oil was discovered at Eakring, trapped in an upfold of Millstone Grit at a depth of 650 metres. Though Eakring was Britain's first substantial oil well, seventeen other discoveries have since been made between Mansfield and the Humber in what is now termed the East Midlands/Lincolnshire oilfield (Taylor and Howitt, 1965). Its production, however, is currently far less than that of Britain's largest onshore field at Wytch Farm, Dorset (see p. 50).

The coarse-grained light brown dolomitic limestone that represents the bulk of the Magnesian Limestone's outcrop in Nottinghamshire is different from the fine-grained yellow Magnesian Limestone of Yorkshire and Durham, but in the East Midlands the Lower Magnesian Limestone escarpment, with its underlying siltstones, forms a conspicuous feature between Nottingham and Bolsover, followed closely by the M1 motorway (Waring, 1965). At its southern end this 160 metre high cuesta is broken up by strike faulting that has caused inliers of Permian Marls to create their own miniature landscape of minor scarps and short vales (Briggs et al., 1985). It was in one such feature, at Cresswell Crags, that Upper Palaeolithic peoples once lived in caves on the gorge sides (Campbell, 1977). Between Nottingham and Mansfield the Permian cover is thin enough for this area to have been the initial section of the concealed coalfield to have been exploited in the mid-nineteenth century. Although the southern part of the main limestone escarpment is rarely broken by river gaps, around Mansfield the headwaters of the Meden and Maun rise on the Coal Measures before flowing eastwards in deep valleys through the limestone and into the Bunter country where they join the major north-flowing subsequent stream of the River Idle which hugs the foot of the Keuper Sandstone scarp. By the time the Magnesian Limestone outcrop reaches the latitude of Doncaster (Coates and Lewis, 1966), where the basal Permian sands have given rise to a glass industry, its cuesta, though still prominent, has fallen in elevation to 110 metres, and here it is increasingly breached by streams flowing eastwards from the Pennine flanks, most notably the Don and the Aire, both of which may have been superimposed from a Triassic sandstone cover (Clayton, 1953a). Much of Welbeck Park and its Abbey occurs on the relatively featureless country created by the narrow outcrop of the Middle Permian Marl, as does Newstead Abbey to the south of Mansfield. Farther south, on the outskirts of Nottingham itself, this dark red Permian Marl has been worked for coarse pottery at Bulwell. Both these sites occupy the valley of the tiny river Leen whose north–south strike valley is highly asymmetrical, with a broad Magnesian Limestone dipslope to the west and a steep scarp capped by Bunter Pebble Beds to the east.

The contrast in topography between the Magnesian Limestone and the Bunter rocks has been described by Straw and Clayton (1979): athough both are porous the former has

> gently sloping plateaux broken by narrow dry valleys that frequently show right-angled bends. The valley sides are cut sharply below the plateau, reflecting the bedding of the limestone. There are no such sharp breaks on the Bunter rocks, for they are practically devoid of bedding . . . resulting in a surface that is everywhere rolling, a succession of smoothly-flowing concave and convex slopes.

Moreover, although the Bunter has a marked absence of surface drainage, because of its porosity, it provides the main water supply for the region because the underlying impermeable layer of the Permian Marl holds the percolating waters in a vast subterranean reservoir. Mostly, the Bunter Sandstones are soft and easily excavated both by physical and by human agencies: the oddly-shaped Hemlock Stone, where the sand grains are cemented by a tenacious barium sulphate (Fig. 7.3), is a product of natural erosion near Bramcote, while human excavations are exemplified in the city of Nottingham by the caves which remain dry because of the rock's high porosity. Some caves have been used as dwellings, and the famous 'Trip to Jerusalem' inn, beneath the Castle, extends into the rock. Nottingham itself was founded on a river-cut bluff of Bunter Sandstone (Smith, 1913) whose wide outcrop extends northwards past Mansfield and Worksop where its light, well-drained soils support large stretches of heathland, gorse, broom and bracken interspersed with great expanses of forest. There is still a considerable amount of primitive oak woodland surviving in Sherwood Forest. In medieval times the whole of the Bunter outcrop was characterized by unenclosed birch and oak woodland with only small patches of enclosed arable. However, clearance throughout succeeding centuries reduced the Forest's extent so that by 1793 a mere 600 hectares of Crown woodland survived and this was sold to a local estate owner

Figure 7.3 The Hemlock
Stone, Bramcote,
Nottinghamshire, where the
grains of the Bunter
Sandstone are cemented by
barium sulphate to produce a
resistant pillar of rock now
isolated by weathering and
erosion. Note the
cross-bedding.

(Boulton, 1965). The poorer lands of the northern part of the Bunter country had
already been systematically purchased by wealthy aristocrats after the dissolu-
tion of the monasteries, and they became the wooded parklands known as the
Dukeries.

The Keuper Sandstones (Elliot, 1961) create a different type of scenery to that
of the Bunter for they occur mainly as thin beds (skerries) especially near the base
of the Marls. Wherever they outcrop they create small but sharp escarpments quite
unlike the rolling Bunter hills. But the main Keuper Sandstone scarp, formed from
the Waterstones, begins in the eastern suburbs of Nottingham and runs northwards through the country to terminate at Gringley on the Hill. The northern
section of the escarpment is virtually unbroken except by wind-gaps that represent
the former courses of the main east-flowing consequent streams, all of which have
subsequently been captured by the piratical River Idle. East of this cuesta the
extensive Keuper Marls (Elliot, 1961) form a broad drift-filled lowland occupied

by the Trent, a zone whose till-derived soils are so impermeable that there is a conspicuous network of surface streams, some of which have short stretches of steep and vigorous flow. The latter are knick-points resulting from a late rejuvenation of the Trent catchment as it cut down to a lower base-level (Clayton, 1953a). Locally, these gorges are known as 'dumbles', as exemplified at Lowdham, Lambley and Gedling.

The Trent itself meanders across a floodplain some 3 kilometres wide between Nottingham and the Humber, a zone of few villages owing to the flood hazard. Though the channel is fringed with natural levees these have been artificially raised, thereby creating difficulties for tributaries endeavouring to reach the main river, as illustrated by the South Muskham stream which parallels the Trent for 8 kilometres before effecting a junction. These damp alluvial river meadows, fringed with alder and willow, drained by ditches and grazed by livestock, have remained virtually unchanged for centuries, although the more elevated staircase of Pleistocene gravel terraces (Clayton, 1953b; Posnansky, 1960; Straw, 1963) has always been given over to arable farming. Here, too, are the villages, occurring at intervals along the valley at Shelford, Gunthorpe, Hoveringham and Bleasby, while Beeston once had a similar position until it was engulfed by the Nottingham suburbs. Farther downstream the villages of the lower Trent become more scattered owing to the paucity of dry gravel patches. Such villages as Burringham and East Butterwick, near Scunthorpe, are merely one street wide because they are built on riverside levees. Today, the lower Trent is dominated by a succession of gigantic thermal power stations, utilizing both the coal from the neighbouring Nottingham coalfield and the cooling water of the River Trent. Across the Humber, at Selby, Britain's newest coalfield supports more enormous power stations around Drax.

The North Midlands and Cheshire

Although the New Red Sandstone passes westwards into Staffordshire, Cheshire and south Lancashire, this northern extension of the Midland plain is narrowed by the low hills of the North Staffordshire coalfield on which the Pottery towns are built. Geologically, these urbanized scarplands are part of the Pennine foothills but the character of the Potteries and their surrounding countryside is essentially Midland. Overlooking the Potteries from the south is a prominent escarpment of Bunter Pebble Beds running transversely across the exposed rocks of the Coal Measures and the rest of the Carboniferous series. The vegetation of the ridge is analogous with that of the much loftier Bunter hill mass of Cannock Chase in central Staffordshire (Palliser, 1976), for large areas of heathland and conifer plantations flourish on their red sandy soils. The nearby Keuper Sandstones have been widely used in the rural churches of north Staffordshire, even though red Coal Measures sandstones were built into most of the Potteries churches. In sharp contrast, not far to the west, towards Shropshire and Cheshire, half-timbered villages stand amid the fertile grasslands of the red clay country where the north Staffordshire and Shropshire hills are only 30 kilometres apart. This so-called Cheshire Gap has acted as an important routeway for centuries, but especially after the Industrial Revolution. The Grand Trunk and Shropshire Union canals first linked the four main rivers of the Trent, Mersey, Dee and

Severn, only to be quickly succeeded by the railways. The main line from London to Crewe took advantage of a glacial meltwater channel which breaches the scarp at Whitmore while the Stoke–Manchester trains follow another such channel at Harecastle, parallel with Brindley's famous canal tunnel (Yates and Moseley, 1958). More recently, the M6 motorway has been routed across the high western rim of the coalfield via a further meltwater channel (Fig. 7.4).

The Bunter escarpment divides the good farming lands on the Keuper Marls of central Staffordshire from the thinner, poorer soils of the north Staffordshire coalfield (Cope, 1954). As one crosses the geological boundary, however, the soil colour and topography hardly change for the hard, red Keele Sandstones, representing the upper barren strata of the Coal Measures, create high ridges around Newcastle-under-Lyme (Fig. 7.4). Separating these are the intervening valleys of the Trent and its tributaries which have been carved along the outcrop of the Coal Measures marls (the Etruria Marls) which separate the Keele Sandstones from the underlying coal-bearing strata (Cope, 1958). It is these local marly clays that formed the basis of Britain's most famous pottery industry. Thus, the siting of the six Pottery towns of Stoke-on-Trent, astride the junction of the Etruria Marls and the Middle Coal Measures, is especially significant, as the bottle-shaped ovens required six times as much coal as clay to produce earthenware (Beaver, 1964). Nowadays the local clay and coal are no longer used and most of the bottle ovens have been demolished, leaving a forlorn industrial legacy of marl pits, piles of broken pottery, abandoned collieries and steel works, only partly ameliorated by some of Britain's most extensive urban reclamation schemes. Nevertheless, there are wild gritstone moors to the east and rich pasturelands of the Cheshire–Shropshire plain just to the west on the almost encircling Trias.

The Cheshire and north Shropshire lowlands are virtually synonymous with a deep basin of Keuper Marl, though the plain is fringed by outcrops of both Bunter and Keuper Sandstones. Dairy farming is the most common land use so that many stock-proof hedgerows have survived modern field amalgamation. The red-brick railway town of Crewe may be contrasted with the ancient city of Chester, with its Roman street plan and pink sandstone walls and cathedral, but the same warm-toned Keuper stones have also been widely used for church construction throughout Cheshire. The lowlands are in fact divided by a conspicuous ridge of Keuper Sandstone which runs north from near Malpas past the fairy-tale Beeston Castle near Tarporley to the imposing red cliffs of Helsby (143 m) overlooking the Mersey. The same sandstone outcrop swings round the central basin of marl, creating isolated rock faces at Nesscliff and Hawkestone Park between Shrewsbury and Wem. Not far from here, in the centre of the basin, even younger rocks occur near Prees, in the form of a small patch of Lias Clay and Marlstone. The Cheshire basin is not noted for its rock exposures because its plains are thickly covered by deep drift deposits mainly of Devensian age for which this is the type-area (named from Deva, the Roman name for Chester) (Worsley, 1970). The maximum ice advance from the Irish Sea basin reached as far south as Wolverhampton more than 31 000 years ago (Morgan, 1973) before retreating to a position farther north marked by a broad moraine that loops from the so-called *kame-kettle* scenery of Ellesmere to Whitchurch (from which it takes its name) and thence in another crescentic curve as far as Madeley on the western outskirts of the Potteries conurbation (Worsley, 1970). To the east of Ellesmere a complex of kettle holes and collapsed *pingos* lies beneath Fenns, Whixall and Bettisfield

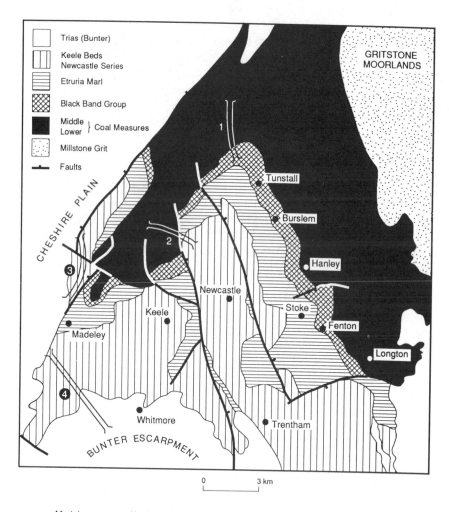

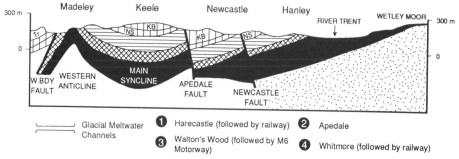

Figure 7.4 The geology of the North Staffordshire coalfield (after S.H. Beaver).

mosses which form the third largest (608 hectare) raised bog in the United Kingdom (see also p. 22). To the south of the moraine, especially near Wellington, the north Telford region of the plain has flat marshy expanses, known as the Weald Moors, related to former pro-glacial lakes near the Wrekin (see p. 131). A contrasting terrain is found near Shrewsbury where northern glacial drifts intermingle with the outwash from a local Welsh ice sheet (Shaw, 1972), thereby creating a hummocky landscape of kettle holes similar to those around Ellesmere, noted above and explained on p. 10. In one such kettle hole the remains of Late Pleistocene mammoths have been discovered at Condover (Coope and Lister, 1987). To the north of the Whitchurch moraine the relief of north Shropshire and south Cheshire is much more diversified by hummocky morainic ridges, small eskers and meltwater channels. Although the Whitchurch moraine itself never rises to more than 150 metres, it serves as a main watershed between the River Weaver, flowing north to the Mersey, and the Tern and Roden that drain southwards to the Severn. One final feature of this broad plain can be seen in the Northwich–Winsford area where scores of small lakes, known as meres and flashes, have formed in subsidence hollows (Wallwork, 1960) due in part to natural solution of the rock-salt beds and more recently enlarged by the subterranean salt-working of the region whose production has always been much larger than that at Droitwich (Wallwork, 1959). In the Keuper Marls salt occurs in beds whose average thickness of 30 metres represents the considerable degree of evaporation that took place in the Triassic salt lakes. Generally, however, industry has not scarred the face of Cheshire and north Shropshire and their damp marly soils have been utilized largely for cattle grazing, once the early woodlands had been cleared and the peat mosses drained. The once extensive Delamere Forest in the north has dwindled almost to nothing, much of its early timber having been taken through the centuries to help construct the impressive half-timbered buildings in such towns as Chester, Nantwich and Shrewsbury, in such villages as Betley (Fig. 7.5) and Hodnet, or in individual buildings such as Little Moreton

Figure 7.5 A half-timbered cottage at Betley on the borders of Cheshire and Staffordshire. Such 'magpie' architecture is typical of the western Midlands and the Welsh border country.

Hall near Congleton. Very much older tree stumps have been revealed in a buried peat layer at the Chelford sand quarry to the west of Macclesfield, whose fine white sands are still worked as a source of industrial silica. Since this deposit is buried by the glacial drifts of the Devensian Irish Sea glaciation and has recently been dated to about 100 000 years ago (Rendell *et al.*, 1991), Chelford is now regarded as the type-site for the earliest Devensian interstadial, when the glacial climate experienced a temporary amelioration (Simpson and West, 1958).

The Welsh border

The borderland is not a true region but a transition zone with poorly defined western limits where it blends almost imperceptibly with the more mountainous Welsh scenery. The eastern limits, on the other hand, have a more precise boundary, for here the very old, hard Lower Palaeozoics of the Welsh Massif plunge abruptly beneath the Triassic rocks of the English Midlands, though in places the junction is masked by a broad band of Carboniferous rocks (Earp and Hains, 1971). Nowhere can this abrupt change be seen more clearly than in the northern limits of the borderland where the Dee turns northwards to its broad but shallow estuary and effectively creates a boundary between Welsh Clwyd and English Cheshire. To the east of Wrexham an anomolous portion of Wales protrudes into the red plains beyond Bangor-is-y-coed, red plains whose soils have been derived not from the underlying bedrock but from the Irish Sea drifts of Devensian age, in the zone where they intermingled with the outwash from the nearby Welsh ice cap (Thomas, 1989).

The Dee estuary marshes are overlooked by the small town of Hawarden, perched at the northern end of a Millstone Grit ridge, near Ewloe's ruined castle, a reminder that this was the base for Norman warriers intent on subduing the Welsh in the mountainlands of Snowdonia some seven centuries ago. The true edge of the Welsh Massif coincides with an outcrop of the Millstone Grit, here known as the Cefn-y-fedw Sandstone, but in this northern border country, wherever the gritstone is broken up by faulting, its place is taken by a broad expanse of shales and sandstones of Coal Measures age despite their being largely devoid of coal seams. The handful of collieries of what used to be termed the North Wales coalfield (North, 1931; Wood, 1954) have long since closed down, leaving few scars on the breezy undulating countryside of stone-walled fields and small woods that lie between Hope and the line of small estuarine coastal towns on either side of the castle town of Flint. From Caergwele southwards, however, the character of the scenery changes markedly, for the Coal Measures between Wrexham and Ruabon have been responsible for a narrow industrial belt that has evolved over the last two centuries. Overlooked abruptly by the uncultivated slopes of Ruabon Mountain (511 m), the coalfield, though no longer productive, has spawned a scatter of urban agglomerations reminiscent of the Midlands. Yet as a reminder that this is Wales, the nearby towering bulk of Cyrn-y-Brain, shrouded in dark forests and moorlands, represents an eroded anticline of Ordovician rocks that are so characteristic of the mountainlands of North Wales. Although remnants of land despoiled by coal-mining survive around Ruabon, it is the exploitation of the Ruabon Marls in the Upper Coal Measures that has produced an even bigger visual impact, for the manufacture of the bright red

Ruabon brick, extensively used throughout North Wales, has left a legacy of old brick pits now lying abandoned between Wrexham and Pen-y-Bont. Not everything is built of brick, however, for the attractive cream-coloured Carboniferous sandstone known as the Cefn Rock (Middle Coal Measures) has been used since medieval times to build some of the older buildings, such as the churches at Ruabon and Wrexham and also, most notably, one of Thomas Telford's masterpieces, the graceful aqueduct of Pontcysyllte which carries a canal across the deep valley of the Dee near Cefn Mawr. Between this hilltop town and Corwen the Dee itself creates a memorable landscape where it leaves the mountainland through a series of deep gorges, which in places take the form of large incised meanders. West of Llangollen Telford's cleverly engineered A5 road follows the river before crossing the 'neck' of an incised meander near Plas Berwyn (Wilkinson and Gregory, 1956). Here, the river has failed to cut through the meander core although the two abandoned meanders, just upstream and downstream from Llangollen, testify to the Dee's ability to straighten its course, probably with the aid of glacial meltwater streams. Since this reach of the river pays no attention to the underlying structure (Wills, 1920) it provides a further example of superimposed drainage at a time when Britain's earliest rivers probably ran eastwards from the western uplands to an incipient North Sea (Linton, 1951). It is impossible to tell the age of the former rock strata from which the drainage was superimposed; some would favour the lowest members of the Carboniferous rocks which here rest unconformably on the older slates and lavas. Their most conspicuous element is undoubtedly the narrow outcrop of Carboniferous Limestone whose startlingly white rocks interject an almost incongruous ribbon of brightness into the dark-toned countryside. At Eglwyseg Mountain its bare crags, towering above Llangollen and the Horseshoe Pass, create one of Britain's most notable limestone escarpments (Tinkler, 1966).

On passing southwards into Shropshire the border scenery changes dramatically, for although the now defunct South Shropshire coalfield drapes around the flanks of the mountainland it is the complex of much older rocks which creates the most prominent landforms that grace the countryside known as the South Shropshire Hills (Cocks, 1989). Here, one feels a sense of the true Welsh Marches, as bracken-clad hills, often with craggy summits, rise abruptly from the gentle English plains, and both sandstone and limestone buildings intermingle with the more traditional black-and-white architecture of the red claylands. In the stretch of countryside ranging from Welshpool through Church Stretton to Ludlow there is an almost textbook correlation between geology and scenery (Toghill, 1990). Sharp-crested hills almost invariably reflect the outcrop of igneous rocks; long straight valleys, with the exception of the Church Stretton rift, are usually eroded where less resistant shales occur; where more resistant gently dipping limestones interrupt the bedded shales a scarp-and-vale landscape can be found.

The igneous rocks which build the jutting hills of the Breiden and Moel-y-Golfa, overshadowing the bend in the Severn between Welshpool and Oswestry, are of the same age as the lava masses of Snowdonia (see p. 177). Farther south, beyond an outcrop of Ludlow Shales (Upper Silurian) from which Welshpool's whale-backed Long Mountain has been carved, another type of igneous rock creates the cone-shaped bulk of Corndon Hill. The junction of the Corndon's resistant dolerite sill with the easily eroded shales into which it has been intruded is marked by a distinct shelf (Blyth, 1944). The mineralization of the region, associated with the igneous activity, caused valuable deposits of lead to be formed in the narrow tract of country between Corndon Hill and Stiperstones. Worked sporadically since Roman times, the mines and shafts are now derelict (Dines, 1958) though the toxic soils of the spoil heaps at Snailbeach still remain devoid of vegetation. Above the line of abandoned workings the prominent ridge of Lower Ordovician quartzite that has been weathered into the dramatic Stiperstones represents the northernmost of the harder rock strata which form a succession of ridges, running in a north-easterly direction and emphasizing the prevailing Caledonian 'grain' of the South Shropshire structures (Dineley, 1960). Not only are the Stiperstones (537 m) an excellent viewpoint but the bizarre shapes of their sparkling white quartzite outcrop also provide an opportunity to study the various stages of tor destruction from the initial disintegration by weathering of the large well-jointed crag of the Devil's Chair to the final litter of hilltop detritus that marks the tor's total decay (Goudie and Piggott, 1981).

On one side of the narrow, faulted and drift-filled trough in which Church Stretton lies (Rowlands and Shotton, 1971), the Longmynd rises steeply to become a smooth-topped moorland. Although its abrupt western edge is virtually unbroken, its eastern flank is deeply cut by narrow, picturesque V-shaped valleys, of which Cardingmill is the best known. Longmynd's generally smooth outline reflects the absence of interbedded lavas among the vertically tilted succession of its Precambrian sedimentaries (to which the name Longmyndian has been given), comprising grey, green, purple and red sandstones with interbedded slates and conglomerates. Across on the other flank of the Church Stretton Valley (Wright, 1968) the narrow line of conical hills is altogether more impressive in shape than the Longmynd (Fig. 7.6), because the sharp-crested summits of the Lawley, Caer Caradoc and Ragleth reflect the presence not only of Cambrian grits (Cobbold, 1927) but also the tough lavas and ashes produced in a Precambrian volcanic episode known as the Uriconian. Of similar age and character is the hog's-

Figure 7.6 Structure of the south Shropshire Hills, looking north-east (see also Fig. 7.7).

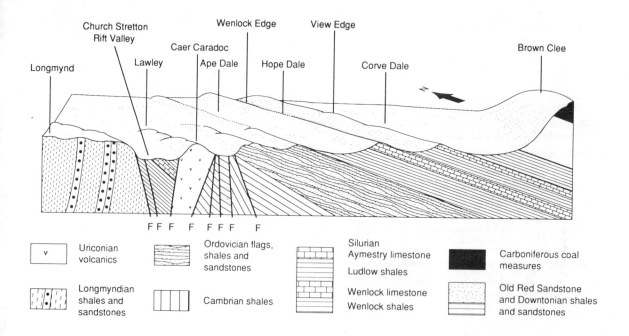

back profile of the Wrekin which, though some 10 kilometres away beyond the Severn, represents a north-eastern extension of this dramatic series of hills (Whittard, 1958). The view from Caer Caradoc eastwards extends across undulating Ordovician sandstone hill country of fields and woodlands into Ape Dale and thence to the long, straight, wooded scarp-face of Wenlock Edge beyond. The heavy clays of Ape Dale, often given over to dairy herds on the wet grassland, are abruptly terminated by the bare grey cliffs and unbroken woodlands of Wenlock Edge whose richly fossiliferous Silurian limestone (Bassett, 1974) runs south-westwards from the Severn Gorge at Benthall to the market town of Craven Arms. On its gentle dipslope the overlying shales have been carved into the discontinuous valley of Hope Dale whose more favoured aspect and fertile soils support mixed farming right up to the crest of the scarp (Fig. 7.7). The north-eastern end of Wenlock Edge has been heavily quarried for building stone, in part to construct the delightful old town of Much Wenlock but more recently for roadstone and aggregate. Overlooking Hope Dale, a second limestone escarpment parallels Wenlock Edge, this time of younger and yellower Aymestry Limestone named from the village south of Ludlow (Alexander, 1936), creating a scarp less steep, less wooded and more broken by stream gaps than its more famous

Figure 7.7 The scarp-and-vale country of south Shropshire, showing (from left to right) the scarp of Wenlock Edge, carved from Wenlock Limestone; the strike-valley of Hope Dale, in Wenlock Shales; and the Aymestry Limestone scarp. All the rocks are of Upper Silurian age.

counterpart (Fig. 7.6). In turn its overlying Silurian shales, which are succeeded by the Downtonian strata of the Old Red Sandstone (Allen and Tarlo, 1963), help form the broader corridor of Corve Dale, a route for the Much Wenlock to Ludlow road with its succession of attractive stone-built hamlets. The Wenlock Limestone diminishes in stature south-westwards, eventually forming a comparatively inconspicuous ridge near Craven Arms and Ludlow, whereas the Aymestry Limestone, by contrast, increases in height until it builds the fine wooded cliff of Norton Camp and View Edge where it is cut through by the Onny near Craven Arms (Holland *et al.*, 1963). Rising south-eastwards from the excellent corn-growing country of Corve Dale is a shelf covered with heavy dark red soil that marks the outcrop of the Old Red Sandstone. Standing out above it are two flat-topped hills, Brown Clee and Titterstone Clee, both outliers of the Coal Measures, though the former is capped by a dolerite sill that gives its summit a cliffed profile when viewed from Ludlow. Thus, from Church Stretton to the Clee Hills an almost complete succession of Palaeozoic rocks is represented.

With so many rocks outcropping in South Shropshire there is a great variety of available building materials, though Ludlow and Much Wenlock have substantial amounts of half-timbering surviving in their urban fabric (Rowley, 1972). But Ludlow Castle is built from yellow-grey Silurian limestone; nearby Stokesay Castle's half-timbering rises from an Old Red Sandstone base, while many farms around Church Stretton have volcanic rocks included in their structure. Near Soudley and Hope Bowdler, and in the Onny Valley near Horderley, much use has also been made of the attractive purple and yellowish-green striped Ordovician sandstone.

To the south of Shropshire the Malvern Hills (Ballard, 1989) act both as a geological and as a scenic boundary, dividing the bright red Triassic plain of the Vale of Worcester from the more undulating, hilly country whose dark red or brown soils are so characteristic of the Old Red Sandstone and older Silurian rocks of Herefordshire. Here Pleistocene ice streams were confined to the valleys with the piedmont lobe of the Wye glacier spreading over the Hereford Basin (Luckman, 1970). The Old Red Sandstone country alternates rapidly between patches of woodland and farmland. It is a dark green bosky landscape of small hills and valleys, laced with hedgerows, apple orchards, hop gardens, holly and oak, and stitched with purple-brown sandstone churches and 'magpie' houses in the peaceful, unspoilt hamlets. Hereford itself, astride the Wye, with its warm rosy sandstone cathedral, is the only large town in one of England's most rural counties. The Silurian limestones, in contrast to the sandstones, tend to form wooded ridges, while the intervening mudstones and shales correspond with the lower cultivated land. It has been seen how the New Red Sandstone's succession of sedimentary rocks includes marls and limestones in addition to its sandstones and conglomerates and, similarly, the Old Red Sandstone strata also include a number of marls and cornstones, all owing their colour and texture to having been formed under continental rather than marine conditions, with many of the beds having been laid down in fresh water. The harder sandstone rocks rise inexorably westwards to form the great escarpment of the Black Mountains which adds such a notable feature to the South Wales scenery, but farther east towards the Malverns the ground is lower and the rich marly soils are more intensively farmed. At intervals this wide expanse of dark red sandstones is interrupted by upfolds that bring older rocks to the surface. For instance, at Woolhope, south-west of Hereford, an anticline has raised both the Wenlock and Aymestry Limestones into a dome that subsequent erosion has fashioned into a hollow centre, where Woolhope village stands, surrounded by a double line of concentric inward-facing limestone scarps (Squirrel and Tucker, 1960). The Lower Silurian sandstone, exposed at the centre of the Woolhope dome, occurs again to the south-east, where it forms the prominent tree-crowned summit of May Hill. One senses that the 'magpie' architecture, so characteristic of the west Midland counties, becomes almost universal in Herefordshire:

> Here a truly remarkable scene meets the eye, where village after village is entirely built of black-and-white houses, primitive and antique in appearance and massively out of plumb, their huge timbers widely spaced, raised on heavy stone bases, their roofs low-pitched and overhanging (Penoyre and Penoyre, 1978).

Standing in splendid isolation above this fertile Marchland country are the breezy Malvern Hills (Penn and French, 1971). Although they are associated with a narrow band of Silurian and Cambrian sedimentaries along the boundary between the New Red and Old Red Sandstones, the true Malverns coincide with a sliver of Precambrian rocks some 12 kilometres long and 1 kilometre wide (Fig. 7.8). Unlike any other Precambrian rocks in England, this combination of foliated granites, sheared pegmatites and the schistose and gneissose banding of their diorites, is otherwise found at the surface only in north-west Scotland. The Malvern Hills' heavily contorted metamorphic rocks, bounded on either flank by north–south faults, rise sharply into a switchback of narrow crests, known

Figure 7.8 The Malvern Hills, carved from ancient Precambrian rocks, separate the rolling Old Red Sandstone landscape of Herefordshire (left) from the New Red Sandstone of the Worcester basin (right).

from north to south as North Hill, Worcestershire Beacon (425 m) Herefordshire Beacon, Hollybush Hill, Raggedstone Hill and Chase End Hill. Many of the cols between the separate summits have been carved along transverse east-west faults, thereby affording routes across the range, such as those at Wyche and Hollybush and, more distinctively, at Wynd's Point where the Great Malvern to Ledbury road climbs through a gap guarded by an Iron Age hillfort on Herefordshire

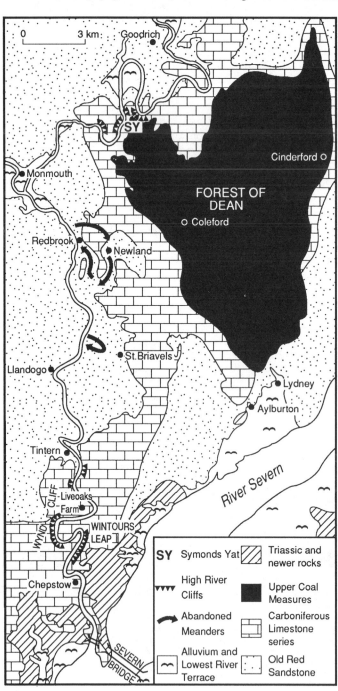

Figure 7.9 Geology and drainage of the Wye Valley and the Forest of Dean.

Beacon. Both the latter summit and that of Chase End Hill lie out of alignment with the other Malvern summits, largely due to thrust-fault patterns (Butcher, 1962). Ground water issuing from the springs and wells on the Malvern Hills slopes, reputed to be the purest in England, led to the growth of Great Malvern as a fashionable nineteenth-century spa.

Completing the picturesque scenery of the Welsh borderland is the southern-most tract bordering on to the Bristol Channel. Here lies the Forest of Dean, claimed to be the most beautiful coalfield in Britain, and crossed by one of Britain's most attractive rivers, the Wye (Dreghorn, 1968). This is largely Carbon-iferous country, the Limestone forming an upland rim round most of the coalfield and extending in a broad belt beyond Chepstow (Fig. 7.9). In terms of its structure the Forest of Dean coalfield is said to be a miniature edition of the South Wales coalfield, but there the resemblance ends for the latter is much higher in elevation, less verdant, more industrialized and more stark than the Forest of Dean coalfield. A royal hunting ground since Saxon times, the Forest comprises mainly oak, beech and sweet chestnut, though stands of conifer are now increasing, replacing the hardwoods felled for both timber and charcoal in earlier centuries (Hart, 1966). As in the Weald, charcoal was first used for smelting the iron ore which occurred in abundance in the coalfield, although the Forest of Dean ores, unlike those of the Weald, are of Carboniferous age. Nevertheless, once Abraham Darby had made his momentous early eighteenth-century innovation at Coalbrookdale near Ironbridge, it became possible to smelt iron by using coking coal. With abundant local coal and limestone (used as a flux) the Forest of Dean became one of Britain's first commercial iron-smelting centres, though Celts and Romans had been the first to work pockets of ore at Ariconium (now Weston-under-Penyard). The remnants of ancient slag heaps and forges, once powered by waterwheels on the Forest's steeply graded streams, can best be seen at the Scowles near Bream. As a whole, this unique land use of smelting, coal-mining, forestry and hunting has produced an intriguing woodland landscape in which small industrial settle-ments have expanded from the initial squatter hamlets of the ironworkers and Free Miners.

The Carboniferous Limestone country is quite different, for here the lower valley of the Wye cuts deeply into the naked rock to create some of England's best-known river gorges. Figure 7.9 illustrates how the relationship is not a simple one, for in its path south of Ross the river recrosses the outcrops of Old Red Sandstone and Carboniferous Limestone several times, and in its great loop at Symonds Yat it leaves the upland only to turn back into it immediately (Fig. 7.10). Such disregard for underlying structures implies that the Wye, like the rivers of South Wales, was first developed on a cover of newer rocks (possibly New Red Sandstone) and was later superimposed on the older rocks once this mantle had been destroyed. Like the deeply incised meanders of the Dee at Llangollen, those of the lower Wye need an explanation, for meanders are more characteristic of rivers winding through broad alluvial plains. Thus, the serpent-like gorges at Symonds Yat and Wynd Cliff near Chepstow, as well as the large abandoned meander of Newlands and that near St Briavels (Fig. 7.9), were all initiated when the river crossed an area of low relief. As sea level fell, in several stages, the chan-nel became incised as the gradient steepened and the river's energy increased (Miller, 1935). The most spectacular gorges occur in the well-jointed limestone for this produces vertical cliffs in certain places. Until this century the lower reaches

Figure 7.10 The Wye at
Symond's Yat, where the river
crosses from Carboniferous
Limestone (foreground) to
Old Red Sandstone (middle
distance) in the form of a
gigantic meander.

above Chepstow were all under broadleaf woodland of which only patches have
survived. The lime-rich soils support not only oak, ash, beech, whitebeam and yew
but also a profusion of spindle and dogwood entwined with traveller's joy. On the
Old Red Sandstone, however, the river is less entrenched, the alluvial meadows are
broader (here stands the beautiful Tintern Abbey), and though the woodlands are
just as lush the wildflowers are less exotic and less numerous on the more acidic
sandstone soils. This lower stretch of the Wye also has a number of ancient and
picturesque castles perched on the riverside crags at Chepstow, St Briavels and
Goodrich, each reflecting the different bedrock from which they were constructed
and all serving as a reminder that this was once the troubled border zone of Wales.

Bibliography

Adlam, B.H. (1974) *The Worcester District*. British Landscapes through Maps no. 17.
  Geogr. Assoc.
Alexander, F.E.S. (1936) The Aymestry Limestone of the Main Outcrop. *Quart. J. Geol.
  Soc.*, **92**, 103–15.

Allen, J..R.L. and Rae, J.E. (1988) Vertical salt-marsh accretion since the Roman period in the Severn estuary, south-west Britain. *Marine Geol.*, **83**, 225–35.

Allen, J.R.L. and Tarlo, L.B. (1963) The Downtonian and Dittonian facies of the Welsh borderland. *Geol. Mag.*, **100**, 129–55.

Ballard, B.W. (1989) *The Malvern Hills: A Student's Guide to the Geology of the Malverns.* Nature Conservancy Council. 73 pp.

Bassett, M.G. (1974) Review of the stratigraphy of the Wenlock Series in the Welsh borderland and South Wales. *Palaeontology*, **17**, 745–77.

Beaver, S.H. (1964) The Potteries: a study in the evolution of a cultural landscape. *Trans. Inst. Br. Geogr.*, **34**, 1–31.

Beckinsale, R.P. and Richardson, L. (1964) Recent findings on the physical development of the Severn Valley. *Geog. J.*, **130**, 87–105.

Bennett, F.W., Lowe, E.E., Gregory, H.H. and Jones, F. (1928) The geology of Charnwood Forest. *Proc. Geol. Assoc.*, **39**, 241–98.

Bishop, W.W. (1958) The Pleistocene geology and geomorphology of three gaps in the Midland Jurassic escarpment. *Phil. Trans. Roy. Soc. B*, **241**, 255–306.

Boulton, H.E. (ed.) (1965) *The Sherwood Forest Book.* Thoroton Society, Nottingham.

Blyth, F.G.H. (1944) Intrusive rocks of the Shelve area, south Shropshire. *Quart. J. Geol. Soc.*, **99**, 169–204.

Bridgland, D.R. and Lewis, S.G. (1991) Introduction to the Pleistocene geology and drainage history of the Lark Valley, in S.G. Lewis, C.A. Whiteman and D.R. Bridgland, *Central East Anglia and the Fen Basin.* Field Guide. Quat. Res. Assoc. 37–44.

Briggs, D.J., Gilbertson, D.D. and Jenkinson, R.D.S. (1985) *Peak District and Northern Dukeries.* Field Guide. Quat. Res. Assoc.

Butcher, N.E. (1962) The tectonic structure of the Malvern Hills. *Proc. Geol. Assoc.*, **73**, 103–23.

Butler, A.J. (1939) The Stratigraphy of the Wenlock Limestone of Dudley. *Quart. J. Geol. Soc.*, **95**, 37–74.

Campbell, J.B. (1977) *The Upper Palaeolithic in Britain.* Oxford University Press.

Clayton, K.M. (1953a) The denudation chronology of part of the Middle Trent basin. *Trans. Inst. Br. Geogr.*, **19**, 25–36.

Clayton, K.M. (1953b) The glacial chronology of part of the Middle Trent basin. *Proc. Geol. Assoc.*, **64**, 198–207.

Coates, B.E. and Lewis, G.N. (1966) *The Doncaster Area.* British Landscapes through Maps no. 8. Geogr. Assoc.

Cobbold, E.S. (1927) The stratigraphy and geological structure of the Cambrian area of Comley (Shropshire). *Quart. J. Geol. Soc.*, **83**, 551–73.

Cocks, L.R.M. (1989) The geology of South Shropshire. *Proc. Geol. Assoc.*, **100**, 505–19.

Coope, G.R., Shotton, F.W. and Strachan, I. (1961) A Late Pleistocene fauna and flora from Upton Warren, Worcestershire. *Phil. Trans. Roy. Soc. B*, **244**, 379–421.

Coope, G.R. and Lister, A.M. (1987) Late-glacial mammoth skeletons from Condover, Shropshire, England. *Nature*, **330**, 472–4.

Cope, F.W. (1954) The North Staffordshire Coalfields, in A.E. Trueman, *The Coalfields of Great Britain.* Arnold. 219–43.

Cope, F.W. (1958) *The Area around Stoke-on-Trent.* Guide no. 8. Geol. Assoc.

Darby, H.C. and Terrett, I.C. (eds) (1971) *The Domesday Geography of Midland England.* Cambridge University Press.

Dineley, D.L. (1960) Shropshire geology: an outline of the tectonic history. *Fld. Stud.*, **1**, 86–108.

Dines, H.G. (1958) The west Shropshire mining region, *Bull. Geol. Survey Gt. Brit.*, **14**, 1–43.

Douglas, T.D. (1981) *Field Guide to the Leicester Region.* Quat. Res. Assoc.

Dreghorn, W. (1967) *Geology Explained in the Severn Vale and Cotswolds.* David and Charles.

Dreghorn, W. (1968) *Geology Explained in the Forest of Dean and Wye Valley.* David and Charles.

Earp, J.R. and Hains, B.A. (1971) *The Welsh Borderland* (3rd edn). Br. Reg. Geol. HMSO. 118 pp.

Edwards, K.C. (1966) *Nottingham and its Region.* Nottingham University Press. 538 pp.

Edwards, W. (1954) The Yorkshire-Nottinghamshire Coalfield, in A.E. Trueman, *The Coalfields of Great Britain*. Arnold. 167–198.

Elliot, R.E. (1961) The stratigraphy of the Keuper Series in Southern Nottinghamshire. *Proc. Yorks. Geol. Soc.*, **33**, 197–234.

Garrett, P.A., Hardie, W.G., Lawson, J.D. and Shotton, F.W. (1958) *The Geology of the Area around Birmingham*. Guide no. 1. Geol. Assoc.

Goudie, A.S. and Piggott, N.R. (1981) Quartzite tors, stone stripes and slopes at the Stiperstones, Shropshire England. *Biuletyn Peryglacjalny*, **28**, 47–56.

Hadfield, C. (1966) *The Canals of the West Midlands*. David and Charles.

Hains, B.A. and Horton, A. (1969) *Central England* (3rd edn). Br. Reg. Geol. HMSO, 142 pp.

Hamblin, R.J.O. (1986) The Pleistocene sequence of the Telford district. *Proc. Geol. Assoc.*, **97**, 365–77.

Harley, J.B. (1964) The settlement geography of early medieval Warwickshire. *Trans. Inst. Br. Geogr.*, **34**, 115–30.

Harrison, M.H., Mead, W.R. and Pannett, T.J. (1965). A Midland ridge-and-furrow map. *Geog. J.*, **131**, 366–9.

Hart, C.E. (1966) *Royal Forest: A History of Dean's Woods as Producers of Timber*. Oxford University Press.

Harwood, D. (1988) Was there a glacial Lake Harrison in the South Midlands of England? *Mercian Geol.*, **11**, 145–53.

Holland, C.H., Lawson, J.D. and Walmsley, V.G. (1963) The Silurian rocks of the Ludlow district, Shropshire. *Bull. Br. Mus. Nat. Hist. (Geol.)*, **8**, 93–171.

Hoskins, W.G. (1957) *Leicestershire*. Hodder & Stoughton. 138 pp.

Johnson, B.C.Z. and Wise, M.J. (1950) The Black Country: 1800–1850. In M.J. Wise (ed.), *Birmingham and Its Regional Setting: A Scientific Survey*. University of Birmingham Press.

Keates, J. (1979) *The Shakespeare Country*. Collins. 320 pp.

Keen, D.H. (1989) *West Midlands*. Field Guide. Quat. Res. Assoc.

Kent, P.E. (1949) A structure contour map of the surface of the buried pre-Permian rocks of England and Wales. *Proc. Geol. Assoc.*, **60**, 87–104.

Linton, D.L. (1951) Midland drainage: some considerations bearing on its origin. *Adv. Sci.*, **7**(28), 449–56.

Luckman, B.H. (1970) The Hereford Basin. In C.A. Lewis, *The Glaciations of Wales and Adjoining Regions*. Longman. 175–96.

Marshall, C.E. (ed.) (1948) *Guide to the Geology of the East Midlands*. Nottingham University Press. 111 pp.

Matley, C.A. (1912) The Upper Keuper (or Arden) Sandstone Group and associated rocks of Warwickshire. *Quart. J. Geol. Soc.*, **68**, 252–80.

Miller, A.A. (1935) The entrenched meanders of the Herefordshire Wye. *Geog. J.*, **85**, 160–78.

Miller, T.G. (1953) *Geology and Scenery in Britain*. Batsford. 244 pp.

Millward, R. and Robinson, A. (1978) *The Welsh Borders*. Eyre Methuen. 256 pp.

Mitchell, G.H. (1954) The Coalfields of the South Midlands, in A.E. Trueman, *The Coalfields of Great Britain*. Arnold. 255–88.

Morgan, A. (1973) The Pleistocene geology of the area north and west of Wolverhampton, Staffordshire, England. *Phil. Trans. Roy. Soc. B*, **265**, 233–97.

North, F.J. (1931) *Coal and the Coalfields in Wales* (2nd edn). University of Wales Press.

Palliser, D.M. (1976) *The Staffordshire Landscape*. Hodder & Stoughton. 283 pp.

Penn, J.S.W. and French, J. (1971) *The Malvern Hills*. Guide no. 4. Geol. Assoc.

Penoyre, J. and Penoyre, J. (1978) *Houses in the Landscape: A Regional Study of Vernacular Building Styles in England and Wales*. Faber. 175 pp.

Pickering, R. (1957) The Pleistocene geology of the south Birmingham area. *Quart. J. Geol. Soc.*, **113**, 223–37.

Posnansky, M. (1960) The Pleistocene succession in the middle Trent Basin. *Proc. Geol. Assoc.*, **71**, 285–311.

Pye, N. (1972) *Leicester and its Region*. Leicester University Press. 603 pp.

Rendell, H., Worsley, P., Green, F. and Parks, D. (1991) Thermoluminescence dating of the Chelford Interstadial. *Earth and Planetary Science Letters.*, **103**, 182–9.

Rice, R. J. (1968) The Quaternary deposits of central Leicestershire. *Phil. Trans. Roy. Soc. B*, **262**, 459–509.

Rice, R. J. (1991) Distribution and provenance of the Bagington Sand and Gravel in the Wreake Valley, northern Leicestershire, England: implications for inter-regional correlation. *J. Quat. Sci.*, **6**, 39–77.

Rose, J. (1987) Status of the Wolstonian glaciation in the British Quaternary. *Quat. Newsletter*, **53**, 1–9.

Rowlands, P. H. and Shotton, F. W. (1971) Pleistocene deposits of Church Stretton (Shropshire) and its neighbourhood. *Quart. J. Geol. Soc.*, **127**, 599–622.

Rowley, T. (1972) *The Shropshire Landscape*. Hodder & Stoughton. 272 pp.

Shaw, J. (1972) The Irish Sea glaciation of northern Shropshire – some environmental reconstructions. *Fld. Stud.*, **4**, 603–31.

Sherlock, R. L. (1947) *The Permo-Triassic Formations*. Hutchinson, London. 367 pp.

Shotton, F. W. (1953) The Pleistocene deposits of the area between Coventry, Rugby and Leamington and their bearing on the topographic development of the Midlands. *Phil. Trans. Roy. Soc. B*, **237**, 209–60.

Shotton, F. W. (1977) *The English Midlands*. INQUA Excursion Guide A2. 10th INQUA Congress, Birmingham. 51 pp.

Shotton, F. W. (1983) The Wolstonian Stage of the British Pleistocene in and around its type area of the English Midlands. *Quat. Sci. Rev.*, **2**, 261–80.

Simpson, I. M. and West, R. G. (1958) On the stratigraphy and palaeo-botany of the Late-Pleistocene organic deposit at Chelford, Cheshire, *New Phytol.*, **57**, 239–50.

Smith, B. (1913) The geology of the Nottingham district. *Proc. Geol. Assoc.*, **24**, 205–40.

Spink, K. (1965) Coalfield geology of Leicestershire and south Derbyshire: the exposed coalfields. *Trans. Leics. Lit. Phil. Soc.*, **59**, 41–98.

Squirrel, H. C. and Tucker, E. V. (1960) The geology of the Woolhope inlier, Herefordshire. *Quart. J. Geol. Soc.*, **116**, 139–85.

Stephens, N. (1970) The Lower Severn Valley, in C. A. Lewis, *The Glaciations of Wales and Adjoining Regions*. Longman. 107–124.

Straw, A. (1963) The Quaternary evolution of the lower and middle Trent. *East Midland Geogr.*, **3**, 171–89.

Straw, A. and Clayton, K. M. (1979) *Eastern and Central England*. Methuen. 247 pp.

Sylvester-Bradley, P. C. and Ford, T. D. (eds) (1968) *The Geology of the East Midlands*. Leicester University Press. 400 pp.

Taylor, F. M. and Howitt, F. (1965) Field meeting in the UK East Midlands' oilfields and associated outcrop areas. *Proc. Geol. Assoc.*, **76**, 195–210.

Taylor, J. H. (1934) The Mountsorrel granodiorite and associated igneous rocks. *Geol. Mag.*, **71**, 1–16.

Thomas, G. S. P. (1989) The Late-Devensian glaciation along the western margin of the Cheshire–Shropshire lowland. *J. Quat. Science*, **4**, 167–81.

Tinkler, K. J. (1966) Slope profiles and scree in the Eglwyseg Valley, North Wales. *Geog. J.*, **132**, 379–85.

Toghill, P. (1990) *Geology in Shropshire*. Swan Hill Press, Shrewsbury, 188 pp.

Tomlinson, M. E. (1925) The River Terraces of the Lower Valley of the Warwickshire Avon. *Quart. J. Geol. Soc.*, **81**, 137–69.

Trinder, B. S. (1973) *The Industrial Revolution in Shropshire*. Phillimore. 455 pp.

Trueman, A. E. (1954) *The Coalfields of Great Britain*. Arnold. 255–88.

Wallwork, K. L. (1959) The mid-Cheshire salt industry. *Geography*, **44**.

Wallwork, K. L. (1960) Some problems of subsidence and land use in the mid-Cheshire industrial area *Geog. J.*, **126**, 191–9.

Waring, L. H. (1965) The basal Permian beds north of Kimberley, Nottinghamshire. *Mercian Geol.*, **1**, 201–12.

Watts, W. W. (1903) Charnwood Forest. A buried Triassic landscape. *Geog. J.*, **21**, 623–36.

Watts, W. W. (1947) *Geology of the Ancient Rocks of Charnwood Forest*. Leics. Lit. and Sci. Soc. 160 pp.

Whittard, W. F. (1958) *Geological Itineraries for South Shropshire*. Guide no. 27. Geol. Assoc.

Wilkinson, H. R. and Gregory, S. (1956) Aspects of the evolution of the drainage pattern of north-east Wales. *Lpool. Manchr. Geol. J.*, **1**, 543–58.

Wills, L. J. (1920) The Geology of the Llangollen district and excursion to Llangollen. *Proc. Geol. Assoc.*, **31**, 1–25.

Wills, L. J. (1924) The development of the Severn Valley in the neighbourhood of Ironbridge and Bridgnorth. *Quart. J. Geol. Soc.*, **80**, 274–314.

Wills, L. J. (1950) *The Palaeogeography of the Midlands* (2nd edn). University of Liverpool Press.

Wills, L. J. (1970) The Triassic succession in the central Midlands in its regional setting. *Quart. J. Geol. Soc.*, **126**, 225–85.

Wise, M. J. (ed.) (1950) *Birmingham and Its Regional Setting: A Scientific Survey*. University of Birmingham Press. 334 pp.

Wood, A. (1954) The Coalfields of North Wales, in A. E. Trueman, *The Coalfields of Great Britain*. Arnold. 244–54.

Worsley, P. (1970) The Chesire–Shropshire lowlands, in C. A. Lewis, *The Glaciations of Wales and Adjoining Regions*. Longman. 83–106.

Worsley, P. (1975) An appraisal of the glacial Lake Lapworth concept, in A. D. M. Phillips and B. J. Turton (eds), *Environment, Man and Economic Change*. Longman. 98–118.

Wright, J. E. (1968) *The Geology of the Church Stretton area*. HMSO. 89 pp.

Yates, E. M. and Moseley, F. (1958) Glacial lakes and spillways in the vicinity of Madeley, north Staffordshire. *Quart. J. Geol. Soc.*, **113**, 409–28.

Wales

8

Wales is an old country, old in its rocks and landforms and also in possessing one of Britain's oldest cultures. Invaded on numerous occasions, it has, nevertheless, retained a cultural identity in its mountainous heartland, a culture that manifests itself in its landscape network of hilly pastures, stone-walled fields, tiny churches, slated villages and whitewashed cottages (Emery, 1969; Thomas, 1977).

Apart from Devon and Cornwall, at markedly lower elevations, Wales is the southernmost bastion of highland Britain, with its mountains being high enough to have spawned distinct ice caps of their own during the Quaternary. Because of this, its uplands have been virtually remodelled by glacial erosion and the debris transported radially outwards to be dumped on the peripheral lowlands (Bowen, 1973). The rugged and bare outlines of the Welsh mountainlands have little in common with the landscapes described in the foregoing chapters and most of the younger sedimentaries that characterize the English lowlands are missing from the Welsh stratigraphic record. Thus, the Liassic shales and limestones of the Vale of Glamorgan are the youngest solid rocks in Wales, if one discounts the deeply downfaulted basin of Oligocene sedimentaries (Wood and Woodland, 1968) submerged beneath Tremadog Bay or the pipe clays of similar age in the tiny basin at Flimston, Pembrokeshire. Nevertheless, sufficient exposures of New Red Sandstone survive in both Glamorgan and Clwyd to suggest that these strata may once have been considerably more widespread. Indeed, some authors have explained the discordant Welsh drainage pattern in terms of superimposition from a cover rock, such as the New Red Sandstone, that has subsequently been worn away from the central massif by denudation.

It has already been seen how southern England's structures bear the imprint of two major mountain-building episodes: the younger rocks have been folded by the Alpine orogeny, while the older pre-Jurassic rocks had already been crumpled by Hercynian fold axes that distort the Mendips and run westwards through the South Wales coalfield into Pembrokeshire (Dyfed) (George, 1970) (see Fig. 1.3). Only the southern third of Wales exhibits east–west folding of this age, the remaining two-thirds being dominated by folding of Caledonian (Silurian–Lower Devonian) age, whose fold axes run very markedly from north-east to south-west. The geological map indicates the contrasting 'grain' of these two different structural regions (see Fig. 1.3) which, after having been tectonically uplifted and worked upon by aeons of weathering and erosion, have been worn down to produce the landforms and landscapes of today (Jones, 1956). Wales has some of Britain's most dramatic and picturesque scenery but although its old hard rocks have in places been carved into bare frost-shattered summits, elsewhere, especially in Mid-Wales, the same rocks produce almost endless vistas of peat-blanketed plateaux. Welsh rainfall, in addition to leaching out most of the nutrients from the upland soils, has also helped maintain perennial rivers which, over millions of years, have incised deep valleys now thickly garlanded with woodlands of oak and alder. It is in these isolated vales and on the more fertile soils of the coastal lowlands in the western peninsulas that Welsh arable farming has managed to maintain a presence, for elsewhere the rain-soaked mountainlands are given over to the ubiquitous sheep or to widespread conifer plantations.

Except for the coalfield areas and a few coastal tracts, the Welsh landscape has changed less rapidly than most of the English lowlands; cultural change in highland Britain is generally at a more leisurely pace. After the Pleistocene ice sheets had disappeared the bare Welsh mountains gradually became clothed with woodland, the succession progressing from early birchwoods to eventual groves of hazel, oak and alder that reached farther up the mountain sides than they do today (Linnard, 1982). The earliest settlers, in Stone Age and Bronze Age times, also began to leave their more modest imprint on the scene, especially in the form of stone megaliths on the coastal margins (Grimes, 1951). But it was not until Iron Age settlers began to construct such large hill fortresses as Tre'r Ceiri in the Llyn Peninsula, along the fringes of the uplands, that major inroads were first made into the Welsh forests. Some writers have claimed that forest destruction during prehistoric times has inadvertently led to soil degradation and to the initiation and spread of blanket bog in the Welsh uplands (Moore, 1973). When settlement finally penetrated the mountain fastnesses during the last millenium, woodland clearance increased its momentum, and many Welsh place names are the only reminder of this vanished heritage: *bedw* (birch), *derw* (oak), *gwern* (alder) and *coed* (woodland), *llwyn* and *gelli* (clumps of trees); equally significant are the names given to tracts of cleared land: *cae* (enclosed fields) and *maes* (open fields). By the time John Leland made his extensive journeys in the 1530s many Welsh lowlands had lost their primeval forests, partly due to clearance for agriculture, partly because grazing by domestic livestock had inhibited natural regeneration, partly through felling to improve security for invading English armies, and, finally, to fuel the earliest metal-working industries that had already appeared (Linnard, 1982). Such industries were to mushroom in succeeding centuries as Welsh lead, zinc, copper and iron were exploited at commercial scales, producing industrial landscapes that completely changed the face of certain regions (Thomas, 1961). Nowhere was this more evident than in South Wales.

South Wales

The last vestiges of the English lowlands taper out westwards into Gwent and Glamorgan, where they coincide with the veneer of Triassic and Liassic rocks which fringe the northern shores of the Bristol Channel. This narrow entry into Wales, across the mouth of the Wye, is commanded at Chepstow by the imposing limestone-built castle on its riverside bluff. Beyond, on both sides of the Usk estuary, are stretches of reclaimed marine alluvium, known as the Wentloog and Caldicott Levels. The tiny villages are located where these marshy coastal grazing lands meet the slightly higher arable land behind the former shoreline. Here one can distinguish between the red fertile marly soils derived from both the Old and New Red Sandstones and the stonier gravels weathered from the Carboniferous Limestone outcrop between Caldicott and Llanwern, where a massive steelworks now dominates the coastal plain. A word is necessary concerning these extensive salt marshes which fringe the Severn estuary hereabouts. Sedimentological, archaeological and historical research has shown that there has been natural vertical salt marsh accretion of some 1.22 metres since Roman times (Allen and Rae, 1988). Additionally, there has been considerable artificial drainage and landfill associated with the industrial development. Farther inland, between

Monmouth and Newport, an outcrop of hard Old Red Sandstone, identical to that which builds the Brecon Beacons, creates a heavily forested north-facing escarpment which separates the lower Usk Valley from the fringing plains of the Bristol Channel. North again, between Abergavenny and Ross, the middle basin of the Usk is underlain largely by less resistant Old Red Sandstone shales and marls whose excellent soils have long supported the finest wheatlands in Wales. They surround an area of thickly wooded hill country built from an inlier of Wenlock Rocks (Silurian) between Usk and Pontypool; (Walmsley, 1959). A similar 'window' of Wenlock flaggy siltstones and mudstones crops out through a cover of Old Red and Triassic sandstones at Rumney, Cardiff, where it forms Penylan Hill, now overrun by the city suburbs.

From this latter viewpoint one can distinguish the scenic features not only of Cardiff but also its surrounding region. To the north the line of hills which marks the southern edge of the coalfield is backed by bare uplands rising to more than 350 metres in height; in that direction the scenery is typically Welsh. Nearer Cardiff, however, and extending westwards as far as the shores of Swansea Bay, lies the Vale of Glamorgan whose scenery is akin to that of the English Midlands because it has been fashioned largely from a covering of Triassic (Thomas, 1969) and Lower Jurassic rocks that hide most of the underlying folds of Palaeozoic strata before tapering out northwards against the bordering ridges of the coalfield itself. Glamorgan's rolling, fertile lowland, with its deep calcareous soils, the most productive farming region in Wales, is more of a coastal platform than a vale, for its gently shelving surface descends southwards from an elevation of 120 metres until it is abruptly terminated by 40 metre sea cliffs (Driscoll, 1958). Between Penarth and Porthcawl these highly fossiliferous and almost vertical coastal cliffs are almost unbroken, except where rivers debouch into the sea. The vale's rock sequence (well exposed at Penarth Head) is an exact replica of that which underlies the Vale of Gloucester, for the horizontal red and green Keuper Marls of the Trias are overlain by the so-called Rhaetic Series (Francis, 1959) comprising Black Shales and marly limestones of the White Lias (Penarth Beds) which in turn are capped by the blue and yellow limestones and clays of the Blue Lias (the lowest beds of Jurassic age). West of Barry Island it is these horizontal Lower Jurassic limestones that are responsible for the lengthy cliffline which gives one of the best exposures of the Blue Lias anywhere in Britain (Trueman, 1922). Although its coastal scenery resembles that of the North York Moors (see p. 124) its settlement pattern differs in so far as the Yorkshire villages, such as Whitby, nestle in every bay and creek because they are fishing centres. The Vale of Glamorgan villages, however, turn their backs on the sea and are located inland because their inhabitants depend almost entirely on farming. Many of these old villages are attractively built of the local grey-blue Lias limestone, sometimes colour-washed and grouped around small grey stone churches with tall square towers. This well-managed landscape of clustered villages set among a patchwork of arable and permanent grass and entwined with a twisting road network that plunges steeply into the deeply cut valleys, is almost entirely a product of Norman settlement and is more a vestige of Norman England than of Celtic Wales. Cowbridge was once the vale's market centre, located on the Roman road of the Portway, its long medieval street of white limestone houses and inns serving a town that was, until the eighteenth century, of greater consequence than Cardiff itself. Although the Romans built a fort near the mouth of the River Taff and the Normans subsequently built a stronghold on the same spot, Cardiff (its Welsh name Caerdydd, meaning 'fort on the Taff') had a population of less than 2000 in 1801. Despite being hemmed in to the north by the limestone and red sandstone border ridges of the South Wales coalfield, Cardiff is ideally located below the narrow gorge at Taff's Well through which the iron and coal could be carried seaward from such iron towns as Merthyr and such coal-mining valleys as the Cynon and the Rhondda. First a canal and then railways were driven through the Taff gorge to serve the coal-exporting docks which sprang up at Cardiff during the nineteenth century (Rees, 1960). Today, however, as coal exports have dwindled and oil imports have expanded, Swansea has taken over the role of South Wales's major port.

At intervals in the Vale of Glamorgan its veil of Mesozoic cover rocks is tattered, for in places the underlying folds of Carboniferous Limestone have been uncovered by denudation. This intermittent exposure of older limestone can be traced westwards past St Brides Major to the extensive stone quarries at Pyle and beneath the sand dunes of Kenfig Burrows and the sandy beaches of Porthcawl (George, 1933), where the prosperous arable farmlands of the vale are finally squeezed out by the edge of the coalfield plateau. From here onwards Swansea Bay is fringed with industry, including the Margam steelworks, Briton Ferry's large petrochemical complexes and Swansea docklands (Balchin, 1971). Before examining the industrial landscapes of South Wales, however, the reappearance of the Carboniferous Limestone outcrop in the attractive peninsula of the Gower must be explained.

The Gower's folded structures are geographically intermediate between the Hercynian folds underlying the Vale of Glamorgan and those which run diagonally out to sea in southern Pembrokeshire (George, 1940). Unlike the Vale of Glamorgan, however, the Gower has no enveloping cover of Trias and Lias, though the 'gash breccias' (see p. 42) of its sea cliffs suggest that Triassic rocks must once have existed before being stripped off by denudation to expose the underlying pattern of east–west trending anticlines and synclines. The anticlinal quartz conglomerates (Old Red Sandstone) rise up as the isolated hills and ridges of Cefn Bryn (186 m), Llanmadog Hill and Rhossili Down (Fig. 8.1). These stony hills, with their sandy soils, support only rough grazing on the associated heathland, whereas the downfolded Carboniferous Limestone, worn down, perhaps by marine agencies during the early Pleistocene, forms relatively level platforms some 130 and 60 metres above sea level (Goskar and Trueman, 1934). The more fertile limestone soils support some of the most prolific cornlands in South Wales and, in addition, provide a haven for an array of lime-loving plants. Moreover, these heavily jointed limestones have been fashioned into the type of limestone scenery already described in the Mendips (p. 19). The narrow, crag-fringed valley between Bishopston and the sea, for example, exhibits a stream which disappears underground before reappearing farther down the valley. It is the southern coastline, however, that gives the Gower its most attractive scenery, for its limestone strata have been carved into a plethora of chasms, arches, caves, cliffs and bays (Bridges, 1987). In contrast to the evenly bedded Liassic cliffs and rather uniform coastal edge of the Vale of Glamorgan, the folding of the Gower's Carboniferous Limestone has created quite spectacular landforms. While the steeply inclined beds produce vertical sea cliffs, the gently dipping ones create enormous slabs covered in masses of yellow gorse. Where faults have dislocated the limestone picturesque bays have formed, sometimes with sand dunes like those at Oxwich.

During the Ice Age ice sheets extended into northern Gower on at least two occasions (Bowen and Henry, 1984) but during the high sea levels of the intervening interglacial (Ipswichian) beach shingle was left high and dry at a number of coastal sites between the Mumbles and Worm's Head, often on raised wave-cut platforms. These Pleistocene beaches extended into some of the peninsula's so-called 'bone' caves in which remains of extinct Ice Age mammals (elephant, rhino, bison, bear, wolf and hyena) have been found associated with skeletons and tools of Palaeolithic man (the Paviland skeleton of the Red Lady is 18 500 years old), some dating back to pre-Ipswichian times (more than 200 000 years ago). Paviland Cave, Minchin Hole and Bacon Hole were all carved by higher Pleistocene sea levels along weaknesses created by faulting.

The South Wales coalfield

The large syncline of the coalfield, contorted by the east-west folds of the Hercynian mountain-bulding episode, is cut off from the Vale of Glamorgan by the steeply upended layers of Old Red Sandstone, Carboniferous Limestone and Millstone Grit that everywhere underlie the Coal Measures and outcrop around their perimeter. In the south their steeply dipping strata give rise to hog's-back scarps known as the border ridges, the southernmost of which is made of steeply folded conglomerates of Old Red Sandstone age (Fig. 8.2). The second, more prominent ridge of Carboniferous Limestone, with its light grey crags, extends westwards from Cefn On to the hill above Castell Goch and to the beautiful Garth Wood. The succeeding linear depression corresponds to an outcrop of shales, the lower part being equivalent to the Millstone Grit of other areas, the upper part

Figure 8.1 Structure of the Gower, South Wales, looking eastwards.

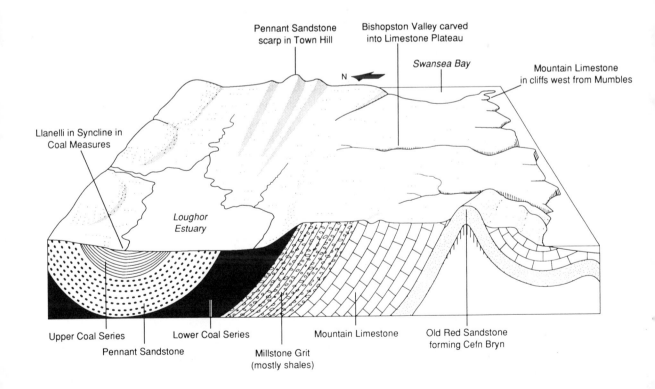

Pennant Sandstone scarp in Town Hill

Bishopston Valley carved into Limestone Plateau

Swansea Bay

Mountain Limestone in cliffs west from Mumbles

N

Llanelli in Syncline in Coal Measures

Loughor Estuary

Upper Coal Series

Pennant Sandstone

Lower Coal Series

Millstone Grit (mostly shales)

Mountain Limestone

Old Red Sandstone forming Cefn Bryn

representing the base of the Coal Measures. The northernmost component of this succession of cuestas at the coalfield rim rises above the gorge at Taffs Well into Garth Hill and Mynydd Rudry, whose dark, barren bracken-covered summits contrast sharply with the wooded ridges farther south. This last escarpment, built from layers of dull grey-green sandstones termed the Pennant Sandstones (or Grits), is generally one's first encounter with the almost horizontal beds which cap many of the coal-bearing strata of the coalfield and which have been the source of most of its building stone (Moore, 1954). Except where these coal-bearing beds have been brought to the surface by folding (as in the Caerphilly Anticline) or where they outcrop extensively along the northern rim, the coal seams of the central coalfield could initially be mined only where rivers had cut deeply down through the Pennant Sandstone to form the well-known mining valleys (North, 1931). Wherever this tough capping of rock forms the surface the land stands high and barren, though many of its former moorland sheep walks have now been blanketed with conifer plantations. Almost imperceptibly, the plateau surface rises northwards from about 300 metres at the border ridges until it forms a steep north-facing escarpment at Craig-y-Llyn (600 m) near the head of the Rhondda valleys (Fig. 8.2). These lonely uplands, rarely crossed by roads, appear as flat-topped tablelands when viewed from the deeply incised, overcrowded mining valleys where river, colliery, railways and roads vie for space on the valley floor and force the bleak rows of terraced houses up on to the valley sides. Here, too, are the colliery spoil heaps, with the steepness of the slopes and the instability of the tips being responsible for much landsliding and slumping, which culminated in the horrifying Aberfan debris-flow disaster of 1966. Natural slope instability is

Figure 8.2 Structure of the South Wales region, looking westwards.

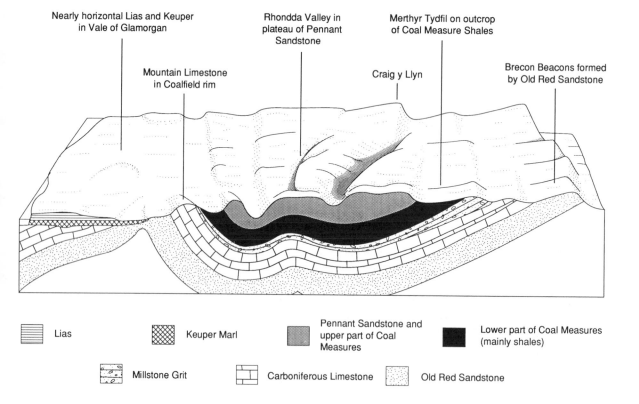

Nearly horizontal Lias and Keuper in Vale of Glamorgan

Mountain Limestone in Coalfield rim

Rhondda Valley in plateau of Pennant Sandstone

Craig y Llyn

Merthyr Tydfil on outcrop of Coal Measure Shales

Brecon Beacons formed by Old Red Sandstone

Lias

Keuper Marl

Pennant Sandstone and upper part of Coal Measures

Lower part of Coal Measures (mainly shales)

Millstone Grit

Carboniferous Limestone

Old Red Sandstone

widespread in the coalfield, however, especially near the springlines which mark the junction of the overlying Pennant Sandstone with the shaly rocks of the Middle Coal Measures (Rouse, 1989). Since 1966 most of the offending South Wales spoil heaps have been cleared and many remedial schemes undertaken. Some of the rivers that occupy such industrialized valleys as the Rhondda Fawr, Rhondda Fach, Cynon, Taff, Rhymney, Sirhowy and Ebbw, rise beyond the northern boundary of the coalfield, but all follow a south-south-east direction to the sea at Cardiff or Newport. In so doing they cross all the complex folds and some of the coalfield faults and therefore offer a good example of superimposed drainage. The presence of neighbouring Mesozoic cover rocks in the Vale of Glamorgan has suggested to some writers that it was possibly the Triassic strata which formerly stretched northwards over the coalfield structures, thereby producing a smooth bevelled surface upon which the parallel drainage pattern was initiated. Others believe that the former cover may have been Chalk, but there is no evidence to support such a supposition (see p. 173).

It will be seen from Fig. 8.2 that the northern limb of the coalfield syncline has a relatively gentler dip and therefore a broader surface outcrop of exposed coal seams than the southern limb. Thus, it was in this northern tract, long before the central mining valleys were exploited, that earliest coal-mining first began to provide coking coal for the long-established Welsh iron industry of the northern edge. By the mid-eighteenth century, when most of the previously widespread broadleaf woodlands of South Wales had been cut down to feed the voracious forges, Abraham Darby's earlier innovation at Coalbrookdale allowed the great Welsh ironmasters, who had set up their works based on charcoal from the woods between Blaenavon and Dowlais, to turn to the excellant outcrop of coking coal which could be dug at the surface as far west as Hirwaun. Since the clayband and blackband iron ores were also at their richest in the Carboniferous rocks east of Merthyr Tydfil, and since both limestone for flux and silica sands for furnace brick-linings were also close at hand, it is no surprise to find that Wales's major iron-working was originally confined to the north-east margin of the coalfield between Pontypool and Aberdare. Today, all mineral extraction has ceased in this area and centuries of iron production have finally terminated, leaving behind a devastated scene of industrial dereliction, now opened up to the gaze of travellers following the head-of-the-valleys main road (Williams, 1975). It must be appreciated that because the nature of the coal itself varies throughout the coalfield, its exploitation has changed as demands have fluctuated. In the far west, near Ammanford, anthracite is most common, while in Mid Glamorgan steam coals predominate until they finally give way eastwards to the bituminous coking coals of Gwent. Overall demand for coal in Britain fell rapidly during the 1960s as less expensive fuel oil began to compete in the energy market. Cheap natural gas from the North Sea also became a competitor while steam railways disappeared, all at a time when Britain's heavy industry was declining. Moreover, because of its peripheral location, less and less Welsh coal has been burned in the power stations of the English Midlands owing to transport costs. Between 1960 and 1980, therefore, two-thirds of the South Wales pits closed down and by 1990 the Rhondda's last coal-mine had ceased production, leaving South Wales facing decades of future industrial land reclamation. Much can be learned from the remarkable success story of the neighbouring Lower Swansea Valley where the remnants of Britain's largest copper, zinc and tinplate complex have recently been tidied up.

Here, during preceding centuries, air pollution had killed both the oak and birch woodland and the heather of the valley sides. Moreover, the topsoil had been lost, to be replaced by toxic waste among the artificial hills of non-ferrous and ferrous slag. Many hectares have now been restored and replanted (Hilton, 1967).

To the west of Neath the coalfield country is less elevated than that farther east, partly because the western Pennant Sandstones contain more numerous shale bands. Thus the rivers have been able to excavate wider valleys in the shale out-crops and have also become more adjusted to the east–west strike as they flow towards Carmarthen Bay. The Amman, for example, has cut a broad strike valley, while other tributary streams entering the Loughor estuary follow the Coal Measures shales, leaving the harder Pennant Sandstones to form such conspicuous ridges as that overlooking Swansea (Trueman, 1924). The latter is breached at several points, most notably where the gorge of the Tawe separates Town Hill from Kilvey Hill (Balchin, 1971). Both the Tawe and its neighbouring river, the Neath (or Nedd), flow in valleys quite different in character from those of the central coalfield. For many kilometres they run from north-east to south-west in virtually straight trenches that have been etched out along belts of crushed and weakened rocks related to lines of major faults (Owen, 1973). Although river rejuvenation has been responsible for the main valley incision it is possible that in the Vale of Neath, at least, a local glacier, nourished by ice from the Brecon Beacons, overdeepened the trunk valley and helped leave hanging valleys from which tributary streams now descend steeply to the valley floor. Such steepness is particularly marked where the valley flanks are cut into Pennant Sandstone, as at Resolven where several torrents have created picturesque waterfalls that plunge through wooded gorges before emerging onto the alluvial floor of the vale. Farther upstream some of the Neath's headwaters rise beyond the coalfield margins but help create a small area of fascinating landforms, reminiscent of those of the northern Pennines, where they cross the narrow northern outcrop of the Carboniferous Limestone (North, 1962). At Ystradfellte, for example, the Mellte plunges into the mouth of the large cave of Porth yr Ogof, surrounded by vertical limestone cliffs, before reappearing some distance down valley (Robertson and George, 1929). Ashwoods cling to these picturesque limestone gorges whose calcareous soils also support such lime-loving plants as bladder fern, green spleenwort, globe flower, meadow cranesbill and saxifrage (Condry, 1981). Progressing northwards from this fertile oasis among the bare moorland pastures, however, the land rises to even loftier eminences as one crosses on to the wide outcrop of the Old Red Sandstone.

The Brecon Beacons and the Black Mountains

The broad expanse of Old Red Sandstone which underlies so much of the border country of Herefordshire, becomes progressively narrower as it is traced westwards into Wales. Nevertheless, the appearance of layers of tough pebbly sandstones (Lower Old Red Sandstone) among its 800 metres of horizontal grits and flaggy mudstones ensures that the landforms to the west of Hay-on-Wye are imposing because of the obdurate nature of these types of rock (termed the Breconian). Indeed, for some 60 kilometres between the English border and the Llandeilo–Ammanford road a gigantic sandstone escarpment looks northwards over the vale of the Towy, across the upper Usk Valley and over part of the middle reaches of the Wye. Though dissected by the same rivers which cut through the coalfield farther south, this imposing sandstone wall, rising up to 886 metres at Pen-y-Fan, (Fig. 8.3) provides one of the most continuous exposures of bare rock in southern Britain and is Britain's only example of a mountainland carved entirely from Old Red Sandstone (North, 1955). In profile the escarpment resembles a great wave, petrified on the point of breaking, and early geologists, unaware of the eroding ability of former British ice sheets, ascribed its formation to normal marine erosion, probably during the biblical Flood. Since then it has been conclusively shown how glacial processes once operated in Britain, helping fashion this southernmost example of an ice-sculptured landscape. Nourished by snow blown from the high plateau tops, small glaciers would have formed on the shaded north-facing slopes and glacier ice would have plucked at the stony cliffs and helped chisel out the amphitheatres we see today. Backed by precipitous frost-shattered walls the armchair-shaped hollows (termed *cwms* in Wales and *corries* in Scotland) are sometimes occupied by tiny lakes such as Llyn-y-Fan Fach and Llyn Cwm Lwch. Glaciers seem to have formed only towards the western end of the scarp because snowfall, like present-day rainfall, is heavier at the Welsh end of the ridge than at its English extremity. Thus the Black Mountains of the English border are devoid of glacial cwms, despite their height (Bowen and Henry, 1984). The entire table-topped sandstone massif is split into four parts by the intervening valleys. Starting in the far west, although the Black Mountain escarpment is carved from Old Red Sandstone its highest summits coincide with a capping of Carboniferous Limestone and Millstone Grit. Carmarthen's Black Mountain is divided from the Fforest Fawr by the headwaters of the River Tawe and in its turn this sharply etched plateau is separated from the loftier Brecon Beacons by the infant River Taff; finally, beyond, the Usk Valley the confusingly named Black Mountains overstep the English border. Considering the redness of their rocks and soils, place

Figure 8.3 View of the northern Old Red Sandstone escarpment of the Brecon Beacons, looking eastwards from Pen-y-Fan.

names in these sandstone mountains are surprisingly devoid of the Welsh term for red (= *coch*), although black (= *ddu*) occurs regularly, perhaps referring to their dark cover of bilberry and heather moor but more likely to their dark shadowy northern precipices.

Because of their remoteness and exposure these bare windswept mountains remained unsettled until the Bronze Age, when tribes brought their cattle and sheep to graze their grassy slopes. Nevertheless, Iron Age hillforts occur only on their flanks mainly along the Usk Valley between Abergavenny and Brecon, an early recognition of the value of this strategic corridor into Mid-Wales, later to be followed by Roman and Norman invaders. It is likely that the high tops have remained treeless throughout historic times (Walker, 1982), with the anomolous Fforest Fawr having derived its name not from woodland but from its importance as a royal hunting domain. For this reason many of the hills have remained unenclosed, with the old county of Brecon possessing more common land than any other Welsh county. Yet their lean soils and high rainfall have meant that these uplands have always been difficult to farm, so that many hill farmers have been attracted to the South Wales industrial valleys, never to return. Today some of the slopes are swathed with Forestry Commission plantations, though several of the valleys have retained natural oakwoods and it is here that the few stone-built settlements occur. Llanthony Priory, for example, in the lonely Vale of Ewyas, which descends from the spectacular and windswept Gospel Pass, is popular as a tourist beauty spot. Farther east, in Herefordshire, is the so-called Golden Valley from which bumper corn harvests have been taken because its fertile soils derive partly from its crumbly 'cornstone' beds (Lower Old Red Sandstone) and partly from its infill of glacial drift.

Pembrokeshire

This south-western extremity of Wales can be divided into two quite different but unequal parts: the northern two-thirds, known as the Welshry, is a Celtic land of Welsh speakers who farm a high, rocky, heath-patched countryside of ancient Lower Palaeozoic sedimentary and igneous rocks folded entirely along Caledonian lines; the southern third, by contrast, is largely an enclave of Viking, Norman and Flemish settlers, speaking virtually no Welsh, who, over the centuries, have made their living from fishing, coal-mining, weaving and farming on the sea-threaded coastal plateaux of the so-called Englishry whose Upper Palaeozoic rocks have been sharply crumpled by Hercynian folding (Owen, 1984). The cultural boundary between north and south, termed the *Landsker*, was originally outlined by the Vikings and later fortified by a chain of Norman castles some of which survive today (John, 1976). Extending in an arc from Newgale on St Bride's Bay to Amroth on Carmarthen Bay (via the fortresses of Roch, Camrose, Wiston and Narberth) the *Landsker* approximates to the junction between the younger southern rock strata and the more ancient northern rocks, that is, those older than the Old Red Sandstone. Such geological subdivisions mean that both coal and limestone are absent from northern (Caledonian) Pembrokeshire but are abundant in the Hercynian tracts of 'Little England beyond Wales'. The poorer soils of the northern hillier country, supporting mainly treeless moorland pastures, also contrast with the more fertile soils of the limestones and sandstones farther south where cornfields and broadleaved woodlands alternate on the shores of the deeply penetrating estuaries.

The great marine inlet of Milford Haven almost isolates southern Pembrokeshire from the rest of the ancient county and here the scenery is more akin to that of the Gower, of which it is a geological extension. Between Tenby and Angle tightly folded structures run along east-south-east to west-north-west axes, with Old Red Sandstone forming the anticlines and the Carboniferous Limestone the synclines. Silurian strata have been exposed in some of the upfolds but the differences in rock hardness have counted for little because the whole area has been planed into an even surface about 80 metres above sea level. Although some have argued that this platform represents an exhumed sub-Triassic surface (see below) others suggest that it is an uplifted Late Tertiary marine abrasion platform (Goskar and Trueman, 1934). Despite the planation, the drainage pattern has clearly become adjusted to the parallel fold axes, likewise the configuration of the deeply indented coastline. The contrasting ability of different strata to withstand modern wave attack has led to the isolation of many stacks and islands on an already crenellated coastline. So remarkable are its coastal landforms that Pembrokeshire has been designated as Britain's only National Park confined almost exclusively to a coastline. As in the Gower, Carboniferous Limestone provides some of the most striking of the coastal features. Tenby, with its elegant pale grey limestone buildings, stands astride a peninsula where the harder limestone adjoins the less resistant shales. A parallel limestone outcrop continues from Caldey Island to form the steeply dipping beds at Lydstep Point and Skrinkle Haven where rubble-filled fissures occur in the limestone sea cliffs (Leach, 1933). The significance of these so-called 'gash breccias', like those in the Gower, lies in the likelihood that they were formed when Pembrokeshire's coastal platforms were buried beneath layers of New Red Sandstone. The same limestone downfold (the Pembroke Syncline) runs diagonally across the peninsula to Pembroke whose imposing Norman castle overlooks the river estuary. A smaller limestone syncline, farther west, has been picked out to form the coastal inlets of Angle and West Angle Bay where the sea has broken through a narrow sandstone anticline that runs all the way to Penally on Carmarthen Bay. The hard conglomerates of this sandstone ridge are followed by an ancient route termed the Ridgeway. Some of the most scenic parts of the coast, however, lie south of the Castlemartin military firing ranges, especially along the limestone cliffs between Linney Head and Stackpole Head. The Long Distance Footpath reveals, in turn, the outstanding wave-cut arch of the Green Bridge of Wales; followed by the 32 metre high pinnacles of the Stack Rocks; then the 45 metre deep shaft of the Devil's Cauldron formed by the coalescence of several fault-guided marine blowholes; and finally the spectacular Huntsman's Leap, a marine fissure also eroded along a fault. In complete contrast to these treeless exposed cliffs, where razorbills and guillemots nest among veritable rock-gardens of tree mallow, sea campion, yellow kidney-vetch, purple rock, sea-lavender and blue carpets of spring squill, are the sheltered beech, ash and sycamore woodlands of the deeply-cut valley containing Bosherston and Stackpole Ponds (Condry, 1981). Generally, however, tree growth is severely limited by the windiness of these western coasts and hedgerows are also rare, usually being replaced by broad turf-capped earth and stone banks.

The northern fringes of the Old Red Sandstone tract of south Pembrokeshire have been invaded by the burrowing waters of one of Britain's greatest natural harbours, that known as Milford Haven (Fig. 8.4), which narrows inland to

Figure 8.4 Milford Haven, Dyfed, looking eastwards. One of the oil terminals can be seen in the middle distance of this deep-water ria.

become the long winding tidal creeks of the Cleddau, one branch of which gives access to Haverfordwest (John, 1972). Such long narrow inlets are drowned valleys or *rias*, formed during the post-glacial (Flandrian) rise of sea level which not only inundated the Fenlands of eastern England but also created the ria coast-line of Cornwall and South Devon, described in Chapter 2. The same submergence flooded all the other Welsh rivers that debouch into Cardigan Bay but because the northernmost valleys, unlike their Pembrokeshire counterparts (John, 1970), had served as outlets for glaciers from the Welsh ice cap their estuaries had already been plugged with glacial drifts, so that the more recent sediments, both marine and fluvial, have filled up these northern estuaries to above present sea level. The deep waters of Milford Haven, by contrast, have, over the centuries, provided a sheltered harbour for fishing fleets, warships and, more latterly, oil tankers, as the national interests have changed. The South Wales coalfield becomes greatly atten-uated as it is traced westwards into Pembrokeshire (Jenkins, 1962), but working of the tightly folded coal seams continued for centuries especially where the anthracite could be easily exported by sea from such tiny harbours as East Hook deep in the recesses of the Cleddau river system (Edwards, 1963). Few signs of the former collieries now remain in the rather featureless Coal Measures tract of country between St Brides Bay and Saundersfoot. Though St Ann's Head and the island of Skokholm, which stand near the mouth of the Haven, are both built of Old Red Sandstone, the first hint of a change in the geology can be found in the picturesque peninsula of Marloes and its continuing line of islands: Middle Isle, Skomer and far-distant Grassholm. Here, beds of Silurian sandstones and silt-stones are interbedded with thick basaltic lavas (known as the Skomer Volcanic Group) (Thomas, 1911); their Hercynian contortions have subsequently been picked out by marine action to create some of the National Park's most notable cliff scenery.

Beyond the *Landsker*, northern Pembrokeshire has been carved from an even older complex of heavily faulted Ordovician and Cambrian shales and mudstones associated with exposures of Ordovician and Precambrian volcanics most of which are of acid, rhyolitic composition, in contrast to the basic basaltic lavas of Skomer. This is the southernmost limit of 'Caledonian' Wales and thus the vulcanicity, mainly of Ordovician age, was characterized not by slowly upwelling basaltic lava flows from fissures (see Chapter 16) but by highly explosive central-vent volcanoes whose products included not only very sticky (viscous) lavas but also thick layers of pumice and ash, referred to as *tuffs*. Moreover, this compli-cated 'layer cake' of interbedded sedimentary and volcanic strata was later to be invaded by many instrusive subterranean flows of magma which squeezed along the bedding planes before cooling and solidifying into rock sheets known as 'sills', later to be exposed as linear outcrops by subsequent erosion. Where the magma cooled rapidly the rocks of the sills have small crystals and are therefore termed 'fine-grained'; where the cooling was slower the larger crystals gave rise to coarse-grained igneous rocks. It is little wonder that wherever the Lower Palaeozoic sedimentary rocks have been underpinned by resistant lavas and bolstered by tough igneous sills they have stood up to the millions of years of denudation more successfully than areas where the igneous rocks are absent. These are the primary reasons why the peninsula of Pen Caer, culminating in Strumble Head, and that of St David's Head (Cox *et al.*, 1930), with its adjoining Ramsey Island, jut boldly into the Irish Sea. In fact every headland from Strumble Head to Ramsey Island is of igneous material and every bay is carved in sedimentary rocks. Their intricate shorelines and pocket-handkerchief beaches of brightly coloured pebbles result from the great diversity of rock types (Elsden, 1905). Similar diversity accounts for the abundance of rare coastal flora on these crumpled sea cliffs: 'Perhaps no stretch of Welsh cliffs has a richer ecology than these of north Pembrokeshire . . . Slopes of every degree of steepness, aspect, dryness and dampness, add to the variety of the scene' (Condry, 1981). Less spectacular in their ecology, but more imposing in their sudden elevation above the planed-off coastal platforms, are the Preseli Hills (536 m) whose mudstones have been armoured by lavas and igneous intrusions (Evans, 1945). Thus they rise like heathery islands above the cultivated network of relatively small fields that characterize the 180 metre coastal plateau. Some modern conifer plantations on the Preselies contrast with the ancient oakwoods which choke the deeply incised river valleys that seam the north Pembrokeshire landscape. It was once thought that some of the valleys which cross the Preselies were created as overflow channels draining a former 'glacial-Lake Teifi' impounded along the northern coastlands by an encroaching ice sheet driving southwards along the floor of the Irish Sea. More recent research has failed to discover traces of such a pro-glacial lake but instead claims have been made that the rather anomolous drainage channels of north Pembrokeshire represent sub-glacial and ice-marginal channels formed along the edges of the Irish Sea ice sheet (Bowen and Gregory, 1965). This Devensian advance, it is thought, extended only as far south as St Ann's Head in west Pembrokeshire during the middle Devensian, thereby leaving most of the county ice-free (John, 1970). The redrawing of the ice limits in south-west Wales has led to the reappraisal of the Banc-y-Warren glacial gravel mounds near Cardigan which had long been regarded as the southern limit of northern ice-sheet glaciation in Wales (Helm and Roberts, 1975).

Central Wales

Figure 8.5 The High Plateau of central Wales south of Pumlumon, showing the deep incision of the headwaters of the River Wye.

Once across the River Teifi and one has entered the Welsh heartland of northern Dyfed and Powys, termed 'Inner Wales' by Emrys Bowen (1957). It is a harsher land of high upland plateaux and seemingly endless stretches of gently undulating moorlands whose acid peaty soils represent countless centuries of weathering of

the almost ubiquitous Silurian shales, mudstones and grits (Jones, 1912). Except where deep valleys bring variety to the scene the land between the Teifi and the Mawddach estuary rises to monotonous plateaux with elevations ranging between 300 and 900 metres. The lack of geological variety has meant that there is a uniformity of both relief and rock colouring, except where the small-scale crags around Llandrindod Wells and Builth Wells signify a patch of Ordovician lavas and igneous intrusions (Jones and Pugh, 1948). The subterranean magma has helped create the mineral springs of these two spa towns. The coastal platforms, too, bring variety especially where they terminate in steep, irregular sea cliffs. Inland, although large tracts remain unenclosed either by drystone wall or by hedgerow, land tenure here was based since time immemorial not on primogeniture, as in England, but on a principle of splitting the holding between all sons, giving a fragmentation which has led to a scatter of tiny farms amid a mosaic of small fields wherever the 'rough and churlish soil' has allowed land improvement. Not surprisingly, these bleak central uplands boast few market towns and are virtually devoid of castles, unlike the countryside of South Wales or the mountainous counties of Gwynedd and Clwyd farther north.

The finest viewpoint in the region is Pumlumon (Plynlimon) whose isolated 740 metre summit and lonely corrie-lake occupy a limited exposure of Ordovician rocks. It is here that the rivers Severn and Wye begin their lengthy journeys, but it is the widespread vistas of moorland and peat bog which catch the eye (Fig. 8.5). Northwards the level plateau stretches to the shoulders of Cadair Idris and Aran Mawddwy whose peaks, like those of Snowdonia, rise sharply above the accordant 520–580 metre surface long known as the High Plateau of Wales. To the south the same unbroken Plateau can be seen extending as far as the Brecon Beacons, truncating *en route* the heights of the Cambrian Mountains and Mynydd Eppynt (Fig. 8.6). There are in fact two other plateau levels in the region, termed by Brown (1960) the Middle Peneplain (365–490 m) and Low Peneplain (215–335 m), respectively, which, owing to their lower elevations, possess greater expanses of improved land than the untamed High Plateau. Early writers believed that these surfaces, which bear no relationship to the geological structure, resulted from wave action, although most modern authors believe that rivers played a major part in their planation. Alternatively, some geologists once believed that the High Plateau may originally have represented an exhumed surface now stripped of its Chalk or New Red Sandstone sediments by forces of denudation. To support such arguments they pointed to the superimposed character of the Welsh drainage pattern which, in general, is indifferent to the grain of the massif (Jones, 1952). Brown (1960) has painstakingly reconstructed the evolution of the Welsh river network in relation to each of the three main upland surfaces (Fig. 8.7), demonstrating how a former radial pattern, developing on a deeply weathered early Tertiary surface, was slowly dismembered by subsequent stream development working along the geological strike as the massif was gradually uplifted in a pulsatory manner by late Tertiary tectonics. Thus the degree of drainage discordance was thought to have decreased progressively over time, leaving only such major rivers as the middle Dee, upper Wye, upper Severn, upper Teifi and Towy (Tywi) as survivals of the initial consequent drainage pattern.

Below the upland plateaux the shores of Cardigan Bay are fringed by coastal platforms reaching some 180 metres in height. Thought by many to be old wave-cut surfaces of early Pleistocene age, these low coastal shelves provide the region

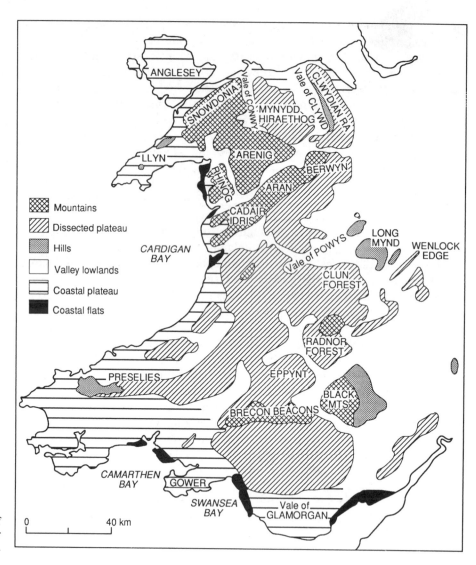

Figure 8.6 The main relief units of Wales (after E. H. Brown).

Legend:
- Mountains
- Dissected plateau
- Hills
- Valley lowlands
- Coastal plateau
- Coastal flats

0   40 km

of Central Wales with its only widespread example of terrain suited to cultivation. Here the farms include both arable and pasture land and grow a surprising amount of corn for such windy and wet coastlands. As one climbs to the uplands, however, the growing season decreases in length and the husbandry rapidly reverts to sheep-rearing. Whereas many valleys of the upper plateaux are wide and open, the coastal platforms are crossed by narrow and deep valleys, often picturesquely wooded, whose incision has been taken as evidence of a relatively late phase of river rejuvenation following Pleistocene uplift; it may be expected in time that the gorge incision will work its way back into the uplands. Some of the gorges have particular charm, such as that at Devil's Bridge where the chasm, with 'woods climbing above woods', has been cut down several hundred metres into the hard Silurian rocks below the higher, wider and older valley which is followed by the A4120 road. The two valleys were formed by different rivers, for the older upper part of the Rheidol was formerly a south-flowing stream on the High Plateau prior

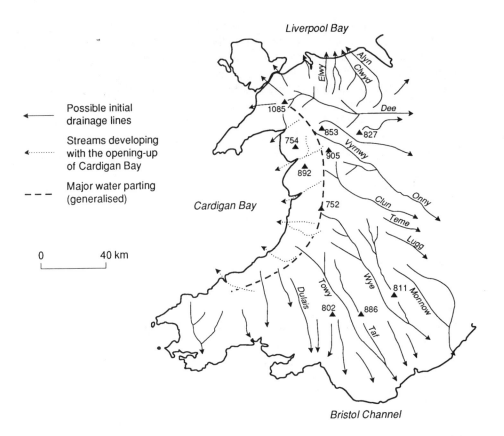

Possible initial
drainage lines

Streams developing
with the opening-up
of Cardigan Bay

Major water parting
(generalised)

0   40 km

Liverpool Bay

Cardigan Bay

Bristol Channel

Heights in
metres

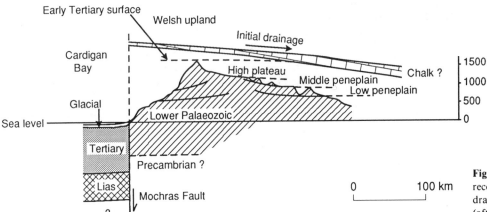

Early Tertiary surface

Welsh upland

Initial drainage

Cardigan
Bay

High plateau

Middle peneplain

Chalk ?

Low peneplain

1500
1000
500
0

Glacial

Lower Palaeozoic

Sea level

Tertiary

Precambrian ?

Lias

Mochras Fault

?

0   100 km

Figure 8.7 Hypothetical
reconstruction of Welsh
drainage evolution
(after E.H. Brown).

to relatively recent capture by a younger, more powerful stream cutting back its
deep valley eastwards across the coastal platforms. The waterfalls, the smoothing
and hollowing effect of turbulent water upon rock, the sharp change of direction
of the river (the elbow of capture) are all classic examples of river piracy.

The upper Teifi Valley also has many attractive features, not least of which is
the renowned Tregaron Bog where a lake once stood impounded by a moraine in

a broad basin that had recently been vacated by the ice sheets. Throughout the suceeding 10 000 years the river has gradually lowered the lake outlet through the moraine, thereby draining the lake and allowing peat to form on the layers of lake muds. Today, the bog is a wilderness of acid peat clothed with various mosses, rushes, cotton grass, deer grass and heather which provide shelter for a profusion of wildlife, strictly protected by the Nature Conservancy Council (Godwin and Conway, 1934). Peat was once cut for fuel amid the tangled thickets of willows, which themselves provide habitats for otters among their roots and for herons in their branches, though it is the kites and hen harriers that bring ornithologists to this primordial solitude of raised bog and fen peat. Below Tregaron and Lampeter the Teifi Valley narrows where it crosses on to the Ordovician rocks and from here to the sea its course becomes a deep picturesque valley with a 'Loire-like loveliness'. The river glides past the steep wooded slopes at Henllan and Newcastle Emlyn, the falls at Cenarth and past Cilgerran Castle on its cliff, until it finally emerges into an attractive estuary below the ancient stone-built town of Cardigan.

Before examining the relatively unspoiled coastline of Cardigan Bay, something must be said of the heavily forested but otherwise deserted tracts of upland enclosed by the headwaters of the Severn, Wye and Teifi rivers, many of which have been dammed to form reservoirs. The ample rainfall, the impermeable nature of the rocks and the occasional presence of narrow defiles for dam sites plus the wide glaciated valleys upstream for the reservoirs themselves, all combine to make ideal locations for water catchment mainly to supply distant cities of England, albeit at the expense of relocation of the sparse rural population. Llyn Brianne, on the upper Towy (Tywi), helps maintain Swansea's water supply; the Elan Valley complex, on the Upper Wye tributaries, serves the voracious demands of Birmingham; Lake Vyrnwy, much farther north on a tributary of the Severn, has supplied Liverpool for almost a century. The two latter reservoirs have aqueducts to carry their waters directly to the cities, while the newer Clywedog dam, on a tributary of the Severn, is used to control river flow, thus alleviating floods and low flows farther downstream.

North of the Teifi estuary the coast of Cardigan Bay swings round to follow a Caledonoid trend (Bowen, 1977). From here northwards as far as New Quay there are long stretches of sea cliffs carved from the folded layers of dark-coloured shales and blue-grey sandstones of Ordovician and Silurian age. Broken only by narrow wooded valleys at such places as Aber Porth, Llangranog and Cwmtyde, this wild rocky coast of Ceredigion is regularly diversified by gentler slopes of coastal screes between its cliff-girt headlands. Condry (1981) describes how these provide sites for 'primroses, cowslips, false oxslips, moschatel, sanicle, wood spurge, wild privet, great horsetail, small scabious, greater knapweed and many other delights'. From New Quay northwards the coastal character changes, for the slowly rising Flandrian transgression has so far (with a few exceptions) failed to reach the boulder-clay-smothered slopes of a former coastline once carved by the waves of a Pleistocene interglacial sea. Thus, the present sea coast of Cardigan Bay comprises wide alluvial flats and marshes interspersed with lengthy stretches of cliffs carved not in rock but in till whose constant erosion supplies the cobbles for the pebbly beaches that abound all the way to the Mawddach estuary. Legends describe how the rising waters of Cardigan Bay once drowned the lost kingdom of Cantref-y-Gwaelod, although it is more realistic to explain the tree stumps of the submerged forests, exposed at low tide, and the remarkable lines of boulders (sarns) extending far out from the coastline, as the result of the Flandrian submergence of a late Pleistocene till-plain seamed with lateral moraines from local Welsh glaciers (Watson, 1970). Beyond the old grey university town of Aberystwyth, with its steep gritstone and tumbled mudstone cliffs (Wood, 1959), the coastline finally descends to a long shingle spit that has grown northwards from Borth to Ynyslas, thereby enclosing a salt marsh on which a raised bog has developed along the southern shores of the Dyfi estuary. Not only is this a renowned site for studying Borth's submerged forest but it also provides opportunities to examine at one site the flora and fauna of a shingle ridge, a sand dune complex, a salt-marsh succession and a coastal peat moor, all in a beautiful mountainous setting (Godwin and Newton, 1938). The River Dyfi's picturesque drowned valley represents the border of Gwynedd, whose very distinctive geology and terrain mark the southern limits of Snowdonia. To the north of Machynlleth the Silurian rocks which have characterized the large stretches of Aberystwyth's hinterland (Jones and Pugh, 1935) give way to Ordovician sedimentaries strongly bolstered by igneous intrusions and volcanics.

North Wales

The mountains of Snowdonia provide one of southern Britain's scenic highlights and as such have been designated a National Park (Condry, 1966). Their fame rests partly on their height, steepness and ruggedness but also on their spectacular waterfalls, river gorges and lakes that occupy the deeply ice-scoured valleys, many of which are clothed with ancient broad-leaved woodlands. Yet the mountainous heartland is surrounded by very different but equally attractive countryside: the probing finger of the Llyn Peninsula, with its knuckly western hills; the rolling low profile of Anglesey, with its chequerboard of arable and pastureland; the less ordered mosaic of plateau farmlands that march eastwards into Clwyd, where a fertile vale divides the Denbighshire moorlands from the heather-clad Clwydian Hills (Milward and Robinson, 1978). Wrapping round all these peninsulas and islands is the Irish Sea whose tidal waters burrow deeply into the mountainland and whose waves have fashioned some noteworthy coastal features all the way from Morfa Dyffryn and Morfa Harlech to the mouth of the Dee.

Snowdonia

The strata of North Wales, well exposed in Snowdonia, comprise some of Britain's oldest sedimentary rocks, dating back to Cambrian times when the earliest fossils appear in the geological record (Challinor and Bates, 1973; Rushton, 1974). Additionally, there are many examples of igneous rocks, illustrating how this region, like that of the Lake District, was a major zone of intermittent volcanism in Lower Palaeozoic times (Howells *et al.*, 1981). It has been established that during this early geological era the earth's large continental plates began to move towards each other and that as a result the intervening ocean basin, known as *Iapetus*, in which thick deposits of mud and sand had accumulated (Woodcock, 1984), began to narrow while volcanic eruptions broke out along their continental margins (Shackleton, 1958; Smith and George, 1961). Because many of the lavas were

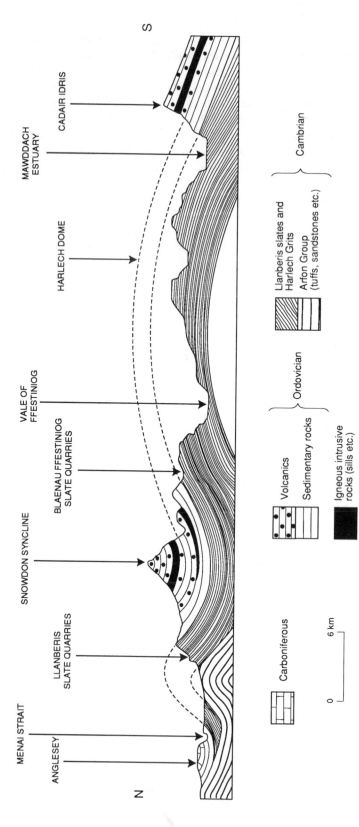

Figure 8.8 Generalized geological section of Snowdonia, North Wales.

extruded on the sea floor they became interbedded within the submarine sediments, as did the extensive flows of volcanic ash, known as ash-flow tuffs or 'ignimbrites', whose modern equivalents are the *nuées ardentes* (glowing clouds) that have caused disasters on certain of the West Indies volcanic islands (for example, on Martinique in 1902). Following the final closure of the primeval *Iapetus* ocean the collision of the continental plates between late Silurian and early Devonian times led to the creation of the Calendonian mountain chain across northern and western Britain. The various strata were crumpled and uplifted as gigantic folds aligned along north-east to south-west axes (see Fig. 1.3). Despite subsequent denudation three of these fundamental structural elements can be distinguished in Snowdonia (Fig. 8.8), though each includes scores of minor folds, faults and igneous intrusions. First, in the north, the unfolded early Cambrian basal sequence of highly contorted tuffs, sandstones and conglomerates (the Arfon Group), lies between the Menai Straits and the mountains (Reedman *et al.*, 1984) and includes the important Llanberis Slates Formation. Second, in the centre, is the main Snowdon syncline of interbedded volcanics and Ordovician sedimentaries that form the highest peaks. Third, and finally, is the greatly denuded remnants of the Harlech Dome whose core is represented by the Rhinogs and whose southern flank comprises the towering Cadair Idris escarpment.

Cadair stands out because of the resistance of its instrusive sills and extrusive lavas and tuffs which, together with the intervening sediamentary strata, dip steeply to the south (Cox, 1925). Thus, its steep northern precipice, which looks northwards across the picturesque Mawddach estuary and the mountains of the Harlech Dome (Matley and Wilson, 1946), is really a gigantic escarpment which has been heavily ice-worn (Watson, 1960). Its great glacier-eroded hollows, in which nestle the tiny lakes of Llyn Cau and Llyn-y-Gader, have often been likened to craters, particularly as depicted in the paintings of Richard Wilson. Today, we know that although volcanic rocks help build the bounding cliffs there are no other remnants of the mighty volcanic cones which once existed hereabouts more than 500 million years ago. To the south of Cadair is the long U-shaped valley of Tal-y-Llyn, holding a lake impounded behind a landslip below the cliffs of Graig Goch. Though considerably straightened and overdeepened by glaciers, the alignment of the valley was primarily determined by the existence of a belt of crushed rocks along the line of the Bala fault (Bassett, 1958). This major fracture extends north-eastwards past Bala Lake, where it is followed by the upper reaches of the Dee, before cutting across the North Wales coalfield north of Wrexham as the Bryneglwys Fault. The horizontal displacement of the fault is about 3 kilometres, as demonstrated by the movement of the rocks of the southern block in relation to those which build Cadair itself. Although the line of the fault is Caledonoid, it may have moved considerably during Hercynian earth movements. Many millions of years later, the Tal-y-Llyn glacier appears to have been of such magnitude that it spilled northwards over the adjacent western ridge, thereby lowering the two cols west of Tal-y-Llyn village as well as those overlooking Abergynolwyn and Dolgoch villages (Watson, 1962). Such a process is termed *ice-breaching* or *glacial diffluence* and in this case it has led to the disruption of the former river system. It would appear that the river which drains the Tal-y-Llyn fault-guided trough must once have flowed directly south-westwards to the sea at Towyn, but now it turns sharply through the ice-breached gorge at Abergynolwyn before joining the Dysynni in its parallel valley; the beheaded and diminutive

Fathew continues to drain the old valley past Dolgoch.

The lowest strata of the Harlech Dome, between the Mawddach estuary and the equally tidal Vale of Ffestiniog, have been stripped of all their Upper Cambrian and Ordovician rocks to reveal the gently dipping but massive beds of coarse-grained Cambrian grits (the Harlech Grits) which build the tabular summits of the Rhinogs (750 m). The semicircular lowland, which can be traced from the Afon Mawddach around the eastern flank of the dome via the Afon Eden and Trawsfynydd Lake (with its nuclear power station) northwards to the Vale of Ffestiniog, has been carved from the less resistant Upper Cambrian shales, flags, mudstones and slates of the so-called Mawddach Group of rocks. Within this group is the Maentwrog Formation whose steeply dipping secondary cleavage has caused considerable land-slipping wherever road cuttings have been engineered. Expensive remedial measures have had to be undertaken, especially in the Vale of Ffestiniog (Hawkins, 1985). It was along the junction between the Harlech Grits and these overlying black Clogau mudstones (Mawddach Group) that mineralization of Devonian age caused the emplacement of Wales's most important gold belt, mined since the mid-nineteenth century (Andrew, 1910). In addition, copper, lead, silver and manganese ores were once worked at various places in the dome, though the rocky hillsides have now been returned to extensive sheepwalks and occasional forestry plantations. The same mixture of Ordovician volcanic and sedimentary rocks which once covered the dome and created Cadair Idris also outcrops along the eastern and northern flanks of the dome, rearing up in a semi-circle of high rugged peaks. The earliest Ordovician rocks are the Arenig volcanic lavas and tuffs which rest discordantly upon various members of the Upper Cambrian sediments and are themselves overlain by the coarse, pebbly Garth Grit (Fearnsides, 1905). From Cadair northwards the wild and isolated summits of the Arans and the Arenigs, where the centre of the North Wales ice cap is thought to have been located (Rowlands, 1979), are succeeded by the brooding Manod and Moelwyns, overlooking Blaenau Ffestiniog, before reaching the majestic line of peaks that marks the north-east to south-west axis of the main Snowdon syncline.

At first it may appear paradoxical that the highest of Snowdonia's mountains have been carved from a downfold, although this has already been explained on p. 3. Suffice to say that the synclinal structure can clearly be seen in the summit of Snowdon itself (Williams, 1927) and also in the cliffs of the Devil's Kitchen behind Llyn Idwal (Williams, 1930). From Snowdon's summit (1085 m) the craggy country, formed largely from the volcanic rocks, can be seen stretching away north-eastwards through the Glyderau (1000 m) and the Carneddau (1062 m), and south-westwards into the Llyn Peninsula. The massif has been profoundly modified by glaciation and divided into discrete blocks by the deep through-valleys carved out by radiating ice streams where they breached the main pre-glacial watershed at a time when the local ice cap had a surface elevation of some 1400 metres (Addison et al., 1990). Snowdon lies between three such glacial troughs: the broad western vale occupied by Llyn Cwellyn; the picturesque southern valley of Nant Gwynant (see Fig. 1.1), with its tree-lined lakes; and its eastern defile, the bare, narrow and awesome Pass of Llanberis. The latter exhibits all the features of glacial erosion (Addison, 1983), including truncated spurs (for example, Dinas Mot, illustrated in Fig. 8.9), striated and polished rock pavements (Gemmell et al., 1986), perched boulders, and the valley lakes of Padarn and Peris occupying the overdeepened floor of the trough where the glacier differentially scoured out the less resistant Llanberis Slates before being forced to override the more resistant tuffs of the bare Padarn ridge. Snowdon's sharply conical profile is the result of the imminent coalescence of its surrounding cwms. The deeply ice-gouged basin of Clogwyn Du'r Arddu is the most dramatic but the staircase of cirques containing the lakes of Glaslyn and Llydaw is the best known, though more intrepid walkers may prefer to reach the summit via the narrow pinnacled and knife-edged ridge (*arête*) of Crib Goch. A similar mixture of volcanics and sedimentaries builds the more flat-topped peaks of the Glyderau and the spectacular hog's-back of Tryfan. The summit of Glyder Fawr is a wilderness of remarkable frost-splintered rocks, with some of the tumbled monoliths achieving lengths of 9 metres. But one of the most rewarding Snowdonian views, so far as glacial features are concerned, is that seen from the head of the Nant Ffrancon. Here, stretching as far as the skyline of the Bethesda slate quarries, the floor of the U-shaped trough carries a patchwork of fields on the marshy flat of a former lake floor. Several tributary streams cascade down the north-east-facing valley side, breaking through the small moraines as they flow from the suite of cwms that hang considerably above the overdeepened trough. On the opposite flank cwms are absent, again illustrating the fact that in the northern hemisphere small cirque glaciers lingered longest on the shaded hillsides facing north-east (see p. 10). In addition to their relative freedom from ablation, these hollows also acted as receptacles for the windblown snow carried over the crests by prevailing south-westerlies. Moreover, there is a tendency for maximum precipitation to fall just over the crests on the leeward slope, not on the windward slope (Unwin, 1973). At Ogwen Cottage the trough ends abruptly and the A5 road climbs up the highly glaciated rock step (Fig. 8.10a) which forms the main viewpoint and over which the river cascades after escaping from the shallow valley lake of Llyn Ogwen. By contrast, occupying a gloomy hollow below the dark synclinal cliffs and deep cleft of Twll Ddu (the

Figure 8.9 The glacially overdeepened valley of the Llanberis Pass, Snowdonia, incised into hard Ordovician volcanic rocks. The truncated spur of Dinas Mot can be seen on the left.

Devil's Kitchen), Llyn Idwal is impounded by a conspicuous moraine marking the extent of the Idwal glacier during the Loch Lomond Stadial at the close of the Ice Age (Gray, 1982). Immediately to the east of the Devil's Kitchen waterfall the steep Idwal Slabs obviously form one limb of the Idwal syncline, while just north of these, four morainic ridges run obliquely down the slope to link with the hummocky moraines which traverse the upper end of the lake, signifying the successive downwasting stages of the Idwal glacier (Fig. 8.10b).

The presence of the Cambrian slate belt in Snowdonia has led to consider-

Figure 8.10 (a) The severely ice-gouged rock step at the head of the Nant Ffrancon, Snowdonia, illustrating a type of roche moutonée. (b) The moraine-encircled Llyn Idwal, Snowdonia, cradled in the glacial cirque of Cwm Idwal. The nearer hummocky moraine, which crosses the Lake was formed during the Loch Lomond stadial. Photograph (a) was taken from a point just beyond the furthest point of the lake.

able spoilation of the scenery of the mountain flanks at places such as Nantlle, Dinorwig, Bethesda and Blaenau Ffestiniog (North, 1946). The different character of the quarries and mines in Snowdonia can be explained by the differences in the folding and varying width of outcrop of the slaty rocks in relation to the regional cleavage due to metamorphism (see Chapter 1). Though Nantlle quarry was the earliest to be worked (Fearnsides and Morris, 1926), probably supplying the floorstones for the Roman forts of Segontium (Caernarfon) and Caer Llugwy (near Capel Curig), the Penrhyn quarry at Bethesda is Britain's largest artificial void. Though production has virtually ceased, its twenty-one galleries still expose the grey, green and purple slates on a face 2 kilometres long and 400 metres high. Surrounding the bleak slate-quarry towns and their overwhelming tips of waste, the mountain flanks are patterned with a maze of drystone walls. This patchwork of tiny fields, stone-built cottages and chapels, represents isolated settlements carved out of the rough hill pastures by quarrymen (Embleton, 1962). It is one of the most distinctive landscapes in Snowdonia, for it has been overlaid on the historic pattern of Welsh land tenure described on p. 173 (Milward and Robinson, 1978). Though many of the cottages and drystone walls have been built largely from glacially dumped boulders cleared from the fields, slabs of rudely fashioned slate have also been widely utilized for fences, doorposts, lintels and steps, in addition to the ubiquitous use of slate as a roofing material.

The great expanse of the Carneddau, from the glacial trough of Nant Ffrancon to the less glacially deepened but lengthy tract of the Conwy valley (Fishwick, 1977) is the least accessible part of Snowdonia because of its dearth of roads. Its tableland boasts the largest extent of mountainland above 1000 metres south of the Scottish Highlands and as such has several sites where periglacial processes are still sufficiently active to produce constantly changing stone polygons and other types of patterned ground (Ball and Goodier, 1970). Its peaks are high but less dramatically shaped and its cwms are deep but more widely spaced than those farther west, though it boasts a notable lake-filled glacial breach at Llyn Cowlyd near Capel Curig. Most of the Carneddau lakes have been utilized for hydro-electric power or local water supplies and some were associated with the former lead and zinc mines now overgrown by Gwydir Forest. This mountain tract is better known where it reaches the coast for it has been steeply cliffed by the sea at Llanfairfechan, Penmaenmawr and Conwy. Here the plutonic and volcanic rocks produce craggy hills of great beauty; owing to their lower elevations (less than 400 m) they have a richer vegetation than the higher peaks, with the deep purple heather and golden gorse of Conwy Mountain providing one of the area's scenic highlights. Nevertheless, the same microgranites which build these coastal headlands have also been heavily quarried for roadstone, severely disfiguring the slopes of Penmaenmawr, which is now also threaded with road and rail tunnels to improve the communication links on this rockbound coast.

The coasts of North Wales

Stone quarries are also found on the western coastal extremities of Snowdonia, especially on the flanks of the majestic igneous pyramid of Yr Eifl in the Llyn Peninsula. All the conical hills which rise abruptly from the 75 metre coastal platform of Llyn are carved from volcanics or igneous intrusions of similar age to those of Snowdonia, while the less elevated ground coincides with the Lower

Palaeozoic sedimentary rocks (Catermole and Romano, 1981). The heathery summit of Carn Fadryn (371 m) is the highest peak, but the vertical sea cliffs between Nefyn and Trefor offer some of the wildest scenery. Here a rare primeval coastal oakwood can be found near to the headland of Carreg-y-Llam, 'the guillemot metropolis of north Wales'. Farther west still, the tip of the peninsula comprises a tract of Precambrian metamorphic and igneous rocks that create a number of low isolated hills all the way to Bardsey Island (Matley, 1928). This is a less frequented part of Wales, with hidden sea coves, fine cliffs and beautifully coloured beach pebbles derived from the Precambrian serpentines and jaspers. The scenery has many similarities to that of Cornwall, even to the heathland and acid-loving vegetation developed on the stony soils of the igneous outcrops. In complete contrast to Cornwall, however, are the numerous examples of lime-loving plants that flourish on the plains and in the bays of the Llyn Peninsula. For these are the areas that are mantled with glacial drifts, many of them highly calcareous because their incorporated shells were dredged up by northern ice sheets as they bulldozed southwards down the floor of the Irish Sea basin. In fact the Llyn Peninsula was a battleground between the northern ice and the glaciers which extended northwards and westwards from Snowdonia's own ice cap, centred over the Arenigs (Whittow and Ball, 1970). From the Glaslyn estuary, for example, a piedmont glacier of Welsh ice extended into Tremadog Bay as far as St Tudwal's peninsula, leaving its lateral moraine (now Sarn Badrig) projecting far into the sea from the cliffs at Harlech. Thus, the boulder clay cliffs between Criccieth and Abersoch have been carved from Welsh drifts only, while farther west the dramatic bay of Porth Neigwl and that in the Nefyn glacial sands have been fashioned exclusively from northern drifts (Campbell and Bowen, 1989). Two classic coastal sites occur in Llyn in terms of Welsh glacial stratigraphy: Dinas Dinlle hillfort on the north coast exhibits massive glacial tectonics indicative of over-riding by ice of an existing suite of glacigenic sediments; Glanllynau, west of Criccieth on the south coast, has an almost complete record of Upper Devensian tills and glacio-fluvial drifts passing up into Late-glacial and Flandrian sediments trapped in a kettle hole complex now truncated by marine erosion (Simpkins, 1974). Much of this unconsolidated Pleistocene material, eroded by the waves of the rising Flandrian sea, has been carried by longshore drift to create the beaches and shingle spits around Tremadog Bay, notably those of Morfa Bychan (near Criccieth), Morfa Harlech and Morfa Dyffryn (north of Barmouth) (Steers, 1939). Of these Morfa Harlech is the most interesting for its recent growth can be estimated by reference to the building of Harlech Castle by Edward I in 1286. Like his other castles at Conwy, Caernarfon and Beaumaris, all located to blockade the Welsh in the mountainland, Harlech was formerly supplied by sea from a harbour which stood at the Water Gate. However, the spit has now lengthened and the dunes and marsh (*morfa* is Welsh for 'marsh') have grown sufficiently to isolate the castle from the sea. Human intervention has also altered the coastline hereabouts, for the Morfa Harlech marshes were enclosed by an embankment in 1808 and the Glaslyn estuary virtually closed off from Tremadog Bay in 1811 by W. A. Madock's embankment, thereby preventing the sea from ever again penetrating into the mountains as far as Aberglaslyn bridge where a tiny harbour once flourished.

The rising post-glacial sea not only overran the drift-covered lowlands which once surrounded the Welsh coast, but also flooded through a complex of glacial meltwater channels near to Bangor to create the narow tide-ripped Menai Straits which now isolate Anglesey from the identical landscape of Arfon between Caernarfon and Bangor. Anglesey is a rolling platform, about 75 metres in elevation, from which a few isolated hills rise to heights of some 200 metres. Its uniformly low level is anomolous because it is composed of some of Britain's oldest and hardest rocks, with the highly contorted metamorphic gneisses and schists of the so-called Mona Complex (Barber and Max, 1979) of the northern fringe being as old as those of the Northern Highlands of Scotland. In addition, granites, slates, sandstones and limestones of Palaeozoic age are also present, almost all conforming to the Caledonian 'grain' that dominates North Wales's structures and landforms (Bates and Davies, 1981). Some believe that Anglesey and Arfon represent a wave-cut platform extending to an ancient sea cliff at the foot of the mountains. An alternative hypothesis is to regard the so-called Menaian Platform as an exhumed surface from which a former cover of New Red Sandstone has been stripped (Embleton, 1964), similar in genesis to the Vale of Glamorgan or somewhat comparable with that of the formation of the Lewisian gneiss platform of north-west Scotland where the Torridonian Sandstone has been removed (see p. 419). More recently, an ingenious hypothesis has suggested that E.H. Brown's Early Tertiary Welsh 'Summit Plain' (1000–1085 m) (see Fig. 8.7) is the tectonically uplifted section of the Anglesey surface, raised in the Upper Miocene some 650 metres along the large Dinorwig fault system (where earthquakes still occur); such a suggestion is based on the vertical displacement of the Eocene igneous dykes between Bangor and Marchlyn Mawr in northern Snowdonia (Battiau-Queney, 1984). Though Anglesey's great variety of rock exposures (from Precambrian to Carboniferous) has been scoured by northern ice moving south-westwards, the intervening hollows are drift-filled, producing soils deep enough to support cultivation of grain crops; Anglesey was renowned as the granary of Wales from Roman to medieval times. But today most of its fields are used for stock-rearing and the wintering of mountain sheep. Its general lack of woodlands, its dwarfed and bent trees, all testify to the windiness of this exposed island, suggesting a bleakness more typical of the Hebrides than of southern Britain. In such exposed situations as Pembrokeshire, the Llyn Peninsula and Anglesey, it is not surprising to find that many of the older single-storey Welsh cottages have deeply recessed windows and a thick covering of mortar over their slated roofs to withstand the gales. Most of Anglesey's cottages are whitewashed and exhibit variants of the Welsh long-house pattern in which living quarters and cattle byre are adjoined. Anglesey's greatest attractions are its coasts. The vast sandy beaches of the east support veritable 'villages' of caravans between the limestone headlands. Its western coast is a wilderness of rocky reefs and sandy warrens on one of whose dune complexes the Forestry Commission has planted an enormous conifer forest at Newborough. The northern coast of older rocks, despite the Wylfa nuclear power station and the Holyhead aluminium smelter, possesses the most striking scenery, akin to that of Pembrokeshire and Cornwall, in which heavily contorted rock cliffs, tiny coves and stacks carry a wide variety of sea birds and some quite rare floral species.

At the easternmost extremity of Anglesey, around Red Wharf Bay, at Penmon Point and the adjacent Puffin Island (Greenly, 1928), layers of gently dipping Carboniferous Limestone create features that are replicated on a grander scale in Great Orme's Head across Conwy Bay. The latter's imposing limestone promontory was termed the 'Botanical Garden of Cambria' as long ago as 1800 because its calcereous soils and limestone cliffs offer habitats to some rare flora, notably *Cotoneaster integrimus*, together with an abundance of bird life. Sheltering beneath the Great Orme's limestone cliffs the planned Victorian resort of Llandudno has developed on the low spit of sand that now joins the former Great Orme island to the mainland in the form of a tombolo (Fig. 8.11). Similar limestone hills, with exposed pavements and wind-stunted woodland, give further diversity to the Creuddyn peninsula between Colwyn Bay and Llandudno, including the smaller headland of the Little Orme (Neaverson, 1937). The River Conwy, which follows a fault-guided trough all the way from Betws-y-coed to Glan Conwy, formerly flowed across the base of the Creuddyn to exit at Penrhyn Bay. Its diversion to the present mouth at Conwy, where it now washes the grey walls of the well-preserved medieval castle town, was probably caused in Pleistocene times by northern ice sheets encroaching on to the north coast of Wales. The marine shells and red Triassic sands dredged up by this ice sheet from the floor of Liverpool Bay contribute to the red calcareous till which is exposed in the low coastal flats from western Anglesey all along the north coast of Clwyd to the point of Ayre.

To the east of the Conwy Valley, whose western valleyside waterfalls mark the eastern edge of the Ordovician volcanic tract of Snowdonia (Fishwick, 1977), the Denbigh Moors (Hiraethog) stretch away as an undulating tract of hill country as far as the Vale of Clwyd. They are composed of shales, flagstones, mudstones and grits of Silurian age (Boswell, 1949), though wherever the Denbigh Grit (Cummins, 1957) occurs it creates bold hills and minor scraps in the generally undulating terrain of drumlins and incised river valleys. Moreover, the gritstone has also been used as an important building stone in towns such as Llanrwst and

Figure 8.11 The former Carboniferous Limestone island of the Great Orme, Llandudno, is seen in the distance, now linked to the mainland by a post-glacial tombolo on which the resort of Llandudno stands. The estuary of the River Conwy opens beyond the dune-fringed coastal spit of Conwy Morfa, now occupied by a caravan park.

also in Conwy's castle and town walls, though both contain occasional volcanic blocks in their fabrics.

The downfaulted Vale of Clwyd, with its floor of New Red Sandstone, intrudes a broad tongue of lowland into the upland scene, creating landscapes more akin to Cheshire than to Wales. Its fertile soils, derived from a thick cover of glacial drift deposited by northern ice sheets which penetrated into the Vale beyond Denbigh (Embleton, 1970), have long supported excellent grasslands as a basis for an important dairying industry, although good grain crops have also been taken from this sheltered and relatively sunny lowland. In complete contrast to Snowdonia, whose large towns lie only on the perimeter, the historic towns of the vale continue inland from the grey Edwardian castle of Rhuddlan on its coastal marshes, past St Asaph's ancient cathedral, to the large market towns of Denbigh and Ruthin (Carter, 1965). The vale is overlooked from the east by the conspicuous fault-line scarp of the Clwydian Hills which rise to 554 metres as the final expression of the Welsh uplands before they descend to the Dee estuary. On these hills a few of the subsidence hollows and solution collapse structures in the Carboniferous Limestone have been found to contain relic deposits of relatively recent sediments of possible Tertiary age (Walsh and Brown, 1971). It seems probable that they were formed in the same way as the Brassington Formation of the southern Peak District (see p. 219). The considerably older mudstones, siltstones and occasional sandstones of the Elwy Group of Upper Silurian rocks (Simpson, 1940) produce landforms and land uses very similar to those of the Denbighshire Moors, though they are more limited in extent. The northern and eastern flanks of the Clwydian Hills are overlapped by a broad tract of Carboniferous Limestone with its typical calcicole vegetation and a plethora of abandoned iron, copper, lead and zinc workings, similar to those which occur in the limestone outcrop between St Asaph, Abergele and Llandulas. Numerous caves in the limestone, on either flank of the vale (such as Cae Gwyn, Pontnewydd and Ffynnon Beuno) have yielded abundant human and other mammalian bones associated with artefacts ranging from Palaeolithic to Neolithic times (Green *et al.*, 1981).

Bibliography

Addison, K. (1983) *Classic Glacial Landforms of Snowdonia*. Landform Guide no. 3. Geog. Assoc. 48 pp.

Addison, K., Edge, M. J. and Watkins, R. (1990) *North Wales Field Guide*. Quat. Res. Assoc. 190 pp.

Allen, J. R. L. and Rae, J. E. (1988) Vertical salt-marsh accretion since the Roman period in the Severn estuary, south-west Britain. *Marine Geol.*, **83**, 225–35.

Andrew, A. R. (1910) The geology of the Dolgelley gold belt. *Geol. Mag.*, **47**, 159–71, 201–11, 261–71.

Balchin, W. G. C. (1971) *Swansea and Its Region*. University of Wales Press. 391 pp.

Ball, D. F. and Goodier, R. (1970) Morphology and distribution of features resulting from frost-action in Snowdonia. *Fld Stud.* **3**, 193–217.

Barber, A. J. and Max, M. D. (1979) A new look at the Mona Complex (Anglesey, North Wales). *J. Geol. Soc. Lond.*, **136**, 407.

Bassett, D. A. (1958) Notes on the faults of the Bala district. *Liverpool and Manchester Geol. J.*, **2**, 1–10.

Bates, D. E. B. and Davies, J. R. (1981) *Anglesey*. Guide no. 40. Geol. Assoc.

Battiau-Queney, Y. (1984) The pre-glacial evolution of Wales. *Earth Surface Processes and Landforms*, **9**, 229–52.

Boswell, P.G.H. (1949) *The Middle Silurian Rocks of North Wales*. Arnold.

Bowen, D.Q. (1973) The Pleistocene history of Wales and the borderland. *Geol. J.*, **8**, 207–24.

Bowen, D.Q. (1977) The Coastline of Wales, in C. Kidson and M.J. Tooley (eds), *The Quaternary History of the Irish Sea*. Geol. Jour. Special Issue no. 7. 223–56.

Bowen, D.Q. and Gregory, K.J. (1965) A glacial drainage system near Fishguard, Pembrokeshire. *Proc. Geol. Assoc.*, **74**, 275–81.

Bowen, D.Q. and Henry, A. (eds.) (1984) *Wales: Gower, Preseli, Fforest Fawr*. Field Guide. Quat Res. Assoc. 102 pp.

Bowen, E.G. (1957) *Wales. A Physical, Historical and Regional Geography*. Methuen. 528 pp.

Bridges, E.M. (1987) *Classic Landforms of the Gower Coast*. Landform Guide no. 7. Geog. Assoc. 48 pp.

Brown, E.H. (1960) *The Relief and Drainage of Wales*. University of Wales Press. 186 pp.

Campbell, S. and Bowen, D.Q. (1989) *The Quaternary of Wales*. Geological Conservation Review. Nature Conservancy Council. 237 pp.

Carter, H. (1965) *The Towns of Wales*. University of Wales Press.

Catermole, P.J. and Romano, M. (1981) *Lleyn Peninsula*. Guide no. 39 Geol. Assoc.

Challinor, J. and Bates, D.E.B. (1973) *Geology Explained in North Wales*. David & Charles. 214 pp.

Condry, W.M. (1966) *The Snowdonia National Park*. Collins. 238 pp.

Condry, W.M. (1981) *The Natural History of Wales*. Collins. 287 pp.

Cox, A.H. (1925) The geology of the Cader Idris range. *Quart. J. Geol. Soc.*, **81**, 539–94.

Cox, A.H., Green, J.F.N., Jones, O.T. and Pringle, J. (1930) The geology of St. David's district, Pembrokeshire. *Proc. Geol. Assoc.*, **41**, 241–50.

Cummins, W.A. (1957) The Denbigh Grits: Wenlock greywackes in Wales. *Geol. Mag.*, **94**, 433–51.

Driscoll, E.M. (1958) The denudation chronology of the Vale of Glamorgan. *Trans. Inst. Br. Geogr.*, **25**, 45–57.

Edwards, G. (1963) The coal industry in Pembrokeshire. *Fld Stud.*, **1**, 33–64.

Elsden, J.V. (1905) The igneous rocks occurring between St. David's Head and Strumble Head. *Quart. J. Geol. Soc.*, **61**, 579–607.

Embleton, C. (1962) *Snowdonia*. British Landscapes through Maps no. 5. Geog. Assoc.

Embleton, C. (1964) The planation surfaces of Arfon and adjacent parts of Anglesey – a re-examination of their age and origin. *Trans. Inst. Br. Geogr.*, **35**, 17–26.

Embleton, C. (1970) North-eastern Wales, in C.A. Lewis (ed.), *The Glaciations of Wales and Adjoining Regions*. Longman. 59–82.

Emery, F.V. (1969) *Wales*. Longman. 139 pp.

Evans, W.D. (1945) The geology of the Prescelly Hills, north Pembrokeshire. *Quart. J. Geol. Soc.*, **101**, 89–110.

Fearnsides, W.G. (1905) On the geology of Arenig Fawr and Moel Llyfnant. *Quart. J. Geol. Soc.*, **61**, 608–40.

Fearnsides, W.G. and Morris, T.O. (1926) The stratigraphy and structure of the Cambrian slate-belt of Nantlle, Caernarvonshire. *Quart. J. Geol. Soc.*, **82**, 250–303.

Fishwick, A. (1977) The Conway Basin. *Cambria*, **4**, 56–64.

Francis, E.H. (1959) The Rhaetic of the Bridgend district, Glamorgan. *Proc. Geol. Assoc.*, **70**, 158–78.

Gemmell, C., Smart, D. and Sugden, D. (1986) Striae and former ice-flow directions in Snowdonia, North Wales. *Geog. J.*, **152**, 19–29.

George, T.N. (1933) The Carboniferous Limestone series in the west of the Vale of Glamorgan. *Quart. J. Geol. Soc.*, **89**, 221–72.

George, T.N. (1940) The structure of Gower. *Quart. J. Geol. Soc.*, **96**, 131–98.

George, T.N. (1970) *South Wales* (3rd edn). British Regional Geology. HMSO. 152 pp.

Godwin, H. and Conway, V.M. (1934) The ecology of a raised bog near Tragaron, Cardiganshire. *J. Ecol.*, **27**, 313–59.

Godwin, H. and Newton, F.N. (1938) The submerged forest at Borth and Ynyslas, Cardiganshire. *New Phytol*, **37**, 333–44.

Goskar, K.L. and Trueman, A.E. (1934) The coastal plateaux of South Wales. *Geol. Mag.*, **71**, 468–79.

Gray, J. M. (1982) The last glaciers (Loch Lomond Advance) in Snowdonia, North Wales. *Geol. J.*, **17**, 111–33.

Green, H. S., Stringer, C. B., Collcutt, S. N. *et al.* (1981) Pontnewydd Cave in Wales – a new Middle Pleistocene hominid site. *Nature*, **294**, 707–13.

Greenly, E. (1928) The Lower Carboniferous rocks of the Menaian region of Caernarvonshire. *Quart. J. Geol. Soc.*, **84**, 382–439.

Grimes, W. F. (1951) *The Prehistory of Wales*. University of Wales Press.

Hawkins, T. R. W. (1985) Influence of geological structure on slope stability in the Maentwrog Formation, Harlech Dome, North Wales. *Proc. Geol. Assoc.*, **96**, 289–304.

Helm, D. G. and Roberts, E. (1975) A re-interpretation of the origin of sands and gravels around Banc-y-Warren near Cardigan, west Wales. *Geol. J.*, **10**, 131–46.

Hilton, K. J. (1967) *The Lower Swansea Valley Project*. London.

Howells, M. F., Leveridge, B. E. and Reedman, A. J. (1981) *Snowdonia*. Geol. Field Guide. Unwin. 119 pp.

Jenkins, T. B. H. (1962) The sequence and correlation of the Coal Measures of Pembrokeshire. *Quart. J. Geol. Soc.*, **118**, 65.

John, B. S. (1970) Pembrokeshire, in C. A. Lewis (ed.), *The Glaciations of Wales and Adjoining Regions*. Longman. 229–65.

John, B. S. (1972) *The Fishguard and Pembroke Area*. British Landscapes through Maps no. 16. Geog. Assoc.

John, B. S. (1976) *Pembrokeshire*. David & Charles. 240 pp.

Jones, O. T. (1912) The geological structure of Central Wales and the adjoining regions. *Quart. J. Geol. Soc.*, **68**, 326–44.

Jones, O. T. (1952) The drainage system of Wales and the adjacent regions. *Quart. J. Geol. Soc.*, **107**, 201–25.

Jones, O. T. (1956) The geological evolution of Wales and the adjacent regions. *Quart. J. Geol. Soc.*, **111**, 323–51.

Jones, O. T. and Pugh, W. J. (1935) The geology of the district around Machynlleth and Aberystwyth. *Proc. Geol. Assoc.*, **46**, 247–300.

Jones, O. T. and Pugh, W. J. (1948) The form and distribution of dolerite masses in the Builth–Llandrindod inlier, Radnorshire. *Quart. J. Geol. Soc.*, **104**, 71–98.

Leach, A. L. (1933) The geology and scenery of Tenby and the south Pembrokeshire coast. *Proc Geol. Assoc.*, **44**, 187–216.

Linnard, W. (1982) *Welsh Woods and Forests: History and Utilization*. Cardiff: Amguedda Geuedlaethol Cymru.

Matley, C. A. (1928) The pre-Cambrian complex and associated rocks of south-western Lleyn. *Quart. J. Geol. Soc.*, **84**, 440–504.

Matley, C. A. and Wilson, T. S. (1946) The Harlech Dome, north of the Barmouth estuary. *Quart. J. Geol. Soc.*, **102**, 1–40.

Milward, R. and Robinson, A. (1978) *Landscapes of North Wales*. David & Charles. 207 pp.

Moore, L. R. (1954) The South Wales Coalfield, in A. E. Trueman, *The Coalfields of Great Britain*. Arnold. 92–125.

Moore, P. D. (1973) The influence of prehistoric cultures upon the initiation and spread of blanket bog in upland Wales. *Nature*, **241**, 350–3.

Neaverson, E. (1937) The Carboniferous rocks between Llandudno and Colwyn Bay. *Proc Liverpool Geol. Soc.*, **17**, 115–35.

North, F. J. (1931) *Coal and the Coalfields of Wales* (2nd edn). National Museum of Wales.

North, F. J. (1946) *The Slates of Wales*. (3rd edn). National Museum of Wales.

North, F. J. (1955) The geological history of Brecknock. *Brycheiniog.*, **1**, 9–77.

North, F. J. (1962) *The River Scenery at the Head of the Vale of Neath*. National Museum of Wales. 101 pp.

Owen, T. R. (1973) *Geology Explained in South Wales*. David & Charles. 211 pp.

Owen. T. R. (1984) Upper Palaeozoic Wales – a review of studies in the past 25 years. *Proc. Geol. Assoc.*, **95**, 349–64.

Reedman, A. J., Leveridge, B. E. and Evans, R. B. (1984) The Arvon Group (Arvonian) of North Wales. *Proc. Geol. Assoc.*, **95**, 313–22.

Rees, J. F. (ed.) (1960) *The Cardiff Region*. University of Wales Press. 222 pp.

Robertson, T. and George, T.N. (1929) The Carboniferous Limestone of the north crop of the South Wales Coalfield. *Proc. Geol. Assoc.*, **49**, 18–40.

Rouse, W.C. (1989) The frequency of landslides in the South Wales Coalfield. *Cambria*, **15**, 167–79.

Rowlands, B. (1979) The Arenig Region: a study in the Welsh Pleistocene. *Cambria*, **6**, 13–31.

Rushton, A.W.A. (1974) The Cambrian in Wales and England, in C.H. Holland (ed.), *Cambrian of the British Isles, Norden and Spitzbergen*. Wiley. 43–121.

Shackleton, R.M. (1958) The structural evolution of North Wales. *Liverpool and Manchester Geol. J.*, **1**, 261–96.

Simpkins, K. (1974) The late-glacial deposits of Glanllynau, Caernarvonshire. *New Phytol.*, **73**, 605–18.

Simpson, B. (1940) The Salopian rocks of the Clwydian range between the Bodfari Gap and Moel Llys-y-coed, Flintshire. *Proc. Geol. Assoc.*, **51**, 188–206.

Smith, B. and George T.N. (1961) *North Wales* (3rd edn). British Regional Geology. HMSO. 96 pp.

Steers, J.A. (1939) Sand and shingle formations in Cardigan Bay. *Geog. J.*, **44**, 209–77.

Thomas, D. (1977) *Wales: A New Study*. David & Charles. 338 pp.

Thomas, H.H. (1911) The Skomer Volcanic Series, Pembrokeshire. *Quart. J. Geol. Soc.*, **67**, 175–214.

Thomas, T.M. (1961) *The Mineral Wealth of Wales and Its Exploitation*. Edinburgh University Press.

Thomas, T.M. (1969) The Triassic rocks of the west-central section of the Vale of Glamorgan. *Proc. Geol. Assoc.*, **79**, 429–39.

Trueman, A.E. (1922) The Liassic rocks of Glamorgan. *Proc. Geol. Assoc.*, **33**, 245–84.

Trueman, A.E. (1924) The geology of the Swansea district. *Proc. Geol. Assoc.*, **35**, 283–308.

Unwin, D.J. (1973) The distribution and orientation of corries in north Snowdonia, Wales. *Trans. Inst. Br. Geogr.*, **58**, 85–97.

Walker, M.J.C. (1982) Early and Mid-Flandrian environmental history of the Brecon Beacons, South Wales. *New Phytol.*, **91**, 147–65.

Walmsley, V.G. (1959) The geology of the Usk inlier (Monmouthshire). *Quart. J. Geol. Soc.*, **114**, 433–52.

Walsh, P.T. and Brown, E.H. (1971) Solution subsidence outliers containing probable Tertiary sediment in north-east Wales. *Geol. J.*, **7**, 299–320.

Watson, E. (1960) Glacial landforms in the Cader Idris area. *Geography*, **45**, 27–38.

Watson, E. (1962) The glacial morphology of the Tal-y-llyn Valley, Merionethshire. *Trans. Inst. Br. Geogr.*, **30**, 15–31.

Watson, E. (1970) The Cardigan Bay area, in C.A. Lewis (ed.), *The Glaciations of Wales and Adjoining Regions*. Longman. 125–45.

Whittow, J.B. and Ball, D.F. (1970) North-west Wales, in C.A. Lewis (ed.), *The Glaciations of Wales and Adjoining Regions*. Longman. 21–58.

Williams, D. (1930) The geology of the country between Nant Peris and Nant Efrancon (Snowdonia). *Quart. J. Geol. Soc.*, **86**, 191–230.

Williams, H. (1927) The geology of Snowdon (North Wales). *Quart. J. Geol. Soc.*, **83**, 346–431.

Williams, M. (1975) *The South Wales Landscape*. Hodder & Stoughton, 271 pp.

Wood, A.A. (1959) The erosional history of the cliffs around Aberystwyth. *Geol. J.*, **2**, 271–9.

Wood, A.A. and Woodland, A.W. (1968) Borehole at Mochras, west of Llanbedr, Merionethshire. *Nature*, **219**, 1352.

Woodcock, N.H. (1984) Early Palaeozoic sedimentation and tectonics in Wales. *Proc. Geol. Assoc.*, **95**, 323–36.

One of the most striking features of the terrain of northern England is the contrast in width of the lowlands on either flank of the Pennines; in the east the land below 30 metres stretches some 90 kilometres from the Pennines to the North Sea, whereas in Lancashire it averages less than half this width. Farther north the contrast between east and west becomes more apparent, for the highland mass of the

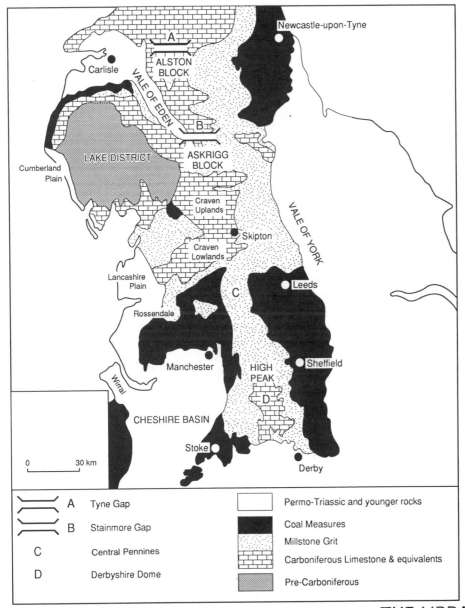

Figure 9.1 The main geological regions of northern England.

Lake District squeezes the Lancastrian and Cumbrian coastal lowlands to insignificance (Fig. 9.1). Only the Solway plain and the Vale of Eden compare in stature with the broad, fertile Vale of York and the Durham–Northumberland lowlands. The western lowlands, almost without exception, coincide with structural basins of New Red Sandstone (and some Coal Measures rocks) which lie within the highland province of old hard rocks that represent the denuded stumps of Caledonian and Hercynian mountainlands (Fig. 9.1). Because they occur within the highland zone, however, the more easily denuded younger rocks have often survived only by virtue of downwarping and downfaulting. The boundaries of these sandstone basins, therefore, are distinguished either by marked unconformities or by boundary faults similar to those which characterize the English Midlands (Taylor *et al.*, 1971). North of the Dee and Mersey the Lancashire countryside displays many similarities to the scenery of the red Midlands and, because of its easily exploited coalfields, also bears many of the selfsame scars and widespread urbanization created by the Industrial Revolution.

Because the plains of the North-West are thickly plastered with glacial material, both boulder clay and glacio-fluvial sands and gravels, the solid rocks rarely protrude at the surface except on the fringes of the uplands. For this reason the pre-glacial drainage pattern has been virtually obliterated on the lowlands where an entirely new river system has developed on the drift cover (Johnson, 1985). Nevertheless, within the Lake District and the Pennines the post-glacial rivers have retained most of their Tertiary courses though these have been greatly modified by glacial and meltwater erosion, especially in the Lake District whose ancient radial network became interrupted by new lake formation in the ice-deepened rock basins. In general, the ubiquitous drift has also created a coastline of low relief, analogous with that of East Anglia (Huddart *et al.*, 1977). At the close of the Ice Age the Irish Sea would have been considerably narrower and shallower, with the coastline of western Britain lying many kilometres west of its present position. It has been demonstrated by Tooley (1978) that between 9200 and 5000 years ago the sea level rose by some 20 metres but in the succeeding 4000 years only by a further 2.5 metres, constantly eroding till headlands and creating the shingle spits, sandbars and sand-dunes that characterize England's north-western coasts. Only at St Bee's Head, around Morecambe Bay and on the Wirral are solid rocks exposed at the coast and they are all flanked by wide valleys deeply filled with glacial drift and Flandrian marine sediments (Tooley, 1980).

The Wirral and the Mersey

The general level of this stubby peninsula of Triassic rocks is about 50 metres, its low platform coinciding largely with occurrences of Bunter Sandstones and Pebble Beds. But since these are usually mantled with glacial drifts which, on the coast at Dawpool, contain thin beds of loess amid the tills (Lee, 1969), the landscape is one of farmland, not hilly heath and forest land as at Cannock Chase (p. 142). Wherever the Keuper Sandstone occurs the Wirral landscape changes, for this hard rock usually creates sudden eminences such as Heswall Hill, Caldy Hill and Bidston Hill, with their red rocks and gorse-clad slopes. Even more striking is the forested ridge of Storeton Hill which shields the industrialization of Merseyside from the pastoral landscapes of central Wirral. In places such as Barnston tiny streams have cut picturesque gorges through the drift, down into the buried sandstone which has been quarried for the few sandstone buildings that have survived the wave of modern brick housing which has surged out from the shipbuilding centre of Birkenhead. The vast suburban estates have engulfed the Wirral's ancient villages and their half-timbered architecture has largely disappeared: the black and white village of Thornton Hough is merely a Victorian copy of a lost heritage.

The unusual shape of the Wirral peninsula has provoked an interesting hypothesis concerning its evolution. It is believed that an old deeply buried river channel between Runcorn and Shotton represents a former course of the Mersey when it is thought to have joined the Dee in pre-glacial times. The present narrow and deep estuary of the Mersey at Liverpool could be a so-called 'ice way' scooped out by an ice sheet driving south-eastwards into the Cheshire Basin, representing, therefore, one of the few *lowland* examples in southern Britain of such intense glacial erosion (Gresswell, 1964). Whatever the truth behind this speculation, there is an undoubted contrast in the character of the Dee and Mersey estuaries. The former widens seawards and is a rapidly silting, marsh-fringed inlet almost infilled with tidal mudflats and salt marshes (Marker, 1967). After the decline of Chester as a port, Parkgate, with its quay and picturesque 'waterfront', once was an embarkation point for Ireland, but now the tide never reaches it because of salt-marsh growth on the Gayton Sands. The Mersey estuary, by contrast, has a tidal flow constricted by the narrow strait between the sandstone hills of Liverpool and Wallasey, thus assisting tidal scour. Here, on the deep waterway, is a landscape of docks, oil refineries and large industrial enterprises (Gresswell and Lawton, 1968). Liverpool has expanded from its shore up on to the Keuper Sandstone ridge of Everton and beyond to the Bunter Pebble Bed hills of Anfield and Walton (Smith *et al.*, 1953). A thin wedge of Bunter Sandstone helps create the ridge on which the cathedrals stand and through which the railway has to tunnel *en route* to Lime Street Station. The famous Olive Mount cutting at Edge Hill is over 3 kilometres long and 25 metres deep (Bathurst *et al.*, 1965).

Inland, the River Mersey has been artificially deepened and channelled to accommodate the Manchester Ship Canal which links this large inland city with the sea (Carter, 1962). Since the river was the historic boundary between Saxon Northumbria and Mercia (from which it could have derived its name) the Mersey was once an ancient frontier zone of impenetrable marshes and whose lowest bridging-point was at Warrington. Though the Mersey lies several kilometres to the south of the Lancashire coalfield, its valley represented the meeting place of Cheshire salt and Lancashire coal (Gregory *et al.*, 1953), so it is not surprising that Runcorn and Widnes became the focus of an important chemical industry (Hardie, 1950), while the nearby post-glacial spread of Shirdley Hill Sand (see p. 194) led to St Helens becoming a centre of glass-making.

The South Lancashire lowlands

Where the marshy expanses of the Mersey merge into the Lancashire coalfield (Trotter, 1954a) a string of collieries once emboldened the skyline in an arc stretching eastwards from St Helens through Wigan, Leigh, Bolton, Radcliffe to Oldham, just to the north of Manchester, which itself is centred on low hills which rise above the drift-covered plain of New Red Sandstone (Jones, 1924) (see

Fig. 9.1). Heavily disturbed by faulting, the Lancashire coal seams were always expensive to work and, since they were mined largely to supply power for the local cotton industry (Ogden, 1927) which has suffered almost complete extinction since 1950, the Lancashire coalfield has itself almost ceased production (Lawton and Smith, 1953). Its contraction has left a ravaged landscape of dereliction, although the colliery waste tips are now being levelled, the mining subsidence hollows (flashes) infilled, and new housing estates are proliferating. Many of the smoke-blackened dwellings have been demolished and the veneer of industrial grime is now disappearing. The coal seams were once widely exposed at the surface, with the result that Lancashire was one of the first centres of the Industrial Revolution. There are thus few vestiges of the pre-eighteenth-century landscape to be seen. A few half-timbered houses have survived, as at Hall-i-th'-Wood at Bolton, to remind us that had it not been for the industrial development, the 'magpie architecture' of the Cheshire plain, which formerly extended into the Lancashire lowlands, would still have been commonplace in a region almost devoid of building stone (Milward, 1955).

Although the Coal Measures extend westwards almost to Ormskirk and Huyton, they are buried beneath a thick cover of drift, so that it is not until one crosses the Upholland ridge, rising some 150 metres above the plain, that a different landscape unfolds to the west. The ridge itself results from a faulted slice of Millstone Grit emerging through the Coal Measures and the low crest gives a good western vantage point for distinguishing the bright green farmlands from the coppiced woodlands and the black soils of the reclaimed mosses that stretch westwards to the coastal dunes of Formby. Although New Red Sandstone makes up the floor of western Lancashire between the Mersey and Morecambe Bay, the solid rocks rarely emerge from beneath their thick covering of glacial and post-glacial deposits. Thus, while the eastern landscape represents the industrial face of eastern Lancashire and is a landscape of defunct collieries, where the cotton industry also thrived throughout the nineteenth and early twentieth centuries (Rogers, 1960), the western tract owes more to the detailed contrasts in soil and drainage characteristics of its extensive drift cover than to the mineral wealth derived from the solid rocks (Fig. 9.2).

As the ice sheets melted, hollows in the undulating blanket of boulder clay eventually became infilled with post-glacial peat. Place names incorporating 'moss' and 'mere' occur frequently in the area today but give little indication of their former meaning except for their association with a mosaic of carefully maintained ditches and drains, where the black peaty soils mark the former hollows. One of the most extensive of the superficial deposits is the wind-blown Shirdley Hill sand (Wilson *et al.*, 1981) which emerges from beneath Downholland Moss and extends east to the slopes of the Upholland ridge. Its enclosed peat layers have been dated to early Boreal times (9000 years ago) though their fossil birch and pine remnants already show signs of artificial clearance during the succeeding millennia of late Mesolithic and Neolithic times (sub-Boreal, 3000–5000 years ago). Farther westwards, below an elevation of 7 metres, many extensive mosses now mark the sites of former reedswamps and alder and oak fens that once grew in the lagoons and tidal flats created by the earliest transgressions of the rising Flandrian sea (see p. 192). The most notable are Downholland Moss, Martin Moss and Altcar Moss (south Lancashire), Lytham Moss (Fylde), Cockerham Moss (Over Wyre) and Silverdale, Heysham and White Mosses (around Morecambe Bay) (Shimwell, 1985). By

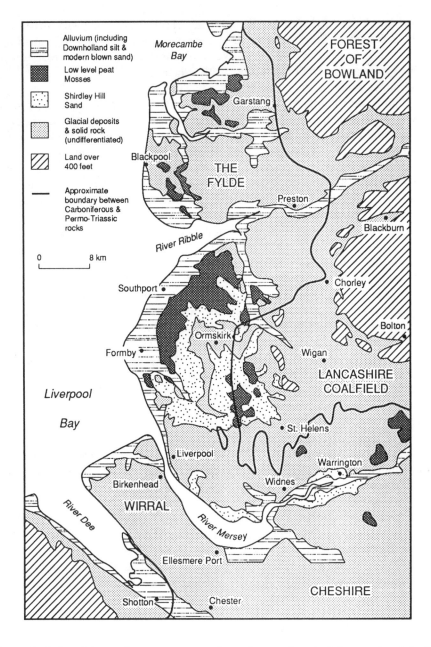

Figure 9.2 Drift map of Lancashire and Merseyside.

the end of the eighteenth century extensive schemes for draining and reclaiming the mosses had already been implemented. But Defoe's 1725 description of the notorious Chat Moss (Birks, 1964), between Liverpool and Manchester, prior to its reclamation, gives an indication of the state of these lowlands prior to their conversion to one of Britain's most fertile arable farming tracts, comparable with those on the highly productive soils of the Fenlands:

> The surface, at a distance looks black and dirty, and is indeed frightful to think of, for it will bear neither horse or man . . . what nature meant by such a useless production, 'tis hard to imagine; but the land is entirely waste.

The mosslands studded with meres, the heavy clay soils of the glacial drift plain and the barren sand dunes along the Irish Sea coast, all contributed to a landscape hardly conducive to early settlement. Not until the draining of the mosses do we see the Victorian resorts of Southport and Blackpool begin to flourish on the coastal dunes (Freeman *et al.*, 1966).

Blackpool was sited where low boulder-clay cliffs emerge from the stretches of post-glacial marshland and blown sand that fringe the stretch of coastal plain know as the Fylde (Old English *gefilde* means 'plain') between the Ribble estuary and Morecambe Bay (Gresswell, 1967). Its undulating surface of boulder clay, with occasional mounds of glacial sand and gravel, is today an ordered landscape of neat fields, well-trimmed hedgerows and carefully enclosed woodlands. It is difficult to realize that this rich farmland, with its verdant pastures carrying a heavy density of livestock, was once a dreary expanse of bleak marshlands similar to those of south-west Lancashire. Its modern dairy herds are more comparable, however, with those of Cheshire, although pigs, sheep and poultry also abound on the fertile grasslands (Smith, 1937). Fleetwood, at the mouth of the Wyre, which drains the Fylde, was once a great fishing port but today its trawlers have been replaced by broad-beamed container ships bound for Ireland. East of here, where the Lune enters Morecambe Bay, the Forest of Bowland and the Namurian grits and shales of the Lancaster fells (Moseley, 1953) effectively terminate the Lancashire plain where it has been inundated by Morecambe Bay itself. Here the ancient town of Lancaster stands amid its drumlins, dominating the historic routeways to the North.

Morecambe Bay and the Cumbrian coast

Mudflats, salt marshes (Gray, 1972) and sandbanks characterize the broad but shallow indentation of Morecambe Bay carved out by the sea from a structural basin of New Red Sandstone that is banked up against the surrounding rim of older Palaeozoic rocks. Though the Triassic rocks are mainly submerged beneath the sea (where they conceal a significant natural gas reservoir) they emerge on the perimeter of the bay near Heysham, but also on the Cartmel peninsula and in Furness (Dunham and Rose, 1948). Elsewhere, the encroaching Flandrian sea has pushed the coastline back to the fringing strata of Carboniferous Limestone which had earlier been tilted by faulting into horst-like wedges with generally northward pointing apices that interdigitate with the older Palaeozoics. Several rivers, most notably the Leven and Kent, debouch into Morecambe Bay, helping create a coastline fretted with marshy creeks and tidal inlets. The alluvial deposits are covered by peat bogs, termed 'mosses', or salt marshes, some of which have been reclaimed (Oldfield, 1960; Dickinson, 1973). It has been suggested that Silverdale Moss, on the southern edge of the Kent estuary, and nearby New Barns Moss, occupy flat-floored, steep-sided limestone solution hollows known as *poljes*, much smaller than their more celebrated Yugoslavian counterparts. By contrast, many of the low headlands are carved from Carboniferous Limestone whose white rocks, grassy hollows and dark green woodlands 'cling like a garland about the hem of the capricious sea' (Edwin Waugh). Whether the capricious sea will be excluded from the bay in the future by an artificial barrage remains to be seen. Sheep and cattle are reared on the lush grasslands of the coastal limestones and on the poorer grazings of the alluvial flats and the salt marshes (Gray, 1972) in the silted-up estuaries, but there are tiny plots of arable on the hummocky land to provide root crops for winter stock feeding. Moreover, on the New Red Sandstone the lighter soils have produced other important pockets of arable on the Cartmel and Furness peninsulas. In the mid-nineteenth century one writer proclaimed the cornfields of the 'rich district of Furness the redeeming feature of Lancashire farming'. Attractive villages such as Cartmel, with its medieval gate-house and priory church, and Beetham, with its ancient water mills, are built largely from the dove-grey Carboniferous Limestone. The tiny coastal village of Silverdale, too, is limestone-built, its straggling houses and old copper-smelting furnace being set in a labyrinth of stone field walls, silver-grey crags and scattered woodlands. The fossiliferous Carboniferous Limestone produces a lime-rich soil on which tormentil, columbine, milkwort and various orchids flourish, as do the native trees of yew, juniper and Scots pine. Arnside Knott is a good viewpoint for Morecambe Bay, its name reminding us that 'knot' means a rounded hill. Indeed, many of the limestone hills hereabouts have been rounded by the passage of ice sheets from the nearby Lake District and their naked limestone pavements are a testimony to the processes of water erosion and solution, termed *karstification* (Ashmead, 1974), as well as to the smoothing and plucking action of glacier ice. Nowhere is this better illustrated than at Hutton Roof and Newbiggin Crags, whose ice-scoured pavements carry patches of wind-blown loess, dating from the Devensian period of the Ice Age. The loess occupies depressions and is identifiable by its heathery cover, a vegetation type not normally associated with Carbon-iferous Limestone. The drift-plugged valleys of the rivers Kent and Lune exhibit a contrasting terrain, for here the ice sheets which scraped the rocky outcrops moulded the glacial drift into whale-backed drumlins. The Lune itself, working along a faultline, has cut headwards through the Lune gorge to capture some of the formerly north-flowing headwaters of the Eden near Tebay (Harvey, 1985). Either glacial ice or meltwater erosion was responsible for this diversion because the deep gorge breaches one of the major pre-glacial watersheds in northern England (between the Pennines and the Lake District), thereby affording passage for the M6 motorway.

Because the Carboniferous Limestone of the Furness peninsula contains rich deposits of haematite iron ore, the landscapes around Dalton, Askam, Barrow and Millom present a very different picture to those on the eastern shores of Morecambe Bay. Though the ores are now exhausted and the blast furnaces closed, the legacy of nineteenth-century industry, with its regimented streets of slate-roofed brick houses, remains. Barrow's formerly important shipbuilding industry has also declined, leaving Vickerstown inhabitants to contemplate the bleak scenery of drumlins, storm beaches, marshy flats and sand-dunes that together make up the slender strip of Walney Island (Grieve and Hammersley, 1971). But in compensation the nearby Duddon estuary, with its wide sweep of yellow sands and sheep-grazed turf, adds to the magnificent backdrop of Lakeland fells, especially that of Black Combe. To the north, the narrow Cumbrian coastal plain is also dominated by industry both ancient and modern. The usual clutter of the worked-out Cumberland coalfield partly disfigures the narrow mountain-girt tract between Whitehaven, Workington and Maryport where a heavily faulted strip of Coal Measures dips away from the mountains north-westwards beneath the Irish Sea (Trotter, 1954b). The dark brown Upper Coal Measures Sandstone, some 300 metres thick, gives way to the south of Whitehaven to the bright red Triassic Sandstone from which the high cliffs of St Bees Head have been carved (Smith *et al.*, 1925). Here, a chemical factory, based partly on the anhydrite of the Triassic rocks, forms a prominent coastal landmark, although not as notorious as the nuclear installations of Sellafield several kilometres farther south. Whitehaven exemplifies the choice of building stone available hereabouts, for while its harbour was built with Coal Measures Sandstone its churches were constructed from the pinker St Bees Sandstone. As one passes northwards towards Silloth the cold, heavy clay soils which mark the boulder clays that overlie the Coal Measures, give way to good alluvial soils on the warplands that lie behind the coastal marshes of Solway Firth (Marshall, 1962). The warplands, developed on extensive marine clays, are clothed with a superb sward of short, springy grass that finds a ready market for lawns and sportsgrounds all over Britain. As in southern Lancashire, there are also several partly drained peaty mosses, such as Wedholme Flow, Bowness Common and Solway Moss, where cattle and sheep graze between the artificial drains of these windswept plains.

The Vale of Eden

The fertile chequerboard field pattern of Edenside contrasts strongly with the land use and scenery of high, barren and drab moorlands of the Pennines to the east. The latter's scarped edge rises sharply from the plain by virtue of a massive fault which has uplifted the hard rocks and lowered the New Red Sandstone to form the Vale of Eden. One is immediately reminded of the Vale of Clwyd and the neighbouring Clwydian Hills in North Wales, where the geology and faulted escarpment structures are almost identical.

On the flanks of Cross Fell, the Pennines' highest peak (823 m), the steep mountain wall is interrupted by a shelf of older Ordovician rocks exposed on the face of the fault-line scarp beneath the capping of Carboniferous limestones and shales which form the edge of the Pennines' tilted plateau. These Ordovician rocks, of similar age to those of the northern Lake District, are part of the 'basement' of northern England which underlies the Pennines. An examination of the composition of the various New Red Sandstones, termed the Penrith Sandstone (Permian), the St Bees Sandstone and the Kirklinton Sandstone (both Triassic), allows a reconstruction of the landscape at the time of their formation about 250 million years ago. Some of the oldest beds are termed *brockrams* (Smith, 1924), which were used by the Romans to aid in the construction of Hadrian's Wall and have subsequently been quarried near Kirkby Stephen and Appleby for local buildings. Initially those rocks were coarse, angular screes or breccias, consisting mainly of Carboniferous Limestone fragments in a matrix of red desert sandstone. By contrast, the overlying Penrith Sandstone is characterized by well-rounded wind-blown sand grains cemented by secondary quartz and it is this bright red sandstone which gives so much character to the urban fabric of the attractive market town of Penrith. The River Petteril, which rises near Penrith and flows north to Carlisle, has picked out the western boundary of this glowing Permian sandstone outcrop and, in working along it as a strike-stream, has left a marked west-facing sandstone scarp which acts as a watershed between the Petteril and Eden rivers that flow parallel all the way to Carlisle. Here the Permian sandstone ridge disappears and it is upon a bluff of Triassic rocks that the old fortified border city of Carlisle was founded. Most of it is brick-built although many of its churches and civic buildings are constructed of New Red Sandstone. Carlisle's surrounding plain coincides with an expanse of Keuper Clays which extend to the coast at Silloth, but are everywhere thickly plastered with glacial drift, though at Great Orton a small tableland stands above the general level due to a very isolated outlier of dark blue shales and limestones of Lower Liassic age. It is the glacial drift, however, coloured red by the underlying rocks, which creates the real scenic character of the Carlisle plain and the northern end of Edenside (Hollingworth, 1931). Both Scottish and Lakeland ice sheets moved southwards up the Vale of Eden, fashioning the drift into parallel ridges and hollows (Huddart, 1971). Some of the ridges break up into drumlins, smooth hillocks, oval in plan and with the 'upstream' ends steeper and blunter than their other slopes. By contrast, glacio-fluvial sands and gravels, produced by melting ice, are often associated with 'kames' and 'deltas' formed in ephemeral ice-ponded lakes (Huddart and Tooley, 1972), all well exemplified in the Brampton area where steeply-sloping gravel hills rise 30 metres above the plain. These sandy ridges are easier to work than the less tractable soils of the boulder clay, so a distinction is clearly visible between the patchy arable lands and the large areas of permanent grassland well known for both dairying and the fattening of cattle. Nevertheless, on both flanks of the vale one passes rapidly from this rich farming country with its woods and hedgerows to the treeless moorlands and poorer-quality grasslands of the Pennines and the Lake District where sheep graze in open pastures occasionally enclosed by drystone walls and where arable land is a rarity.

The Lake District

The scenery of Lakeland is familiar to so many that it is almost unnecessary to praise its quality (Griffin, 1968); suffice to say that as early as 1810 Wordsworth was confessing that he did not know 'any tract of country in which, in so narrow a compass, may be found an equal variety in the influences of light and shadow upon the sublime and beautiful features of the landscape'. In some ways it is this compactness which is so appealing, for within its 50 kilometre diameter the Lake District boasts craggy cliffs, bare fells, deep ravines, tumbling waterfalls, impressive woodlands and, above all, a wonderful variety of lakes. Because of its heavy rainfall and high relief there are few tracts of cultivated land within the uplands themselves, but where the valleys open out on to the surrounding lowlands the improved lands become widespread and it is around the perimeter that the old market towns of Kendal, Penrith and Cockermouth are situated.

The general make-up of the region's geology can be described briefly as a denuded massif of early Palaeozoic rocks surrounded by a rim of Carboniferous and New Red Sandstone strata which dip away from it on all sides (Cumberland Geological Society, 1982; Hollingworth, 1954). In detail, however, the central core of ancient rocks is quite complex for it encompasses not only a variety of sedimentaries but also an important group of volcanics and some significant igneous intrusions (Moseley, 1978). Indeed, Bott (1978) expounded a theory to explain that Lakeland has long remained an upland area because of the emplacement of an enormous granite batholith during the Caledonian mountain-building episode some 400 million years ago (Fig. 9.3a). Extending at depth from Durham to the Isle of Man, this batholith is comparable in size with that underlying South-West England (Chapter 2), although in the Lake District masses of granitic magma invaded the roots not of a Hercynian but a Caledonian mountain range (Brown *et al.*, 1964) whose subsequent denudation has unroofed parts of the granite in the relatively small exposures (from west to east) of the Eskdale Granite, the Ennerdale Granophyre (Rastall, 1906), the Skiddaw Granite and the Shap Granite (Grantham, 1928).

A study of Fig. 9.3c will show how Lakeland's oldest sedimentary rocks are the Skiddaw Group (Jackson, 1978), a series of dark slates interbedded with occasional flags and grits, all of Lower Ordovician age, that is, similar to those of Snowdonia. Because they have since been subjected to a low-grade metamorphic episode, however, these sedimentaries now exhibit a distinctive cleavage which, together with their shaly nature, means that the Skiddaw Group weathers quickly into easily transported rock slivers that clothe the mountain slopes with aprons of debris. Thus, the uniformly smooth cones of the mountains to the north of Keswick give a distinctive skyline when viewed from Derwentwater, with Skiddaw (931 m) and Saddleback (868 m) dominating the view. The few crags occurring in the Skiddaw Group of rocks (Goat Crags in the Grasmoor mountain group, for example) have been carved either from gritstone bands or from sedimentary rocks hardened in the metamorphic aureole around the fringes of the granitic intrusions. Some 250 years ago Skiddaw was one of the first British mountains to have been climbed for the sake of its scenery, and the intrepid visitors were stirred by this 'stupendous mountain' with its 'chasms and enormous depths'. Because the slaty cleavage is different from that in North Wales, the Skiddaw Slates are useless for large-scale commercial exploitation and, although they are suitable for drystone walls and some vernacular building the Skiddaw Slate country is, therefore, devoid of the vast slate quarries that so disfigure the slate belt of Snowdonia. Instead, the area has a few small mines following the mineral veins formed in association with the granitic intrusions (Shaw, 1970). Although the copper mines are now closed and the barytes mine at Force Crag worked only sporadically, the graphite vein at Keswick (now worked out) supplied the famous pencil works which continues to thrive, but on imported raw material.

A curved line drawn roughly from central Ullswater westwards through southern Derwentwater to Ennerdale separates the smoothly profiled fells of the Skiddaw Group of northern Lakeland from the broken, irregular outlines of the central tract of mountains carved from the Borrowdale Volcanic Group of rocks (Upper Ordovician), as illustrated in Fig. 9.3c. This is the heart of the Lake District and contains most of its highest summits, but it is largely the ruggedness of the terrain which gives central Lakeland its special character. In terms of its geological history, the lengthy period of Ordovician explosive vulcanicity, like that in Snowdonia, marks the final collision of two primeval tectonic plates 500 million years ago which led to the development of a volcanic island-arc system analagous with those of the modern West Indies or the Aleutians. As the descending oceanic plate was overridden by its continental counterpart (at a junction termed a *subduction zone*) the rock-melting caused magma to surge upwards through the crust where it burst out as lava flows, ranging in mineral composition from basaltic (basic) to rhyolitic (acidic), all associated with extensive pyroclastic deposits ejected from the volcanic vents. Particularly common are the welded tuffs, known

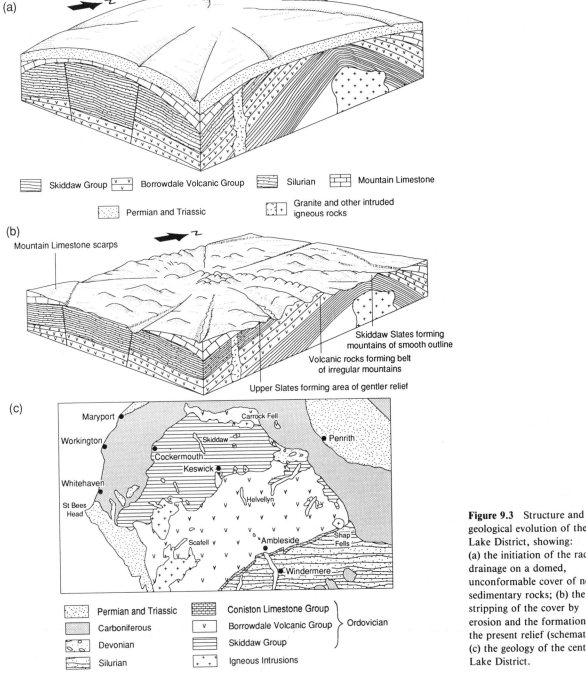

(a)

Skiddaw Group   Borrowdale Volcanic Group   Silurian   Mountain Limestone

Permian and Triassic   Granite and other intruded igneous rocks

(b)

Mountain Limestone scarps

Skiddaw Slates forming mountains of smooth outline

Volcanic rocks forming belt of irregular mountains

Upper Slates forming area of gentler relief

(c)

Maryport   Carrock Fell

Workington   Skiddaw   Penrith

Cockermouth
Keswick

Whitehaven

St Bees Head

Helvellyn

Scafell   Ambleside   Shap Fells

Windermere

Permian and Triassic   Coniston Limestone Group

Carboniferous   Borrowdale Volcanic Group   } Ordovician

Devonian   Skiddaw Group

Silurian   Igneous Intrusions

Figure 9.3 Structure and geological evolution of the Lake District, showing: (a) the initiation of the radial drainage on a domed, unconformable cover of newer sedimentary rocks; (b) the stripping of the cover by erosion and the formation of the present relief (schematic); (c) the geology of the central Lake District.

as *ignimbrites*, whose ejected fragments became fused together while they were still hot. Because the volcanoes erupted on the sea floor it is not surprising that, as in Snowdonia, the volcanic strata are interbedded with layers of sediment, ranging in texture from coarse grits to fine muds (Green, 1919). The latter have often been converted into true slates by enormous pressures, but paradoxically, the well-known green 'slates' of Honister Crag (Fig. 9.4) above Buttermere, that are still being sporadically worked for wall-cladding material and for other ornamental purposes, are not true slates but a well-cleaved, fine-grained volcanic ash (Clark, 1964).

In general, the lavas, ignimbrites and volcanic intrusive rocks (dykes and sills) stand out as crags and cliffs while the less resistant volcanic ash beds and finer-grained sedimentary rocks have been worn down into valleys and combes, though this is not invariably true (Moseley, 1986). Wherever well-developed joint-planes cut through the tougher outcrops they have often been sculptured into spectacular rock faces beloved by climbers, occurring especially where glacier ice has steepened the valley sides or the back-walls of the cirques. Though all the fells have been ice-scoured and frost-shattered, it is never difficult to pick out the volcanic terrain because all its eminences are knobbly, bony and gnarled by comparison with the smoother lines of the surrounding sedimentary rocks (Fig. 9.5). Most of Lakeland's highest and best-known summits belong to this volcanic country including Helvellyn (Hartley, 1942), Scafell (Oliver, 1961), Great Gable and the

Figure 9.4 Honister Crag at the head of the U-shaped glacial valley above Buttermere in the Lake District. The so-called 'slate' quarry, in the face of the Crag on the left, is more strictly working a fine-grained volcanic ash.

Langdale Pikes (Hartley, 1932). Great Gable (899 m), with its screes, crags and pinnacles (for instance, Napes Needle) is one of the region's finest viewpoints because it stands at the head of Wasdale, arguably Lakeland's most dramatic and primitive valley. When early visitors spoke of the lakes 'as beauty lying in the lap of Horrour' they may well have had in mind the silvery expanse of Wastwater, Lakeland's deepest lake, set amid its rugged amphitheatre of towering peaks (Firmin, 1957). Wasdale's glacially deepened trough, its remarkable suite of screes descending into the lake, its ice-scraped rocks and tiny cluster of fields around the lonely trough's end of Wasdale Head, all combine to create an unforgettable panorama. In contrast to this stark, treeless upland valley, Wasdale's lower reaches, below Nether Wasdale village, exhibit some of the Lake District's best surviving examples of natural broadleaf woodland that was once more widespread. Ash and oak woodlands flourish on either bank of the River Irt, although more modern conifer plantations are now more commonplace in other western valleys such as Ennerdale, completely changing its character over the last sixty years. Many of Lakeland's central valleys also retain vestiges of the natural broadleaf woodland cover (Pearsall, 1921), especially around Rydal Water and Grasmere, though there has been considerable tree-planting hereabouts since

Figure 9.5 A view of the type of rugged terrain carved from the Borrowdale Volcanic Series in the Lake District.

the nineteenth century in order to counteract the wholesale forest clearance of previous centuries. When Defoe visited the region early in the eighteenth century he recorded how the land seemed 'all barren and wild, of no use or advantage either to man or beast'. A century later, however, Lakeland's earliest botanists and its celebrated Romantic poets were eulogizing over the region's sylvan beauty, its diverse mountain plants (Ratcliffe, 1960) and the picturesque charm of the gorges and waterfalls. Visiting Stockgill Force near Ambleside, Keats remarked upon 'the tone, the colouring, the slate, the moss, the rockweed', all elements that characterize the sudden transition into southern Lakeland's gentler park-like country of lower relief that replaces the stark Borrowdale volcanic tract lying north of a line drawn from Ambleside through Coniston to the Duddon Valley. The scenic change is particularly noticeable where the rugged Tilberthwaite and Coniston Fells form the edge of the true mountainland between Lake Windermere and the town of Coniston (Hartley, 1925).

The rocks forming the southern part of the Lake District are somewhat like those of the Skiddaw range, but whereas the latter are older than the volcanic rocks, those south of Ambleside are newer sedimentaries of Silurian age (Ingham *et al.*, 1978). One of the most interesting is the Coniston Limestone which has an influence on the scenery out of all proportion to its width of outcrop (see Fig. 9.3c). Stretching north-eastwards as a narrow band from the Duddon Valley through Coniston, Tarn Hows and Waterhead to beyond Troutbeck, its interest lies in its effect on the vegetation; in a region of acid soils the limestone, which is really a lime-rich fossiliferous mudstone, supports lime-loving plants and an altogether lusher and greener ground cover than elsewhere (Pearsall and Pennington, 1973). The limestone does not create strong topographic features but instead marks an important boundary between the rugged volcanic country of the central fells and the more subdued topography of the Silurian rocks further south. These southward-dipping shales, mudstones and sandstones originated in the same manner as those of the Skiddaw Group, as muddy and gritty sediments on the sea floor. But because they weather more easily than the Skiddaw rocks and form better soils, the hills are lower and their profiles more rounded than those of the north. Moreover, they support more flourishing farmlands and broadleaf woodlands than the Skiddaw sedimentaries which instead carry stretches of bog, moorland, scrawny pastures and scattered coniferous plantations. Thus, southern Lakeland possesses far more pastoral charm despite the fact that it contains the Lake District's main commercial slate belt in a narrow tract extending from the Duddon Valley north-eastwards through the Tilberthwaite Fells, Elterwater and Ambleside to the Kirkstone Pass (Milward and Robinson, 1970). Surprisingly, this slate belt possesses little of the bare austerity of the Snowdonian slate country, where recent studies have shown that no less than 80 per cent of Snowdonia's broad-leaf woodlands are failing to regenerate, largely due to livestock grazing in a region where some two-thirds of the wooded areas are unenclosed. By contrast, because the Lakelander has remained predominantly a farmer who has enclosed his fields, and because the slate industry has played a comparatively minor role by comparison with that of North Wales, the woodlands are more thriving and the Lake District quarries are not so scenically intrusive except around Elterwater village. Lakeland slates are generally blue-grey in colour, save those near to Ambleside which have a greenish-grey hue. These roofing slates, formerly termed Westmorland Slates, are thicker and heavier than Welsh slates, thereby necessitating heavier roof beams to withstand their weight. The flaggy stone left as a by-product of the roofing-slate industry makes an excellent building material for cottage and drystone wall alike. Although many rural cottages and farms have been liberally coated with whitewash, the towns and villages retain a certain dourness due to their untreated flagstone walling, except where slate-hanging adds an attractive dimension in villages such as Hawkshead. A discerning analysis of the relationship between Lakeland landscape and its architecture is that of Wordsworth, who noted that the cottages,

> of rough unhewn stone, are roofed with slates which were rudely taken from the quarry before the present art of cutting them was understood, and are therefore rough and uneven in their surface, so that both the coverings and sides of the houses have furnished places of rest for the seeds of lichens, mosses and flowers. Hence buildings which in their very form call to mind the presence of nature, do thus, clothed in part with a vegetable garb, appear to be received into the bosom of the living principle of things as it acts and exists among the fields and woods.

Nowhere are these woodlands more beautifully displayed than along the lakeshores, especially those of Windermere, Grasmere, Ullswater, Derwentwater and Buttermere, though it is more important to understand how the lakes themselves were formed. In any explanation of the Lake District's water bodies and river systems it is essential to start with an examination of the regional structure. The concentric disposition of the Carboniferous and New Red Sandstone rocks in North-West England led early geologists to postulate that since they currently outcrop in a peripheral ring around the older Lakeland Palaeozoic rocks they must once have covered them completely. The structural relationship is one of marked unconformity, as illustrated in Fig. 9.3a, suggesting that, first, the Carboniferous Limestone was laid down unconformably across an updomed but severely folded and denuded massif of older rocks; second, the whole area was domed once more, this time by Hercynian uplift which caused considerable erosion of both the limestone and of the older Lakeland rocks; and third, a layer of Permian and Triassic sedimentaries was deposited unconformably across this freshly denuded surface. The final episode appears to have been one of tectonic uplift in mid-Tertiary times to create the elongated dome from which the present Lake District landscape has been carved. Most writers (Monkhouse, 1972) are agreed that the radial drainage pattern was initiated on the dome's cover of younger rocks and that in wearing away the latter, thereby exposing the primeval 'core' that now forms the central fells, the rivers gradually became superimposed upon these older underlying rocks (see Fig. 9.3b). Some authors have suggested that there is no true radial pattern but merely a structurally guided set of north- and south-flowing rivers diverging from a central axis that extends eastwards from Great Gable, through the Langdale Pikes, Dunmail Raise and the Kirkstone Pass to Shap. Although a few valleys are aligned along anticlinal axes (for example, Ullswater) or faults (Thirlmere) the radial pattern is convincing enough to suggest that superimposition from an uplifted cover of younger strata is still the most likely explanation. By the onset of the Ice Age the river pattern had been long established but there seems little doubt that glaciers and glacial meltwaters have played a major role in emphasizing the remarkably incised valley pattern that exists today.

The Lake District mountains probably acted as an ice-dispersal centre at various times during the stadials of the Pleistocene but, with one exception in Mosedale Beck (Boardman, 1982), the only surviving glacial and periglacial deposits date almost exclusively from late-Devensian times (after 28 000 years ago). Moreover, although the glacial troughs and cirques may well have been initiated during earlier glacial advances the features seen today were probably fashioned largely by Devensian glaciers (Boardman, 1988). The latter, moving radially outwards, came into contact with Scottish ice sheets which divided around the Lake District to pass down the Cumbrian coast and southwards along the Vale of Eden. That their ice margins oscillated is shown by the intermingling of erratics from both Scottish and Lake District sources. For example, boulders of Criffel granite from southern Scotland are found at elevations up to 300 metres on the western Lakeland fells, while at the foot of Ennerdale erratics from the Borrowdale Volcanic tract occur in a local till that overlies a northern red boulder clay containing pebbles of coal and St Bees standstone. During the maximum extent of the Ice Age the British ice sheets would have been thick enough to bury the Lake District summits to a depth of some 700 metres, demonstrating that considerable glacial scouring and erosion of its soils and regolith must have occurred. Only during the last phases of the Devensian would the rugged peaks have stood starkly above the glacier-filled valleys and it was then that their summits and flanks would have begun to be riven by frost action, a process that continues today. It was in this manner that the severely denuded dome received its final sculpturing by both glacial and periglacial processes, long before its famous lakes appeared.

Part of the Lake District's original dome-like profile can still be seen in such smooth mountain ridges as Helvellyn (949 m) and High Street (828 m), although their flanks are deeply scarred with cirques (Clough, 1977) and trenched by glacial troughs. Some of the ice-eroded hollows are occupied by tiny lakes or tarns, often impounded by cirque moraines dating from the Loch Lomond Stadial (Sissons, 1980): Blea Water, beneath the eastern face of High Street; Goat's Water, under the frowning cliffs of Dow Crag; Stickle Tarn, amid the Langdale Pikes; and, most striking of all, Red Tarn, encompassed by Helvellyn's twin eastern arêtes of Swirral Edge and Striding Edge. As in Snowdonia, the majority of the cirques face north-east, an aspect favouring the retention of ice and snow (Temple, 1965), but the glacier-steepened cliffs elsewhere in the Lake District often owe their form and location more to the direction of ice movement and the character of the rocks than simply to aspect. Thus, Great Gable's pinnacled ridge faces south, as does Gimmer Crag in Langdale, while the awesome precipices of Pillar Rock and Scafell Pinnacle look due north – all of them having been carved from well-jointed Borrowdale Volcanics.

Apart from its rugged mountains, the Lake District is also renowned for its remarkably ice-scoured valleys, some of which have been so overdeepened that lengthy but narrow post-glacial lakes have subsequently formed on their valley floors. Apart from Wasdale, described above, the most spectacular U-shaped valleys are Ennerdale, Honister (see Fig. 9.4), Borrowdale, Langdale and Grisedale. Farther downvalley from the jutting prow of Honister Crag, the twin lakes of Buttermere and Crummock Water were obviously once a single water body but have since been separated by a post-glacial stream delta. Sombre Borrowdale has picturesque Derwentwater at its northern end, located where the glacial trough broadens out on crossing from the volcanic rocks into the more easily eroded Skiddaw sedimentaries. The River Derwent, which drains from the northern end of the lake at Portinscale, passes through Bassenthwaite Lake before meandering to the Irish Sea at Workington. Ullswater's serpentine form illustrates how its entrenched upper end, overlooked by high fells, occurs in the rugged volcanic tract (Moseley, 1960), while its lower reaches thread through the less elevated hill country of Skiddaw slates and mudstones. Both Thirlmere and Hawes Water can be dismissed because both have been artificially enlarged to serve as reservoirs, the latter having inundated a former village in the glacial trough of Mardale. But Coniston Water and Windermere are both natural 'finger' lakes occupying long narrow valleys in the gentle, undulating fell country of the Silurian rocks in southern Lakeland. Windermere, at 17 kilometres England's longest lake, is not only renowned for its beautiful islands and woodlands but also for the fact that its sediments provide the type-site for the Pleistocene's last short interlude of climatic warming, the so-called Windermere Interstadial, prior to the final cold phase of the Ice Age during the Loch Lomond Stadial (Coope and Pennington, 1977). During the latter's frigid phase, some 10 000 to 10 500 years ago, some 64 glaciers became re-established in the Lakeland cirques, with some advancing to leave moraines in such valleys as Langdale; in all they extended over an area of 55 km^2 (Sissons, 1980). As modern tourists visit the enormous perched block of the Bowder Stone above Borrowdale, marvel at the tumbling Falls of Lodore on Derwentwater's ice-steepened shore, or drive rapidly across one of the two deep glacial breaches through the main pre-glacial drainage divide at Dunmail Raise (Fig. 9.6) (the Kirkstone Pass is the other), how many of them realize that all were created by ice action?

Figure 9.6 Grasmere and the glacial breach of Dunmail Raise carved through the Lake District's main pre-glacial watershed. The slopes on the right rise to the summit of Helvellyn.

Several centuries after the glaciers had gone, during which time vegetation had re-established itself on the fells (Walker, 1965), primitive Stone Age arrivals soon discovered that certain of Lakeland's volcanic rocks could be fashioned into artefacts, with the stone-axe 'factories' on the slopes of Great Gable, Scafell and the Langdale Pikes sending their products all over Britain. Yet the austere mountainland remained almost devoid of settlement even in the succeeding Bronze Age, notwithstanding the two well-preserved stone circles of Castlerigg (near Keswick) and Swinside (near Millom) both of which are peripheral to the central fells. During Roman times Lakeland was part of their military zone; a Roman road climbs steadily along High Street's summit ridge, while another strikes westwards from Ambleside across the windy western fells and past the ruins of Hard Knott fort before reaching the former coastal stronghold at Ravenglass. Nevertheless it was the Norsemen who finally settled the Lake District and many place names testify to these Viking colonists. The term *thwaite*, for example, means 'clearing in a forest', and even today Stonethwaite in Borrowdale conveys the difficulties involved in taming this boulder-choked valley, for the Vikings were sufficiently astute to place their hamlets on poorer ground in order to reserve the fertile soils for their arable plots and hay meadows. They also had an eye for water supply and safety, as exemplified by the village of Troutbeck, strung out along a valleyside springline and above the winter flood level.

Today many Lakeland cottages and farmhouses still occupy these early sites, possibly built with some of the stones first cleared from their tiny fields by the Norsemen. The oldest of the buildings is the longhouse in which dwelling, byre and barn were all constructed under one roof. The rubble stone was generally uncoursed and laid without mortar except for the more vulnerable chimney stacks, some of which were distinctively circular to avoid having to make difficult corners with bulky volcanic stones. Although many modern farmhouses have been whitewashed it is the untreated masonry of the outhouses that conveys Lakeland's true character. 'They may rather be said to have grown than to be erected – to have risen, by an instinct of their own, out of the native rock – so little is there in them of formality, such is their wildness and beauty'. Thus wrote Wordsworth, and it is appropriate to let him have the final word.

Bibliography

Ashmead, P. (1974) The caves and karst of the Morecambe Bay area. In A. C. Waltham (ed.), *The Limestones and Caves of North West England*. David and Charles. 201–26.

Bathurst, R. G. C., Harper, J. C., Eagar, R. M. C. *et al.* (1965). *Geology Around the University Towns: Liverpool*. Guide no. 6. Geol. Ass.

Birks, H. J. B. (1964) Chat Moss, Lancashire. *Mem. Proc. Manchr. Lit. Phil. Soc.,* **106,** 1–45.

Boardman, J. (1982) Glacial geomorphology of the Keswick area, northern Cumbria. *Proc. Cumbs. Geol. Soc.,* **4,** 115–34.

Boardman, J. (1988) *Classic Landforms of the Lake District*. Classic Landform Guide no. 8. Geog. Ass.

Bott, M. H. P. (1978) Deep Structure, in F. Moseley (ed.) *The Geology of the Lake District*. Yorks. Geol. Soc. Occasional Publications, Leeds, no. 3.

Brown, P. E., Miller, J. A. and Soper, N. J. (1964) Age of the principal intrusions of the Lake District. *Proc. Yorks. Geol. Soc.,* **34,** 331–42.

Carter, C. F. (ed.) (1962) *Manchester and its Region*. Manchester University Press. 265 pp.

Clark, L. (1964) The Borrowdale Volcanic series between Buttermere and Wasdale, Cumberland. *Proc. Yorks. Geol. Soc.,* **34**, 343–56.

Clough, R. McK. (1977) Some aspects of corrie initiation and evolution in the English Lake District. *Proc. Cumbs. Geol. Soc.,* **3**, 209–32.

Coope, G.R. and Pennington, W. (1977) The Windermere Interstadial of the Late Devensian. *Phil. Trans. R. Soc. B,* **280**, 337–39.

Cumberland Geological Society (1982) *The Lake District.* Unwin. 136 pp.

Dickinson, W. (1973) The development of the raised bog complex near Rusland in the Furness district of north Lancashire. *J. Ecol.,* **61**, 871–86.

Dunham, K.C. and Rose, W.C.C. (1948) Permo-Triassic geology of South Cumberland and Furness. *Proc. Geol. Assoc.,* **60**, 11–40.

Firmin, R.J. (1957) The Borrowdale Volcanic series between Wastwater and Duddon Valley. *Proc. Yorks. Geol. Soc.,* **31**, 39–64.

Freeman, T.W., Rogers, H.B. and Kinvig, R.H. (1966) *Lancashire, Cheshire and the Isle of Man.* Nelson. 308 pp.

Grantham, D.R. (1928) The petrology of the Shap Granite. *Proc. Geol. Assoc.,* **39**, 299–331.

Gray, A.J. (1972) The ecology of Morecambe Bay. 5. The Saltmarshes of Morecambe Bay. *J. Applied Ecol.,* **9**, 207–20.

Green, J.F.N. (1919) Vulcanicity of the Lake District. *Proc. Geol. Assoc.,* **30**, 153–82.

Gregory, S., Lawton, R. and Learmonth, A.T.A. (1953) The Middle Mersey and the Chemical Area, in W. Smith, F.J. Monkhouse and H.R. Wilkinson (eds), *A Scientific Study of Merseyside.* Liverpool University Press. 251–67.

Gresswell, R.K. (1964) The origin of the Mersey and Dee Estuaries. *Geol. J.,* **4**, 77–86.

Gresswell, R.K. (1967) The geomorphology of the Fylde, in R.W. Steel and R. Lawton (eds), *Liverpool Essays in Geography.* Longman. 25–42.

Gresswell, R.K. and Lawton, R. (1968) *Merseyside.* British Landscape through Maps no. 6. Geog. Assoc. 33 pp.

Grieve, W. and Hammersley, A.D. (1971) A re-examination of the Quaternary deposits of the Barrow area. *Proc. Barrow Natural Field Club,* **10**, 5–25.

Griffin, A.H. (1968) *The Roof of England.* Hale.

Hardie, D.W.F. (1950) *A History of the Chemical Industry in Widnes.* ICI General Chemicals Division.

Hartley, J.J. (1925) Borrowdale Volcanic Series between Windermere and Coniston. *Proc. Geol. Assoc.,* **36**, 203–36.

Hartley, J.J. (1932) The volcanic and other igneous rocks of Great and Little Langdale, Westmorland. *Proc. Geol. Assoc.,* **43**, 32–69.

Hartley, J.J. (1942) The geology of Helvellyn and the southern part of Thirlmere. *Quart. J. Geol. Soc.,* **97**, 129–62.

Harvey, A.M. (1985) The river systems of North West England, in R.H. Johnson (ed.), *The Geomorphology of North West England.* Manchester University Press. pp. 122–42.

Hollingworth, S.E. (1931) Glaciation of Western Edenside and adjoining areas and drumlins of Edenside and the Solway Basin. *Quart. J. Geol. Soc.,* **90**, 281–359.

Hollingworth, S.E. (1954) The geology of the Lake District. *Proc. Geol. Assoc.,* **65**, 385–402.

Huddart, D. (1971) Textural distinction of Main Glaciation and Scottish Readvance tills in the Cumberland lowland. *Geol. Mag.,* **108**, 317–24.

Huddart, D. and Tooley, M.J. (eds) (1972) *The Cumberland Lowland Handbook.* Quat. Res. Assoc.

Huddart, D., Tooley, M.J. and Carter, P.A. (1977) The coasts of North West England, in C. Kidson and M.J. Tooley (eds), *The Quaternary History of the Irish Sea.* Geol. Jour. Special Issue no. 7. 119–54.

Ingham, J.K., McNamara, K.J. and Rickards, R.B. (1978) The Upper Ordovician and Silurian rocks, in F. Moseley (ed.), *The Geology of the Lake District.* Yorks. Geol. Soc. Leeds. Occ. Publication no. 3. 121–45.

Jackson, D.E. (1978) The Skiddaw Group, in F. Moseley (ed.), *The Geology of the Lake District.* Yorks. Geol. Soc. Leeds. Occ. Publication no. 3. 79–98.

Johnson, R.H. (ed.) (1985) *The Geormorphology of North West England.* Manchester University Press. 421 pp.

Jones, O. T. (1924) The origin of the Manchester Plain. *J. Manchr. Geog. Soc.,* **39**, 40, 89–124.

Lawton, R. and Smith, W. (1953) The West Lancashire Coalfield, in W. Smith, F. J. Monkhouse and H. R. Wilkinson (eds), *A Scientific Study of Merseyside.* Liverpool University Press. 268–77.

Lee, M. P. (1969) Loess from the Pleistocene of the Wirral Peninsula, Merseyside. *Proc. Geol. Assoc.,* **90**, 21–26.

Marker, M. E. (1967) The Dee estuary: its progressive silting and saltmarsh development. *Trans. Inst. Br. Geogr.* (NS), **2**, 490–7.

Marshall, J. R. (1962) The morphology of the Upper Solway salt marshes. *Scot. Geog. Mag.,* **78**, 81–99.

Milward, R. (1955) *Lancashire. An Illustrated Essay on the History of the Landscape.* Hodder & Stoughton.

Milward, R. and Robinson, A. (1970) *The Lake District.* Eyre & Spottiswoode.

Monkhouse, F. J. (1972) *The English Lake District.* British Landscape through Maps no. 1. Geog. Assoc. 24 pp.

Moseley, F. (1953) The Namurian of the Lancaster Fells, *Quart. J. Geol. Soc.,* **109**, 423–54.

Moseley, F. (1960) The succession and structure of the Borrowdale Volcanic rocks south-east of Ullswater. *Geol. J.,* **4**, 127–42.

Moseley, F. (ed.) (1978) *The Geology of the Lake District.* Yorks. Geol. Soc. Leeds. Occ. Publication no. 3.

Moseley, F. (1986) *Geology and Scenery in the Lake District.* Macmillan. 112 pp.

Ogden, H. W. (1927) The geographical basis of the Lancashire cotton industry. *J. Manchr. Geogr. Soc.,* **43**, 8–30.

Oldfield, F. (1960) Late-Quaternary changes in climate, vegetation and sea-level in Lowland Lonsdale. *Trans. Inst. Br. Geogr.,* **28**, 99–117.

Oliver, R. L. (1961) The Borrowdale volcanic and associated rocks of the Scafell area, Lake District. *Quart. J. Geol. Soc.,* **117**, 377–417.

Pearsall, W. H. (1921) The development of vegetation in the English Lakes. *Proc. Roy. Soc. B.,* **92**.

Pearsall, W. H. and Pennington, W. (1973) *The Lake District.* Collins.

Rastall, R. H. (1906) The Buttermere and Ennerdale granophyre. *Quart. J. Geol. Soc.,* **66**, 116–41.

Ratcliffe, D. A. (1960) The mountain flora of Lakeland. *Proc. Bot. Soc. Br. Isles.* **4**.

Rogers, H. B. (1960) The Lancashire cotton industry in 1840. *Trans. Inst. Br. Geogr.,* **28**, 135–53.

Shaw, W. T. (1970) *Mining in the Lake District.* Clapham.

Shimwell, D. (1985) The distribution and origins of the lowland mosslands. In R. H. Johnson (ed.), *The Geomorphology of North West England.* Manchester University Press. 299–312.

Sissons, J. B. (1980) The Loch Lomond Advance in the Lake District, northern England. *Trans. Roy. Soc. Edinb. Earth Sci.,* **71**, 13–27.

Smith, B. (1924) On the west Cumberland brockram and associated rocks. *Geol. Mag.,* **61**, 289–308.

Smith, B., Dixon, E. E. L., Eastwood, T. *et al.* (1925) Sketch of the geology of the Whitehaven District. *Proc. Geol. Assoc.,* **26**, 37–75.

Smith, W. (1937) The agricultural geography of the Fylde. *Geography,* **22**, 29–43.

Smith, W., Monkhouse, F. J. and Wilkinson, H. R. (eds) 1953. *A Scientific Study of Merseyside.* Liverpool University Press. 299 pp.

Taylor, B. J., Burgess, I. C., Land, D. H. *et al.* (1971) *Northern England* (4th edn). British Regional Geology. HMSO. 121 pp.

Temple, P. H. (1965) Some aspects of cirque distribution in the west-central Lake District, northern England. *Geogr. Annalr.,* **47A**, 185–93.

Tooley, M. J. (1978) *Sea-Level Changes. North West England during the Flandrian Stage.* Clarendon Press. 232 pp.

Tooley, M. J. (1980) Solway lowlands, shores of Morecambe Bay and south western Lancashire, in W. G. Jardine (ed.), *Field Guide: Western Scotland and North West England.* INQUA Sub-Commission on shorelines of North West Europe. 71–110.

Trotter, F. M. (1954a) The Lancashire Coalfield, in A. E. Trueman, *The Coalfields of Great Britain*. Arnold. 199–218.

Trotter, F. M. (1954b) The Cumberland Coalfield, in A. E. Trueman. *The Coalfields of Great Britain*. Arnold. 314–24.

Walker, D. (1965) The post-glacial period in the Langdale Fells, English Lake District. *New Phytol.*, **64**, 488–510.

Wilson, P., Bateman, R. M. and Catt, J. A. (1981) Petrography, origin and environmental deposition of the Shirdley Hill Sand of south west Lancashire, England. *Proc. Geol. Assoc.*, **92**, 211–30.

The Pennines and North-East England

10

If the English Midlands epitomize New Red Sandstone country and the stone belt is the realm of the British Jurassic then, geologically speaking, the Pennines and the North-East are the Carboniferous province of England. Rocks of the Carboniferous succession outcrop over a greater geographical area than any other system in Britain; the variation of the facies is unrivalled; its range of scenery is remarkably diverse and, since its Coal Measures are one of Britain's most valuable resources, more is known about the Carboniferous strata than any other British succession. Of equal importance is the fact that the Pennines represent the largest tract of upland scenery in England and thereby contain England's most widespread moorlands and some of its most extensive conifer plantations. This highland backbone, however, is relatively narrow, for the Irish Sea and the North Sea are only 120 kilometres apart, confining the lowlands to relatively narrow coastal plains in Cumbria and Northumberland. The upland spine and its foothills have played a significant role not only by providing cave sites for some of Britain's first inhabitants (Campbell, 1969; Briggs *et al.*, 1988) but also by creating a barrier to divide the subsequent phases of human colonization into distinctive eastern and western patterns: Yorkshire, Northumberland and Durham have retained their Anglo-Saxon dialects and place names while the western coastlands, described in Chapter 9, carry a mixture of early British and Norse cultural foundations. Finally, one is reminded that the creation of the nearby Scottish Border should not allow anyone 'to underestimate the affinities of the people of North England with the Scots, affinities which have been emphasised by circumstances of physical geography, as well as of historical development, that are very different from those farther south' (Smailes, 1961).

In the Peak District of the southern Pennines it is possible to retain the conventional division of the Carboniferous succession into the older Carboniferous Limestone, the intermediate Millstone Grit and the younger Coal Measures. Farther north, however, this simple classification is inappropriate, except in terms of fossil content, for there the patterns of sedimentation were significantly different. In northern England both the thickness and the surface outcrop of the limestone, often termed Mountain Limestone, are reduced as its upper layers become increasingly interbedded with sandstones and shales, illustrating how the initial deep-sea conditions became gradually replaced by shallower water and by coastal environments (Rayner, 1953). This complex interbedding continues upwards through the succession into the Middle Carboniferous strata, so that north of Skipton the typical Millstone Grit of the Peak District becomes more shaly and less distinctive than that farther south. In fact, the boundary between the Mountain Limestone and its overlying gritstone is here replaced by the so-called Yoredale Succession, made up of a rhythmic sequence (termed a *cyclothem*), repeated up to eleven times, of limestone, shale, sandstone and grit, and coal (in ascending order) (Hudson, 1924). In short, this is an indication of the way in which the Carboniferous maritime geography changed periodically from clear-water oceans (limestones), through increasingly muddy seas (shales), to estuaries and deltas (current-bedded sandstones and grits) which finally bore the Coal Measures swamps. Strictly speaking, for the Pennines as a whole, the geologist prefers to base the Carboniferous terminology on overseas nomenclature which gives the following succession: Carboniferous Limestone (*Dinantian*), Millstone Grit and Shale (*Namurian*), Coal Measures (*Westphalian*) (Edwards and Trotter, 1954; Taylor *et al.*, 1971). One would do well to remember that in Scotland the Carboniferous stratigraphy is even more complex because of the contemporaneous volcanic outbursts (missing in most of England) and the paucity of zone fossils. Since Northumberland also suffers from the latter handicap, cross-border correlations are far from simple. Instead of the relatively simple Carboniferous Limestone succession, for example, the Scottish Dinantian comprises a thick basal sandstone with cementstones and oil shales (known as the Calciferous Sandstone Series). Moreover, the Scottish Carboniferous Limestone not only spans the Dinantian–Namurian boundary but also contains important coal seams which are much older than the Westphalian. Thus, the respective 'Limestone Groups' of northern England and Scotland do not mean the same thing.

Although it has been demonstrated how Hercynian folding in southern Britain can be traced in such east–west structural lines as those found in the Mendips, South Wales and the South-West Peninsula, the apparently contradictory north–south structural alignment of the Pennines is also of this age (Edwards and Trotter, 1954). But it is really the underlying structures, beneath the Carboniferous cover rocks, that have been largely responsible for the geological layout of the backbone of England. Such early Palaeozoic basement massifs as the Alston Block (Trotter and Hollingworth, 1928) and the Askrigg Block, for example, which are buried beneath the northern Pennines, and to a lesser extent the Derbyshire Dome which underlies the Peak District, have all played an influential part both in the regional sedimentation and structural development over a considerable period (see Fig. 9.1). Moreover, the Stublick faults, the Pennine and Dent faults (Turner, 1927), which define the northern and western margins, respectively, of the northern Pennines, together with the North Craven fault which divides the northern Pennines from the uplands farther south, have all suffered periodic displacements as the Pennines have been uplifted in succeeding tectonic episodes (Turner, 1935) including that of the Alpine mountain-building phase. One result of this continuing differential uplift and its associated marginal downfaulting has been the contrasting amounts of deposition of the older Carboniferous sediments and of any younger cover rocks that may have been laid down both in northern England and in southern Scotland (Fig. 10.1). One can now begin to understand why subsequent erosion has produced different types of scenery in different parts of the Pennines, as the overlying Coal Measures and the sandy or gritstone strata have been variously stripped away from the Pennine 'arch' as it has been tectonically raised by a series of pulsatory uplifts since late Palaeozoic times, after the emplacement of the Weardale granite (Bott, 1967) (see p. 200). Broadly speaking, this prolonged denudation, combined with downfaulting on the mountain flanks, has left the coalfields surviving only on the western and eastern lowland margins (see Fig. 9.1). The Pennine foothills, by contrast, are generally characterized by inward-facing scarps made of grits and sandstones, that look across broad expanses of Carboniferous Limestone in those central areas where the upper Carboniferous rocks were relatively thin

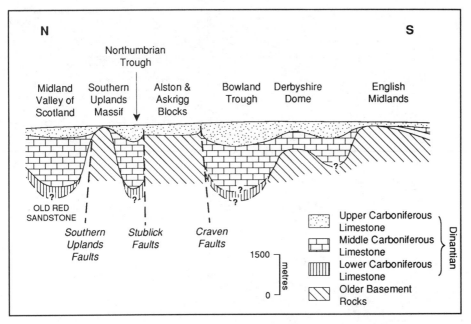

Figure 10.1 Generalized section of the Dinantian (Carboniferous) sedimentation and structures of northern England and Southern Scotland.

and where the older limestones have been fairly quickly exposed above the crests of the underlying ancient blocks. Nowhere is this better exemplified than in the Peak District.

The Peak District

This enclave of spectacular scenery, lying within one hour's drive of a quarter of Britain's population, is one of the best-known and most loved areas of the British uplands (Edwards, 1962). Covering an area of about 1800 km², the Peak District is a region of marked contrasts, ranging from the high windswept moorland plateaux down to the pretty, wooded dales and their intimate settlements (Milward and Robinson, 1975). The gradual wearing down of the Carboniferous rocks of the Derbyshire Dome has produced a relatively simple pattern in which the oldest Mountain Limestone is now exposed in the central area where its pale rocks, fairly fertile soils and lime-loving vegetation create the tract known as the White Peak or Low Peak. Surrounding this limestone exposure are concentric tracts of almost treeless moorlands, coinciding with the acidic soils of the shales, gritstones and sandstones of the Millstone Grit Series, all of which once covered the limestone but now dip outwards to pass beneath the flanking Coal Measures (Fig. 10.2). Indeed, the vegetation of the Peak gives a fair reflection of its geology (Moss, 1913). The structure of the arch is not symmetrical, for the western margins are generally steeper and disturbed by folds in Cheshire and north Staffordshire. In complete contrast to the White Peak are the landforms of the more northerly tract where the limestone has not been uncovered and where the hard arenacous rocks, with their acid soils, form the dissected moorland plateau of Kinderscout and its associated gritstone edges. This is variously known

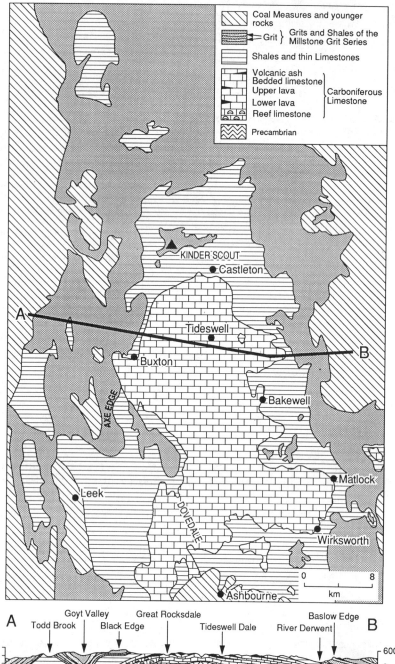

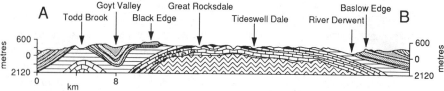

Figure 10.2 Geology and structure of the Peak District (based on material prepared by the British Geological Survey).

as the High Peak or the Dark Peak because of its absolute height and its more sombre colouring (Cope, 1958).

The Carboniferous Limestone Series constituting the White Peak can be subdivided into three distinct facies, each indicative of a different type of depositional environment (Simpson, 1982). The most common is the so-called *shelf* limestone, a pale grey, well-bedded, fine-grained but hard lime-rich mud. It is packed with broken pieces of calcareous shells and skeletons of marine organisms all held together by a finely crystalline calcite cement. The next most common limestone facies is the *basin* limestone, darker in colour than the shelf limestone and with its thinner beds having many partings of shale or mudstone because its depositional environment contained deeper, muddier water. The least common type is the *reef* limestone which, as its name suggests, is very rich in fossils, particularly corals, though calcareous algae are also abundant (Bond, 1950). Because the reef limestone is virtually devoid of bedding, its structure tends to resist weathering better than the other limestones, thereby leaving it projecting as a 'reef knoll' in the landscape. Varying in width from a few metres to several hundred metres across, reef knolls are found around Dovedale and Castleton, but are particularly well exposed in the 'knoll country' of the Craven Uplands of the North Pennines (see p. 227).

Before examining the limestone scenery of the White Peak (Dalton *et al.*, 1988), an explanatory word is necessary concerning the sporadic volcanic activity that took place hereabouts during the deposition of the Carboniferous Limestone Series. Some of the shelf limestones, for example, were overwhelmed by basaltic lava flows that have formed dark grey-green, finely crystalline rocks whose iron-rich silicates have been weathered into soft, crumbly material surrounding grey-brown lumps of less decomposed basalt. Additionally, some thin beds of volcanic ash, now represented by thin partings of grey-green clay between the limestones, together with some thicker sills of dolerite, also occur. All of these dark-coloured rocks are termed *toadstones* (Bemrose, 1907) which, unlike the limestones, act as impermeable barriers to groundwater flow, thereby influencing patterns of subterranean drainage and cave development. Where their layers are steeply inclined and exposed on valley sides, landslips are liable along their water-lubricated surfaces, including the rock slide at Peter's Stone crag in Cressbrookdale. Moreover, because they weather more rapidly than the surrounding limestone, toadstones often coincide with topographic depressions. The volcanic phase also initiated widespread mineralization in the White Peak and subsequent ore extraction has left significant scars on the limestone landscape, now marked by lines of trees along the so-called 'rakes' (Ford and Rieuwerts, 1975). Furthermore, the spa towns of Buxton and Matlock owe their location to natural hot springs which, like the lead and zinc lodes, have been known since Roman times.

The gently rolling plateau of the limestone is deeply dissected by the rivers Manifold (Prentice, 1950), Dove and Wye and their associated network of dry valleys. It has been claimed that since the main rivers manage to cross the porous limestone tract only because their headwaters rise on the less permeable neighbouring Namurian rocks, the whole drainage system must have been initiated on a former cover of such rocks, only becoming superimposed on to the limestone surface as these more impermeable shales and grits were slowly removed. Subsequent incision of the trunk streams into the limestone appears to have helped in lowering the regional water table sufficiently to leave the tributary valley networks (which rise only on the limestone) high and dry (Fig. 10.3). Perhaps this may explain why some of these tributary valleys now 'hang' above the incised gorges. Nowhere is this better exemplified than at Lathkilldale, east of Monyash.

The origin of the plateau surface, that cuts discordantly across the limestone folds, has been the subject of considerable discussion (Jones and Charsley, 1985). While some believe it to be simply the exhumed sub-Namurian surface stripped of its shales and grits, others think it is a sub-Permo-Triassic surface, pointing by way of confirmation to the Weaver Hills where the New Red Sandstone lies

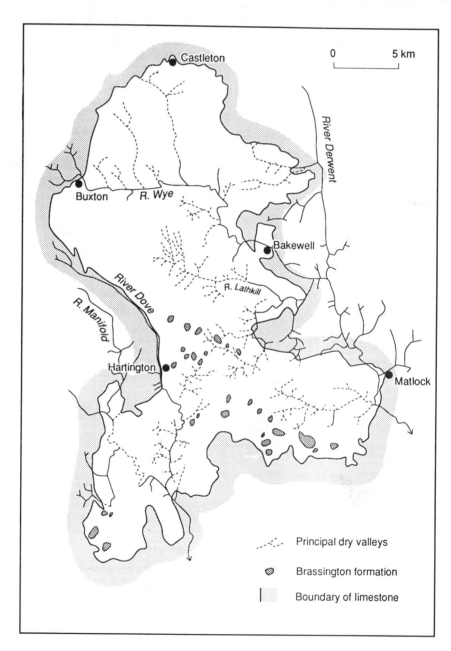

Figure 10.3 Dry valley location and the distribution of the Brassington Formation on the Carboniferous Limestone of the Peak District (after A. Straw and K. Clayton).

directly on the limestone to the west of Ashbourne (Kent, 1957). Because both of these exhumed surfaces exhibit extremely uneven terrain, however, a third alternative has been outlined. In this explanation, the Peak District Upland Surface is believed to be closely associated with the Brassington Formation, a number of scattered Tertiary sediments that have survived in deep subsidence pockets on the limestone outcrop around Brassington village. These Neogene gravels, sands and clays owe their remarkable preservation to some 250 metres of subsidence following subterranean solution and karstic collapse of the limestone (Walsh *et al.*, 1972). It is claimed, therefore, that the upland surface has been worn down by quite an appreciable amount since the formation of the Late Tertiary surface (Fig. 10.3), as the limestones have been slowly uncovered and lowered by solution (Pitty, 1968). Among other distinctive features in the Brassington area are a collection of limestone tors that are found only where the limestone has been converted into dolomite. Dolomitization of this southern tract of the White Peak limestone probably occurred when magnesium-rich solutions from a former cover of New Red Sandstone infiltrated the upper beds of limestone to produce a type of Magnesian Limestone: $(CaMg) CO_3$. The rock pinnacles, 15 metres high, are best seen at Rainster Rocks, west of Brassington village.

Completely different types of limestone pinnacle and other spectacular rock forms are found on the valleysides of some of the river gorges, most notably in Dovedale, whose praises popular guide books regularly sing: 'There is no river in England to compare with the Dove [yet] in spite of its peerless beauty it is the most modest of rivers, hiding itself in a deeply cleft passage of which the whereabouts cannot readily be perceived' (Mee, 1937). The 'deeply cleft passage' in the limestone rocks of Dovedale (Parkinson, 1950), with its Reynard's Cave and monoliths of Ilam Rock, Jacobs Ladder and Tissington Spires, was created partly by frost and partly by swollen waters from melting Ice Age glaciers. But none of these spectacular features could have been sculptured without the existing network of underground drainage that had already been carved out of the massively jointed Mountain Limestone (Cope, 1976). In fact, the downcutting river Dove has merely opened up the maze of underground karstic features. Despite its thin, dessicated soils, Dovedale supports one of England's finest Mountain Limestone woodlands, a rich primary mixture of ash, lime, wych-elm and yew, contributing to Dovedale's status as a site of special scientific interest (Balme, 1953; Merton, 1970). Limestone is used exclusively in the centre of the White Peak to build such attractive villages as Wetton, Ilam and Miller's Dale, but it is such ancient hamlets as Monyash, Flagg and Alstonefield which, set high on the grassy uplands, really convey the isolated nature of the enclosed plateaux and their limestone strata (Shirley, 1959). Here, there are chequerboards of drystone field walls laid out geometrically during the eighteenth-century enclosure acts. Near Castleton, however, a group of narrow, linear fields are bounded by walls that have a flattened S-shaped plan, indicating that they follow the Domesday strip-fields as survivals of feudal land tenure. As far as earlier settlements in the White Peak landscape are concerned, it appears that the earliest colonization, in Neolithic times, was confined entirely to the limestone, as exemplified by the henge of Arbor Low (Briggs *et al.*, 1988) and the chambered tombs of Green Low and Minninglow. Not until the Bronze Age did settlement spread onto the surrounding gritstone, although by the Iron Age

human occupation was again restricted to the limestone, an indication of the
significantly higher fertility of the limestone soils (Pigott, 1965), in contrast to
the less favourable acidic podzols of the surrounding Namurian rocks. Because of
water supply difficulties villages on the limestone are often linear in plan when
sited along the narrow floor of a dry valley, as at Chelmorton (Roberts, 1987).
Where lead-mining intervened, however, the linear pattern was lost, as at Bradwell
and Winster.

Between the limestone perimeter and the gritstone edges occur outcrops of
Namurian shales (see Fig. 10.2), and it is this ring of weaker beds that has played
an important role in fixing the position of some of the region's major rivers.
This is particularly true along the broader eastern shale outcrop which is followed
for a great distance by the Derwent, its wooded valley overhung by an almost
continuous line of west-facing gritstone scarps, most notably those of Stanage
Edge and Millstone Edge near Hathersage (Fearnsides, 1932). These gritstone
moorlands descend eastwards to the city of Sheffield (Linton, 1956), located
where several moorland dipslope streams converge to form the river Don. Nothing
could be more contrasting, in terms of scenery, between the heavily industrialized
valley between Sheffield and Rotherham and the upspoiled countryside of the
River Derwent. Scarcely one scarpslope tributary joins the Derwent's left bank
from these same gritstone moorlands, in contrast to the many tributaries,
including the Wye, which descend through limestone dales to join the Derwent's
right bank. Between Baslow and Rowsley the Derwent meanders through the
landscaped park of Chatsworth whose stately house, like the Crescent at Buxton,
was built from the Kinderscout Group of the Millstone Grit, one of northern
England's finest building stones.

Southwards, where the Derwent emerges from Darley Dale, its character
changes from a broad valley floor with an established floodplain developed on
the shales, to a narrow high-sided gorge as it encounters the eastern flank of
the Carboniferous Limestone outcrop (see Fig. 10.3). From Matlock to Cromford,
4 kilometres downstream, the Matlock gorge, with its celebrated 120 metre vertical
cliff of High Tor developed in a reef limestone, has limestone features comparable
with Dovedale but on a much grander scale. Like the course of the Dove, which
switches from shale to limestone and back again, the anomolous course of the
Derwent has also to be explained. Although simple superimposition on to the
limestone from a cover of Namurian rocks now stripped away (see p. 218) may
satisfactorily explain the vagaries of the Dove, the Derwent's evolution appears
to be a combination of both superimposition and river capture. Research has
shown that the pre-glacial course of the Derwent southwards from Curbar lay
not through Chatsworth but in a great western loop via Bakewell and the present
course of the Wye, thereby following the limestone–Namurian shale boundary,
before joining the modern north–south valley at Rowsley. It is suggested that since
the so-called Pilsley Terrace (60 metres above the floodplain), which follows this
western route, is missing in the Chatsworth tract of its modern valley, the Derwent
may have found this older western loop blocked by ice or glacial infill and may
thereby have been forced to follow a completely new direct Baslow–Rowsley
valley excavated by glacial meltwaters (Straw, 1968). It is further claimed that
the lower Hathersage Terrace, which runs along the length of the Derwent Valley
through Chatsworth Park, was produced by the post-glacial Derwent after it
had discovered the newly carved valley (Waters and Johnson, 1958).

One of the most popular tourist areas in the Peak District occurs around Castleton, where the northern fringes of the White Peak limestone (Shirley and Horsfield, 1940) disappear beneath the shales and grits of the High Peak moorlands (see Fig. 10.2). The junction is marked by the Hope Valley and Rushup Vale, each with its distinctive southern flank developed on limestones and its northern flank rising steeply on the Namurian shales, sandstones and grits to the hillfort-crowned Mam Tor (Preston, 1954) and Rushup Edge, respectively. The subterranean flow from Rushup Vale finds its way ultimately eastwards to the topographically distinct Hope Valley. As they cross on to the limestone the south-flowing streams from Rushup Edge disappear underground in a series of 'swallets' or sinks, as seen at Little Bull Pit. All reappear at the surface as a combined stream in the Hope Valley, having passed through one of the Peak District's most extensive cave networks including that of the Speedwell Cavern. However, the Peak Cavern, Treak Cliff and Blue John Caverns, all with their various stalactites and stalagmites, appear to belong to quite different drainage systems (Ford, 1986). Castleton village, supplied by waters emerging from the Peak Cavern, was once a centre for lead-mining and production of the ornamental fluorspar known as Blue John stone, although today Castleton survives largely on tourists who, in addition to visiting the caverns, also walk through the dry limestone valley of the Winnats Pass, possibly cut to its present form by glacial meltwater or when the ground water was frozen by permafrost during the Upper Pleistocene. The present gorge, however, is merely the latest manifestation of a complex history, for it follows an inter-reef channel of Lower Carboniferous age that later became infilled with Namurian shales. Another well-known Castleton feature is the towering peak of Mam Tor (517 m) whose sandstone-capped escarpment (Allen, 1960) is constantly being undermined by the removal of the underlying Edale shales. Because of its instability the eminence is known as the 'Shivering Mountain', beneath whose face is one of Britain's most notorious landslides. Below the landslip scar (105 metres high), the jumble of slipped material and rotational blocks, together with the hummocky, marshy toe of the landslip, combine to cover an area 1000 metres long and 550 metres wide, active enough to have destroyed the A625 main road.

To the north, the valley of Edale, formed along the axis of an anticline within the Kinderscout Group of interbedded grits and shales (Hudson and Cotton, 1945), also exhibits a number of landslides, especially on its steeper, north-facing slopes. Wherever the massive Kinderscout Grit outcrops it forms escarpment crags, some of which have been fashioned into valleyside tors (Cunningham, 1965; Palmer and Radley, 1961) with associated blockfields, all evidence of prolonged periglacial activity during the Devensian, when it appears that Edale itself escaped invasion by glaciers (Briggs *et al.*, 1988). Thus, Edale is thickly mantled with periglacial valley-fill deposits whose bright green fields contrast with the surrounding sombre-coloured peats which blanket the surrounding tablelands of Edale Moor and the summit plateau of Kinderscout (650 m), described by Defoe as the 'most desolate, wild and abandoned country in all England'. Edale village marks the southern end of the Pennine Way, the northern limit of which terminates across the Scottish border. Although its route misses out on the attractive tree-lined lake scenery of Derwent Dale, with its large system of reservoirs to supply industrial south Yorkshire cities, and also avoids the dramatic landslipped gritstone pinnacles of Alport Castles (England's largest inland landslip), possibly undermined by Pleistocene valley glaciers and shattered by frost weathering (Tufnell, 1969), this high-level footpath passes through Britain's best-known gritstone scenery.

The central Pennines

In the Central Pennines, in the area bounded by the cities of Sheffield and Manchester and by Bradford and Burnley, the Millstone Grit is almost 2000 metres thick, if one includes the many incorporated shaly layers. Its current-bedding demonstrates how it was laid down by powerful currents in shallow water, for in places conglomerates or pebble beds occur among the normal grits (Gilligan, 1920). Even the grit bands are of very coarse texture, appearing almost crystalline because of their abundance of quartz and feldspar crystals. Since these are also important constituents of granite, it is hardly surprising that some grits have been mistaken for granite, most notably by Charlotte Brontë in *Jane Eyre*. In fact the grits were probably derived from some distant granite mass that was undergoing denudation at the time of their deposition.

From most high viewpoints the uncompromising darkly-weathered grit dominates the upland skylines, a scene of unspoiled 'heath-clad showery hills' where peat bogs stain the brooks and 'silence dwells o'er flowerless moors'. Yet these apparently featureless moorlands are regularly trenched by swift-flowing streams and bounded by ice-steepened and frost-riven scarps which loom darkly over valleyside villages and valleyfloor factory towns. The imprint of the Industrial Revolution is written large in these central Pennine dales (Raistrick, 1970), for this is where moorland sheep and torrential stream power provided the original resources for Yorkshire's famous woollen industry. Although it has been claimed that in Mesolithic times the Pennines were heavily wooded (Tallis and Switsur, 1983), today the poorly drained expanses of the plateau tops are mantled with bogs where erosion has channelled the peat into 'hags' separated by deep gulleys (Phillips *et al.*, 1981; Tallis, 1985) and where the lugubrious countenance of the moorland is scarcely lightened by the patches of white cotton grass (*Eriophorum*) and the gradually diminishing remnants of heather and gorse. Curiously, the bright green sphagnum moss, a typical component of blanket bogs (Conway, 1954), is also rare, probably because of the centuries of continuous grazing and periodic burning followed by the insidious effects of industrial pollution. Add to this the dearth of trees on the high moors, taken mainly for fuel or simply inhibited by air pollution, then the gritstone uplands now offer a prospect even starker than that chronicled by the Brontës some 150 years ago. The gritstone tops are not all boggy, however, for in areas of lower rainfall and steeper slopes the soils are drier and sandier. Consequently, a distinction can be made between the wet 'mosses' and the drier 'moors' especially in the distribution of place names. Research has shown that in areas above 365 metres, with rainfall between 1400 and 1600 millimetres, mosses abound, while at altitudes of 213 to 365 metres, with rainfall less than 1400 millimetres, moors heavily outnumber mosses among the place names.

The edges of all these relatively smooth Pennine tablelands are etched with black escarpments where the grit's well-developed current-bedding and jointing (Fig. 10.4a) has allowed frost, wind and rain to sunder the cliffs into a chaos of

Figure 10.4 (a) The Millstone Grit escarpment of Hen Cloud and the Roaches on the western edge of the Peak District. Beyond lies the New Red Sandstone basin from which the Churnet Valley has been carved near Leek, Staffordshire. (b) The current-bedded and well-jointed gritstone of the Roaches has been weathered into bizarre shapes.

slabs, clefts and buttresses (Tufnell, 1969), like those seen at Hen Cloud, Ramshaw Rocks and the Roaches (Fig. 10.4b) near the Leek–Buxton road. Where the flat-bedded strata have been slowly whittled away, particularly during the severe periglacial climate of the Pleistocene Ice Age (Boardman, 1985), gritstone tors have been created, one of which was later to be fortified by early man into the brooding hillfort known as Carl Wark, near Hathersage (Preston, 1954). Not surprisingly, many of the natural escarpments have been quarried for centuries to provide building stone and millstones for grinding corn, to serve such ancient water mills as that surviving at Nether Alderley in Cheshire. Sadly, these superb grindstones are no longer in demand and the once famous Millstone Edge quarry near Sheffield, littered with hundreds of half-finished millstones, is a veritable graveyard of rural industry (Radley, 1966). The earliest Pennine dwellings reflect the former dominance of their livestock husbandry because the typical farmhouse evolved, like that of the Lake District, into a longhouse in which byre, barn and residential quarters were all beneath one lengthy roof. Their long, squat profiles are commonplace on the moors around Halifax and Huddersfield, where their roughly squared, unornamented masonry illustrates the difficulties of fashioning and carving the tough Millstone Grit. These sturdy dwellings, like those of the Yorkshire Dales farther north, were originally roofed with thick sandstone slabs, darker and heavier than the 'slates' of the Jurassic stone belt. Those known in West Yorkshire as 'thackstones' were quarried almost exclusively at Elland near Leeds. The blue-grey flagstones found both on the roofs and the older pavements of east Cheshire and north Staffordshire hill towns often came from Kerridge quarry at Macclesfield, while the Lancashire side of the Pennines sought its flagstones from the Rossendale quarries.

Hereabouts, the Pennine chain narrows into a 'wasp waist' squeezed between the industrialized towns of Lancashire and Yorkshire which sprawl along their flanking coalfields (see Fig. 9.1). Thus, although odd villages like Mankinholes, astride its ancient packhorse route, appear relatively remote, most hilltop villages, such as austerely handsome Heptonstall, usually look down on industrial valley towns like Marsden, Todmorden and Hebden Bridge. The moorland slopes around the Calder Valley carry a settlement pattern virtually unique in Britain. Because of the abundance of surface water, clustered villages were unnecessary so that the early domestic woollen industry grew up in a scattering of isolated dwellings each characterized by its long line of 'weavers' windows'; only the early fulling mills were located in the valley bottoms near the rivers and canals. Writing in 1724, Defoe described these gritstone moorlands as 'spread with houses, and that very thick . . . in short, one continued village'.

The majority of West Yorkshire's dales, such as Calderdale, Airedale and Wharfedale, have served as important Pennine routeways since earliest times, but the river gradients are generally too steep to have allowed them to contribute significantly to water transport during the Industrial Revolution, hence the presence of three historic trans-Pennine canals, paralleling the rivers Colne, Calder and Aire. Waterfalls are quite numerous in the tributary valleys, especially where horizontal gritstone bands overlie softer shale beds. The Lumb Falls near Hebden Bridge and those in Marsden Clough at Holmbridge near Huddersfield, are both caused by an outcrop of the Kinderscout Grit (Collinson, 1969). The Dolly Folly Falls near Meltham, by contrast, are due to faulting, the falls being formed where a 10 metre band of grit, termed the Huddersfield White Rock, has been downthrown, thereby bringing less resistant shales into contact with the fault face of the grit on the upthrow side. With the exception of Keighley, the larger settlements of West Yorkshire are located farther east, where the dales open out as they cross on to the less resistant Coal Measures. Once coal had replaced water power, the woollen industry shifted from the rural uplands to such lowland coalfield towns as Leeds, Bradford and Huddersfield, though most of their giant mills are now closed (Beresford and Jones, 1967).

The elevation of the Yorkshire coalfield is much below that of the gritstone moorlands, yet it is crossed by several prominent north–south edges due to eastward-dipping sandstone bands intervening between the grey Namurian shales and those of the Coal Measures. For example, the outcrop of the so-called Rough Rock between Holmfirth and Huddersfield and northwards to beyond Halifax, marks not only the geological boundary between the Namurian and Westphalian but has also been picked out by erosion to create the west-facing scarps of Hade Edge, Crosland Edge and Sentry Edge. This tract also marks the transition zone where upland sheep farming gives way to the mixed dairy farming of the Pennine foothills and lower dales, a land use which itself is replaced by a broad belt of arable below the 100 metre contour. These arable lands extend far beyond the eastern margin of the coalfield where they not only coincide with the better-drained soils of the Magnesian Limestone outcrop but also stretch eastwards across the fertile Vale of York. It is noteworthy that the relatively small medieval castle and market towns of Pontefract and Knaresborough, sited astride the Magnesian Limestone cuesta, have histories which considerably pre-date the larger cities of the coalfield. The elegant stone-built spa towns of Ilkley and Harrogate (Hudson *et al.*, 1938), by contrast, are largely creations of the mineral waters associated with the gritstone outcrop.

Where the Pennines are at their narrowest, between Huddersfield and Rochdale, the Pennine upfold is asymmetrical, with the dips to the west being steeper than those to the east. Accordingly, the relatively gentle dipslopes and the widely spaced scarps of the Yorkshire flanks are replaced by much steeper dips and more crowded scarps on the Lancashire side. Moreover, the western structures of the Pennines are far more disturbed by folding and faulting. Consequently, the transition from gritstone upland to the industrial cotton towns of Nelson, Burnley, Rochdale and Oldham, spread along the Lancashire coalfield margin, is much more rapid. Hence, the terrain contrasts are also greater, with the west 'wall' of the Pennines towering high above the Greater Manchester lowland conurbation. Here, during the Pleistocene, the thick Scottish ice sheets, reinforced by Lake District ice, were deflected southwards by the Pennine mass and their coursing meltwaters forced to cut deep marginal channels along the western moorland slopes at many locations between the Cliviger Gorge (near Burnley) and the Rudyard Gorge (near Leek) (Johnson, 1965). A little to the west of the central Pennines a smaller but topographically similar upland, termed the Forest of Rossendale, juts out into Lancashire and divides its coalfield into northern and southern parts (see Figure 9.1). The Coal Measures dip away from Rossendale's central outcrop of Namurian rocks, indicative of its anticlinal structure the axis of which runs from north-east to south-west, unlike the north–south structural alignment of the true Pennines. Nevertheless, its grits, shales and flags (Pendleside Grit, Kinderscout Grit, Haslingden Flagstones and the Rough Rock) are virtually identical with those of the neighbouring Pennines and, therefore, create similar moorland scenery. In the central area of Rossendale the beds are practically horizontal, each step of its terraced landscape corresponding to a gritstone outcrop. Near the borders of the upland, however, in the direction of both Accrington and Rochdale, the outward angle of dip increases, giving rise to a succession of sharp cuestas trenched by narrow river valleys with their numerous waterfalls. As in the case of Yorkshire's early woollen industry, many of the

Rossendale falls were harnessed to provide power for some of the first cotton-spinning mills.

The northern Pennines

At Skipton the geology changes (see Fig. 9.1), for the structure of the northern Pennines is less simple than that to the south (King, 1976). The arch of the central Pennines, which becomes progressively asymmetrical northwards, is suddenly broken along its western margin by the Craven and Dent faults. This break at the crest of the arch has caused an uplift of the western flanks of the Pennines, the highest points of which now occur near the western margins overlooking both Ribblesdale and the Vale of Eden. Erosion has worked more swiftly, therefore, on the rocks of this uplifted western flank, and has proceeded to uncover not only the Carboniferous Limestone but also some older Palaeozoic and even Precambrian strata. This degree of denudation means that the newer formations of the Carboniferous (Namurian and Westphalian) are now restricted in their outcrop to the long, eastward-dipping slopes of the eastern flanks. In a few places the Millstone Grit has survived but, in general, to the north of Skipton the true Millstone Grit outcrop is narrow and ill defined, and here the landscape is now dominated by the Carboniferous Limestone together with its almost horizontal capping of Yoredale rocks (see p. 213). It must also be remembered that the geology and scenery of the northern Pennines have been strongly influenced by the presence of the underlying Palaeozoic massifs of the Alston Block and the Askrigg Block (Figs 9.1 and 10.1). These basement blocks were probably established by Caledonian folding in Silurian times but their presence had a significant effect on the Dinantian and Namurian sedimentation as the Pre-Carboniferous floor was being uplifted by Hercynian earth movements (Johnson, 1967). Thus, the Lower Carboniferous sediments, some 1828 metres thick south of the Craven Faults, thin to less than 520 metres when traced over the Askrigg Block and the Alston Block (Bott and Johnson, 1967). Though this explains in part the virtual disappearance of the Millstone Grit, there is no evidence that the buried blocks had any effect on the deposition of the Coal Measures farther east.

To the north-west of Keighley and Ilkley the gritstone moorlands of the Brontë country give way to less austere scenery around Skipton, an area known as the Craven Lowlands (see Fig. 9.1). On the solid edition of the Geological Survey maps the Craven Lowlands, some 180 metres above sea level, are depicted as belonging to the Carboniferous Limestone series, but in fact their underlying rocks are mainly downfaulted Yoredales quite sharply folded into a number of north-east to south-west anticlines arranged *en echelon*. Since the surface is thickly mantled with glacial deposits, however, the solid geology has little effect on the lowland scenery. The most striking landforms of these lowlands are the myriad of drumlins found between Skipton, Settle and Bolton-by-Bowland, and through which the Leeds–Liverpool Canal winds its tortuous way. The watershed position of the area is illustrated by the fact that it is drained westwards by the Ribble and eastwards by the Aire. The whole area is devoted to cattle and sheep rearing, so that permanent grasslands prevail with scarcely an arable field in sight, though oats and barley were grown two centuries ago, according to Arthur Young's account of 1770.

The Craven Lowlands are terminated abruptly northwards by the three great fractures known as the Craven Faults whose southerly downthrows delimit the Craven Uplands of the Askrigg Block by means of a sequence of notable fault-line scarps (Edwards and Trotter, 1954) (see Fig. 10.1). The earliest fracture, the Mid-Craven Fault initiated in the early Carboniferous, extends from Burnsall through Malham, where it helps create spectacular scenery, and westwards to Settle. The main or North Craven Fault, belonging to a later period of Hercynian earth movements, runs from Pateley Bridge through Stainforth to near Ingleton. The South Craven Fault is thought to be more recent, possibly moving during the Alpine earth movements to create the remarkably sharp fault-line scarp of Giggleswick Scar to the west of Settle.

The landscapes of the Craven Uplands are some of the most distinctive in Britain because they have been carved from an almost horizontal, 130 metre thick layer of Mountain Limestone (the virtually pure light-grey Great Scar Limestone) which is topped by a number of striking tabular summits hewn from the overlying Yoredale strata of alternating sandstones, shales and thin limestones. Furthermore, the existence of a large submarine bank along the southern edge of the Askrigg Block in Lower Carboniferous times assisted in the formation of a belt of lenticular reef limestones (Bond, 1950) whose 'knolls', exhumed by erosion, now form prominent rounded hills in a curving tract extending from Clitheroe through Settle to Malham and Burnsall (Parkinson, 1935). The highest Millstone Grit-capped summits of the Craven Uplands, Whernside (737 m), Ingleborough (723 m) and Pen-y-Ghent (693 m), rise like truncated pyramids above the gleaming limestone plateaux, having been fashioned by rivers and glaciers from a once continuous cover of impermeable Yoredales. Streams still descend steeply from their shaly summits until they cross on to the plinth of porous limestone where they rapidly disappear into shafts known as 'potholes' (Sweeting, 1950). The

Figure 10.5 Structure of the Ingleborough area, looking north-west.

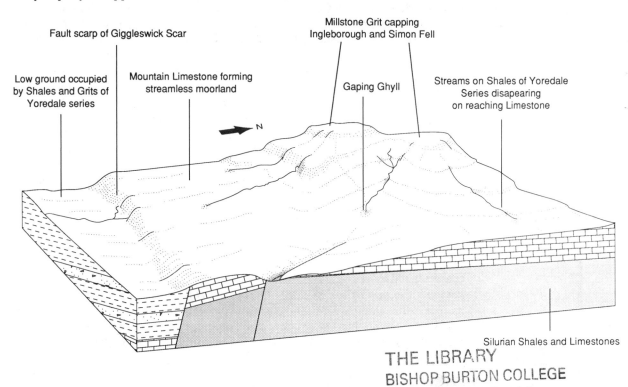

Fault scarp of Giggleswick Scar

Millstone Grit capping Ingleborough and Simon Fell

Low ground occupied by Shales and Grits of Yoredale series

Mountain Limestone forming streamless moorland

Gaping Ghyll

Streams on Shales of Yoredale Series disapearing on reaching Limestone

N

Silurian Shales and Limestones

most renowned is Gaping Gill (or Ghyll), on the flanks of Ingleborough, where the Fell Beck plunges vertically for some 110 metres (Fig. 10.5). Finally, all the underground streams eventually reappear in the valleys far below, either as a quiet 'rising' in a dark placid pool or as a brook issuing from a cave mouth, like that at Clapham Beck Head or at Malham Cove (Waltham, 1970). The latter's enormous amphitheatre, with its 100 metre cliff of naked limestone (Fig. 10.6a), requires a special explanation for precipices of this magnitude are rare in Britain apart from some sea cliffs and the glacially eroded mountainlands (Clayton, 1981). Above the cove a dry valley can be traced back across the North Craven Fault to lonely Malham Tarn, sited on a narrow outcrop of Silurian slate belonging to the otherwise buried Askrigg Block. It is clear that a stream once occupied the now waterless Watlowes Valley, probably during the periglacial conditions of the Ice Age when all underground water would have been frozen by permafrost and the frigid cave network sealed by ice. Surface waters from the melting ice sheets of the uplands would have been forced to carve out an overland route to the cove's faulted escarpment (North Craven Fault) over which they must have plunged as a mighty waterfall. Once the climate had ameliorated in post-glacial times the drainage would have returned underground once more (Smith and Atkinson, 1977). At neighbouring Gordale Scar the limestone roof of a similar subterranean cave system has collapsed to create an awesome chasm of thundering waterfalls and overhanging walls of bare limestone (O'Connor *et al.*, 1974).

The almost horizontal disposition of the Craven limestones has helped create other noteworthy landforms, in which white valleyside cliffs, or *scars*, have been chiselled out by moving ice; Kilnsey Crag, Raven Scar and Twisleton Scars are among the most remarkable. Above them rise staircases of grassy 'treads' and starkly white 'risers'. In places the glacial scouring and subsequent solution of the limestone have combined to produce horizontal limestone pavements (Fig. 10.6b). It is noteworthy that the Carboniferous Limestones of Mendip and the White Peak have no limestone pavements and, since both appear to be unaffected by glacial erosion, it would seem that ice action is a prerequisite for the initial stripping of true limestone pavements (Williams, 1966). Among the many examples, one of the best known is that above Malham Cove, with its scrubbed surface criss-crossed by deep fissures, termed *grikes*, where rainwater has widened the joints and left the intervening rock as a mosaic of pedestals known as *clints*. Seemingly devoid of vegetation, in fact these clefts carry a rich lime-loving flora, protected from the vagaries of wind, sheep and man. Indeed, it has been claimed that the impact of people and their domestic livestock has probably been one of the major factors responsible for the loss of many of the Pennines forests during post-glacial times, although some writers think only in terms of climatic change (Turner and Hodgson, 1979). The bright green calcicole grasslands of the Craven Uplands limestone tracts, dominated by sheep's fescue (*Festuca ovina*), survive despite the heavy rainfall because the limestone's porosity prevents the accumulation of acid humus in the soil. By contrast, the more impermeable Yoredales are characterized by mat-grass (*Nardus stricta*), purple moor-grass (*Molinia caerulea*), heather (*Calluna vulgaris*) and bracken (*Pteridium aquilinium*) whose acidic moorlands and wetter grasslands bring a considerably darker tone to the upland peaks, producing scenery much more comparable to the gritstone moors of the central Pennines. The limestone plateau to the east of Ingleborough has a

Figure 10.6 (a) The vertical cliff of Malham Cove, central Pennines, carved from Carboniferous Limestone, was once the site of a large waterfall during the Pleistocene Ice Age. (b) The ice-scoured limestone pavement above the cliffs of Malham Cove. Both grikes (fissures) and clints (pedestals) can be seen.

scattering of large Yoredale boulders distributed as glacial erratics during the Ice Age. Because they have protected the underlying limestone from rainfall they now perch on pedestals up to 30 centimetres high, making it possible, therefore, to calculate that since they were dumped some 12 000 years ago the limestone surface has been lowered at an average rate of about 25 millimetres every 1000 years. Further calculations suggest that such limestone surfaces may have been lowered by as much as 80 metres during the 1.6 million years of the Pleistocene (Pitty, 1968).

Notwithstanding the remarkable character of the Craven Uplands, many would contend that the most attractive scenery is to be found on the eastern flanks of the Askrigg Block, namely the east-flowing river valleys which gave J. B. Priestley cause to proclaim that he had 'never seen a countryside to equal in beauty the Yorkshire Dales'. All have karstic limestone scenery in their upper reaches, while one (Airedale) flows from limestone Malham to gritstone Ilkley and onwards to the industrial West Riding. Wensleydale and Swaledale are different from Airedale because their limestone valleysides are more conspicuous and their drystone fieldwalls give a unique character to their scenery (King, 1960). Andrew Young found that Swaledale 'owes much to its walls . . . dragging up the fields and drawing down the fells, they bind them in unity. They cover the steep uneven slopes with their wavering parallelograms'. Although outliers of the Yoredales have survived between Swaledale and Wensleydale (Moore, 1958), it is the glittering limestone that has been used in all the older buildings except for the thick Yoredale roofing flags, quarried at Penhill in Wensleydale, and whose weight has bowed the roof beams of farm and barn alike. The lichen-crusted isolated field barns, with hayloft above the livestock byre below, are reminiscent of Alpine rather than Pennine landscapes. But the settlement patterns are largely Scandinavian, as illustrated by such Norse names as Healaugh, Low Whita and Thwaite in Swaledale, and Hardraw, Swinthwaite and Aysgarth in Wensleydale. Unlike the White Peak of Derbyshire, the Dales have no settlements on their limestone uplands, instead the villages crowd along the valley springlines or at river crossings. Interestingly, it has been shown by Smailes (1961) how the character of the valleys themselves is reflected in their nomenclature. Thus, the broad pre-glacial trunk valleys are always 'dales'; the open, mature tributaries are often termed 'hopes'; the deeper post-glacial gorges are 'denes' or 'gills' depending on whether they relate, respectively, to Anglian or Scandinavian place names, while narrow cleft-like gullies and most streamless meltwater channels are often known as 'cleughs'.

To the north, the Alston Block is delimited from its neighbouring uplands by the trans-Pennine glacial breaches of Stainmore (in the south) and the Tyne Gap (in the north) (Fig. 10.7). Both served as former routeways for Scottish and Lake District ice sheets which crossed northern England's main watershed as shown by the fans of erratics which spread from their eastern exits, and by the marked patterns of drumlins which converge from Edenside into their narrow western entrances (Trotter, 1929b; Mitchell, 1991). Stainmore, carved along a zone of faulting and a transverse syncline, is today followed by the remains of a Roman road which climbs gently up its eastern dipslope from Barnard Castle before dropping steeply down to the Vale of Eden (see Fig. 9.1). This topographic asymmetry reflects the structure of the Alston Block for it is a fairly simple tilted massif uplifted in the west along the main Pennine Fault Zone to produce the

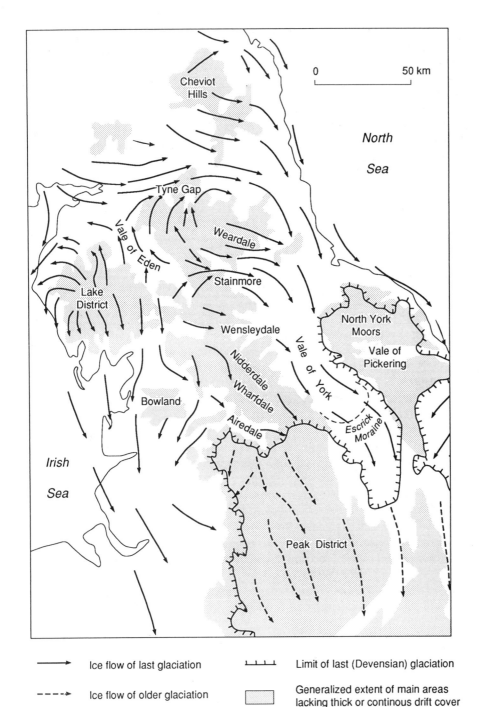

→ Ice flow of last glaciation	⊥⊥⊥ Limit of last (Devensian) glaciation
‑ ‑ ‑→ Ice flow of older glaciation	▢ Generalized extent of main areas lacking thick or continous drift cover

Figure 10.7 The glaciation of northern England (after C. Embleton).

fault-line scarp on which stands Cross Fell (893 m) overlooking Edenside (see p. 198). The surface gradient of the eastern slopes is almost parallel with the regional dip of the Yoredales which decline eastwards to pass beneath the strata of the Durham coalfield. It was upon this dipslope that a group of east-flowing consequent rivers developed to match those of the Yorkshire Dales (Trotter,

1929a): the Tees runs directly through the industrial tract of Teeside (Warren, 1968) to the North Sea at Middlesborough without crossing the coalfield; the Wear, more circuitously, glides in incised meanders past the attractive cathedral city of Durham (Gibby and Drury, 1970), as it proceeds across the southern half of the coalfield (Johnson, 1973) and through the Magnesian Limestone cuesta to Sunderland (Dewdney, 1970). The South Tyne river, however, descends from the Tyne Gap to join a complex series of other Tyne headwaters (including the North Tyne) which, having captured the upper reaches of the Wansbeck and Blyth rivers, now all debouch at Tynemouth to create a classic example of river piracy. Several studies have suggested that the Northumbrian rivers, like their east-flowing Scottish counterparts, were all related to periodic uplift in western Britain and the gradual development of a dominantly eastward-flowing set of consequent streams (Sissons, 1960). There is little doubt, however, that many of the more intricate details of the stream patterns were initiated during the Pleistocene, when considerable glacial disruption occurred (Sissons, 1958).

The gentler eastern slopes of the Alston Block are generally heather-covered on the poor acid soils of the Yoredales, in contrast to the mat grass/fescue grassland of the steeper western scarp. On the drier sandstone plateaux *Rhacomitrium* heath is interspersed with the fescue grasslands but, more frequently, the poorly drained uplands are draped with blanket bog, especially where they are thickly mantled with boulder clay. Upper Teesdale, however, is a different story for, as J. G. Baker wrote in 1868, there 'is probably no ground in Britain that produces so many rare species within a limited space as Widdy Bank Fell'. These include the very rare spring gentian (*Gentiana verna*), Teesdale violet (*Viola rupestris*) and bog sandwort (*Minuartia stricta*). It is generally agreed that the so-called 'Teesdale assemblage' are relics of a vegetation type that was once widespread in parts of upland Britain at the end of the Ice Age (Pigott, 1956). They are restricted to the so-called 'sugar limestone', a crumbly crystalline limestone that has been changed into a marble by contact with the hot magma of the Whin Sill.

Though this Carboniferous magma (Fitch and Miller, 1967) never reached the surface, its extensive sheets of dolerite became squeezed between the limestone strata in the form of a gigantic sill, producing an intrusive black igneous step in the gentle white staircase of Pennine limestones. 'Whin' and 'Whinstone' are, in fact, quarryman's terms for any dark-coloured rock such as dolerite or basalt. Wherever erosion has exposed the sill at the surface it often forms a vertical cliff some 15–30 metres in height and such a feature extends intermittently for more than 150 kilometres in northern England as a broken curving line from Upper Teesdale, through Cross Fell and eastwards across the Tyne Valley (where it is crowned by Hadrian's Wall) before reaching the Northumberland coast and the Farne Islands (Fig. 10.8). After flowing for some distance across featureless moorlands the infant River Tees first encounters the Whin Sill at Cauldron Snout where the meandering stream in its broad limestone valley is suddenly transformed into a torrent as it descends over the dark igneous rock in a series of cascades. Not far downstream it again crosses the sill but here it plunges some 20 metres in one spectacular leap at High Force, one of England's largest and most spectacular waterfalls. The dark, vertically jointed dolerite has withstood the constant attack of the peat-stained waters much more successfully than have the bedded limestones beneath. Where the base of the waterfall has quarried away at these lower, less resistant beds it has undermined the sill to leave it precariously

Figure 10.8 Hadrian's Wall sited along an outcrop of the Whin Sill near Housesteads, Northumberland.

overhanging. Periodically, masses of black whinstone crash into the boulder-strewn gorge, causing the waterfall to retreat gradually upstream.

The most important of the Carboniferous Limestone beds is the 20 metre thick Great Limestone which has not only been quarried extensively at such places as Stanhope in Weardale but also contains significant veins of lead and zinc (Dunham, 1944). In the so-called 'Lead Dales' of Teesdale, Weardale and Allendale (a tributary valley of the River Tyne system) the mineralized area, created by the completely buried Weardale Granite – (now dated to Devonian times, some 362 million years ago (Bott, 1967) – is confined to the upper valleys, but the smelting centres were often sited outside the mining areas, lower down the valleys. The veins are thin in the shales, thicker in the better-jointed sandstones but best developed in the limestones whose wide fissures facilitated ore emplacement. When the mines were in production during the eighteenth and nineteenth centuries it was a policy for the mine-owners to provide agricultural small-holdings for the lead miners. Thus, the limits of improvement were pushed unusually high into the moorland zone, well above 500 metres, although hay was virtually the only crop in this irregular pattern of stone-walled fields (Smailes, 1961). The ruined smelt-mills today form conspicuous features in the upper dales, although many of the dispersed farmsteads have survived. Weardale finally opens out on to the Durham coalfield but in the mid-nineteenth century the blast-furnaces set up at Tow Law and Consett farther north, both on the western edge of the coalfield, were based not on Coal Measures ores but on iron deposits from the Pennine limestone. For example, iron ores from as far afield as the isolated town of Alston were once smelted at Stanhope, using locally quarried limestone for flux.

The North-East coalfield and the coastlands

Despite the large extent of the Coal Measures outcrop (being almost 50 kilometres wide in Co. Durham) the original rural landscape, with its livestock farming patterns, has not everywhere been obscured by the normally ubiquitous industrial overlay. In fact, the presence of thick sandstones among the softer shales and marls of the Coal Measures brings considerable diversity to the coalfield scenery (Hickling *et al.*, 1931). In western Durham the easterly dip of the sandstone beds is so low that these sandstones frequently add almost horizontal cappings to the tabular hills (termed *laws*). In particular, a group of sandstones which occur just above the most important coal seams of the Middle Coal Measures is responsible for some of the highest ground in the coalfield. They create the steep hills of Newcastle before extending southwards past Hollinside (244 m) near Lanchester to Broom Hill (287 m) east of Tow Law.

Where the coalfield reaches the Northumberland coast between Tynemouth and Amble the outcropping cliffside seams have been continuously eroded by the waves to provide copious supplies of 'sea-coal', used by salt-panners and fisher folk from time immemorial. By the mid-sixteenth century the depletion of England's timber resources had begun to threaten a fuel shortage, especially in London, which meant that coal had to be adopted as a domestic fuel. Henceforward the easily worked outcrops on the banks of the navigable Tyne were to provide London with its nearest water-transported supply, but having supplied most of South-East England's coal since Elizabethan times many of the thicker seams of the North-East coalfield are, not surprisingly, now exhausted. It is noteworthy that in Northumberland steam coals and house coals are more prevalent, while in Durham coking and gas coals are more common (Hopkins, 1954). With the demise of 'town' gas production in favour of North Sea natural gas, however, coal extraction from the exposed western parts of both the Durham and the Northumberland coalfields has now ceased. Today, coal is mined almost exclusively near to the eastern coast, either from a few pits around Ashington and Morpeth at the northernmost extremity of the exposed coalfield, or from the very productive seams buried beneath thick layers of Permian Sandstone and Magnesian Limestone around Easington in eastern Co. Durham (Reid, 1970). The main folding of the Coal Measures must be of post-Westphalian and pre-Permian age, because the gently dipping Coal Measures of the western limb of the coalfield suddenly give way to steeply folded anticlines and synclines where they pass unconformably beneath the virtually flat-lying cover of Permian rocks (Smith, 1970). Of these the Magnesian Limestone is the most conspicuous of the strata, its yellowish-brown dolomitic limestone occupying a triangular-shaped area that lies between the towns of Darlington, Hartlepool and South

Shields (Trechmann, 1925). Its western edge creates a marked escarpment facing across the worked-out exposed coalfield and, because of its cavernous nature, due to the action of underground waters, large tracts of the limestone surface are waterless. It may once have been crossed by major rivers draining eastwards from the Alston Block, but if so they have been captured by the middle portion of the Wear, which from Bishop Auckland to Chester-le-Street is evidently a subsequent stream flowing northwards along the foot of the Magnesian Limestone scarp (Beaumont, 1970). At the coast the same limestone gives rise to steep rocky seacliffs which are in marked contrast to those formed by boulder-clay-capped Coal Measures to the north of Tynemouth. In such places as Marsden sea stacks have been fashioned by wave erosion along vertical joints in the yellow dolomitic limestone. Elsewhere, the few coastal streams have eroded deep gorges or 'denes' where they have cut down through the thick drift cover and into the underlying limestone, although some of the bays mark the exits of deep but buried Pleistocene stream valleys now plugged with boulder clay derived, it is thought, partly from Scandinavian ice but mainly from the west and north (Raistrick, 1931). The so-called Scandinavian drift at Warren House Gill near Horden, Co. Durham, is overlain by a loess-like material claimed to be of inter-glacial age, possibly originating during the Ipswichian interglacial (Trechmann, 1915), when the nearby 27 metre Easington raised beach may also have been formed. Ice-flow directions in the Durham coastlands seem to have been very complex, for the local glaciers emerging from the Yorkshire Dales (Raistrick, 1926) and from Teesdale (Agar, 1954) were joined by trans-Pennine ice flowing through Stainmore, before being deflected southwards by the inferred presence of the Scandinavian ice sheet in the North Sea Basin (Beaumont, 1968) (see Fig. 10.7).

It appears that in addition to the Cheviot, the Carter Fell and Cross Fell ice caps (Raistrick, 1926) of the northern Pennines ice sheets from the Lake District and western Scotland periodically advanced and retreated across the main watershed, by way of Stainmore and the Tyne Gap, on several occasions (see Fig. 10.7) (Raistrick, 1934). In Tynedale it has been shown how the glacial and glacio-fluvial sediments have subsequently been turned into terraces in post-glacial times by river action. Recent research has demonstrated, moreover, that the waste products of the metalliferous mining have had equally dramatic effects on the sediment supplied to the rivers of this area, but this time during the nineteenth century. At that time this region was Britain's main lead and zinc producer and the copious waste material has caused massive valleyfloor aggradation and a change from a meandering to a braided river channel pattern (Macklin and Rose, 1986). Post-glacial valleyfills of this type found elsewhere in Britain have usually been caused by deforestation related to the advent of agriculture and, although most of the natural tree cover of the north Pennines is known to have disappeared by the close of the Roman occupation, these northern alluvial deposits have not as yet been linked to forest clearance which must, nevertheless, have induced increased soil erosion and sediment production in these northern valleys.

The Tyne Corridor or Gap is a valley eroded along the axis of a synclinal trough that separates the Alston Block of the Pennines from the Bewcastle and Cheviot domes of the border (see Fig. 9.1). Along its southern edge the east–west Stublick Faults, which also delimit the northern edge of the Alston Block, are not manifested by a fault-line escarpment, unlike their western counterparts below Cross Fell. The northern side of the Tyne Corridor is marked, instead, by a moderately dipping succession of Dinantian and Namurian limestones, shales and sandstones into which the Whin Sill has been intruded (Johnson, 1959). Such structures have been fashioned into a distinctive cuesta-type of landscape, characterized by lengthy southerly-descending dipslopes and steep but low north-facing scarps (see Fig. 10.8). A ribbon of farmland continues right through the Tyne Gap but, more surprisingly, there is evidence of former coal-mining activities as far west as Haltwhistle, for hereabouts the Lower Dinantian Limestone series include several seams of workable coal. The collieries were sited within easy reach of the railway through the Tyne Gap. Today, the greatest extraction industry is in the dolerite of the Whin Sill, quite extensively quarried for roadstone at Haltwhistle and the Nine Nicks of Thirlwall. Sadly, important sections of the Sill escarpment and also parts of Hadrian's Wall itself have been destroyed in the quarrying process. Near Hexham the line of the Sill crosses the North Tyne and from here westwards Hadrian's Wall sits atop the sharply etched escarpment. Commenced in AD 123, this northern bulwark of Roman Britain was constructed largely from Carboniferous sandstones and limestones but also included occasional blocks of whinstone. For centuries after the Romans' departure its stone-work was plundered both for farmstead and field wall, but particularly for incorporation into the solitary 'peel towers' which served as fortified farms during the border warfare of the Middle Ages. Northwards, the deserted countryside stretches away over unbroken vistas of pastureland until the great forests of Wark and Kielder spread across these lonely Border lands. The place names from Hexham westwards are suggestive of Celtic survivals in this bleak hill-farming country, but eastwards, where the terrain is lower, the climate milder and the soils less heavy, the Saxon settlers were able to plough the lowlands of Northumbria and there the place names reflect this later period of settlement (Fraser and Emsley, 1978). It is through these lowlands that the Whin Sill marches to the coast where it forms a line of columnar sea cliffs between Alnwick (Westoll *et al.*, 1955) and Bamburgh before disintegrating into the scatter of bird-haunted reefs and stacks known as the Farne Islands. Here the vertically jointed dolerite has created a multitude of nesting sites for thousands of guillemots, kittiwakes, shags and puffins, while the whinstone reefs support one of Britain's largest grey seal breeding grounds. The much altered but still imposing Bamburgh Castle on the whinstone crag above the dune-fringed beach is perhaps the best known of Northumberland's coastal castles, although the ruined fortress of Dunstanburgh is even more atmospheric as it perches on its dolerite promontory.

To the north of Hadrian's Wall the Carboniferous Limestone, which helps give the Alston Block some of its finest scenery, begins to diminish in thickness as it becomes interleaved with beds of sandstone and shale. Eventually, to the east of the Cheviot's igneous dome the character of the limestone changes (Hickling *et al.*, 1931). Some 350 million years ago this region appears to have been a Cheviot island surrounded by shallow seas. Beach pebbles of that time have been transformed into the basal conglomerates of the Dinantian that are exposed at such places as Windy Rigg and Roddam Dene. Between the beach shingle ridges of the Lower Carboniferous coastline muddy deltas must have witnessed a mixing of clay and limestone as the tides ebbed and flowed; these clayey limestones are today known as *cementstones*, outcrops of which can be viewed in the 45 metre deep gorge of the Coquet above Alwinton. The next beds of rocks to be laid down in this Lower Carboniferous (Dinantian) succession were very different in character for they were composed of current-bedded sands and grits which accumulated to thicknesses of 100 metres and are now exposed as the Fell Sandstones (Robson, 1956). Each of these different rock layers forms concentric strips around the eroded Cheviot Dome and because of their differing resistance to erosion they have now been etched into a series of concentric vales, on the shales and cementstones, and inward-facing scarps mainly on the Fell Sandstones (Shiells, 1964). The easterly dipping cuesta of these tough sandstones has produced a broad line of hills which sweeps in a curve southwards from Berwick. It rises in elevation as it is traced south past the attractive stone castle town of Alnwick and the picturesque village of Rothbury to the thickly forested plateau of Simonside (429 m). This cuesta shuts off the Cheviot Hills from the Northumberland coast and is crossed by only two rivers, the Aln and the Coquet, where the sandstone outcrop is affected by faults. In addition to the fortifications at these two river gaps, castles are commonplace along the ridge, from Chillingham Castle in the north to Chipchase Castle in the south (Newton, 1972). The Fell Sandstone escarpment overlooks a broad curving vale that can be traced northwards to the valley of the Tweed. Apart from the coastal route this vale, swinging around the eastern flanks of the Cheviot and drained mainly by the north-flowing River Till, has served as a strategic border routeway, as testified by the number of its battle sites, including Flodden. The radial drainage pattern of the Cheviot Hills has been considerably modified since its inception on the flanks of the uplifted igneous dome. Originally spawned on a thick cover of Carboniferous rocks the initial consequents would have traversed the entire dipslope in the same manner as the modern Aln and Coquet. Owing to the comparative ease with which their tributary streams could erode the cementstones, however, they were able to excavate a vale along the curvilinear regional strike and develop into piratical streams that have captured the headwaters of many of the consequents. In the north the Till has led off the College Burn, Harthope Burn and the Breamish to join the Tweed; in the south the North Tyne has captured the Rede which originally formed the headwaters of the Wansbeck. Dense carpets of heather survive on the podzols of the Fell Sandstone plateau except where the estates of the great landowners intervene. The regular settlement pattern, the straight roads and regimented woodlands all suggest a relatively recent overlay of a planned landscape rather than one that has evolved naturally through the centuries.

Contrastingly, the settlement patterns of the Cheviot Dome exhibit a greater antiquity for they consist largely of clustered hamlets around a fortified stone farmhouse set amid widespread upland grazings the fertility of which is governed entirely by the character of the terrain, geology and soils. The better-drained lower slopes of the base-rich andesites, though their soils are leached, carry good pastures of sheep's fescue and bent, especially on the Cheviot's southern slopes where large flocks of sheep are to be found. These palatable grasses are replaced at higher altitudes, especially where the drainage is poorer, by mat grass and purple moor grass, a typical grassland of wet, heavily leached soils, whose grazing potential is considerably less. Thus, many of these 'prairies' have been afforested with conifer plantations. A century ago heather moors were much more extensive on the more acidic soils of the Cheviot Granite but these have declined as sheep grazing has expanded to replace grouse moor management. Among the most characteristic features of the Cheviot Hills' sheep today are the large flocks of white-faced 'Cheviots' on the lower grasslands (the Whitelands) and the hardier 'Blackfaces' on the windswept heather moors of the summits (the Blacklands).

The geology of the Cheviot Hills is very different to that of the rest of the Pennines, for here is a massif carved from a pile of Lower Old Red Sandstone volcanics subsequently invaded by the large Cheviot Granite. This intrusion appears to have led to doming, uplift and the creation of a radial dike-swarm of fine-grained pink felsite as magma was forced into tensional cracks in the crustal upwarp. A waterfall, the Linhope Spout, has formed where a tributary of the upper Breamish cascades over one such resistant dike. The volcanic activity was explosive judging by the amount of pyroclastic material associated with the lava flows most of which were base-rich andesites whose purple-grey and pink pebbles can be found in every streambed. Some of the 'glassy' andesites, however, are an attractive black colour with red veining. The unroofed granite, at the centre of the dome, forms the highest hills of Hedgehope and the Cheviot itself (816 m). Despite its elevation the scenery is lacking in the grandeur one might expect from volcanic terrain, and rock exposures are rare except in the stream-eroded gorges. This is partly explained by the thick solifluction sheets of till, head and regolith which may have been formed during the Loch Lomond stadial. An exception to this occurs on the metamorphic aureole where the granite came into contact with the andesite and baked it into a tougher, darker rock with larger crystals of mica and feldspar. This circle of harder metamorphic rock has subsequently been fashioned into tors, such as those at Long Crag and Housey Crag above the Harthope Burn. The only other Cheviot topographic features of note were a product of the Ice Age (Derbyshire, 1961). Streamless meltwater channels, produced beneath or marginal to the ice sheets, score the hillsides below Yeavering Bell and in the Harthope Valley, while the Newcastle–Coldstream road (A697) follows such a channel at Powburn (Clapperton, 1971). Otherwise, the Cheviots boast only a single glacial cirque, the Bizzle, surrounded by the ubiquitous grass-covered slopes.

Bibliography

Agar, R. (1954) The glacial and post-glacial geology of Middlesborough and the Tees estuary. *Proc. Yorks. Geol. Soc.*, **29**, 237–53.
Allen, J. R. L. (1960) The Mam Tor Sandstones: a 'turbidite' facies of the Namurian deltas of Derbyshire, England. *J. Sedimentary Petrology*, **30**, 193–208.
Balme, O. E. (1953) Edaphic and vegetational zoning on the Carboniferous Limestone of the Derbyshire Dales. *J. Ecol.*, 41.
Beaumont, P. (1968) *A History of Glacial Research in Northern England from 1860 to the Present Day*. Univ. of Durham Occ. Paper no. 9.
Beaumont, P. (1970) Geomorphology, in J. C. Dewdney (ed.) *Durham County and City with Teeside*. University of Durham Press. 26–45.
Bemrose, H. H. A. (1907) The Toadstones of Derbyshire: their field relations and petrography. *Quart. J. Geol. Soc.*, **63**, 241–81.
Beresford, M. W. and Jones, G. R. J. (1967) *Leeds and its Region*. Leeds University Press. 298 pp.
Boardman, J. (1985) *The Periglacial Landforms of Northern England*. Field Guide. Quat. Res. Assoc. 82 pp.

Bond, G. (1950) The nomenclature of Lower Carboniferous 'Reef' Limestones in the North of England. *Geol. Mag.*, **87**, 267–78.

Bott, M.H.P. (1967) Geophysical investigations of the northern Pennine basement rocks. *Proc. Yorks. Geol. Soc.*, **36**, 139–68.

Bott, M.H.P. and Johnson, G.A.L. (1967) Controlling mechanism of Carboniferous cyclic sedimentation, *Quart. J. Geol. Soc.*, **122**, 421–41.

Briggs, D.J., Gilbertson, D.D. and Jenkinson, R.D.S. (1988) *Peak District and Northern Dukeries*. Field Guide. Quat. Res. Assoc. 221 pp.

Campbell, J.B. (1969) Excavations at Creswell Crags. *Derbys. Archaeol. J.*, **89**, 47–58.

Clapperton, C.M. (1971) The location and origin of glacial meltwater phenomena in the eastern Cheviot Hills. *Proc. Yorks. Geol. Soc.*, **38**, 361–80.

Clayton, K.M. (1981) Explanatory description of the landforms of the Malham Area. *Fld Stud.*, **5**, 389–423.

Collinson, J.D. (1969) The sedimentology of the Grindslow Shales and the Kinderscout Grit: a deltaic complex in the Namurian of northern England. *J. Sedimentary Petrology*, **39**, 194–221.

Conway, V.M. (1954) Stratigraphy and pollen analysis of southern Pennine blanket peats. *J. Ecol.* **42**, 117–47.

Cope, F.W. (1958) *The Peak District, Derbyshire*. Guide no. 26. Geol. Assoc. 26 pp.

Cope, F.W. (1976) *Geology Explained in the Peak District*. David and Charles. 192 pp.

Cunningham, F.F. (1965) Tor theories in the light of south Pennine evidence. *East Midland Geogr.*, **3**, 424–33.

Dalton, R., Fox, H. and Jones, P. (1988) *Classic Landforms of the White Peak*. Classic Landform Guides no. 9. Geog. Assoc. 48 pp.

Derbyshire, E. (1961) Sub-glacial col channels and the deglaciation of the north eastern Cheviots. *Trans. Inst. Br. Geogr.*, **29**, 31–46.

Dewdney, J.C. (ed.) (1970) *Durham County and City with Teeside*. University of Durham Press. 522 pp.

Dunham, K.C. (1944) The genesis of the north Pennine ore deposits. *Quart. J. Geol. Soc.*, **90**, 689–720.

Edwards, K.C. (1962) *The Peak District*. Collins. 240 pp.

Edwards, W. and Trotter, F.M. (1954) *The Pennines and Adjacent Areas* (3rd edn). Brit. Reg. Geol. HMSO. 86 pp.

Fearnsides, W.G. (1932). The valley of the Derbyshire Derwent. *Proc. Geol. Assoc.*, **43**, 153–78.

Fitch, F.J. and Miller, J.A. (1967) The age of the Whin Sill. *Geol. J.*, **5**, 233–50.

Ford, T.D. (1986) The evolution of the Castleton cave systems and related features, Derbyshire. *Mercian Geol.*, **10**, 91–114.

Ford, T.D. and Rieuwerts, J.H. (1975) *Lead Mining in the Peak District*. Peak Park Planning Board.

Fraser, C. and Emsley, K. (1978) *Northumbria*. Batsford. 208 pp.

Gibby, C.W. and Drury, M.P. (1970) Durham City, in J.C. Dewdney (ed.), *Durham County and City with Teeside*. University of Durham Press. 511–22.

Gilligan, A. (1920) The petrography of the Millstone Grit of Yorkshire. *Quart. J. Geol. Soc.*, **75**, 251–94.

Hickling, H.G.A., Carruthers, R.G., Dunham, K.C. *et al.* (1931) The geology of Northumberland and Durham. *Proc. Geol. Assoc.*, **42**, 217–96.

Hopkins, W. (1954) The coalfields of Northumberland and Durham. In A.E. Trueman, *The Coalfields of Great Britain*. Arnold. 289–313.

Hudson, R.G.S. (1924) On the rhythmic succession of the Yoredale Series in Wensleydale. *Proc. Yorks. Geol. Soc.*, **20**, 125–35.

Hudson, R.G.S., Versey, H.C., Edwards, W. and Raistrick, A. (1938) The geology of the country around Harrogate. *Proc. Geol. Assoc.*, **49**, 293–352.

Hudson, R.G.S. and Cotton, G. (1945) The Carboniferous rocks of the Edale anticline, Derbyshire. *Quart. J. Geol. Soc.*, **101**, 1–36.

Johnson, G.A.L. (1959) The Carboniferous stratigraphy of the Roman Wall district in western Northumberland. *Proc. Yorks. Geol. Soc.*, **32**, 83–130.

Johnson, G.A.L. (1967) Basement control of Carboniferous Sedimentation in northern England. *Proc. Yorks. Geol. Soc.*, **36**, 175–94.

Johnson, G.A.L. (1973) *The Durham Area*. Guide no. 15. Geol. Assoc. 32 pp.

Johnson, R.H. (1965) The glacial geomorphology of the west Pennine slopes from Cliviger to Congleton, in J.B. Whittow and P.D. Wood (eds), *Essays in Geography for Austin Miller*. University of Reading. 58–93.

Jones, P.F. and Charsley, T.J. (1985) A re-appraisal of the denudation chronology of south Derbyshire, England. *Proc. Geol. Assoc.*, 96, 73–86.

King, C.A.M. (1960) *The Yorkshire Dales*. Landscapes through Maps no. 2 Geog. Assoc. 29 pp.

King, C.A.M. (1976) *Northern England*. Methuen. 213 pp.

Kent, P.E. (1957) Triassic relics and the 1000-foot surface in the southern Pennines. *East Midland Geogr.*, 8.

Linton, D.L. (ed.) (1956) *Sheffield and its Region*. Oxford University Press, 334 pp.

Macklin, M.E. and Rose, J. (1986) *Quaternary River Landforms and Sediments in the Northern Pennines*. Field Guide. Quat. Res. Assoc. and Brit. Geomorph. Res. Gp. 88 pp.

Mee, A. (ed.) (1937) *Derbyshire, The Peak Country*. Hodder and Stoughton.

Merton, L.F.H. (1970) The history and status of woodlands of the Derbyshire limestone. *J. Ecol.*, 58, 723–44.

Milward, R. and Robinson, A. (1975) *The Peak District*. Eyre Methuen. 301 pp.

Mitchell, W.A. (ed.) (1991) *Western Pennines*. Field Guide. Quat. Res. Assoc. 124 pp.

Moore, D.G. (1958) The Yoredale Series of Upper Wensleydale and adjacent parts of North West Yorkshire. *Proc. Yorks Geol. Soc.*, 31, 91–148.

Moss, C.E. (1913) *Vegetation of the Peak District*. Cambridge University Press.

Newton, R. (1972) *The Northumberland Landscape*. Hodder & Stoughton. 256 pp.

O'Connor, J., Williams, D.S.F. and Davies, G.M. (1974) Karst features of Malham and the Craven Fault Zone, in A.C. Waltham (ed.), *The Limestones and Caves of North-West England*. David and Charles. 395–409.

Palmer, J. and Radley, J. (1961) Gritstone tors of the English Pennines. *Zeitschrift für Geomorphologie*, 5, 37–52.

Parkinson, D. (1935) The geology and topography of the Limestone knolls in Bolland (Bowland), Lancashire and Yorkshire. *Proc. Geol. Assoc.*, 46, 97–120.

Parkinson, D. (1950) The stratigraphy of the Dovedale area, Derbyshire and Staffordshire. *Quart. J. Geol. Soc.*, 105, 265–94.

Phillips, J., Yalden, D. and Tallis, J.H. (1981) *Peak District Moorland Erosion Study: Phase I*. Report Peak Park Joint Planning Board.

Pigott, C.D. (1956) The Vegetation of Upper Teesdale in the northern Pennines. *J. Ecol.*, 44, 545–86.

Pigott, C.D. (1965) The structure of limestone surfaces in Derbyshire. *Geog. J.*, 131, 41–4.

Pitty, A.F. (1968) The scale and significance of solutional loss from the limestone tract of the Southern Pennines. *Proc. Geol. Assoc.*, 79, 153–78.

Prentice, J.E. (1950) The Carboniferous Limestone of the Manifold Valley region, north Staffordshire. *Quart. J. Geol. Soc.*, 106, 171–209.

Preston, F.L. (1954) The hillforts of the Peak. *Derbys. Archaeol. J.*, 74, 1–31.

Radley, J. (1966) Peak millstones and Hallamshire grindstones. *Trans. Newcomen Soc.*, 36, 165–74.

Raistrick, A. (1926) The glaciation of Wensleydale, Swaledale and the adjoining parts of the Pennines. *Proc. Yorks. Geol. Soc.*, 20, 366–410.

Raistrick, A. (1931) The glaciation of Northumberland and Durham. *Proc. Geol. Assoc.*, 42, 281–91.

Raistrick, A. (1934) The correlation of glacial retreat stages across the Pennines. *Proc. Yorks. Geol. Soc.*, 22, 199–214.

Raistrick, A. (1970) *West Riding of Yorkshire*. Hodder & Stoughton. 191 pp.

Rayner, D.H. (1953) The Lower Carboniferous Rocks in the North of England: a review. *Proc. Yorks Geol. Soc.*, 28, 231–315.

Reid, W. (1970) The coal mining industry, in: J.C. Dewdney (ed.), *Durham County and City with Teeside*. University of Durham Press. 294–302.

Roberts, B.K. (1987) *The Making of the English Village*. Longman. 237 pp.

Robson, D.A. (1956) A sedimentary study of the Fell Sandstones of the Coquet Valley, Northumberland. *Quart. J. Geol. Soc.*, 112, 241–62.

Shiells, K. A. G. (1964) The geological structure of north east Northumberland. *Trans. R. Soc. Edinb.*, **65**, 447–81.

Shirley, J. (1959) The Carboniferous Limestone of the Monyash-Wirksworth area, Derbyshire. *Quart. J. Geol. Soc.*, **114**, 411–31.

Shirley, J. and Horsfield, E. L. (1940) The Carboniferous Limestone of the Castleton-Bradwell district, Derbyshire. *Quart. J. Geol. Soc.*, **96**, 271–99.

Simpson, I. M. (1982) *The Peak District*. Unwin. 120 pp.

Sissons, J. B. (1958) Sub-glacial stream erosion in southern Northumberland. *Scot. Geog. Mag.*, **74**, 163–74.

Sissions, J. B. (1960) Erosion surfaces, cyclic slopes and drainage systems in southern Scotland and northern England. *Trans. Inst. Br. Geogr.*, **28**, 23–38.

Smailes, A. E. (1961) *North England*. Nelson. 324 pp.

Smith, D. B. (1970) Permian and Trias, in *The Geology of Durham County*. Trans. Nat. Hist. Soc. Northumberland.

Smith, D. I. and Atkinson, T. C. (1977) Underground flow in cavernous limestones with special reference to the Malham Area. *Fld Stud.*, **4**, 597–616.

Straw, A. (1968) A Pleistocene diversion of drainage in North Derbyshire. *East Midland Geogr.*, **4**, 275–80.

Sweeting, M. M. (1950) Erosion cycles and limestone caverns in the Ingleborough district. *Geog. J.*, **115**, 63–78.

Tallis, J. H. (1985) Erosion of blanket peat in the southern Pennines: a new light on an old problem, in R. H. Johnson (ed.), *The Geomorphology of North West England*. Manchester University Press. 313–36.

Tallis, J. H. and Switsur, V. R. (1983) Forest and moorland in the south Pennine uplands in the mid-Flandrian period. I. Macrofossil evidence of the former forest cover. *J. Ecol.*, **71**, 585–600.

Taylor, B. J., Burgess, I. C., Land, D. H. *et al.* (1971) *Northern England* (4th edn). British Regional Geology. HMSO. 121 pp.

Trechmann, C. T. (1915) The Scandinavian Drift of the Durham coast and the general glaciology of south-east Durham. *Quart. J. Geol. Soc.*, **71**, 53–82.

Trechmann, C. T. (1925) The Permian Formation in Durham. *Proc. Geol. Assoc.*, **42**, 246–52.

Trotter, F. M. (1929a) The Tertiary uplift and resultant drainage of the Alston Block and adjacent areas. *Proc. Yorks. Geol. Soc.*, **21**, 161–80.

Trotter, F. M. (1929b) The glaciation of eastern Edenside, Alston Block and the Carlisle Plain. *J. Geol. Soc. Lond.*, **88**, 549–607.

Trotter, F. M. and Hollingworth, S. E. (1928) The Alston Block. *Geol. Mag.*, **65**, 433–48.

Tufnell, L. (1969) The range of periglacial phenomena in northern England. *Biuletyn Peryglacjalny*, **19**, 291–323.

Turner, J. S. (1927) The Lower Carboniferous succession in the Westmorland Pennines and the relations of the Pennine and Dent faults. *Proc. Geol. Assoc.*, **38**, 339–74.

Turner, J. S. (1935) Structural geology of Stainmore, Westmorland, and notes on the late-Palaeozoic (late-Variscan) tectonics of the North of England. *Proc. Geol. Assoc.*, **46**, 121–51.

Turner, J. and Hodgson, J. (1979) Studies in the vegetational history of the northern Pennines, I. Variations in the composition of the Early Flandrian forests. *J. Ecol.*, **67**, 629–46.

Walsh, P. T., Boulter, M. C., Ijtaba, M. and Urbani, D. M. (1972) The preservation of the Neogene Brassington Formation of the southern Pennines and its bearing on the evolution of upland Britain. *Quart. J. Geol. Soc.*, **128**, 519–59.

Waltham, A. C. (1970) Cave development in the limestone of the Ingleborough district. *Geog. J.*, **136**, 574–85.

Warren, K. (1968) The shaping of the Teeside industrial region. *Adv. Sci.*, **25**, 185–99.

Waters, R. S. and Johnson, R. H. (1958) The terraces of the Derbyshire Derwent. *East Midland Geogr.*, **2**, 3–15.

Westoll, T. S., Robson, D. A. and Green, R. (1955) A guide to the geology of the district around Alnwick, Northumberland. *Proc. Yorks. Geol. Soc.*, **30**, 61–100.

Williams, P. W. (1966) Limestone pavements. *Trans. Inst. Br. Geogr.*, **40**, 155–72.

Young, A. (n.d.) *A Prospect of Britain*. Harper and Bros. 200 pp.

The Scottish Border Country and Galloway

11

The crestline of the Cheviot Hills and the lower reaches of the River Tweed are followed largely by the border itself, though the landforms hardly change as one passes from England into Scotland. Nevertheless, once across the Tweed the cultural landscapes become distinctively Scottish in what is known as the Border Country.

The Border Country

The grey, walled town of Berwick-upon-Tweed, described by Burns as 'an idle town, rudely picturesque', is really a Norman foundation but has long served as a focus for the Scottish road pattern of the Tweed basin (White, 1973).

All the main roads radiating from Berwick swing gradually round in a south-westerly direction as they cross the farmlands of the Merse of Berwickshire, because they follow the 'grain' of the Merse landforms produced by ice sheets as they moved down the valley of the Tweed. The ice was powerful enough to smooth any rock outcrops into low whaleback hills and to fashion the thick boulder clay into a fluted topography with streamlined hillocks, or 'drumlins', whose long axes reflect the direction taken by the former ice sheet. The fertile clay loams of the Merse support a flourishing agricultural economy, so that the Tweed Basin is renowned for its large mixed farms – areas of over 200 hectares are not uncommon – on some of Scotland's richest soils. The landscape is a prosperous one, with neat hedgerows of beech and thorn dividing the extensive cornfields from the sheep- and cattle-crowded pastures.

For the last 48 kilometres of its course below Kelso the Tweed meanders across this farming landscape, scarcely coming into contact with the solid rock which is hidden beneath the glacial drifts. In terms of its structure the Merse is a basin of Upper Palaeozoic strata (mainly Carboniferous) surrounded on three sides by older harder rocks which form a semi-circle of uplands. To the north the Silurian and Ordovician rocks of the Lammermuir Hills separate the Tweed Basin from the Midland Valley; to the west, a curving highland of various Palaeozoic sedimentary and volcanic rocks (Eckford and Ritchie, 1939) creates a high gathering-ground for the waters of the Tweed catchment; and, to the south, the long line of the Cheviot Hills forms an appropriate upland barrier for the border itself to follow (Robson, 1977). The lowland of the Merse corresponds to a downfold of Old Red Sandstone and overlying Carboniferous rocks, forming an eastward-tilted syncline which descends towards the North Sea. Thus the youngest rocks, the Carboniferous Limestones, occur near the coastal margin, giving way inland to the older Calciferous Sandstones of Lower Carboniferous age, equivalent in character to the Fell Sandstones and Cementstones of Northumberland. These calcareous sandstones, of creamy-brown colour, are deeply buried beneath the drumlins of the Merse, but the tilt or dip of their bedding-planes raises them high enough to appear at the surface around the flanks of the Tweed Basin. Here they have been sporadically quarried for building stone, since they provide a splendid freestone which has been used in many local buildings, including those of Duns, Coldstream and Kelso.

On both western and northern flanks the geology of the central basin of the Lower Tweed changes from the Carboniferous Limestones and Calciferous Sandstones to the older, more brightly coloured arenaceous rocks which make up the Old Red Sandstone succession of south-east Scotland (Greig, 1971). In the Lower Old Red Sandstone, between Eyemouth and Reston, conglomerates and grits are abundant, especially at the base of the succession, but these are succeeded upwards by the more widespread softish red sandstones. Among the conglomerates are pebbles of Silurian greywacke, slate, chert and jasper which give some indication of the type of landmass from which the materials were eroded during the deposition of the Old Red Sandstone. It will be seen later that this period of geological time also witnessed a prolonged episode of vulcanicity, when hundreds of metres of lavas were poured out from volcanoes, some remnants of which can still be seen in the Scottish landscape. Even older Ordovician slates and shales crop out in a narrow band along the northern flanks of the Lammermuir Hills, but by far the most extensive strata are the Silurian shales, grits and flagstones which stretch from Peebles to Hawick. All have subsequently been intensely folded and uplifted by the Caledonian mountain-building episode. Countless minor crumples and faults have affected these older rocks in detail, although in general two primary fold axes can be distinguished: in the north an upfold affects the Ordovician rocks, but this gives way southwards, in the Silurian area, to a complex downfold (Figure 11.1). Since these primary folds are composed of numerous parallel minor flexures it is preferable to refer to them as an *anticlinorium* and a *synclinorium*, respectively, instead of using the terms 'anticline' and 'syncline' (McKerrow, 1987).

The convoluted folding of the older rocks is best seen in the coastal cliffs around St Abb's Head, which some regard as the finest stretch of coastal scenery in southern Scotland. Southwards towards Berwick, however, where the Carbon-

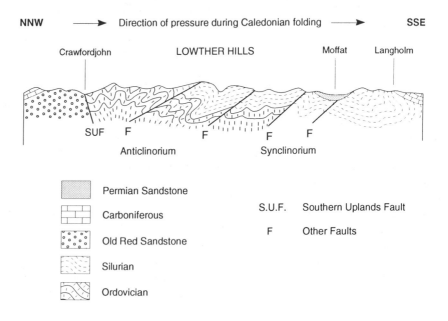

Figure 11.1 Generalized geological section of the Southern Uplands.

iferous rocks of the Tweed Basin reach the coast, the high, rugged cliffs of contorted older rocks near Eyemouth give way to the gently dipping Lamberton Limestone which creates a rather featureless coastline.

So far as historical geology is concerned, Siccar Point must take its place as one of the most important sites of scientific interest in the British Isles, for it was here in about 1790 that Dr James Hutton became the first person to grasp the concept of a geological unconformity (Craig, 1960). In his famous treatise, *Theory of the Earth* (1795), Hutton describes how:

> At Siccar Point we found a beautiful picture of this junction [between the underlying Silurian and overlying Old Red Sandstone] washed bare by the sea. The sandstone strata are partly washed away and partly remaining upon the ends of the vertical schistus; and in many places points of the schistus are seen to stand-up through among the sandstone, the greatest part of which is worn away.

It seems true to say that from this world-famous section, and from similar ones in the banks of the Jed at Jedburgh and in the Isle of Arran, Hutton was able to construct the principles of the cycle of erosion and sedimentation which are fundamental to the study of earth science. In recognizing the orderly system by which the earth's surface was worn down and the material then transported to the ocean floor, there to be stratified and finally uplifted to form a new landmass, Hutton was challenging the entire philosophy of the so-called Catastrophists, who saw all geological phenomena in terms of the catastrophic biblical Flood.

From the sea cliffs at Siccar Point there are splendid views north-westwards towards Dunbar. Near at hand, at Pease Bay, the Upper Old Red Sandstone can be seen grading upwards into the greyish sandstones of the Lower Carboniferous series. Beyond stands the finger of Barns Ness lighthouse on its platform of Carboniferous Limestone, while in the distance the volcanic plugs of North Berwick Law and the Bass Rock faintly puncture the horizon. The Lammermuirs slope steeply seawards hereabouts, but the coastline is generally low-lying where the Southern Uplands Fault crosses the coast and marks the northern boundary of the Southern Uplands and of the Border Country. To the north lies the Midland Valley of Scotland (see Chapter 12) with its urbanized and industrialized landscapes cut off from the borderlands by the steep northern face of the Lammermuir Hills. This abrupt termination of the Lammermuirs, between Dunbar and the Soutra Pass, represents a fault-line scarp where the Southern Uplands Fault has brought the harder Ordovician rocks against the relatively softer Upper Palaeozoic sandstones of the Midland Valley. The adjoining Moorfoot Hills, to the west of the Soutra Pass, are the only other clear example of a fault-line scarp in association with the Southern Uplands Fault, for elsewhere along its length much tougher conglomerates, grits and volcanics lie directly against the hard rocks of the Southern Uplands. Farther south-westwards, therefore, in Lanarkshire, the northern edge of the Southern Uplands is not so clearly defined.

Southwards, across the Soutra Pass, the rolling summits of the Lammermuirs can be seen stretching away to the eastern horizon, their tawny-coloured grasslands unbroken by major rock outcrops and diversified only by the dark lines of forestry plantations. The Leader, flowing south to join the Tweed, has here taken advantage of a narrow tongue of Old Red Sandstone to carve out the attractive valley of Lauderdale. The rich, red, sandy soils and the mature

woodlands of the hillslopes in prosperous Lauderdale give more than a hint of
Welsh rather than Scottish border country although the little town of Lauder, with
its tolbooth and its Scottish harling (a type of stucco) on the kirk walls, soon
removes all doubt as to the true location on the edges of Tweedsdale.

Where the middle reaches of the Tweed, and its tributaries the Gala, Yarrow,
Ettrick and Teviot, have cut deep trenches into the Silurian rocks (Linton,
1933), they have allowed ribbons of farmland from the Berwickshire lowlands to infiltrate deeply into the Southern Uplands. Above the woodlands of the valleysides
some of the ploughed fields extend even to elevations of 360 metres – the highest
improved land in all Scotland. Within this well-wooded and cultivated foothill
zone the towns of Selkirk, Galashiels, Melrose and St Boswells cling to the
steep valleysides above their tree-lined water-courses. Most of these towns have
developed as part of the tweed and knitwear manufacturing complex that has
brought fame to the Scottish borders, utilizing the well-known Cheviot hill sheep
and the availability of water power for the earliest looms. The stone-built houses,
a mixture of dark Silurian greywackes and ruddy Old Red Sandstone, reflect
the location of these towns astride a geological boundary, although the brick
mill chimneys bring a note of Victorian harshness into the townscapes of mellow
Scottish stone. Long before woollen spinning and weaving had reached commer-

Figure 11.2 The Eildon
Hills. The steep moorland
slopes of the Eildon laccolith
contrast with the farmlands
on the sedimentary rocks of
the Tweed Valley. Note the
hill-fort structures on the
farthest summit.

cial levels, however, these valleys were famed as ecclesiastical centres, as their picturesque abbey ruins so clearly demonstrate.

From almost any viewpoint in the Middle Tweed Basin the triple summits of the Eildon Hills dominate the skyline, and they remain as scenically stimulating today as they must have been to the Iron Age peoples (who built a hillfort on the northern summit) and to the Romans (who placed the aptly named fort of Trimontium at their feet) (Fig. 11.2). But it was Sir Walter Scott who brought most fame to these conical eminences, for the graceful lines of his 'delectable mountains' stimulated some of his greatest writings from his home of Abbotsford, a short distance away. The hills are best seen from the east, from the so-called Scott's View near Melrose, where their shapely, heather-clad summits rise above the neatly ordered fields and woodlands of the Tweed. The Eildons are regarded as the remnant of an enormous composite laccolith, made up of several sheets of mainly acidic lava which have invaded the bedding-planes of the sedimentary Old Red Sandstone (Fig. 11.3). Fed by volcanic vents from deep-seated magma chambers, the lavas, of Carboniferous age, caused the horizontal sandstones to become updomed, but without enabling the fluid igneous material to break out at the surface as a sub-aerial lava flow. Once the intrusive material had cooled and hardened into individual sheets of igneous rocks it remained interbedded with the sedimentary rocks until denudation destroyed the overlying cover and exposed the ancient laccolith (Eckford and Manson, 1960). Sills, or sheets of intrusive igneous rocks, are common around Melrose and have helped form such eminences as Black Hill, White Hill and Bemersyde Hill. Mention should also be made of the large volcanic neck of Chiefswood, which lies between the town and Abbotsford (Fig. 11.3). Although of no great topographical significance, this oval igneous mass, some 3 kilometres long, represents an ancient volcanic vent but it is no use looking for a great Vesuvian cone in the landscape, for the ash and lava cone (if it ever existed) has long since disappeared. Only the walls of the vent have survived, together with the infilling of volcanic agglomerate which can be viewed in the workings at Quarry Hill. Angular fragments of the surrounding sedimentary rocks (Silurian and Old Red Sandstone), shattered by the explosive forces, can be seen mingling with pieces of igneous rock which fell back into the former vent (chiefly basalt, trachyte and quartz-porphyry).

The largest town of the Borders, Hawick, is located in Teviotdale, overlooked from the south by hills carved from Silurian rocks of Wenlock age (Warren, 1964). As with its associates farther north, Hawick's sandstone buildings are interrupted by the alien brick chimneys of its woollen mills. In a side valley, on the Jed, the historic town of Jedburgh is, however, a good deal more romantic, with its fine abbey ruin of grey, red and yellow sandstone (MacGregor and Eckford, 1948) surrounded by tall stone houses with steep slate roofs. Excellent exposures of the Old Red Sandstone can be seen in the river cliffs at Jedburgh, including one of Hutton's famous unconformities. But it is not the red rocks and soils of this area which take the eye for there are several conical hills whose steep-sided summits have been carved from a variety of igneous rocks, formed during Carboniferous times. The former volcanic vents which form the Minto Hills, Troneyhill and Ancrumcraig were filled only with agglomerate, but the high summits of Rubers Law, Black Law and Lanton Hill have vents infilled with both agglomerate and basalt. Finally, Dunion Hill and the oddly named Fatlips Crags have only plugs of basalt beneath their prominent summits.

The border hills

The Scottish flank of the Cheviot (see Chapter 10) is little more than a peat-covered dome and it is difficult to understand why Daniel Defoe, on his visit there, ventured upwards with trepidation, afraid that there would not be sufficient room for himself and his guides on the summit. One of the most striking scenic features is the way many of the Cheviot's hillslopes, spurs and drainage divides are indiscriminately cut through by deep, virtually streamless channels. These obviously bear little relationship to the present drainage pattern, and one is forced to turn to the Pleistocene Ice Age to seek an explanation of their form. Although earlier writers have invoked ice-impounded lakes to explain them as glacial 'spillways' carved by overflowing lake waters, more recent research has suggested that these channels were formed entirely sub-glacially. Thus, glacial meltwaters, running under enormous pressures beneath a downwasting ice sheet, had sufficient energy to carve this branching and twisting channel network. The streams reworked much of the englacial detritus, ultimately leaving it as bedded sands and gravels along the valley floors and hill slopes. The ice sheet responsible for the majority of the channels and the glacio-fluvial landforms was generated from the Southern Uplands, so the ice moved across the northern slopes of the Cheviots and down the Tweed Basin.

Figure 11.3 Geology of the Eildon Hills laccolith (after R.J.A. Eckford and W. Manson).

The associated glacio-fluvial sand and gravel formed kames and eskers (see p. 251) in a complex system which can be traced down Teviotdale to Eckford

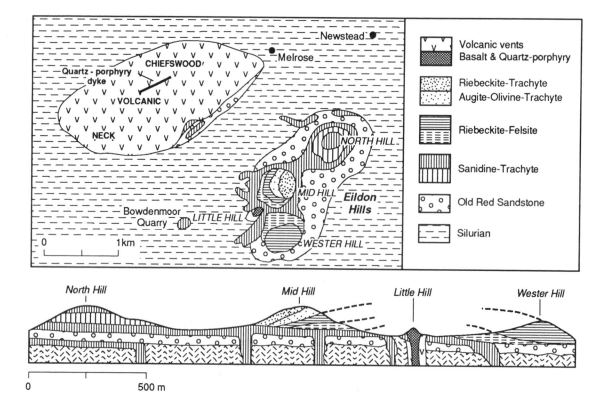

and thence up the Kale Water Valley, past Morebattle and into the meltwater-modified valley of the Yetholms. Here, river diversion has left an old abandoned channel of the Bowmont Water, now occupied by the marshy hollow of the Stank and Yetholm Loch. The attractive villages of Town Yetholm and Kirk Yetholm are built of a mixture of Carboniferous Sandstone and black Cheviot lavas but, as if to demonstrate the proximity of England, several of the cottages have retained their thatch.

The central part of the border hills is in reality the main massif of the Southern Uplands, which separate the Solway plains of England from the Midland Valley of Scotland. Their major geological structures, of complex Caledonian folds with an orientation from north-east to south-west, remain in general the same as those described above (p. 244), but here in the Lowther and Tweedsmuir Hills the elevations are somewhat greater. Between the towns of Peebles and Moffat, for example, more than a dozen summits approach or exceed 750 metres. These high summits are remnants of a once higher surface that has been almost totally destroyed, leaving them standing above the general level of the dissected surface of the main plateau, the gently rolling level of which ranges between 450 and 600 metres. The residual hills stand above the plateau partly because they coincide with outcrops of massive grits, which occur within the complex succession of folded Lower Palaeozoic sediments. Yet only in a few places can these uplands be compared with the grandiose scenery of the Lake District or North Wales, built from sedimentary rocks of similar age. The reason seems to lie in the fact that the central Southern Uplands lack many of the hard igneous intrusions and interbedded volcanic rocks which help form the rugged peaks of Cumbria and Snowdonia. Instead they are composed of Lower Palaeozoic greywackes, flags and mudstones which, because of their highly folded thin bedding, usually occur as steeply inclined narrow outcrops, thereby excluding major structurally controlled features. Only where glacial overdeepening has intervened do the landforms take on the stature of their Lake District neighbours.

One such valley can be found where the Yarrow Water meanders through the uplands known as the Ettrick Forest. Upstream from the picturesquely wooded stretches around Selkirk, the Yarrow valley penetrates deeply into the highest hills. These are mirrored in St Mary's Loch and Loch of the Lowes, once a single valley lake but now divided by a delta on which stands Tibbie Shiel's Inn. The lakes occupy a true rock basin, where the valleyfloor has been glacially overdeepened by the same ice sheet which breached the main pre-glacial watershed of the Southern Uplands at the head of the valley. Thus the main road now climbs easily out of the valley of the Yarrow Water and across the high col at Birkhill, before descending south-westwards into Moffatdale. Immediately the character of the scenery changes and one could be in a typical Lakeland or Welsh glacial valley. At the upper end is Dobb's Linn, where a waterfall plunges over the vertical Silurian grits in a series of steps (Strachan, 1960). It was from the exposed rocks in the cliffs of the gorge that Charles Lapworth, in the late nineteenth century, worked out the complex stratigraphical succession and the structures of this region, while employed as the local schoolmaster. It was here also that Lapworth, later to become an eminent professor of geology, identified many of the fossils known as graptolites, which lived in the Silurian seas some 400 million years ago. Farther down Moffatdale, where the valley takes on the characteristic U-shape of glacial terrain, is the Grey Mare's Tail, where a superb waterfall cascades from a textbook example of a hanging valley (Fig. 11.4). The stream, falling some 200 metres to the valleyfloor, is known as the Tail Burn and drains the moraine-impounded Loch Skene, which lies in a corrie-girt upland basin (Cornish, 1981). The large glacier of Moffatdale succeeded in lowering the main valley more than the tributary valleys which have, as a result, been left 'hanging' at their point of confluence. Such glacial overdeepening was assisted in this instance by the presence of a major fault, which can be traced for 64 kilometres past St Mary's Loch to Moffat. The shatter-belt associated with the faulting has not only assisted erosion but also accounts for the remarkable straightness of Moffatdale itself.

To the north of Moffatdale the northern valleys of the Tweedsmuir Hills are drained by the headwaters of the Tweed, which first flows north-eastwards along the axes of the Caledonian folding before turning eastwards at Peebles. Thence, for the next 32 kilometres of its course, the Tweed cuts discordantly across the major structures of the Southern Uplands (Linton, 1933). One interesting effect of these contrasting reaches of the Tweed is the way in which the character of the valley changes: where it lies parallel with the strike it is often broad, with spur ends truncated, but in its discordant reaches the valley is irregular and constricted. At Drumelzier the northern hills are broken by the Biggar gap, a remarkably wide, flat valley that may once have carried the waters of the upper Clyde eastwards to the Tweed (Linton, 1934). Its strategic importance as the

Figure 11.4 The Grey Mare's Tail in the border hills. The Tail Burn stream descends from a hanging valley into the glacially overdeepened valley of Moffatdale.

only major east–west routeway in the Southern Uplands is demonstrated by the abundance of hillforts and pele towers in the district. The slated roofs of Peebles, and indeed those of old Edinburgh and of many border towns, were almost certainly constructed from the Silurian slates of nearby Stobo, which once possessed the largest slate quarry in southern Scotland.

The Peebles area is more significant, however, for its large number of glacio-fluvial landforms. Since the Carlops district (Sissons, 1963) and the Eddleston Valley were among the first sites in the British Isles where subglacial, englacial and marginal drainage channels were recognized, they are worthy of examination. Today the Eddleston Water runs southwards to join the Tweed at Peebles, but the pattern of meltwater channels has shown that at one period in the Pleistocene the meltwaters of the Southern Uplands ice sheet escaped towards the Midland Valley near the northern end of the Eddleston Valley, at an altitude of almost 300 metres, because the Tweed Valley was buried beneath the ice. The outwash from the icesheet created a number of kame terraces which can be traced northwards to the former outlet, although the modern drainage of the Eddleston Water flows in the opposite direction. Subsequent work in the upper Tweed Valley by Price (1960; 1963a; 1963b) has shown that hundreds of glacial meltwater channels exist in this area, making Peebles an important centre for the study of phenomena associated with the downwasting of ice sheets.

The complex folding of the Ordovician and Silurian sedimentaries, which form the central massif of the Southern Uplands, is here diversified by the presence of basins of Coal Measures and of New Red Sandstone, while in the south-east Carboniferous Sandstones and Limestones reappear, together with a suite of Carboniferous volcanic rocks near Langholm (Elliot, 1960). Between Annan and Gretna an extension of New Red Sandstone rocks stretches northwards from the neighbouring Vale of Eden and the Solway plain (Barrett, 1942), although in Scotland the New Red Sandstone is represented largely by the Permian system rather than by the Trias. These Permian rocks are made up of dune-bedded sandstones and breccias which indicate that they were formed under desert conditions. The breccias, sometimes referred to as 'brockrams', are in reality fossil screes of greywacke, basalt and sandstone which formed on the surrounding slopes of the desert basins some 280 million years ago.

It has been described above how the primary drainage of the Eastern and Middle Marches of the Border Country has been integrated by the Tweed, which carries the rivers eastwards to the North Sea. To the west of the high hills around Loch Skene, however, the drainage is related to the Solway Firth, so that here the valleys of the Nith, the Annan and the Esk run from north to south and have long been used as important routes across the Southern Uplands.

The major watershed between the Solway drainage and that of the Midland Valley lies along the faulted northern edge of the Southern Uplands. Indeed, the headwaters of the Nith rise to the north of the Southern Uplands Fault and look as if they belong to the Ayrshire rivers rather than to the Solway system. It has been demonstrated, in fact, that the Nith drainage is a composite one, having captured some of the headwaters of both the Lugar Water and the Clyde. It becomes clear that the Nith headstream once flowed northwards through the New Cumnock gap, but was later captured by the reach which had adjusted itself to the synclinal structure of the Sanquhar coal basin (George, 1955). Nevertheless it is equally clear, from a study of the river pattern in the lead-mining country around Wanlockhead, that the Sanquhar basin itself was once drained by the headwaters of the Clyde. The elbow of capture and the marshy wind-gap of Crawick Moss bear mute testimony to the former river course.

A general correspondence can also be seen between the alignment of Annandale and the structural basins of newer rocks. While the Nith took advantage of both Carboniferous and Permian outliers, Annandale is related only to the Permian sandstone basins of Moffat and Lochmaben. At the head of the Annan, a few miles above the town of Moffat, a most remarkable trough, known as the Devil's Beef Tub, sunders the uplands between the Lowther and Tweedsmuir Hills. Although glacial erosion has played no small part in its excavation, the Beef Tub represents the ancient floor of the pre-Permian valley which has been re-excavated by the headwaters of the Annan, necessitating the partial removal of the Permian sandstones which still occupy the lower reaches of the valley (see Fig. 11.1). The same bright red sandstones have been extensively used in the local buildings, especially in the attractive town of Moffat.

The valley of the Esk, lacking the more easily eroded Permian rocks, is different in form from those of the Annan and Nith. The river has been more constricted in its journey across the Silurian rocks, so that its valley remains narrow right down to where England meets Scotland near Canonbie, where the New Red Sandstone reappears to form the Solway plain. Unlike the more fertile New Red Sandstone soils of the Solway plain, however, the soils of this western marchland become thinner and stonier on the hillslopes, despite the thick drift infilling of the valleys. The differences in soil quality and depth are reflected in the contrasting vegetation of the southern hills. Bracken abounds on the lower, steeper slopes where the soils are deeper, while on the better-drained land, known as 'white land', extensive grasslands flourish, with sheep's fescue, sweet vernal grass and bent most common. But where drainage conditions are poor, especially on the plateaux and spurs, sedges and rushes occur in association with the deep layers of peat that mantle the hilltops. Where heather has carpeted the rapidly eroding peat-hags, the colour of the hills takes on a darker hue: such areas have been given the name 'black land' (Tivy, 1964).

Along the border itself runs Liddesdale, different from Eskdale in its geology and landforms, and hence in its character. Near its head stands the grim castle of Hermitage but here also are the extensive conifer forests which appear to have spilled over the border from Redesdale and Kielder. Nevertheless, some natural woodlands have survived in the valleys, where trim beech hedges replace the stone field boundaries of the uplands. At Canonbie the River Liddle, having left the Silurian uplands, is cutting into red sandstones, but these are the barren red Coal Measures which herald the tiny Canonbie coalfield, where production has long ceased. The valley has now opened out on to the broad Solway plain, and the red sandstone farmsteads and the pele tower of Kirkandrews reflect not only the reappearance of the New Red Sandstone but also the proximity of the English border. As if to demonstrate the impending transition between England and Scotland the Permian rocks give way to the Trias within the New Red Sandstone succession between Annan and Gretna (Barrett, 1942). The Trias was once used as a building stone here, although it was soon discovered that its weathering qualities were greatly inferior to those of the Permian sandstones.

Jutting westwards into the Irish Sea, the peninsula of Galloway is the most clearly defined of all the regions of lowland Scotland. It is bounded on three sides by the maritime waters of the Solway Firth, the Firth of Clyde and the North Channel, the last of which separates it from the neighbouring coast of Ulster, a mere 32 kilometres away.

The landscape of Galloway exhibits a contrast between the neat orderliness of its rolling farmlands and the wilderness of its forests and moorlands – between the bright green pasturelands of the lowlands, one of the richest dairying regions in Britain, and the dark green conifer forests and rock-strewn summits of its mountainous heartland. Although it was overrun by ice sheets, bare ice-scrubbed rocks are uncommon in the Galloway lowlands, and the true crofting landscapes of northern Scotland, with their pocket-handkerchief plots, are therefore absent. Instead, there is a lowland scene of pastoral prosperity, patterned with well-timbered hedgerows and neat white farms, flourishing on the ubiquitous glacial drifts. Nevertheless, inland the rock basins, peaty hollows, lochs and glacial valleys of the Merrick (843 m), the highest peak of the Southern Uplands, are more reminiscent of the Western Highlands.

The town of Dumfries, the largest in the Southern Uplands, is the traditional gateway to Galloway and controls an important crossing-point of the Nith. It is located in the centre of the largest of southern Scotland's Permian basins, and the warm red sandstone from the neighbouring Locharbriggs quarry has left its imprint not only on the architecture of this town, but also on Glasgow and other urban settlements of the lowlands, for Locharbriggs once provided about half the freestone used for building in Scotland. The Permian sandstones, like those of the Trias in England, are also important for their water-bearing qualities, and in earlier years some of the Dumfries manufacturing industries were based on the high-quality artesian water of the Permian basin (Craig, 1965). The basin is not only a structural feature; it is, like the neighbouring Lochmaben Basin, also a topographic hollow. Its southern end passes beneath the waters of the Solway Firth, and it has been suggested that the Solway coastline was determined very largely by the drowning of similar basins of relatively softer rocks. It is true that between the Nith and Abbey Head the coastline coincides almost exactly with the northern limit of a submerged trough of Carboniferous and New Red Sandstone, so that the older, harder rocks of Criffell and Bengairn rise steeply from the low coastal fringe. Furthermore, to the west, Loch Ryan, the Stranraer lowland and much of Luce Bay have manifestly been carved from a partly submerged basin of Permian sandstone; Wigtown Bay may have a similar relationship. Thus, the coastal landscapes comprise old, hard rock headlands separated by bays which probably owe their origin to the presence of softer rocks, now largely inundated by the sea. In detail, however, the character of the Solway coast owes much to the variety of superficial deposits, which range from those of glacial derivation, through the suite of raised beaches, to the extensive post-glacial peat mosses and estuarine deposits.

The Solway shores are perhaps most famous for their marshes, whose wide, lonely expanses provide a quiet solitude but one quite unlike that of the mountainous heartland of Galloway. The sinuous channel networks of the salt marshes, uncovered during every low tide, interlace the gleaming bronze mudflats treasured by the ornithologist and marine biologist but disliked by tourists in search of firm sandy beaches. And yet these coastal flats, with their characteristic flora of glasswort (*Salicornia stricta*), sea mannagrass (*Puccinellia maritima*), sea pink (*Armeria maritima*) and sea aster (*Aster tripolium*), are in fact more sandy than the majority of British coastal marshes, being made up almost entirely of fine-grained marine sands.

The most extensive of the coastal marshes, Lochar Moss, reclaimed only at its fringes, was once the scene of commercially mechanized peat-cutting for industrial and domestic fuel. Although peat has horticultural value, however, its mechanical extraction is no longer economically competitive, while even hand-dug peat is rarely burned on the Solway coast today.

At both Lochar Moss and Moss of Cree, near Wigtown, the peat bogs have accumulated on layers of marine clays and sands which belong to the well-marked post-glacial raised beach that fringes the Solway coastline (Jardine, 1964). In a few places the raised beach deposits themselves rest on buried peaty material and on a few tree stumps (appearing at low tide in a position of growth), which demonstrates that an old post-glacial landsurface, similar to that of south-west Lancashire (Chapter 9) has been subsequently inundated by a rise in sea level. This post-glacial rise was a world-wide phenomenon, as water returned to the oceans from the melting ice sheets. But why is it that the raised post-glacial shorelines of the Solway Firth stand as high as 7.6 metres above present Ordnance Datum? It must be remembered that when the Scottish ice sheet was present in this region the land became locally depressed by the excessive weight of the ice. Depression of the earth's crust of this type is called *isostatic downwarping*, and in the British Isles it reached its greatest magnitude in western Scotland, where the ice sheets were thickest. With the disappearance of the ice, however, the land began to recoil and return to its former level, as the excess weight was removed. Nevertheless, the rate of land recovery in north-western Britain is known to have been outpaced for a short period of time, some 8000 years ago, when the post-glacial sea level rose even more rapidly. Thus, for several centuries a post-glacial marine transgression of western Scotland inundated the early Flandrian forests and flooded a few kilometres inland, where the waves cut cliffs and left their marine clays and sands on the newly emerged land surface. But this transgression was short-lived and by 3500 years ago the rate of recovery of the land was greater than the rise in sea level, so that the sea receded from the clifflines, leaving the post-glacial marine clays and raised beaches high and dry. The importance of the post-glacial raised beach in the Galloway landscape lies in its effect on coastal settlement and land use, for the raised shoreline had added many square kilometres of low marshland to the coastal fringe, especially in the large bays and estuaries of the Solway coast. Overlooking the coast is the granite hump of Criffell (575 m), its rocky footslopes patterned with stone walls constructed largely from the numerous erratic boulders of granite dumped indiscriminately by former ice sheets but now cleared from the fields. The Criffell Granite represents only one, albeit the largest, of the Caledonian igneous intrusions which contribute significantly to the relief of Galloway (Bott and Masson-Smith, 1960).

For an understanding of the granitic emplacements in the Southern Uplands, one must first take into account the sequence of events in Scotland during the Caledonian orogeny, and especially the Caledonian igneous activity. During the prolonged earth movements of Lower Palaeozoic times igneous activity was widespread in the British Isles, but especially in Scotland. At the outset a distinction must be made between the so-called 'metamorphic' Caledonian belt of Highland Scotland and the 'non-metamorphic' Caledonian belt of the Scottish lowlands, south of the Highland Border Fault. Five major groups of Caledonian intrusions (in approximate order of age) have been recognized: first came the *migmatites* of the Highlands (sometimes termed the Older Granites), which were intimately connected with the folding and metamorphism of the Moinian rocks; next, the post-Cambrian alkaline intrusions of Assynt, in the Northern Highlands; third, the basic intrusions (especially gabbro) of north-east Scotland, which post-date the deformation of the Dalradian rocks of the Highlands; fourth, the so-called Newer Granites, the only group well represented in the less metamorphosed rocks of the lowlands (including all the Southern Uplands granites); finally came the last group of intrusions, known as *ring complexes*, which post-date the Caledonian folding and are best seen around Ben Nevis (see Chapter 15), although the Cheviot Granite is probably of the same age.

The Galloway granites were not formed from ring complexes, nor were they associated with metamorphic processes as were the Highland migmatites. Instead they were formed relatively simply, like the Hercynian granites of South-West England (Chapter 2), by magmatic injection from below into the existing sedimentary sequence. Since it was intruded at depth as a batholith, the molten magmatic material cooled slowly to form quite large crystals, compared with, for example, the finely crystalline texture of extrusive lavas. The varying proportions of the constituent minerals of quartz, feldspar, and mica, biotite or hornblende, result in different types of granite, although the true granite (in its strictest sense) is very acid, with a high percentage of quartz and a small proportion of biotite.

The Criffel Granite forms an elevated tract of land some 24 kilometres in length and is composed of three granodiorites and a quartzdiorite (Fig. 11.5). It varies in texture from a coarse-grained quartz-porphyry at the centre to a fine-grained variety at Auchencairn, although the main summits of Criffell and Bainloch Hill are formed from a medium-grained granodiorite (Phillips, 1956). At Bengairn, however, it is associated with a grey quartzdiorite which is very similar to granite (MacGregor, 1937). Although Criffell stands out as an upland because the granite has apparently resisted forces of denudation more successfully than the fringe of Carboniferous and the more extensive tract of Galloway's Silurian rocks (Craig and Walton, 1959; Weir, 1968), the upland is not simply coincident with the limits of the granitic outcrop. Not only is there granite beneath some of the lowlands, but the metamorphic aureole has also played no part in the relief hereabouts, in contrast with that of the Loch Doon Granite. The coast road swings along the southern slopes of the granitic hills, which hereabouts have been heavily planted by the Forestry Commission, and across gorse-covered, ice-scrubbed rock exposures before reaching the light grey granite town of Dalbeattie. On Craignair Hill, to the west of the town, the quarries form a conspicuous scar. They have been worked since 1824, to build not only the Liverpool docks, but also those at Birkenhead, Newport and Swansea. Easily exported by boat on the Urr Water, this coarse, grey granite with white to pale pink feldspars was also used in the King George V Clyde Bridge at Glasgow.

Once the granite country is left behind, the landscape appears to soften in texture, partly by virtue of the great spreads of glacio-fluvial deposits in the

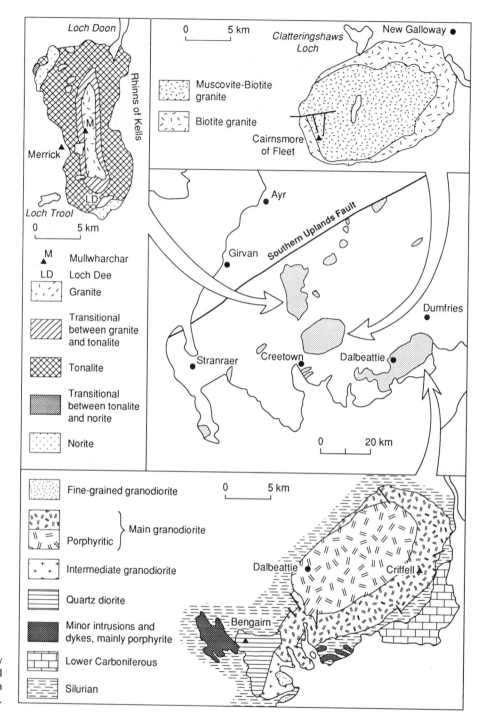

Figure 11.5 The Galloway Granites (based on material prepared by the British Geological Survey).

lower Dee Valley and partly because of the change in the agricultural scene. Here 50 to 75 per cent of the improved land is under grass; the thicker drifts and the mild climate support some of the most productive dairy farms in Scotland. Cropping has never played an important role in Kirkcudbrightshire, but there has been a significant change from beef-cattle rearing to dairying since modern transport has helped the Galloway creameries supply the dense industrial settlements of the Midland Valley. To some, however, the true Galloway is the mountainous interior – the grey Galloway of misty hills, 'of brown bent and red heather, of green knowe and grey gnarled thorn' (S. R. Crockett). These are the 'High Moors' of Galloway, but they are mainly 'grass moors', in contrast with the heather moors of the Highlands. It is partly because of the dominance of grassland that sheep-rearing has been practised so extensively in both Galloway and the Border Country. There is, however, evidence that the Galloway hills were not always grasslands and moorlands: in earlier post-glacial times most of the lower hillslopes carried forests of oak, birch or pine, remnants of which are now entombed beneath the peat bogs. Sheep-grazing on the southern 'grass moors' has itself been an important factor in both the partial suppression of the heather and the disappearance of this original forest cover, though climatic change was even more important (Fenton, 1935).

It has been shown that the higher rainfall and humidity of the west, together with its greater cloudiness and exposure, are more conducive to peat growth than conditions in the border hills farther to the east (Tivy, 1954). In the Galloway mountains, therefore, peat bogs are common, even on the valley floors (where they are known as 'flows'), and Galloway's peat deposits are exceeded in magnitude only by those of Caithness and Sutherland. By contrast, the eastern hills of the Border Country lie in something of a rain-shadow, so that on their drier grasslands purple moor grass (*Molinia caerulea*), bog myrtle (*Myrica gale*) and deer sedge (*Scirpus caespitosus*) are not as common as they are on the wetter Galloway mountains. It has already been described how rock outcrops are rare in the smooth scenery of the border hills, but in Galloway's interior the erosive powers of the ice sheets have left many rocky knolls to break up the vegetation cover. These contrasting environments mean that there are further land-use differences between the border hills and Galloway. In the latter improved land extends only to a height of a mere 150 metres; the productive sheep-runs of the border hills require 1 hectare per ewe, while in Galloway, restricted by rock outcrops, 2 hectares per ewe are needed; much more forestry has been introduced on these wetter peaty soils than on the more easterly of the Southern Uplands. Thus, the high mountains of the Merrick and the Rhinns of Kells stand with their feet in the forests, most of which have been planted since 1920 (Fig 11.6). The Glen Trool Forest Park, with over 50 000 hectares of plantations, is the second largest forest in Scotland. Of its coniferous trees, Norway spruce prefers the more fertile, sheltered sites while Sitka spruce will tolerate the poorer soil and the more exposed locations.

A glance at a geology map (Fig. 11.5) will suggest that the Galloway mountains are all associated with granitic outcrops, and in the case of the Cairnsmore of Fleet (711 m) it is true to a certain extent (Parslow, 1968). In this upland, all the major summits around the lonely glacial trough of Loch Grannoch are found within the granite margins. In much the same way, however, as the Southwick Water has hollowed out the centre of the Criffell Granite upland, so the Big Water of Fleet has lowered the central outcrop of the Cairnsmore of Fleet Granite. It seems unlikely that the slightly different mineralogical composition of the innermost granite has been the sole cause in the fashioning of the central amphitheatre, for ice erosion has clearly played a significant part in the shaping of these landforms. This is not true, however, in the case of the Loch Doon 'Granite' (Gardiner and Reynolds, 1932) where petrological differences between the granite margins and the surrounding country rock have clearly played a major part in the formation of this central massif. Here, the hour-glass shaped intrusion of the 'granite' occupies an area extending from Loch Doon to Loch Dee, a distance of almost 19 kilometres, but few of the highest summits coincide with the granite outcrop. Only in the ridge of Mullwharchar (692 m) does the white central granite play a major part in the relief of the area. The surrounding mountains of Shalloch on Minnoch, the Merrick and the Rhinns of Kells are all found not on the granite but on or just outside its metamorphic aureole (Fig. 11.5) whose altered rocks must once have roofed the massive intrusion, but which have now been worn away. The sedimentary strata of Lower Palaeozoic greywackes, shales and flagstones have been changed into tough quartzitic schists and mica schists by contact metamorphism, as with all the Galloway granites, but only around the Loch Doon 'Granite' does the resistance of the aureole create such a conspicuous ring of highlands. Loch Doon and its rivers coincide everywhere with the concentric outcrop of a tonalite granite, a more basic rock with plagioclase feldspar, which

Figure 11.6 The Merrick, Galloway, carved from the metamorphic aureole surrounding the Loch Doon granite, rises above the conifer forest plantations of Glen Trool.

must be less resistant to denudation than either of its adjoining rocks.

A great deal of the denudation must have been the work of Pleistocene ice sheets, which appear to have overridden all of the Galloway Highlands and carried their erratics great distances. For example, Loch Doon Granite erratics have been found on the summits of the Merrick and the Cairnsmore of Fleet, in addition to the Mull of Galloway and the south Ayrshire hills. Granite blocks from Cairnsmore of Fleet and Criffell have been picked up in the drifts of the Solway plain, along the Cumberland coast and in North Wales. During the Loch Lomond stadial only the granite-cored uplands of Loch Doon, Cairnsmore of Fleet and Cairnsmore of Carsphairn (797 m) continued to nourish small ice caps. The signs of glacial activity are most numerous around the Merrick and the Rhinns of Kells, whose northern and eastern faces are fretted with corries. In the north, Loch Doon itself occupies a glacially overdeepened trough, while in the south Loch Trool (the Gaelic *Gleann t'struthail* means 'glen of the river-like loch') infills an equally impressive U-shaped valley.

Despite the enormous amount of glacial modification, it has been suggested that the present drainage system of Galloway originated in mid-Tertiary times, since when drainage modifications have been the result of adjustment to structure and a certain amount of river capture (Jardine, 1959). Although the initial watershed between the Midland Valley and the Solway Firth was along the northern anticlinorium of Ordovician strata, local centres of radial drainage, such as that on the Loch Doon Granite, were also operative. Here, near Loch Doon, it appears that the headstreams of Water of Deugh and Carsphairn Lane once flowed northwards through the valley now occupied by this narrow loch, but were subsequently turned southwards past Carsphairn by river capture around Lamford Hill. A similar diversion appears to have taken place farther down the valleys of the Ken and Dee, where a former south-easterly course past Castle Douglas to Orchardton Bay on the Solway has been replaced by a south-westerly flow to Kirkcudbright Bay. More recently the river flow of the Galloway uplands has been considerably modified by man: although Loch Doon normally discharged its water northwards to the Ayrshire coast, it is now diverted through a kilometre-long tunnel to the River Dee, and thence by a succession of power stations southwards to the artificially deepened Loch Ken and the Solway.

In contrast with the wild moorland landscapes of the uplands of Galloway, the lowlands of Wigtownshire possess a pastoral calm and an agricultural orderliness. The rolling, drift-covered landscape also exhibits a uniformity of colour, for the emerald green of the permanent grassland gives more than a hint of an Irish scene, which the numerous drumlins do nothing to dispel.

Apart from the Permian basin around Stranraer (with its narrow margin of Millstone Grit) Wigtownshire is everywhere composed of Caledonian folded sedimentaries of Ordovician and Silurian age. In the north the Ordovician greywackes and shales form a broad anticlinorium which manifests itself in an area of low hills known as the Moors. In the south, Silurian rocks of very similar character underlie the thick glacial drift in the area known as the Machars. The third of the physiographic regions created by these Lower Palaeozoic rocks lies to the west of the Stranraer lowland and creates the distinctive promontories of the Rhinns.

The broad peninsula of the Machars (Gaelic for 'flat lands'; cf. *machair* of the Hebrides), terminating in the blunt nose of Burrow Head, is often called

'Scotland's dairy farm', where 75 per cent of the improved land is under permanent grassland, partly by virtue of the dampness of these western peninsulas and partly because of the heavy soils of the boulder clay, which itself has been moulded into a southward-trending drumlin swarm. Near Wigtown the drumlin hills are of massive proportions, their whale back form often heightened by the hedgerows which follow the crestline of the hills.

Westwards lie the Rhinns (the Gaelic word *Roinn* means 'promontory'), whose southernmost tip, the Mull of Galloway, is sometimes referred to as the Land's End of Scotland. The analogy is, perhaps, appropriate, since a few miles to the north a small granitic intrusion creates steep, castellated coastal cliffs near Langgantalluch Head and Crammag Head. The narrow promontory of the Mull itself is almost insular, and the distribution of the raised beaches hereabouts suggests that during the higher sea levels of late-glacial times the Mull of Galloway was an island. Northwards, past the attractive whitewashed town of Portpatrick, which climbs the rocky cliffs behind its tiny harbour, the coastline of the northern promontory of the Rhinns is more complex because the frequent intercalations of Lower Silurian shales and mudstones among the folded beds of massive grey-wackes have produced a profusion of minor bays and clefts among the headlands and ribs of harder rocks (Kelling, 1961; Lindstrom, 1958).

Because the Permian-floored isthmus between Luce Bay and Loch Ryan is mantled with a variety of raised-beach deposits one can only infer that the whole of the Rhinns promontory was an island during late-glacial and early post-glacial times. Along the Luce Bay coast the southern end of this lowland is fringed by the most extensive sand-dune formation in Galloway, with some of the dunes reaching more than 15 metres in height. Heather has begun to colonize the older, innermost dunes, but the outermost dunes remain relatively mobile, occasionally revealing the remnants of Mesolithic sites. The middens and artefacts are found at about 15 metres OD, in association with one of the higher raised beaches, and may represent strand-looping activities by very primitive inhabitants who depended entirely on hunting and primitive fishing some 8000–5500 years ago. In contrast with the ancient archaeological remains and lonely shores of Luce Bay, the shores of Loch Ryan display a bustle which accords with their former importance as a naval base and the present function of Stranraer as a cross-channel port to Ireland.

Bibliography

Barrett, B. H. (1942) The Triassic rocks of the Annan Basin, Dumfrieshire. *Trans. Geol. Soc. Glasgow*, **20**, 161–79.

Bott, M. H. P. and Masson-Smith, D. (1960) A gravity survey of the Criffell granodiorite and the New Red Sandstone deposits near Dumfries. *Proc. Yorks. Geol. Soc.*, **32**, 317–32.

Cornish, R. (1981) Glaciers of the Loch Lomond Stadial in the western Southern Uplands of Scotland. *Proc. Geol. Assoc.*, **92**, 105–14.

Craig, G. Y. (1960) Grantshouse, Siccar Point, Cove and Cat Craig, in G. H. Mitchell, E. K. Walton and D. Grant (eds), *Edinburgh Geology: An Excursion Guide*. Edinb. Geol. Soc. 89–101.

Craig, G. Y. (1965) Permian and Triassic, in G. Y. Craig (ed.), *The Geology of Scotland*. (1st edn). Oliver & Boyd. 383–400.

Craig, G. Y. and Walton, E. K. (1959) Sequence and structure in the Silurian rocks of Kirkudbrightshire. *Geol. Mag.*, **96**, 209–20.

Eckford, R. J. A. and Manson, W. (1960) Eildon Hills, in G. H. Mitchell, E. K. Walton and D. Grant (eds), *Edinburgh Geology: An Excursion Guide*. Edinb. Geol. Soc. 102–114.

Eckford, R. J. A. and Ritchie, M. (1939) The igneous rocks of the Kelso District. *Trans. Edinb. Geol. Soc.*, **13**, 464–72.

Elliot, R. B. (1960) The Carboniferous volcanic rocks of the Langholm District. *Proc. Geol. Assoc.*, **71**, 1–24.

Fenton, E. W. (1935) The influence of sheep on the vegetation of hill grazings in Scotland. *J. Ecol.*, **25**, 424–30.

Gardiner, C. I. and Reynolds, (1932) The Loch Doon 'Granite' area, Galloway. *Quart. J. Geol. Soc.*, **88**, 1–34.

George, T. N. (1955) Drainage in the Southern Uplands: Clyde, Nith, Annan. *Trans. Geol. Soc. Glasgow*, **22**, 1–34.

Greig, D. C. (ed.) (1971) *The South of Scotland* (3rd edn). British Regional Geology. HMSO. 125 pp.

Jardine, W. G. (1959) River development in Galloway. *Scot. Geog. Mag.*, **75**, 65–74.

Jardine, W. G. (1964) Post-glacial sea-levels in south west Scotland. *Scot. Geog. Mag.*, **80**, 5–11.

Kelling, G. (1961) The stratigraphy and structure of the Ordovician rocks of the Rhinns of Galloway. *Quart. J. Geol. Soc.*, **117**, 37–75.

Lindstrom, M. (1958) Different phases of tectonic deformation in the Rhinns of Galloway. *Nature*, **182**, 48–9.

Linton, D. L. (1933) The origin of the Tweed drainage system. *Scot. Geog. Mag.*, **49**, 162–75.

Linton, D. L. (1934) On the former connection between the Clyde and the Tweed. *Scot. Geog. Mag.*, **50**, 82–92.

MacGregor, M. (1937) The western part of the Criffell–Dalbeattie Igneous Complex. *Quart. J. Geol. Soc.*, **93**, 457–84.

MacGregor, A. G. and Eckford, R. J. A. (1948) The Upper Old Red and Lower Carboniferous sediments of Teviotdale and Tweedside and the stones of the Abbeys of the Scottish Borderland. *Trans. Edinb. Geol. Soc.*, **14**, 230–45.

McKerrow, W. S. (1987) The Southern Uplands controversy. *J. Geol. Soc. Lond.*, **144**, 753–6.

Parslow, G. R. (1968) The physical and structural features of the Cairnsmore of Fleet granite and its aureole. *Scot. J. Geol.*, **4**, 91–108.

Phillips, W. J. (1956) The Criffel–Dalbeattie Granodiorite Complex. *Quart. J. Geol. Soc.*, **172**, 221–39.

Price, R. J. (1960) Glacial meltwater channels in the Upper Tweed drainage basin. *Geog. J.*, **126**, 483–89.

Price, R. J. (1963a) The glaciation of part of Peeblesshire. *Trans. Edinb. Geol. Soc.*, **19**, 326–48.

Price, R. J. (1963b) A glacial meltwater drainage system in Peeblesshire. *Scot. Geog. Mag.*, **79**, 133–41.

Robson, D. A. (1977) The structural history of the Cheviot and adjoining regions. *Scot. J. Geol.*, **13**, 255–62.

Sissons, J. B. (1963) The glacial drainage system around Carlops, Peeblesshire. *Trans. Inst. Br. Geogr.*, 95–111.

Strachan, I. (1960) Dobb's Linn, Moffat, in G. H. Mitchell, E. K. Walton and D. Grant (eds), *Edinburgh Geology: An Excursion Guide*. Edinb. Geol. Soc., 144–51.

Tivy, J. (1954) Reconnaissance vegetation survey of hill grazings in Scotland. *Scot. Geog. Mag.*, **100**, 21–33.

Tivy, J. (1964) The Scottish Marchlands, in J. A. Steers (ed.), *Field Studies in the British Isles*. Nelson. 330–43.

Warren, P. T. (1964) The stratigraphy and structure of the Silurian (Wenlock) rocks south-east of Hawick, Roxburghshire, Scotland. *Quart. J. Geol. Soc.*, **120**, 193–218.

Weir, J. A. (1968) Structural history of the Silurian rocks of the coast west of Gatehouse, Kirkcudbrightshire. *Scot. J. Geol.*, **4**, 31–52.

White, J. T. (1973) *The Scottish Border and Northumberland*. Eyre Methuen. 253 pp.

The narrow waist of central Scotland, squeezed between the North Sea and the Firth of Clyde, possesses one of Britain's most complex tracts of geological structures, more complicated than anything so far encountered even in the tightly folded structures of Pembrokeshire or in the volcanic intricacies of Snowdonia. It is termed the Midland Valley, although it has been pointed out that the term 'valley' is a misnomer when used to describe the structural unit contained between the Highland Boundary Fault and the Southern Uplands Fault (Cameron and Stephenson, 1985). Apart from the fact that it includes peaks higher than many of the Pennines – for example, Ben Cleugh (720 m) – it has a surprisingly small amount of land below 120 metres, which is the usual upper limit of improved land hereabouts. Its isolated hill masses, such as the Campsies and the Ochils, break up the lowlands into disparate basins and create sub-regions within the apparent unity of the Midland Valley itself. Three distinct regions can be identified. The first is the western region, where the Carboniferous basins of Ayrshire and Lanarkshire are linked by the Clyde and integrated by the overwhelming presence of the Glasgow conurbation. The region also includes the mountainous coastlands and islands of the Firth of Clyde, where younger sedimentary and igneous rocks make significant contributions to the scenery. The second is the eastern region, with the Midlothian and Fifeshire coalfields, cradled around the Firth of Forth and the citadel of Edinburgh. Finally, in the north the extensive tracts of Old Red Sandstone are furrowed by the great corridors of Strathmore and the Tay, which broaden towards the north-eastern coastlands and appear to turn their backs on the rest of the Lowlands. For this reason the northern region is treated in a separate chapter (Chapter 13). Lower Palaeozoic and older rocks are virtually invisible in the Midland Valley because they have been let down *en masse* between two major parallel fault systems to form what was once termed a 'rift valley'. Consequently, except for a few minor exposures, the older rocks are now deeply buried below layers of Upper Palaeozoic sandstones, limestones, shales and coals, which now form the floor of the so-called valley (George, 1960). On either flank, beyond the faults, the older rocks remain as massive upstanding blocks, from which the Southern Uplands and the Highlands have subsequently been carved (Fig. 12.1).

The great parallel fracture systems of the Southern Uplands Fault and the Highland Boundary Fault were initiated during the instability associated with the period of Caledonian mountain-building in early Palaeozoic times (Kennedy, 1958). A prolonged episode of tectonic uplift was terminated when the centre of a gigantic arch of updomed crustal rocks began to crack along lines of weakness which followed the north-east to south-west Caledonian 'grain'. As a result, a vast strip of land, some 80 kilometres in width, was gradually lowered to create an elongated basin in which Old Red Sandstone, Carboniferous and Permian rocks were later to be deposited. The continuing tectonic instability also manifested itself in the form of widespread vulcanicity throughout these depositional episodes (Francis, 1968). In fact many of the major landmarks in the Midland Valley are related to the igneous phenomena of Upper Palaeozoic age, since,

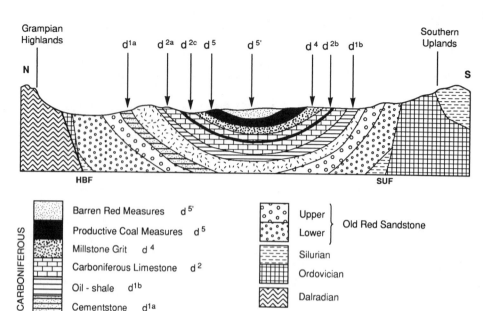

Figure 12.1 Geological section of the Midland Valley of Scotland (based on material prepared by the British Geological Survey). (See also Fig. 12.2.)

CARBONIFEROUS

Barren Red Measures	$d^{5'}$
Productive Coal Measures	d^5
Millstone Grit	d^4
Carboniferous Limestone	d^2
Oil - shale	d^{1b}
Cementstone	d^{1a}
Lavas	

Upper / Lower	Old Red Sandstone
Silurian	
Ordovician	
Dalradian	
HBF	Highland Boundary Fault
SUF	Southern Uplands Fault

together with the Old Red Sandstone grits and conglomerates, these are its most resistant rocks.

Post-Carboniferous earth movements (of Hercynian age) have folded and faulted the thick layers of Upper Palaeozoics and have succeeded in separating the coal-bearing beds into distinct basins which have now become isolated from each other as a result of the denudation of the Carboniferous rocks from the intervening anticlines. One should remember, however, that the Scottish Carboniferous is not as simple as the succession found in England and Wales (Francis, 1965; MacGregor, 1930). Of the two major coal-bearing strata in Scotland, the Lower Coals occur in the so-called Carboniferous Limestone Series, in which sandstones are common and limestones are few. The Upper Coals are found, appropriately enough, in the Coal Measures, but even here there is a very small proportion of coal and many shales and clays. To complete the picture of apparent confusion in the Scottish Carboniferous succession, the so-called Millstone Grit (Muir, 1963), which divides the Upper and Lower Coals, has very few gritstones but many valuable fireclays (Fig. 12.2).

In the western part of the Midland Valley, coalfields have survived in two major downfolds, namely the Lanarkshire Basin and the Ayrshire Basin. These are separated by a ridge of low hills in Renfrewshire, where an upfold of older rocks capped by Lower Carboniferous lavas has introduced a wide tract of featureless moorland between the once colliery-dotted plains.

Ayrshire

Because of its eastern rim of lava plateaux (Whyte and Macdonald, 1974), the Carboniferous basin of central Ayrshire appears to turn away from the Midland

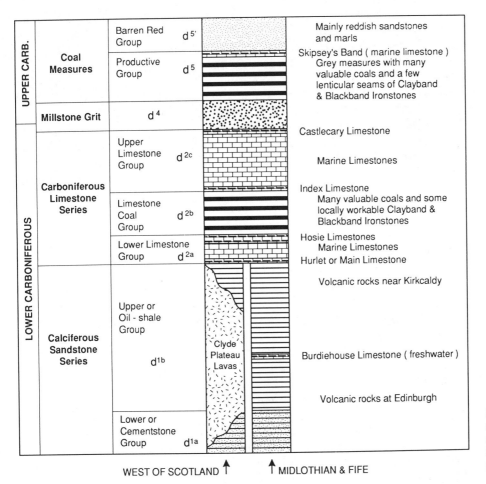

UPPER CARB.	Coal Measures	Barren Red Group	d 5'		Mainly reddish sandstones and marls
		Productive Group	d 5		Skipsey's Band (marine limestone) Grey measures with many valuable coals and a few lenticular seams of Clayband & Blackband Ironstones
	Millstone Grit		d 4		Castlecary Limestone
LOWER CARBONIFEROUS	Carboniferous Limestone Series	Upper Limestone Group	d 2c		Marine Limestones
		Limestone Coal Group	d 2b		Index Limestone Many valuable coals and some locally workable Clayband & Blackband Ironstones
		Lower Limestone Group	d 2a		Hosie Limestones Marine Limestones Hurlet or Main Limestone
	Calciferous Sandstone Series	Upper or Oil - shale Group		Clyde Plateau Lavas	Volcanic rocks near Kirkcaldy
			d 1b		Burdiehouse Limestone (freshwater)
					Volcanic rocks at Edinburgh
		Lower or Cementstone Group	d 1a		

WEST OF SCOTLAND ↑   ↑ MIDLOTHIAN & FIFE

Figure 12.2 Carboniferous succession in central Scotland (based on material prepared by the British Geological Survey).

Valley to face westwards to the sea. In fact, long before the coal seams were exploited its earliest settlements were almost certainly linked with fishing at the coast, where the older towns survive today as ports and holiday resorts. The light, free-draining sandy soils of the raised beaches, together with the dune sands of the coast, have long provided a basis for subsistence farming, but the same soils, with liberal dressings of seaweed manure, today offer a greater cash reward by supporting excellent early potatoes. Inland, on the heavier soils of the northern shales and lavas, and especially where the glacial tills are thickest, the land is given over to permanent grassland for the famous Ayrshire dairy cattle. Even where the lighter loams of the Permian sandstones of Kyle allow sporadic fields of grain and root crops, these are utilized largely as fodder for the herds. Thus the amphitheatre of the Ayrshire lowlands gives an overall impression of greenness – grassland occupies some 70 per cent of the improved land. It seems likely, further- more, that central Ayrshire may always have presented a verdant picture, for its district name of Kyle appears to be derived from the Gaelic *coille*, meaning 'woodland'. Most of the woods have now disappeared, however, replaced in part by scattered pitheads which formerly rose above the open farming land. Unlike many of their English counterparts, some of these Ayrshire coal-mining villages have remained small, with few developing into towns and several reverting to pastoral activities as their collieries closed down. The most recently worked coal seams occur in the southern half of the coalfield in the so-called Mauchline Basin, where the productive Coal Measures are deeply buried beneath thick layers of Carboniferous Barren Red Measures, Permian sandstones and their associated basaltic lavas. It is easy to understand how the easy accessibility of both the Lower and Upper Coals, which emerged at the surface to the north of Kilmarnock, led to their early exploitation and exhaustion. Conversely, the deeper coals, in the centre of the basin to the east of Ayr, were left until modern mining methods were able to extract them from depths of more than 600 metres (MacGregor, 1954).

Included within the Coal Measures are ironstones, which gave an early basis for an iron industry in Ayrshire during the Industrial Revolution. No less than forty-eight blast furnaces were once operative here, and these in turn encouraged engineering in those towns which did develop on the coalfield.

Capping the low plateau country of Kyle, above the buried coalfield, is the 450-metre thick Mauchline Sandstone. Because of its excellent qualities as a building stone, this bright red sandstone has been quarried for many years and widely exported through the Ayrshire ports. Equivalent in age to the Permian sandstones of Dumfries and Penrith, this sandstone is best displayed at the Ballochmyle Quarries at Mauchline, where its large-scale dune-bedding and wind-rounded quartz grains testify to its formation in a Permian desert environment.

Around the Carboniferous basin a discontinuous rim of Old Red Sandstone (Patterson, 1949), bolstered by lavas and igneous intrusions of similar age, creates a perimeter of moorland hills wherever it occurs. This is especially true where this semicircle of harder rocks meets the Firth of Clyde, so to understand the diversity of the Ayrshire scene it would be instructive to traverse this western coastline from south to north. Although the Southern Uplands Fault demarcates the structures of the Midland Valley from those of the Southern Uplands, the boundary in south Ayrshire is less obvious than elsewhere along this important fracture, since Ordovician sedimentary rocks are found both north and south of the fault in the Carrick area, a distribution not found elsewhere in southern Scotland. Moreover, these sediments have been invaded by thick layers of ultra-basic igneous rocks, including serpentine, and also swamped by volcanic lavas, ashes and tuffs of Ordovician age. The igneous rocks have helped to bolster the resistance of the Ordovician sedimentaries so that today the high coastal headlands and moorlands between Ballantrae and Girvan appear to have closer affinities with the upland landscapes of Galloway than with those of the Midland Valley.

North of Glen App, which has been carved along the line of the Southern Uplands Fault, and beyond the little town of Ballantrae, set in its tiny basin of New Red Sandstone among the sharp volcanic hills (Balsillie, 1932), it is only a short distance to the neat and bustling town of Girvan (Williams, 1959). Here the coastline becomes less rugged as blown sand, raised beaches and glacial drift combine to produce the gentle curves of Ayrshire's southern shores. Nevertheless, between Girvan and Ayr the Lower Old Red Sandstone hills thrust their steep, thickly wooded slopes seawards, constricting the narrow coastal plain near

Turnberry, whose famous golf course is on the dune sands which have accumulated on the lowest raised beach. To the north, where the basaltic and andesitic lavas reach the coast, the cliff scenery become more rugged and the hinterland more wild, rising inland to the moorlands of Brown Carrick Hill (287 m). The 60-metre cliffs at the Heads of Ayr are carved from a volcanic agglomerate marking the site of a former vent which has drilled through the surrounding Calciferous Sandstones (or cornstones), representing the basal members of the Carboniferous succession. Where the River Doon crosses from the sandstone hills on to the Coal Measures, is the tiny village of Alloway, famous as the birthplace of Robert Burns. Yet, paradoxically, Ayrshire remains the most English-looking of the Scottish counties. Perhaps it is the regularity and orderliness of its field patterns, with their neatly trimmed hedges, that reminds one of the English Midlands. Or is it the unspoiled villages and the attractive farm cottages with their thatched roofs, a feature once common but now so rare in Scotland? Nevertheless, the absence of trees in the Ayrshire hedgerows confirms that this is the windswept western seaboard of Scotland. Here also is a remarkable collection of raised beaches and dunes fronted by lengthy sweeps of sandy foreshore. There are rocky dolerite sills which form headlands at Prestwick, Troon (the Celtic word *Trwyn* means 'promontory') and Saltcoats, but in general the bays exhibit smooth curves which are orientated at right angles to the approach routes of the dominant marine waves. Here the coastal dunes have been carried some distance inland by the prevailing winds but are now largely fixed by marram grass and the famous golf courses of Troon and Prestwick. These, like that at Turnberry, owe their velvet sward to the light, coarse sands, which are poor in organic matter and mineral plant nutrients but will support fine-bladed grasses on their acid soils.

The islands of the Firth of Clyde

In good visibility, no one travelling along the Ayrshire coast can fail to be impressed by the islands which dominate the western horizon. Ailsa Craig, Arran, Holy Island, Bute and the Cumbraes are names which conjure up romantic visions to seamen and tourists alike, for their craggy hills and rocky cliffs bring a touch of the Highlands, and especially the Hebridean Highlands, deep into lowland Scotland. Their height, ruggedness and steepness are primarily a reflection of their igneous character, although the age of the igneous episode is, in the main, different from that of any so far encountered, for some of them were formed by Tertiary igneous activity (Stewart, 1965).

The smallest but most remarkable of the islands, Ailsa Craig, stands 14.5 kilometres west of Girvan. Although only 1.5 kilometres in diameter, its summit attains a height of 340 metres with a grassy dome-like top surrounded by vertical cliffs up to 150 metres in height. Yet curiously, these coastal cliffs stand beyond high-water mark (except at Stranny Point) and are fronted by a talus slope in some places and by a post-glacial raised beach along the eastern margin. This has led to the suggestion that the cliffs are fossil features which, like the caves, were most probably fashioned by waves during the post-glacial submergence. With the exception of Water Cave in the south-west corner, the majority of the caves have been carved along dolerite dykes that slice through the granitic rock which builds the remainder of the island.

The main rock is a very fine-grained microgranite in which the hornblende takes the form of a mineral known as riebeckite. The fine-grained rock has a well-marked vertical joint pattern and, since denudation has picked this out, the coastal cliffs often exhibit a columnar structure comparable with that on Staffa (see p. 384). The speckled bluish-grey colouring of the granite has proved to be an invaluable marker for the glacial erratics which have been found in the coastal drifts of Cumberland and Wales. The microgranitic boss is thought to be the basal remnant of a volcanic vent which once functioned here, although there appears to be some disagreement about the age of its formation – Tertiary is the more usually accepted date, but a Carboniferous age has also been postulated. In addition to creating the towering cliffs, which house the second largest gannetry in Scotland (St Kilda has the largest), the tough microgranite has been used in the manufacture of curling-stones for Scottish sportsmen, although the quarries, on the north coast of the island, are no longer worked.

To the north of Ailsa Craig, and echoing on a more majestic scale the spectacular steepness of its cliffs, lies the much larger island of Arran (McLellan, 1970). Its rugged grandeur is very largely due to its geological structures; no other British island exhibits such geological complexity for its size (MacGregor *et al.*, 1972; Tomkieff, 1961). Its 427 square kilometres are cut into two parts by the Highland Boundary Fault, with the northern area exhibiting the geology and scenery of the Highlands and the larger southern part being more typical of the lowlands. The variety of its rocks, ranging in age from Precambrian through Palaeozoic and Mesozoic formations to the widespread Tertiary igneous phenomena, together with the diversity of its scenery, make Arran a geologist's paradise, for in a sense it represents a microcosm of Scottish geology.

The contrasts in geology and lithology between north and south Arran are fundamental to an understanding of the topographic differences, which in turn have influenced the vegetation and land use of the two parts. In the north the older, harder Highland rocks, together with the massive Tertiary granitic intrusion, have been fashioned into a deeply dissected highland massif, with rugged peaks rising to almost 900 metres separated by deep glacial valleys such as that of Glen Rosa (Fig. 12.3). The southern portion of the island contains a greater variety of younger, less resistant sedimentary rocks which, despite their scattering of tough igneous intrusions, have produced a much lower undulating plateau surface, rising to 500 metres in height.

In north Arran the steepest slopes coincide with the edge of the granite pluton and, since this occurs within a short distance of the coast, there is space for only a narrow ribbon of coastal plain before the boulder-strewn slopes sweep steeply upwards to the highest peak, Goat Fell (874 m) – the Gaelic name is *Gaoth Bheinn*, meaning 'Mountain of Winds'. In Scotland only the islands of Rhum and Skye have similar high peaks in close proximity to the water's edge, and it is not by chance that all these examples of high insular mountains occur where they do, for they all coincide with massive plutonic intrusions of Tertiary age whose location straddles the north-western seas of the British Isles. The steepness of the slopes, the heavy rainfall and the acidity and thinness of the soils both on the Arran granite and on its metamorphic aureole have limited cultivation and improved pastureland to the narrow coastal margin, where raised beaches overlie the fringe of sedimentary and metamorphic rocks. The remainder of the northern

Figure 12.3 Glen Rosa, Isle of Arran, whose ice-deepened U-shaped valley is surrounded by Arran's highest granite peaks. The A'Chir ridge of Beinn Tarsuinn (left), and the cloud-dappled summit of Cir Mhor (centre) are notched and gullied by invading dykes. Goat Fell is seen to the right of the ice-breached col of the Saddle at the head of the glen.

portion is left as rough moorlands occupied only by deer and sheep. Thus the landscape is one of large-scale grazing farms with irregular field boundaries and a few settlements clustered into the ancient pattern of the 'clachan' (see below).

The southern end of the island has a widespread exposure of New Red Sandstone, the general dip of which is towards the south-west. It is not a simple pattern, however, for numerous Tertiary sills, dikes and other intrusions introduce a ruggedness and lithological complexity into the structures of south Arran. The topography, soils and land use often reflect these geological contrasts, with the improved land being found mainly on the New Red Sandstone and the raised beaches, while the igneous rocks are left mostly as barren moorland. Nevertheless, the better-drained base-rich soils on the dipslopes of some of the basaltic sills can aid farming in a region where waterlogging and soil acidity are widespread away from the lighter soils of the raised beaches. Forests are not common on Arran except around Brodick on the sheltered east coast, and, apart from stunted alder, trees are virtually absent from the gale-lashed southern and western coasts. This is partly because of the windward location but is also connected with the inhibiting effect of grazing in the extensive sheep runs of the island. In the southern portion of Arran there is greater regularity of field patterns than in the north, for the less difficult environment of the south was more conducive to the introduction of agricultural improvements during the eighteenth and nineteenth centuries. In Arran, therefore, the irregular field boundaries and the cultivation rigs associated with the ancient system of land tenure known as 'run-rig' (the infield-outfield system) have survived only in the north, having been lost beneath the geometric field patterns of the enclosure movement farther south. Similarly, in the south the clustered settlement known as the 'clachan' has been replaced by dispersed cottages or by the non-agricultural villages of the eastern seaboard (Storrie, 1967a). In a sense these contrasting agricultural landscapes symbolize Arran's position astride Highland and lowland Scotland.

The line of the Highland Boundary Fault across the island is not a simple one, since the intrusion of the Arran granite caused a certain amount of deformation during the updoming of the country rocks (Figure 12.4). Apart from the granite itself, the rocks to the north and west of the fault are composed almost entirely of Dalradian schists, while to its south and east the sedimentaries range in age from Ordovician to Trias. On the narrow coastal margin of north-east Arran a fringe of Old Red Sandstone and Carboniferous formations can be seen in the coastal cliffs between Corrie and Loch Ranza. Among the Carboniferous strata, which have been folded into a large anticline, it is possible to recognize basal conglomerates, calciferous sandstones and a thick limestone (the Corrie Limestone), but it is the presence of Coal Measures which is perhaps the most interesting discovery, although the collieries at the Cock of Arran have long since ceased production. In geological circles, however, the coast between the abandoned mines and Loch Ranza is better known for yet another of Hutton's famous unconformities. In this instance the Upper Palaeozoic cornstones can be seen to overlie steeply dipping Dalradian schists. This unconformity was in fact the first of the three to be discovered by Hutton (see p. 245).

As these Old Red Sandstone and Carboniferous rocks are traced southwards past the frowning steeps of Goat Fell, their narrow outcrop swings westwards across the waist of the island (Friend *et al.*, 1963), parallel with the edge of the granite pluton and the Highland Boundary Fault (see Figure 12.4). The reason for the change in direction of the strike of these sedimentary rocks must be sought in the displacement caused by the granitic magma. As the granite was intruded it caused an updoming of the country rocks, as is shown by the steep outward dips not only of the Palaeozoic rocks near Brodick but also of the schists on the western flanks of the gigantic intrusion (see Figure 12.4).

South of the so-called String Road, which crosses the waist of the island between Brodick Bay and the west coast, it appears at first sight that the geological succession is becoming less complex as the Carboniferous series dip southwards to pass beneath the Permian and Triassic sandstones (Gregory, 1915). But the uplands around Glen Craigag have been carved not from uncomplicated Palaeozoic and Mesozoic sedimentaries but from a most remarkable jumble of igneous rocks known as a 'ring complex'. This is the well-known Central Ring Complex of Arran, and to understand its formation one must now look briefly at the history of Tertiary igneous activity in western Scotland, though most of these igneous phenomena will be discussed in more detail in Chapter 16.

The Tertiary igneous rocks of Scotland, like those of north-east Ireland, form part of the so-called Brito-Icelandic or Thulean province, which also includes the Faroes. It has been suggested that the enormous thicknesses of basaltic lavas which have survived in many parts of this province were once part of a continuous land surface that has now been fragmented as the Atlantic Ocean slowly widened. In addition to the thick piles of basaltic lava there are numerous intrusive bodies

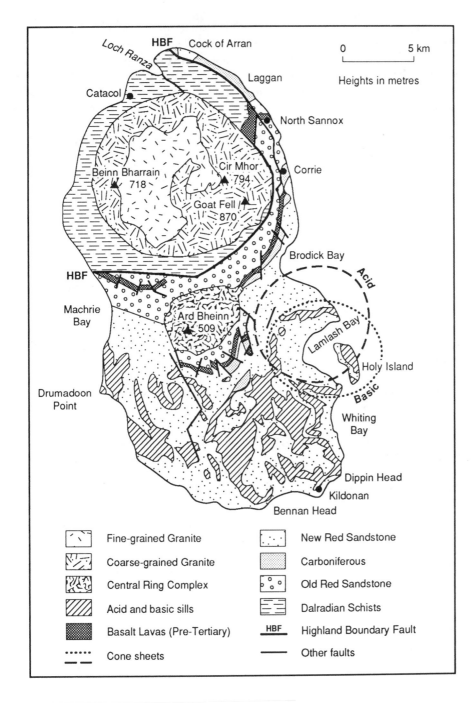

HBF Cock of Arran
Loch Ranza
Laggan
Catacol
North Sannox
Beinn Bharrain ▲ 718
Cir Mhor ▲ 794
Corrie
Goat Fell ▲ 870
HBF
Brodick Bay
Acid
Machrie Bay
Ard Bheinn ▲ 509
Lamlash Bay
Holy Island
Drumadoon Point
Basic
Whiting Bay
Dippin Head
Kildonan
Bennan Head

0   5 km
Heights in metres

Fine-grained Granite

Coarse-grained Granite

Central Ring Complex

Acid and basic sills

Basalt Lavas (Pre-Tertiary)

Cone sheets

New Red Sandstone

Carboniferous

Old Red Sandstone

Dalradian Schists

HBF   Highland Boundary Fault

Other faults

Figure 12.4 Geology of the Isle of Arran (based on material prepared by the British Geological Survey and S. I. Tomkieff).

ranging in character and size from the large plutons, such as the Arran granite, through ring complexes and sills to the more extensive dyke swarms. The mineralogical composition of the igneous rocks also exhibits variety, with ultrabasic, basic and acid intrusives all being represented by one or other of the Scottish centres.

Although some modern geologists would dispute his views, Harker (1918) considered that when studying the Scottish Tertiary igneous rocks one could trace a sequential progression from an early volcanic phase (associated with outpourings of mainly basaltic lavas) through a plutonic phase to a final phase of minor intrusions, all this being associated with a change from basic to acid activity. By contrast, recent research (Walker, 1975) suggests that the basic to acid sequence is misleading, for in some cases there is evidence to show that acid bodies were formed before the basic ones (for instance, in Rhum). Nevertheless, the simple sequence of events outlined by Harker will serve to demonstrate the different types of igneous activity, even though in places both volcanic and plutonic activity may have occurred simultaneously.

The Tertiary igneous activity of western Scotland can be divided into five main episodes which correspond fairly closely with those recognized in Northern Ireland. First, there came the outpouring of basaltic lavas, but, since few have survived in the Arran landscape, these can best be studied in Mull and Skye. Associated with the formation of thick piles of basaltic lavas there was a period of explosive activity during which gigantic central vent volcanoes were created. As magmatic material was created at depth, so the volcanic gases built up enormous pressures, being ultimately released at areas of weakness in the crust where volcanic pipes, necks or vents can now be seen in the landscape. Such vents were drilled through the crust by the same explosions which threw out ash, dust and lava fragments to build the volcanic cones and craters. Only the plugs of lava which cooled slowly in the vents, often forming a hard dolerite or felsite, remain to form steep-sided hills in an otherwise rolling plateau landscape. Several examples of such landforms in the Border Country (see Chapter 11) have already been described, although those igneous rocks were of Palaeozoic age. Where cooling was rapid the rocks exhibit a small or finely grained crystalline structure, as noted in the microgranite (or riebeckite) of Ailsa Craig (see p. 268). If, however, the cooling was slow, as with the rocks which solidified at great depth (hence the term 'plutonic rocks'), then the crystals are generally large or coarse, as in the porphyritic granites.

The sequence of events which led to the formation of the Central Arran ring complex is extremely complicated, but an attempt will be made to explain the main structures (King, 1955). Shortly after the emplacement of the main Arran Granite, a local doming took place in the sedimentary rocks in the centre of the island. This uplift resulted in the creation of a circular fracture, about 5 kilometres in diameter, which sliced right through the sedimentary rocks and the plateau basalts which must then have covered them. *Cauldron subsidence* (of over 900 metres) then followed, producing an enormous surface depression or caldera, the amphitheatre of which was to act as a receptacle for further lava extrusion from the volcanic cones which later erupted on its floor. One interesting point which emerges from a study of the geology of the Central Ring Complex is the presence of large masses of Rhaetic, Lias and Cretaceous sedimentaries within the caldera complex, suggesting that these must have helped build the cover of sedimentary rocks before the igneous activity occurred. Since these Mesozoics are no longer found on Arran, they must subsequently have been destroyed elsewhere on the island. The early basaltic lavas have also virtually disappeared, buried by great thicknesses of later volcanics which have covered the collapsed floor of the caldera. Four volcanic cones appear to have developed on the caldera floor, and these emitted a variety of both basic and acid lavas throughout their short-lived history, together with pyroclastic rocks of similar composition (Figure 12.4). Both during and after this explosive phase, continuing subsidence along the outer ring fracture and along a subsidiary inner fracture allowed granite to rise into the caldera complex, where it solidified as a peripheral *ring dyke* and as a central body. Subsequent denudation has lowered the entire ring complex, but some of the harder igneous rocks have resisted the lowering more successfully than others, creating the upland peaks surrounding Glenn Craigag: Ard Bheinn and Creag Dubh, for example, were formed from rocks in the vents of two of the former volcanoes, whilst Cnoc Dubh and Beinn Bhreac are carved from the granite of the peripheral ring.

The third episode in the Tertiary igneous history of Scotland is the period of sill formation which is thought to mark a declining phase in the volcanic activity. Like the Whin Sill described in Chapter 10, the igneous intrusion is left protruding as a prominent scarp face in the local scenery. In southern Arran the Tertiary sills are interbedded with the less resistant New Red Sandstone, forming numerous scarps, terraces and 'sills' of waterfalls (hence their name). Three varieties have been recognized in south Arran. The coarsest and most massive are those formed from quartz-porphyry, well illustrated in the south-west by the conspicuous cliffs at Drumadoon Point, Brown Head and Bennan Head. The second group of sills is that of the finer-grained quartz-dolerite intrusions, which help form some of the scarps in south-east Arran, such as Cnoc na Garbad (76 metres thick), Auchenhew Hill and many waterfall steps of Glenashdale. The final group, composed of gabbro-like material, termed crinanite, occurs around Lamlash in the form of a broken circle. Since these sheets of basic igneous rocks cut across the bedding of the Permian sandstones and form a circle centred on Lamlash Bay, they have been interpreted by Tomkieff (1961) as a *cone-sheet* complex (see Fig. 12.4). Lamlash Bay has in part been created from the eroded centre of the sedimentary rocks within the cone-sheet complex, while the massive rampart of Holy Island (314 m) is thought to have been formed from an invading 'ring dyke' of riebeckite-trachyte, similar in composition to that of Ailsa Craig.

The two other igneous episodes of Scottish Tertiary history are represented by the intrusion of the narrow, vertical, linear sheets known as dykes, and of the deep-seated plutonic masses of granite and gabbro. Although dykes can be seen clearly along the shore platforms of southern Arran, they can best be described in detail in Mull and Skye, where they produce more spectacular land-forms. Moreover, the mechanisms of plutonic activity, and in particular that of granite emplacement, have already been touched upon in previous chapters (see pp. 33 and 255).

The Arran Granite is the second largest Tertiary granite outcrop in the British Isles, inferior in size only to that of the Mourne Mountains of Ireland, whose age of 58 million years it nevertheless equals. It is in fact composed of two types of granite: coarse granite makes up the outer part of the circular intrusion and helps form the sharper and higher peaks of the eastern and western margins (see Figure 12.4); fine-grained granite has invaded the central area of the coarser granite but has proved less resistant to denudation, thereby coinciding with the lower, rounded mountains around Loch Tanna and parts of Glen Iorsa. The granite is grey in colour because of its mixture of white feldspar, black mica and glassy quartz and is criss-crossed with a maze of dykes and veins of various sizes, which are composed of greenstone, aplite, porphyry or basalt. These invading dykes and veins either stand out as ribs or show as notches or channels in the rocky landscape, depending on their relative hardness in relation to the surrounding granite (see Fig. 12.3). The jointing in the granite has also helped create the serrated appearance of the ridges which run steeply up to the summits from Glen Rosa and Glen Sannox. But the generally rugged appearance of these northern hills is due largely to the action of glaciers and frost weathering during Pleistocene times. Since it is near to the high mountain areas of the south-west Grampians, it is no surprise to discover that Arran, together with the other islands in the Firth of Clyde, was overwhelmed by ice sheets from the Scottish Highlands on several occasions. But, because of its high mountains, it also served as a local ice centre in its own right, this being particularly significant during the last 3000 years of the Pleistocence, when its own ice limits can be correlated not only with those of the Scottish mainland but also with the remarkable series of late-glacial shorelines which occurs around the Firth of Clyde. Although there has been some criticism of his work, a comprehensive study of the island's late-glacial history by Gemmell (1973) has shown that the highest of the raised shorelines (the so-called '100-foot' raised beach of the Geological Survey) occurs at 27 metres in south Arran and at 33 metres in north Arran, the tilt thought to be a result of differential post-glacial isostatic uplift. Even more significant, however, is the fact that this highest strandline is missing from Arran's northern coast between Corrie and Catacol Bay, suggesting that Highland ice sheets were still present in northernmost Arran at that time (c. 13 000 years ago), inhibiting beach formation in this tract. An intermediate raised shoreline (the so-called '50-foot' beach) is also uptilted from south to north (17–23 metres), but since it occurs sporadically all round the island it suggests that by about 12 500 years ago the mainland ice had disappeared and that the sea had access to the entire Arran coast, except for the mouths of some northern valleys which still contained local glaciers. By 10 800 years ago, after a short ice-free phase, valley glaciers reappeared in northern Arran, leaving fresh morainic evidence in all the major glens, but being especially well marked in Glen Iorsa and Glen Rosa. By 10 300 years ago, however, this local glacial equivalent of the so-called 'Loch Lomond Readvance' had disappeared, leaving Arran free of ice and with a rising sea level ready to fashion the post-glacial raised beaches all round the island. These raised beaches were not only to provide a foothold for the earliest Mesolithic settlers but were also later to be used for the ancient practice of 'run-rig' subsistence farming, characteristic of the western isles of Scotland. In such steep and harsh environments the raised beaches were often the only tracts of flat and fertile land available, and it is still fascinating to discover at Balliekine, in north-west Arran, survivals of these unconsolidated field strips and their sprawling clachan (Storrie, 1967b).

The Isle of Bute contrasts scenically with Arran in nearly all respects, not least because of its lack of high mountains. Having no land over 300 metres, Bute is distinguished by extensive areas of grassland and woodland, except on its northern moorlands (Munro, 1973). Yet, like Arran, Bute stands astride the Highland Boundary Fault, which can be traced south-westwards across the island from Rothesay, past Loch Fad, to Scalpsie Bay. The fault helps divide Bute into two main geological tracts, each with its own distinctive scenery. In the northern two-thirds of the island the Dalradian schists, grits and phyllites have weathered into poor, acid soils capable of supporting only moorlands. Nevertheless their steep, rocky northern coasts are fringed by rich woodlands which play no small part in the picturesque scenery of the famous Kyles of Bute which separate Bute from the mainland shore of Cowal. Between Kames Bay and Ettrick Bay the barren northern moorlands are broken by a belt of improved land which coincides with an isthmus now floored with raised beaches. The indentation which has produced these beautiful sandy bays appears to be related to the differential erosion of the less resistant Dunoon Phyllites, which here crop out as a wide band within the Dalradian succession.

South-east of Loch Fad the Highland rocks are replaced by the Carboniferous sandstone and Old Red Sandstone of lowland Scotland, and the resultant change in the landscape is most marked. The moorlands give way to a tract of cultivated fields and thick woodlands, especially on the sheltered eastern coast where most of the settlement is located. Rothesay's Victorian villa-fringed promenade has long been the 'Margate' of Clydeside, being the steamer terminus for the traditional Glaswegian day trip. South of Kilchattan Bay, however, the woodlands and fields turn to rough moorlands once more, for here the Old Red Sandstone has been buried beneath basaltic lavas of Carboniferous age, which in turn have been cut by Tertiary sills, similar to those of south Arran. Where the sandstone emerges from beneath the igneous rocks it is picked out by a scrub of elder, birch and rowan, but on the lavas and sills the ubiquitous bracken holds sway.

The scenery of this southernmost peninsula of Bute is very similar to that of Little Cumbrae Island, which lies three kilometres to the east. It is not surprising to find, therefore, that the mossy turf and bracken of Little Cumbrae mantle a rocky tract of Carboniferous lavas similar not only to those of south Bute (Tyrell, 1926) but also to the extensive lava tracts of the nearby Ayrshire mainland. While Little Cumbrae is deserted because of its thin soils and poor grazing, the same is not true of its neighbour, Great Cumbrae. This well-farmed island, composed almost entirely of Old Red Sandstone and white Carboniferous cornstones, mirrors both the improved lands of south-central Bute and the Largs–Ardrossan coastlands of Ayrshire, whose geological structures it repeats. The almost featureless plateau of Great Cumbrae, where woodlands often mark the poorer soils, is diversified only by dykes and sills of igneous rocks which form prominent ridges smothered in gorse, bracken and scrubby trees (Sutherland, 1926). As in Arran and Bute, the cultivated land is found mainly on the flatter and better-drained areas of raised beach.

Clydeside

From Greenock eastwards the Firth of Clyde's scenic character changes most dramatically, for here begins the man-made urban sprawl of Clydeside and its attendant industrialization – a landscape which some would judge to be more typical of the Midland Valley than that of Ayrshire. The reason may be that the Carboniferous basin of central Scotland (Lanarkshire–Stirlingshire) possessed certain advantages of industrial location denied to Ayrshire, not least the presence of the rivers Clyde and Forth. But, before turning to examine the geological and topographical factors which led to the growth of Glasgow and its industrial region, it is important to look at the encircling rim of uplands which overlooks Glasgow from the south, west and north.

Stretching north-westwards from the Southern Uplands through the Eaglesham Heights (376 m) and the Hill of Stake (552 m), a line of drab, moorland plateaux acts as a divide between the Ayrshire and Lanarkshire basins. In the far south near Lesmahagow the hills are made of Silurian greywackes and shales which have been exposed at the crests of two small anticlines. This is one of the few examples of Lower Palaeozoic strata within the Midland Valley 'rift'. In the main, however, these tablelands have been carved from an extensive occurrence of Lower Carboniferous lavas – the so-called Clyde Plateau lavas – which are over 600 metres in thickness. It has been calculated that they formerly covered an area of at least 1500 square kilometres, so their former limits have either been buried by subsequent sedimentary deposition or destroyed by denudation (MacGregor, 1948).

The uplands of this Carboniferous lava plateau extend north-eastwards across the Clyde into Dunbartonshire and Stirlingshire, where the prominent Kilpatrick Hills (401 m) and the Campsie Fells (578 m) overlook Clydeside from the north (Whyte and Macdonald, 1974). The numerous flows of lava, which were extruded one upon the other, can be seen in profile along the southern flanks of the Campsies. Here, erosion along the line of the Campsie Fault has left the tiers of no less than 30 lava flows to form the cliffs and steep heathery slopes of the Kilsyth and Strathblane Hills (Figure 12.5). These are a good example of a fault-line scarp, with the downthrow of the Carboniferous sediments to the south of the fault helping explain the wooded lowlands of Strathblane. A scarp of this type (with the downthrow block forming the lower ground) will not always result from a fault movement of similar character. A fault-line scarp will form only when differential erosion is able to pick out differences between hard and soft rocks which have been brought together by faulting. In this instance the tough Campsie lavas on the upthrow side are in juxtaposition with the less resistant Carboniferous sandstones and limestones of the downthrow side (Fig. 12.5 section c–d). As if to illustrate the complexity of the structure, exactly the opposite topographic phenomenon has resulted a short distance to the west along the same Campsie Fault (Fig. 12.5, section a–b). Here the lavas occur to the south of the fault, on the downthrow side, but owing to their toughness have formed the north-facing fault-line scrap of the Kilpatrick Hills.

In addition to their steep basalt escarpment, the Campsie Fells are noted for a series of prominent conical hills, especially along their northern face near Fintry (Fig. 12.5). Such landmarks as Dumgoyne (427 m), Garloch Hill (543 m) and the cliffs north of Earl's Seat (578 m) have all been carved from volcanic vents, of similar age and character to that at the Heads of Ayr (see p. 267). Within Strathblane itself, the wooded pinnacle of Dumgoyach and the smaller knob of Dunglass are equally impressive examples of volcanic necks, but the best known is at Dumbarton where the pinnacled rock has long provided a defensive site on the narrow waters of the Clyde (Fig.12.6). Claimed by some as the birthplace of St Patrick (note the adjoining Kilpatrick Hills), Dumbarton has an antiquity greater than that of Glasgow itself. Standing at the mouth of the Vale of Leven, Dumbarton could claim a strategic significance on Clydeside, for here the great river estuary is narrowed as it cuts through the hard basaltic rim of the Renfrew

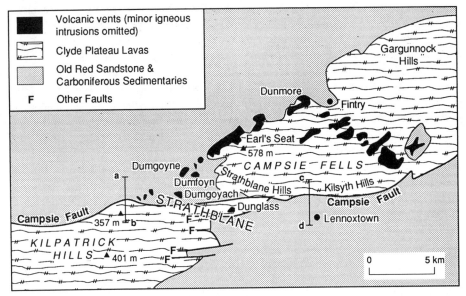

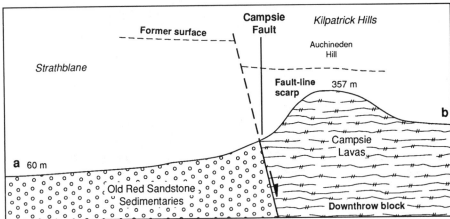

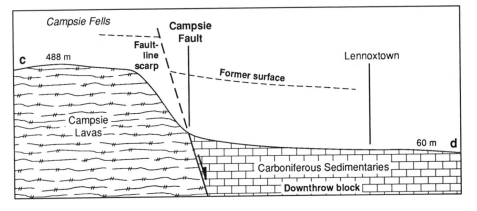

Figure 12.5 Structure of the fault-line scarps of the Campsie Fells and the Kilpatrick Hills near Glasgow.

Heights and the Kilpatrick Hills (Browne and McMillan, 1984). The proximity of the lava hills has both helped and hindered the development of the Clydeside towns hereabouts. The rocky reefs of the Dumbuck ford long frustrated the attempts of ocean-going vessels to sail upstream to Glasgow, thus leading to the creation of such outports as Greenock and Port Glasgow. The same hard rocks which formed the reefs also caused a contraction of the channel downstream, resulting in deep tidal water along the southern shore. Nevertheless, the lava plateaux finally played an inhibiting part in the history of Greenock and Port Glasgow, for the narrow coastal terraces on which these towns were built are not conducive, because of their constricting hillslopes, to the establishment of large cities or great dockyards. To find such space for development one has to travel upstream to Glasgow and Clydebank which, once freed of their offending reefs and shoals, were able to expand on the extensive flats of the so-called Howe of Glasgow.

Figure 12.6 Dumbarton Rock, a prominent volcanic neck rising sharply from the mudflats of the Clyde estuary, was an ancient defensive settlement long before neighbouring Glasgow was founded.

To the east of the lava plateaux there is a clear relationship between the topographic amphitheatre or Howe (the word *howe* means 'hollow place'), in which Glasgow has grown, and the geological structure of the Lanarkshire part of the Carboniferous basin of central Scotland (George, 1958). Although the synclinal basin of the so-called Central Coalfield is diversified by some hardrock ridges, generally related to the Upper Carboniferous Millstone grits and sandstones (Muir, 1963), there is a general coincidence between the downfolded limestones, shales and coals, on the one hand, and the low-lying basin of the Middle Clyde, on the other (Basset, 1958; Bluck, 1973). Owing to the thick layers of glacial drift and alluvial deposits, however, the detailed effects of solid geology on the topography are masked within the basin itself. Nevertheless, by careful study of the colliery waste tips (bings) it is possible to demonstrate the approximate geological boundaries: the Lower Coals in the Carboniferous Limestone Series (see Fig. 12.2) occur on the western flank of the coalfield, creating a line of mining towns from Johnstone, through Glasgow, Kirkintilloch and Kilsyth, to Denny and Stirling; the Upper Coals of the younger Productive Coal Measures outcrop nearer the centre of the basin, from Hamilton and Motherwell to Armadale (MacGregor, 1954). Between the Upper and Lower Coals both the Upper Limestone Group (which includes several thin limestone beds and many thick layers of shale) and the Millstone Grit intervene in the lithological succession, as shown in Fig. 12.2. Since neither of these contains coal seams of any significance, their line of outcrop in the Carboniferous basin has created a 'barren' zone in the coalfield, where pit-heads and spoil-heaps are absent from the landscape.

It took many millions of years of subsequent denudation to destroy any post-Carboniferous rocks which might have been deposited in the Midland Valley and to hollow out the basin of Strathclyde. The final touches must have been provided by the Pleistocene ice sheets, which ultimately lowered the less resistant rocks during several periods of selective glacial erosion. One can reconstruct the direction of former ice movement not only from the drumlins of the Glasgow district but also from the distribution of the distinctive erratics from the Glen Fyne Granite, which is located near the northern end of Loch Lomond. Thus we have evidence that Highland ice sheets advanced south-eastwards across the Howe of Glasgow before moving up the Clyde Valley. In the process the ice left thick layers of till to obliterate the former drainage pattern and infill the pre-glacial rock basins (McLellan, 1969). Borings have revealed the pre-glacial Clyde Valley as a buried rock-cut strath now lost beneath some 90 metres of glacial infill. Consequently the post-glacial river, having been unable to rediscover its former valley (except in a few places), has now cut a new course in the easily eroded superficial deposits. Where the Clyde and its tributaries have succeeded in downcuttting to the old pre-glacial land surface they have carved out spectacular rock gorges. The most famous of these is near Lanark, where the Clyde follows a narrow gorge 30 metres deep, below its well-known series of falls (see p. 281).

Glasgow itself is built on a cluster of drumlins, with many of the famous buildings, including the University, located on their crests. Not only have the drumlins affected the local drainage, as in the case of the meandering River Kelvin, but they have also influenced the layout of the city streets. In the city centre the street-plan of the Park drumlin, east of the University, is a most striking example of this topographic influence, while Sauchiehall Street makes use of a low col between the drumlins to maintain its alignment. After the withdrawal of the ice sheets a rising sea level broke into the Howe of Glasgow to leave both late-glacial and post-glacial raised beaches wrapped around the footslopes of the drumlin hillocks. Where the Clyde subsequently carved its meandering channel through these terraces it created the diversified relief on which Scotland's largest city was to be gradually erected (Miller, 1970).

Despite the presence of Mesolithic hunters and fishermen on the neighbouring shores of the Firth of Clyde, the thickly wooded clay soils of the inland basin were apparently unattractive to these early settlers. The same situation seems to have prevailed during the advent of the Neolithic agriculturalists about 4000 years ago, for they also settled only along the western coasts, utilizing the lighter soils around the Firth of Clyde and leaving their enormous megalithic tombs of so-called Clyde-Carlingford type. Similarly, the succeeding Bronze Age settlers, known as the Beaker Folk, settled only along the western coastlands, penetrating no farther inland than Dumbarton Rock. Even the Iron Age settlements avoided the thickly wooded mid-Clyde Valley and the Howe remained a virtual no man's land until Roman times, when the area was probably reclaimed and cleared during the building of the neighbouring Antonine Wall. This northern bulwark of the Roman Empire was only briefly held against the marauding Highlanders, the Midland Valley finally being given up in AD 196 when the legions retreated to Hadrian's Wall. Eventually, as the post-Roman kingdom of Strathclyde evolved, the Howe became something of a crossroads, where the Clydesdale routes to the Firth met those from Ayrshire and the Lothians. There appear to have been many sandy islets in the river hereabouts, and these provided both a bridging-point and a ford at the centre of the Howe, later to become the focal point of Glasgow (Miller and Tivy, 1958).

Clydesdale

As one follows the Clyde upstream there is no immediate change in the cultural landscape, as the scene remains one of industrial wasteland – factories, collieries and steelworks – now overlaid by a veneer of new housing estates and motorway networks (Lea, 1980). All of the collieries of Hamilton, Motherwell and Airdrie have closed down and the threat of closure hangs over Ravenscraig's steelworks. Despite the fact that the iron industry was one of the earliest industrial enterprises in early nineteeth-century Lanarkshire, the local ores proved too acidic for use in the steel-making which subsequently developed here. Their earliest Scottish exploitation was in the shallow surface workings of the Central Coalfield, where the iron nodules, which had sufficient combustible carbonaceous material to render them self-calcining, were known as the 'blackband ironstones'. These, at first rejected by the coal-miners as 'wild coal', were discovered near Airdrie in 1801, but it was not until about 1830 that the invention of the blast furnace allowed them to be fully utilized. Before then, iron ores were imported from Cumberland and Lancashire to be smelted on the shores of Loch Etive and Loch Fyne, where wood-charcoal could easily be provided from the Highland forests. Before the discovery of the blackband ores the clayband ironstones had been smelted by using local coking coal, first used in Scotland at the famous Carron furnaces in 1759 (see p. 291). Today, iron-ore extraction in the Midland Valley has ceased and all the local geological factors which helped locate the Lanarkshire iron industry are now virtually meaningless.

Throughout this Scottish 'Black Country' the Clyde cuts a swathe of open space, allowing the rural greenery to invade the urban and industrial sprawl, and, since Clydesdale has long been historically important, it is not surprising to find stately homes, ruined castles and pit-mounds cheek by jowl. For instance, the famous Bothwell Castle overlooks abandoned coal tips. William Lithgow spoke of Lanarkshire in 1640 as a land of 'orchards, castles, towns and woods planted side by side', and even by Cobbett's time Clydesdale was still a pleasant country-side. Above Hamilton and Wishaw, because of the sheltered nature of the Clyde Valley, this area has come to be known as the Orchard Country. The orchards can best be seen from Crossford Bridge or the bridge at Garrion, where they rise in tiers above the loitering and twisting Clyde. Although the valley is narrow and often wooded, the low river terraces are flanked by thick deposits of glacio-fluvial material which nourish the strawberry plants, raspberry canes and plum, pear and apple trees which cling even to the steepest banks in their tiny plots. Acres of greenhouses can also be seen climbing up the valleysides, for this is also an important location for tomato-growing.

The tributary streams, often flowing in rock gorges such as those of the Nethan and the Lee Burn in the Carboniferous limestones and sandstones near Crossford, join the Clyde by steep gradients, as if to herald the famous Clyde Falls. At Lanark the Clyde flows across a broad outcrop of Old Red Sandstone which serves to separate the reach of the Upper Clyde from that of the Lower Clyde and here the river tumbles some 9 metres over the Stoneybyres Falls. Three kilometres upstream the gorge becomes narrower until the majestic 27 metre stepped falls at Corra Linn are reached, and a little farther up the chasm the smaller Bonnington Linn completes the sequence. All the gorges and waterfalls have been carved from gently dipping greywackes of Lower Old Red Sandstone age, and they combine with the ancient oak and ash woods and the 'time-cemented tower' of Corehouse Castle on the cliff edge to produce a romantic scene celebrated alike by Wordsworth's pen and Turner's brush. Corra Linn is the best-known landmark because of its high fall of water, the power from which was utilized early in the Industrial Revolution by Richard Arkwright and David Dale. By running the turbulent waters in a subterranean aqueduct through the greywackes, they were able to harness the power of the Clyde to their cotton-spinning mill, set up in 1783 at New Lanark and at that time the largest in Britain. Later this important stone-built mill was incorporated into the famous indus-trial village planned by Robert Owen as an early experiment in practical social-ism. To seek an explanation for the location of the Clyde Falls it is necessary to examine both the tectonic and the erosional history of the Upper Clyde. Its head-waters, which rise high up in a mossy hollow on Clyde Law in the Southern Uplands before flowing through the metal-mining district near Leadhills (Temple, 1956), have not only been regionally uplifted but also subjected to major river capture.

Upstream from Bonnington Linn the Upper Clyde occupies a wide, fertile strath as far as Lamington, where it leaves the inner recesses of the Lowther Hills. Throughout this entire reach the river is a sluggish, meandering watercourse with little change of gradient, and it appears to have been adjusted to a base level of some 168 metres above present sea level (Fig. 12.7b). It has already been noted, however, that near Lanark the character of the valley changes as the river tumbles into a series of gorges before entering the Lower Clyde section of its course, which is adjusted to sea level near Glasgow. Such a change in river character is a result of rejuvenation by tectonic uplift of the river system. This drastic interference with the river's normal equilibrium when, theoretically, it is just able to transport its load, means that the river is given increased energy. In turn this manifests itself in rapid downcutting of the channel into its former valley in an attempt to restore the smooth, long profile of equilibrium, theoretically hyperbolic in form (Fig. 12.7a). Thus the Upper Clyde reflects the former profile of the river, before the regional uplift of some 168 metres, while the Lower Clyde represents the episode of downcutting to a new base level due to increased energy rejuvenation (Fig. 12.7b). The sudden change of gradient between the two stretches is known as a *knick point*, with the Lanark Falls marking the change from the old to the new profile. Since the river is constantly working to smooth out its profile and regain equilibrium by removing irregularities in its course, knick points tend to move upstream. Such headward recession is relatively rapid in the more easily eroded rocks, but once the waterfalls reach a hard-rock band there is a slowing-down of their upstream retreat: hence the Lanark Falls are now 'held' on the hard outcrop of Old Red Sandstone.

It now remains to explain the somewhat anomalous drainage pattern of the Clyde above Lanark where, more than a century ago, Archibald Geikie pointed to a pre-glacial connection between the Clyde and the Tweed. The finest viewpoint in Upper Clydesdale is undoubtedly the summit of Tinto Hill (707 m), from which the remarkably circuitous route of the Clyde from Lamington to Lanark can be seen. The view eastwards from Tinto Hill leaves little doubt that the wide, flat through-valley of the so-called Biggar Gap must have played a significant part in the evolutionary history of the Upper Clyde, as was pointed out by Geikie, who concluded that all the Clyde headwaters once followed this remarkable gap to the Tweed, 'thus entering the sea at Berwick instead of at Dumbarton'. The mechanisms of this major river capture are outlined in Fig. 12.7c. It seems that the former watershed between Clyde and Tweed lay near Lanark, and that the Lower Clyde, working along the less resistant strata of the Lanarkshire Carboniferous basin, also had a shorter route to the sea. These two advantages allowed it to capture the headwaters of the east-flowing Tweed drainage one by one (Linton, 1934). First, what was to be the River Douglas, utilizing a structural syncline, cut off any of the Tweed headstreams which might have risen to the west of the Tinto Hills. Later, the Medwin tributary of the Clyde cut back eastwards into the outcrops of Calciferous Sandstone, thus beheading a series of south-flowing Tweed tributaries in the vicinity of Carstairs and Carnwath. These include the Mouse Water, the Dippool Water, the North Medwin and the Tarth, all of which now turn through a right angle and flow to the Lower Clyde. Finally, the Upper Clyde itself was captured near Symington, leaving the former trunk route of the Biggar Gap virtually streamless and the Tweed robbed of some 388 square kilometres of its former drainage basin. During the Ice Age the Biggar Gap was followed at various times by glaciers and glacial meltwaters.

In the central section of the Midland Valley, the very heartland of the Scottish nation, the divide between the Clyde and Forth is ill defined. Nevertheless, the contrasts between west and east soon become apparent in the landscape –

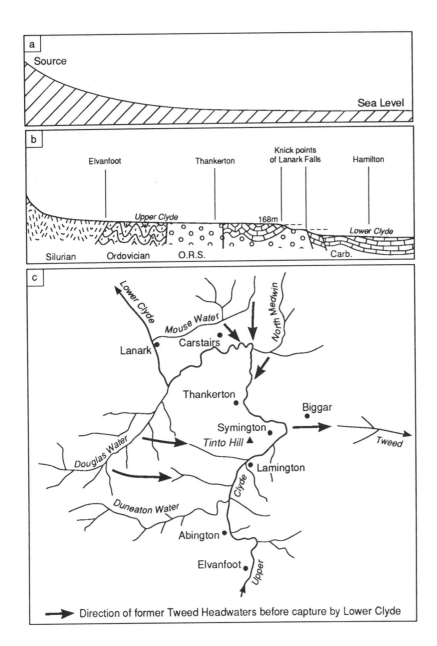

Figure 12.7 Evolution of the River Clyde drainage (after D. L. Linton and T. N. George). (a) Hypothetical curve of the long profile before rejuvenation. (b) Present river profile related to geology. (c) Hypothetical reconstruction of former drainage directions in the basin of the Upper Clyde.

contrasts that seem to be epitomized in the differences of character between the cities of Glasgow and Edinburgh (Lindsay, 1956). In contrast to the long, narrow estuary of the Clyde, the Firth of Forth widens rapidly seawards, bringing the presence of the North Sea and its persistent coastal fog or 'haar' deep into the central valley. The Clyde's overwhelming backdrop of Highland fantasies is also missing here, for the bordering hills of the Lammermuirs and the Ochils stand discreetly back from the Forth. Yet the very flatness of the Forth carselands and the coastal tracts of Fife and the Lothians serves only to magnify the small but craggy igneous outcrops which dot the eastern plains. The importance of these isolated crags as defensive sites will be emphasized when noting the location of Edinburgh itself, sited at the only place where the upland hills approach the Firth, thus restricting the Lothian coastal plain. Farther upstream, Stirling was also founded at a strategic gap where the Forth breaks through the hard rock barrier of the Ochils and the Gargunnock Hills.

Despite the coalfields of the Lothians and Fifeshire, these eastern landscapes do not bear the imprint of industrialism quite so heavily as those of Ayrshire and Lanarkshire, perhaps because the eastern farmlands permeate the scattered industrial areas more easily than they do the massive conurbation along the Clyde. But it is also by geological, topographical and climatic contrasts that one is able to define the differences between the eastern and western regions of the Midland Valley. For example, the extensive lava plateaux of the west create not only unproductive rush-choked uplands but also poor, waterlogged soils. Such plateaux are less widespread in the east, where broad basins of mainly Carboniferous rocks have helped produce the more fertile soils which characterize the wider coastal plains. Here, too, the glacial drifts are more widespread, as are the extensive marine clays associated with the raised shorelines, and where these have been drained some excellent farmlands have been created. The lower rainfall of these eastern tracts has led to a greater emphasis on arable farming, so that the endless grassland and fodder crops of Ayrshire's dairying region are here replaced by a more satisfying chequerboard pattern of yellow grain-fields interspersed among various shades of green. But the westerly prevailing winds are still channelled through the corridors of the Midland Valley, so even in the Lothians shelter-belts of trees along the field boundaries are a common sight (Millman, 1975).

The geological and topographical differences noted above are also evident within the region itself, enabling one to distinguish three separate divisions: the Lothians to the south of the Forth; the area of the Middle Forth (including the Ochils); and the peninsula of Fife and Kinross, between Forth and Tay.

The Lothians

The ancient province of Lothian is neatly cradled between the Southern Uplands and the Firth of Forth, and though its southern limits extend upwards into the Lammermuirs and Moorfoots, these hill masses lie beyond the Southern Uplands Fault and have been treated elsewhere (see Chapter 11). The remainder of the Lothians is not all lowland, however, for the high ridge of the Pentland Hills thrusts its shoulders into the fringes of Edinburgh to remind us that the term Midland 'Valley' is something of a misnomer (Finlay, 1960). As in other parts of the Central Lowlands, such isolated hill masses divide the drift-covered plains into a number of basins; in this case the Pentlands act as a substantial barrier between East and West Lothian. The hill masses themselves are often structurally controlled, with the Moorfoots and the Pentlands both exhibiting fault-line scarps. Not all the topographic contrasts are related to faulting, however: a comparison between the relief map and the geological map will show that, while the lowlands generally coincide with rocks of Carboniferous age, the hills are carved from a variety of pre-Carboniferous rocks which appear to have resisted denudation more successfully than the Carboniferous sedimentaries.

Generally speaking the thin, acid soils of many Scottish hills are too deficient in phosphate to support anything but peat and heather moor. But, because of the basalts and basic tuffs which crop out, the northern end of the Pentlands possesses soils with a higher content of mineral salts than usual and is thus conducive to the growth of such grasses as *Agrostis* and *Festuca ovina*. The resulting sward is kept closely grazed by the Blackface sheep which wander across the treeless slopes; no woodland could survive such longstanding grazing pressure. Nevertheless, remains of birch and Scots pine in Boghall Glen suggest that forests once flourished on parts of the Pentlands, perhaps on the more acid soils of the Old Red Sandstone which forms their north-western and south-western flanks. It is recorded that juniper and heather also reached far down the slopes in earlier centuries, but burning and grazing have reduced such vegetation to a fraction of its former extent.

The structure of the Pentlands is that of a denuded anticline, in which the stripping of the former Carboniferous strata has revealed a complex mixture of Old Red Sandstone sedimentaries and lavas and a few highly folded Silurian rocks (Campbell, 1927). The latter form the core of the anticline and represent one of the few exposures of Lower Palaeozoic rocks within the Midland Valley proper (Fig. 12.8). Among the volcanic rocks, which attain a thickness of some 1800 metres at the northern end of the hills, no less than ten distinct groups of lava flows have been recognized. These range from the lower basalts and andesites of Warklaw Hill, up through the trachytes between Carnethy and Scald Law (579 m) summits, to the uppermost basalts and andesites, including the attractive porphyrite of Carnethy (Mykura, 1960). As it is traced northwards, the Upper Old Red Sandstone thins considerably before disappearing beneath the Basal Carboniferous Beds in the southern suburbs of Edinburgh. Here, in Craigmillar Quarry, the Old Red Sandstone has been widely exploited for its fine-quality freestone, which has contributed greatly to many of the buildings in the Edinburgh townscape. In addition, the same formation has served as a source of pure water supply for the city's brewing and paper-making industries.

Seen in profile, the Pentlands appear to be steeper along their eastern than on their western flanks. This is because on the eastern side the Pentland Fault has brought the relatively harder Old Red lavas directly against the more easily denuded Carboniferous rocks of the Midlothian coalfield without the intervention of the Old Red Sandstone. The fault-line scarp thus produced can be traced north-eastwards through Carlops to Straiton with the fault itself continuing beneath the city to the Forth at Portobello. At first glance the alignment of the Pentland Hills is seen to conform with the Caledonian trend lines (of Middle Old Red Sandstone age). Taken in association with the neighbouring syncline of the Midlothian coal basin, however, the direction of folding is seen to swing round into a more northerly alignment as it is traced across the Forth into Fife (see Fig. 12.8). Since the Carboniferous rocks themselves are also folded, one is dealing not with an episode of Caledonian folding but with one of Hercynian age which came later, in Carbo-Permian times. It has been shown how the structural framework of the Midland Valley is Caledonian (as demonstrated by its boundary faults), but within this framework many of the important folds and faults were created by a phase of Hercynian compression. During this ensuing

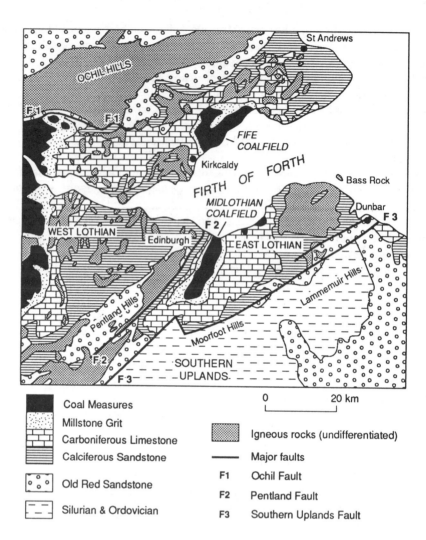

Figure 12.8 Geology around the Firth of Forth (based on material prepared by the British Geological Survey).

period of mountain-building the pressure was exerted from a southerly direction, and this has manifested itself in two sets of Hercynian structures: first, those with a 'normal' east–west trend, such as in the Ayrshire Coalfield, the Glasgow–Airdrie syncline, the Campsie Fault and the Ochil Fault; and second, those in which the underlying Caledonian structures have influenced the folding and faulting, causing them to take on a 'Caledonoid grain'. The best examples of the latter type are found in the Midlothian syncline and in the Pumpherston anticline of West Lothian, which affects the oil-shale workings (see p. 290).

East of the Pentland Hills the Lothian plains stretch uninterruptedly to the North Sea at Dunbar. Here is some of the finest arable land in Scotland, where crops of barley and wheat flourish on the thick glacial drifts – wheat preferring the heavier soils of the boulder clay (mainly derived from Carboniferous rocks), while barley is grown more successfully on the equally basic but lighter soils of the glacio-fluvial drifts. The large, regular, square fields with their scattered settlements and individual holdings create a landscape similar to that of Berwickshire, where the 'rationalized' field pattern has led to equally efficient farming. This, then, is a typical landscape of 'improvement', where the traditional Scottish custom of 'run-rig' was abolished early as the mosses were drained and the ancient oak woods cleared (Ogilvie, 1951). Only at Roslin Glen and in the park of Dalkeith House have sufficient oak woods survived to remind one that, prior to the eighteenth century, the view eastwards from the Pentlands would have been very different. Only at the foot of the Lammermuirs are there remnants of the old fields, with the twisting road patterns and the few ancient villages being located on the poorer, more acid soils of the upland fringe because, on the tops of the Lammermuirs the hill settlements have been progressively abandoned during the last century (Parry, 1976). It is no surprise to discover, therefore, that the surviving hillfoot villages – Gifford with its beechwoods, the sandstone and pantiled cottages of Garvald, the grass-fringed street of Stenton – are part of a Conservation Area. From these vantage points, the dark, isolated igneous hill masses of the Lothians dominate the view.

The southernmost of these hills, Traprain Law (221 m), rises abruptly above the valley of the Tyne, which follows a gorge overdeepened by glacial meltwaters across the hard rock-band of Carboniferous basalts, some of which have been quarried for use as a building stone at East Linton. The prominent cliffs and dome-like summit of the Law demonstrate very clearly the shape of the phonolitic igneous rock which was intruded into the Calciferous Sandstones in the form of a laccolith (MacGregor and Ennos, 1922). The sedimentary rocks, formerly up-arched by the intrusion, have now been eroded from the dome, leaving the fine-grained, well-jointed igneous rock clearly exposed. On the summit the remains of a hillfort indicate that there was an important defensive settlement here between AD 100 and 400. Traprain Law provides a good viewpoint for the other Lothian igneous hills: to the west are the Garleton Hills (180 m), formed largely from Carboniferous tuffs and trachytic lavas; immediately to the north is the wooded Pencraig Hill, also a laccolith but more subdued than Traprain Law, while away in the distance the prominent crags of North Berwick Law and the Bass Rock dominate the northern coastline. North Berwick Law (187 m) is a particularly precipitous crag, its red-mottled trachytic intrusion rising incongruously above the flat farmlands which occupy the Carboniferous sandstones of the coastal plain. Several of the nearby sea cliffs have been carved from associated volcanic rocks, including agglomerates occupying vents which have been drilled through the older rocks (Francis, 1962). The most interesting of the vents is that upon which the picturesque Tantallon Castle stands, for here can be seen not only the so-called 'bread-crust' type of volcanic bombs, bedded dark-green basaltic tuffs and a variety of pyroclastic rocks, but also a large mass of sandstone which appears to have been deposited in a hollow within the temporarily quiescent Carboniferous volcano. The famous Bass Rock, a few miles off shore, has a similar structure to that of North Berwick Law, its fortress-crowned cliffs having been carved from an intrusive plug of trachyte which, like North Berwick Law, formerly supplied a volcanic vent.

Although Traprain Law and North Berwick Law were intruded into the Carboniferous strata in somewhat different ways, their subsequent history in the Ice Age is strikingly similar, for both exhibit the landform known as a crag-and-tail. Nowhere else in Scotland are there such superb examples of this phenomenon as in the Lothians: in addition to the two mentioned above, crag-and-tail features may be seen at Dechmont Law (West Lothian), Blackford and Craiglockhart Hills (Edinburgh) and – classic examples – at Calton Hill and Castle Rock, right in the city centre. It is known that ice sheets, moving in an easterly direction down the Forth, helped create these singular landforms, with the igneous 'crag' being overridden by ice but helping to protect the leeward 'tail' from such intense erosion. Thus the western faces of these crags are usually precipitous, while their eastern slopes taper off more gently into the tail itself. There is a mistaken belief that the tail is composed of glacial drift, despite the correct observation made by Archibald Geikie more than a century ago that the tail is composed very largely of solid rock, often with only a veneer of drift. Thus, it is an erosional and not a depositional feature.

Glacial erosion has also helped smooth off the irregularities of the sedimentary rocks in the Lothians, so that the landscape of today, despite its covering of glacial drifts, is very largely an erosional one glacially moulded into tapering streamlined ridges. The 'fluted' drift landscape of East Lothian, made up of kames, drumlins and kame terraces, combines with the ice-moulded ridges and depressions to create a regular east-north-east alignment (Sissons, 1958). The effect of this alignment on the drainage pattern is very clear, especially in the case of the Tyne, but even more striking is the way in which many of the Lothian streams occupy valleys that were almost entirely excavated by glacial meltwaters.

In the Midlothian coalfield the relatively new collieries of Bilston Glen and Monktonhall have been designed to exploit the very deep reserves of the Lower Coals (Carboniferous Limestone Series) which occur at the base of the Midlothian Carboniferous syncline (McAdam, 1951). Earlier collieries mined only the easily accessible Upper Coals and the steeply dipping linear outcrops of the Lower Coals (the Edge Coals), where these occur on the fringes of the basin (see Fig. 12.8), but these had been worked out by the mid-twentieth century. The coastal fringes of the Forth have long been known for their salt manufacture, especially those around Prestonpans, which derived its name from the coastal salt pans. Sea water provided the major raw material, and although peat and timber were originally used in the evaporating process the abundant coal outcrops, both here and in Fife and West Lothian, became more important in the ultimate location of the Scottish salt industry in a region which lacks the brine deposits of the English Trias (Adams, 1965).

When compared with the mining and industrial landscapes around Tranent and the Esk Valley, the coastal marshes and sand dunes around Aberlady Bay present a picture of rural serenity. Here is the most important area for market gardening in Scotland, accounting for more than half the acreage of vegetables and for over 60 per cent of their production. The reason for the location of the market gardens is the combination of the sandy and gravelly soils of the raised beaches (which have lime-rich mixtures of marine shells) with a favourable climate and the proximity of the Edinburgh markets.

Generations of writers and artists have tried to recapture the qualities of Edinburgh, often referred to as the 'Athens of the North'. The profusion of igneous hill masses within the city boundary is the main reason for Edinburgh's distinctive character: the abrupt changes of level give splendid vistas and viewpoints at every turn (Scott-Moncrieff, 1947). Two other factors have also played a part in the creation of this urban masterpiece. First, Edinburgh is built almost entirely of the creamy local Craigleath Sandstone, which gives it an air of congruity rare in most British towns away from the Cotswold stone belt. Second, the city was fortunate in its eighteenth- and nineteenth-century architects and planners, who built with vision, grace and good sense. But it is to the ancient 'wynds' and 'pends' of the Old Town that the tourist will keep returning, where the names Grassmarket, Lawnmarket and Cowgate are redolent of the Middle Ages, and where the street canyons of the High Street are an early example of high-density urban housing (Malcolm, 1951). The Castle Hill and High Street axis continues eastwards to Holyrood House as the Royal Mile and is, perhaps, the best-known example of a crag-and-tail in geological literature. The basalt plug on which the Castle is built has been greatly oversteepened by ice sheets (Price and Knill, 1967) which were then deflected along the northern and southern faces. To the north the ice bulldozed the softer sedimentaries to form the Waverley depression, later to become a marshy, lake-filled hollow, and then to be drained and reclaimed for the Princes Street gardens and the railway tracks (Fig. 12.9).

Figure 12.9 Edinburgh. The Castle on its igneous crag stands in the centre of the view with the wooded Princes Street gardens and Waverley railway station occupying a former marshy ice-deepened valley. The sill of Salisbury Crags and the ancient volcano of Arthur's Seat rise beyond the city.

South of the Castle Rock the ice similarly excavated the depression now occupied by Cowgate and the Grassmarket (Sissons, 1971). Between these hollows stands the tail of the Royal Mile, 'whose ridgy back heaves to the sky' (Scott), inspiring the analogy of spine and ribs much used in descriptions of the Old Town street pattern. Near the Portcullis gate of the Castle the actual junction of the basalt plug of the crag with the grey Carboniferous marls of the tail may be seen (Tait, 1945), while the north-western cliffs of the crag exhibit glacial grooving and striae. But the crag-and-tail of Blackford Hill, some 3 kilometres to the south, is even more significant in this respect, for it was here in 1840 that the eminent Swiss geologist, Louis Agassiz, recognized the grooving in the overhanging andesite cliff as the work of a former ice sheet – the first such recognition in Scotland.

It is little wonder that Edinburgh has been the home of many notable geologists, considering the wealth of geological phenomena both in and around the city. The well-known landmark of the Salisbury Crags sill, for example, provided Hutton with irrefutable evidence to support his hypothesis of magmatic intrusion during the prolonged Neptunist–Plutonist arguments of the eighteenth century. Immediately to the east of this prominent escarpment the remnants of the long extinct Carboniferous volcano of Arthur's Seat (251 m) dominate the city (Black, 1966). The complex structure of the volcano includes no less than thirteen lava flows, extruded variously from five vents: the Lion's Head (forming the summit crag); the extensive Lion's Haunch (composite basalt and vent agglomerate); the smaller Crags Vent (agglomerate); and the basalt-filled vents of Pulpit Rock and Castle Rock. Remnants of the former ash/lava cone can be seen at Whinny Hill and Calton Hill, from which exposures it was possible to elucidate the geological history of the volcano.

Immediately to the west of Edinburgh lies a wide expanse of Lower Carboniferous Sandstone which includes the Oil-Shale Group (Parnell, 1984). This tract was for a short period the most important oil-producing area in the world, as witnessed by the many truncated cones of spent shales – the well-known red shale 'bings' (derived from *beinn*, meaning 'hill') of West Lothian – which dominate the skyline around the new town of Livingston. The thick brown shales found in association with the coal never offered as good a yield as the cannel coal but, in contrast with the limited coal reserves, the extent of the oil shales was sufficient to produce 25 million gallons (112 million litres) of crude oil per year in the late nineteenth century. Thus the towns of Mid Calder, West Calder, Broxburn and Pumpherston grew in size, while the Bathgate works also produced ammonium sulphate, paraffin and candles. During the twentieth century, however, imported liquid oil became cheaper to produce than shale oil, leading to a final closure of the West Lothian oil-shale mines in 1962. The nearby Grangemouth refinery, located there originally because of the proximity of the shale oil, has grown into a massive petrochemical complex on the banks of the Forth, now dependent on ocean-going tankers for its supplies (Chapman, 1974). The oil shales belong to the Calciferous Sandstone Series of the Lower Carboniferous and appear to have been deposited by a special type of alternating lagoonal and estuarine sedimentation in a restricted basin. Decaying plant and animal remains in the lagoons supplied the carbonaceous matter which ultimately impregnated the shallow-water mud-flats. Sun-cracks suggest that dessication was intense, but occasional marine bands indicate periodic incursions of the sea. A freshwater limestone, the Burdiehouse Limestone, is also present, a further indication of the rapidly changing environmental conditions of the time.

The sedimentary rocks have been invaded by numerous dolerite sills and dykes which, like the Bathgate lava hills, produce prominent ridges in the otherwise featureless drift-covered landscape. Because of the thick boulder clays, often moulded into drumlins, the soils are generally heavier and more poorly drained than in East Lothian. This has been aggravated not only by the ubiquitous marls and shales of the bedrock but also by the widespread hollows caused by underground mining subsidence. These factors, together with the higher rainfall, mean that there is a greater proportion of permanent grassland in the West Lothian landscape (some 50 per cent), and the spread of rushes remains a perennial problem for the dairy farmer. More than a century ago these pastures were won from the mossy wastes by new drainage techniques and by chemical improvement of the soil with lime produced by burning the Burdiehouse Limestone with local cannel coal in newly erected limekilns, now left standing forlornly among the hayfields. But the Calciferous Sandstones here descend westwards beneath the Carboniferous Limestone and the coal-bearing rocks of the Upper Carboniferous Central Coalfield. Thus the rural scene soon gives way to the industrial sprawl of the Carron Valley and the extensive carselands of the Middle Forth.

No other area in Scotland has a nodality to equal that of the narrow corridor of lowland which separates the volcanic heights of the Ochils from those of the Gargunnock Hills (Francis, 1960). The town of Stirling has been founded at the veritable crossroads of Scotland, where the Forth leaves the Old Red Sandstone of the Menteith basin to follow the narrow gap to the Firth. The Middle Forth is, therefore, something of a transition zone at the very centre of the Midland Valley (Timms, 1974); its coal-mines and blast furnaces echo the landscapes of the Lanarkshire coalfield, of which this is the northern extension; its agriculture continues the trend already noted in West Lothian where arable farming becomes increasingly subordinate to dairying as one moves towards the more humid west; and its architecture is already beginning to include the typical pantiles and Low Countries building style which dominates the Fife towns and villages farther east. Only the River Forth gives unity to this narrow zone which spans parts of the old counties of Stirlingshire, Clackmannanshire, Perthshire and Fife – a unity now recognized in the creation of the Central administrative region of Scotland.

The industrial district around Falkirk is notable as the cradle of the Industrial Revolution in Scotland and its landscape still bears the scars of this long-term exploitation of the local resources. It all started when the blast furnaces at Carron began to utilize the neighbouring 'splint' coals and clay band iron ores of the Coal Measures to produce the first Scottish pig-iron in 1759 (Warren, 1965). The scarcity of coking coal meant that the 'splint' coals were fed raw into the furnaces, replacing charcoal and the water power of the River Carron, and building up a local industry which was producing some 27 per cent of British pig-iron by 1850. Scottish iron-ore mining has now ceased, so the Scottish steel industry, which has moved south to Motherwell, is now dependent on Furness and Cleveland ores. But Falkirk has retained some important metal industries, including the manufacture of iron castings and aluminium sheeting. Coal-mining has also survived, especially in Clackmannanshire, where the scattered new collieries among the conifers of Devilla Forest now supply most of the needs of the gigantic thermal power stations of Kincardine and Longannet. Both of these are situated on the banks of the Forth because of their voracious demand for enormous quantities of cooling water.

Above Kincardine the Forth narrows considerably, and until the building of the Forth Road Bridge this was the lowest bridging-point on the river. It is in this section, upstream as far as the Lake of Menteith, that the carselands of the Forth may best be studied. Today the scene is one of pastoral serenity, with the river winding at its leisure through crops of hay and corn and the widespread permanent pastures which characterize the heavy soils of these claylands. It is difficult to realize, therefore, as one looks down on this riparian landscape from Stirling Castle or Wallace's Monument, that the formation of the Forth glacial deposits, the raised shorelines and their overlying peat mosses represents some of the most complex chapters in the Quaternary history of Scotland so far encountered.

The traditional view of Scottish raised beaches sees them as having three simple shorelines – the so-called 100-foot (30 metre), 50-foot (15 metre) and 25-foot (8 metre) beaches – with the two highest belonging to the late-glacial period and the lowest being of post-glacial age. Painstaking work by Sissons (1962) has demonstrated that such a viewpoint can no longer be upheld. In its place he and his colleagues have erected a complex picture of fluctuating sea levels, ice-front advances and retreats and alternating periods of glacio-fluvial, estuarine and marine sedimentation, the formation and ultimate dislocation of raised shorelines by periods of non-uniform uplift (Sissons, 1972), together with concluding episodes of post-glacial peat growth. The story is a long and complicated one and took place not only in the valley of the Forth but also in that of the neighbouring Tay (Sissons *et al.*, 1965).

As the Scottish ice sheets withdrew westwards from the North Sea coastlands, rising sea levels left the oldest late-glacial beaches in East Lothian and east Fife (Cullingford and Smith, 1966), and because of isostatic readjustment these beaches have the greatest tilt from west to east (see p. 254). To the west of Stirling, in the Carse of Stirling, these terraces disappear, to be replaced by a wide plain of flat carse clays and peat mosses some 100 square kilometres in extent. It is now known, however, that these innocuous meadowlands hide an even more complex sequence of sediments related to buried channels, and buried beaches and peats, discovered only from borehole data (Fig. 12.10) (Sissons, 1966).

The so-called High, Main and Low Buried Beaches of Fig. 12.10 were created partly from the glacio-fluvial outwash of a later ice advance (the Loch Lomond Readvance) which built the Menteith Moraine near Arnprior some 10 300 years ago. The Lake of Menteith is in fact impounded behind the kames of this morainic belt, occupying a gigantic kettle hole left after the melting of an enormous ice block. The intermittently falling sea level of these times was responsible for the formation of the three buried raised beaches between 9500 and 8800 years ago (Sissons and Brooks, 1971). It was upon these abandoned shorelines that forests of alder and birch began to grow, indicating the passage from late-glacial into post-glacial times. The remains of the trees became entombed in peat deposits (Sissons and Smith, 1965), the appearance of reeds in the upper layers of which suggests that there was a return to an estuarine environment when the forests were drowned by the major post-glacial marine transgression around 8500 years ago. This is the reason for the widespread blanket of stiff blue carse clays, which are simply uplifted fossil mudflats formed at the edge of the so-called

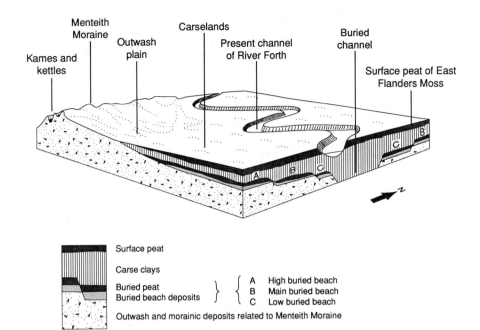

Kames and kettles

Menteith Moraine

Outwash plain

Carselands

Present channel of River Forth

Buried channel

Surface peat of East Flanders Moss

Surface peat

Carse clays

Buried peat
Buried beach deposits

A   High buried beach
B   Main buried beach
C   Low buried beach

Outwash and morainic deposits related to Menteith Moraine

Figure 12.10 The superficial deposits of the Carse of Stirling (after J. B. Sissons).

Flandrian Sea in much the same way as the present tidal flats have formed at the edge of the modern shorelines. The surface of this main post-glacial raised shoreline can be seen to descend downstream across the Carse of Stirling from a height of 15 metres at West Flanders Moss to 13 metres at Stirling – and this is the so-called '25-foot' post-glacial beach! When it is traced down the Firth (at Leith it is about 9 metres), its character changes from carse clays at Aberlady Bay to sands and shingles at Dunbar. As in the case of the older beaches, the Main Post-glacial Shoreline is associated with other beaches at slightly lower elevations. As the sea level gradually descended towards its present position in a series of intermittent halts, so the peat bogs continued to grow in thickness on the carselands of the Middle Forth, and these remained undrained until the agricultural improvements of the late eighteenth century. Apart from peat-cutting for fuel by the inhabitants of the peripheral villages, the mosses of Flanders and Blairdrummond remained virtually untouched until 1767, with ploughland being restricted to the Old Red Sandstone outcrops on the margins of the Vale of Menteith. Extensive draining, ploughing and liming of the peatlands have, however, since led to the reclamation of Blairdrummond Moss, which today produces high-quality crops, although Flanders Moss survives as a reminder of the former landscapes of these parts.

Stirling Castle, high on a dolerite crag, symbolizes the military significance of the Stirling gap, while across the silvery meanders of the Forth the conspicuous Wallace Monument, at the foot of the Ochils, rises from another eminence of intrusive dolerite (Fig. 12.11). Stretching for more than 40 kilometres from south-west to north-east, the Ochil Hills rise to considerable elevations (for instance, Ben Cleuch reaches 720 metres), their plateau-like crests seamed with deeply cut valleys, including the remarkable glacial trough of Glen Eagles (Soons, 1958). From any southerly viewpoint their most striking feature is the conspicuous

Figure 12.11 The Ochil Hills and the Forth Valley as Stirling. The Ochil Fault separates the resistant Ochil lavas, of Old Red Sandstone age (left), from the Carboniferous sedimentary rocks of the Forth Valley (right). Note the Wallace Monument standing on a dolerite crag in the centre of the view.

scarp which runs for some 32 kilometres from Blairlogie eastwards to beyond Dollar. This straight mountain front, illustrated in Fig. 12.11, rises steeply from the Clackmannan plain, the abrupt change of slope coinciding with the line of the Ochil Fault, which extends for nearly 90 kilometres from the Clyde to central Fife and exhibits a southerly downthrow of some 3000 metres. Such a displacement has brought resistant Lower Old Red Sandstone andesitic lavas into juxtaposition with Carboniferous sediments. The latter now form the lowland of the Clackmannan coal basin, while the lavas build the 500 metre fault-line scarp of the Ochils. But, as if to demonstrate that there are exceptions to the broad association of uplands with the more resistant rocks, the relatively low plain of Kinross, to the west of Loch Leven, has been levelled across identical andesitic lavas. Furthermore, the Ochil Fault is here found at the Cleish Hills and is therefore not responsible for the continuation of the southern scarp-face of the Ochils to the east of Dollar. It has been suggested that many of the river valleys of the Ochils have been carved along lines of structural weakness, possibly related to a Hercynian fault mosaic which followed earlier trends of Caledonian (north-east to south-west) and even older (north-west to south-east) structures (Read, 1927). But some of the streams appear not to have been influenced either by structure or by glaciation (of these, the east-flowing headwaters of the Devon are the most important). To explain this and similar anomalies the process of superimposition from a former cover of Carboniferous sedimentary rocks has been invoked.

In the Fife peninsula the predominantly west-south-west to east-north-east grain of the Carboniferous, the Old Red Sandstone and the volcanic and intrusive rocks has produced a relatively simple pattern of alternating upland and lowland zones (MacGregor, 1973) allowing the following tracts to be recognized (see Figure 12.8): first, in the south, the Carboniferous coastlands along the Forth, including the Fife coalfield; second, the line of prominent igneous hills which forms the boundary between Fife and Kinross; third, the Old Red Sandstone corridor known as the Howe of Fife, drained by the river Eden; fourth, the low Carboniferous Sandstone plateau of the East Neuk, with its fringe of picturesque fishing villages; and finally, the northern ridge of volcanic hills which cuts off the major part of Fife from the Firth of Tay (Balsillie, 1927).

The Fife scenery, therefore, exhibits a remarkable diversity: its rich, rolling farmlands being interspersed with derelict coalfield clutter, its wooded parks of the great estates, picturesque lochs and heathery hills, all being encircled by coastal dunes and rocky cliffs, whose pretty fishing villages are reminiscent of those in Cornwall. Because its soils are fertile clays and loams, developed mainly from sandstones and limestones, and because the climate of the coastal plateaux is as favourable as that of the neighbouring Lothians, Fife has the highest proportion of arable land of all the Scottish counties. Since much of this is devoted to wheat, especially in the coastlands, and since the igneous hills of the interior have remained as patches of moorland, it is easy to understand the traditional description of Fife as a 'beggar's mantle fringed with gold'. In earlier centuries such a description would have been even more appropriate than today, for the centrally located Howe of Fife was once a badly drained basin of forest and marshland. Recent reclamation, however, has made its potentially fertile soils some of the most productive in Scotland. Much of the charm of Fife is to be found in its towns and villages, where the influence of Dutch and Flemish architecture is manifest in the curved gables and high-pitched roofs. Culross, for example, rising in tiers above the banks of the Forth, is noted for the rosy pantiles of its whitewashed houses, which bring a pleasant relief from the more usual slates. Dunfermline, by contrast, is a city of grey stone, with its massive Norman abbey echoing the dignity of Durham Cathedral. The same stream which initially gave security eventually supplied water power for milling, so that modern Dunfermline is dominated by its linen mills and silk factories. Kirkaldy, too, is an industrial town, but its growth has depended on linoleum as well as linen (Turner, 1966). Its initial development was restricted by the narrow raised beaches, so its nick-name 'the Lang Toon' was more understandable in the past than it is now that its suburbs have stretched away from the coastal margin. The contrasting character of the Kirkcaldy collieries reflects the changing history of the Fife coalfield (McNeill, 1973). To the east of the town, the older Frances Colliery only touched the fringes of the coal reserves, having retained methods traditional since the seventeenth century. To the west, however, the massive Seafield Colliery, using modern technology, was able to exploit the considerable reserves which exist beneath the Firth of Forth. Inland, where coal-mining has ceased, the bings can be seen dotting a countryside which has been badly scarred by decades of coal-mining and surface subsidence, especially in the Cowdenbeath–Lochgelly area (Goodwin, 1959).

Cutting through the Carboniferous sedimentary rocks are numerous igneous intrusions, including many basic sills. These fine-grained, olivine-rich rocks are responsible for the majority of the smaller ridges of southern Fife; they also create the well-known islands of Incholm and the Isle of May at opposite ends of the Firth. The highest hills of Fife have been carved from thick sheets of quartz-dolerite, locally pierced by volcanic necks and agglomerate-filled volcanic vents. In the west are the largely forested Cleish Hills (379 m), while Benarty Hill (345 m) stands isolated in the centre. But it is the Lomond Hills, farther east, which are the most prominent, with their volcanic necks rising dramatically above the flat farmlands of the Howe of Fife: West Lomond reaches 522 metres, and East Lomond 425 metres.

Between the steep northern slopes of the Lomond Hills and the volcanic uplands of northern Fife the grits and conglomerates of Upper Old Red Sandstone age have been picked out by denudation to form a narrow strath known as the Howe of Fife, which continues westwards as the Loch Leven basin. Considering its large size, it is remarkable that Loch Leven does not occupy a glacially eroded rock basin, but investigation has shown that, like the Lake of Menteith, it rests in a hollow within the glacio-fluvial deposits. By comparison with the widespread boulder clay of southern Fife, this Old Red Sandstone vale is thickly infilled with glacial outwash – the corridor must have acted as a major outlet for glacial meltwaters during the waning of the ice sheets. Like the Loch Leven basin, the Howe of Fife once boasted a loch at its centre, but this was finally drained in 1745. Today the basin is partly under arable farming (the light, sandy soils favouring sugar-beet) and partly under forests which have flourished here for centuries, for this was an ancient royal forest, the ruined palace of Falkland testifying to its earlier importance. The former forests and marshes at the centre of the Howe have meant that the village and town settlements are restricted to the perimeter, generally on encircling bluffs of boulder clay. Of these settlements, Auchtermuchty is by far the most interesting, for it retained its thatched roofs much longer than most other Scottish towns.

The coastal plateaux of the East Neuk are composed largely of Calciferous Sandstone, although Carboniferous Limestone and Millstone Grit occur along the western margins. But the sedimentary rocks are thickly mantled with glacial drift so that the only occurrences of solid rock which can be seen, apart from the coastal cliffs and platforms, are the conical hills of the Laws. Like their Lothian counterparts, such eminences as Largo Law (290 m), Kellie Law (182 m) and the oddly named Bungs of Cassingray (211 m) are all carved from igneous rocks, generally volcanic necks and vent agglomerates. These basic volcanics and the Lower Carboniferous rocks through which they have been injected have combined to produce fertile loamy soils, with a high proportion of phosphate of lime owing to the presence of the mineral apatite, derived from the underlying igneous rocks. Thus, all but the highest craggy hills have been farmed, making the East Neuk one of the most prolific areas of mixed farming in Scotland. Cattle and sheep are fattened on the rich grasslands of the interior, where beech- and ash-fringed lanes lead to attractive stone-built farmsteads. The coastal margin is even more attractive, for here we can find a collection of fishing villages which are as picturesque as anything in Britain. Such places as Crail, Anstruther, Pittenweem, St Monance and Elie have retained much of their old-world charm, with their tiny harbours and stone quays crouching below steep, cobbled streets, crow-stepped gables and a profusion of chimneys on pantiled roofs. In this area building-stone was plentiful, so brick was rarely used. Woodlands are uncommon in this well-farmed landscape, generally surviving only in the narrow rocky ravines or 'dens', where the streams have cut down through the ubiquitous drifts. An important exception to the coastal treelessness of east Fife is the extensive Tentsmuir Forest on the dunes to the north of St Andrews Bay, where the land is of no use for farming. The same conditions might have existed on the sandy peninsula of Out Head which juts north from St Andrews itself, but here the dunes have been developed to make the most famous golf course in the world, that of St Andrews, where an ancient castle, university and cathedral, are grouped round a stone-built harbour.

Bibliography

Adams, I. H. (1965) The salt industry of the Forth Basin. *Scot. Geog. Mag.*, **81**, 153–62.

Balsillie, D. (1927) The igneous geology of eastern Fife. *Proc. Geol. Assoc.*, **38**, 463–9.

Balsillie, D. (1932) The Ballantrae Igneous Complex. *Geol. Mag.*, **69**, 107–31.

Bassett, D. A. (1958) *Geological Excursion Guide to the Glasgow District*. Geol. Soc. Glasgow. 104 pp.

Black, G. P. (1966) *Arthur's Seat: A History of Edinburgh's Volcano*. Oliver & Boyd. 226 pp.

Bluck, B. J. (ed.) (1973) *Excursion Guide to the Geology of the Glasgow District*. Geol. Soc. Glasgow.

Browne, M. E. and McMillan, A. A. (1984) Shoreline inheritance and coastal history in the Firth of Clyde. *Scot. J. Geol.*, **20**, 119–20.

Campbell, R. (1927) The geology of the Pentland Hills. *Proc. Geol. Assoc.*, **38**, 407–14.

Cameron, I. B. and Stephenson, D. (eds) (1985) *The Midland Valley of Scotland* (3rd edn). Br. Reg. Geol. HMSO. 172 pp.

Chapman, K. (1974) The structure and development of the oil-based complex at Grangemouth. *Scot. Geog. Mag.*, **90**, 98–109.

Cullingford, R. A. and Smith, D. E. (1966) Late-glacial shorelines in eastern Fife. *Trans. Inst. Br. Geog.*, **34**, 31–51.

Finlay, I. (1960) *The Lothians*. Collins. 178 pp.

Francis, E. H. (1960) The Ochils from Stirling, in G. H. Mitchell, E. K. Walton and D. Grant (eds), *Edinburgh Geology: An Excursion Guide*. Edinb. Geol. Soc. 198–205.

Francis, E. H. (1962) Volcanic neck emplacement and subsidence structures at Dunbar, south-east Scotland. *Trans. R. Soc. Edinb.*, **65**, 41–58.

Francis, E. H. (1968) Review of Carbo-Permian volcanicity in Scotland. *Geol. Rundschau*, **57**, 219–46.

Francis, E. H. (1965) Carboniferous, in G. Y. Craig (ed.), *Geology of Scotland*. (1st edn). Oliver & Boyd. 309–57.

Friend, P. F., Harland, W. B. and Hudson, J. D. (1963) The Old Red Sandstone and the Higland Boundary in Arran, Scotland. *Trans. Edinb. Geol. Soc.*, **19**, 363–425.

Gemmell, A. M. D. (1973) The deglaciation of Arran, *Trans. Inst. Br. Geog.*, **59**, 25–39.

George, T. N. (1958) The geology and geomorphology of the Glasgow district, in R. Miller and J. Tivy (eds), *The Glasgow Region*. Glasgow University Press. 17–61.

George, T. N. (1960) The stratigraphical evolution of the Midland Valley. *Trans. Geol. Soc. Glasgow*, **24**, 32–107.

Goodwin, R. (1959) Some physical and social factors in the evolution of a mining landscape. *Scot. Geog. Mag.*, **75**, 3–17.

Gregory, J. W. (1915) The Permian and Triassic rocks of Arran. *Trans. Geol. Soc. Glasgow*, **15**, 747–87.

Harker, A. (1918) Some aspects of igneous activity in Britain. *Quart. J. Geol. Soc.*, **73**, lxvii–xcvi.

Kennedy, W. Q. (1958) The tectonic evolution of the Midland Valley of Scotland. *Trans. Geol. Soc. Glasgow*, **23**, 106–33.

King, B. C. (1955) The Ard Bheinn area of the Central Igneous Complex of Arran. *Quart. J. Geol. Soc.*, **110**, 323–54.

Lea, K. J. (1980) Greater Glasgow. *Scot. Geog. Mag.*, **96**, 4–17.

Lindsay, M. (1956) *The Lowlands of Scotland*. Hale. 308 pp.

Linton, D. L. (1934) On the former connection between the Clyde and Tweed. *Scot. Geog. Mag.*, **50**, 82.

MacGregor, A. G. (1948) Problems of Carbo-Permian volcanicity in Scotland. *Quart. J. Geol. Soc.*, **104**, 133–53.

MacGregor, A. G. and Ennos, F. R. (1922) The Traprain Law Phonolite. *Geog. Mag.*, **59**, 514–23.

MacGregor, A. R. (1973) *Fife and Angus Geology: An Excursion Guide*. Scottish Academic Press. 281 pp.

MacGregor, M. (1930) Scottish Carboniferous stratigraphy: an introduction to the study of the Carboniferous rocks of Scotland. *Trans. Geol. Soc. Glasgow*, **18**, 442–558.

MacGregor, M. (1954) The Coalfields of Scotland, in A. E. Trueman (ed.), *The Coalfields of Great Britain*. Arnold. 325–81.

MacGregor, M., Herriot, A. and King, B. C. (1972) *Excursion Guide to the Geology of Arran*. Geol. Soc. Glasgow. 199 pp.

Malcolm, C. A. (1951) The Growth of Edinburgh c.1128–1800, in A. G. Ogilvie (ed.), *Scientific Survey of South-east Scotland*. Edinburgh University Press. 65–72.

McAdam, R. (1951) Mining, in A. G. Ogilvie (ed.), *Scientific Survey of South-East Scotland*. Edinburgh University Press. 113–19.

McLellan, A. G. (1969) The last glaciation and deglaciation of Lanarkshire. *Scot. J. Geol.*, **5**, 248–68.

McLellan, R. (1970) *The Isle of Arran*. David and Charles. 269 pp.

McNeill, J. (1973) The Fife coal industry. *Scot. Geog. Mag.*, **89**, 81–94.

Miller, R. (1970) The new face of Glasgow. *Scot. Geog. Mag.*, **86**, 5–15.

Miller, R. and Tivy, J. (eds) (1958) *The Glasgow Region*. Glasgow University Press. 325 pp.

Millman, R. N. (1975) *The Making of the Scottish Landscape*. Batsford. 264 pp.

Muir, R. O. (1963) Petrology and provenance of the Millstone Grit of Central Scotland. *Trans. Edinb. Geol. Soc.*, **19**, 439–85.

Munro, I. S. (1973) *The Island of Bute*. David and Charles.

Mykura, W. (1960) The Pentland Hills, in G. H. Mitchell, E. K. Walton and D. Grant (eds), *Edinburgh Geology: An Excursion Guide*. Edinb. Geol. Soc. 175–87.

Ogilvie, A. G. (ed.) (1951) *Scientific Survey of South-East Scotland*. Edinburgh University Press.

Parnell, J. (1984) Hydrocarbon minerals in the Midland Valley of Scotland with particular reference to the Oil Shale Group. *Proc. Geol. Assoc.*, **95**, 275–85.

Parry, M. L. (1976) The abandonment of upland settlement in southern Scotland. *Scot. Geog. Mag.*, **92**, 50–60.

Patterson, E. M. (1949) The Old Red Sandstone rocks of the West Kilbride–Largs district. Ayrshire. *Trans. Geol. Soc. Glasgow*, **21**, 207.

Price, D. G. and Knill, J. L. (1967) The engineering geology of Edinburgh Castle Rock. *Geotechnique*, **17**, 411–32.

Read, H. H. (1927) The western Ochil Hills. *Proc. Geol. Assoc.*, **38**, 492–4.

Scott-Moncrieff, G. (1947) *Edinburgh*. Batsford. 112 pp.

Sissons, J. B. (1958) The deglaciation of part of East Lothian. *Trans. Inst. Br. Geog.*, **25**, 59–77.

Sissons, J. B. (1962) A re-interpretation of the literature on late-glacial shorelines in Scotland, with particular reference to the Forth area. *Trans. Edinb. Geol. Soc.*, **19**, 83–99.

Sissons, J. B. (1966) Relative sea-level changes between 10 300 and 8300 BP in part of the Carse of Stirling. *Trans. Inst. Br. Geog.*, **39**, 19–29.

Sissons, J. B. (1971) The geomorphology of central Edinburgh. *Scot. Geog. Mag.*, **87**, 185–96.

Sissons, J. B. (1972) Dislocation and non-uniform uplift of raised shorelines in the western part of the Forth Valley. *Trans. Inst. Br. Geog.*, **55**, 145–59.

Sissons, J.B. and Brooks, C.L. (1971) Dating of early postglacial land and sea-level changes in the western Forth Valley. *Nature Physical Science*, 234(50), 124–7.

Sissons, J.B., Cullingford, R.A. and Smith, D.E. (1965) Some Pre-Carse valleys in the Forth and Tay Basins. *Scot. Geog. Mag.*, 81, 115–24.

Sissons, J.B. and Smith, D.E. (1965) Peat bogs in a post-glacial sea and a buried raised beach in the western part of the Carse of Stirling. *Scot. J. Geol.*, 1, 247–55.

Soons, J.M. (1958) Landscape evolution in the Ochil Hills. *Scot. Geog. Mag.*, 74, 86–97.

Stewart, F.H. (1965) Tertiary igneous activity, in G.Y. Craig (ed.), *Geology of Scotland*. (1st edn). Oliver & Boyd. 417–65.

Storrie, M.C. (1967a) Landholding and population in Arran from the late eighteenth century. *Scottish Studies*, 11.

Storrie, M.C. (1967b) Balliekine, Arran: Survivor of two revolutions. *Folk Life*, 5.

Sutherland, D. (1926) The vegetation of the Cumbrae Islands and South Bute. *Scot. Geog. Mag.*, 42, 272–86 and 321–28.

Tait, D. (1945) Geological notes on (a) the Nor'Loch and (b) the Fore Well in Edinburgh Castle. *Trans. Edinb. Geol. Soc.*, 14, 28–33.

Temple, A.K. (1956) The Leadhills–Wanlockhead Lead and Zinc deposits. *Trans. R. Soc. Edinb.*, 63, 85–113.

Timms, D.W.G. (ed) (1974) *The Stirling Region*. Stirling University Press. 283 pp.

Tomkieff, S.I. (1961) *Isle of Arran*. Guide no. 32. Geol. Assoc. 35 pp.

Turner, W.H.K. (1966) The concentration of the jute and heavy linen manufacturing industry in east central Scotland. *Scot. Geog. Mag.*, 82, 29–45.

Tyrell, G.W. (1926) The igneous rocks of the Cumbrae Islands, Firth of Clyde. *Trans. Geol. Soc. Glasgow.*, 16, 244–56.

Walker, G.P.L. (1975) A new concept of the evolution of the British Tertiary intrusive centres. *J. Geol. Soc. Lond.*, 131, 121–41.

Warren, K. (1965) Locational problems of the Scottish iron and steel industry since 1760. *Scot. Geog. Mag.*, 81, 18–37.

Whyte, F. and Macdonald, J.G. (1974) Lower Carboniferous vulcanicity in the northern part of the Clyde Plateau. *Scot. J. Geol.*, 10, 187–98.

Williams, A. (1959) A structural history of the Girvan district, south west Ayrshire. *Trans. R. Soc. Edinb.*, 63, 62–7.

Tayside, Strathmore and the north-eastern coastlands

13

To travel through Strathmore in springtime is a revelation, for the rich red soils and the vernal green of this sandstone vale create a picture more reminiscent of Herefordshire than of a Highland border county. Burns wrote of 'the fine, fruitful, hilly, woody country round Perth' and of 'the rich harvests and fine hedgerows of the Carse of Gowrie'.

The Lower Tay region is relatively simple to define in terms of its physiography, being bounded on most sides by major physical features. In the north the prominent scarp of the Highland Front parallels the Highland Boundary Fault; in the east the coastline of the North Sea is a no less distinctive boundary; while to the south the bulky line of the Ochils divides Tay from Forth. Only in the west is the boundary less certain, for south of Strathearn the watershed between the Allan Water and the Earn is low and ill defined. In the case of its geology, broadly speaking, as one moves away from the central coal basins the Midland Valley rocks get progressively older as they are traced towards the bounding faults. Thus, in the case of the Lower Tay, the lowland which stretches north-eastwards from Dunblane to the North Sea at Montrose is devoid of Carboniferous rocks and corresponds very largely with the Strathmore syncline. This asymmetric downfold, some 4500 metres in depth, affects a great thickness of Lower Old Red Sandstone which was folded and faulted along a north-easterly axis in mid-Devonian times (Fig. 13.1). The north-western limb of the syncline is almost vertical, while between the downfold and the Highland Boundary Fault a steep anticline brings a narrow strip of Lower Palaeozoic rocks up to the surface in Angus and Kincardineshire. Such mid-Devonian earth movements also resulted in the metamorphic rocks of the Highland massif being driven south-eastwards

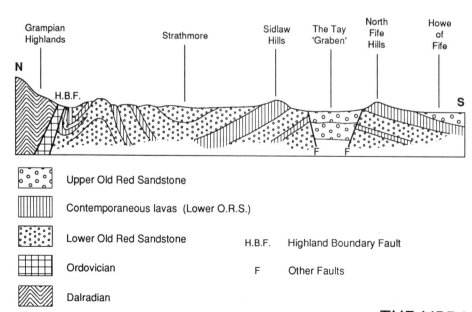

Upper Old Red Sandstone

Contemporaneous lavas (Lower O.R.S.)

Lower Old Red Sandstone   H.B.F.   Highland Boundary Fault

Ordovician   F   Other Faults

Dalradian

Figure 13.1 Generalized geological section of Strathmore and the Firth of Tay.

THE LIBRARY
BISHOP BURTON COLLEGE
BEVERLEY HU17 8QG
TEL: 0964 550481 Ex: 227

towards the downfaulted Old Red Sandstone of the Midland Valley. Thus the Highland Boundary Fault can be regarded for much of its length as a steeply inclined reversed or thrust fault (Fig. 13.1), although the fault appears to be normal near the Firth of Clyde.

There seems little doubt that the Highland Boundary Fault was not initiated by the mid-Devonian earth movements, for it seems to have been in existence earlier in Palaeozoic times when the Caledonian mountain-building episodes first created the Grampian massif in central Scotland. From these early highlands powerful rivers must have flowed southwards, carrying detritus into the lower basins of the incipient Midland Valley. As they crossed the forerunner of the modern Highland Line their flow would have been checked by the sudden easing of the gradient. Thus, enormous fans and deltas of coarse material from the Highland metamorphics mark the geological boundary, and today these form the conglomerates and coarse grits of the Lower Old Red Sandstone. The finer sediments of sand and mud were light enough to be carried farther into the basin, so that the conglomerates give way southwards to the ubiquitous thick brown sandstones which floor the Strathmore lowland. Because these thick sandstones contain layers of thin calcareous cornstones and lacustrine marls, there must have been periodic episodes of dessication during their formation (Waterston, 1965).

The Upper Old Red Sandstone is less widespread than the Lower and occurs only as a limited outcrop around the Firth of Tay, where it lies on the Lower with a marked unconformity, the Middle Old Red being unrepresented in the Midland Valley. It can also be distinguished from the Lower by virtue of its brighter redness and its greater irregularity of bedding. The latter can be explained by the more rapid change of palaeoenvironments following the mid-Devonian earth movements, which must have had an important influence on the patterns of deposition. Thus, coarse conglomerates merge into purple, green and mottled marls and chemically precipitated cornstones, while the wind-polished pebbles, sun-cracks and wind-rounded sand-grains indicate a much more arid climate than hitherto existed. Another distinction between the Lower and Upper Old Red series is the absence of volcanic or intrusive rocks in the younger sandstones. It will be shown that the Lower Old Red Sandstones are frequently interbedded with thick lava flows which have helped form both the Ochils and the Sidlaw Hills because of their general resistance to denudation. They are mainly basaltic lavas in which the formerly gas-filled cavities subsequently became lined with secondary minerals such as calcite and quartz. Erosion has now carried many of the chalcedonic stones into the local rivers, where they are treasured as 'Scotch pebbles', famed for their distinctive concentric agate banding.

The Lower Tay region can be divided into three distinctive districts, each of which is delimited very largely on geological grounds: first, the western lowlands of Strathearn; second, the Firth of Tay, confined in its rift valley between the Sidlaws and the North Fife Hills (see Fig. 13.1); and finally, the synclinal, sandstone lowland of Strathmore which opens out on to the eastern coastlands.

Strathearn and Perth

One of the traditional routes from the heavily populated Scottish heartland to the Highlands lay north-eastwards via Stirling Bridge and past Dunblane Cathedral into the prosperous farmlands of Strathallan, which skirt the north-western flanks of the Ochils. Here is a landscape of regular field patterns, neatly manicured hedgerows, shelter-belts and dark clumps of conifers, all dotted with neat farms and rolling woodlands and backed by the often snow-clad peaks of the Highlands. It is a countryside of extensive estates, country houses and baronial castles. Near to Crieff, for example, the formal gardens of Drummond Castle are a miniature Versailles, approached through verdant avenues of beech and lime. The hummocky drift around Auchterarder, on which Gleneagles golf course has been sited, can be traced eastwards into the widespread Strathearn glacio-fluvial outwash plain, both having been formed during the decay of the main Devensian ice sheet (Browne, 1980). The contrast in form between the hard rock landforms of the volcanic Ochils and the relatively soft rock features of the Strathallan–Strathearn lowland is noteworthy (Linton, 1962). An ice sheet moving generally eastwards towards the Firth of Tay not only moulded and truncated the spurs of the Ochil northern slopes to an elevation of some 274 metres, but also succeeded in pushing a lobe of ice forcibly into the valley of Glen Eagles. Ice erosion was sufficiently powerful to lower the pre-glacial watershed by 230 metres near St Mungo's so that today the summit col of the Glen Eagles through-valley is 1 kilometre farther south and at a considerably lower elevation than before. Such breaching of a pre-glacial watershed by ice is known as *glacial diffluence* (Linton, 1951a). The spectacular steep-sided form of Glen Eagles is largely a result of the resistance shown by the Ochil igneous rocks; by comparison the sandstones of Strathallan and Strathearn were more easily eroded.

The Devensian ice sheet, which sent a lobe through the Forth gap at Stirling, is the same one that swung round the western end of the Ochils before entering the basin of the Tay via Strathearn. A well-known drift section in the river bank of the Almond, 3 kilometres north-west of Perth, together with other evidence, has suggested to some authors (Simpson, 1933; Sissons, 1963–4) that this was created by a major ice readvance (once termed the Perth Readvance), although it is now believed that the kame-and-kettle zone near Perth may represent only a stillstand in the general retreat from the maximum extent of the last major glaciation in Scotland (Patterson, 1974).

Where the Tay breaks through the line of the hard volcanics of the Sidlaws, the narrow gap (once thought to be due to superimposed drainage) was selected, in much the same way as at Stirling, for the location of a major town. Perth's medieval street-plan and original street names remain as a testimony to the town's antiquity and its commercial importance when it commanded the lowest bridging-point of the Tay. The river water was not only used for milling: its softness (due to the dearth of calcareous minerals in its catchment) has made Perth the site of important bleaching, dyeing and whisky-distilling industries. The location of the nearby linen mills on the Tay, Ericht and Almond was determined by the narrow zone of rapids and cataracts where the rivers, having already crossed the Highland Line, had commenced downcutting into the lowland sandstones of Strathmore (Turner, 1957; 1958). The cataracts themselves, such as that at the Linn of Campsie, near Stanley, occur where the Tay is busily engaged in lowering one of the tough igneous dykes which slice through the Old Red Sandstone hereabouts.

Tayside

The structural history of this tract is noteworthy because it is the best example of a true rift valley in Scotland, if not in the whole of Britain. It has already been seen how the massive lava flows and associated volcanics of Old Red Sandstone age helped to build the Ochil Hills which lie to the south of the Firth of Tay. Rocks of the same type also contribute to the stature of the Sidlaw Hills to the north of the estuary. The tilt of the Ochil lavas is to the south-east and that of the Sidlaw lavas to the north-west, which demonstrates that they are in fact the opposing limbs of an anticline, known as the Tay Anticline (see Fig. 13.1). One could conclude that the lavas of the intervening crest of the arch have been removed by denudation, but the steep, river-facing slopes of the Ochils and the equally steep Braes of the Carse across the valley have been shown to be parallel fault-line scarps at the borders of a rift valley or 'graben'. Thus, the missing volcanics from the highest point of the upfold have not been destroyed but merely downfaulted, being now buried by a layer of Upper Old Red Sandstone, to say nothing of the Pleistocene and post-glacial infill (see Fig. 13.1).

Much of the superficial material within the Firth of Tay is of post-glacial age, forming the well-known Carse of Gowrie, a flat stretch of marine clay, lying between the Sidlaws and the reed-fringed estuary, and one of the richest and most fertile tracts in Scotland. Near the river banks themselves, in both the Tay and the Lower Earn valleys, the soils get heavier and cattle pastures are therefore more prevalent. But it is for its wheat, barley, sugar-beet, peas, beans and soft fruits that the Carse is best known, so it is little wonder that nearby Dundee has an important preserving and canning industry. There has been a tendency to compare the carselands of the Tay and Forth with the English Fenlands because of their similar land-use patterns. The analogy is inappropriate, however, for, as Sissons (1966) has pointed out, the Fenlands are at sea level while these Scottish carselands have been raised a long way above sea level by post-glacial isostatic warping. Thus, they are rarely flooded by their rivers, even during the highest floods, and now stand high and dry above the incised river channels. Nevertheless, the Carse has not always been dry, for there is evidence to show that until the draining and agricultural improvements of the eighteenth century the land surface was sprinkled with pools and marshes because of the impeded drainage of the uplifted marine clays of this post-glacial raised beach. The numerous place names with the prefix 'Inch' (island), such as Inchmartin and Inchmichael, show where there were dry sites on the Carse prior to the drainage schemes. Curiously, unlike the carse clays of the Forth which they resemble in every other way, the clays of the Carse of Gowrie seem never to have carried a major cover of peat on their surface, so there is no history of peat-cutting around the Firth of Tay. Above the main post-glacial raised beach of the Earn and Tay (Morrison *et al.*, 1981), which rises in elevation as it is traced upstream from 8.5 metres at Dundee to 11 metres near Bridge of Earn, several conspicuous river terraces can be seen. Foremost of these is the one on which Newburgh is located and which declines in elevation eastwards until it disappears beneath the post-glacial carse clay as a buried raised beach. Like their counterparts in the Forth, these represent late-glacial features created from the outwash of a decaying ice sheet, their staircase of terraces having been carved by the frequently rejuvenated river during the pulsatory uplift of the land as the weight of the ice cap was gradually reduced.

The old city of Dundee (Jones, 1968) was located on a bench of dolerite which provided a dry platform above the marshes of the post-glacial raised beach and the valley of the Scouring Burn. This and the neighbouring Dens Burn now flow underground in culverts, but formerly provided the important advantages of power and bleaching ability in the early years of Dundee's jute and textile industry (Lenman and Gauldie, 1968; Turner, 1966). Of similar importance was the occurrence of local wells, aligned along the junction of the Old Red Sandstone and the intrusive dolerite.

Some 8 kilometres to the north of the city the Sidlaws rise abruptly above the low plateaux of Old Red Sandstone, which hereabouts are interspersed with prominent basic igneous hills carved from a variety of petrographic types (Scarth, 1968). The Sidlaw Hills themselves reach only modest heights (455 m) in comparison with the Ochils, due partly to the fact that the Ochil–Sidlaw lava group becomes less thick as it is traced north-eastwards away from the major volcanic centre near Stirling. Thus, a thickness of nearly 2000 metres in the western Ochils declines to 900 metres in the western Sidlaws (Harry, 1956) and a mere 200 metres on the Angus coast. Nevertheless, the sudden thickening of the basaltic lavas near Montrose suggests that a separate volcanic centre must have functioned here in Lower Old Red times, although no vents have been found (Harry, 1958). Because of their base-rich rocks the soils of the Sidlaws, like those of the Ochils, contain important nutrients such as calcium, phosphorus and potassium, so that montane grasslands are more widespread than on the more acid soils of the granitic Highlands farther north. But heather moor is still very extensive on the Sidlaws, and hardy Blackface sheep compete with forestry plantations for the remaining rough grazing. One hilltop which has survived the extensive afforestation is that of Dunsinane in the western Sidlaws, from which it is possible to look across the expanse of Strathmore to the equally famous Birnam Wood, immortalized by Shakespeare in Macbeth.

Strathmore

Where the Tay enters Strathmore at the Pass of Birnam this great sandstone vale is some 13 kilometres wide, a width it retains virtually intact north-eastwards through Angus into Kincardineshire for a distance of nearly 80 kilometres. Its dark brown sandstones, grits and conglomerates are virtually identical with those of similar age in South Wales and the Welsh borderland. It is paradoxical, therefore, that in the latter region the Old Red Sandstone of, for example, the Brecon Beacons is one of the most resistant formations in the area, while in Strathmore the sandstone coincides with a zone of lowland. The explanation lies not only in downfaulting along the Highland Boundary Fault but also in the juxtaposition of the even more resistant Dalradian rocks to the north and the tough Sidlaw volcanics to the south. It must be remembered, however, that within the Old Red Sandstone certain formations are extremely hard, so that some hill masses have survived even to the south of the Highland Boundary Fault. The most prominent of these is Uamh Beag (662 m), overlooking Strathalan from the north-west and owing its bulk to the resistance of the Old Red basal conglomerates, known as the Dunnottar Group, which in places achieve thicknesses of over 2000 metres. The Dunnottar conglomerates also form the distinctive line of low foothills which stretch north-eastwards from Blairgowrie through the Hill of Alyth (295 m) and Tullo Hill (314 m) to Edzell on the North Esk. Between these foothills and the Grampians themselves a narrow, discontinuous linear valley separates the basal Old Red Sandstone conglomerates from the Highland Boundary Fault. Here differential erosion has picked out a narrow outcrop of less resistant Ordovician faulted wedges and Downtonian (Lower Old Red/Upper Silurian) rocks which occur at intervals along the Highland Boundary Fault (see Fig. 13.1).

The soils of Strathmore are normally fertile red loams renowned for their high yields of hay, corn and root crops. In addition, the sheltered south-facing slopes of the vale, especially around Kirriemuir and Blairgowrie, support intensive soft-fruit growing, mainly raspberries and peas. It is wrong, however, to look for a direct relationship between the solid geology and the land use, for, except on the highest hills, the land surface carries a thick layer of glacial drift, derived partly from the Highlands and partly from Strathmore itself. Thus, it is important to know something of the glacial history of this region. Three sources of glacial drift have been recognized, although the very fertile shelly clays of the eastern coastlands around Montrose are of only limited extent. More important are the widespread bright red drifts of Strathmore, derived from a major ice sheet which moved north-eastwards down the vale. Along the Highland border there are signs of a third source of superficial materials, for here a locally restricted south-easterly advance of Highland ice brought grey ground-moraine from the Grampians, together with a good deal of glacio-fluvial outwash during the melting phase of the main Devensian ice sheet.

Sissons (1966) has drawn attention to the extensive 'sandur', or plains of outwash, which occur in Strathmore at the mouths of most of the Highland glens. To the south of Blairgowrie, for example, the moors, woods and golf course between Muirtown and Rosemount indicate the gravelly soils of a sandur, interrupted by the 'myres' and lochs which occupy some of the numerous kettle holes. Similarly, around Edzell the forests and abandoned airfield are located on the flat surface of an outwash plain created by the Pleistocene forerunner of the North Esk river system. Here the modern river now follows a channel through a magnificent suite of five terraces, eroded by former meltwater streams in the glacial outwash sands and gravels. Old channels and linear depressions can clearly be seen along the feet of the erosional bluffs which delimit the terrace fronts. As this outwash is traced downstream its surface declines gently southwards away from the mountain front, while at the same time the coarseness of the deposits progressively lessens. An analogy is at once apparent between this glacial outwash of Pleistocene age and the lithology of the Strathmore Old Red Sandstone itself, where the conglomerates are gradually replaced by finer sediments as they are traced away from the Highland border (see p. 302). Although the climatic conditions of the two palaeoenvironments were vastly different, the principles of sedimentation are fairly similar. If, however, one traces the glacio-fluvial outwash upstream into the glens themselves it can be seen to emanate from a tumbled terrain of kames and dead-ice hollows which mark a downwasting stage of the former glaciers emerging from the valleys of the Bran, Tay and Ericht which once combined to form a piedmont ice lobe in western Strathmore and left their grey Highland till above the red sandstone till of the vale. Farther east, however, the glaciers failed to emerge from Glen Prosen, Glen Clova and Glen Esk during this particular glacial episode.

Wherever the ice sheets left extensive sandur plains or tumultuous kame-and-kettle topography the land use of Strathmore changes in no uncertain fashion. From the cornfields and cattle-grazed pastures of the damper claylands the landscape alters abruptly to gorse- and heather-clad moorlands and conifer plantations on the well-drained sands and gravels. One of the best examples can be seen to the north of Glamis Castle, where a tract of pine-studded 'muirs and myres' interrupts the rich farmlands between Kirriemuir and Forfar. One interesting point relating to these two sandstone-built market towns is that two of the world's most eminent geological pioneers were born there – John Playfair at Forfar and Charles Lyell near Kirriemuir.

Beyond Brechin, Strathmore tapers into a hill-girt basin known as the Howe of the Mearns. That this extensive lowland trough fails to reach the sea at Stonehaven is due to the increasing importance of the volcanic rocks in the succession as the Strathmore syncline is traced north-eastwards. Thus the line of hills along the southern flank near Laurencekirk and the vale's culminating Bruxie Hill (216 m) at the eastern end are built from lavas. Nevertheless, the larger Strathfinella Hill (414 m), which overlooks the Howe from the north, has been carved from an outcrop of the Dunnottar Group conglomerate (see p. 305), near the type-site of this resistant rock, where, on the nearby coast of Kincardineshire, the ruined Dunnottar Castle stands atop its 50 metre cliff.

The coasts of Angus (Rice, 1962) and Kincardineshire exhibit an interesting variety of forms which are related to the alternating igneous and sedimentary rocks within the Old Red Sandstone succession. The harder basaltic lavas, intrusive dykes, Old Red conglomerates and coarse grits are the chief cliff-formers, while the relatively soft sandstones, shales and superficial deposits correspond with the lower and less spectacular coastlines. To the north of the Tay estuary lies the large triangular raised-beach foreland of Buddon Ness, whose dunes and shingle ridges help build the renowned Carnoustie golf links. Northwards from here the coast is generally low and featureless to beyond Arbroath, where the appearance of the igneous rocks brings an irregularity to the cliff scenery. Around the sea stack of the Deil's Heid are outstanding examples of how the jointing of the Upper Old Red Sandstone has influenced wave erosion. The fine blow-hole of Graylet Pot, which terminates a narrow 90 metre sea cave, is one of the more noteworthy features of the high conglomeratic cliffs on which Lud Castle is precariously perched. Between here and Montrose the main exposures of the Ochil–Sidlaw lava group reach the North Sea and, since the coastline has been cut obliquely across their various outcrops, the result is a series of alternating bays and headlands. Red Head, with its 75 metre basaltic lava cliffs, is succeeded by the beautiful curving sandy beach of Lunan Bay. The dunes and raised beaches (Cullingford and Smith, 1980) of this attractive haven have been derived from the unconsolidated glacial and glacio-fluvial deposits infilling the broad Lunan Valley, which itself corresponds with the outcrop of the less resistant red, grey and blue shales and flagstones of the so-called Carmyllie Group of the Lower Old Red succession. Northwards, however, the axis of the major Tay Anticline (see p. 304) brings andesites and basalts back into the picture to create rugged but unspectacular sea cliffs around Fishtown of Usan. The Kincardineshire coast in general repeats the pattern, although its cliffs and raised beaches have the added attraction of the St Cyrus salt marsh and dune complex, a National Nature Reserve.

Before leaving the Midland Valley of Scotland and crossing the important boundary fault into the Highlands, mention should be made of the drainage pattern of this transition zone. Few regions have excited so much interest from geologists and geomorphologists as that consisting of the basin of the Tay and its neighbouring streams, probably because of the general discordance exhibited between the rivers and the underlying structural trends. While the general structures run from south-west to north-east (as the Caledonian 'grain'), the drainage is largely from the west or north-west, showing scant regard for the structural 'grain'. Many of the earliest writers (including Sir Archibald Geikie (1901), Sir Halford Mackinder (1902) and Messrs Peach and Horne (1930)) believed that all the major consequent streams were extremely ancient and originally followed south-easterly courses across an uplifted and tilted peneplain from the North-West Highlands to the ancient Rhine delta. They believed that during this period the Midland Valley was apparently unexcavated, while virtually ignoring the easterly-flowing anomalous rivers. Later writers, such as Bremner (1942) and Linton (1951b), formulated a completely new hypothesis in which they asserted that the former drainage was an easterly-flowing one, initiated on a tilted cover of Chalk strata which was subsequently eroded (Figure 13.2a). In this hypothesis the south-easterly flowing drainage components were regarded merely as secondary developments (generally known as 'subsequent streams') related to the gradual excavation of Strathmore and the Tay graben. In both hypotheses a great deal

Figure 13.2 Hypothetical reconstruction of drainage evolution in Scotland (a) after D. L. Linton; (b) after J. B. Sissons.

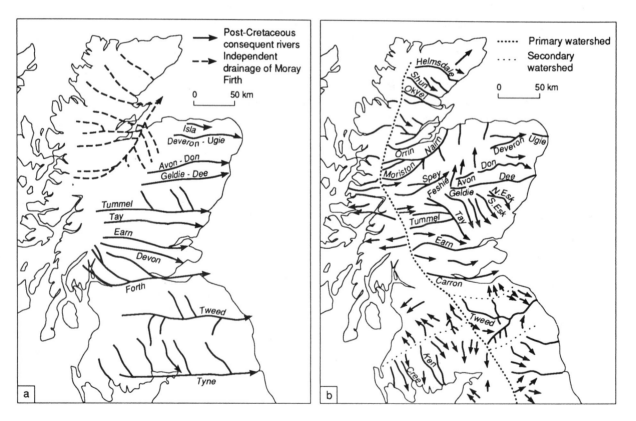

of stress was laid on the concept of superimposition from former 'cover' rocks which have now disappeared, leaving the streams partly adjusted to the underlying structures and partly discordant and therefore 'superimposed' (Linton, 1940). Although it is tempting to regard the anomalous Perth gap and the discordant nature of the North and South Esk as products of superimposition on to the resistant lavas from a former blanket of Upper Old Red Sandstone (as suggested by Geikie), an alternative explanation has been offered by Sissons (1966), who believes that the present-day pattern is not so far removed from that of the initial drainage after all (Fig. 13.2b). The latter may well have developed on a gradually emerging landmass in which the greatest uplift was in the west. This gentle but pulsatory uplift was accompanied by local warping, so that as the consequent streams developed upon the successively emerging coastal platforms during Late Tertiary times they extended themselves seawards in a variety of directions, but always down the steepest slopes. Thus the former drainage was accordant with the earlier coastlines, but became gradually more discordant with some of the underlying structural lines as the rivers incised themselves, much as the present eastern coastline hereabouts is discordant with the local structures.

The north-eastern coastlands

Kincardineshire is little more than a transition zone at the junction of three distinct topographical regions, Strathmore, the Grampians and the north-eastern coastlands. Nothing reflects this transitional character better than the agricultural landscape, for among its mixed farming-patterns the barley and potato crops remind one of Strathmore, the sheep-rearing of the Grampian Mountains and the beef-cattle of the Buchan lowlands (O'Dell and Mackintosh, 1963). As one journeys northwards from the Howe of the Mearns the colour of the ploughed fields changes from bright red to greyish-brown, as the drier, less stony and more fertile red soils of Strathmore give way northwards to heavier, wetter, stonier and more acid soils. In fact, one is leaving the lowlands of Scotland and crossing the Highland Boundary Fault. Since this brings the tougher Dalradian grits, schists and gneisses suddenly into the scene, it is not only the agricultural landscape which reflects the transition. The terrain also changes as the long shingly bay of Stonehaven is left behind and the roads climb 60–90 metres on to the wind-swept, almost treeless clifftop of the Kincardineshire plateau (Macgregor, 1948). Here the foothills of the Grampians reach the North Sea coast, hindering coastal communications and settlement alike. The villages are either clustered along the rock-bound coast or hidden in the narrow and often tree-lined valleys which entrench the plateau. The trim whitewashed fishing village of Muchalls, with its smugglers' cove, vies with Portlethen as a tourist attraction, but the clifftop village of Findon is more renowned because of its associations with smoked 'Finnan' haddock. In the coastal cliffs between Stonehaven and Aberdeen one can see how the rock structures have influenced the formation of the stacks, cliffs, arches and 'yawns' (a type of *geo*). Not only have the textural differences within the metamorphosed Dalradian rocks been etched out by wave attack, but glacial drifts and linear igneous dykes have also played an important part in creating such landmarks as the Bridge of One Hair, Castle Rock of Muchalls and features with such distinctive names as Arnot Boo and Blowup Nose.

In general, the north-eastern corner of Aberdeenshire, right round to the Moray Firth, is something of a paradox because although its geology is clearly that of Highland Scotland, the countryside to the north of Aberdeen belies this fact. Its extensive coastal lowlands, with some of the richest beef-cattle farming in Britain, are underlain by structures in which 'the complex basement has behaved under erosion almost as if it were homogeneous'. And yet rocks which make no major contribution to positive relief in places like Buchan can, as they are traced inland, create some of the highest mountains in Britain (Walton, 1963a).

Aberdeen and its rivers

The granite city of Aberdeen grew from the gradual coalescence of twin burghs, originally located on the neighbouring rivers of Dee and Don. The first settlements were greatly influenced by a north–south kame-like ridge of glacio-fluvial sands and gravels, once thought to belong to an Aberdeen glacial limit (Clapperton and Sugden, 1972), and which later separated the dunes and raised beaches of the coast from a series of waterlogged hollows which lay to the west of the present Gallowgate. The fishing village of New Aberdeen was to spring up at the southern end of the ridge, where the Den Burn creek of the Dee estuary provided a sheltered haven away from the currents and shifting sandbanks of the main river (Walton, 1963c). After extensive reclamation and dredging, this site of Footdee now forms the nucleus of Aberdeen's important harbour complex. In contrast, the estuary of the Don is constricted and shallow and its outlet is variable, so its port facilities have never been significant. It was here, nevertheless, around the large meander at Seaton Park where the Don cuts through the northern end of the ridge, that the ancient burgh of Old Aberdeen grew up. On the better-drained gravel slopes of the ridge to the east of Old Aberdeen Loch St Machar's Cathedral was built, to be followed by the Chanonry (the ecclesiastical quarter) and the sixteenth- to nineteenth-century University 'village' (Coull, 1963). Today Aberdeen is the centre for the North Sea oil industry (Smith *et al.*, 1976).

Up to and during Victorian times most of Aberdeen's buildings were constructed of solid granite, but because of rising costs many of the later houses of the inner suburbs are only granite-faced. Finally, as costs became prohibitive and granite quarries closed down, the outer suburbs, such as Craigiebuckler, were built of non-granitic materials, much as clay tiles have replaced slates as a roofing fabric. The first major quarry appears to have been opened in 1604 to supply mainly door lintels and window sills, but the middle of the eighteenth century saw the opening of the famous quarry of Rubislaw, from the granite of which more than half of Aberdeen was built. The city suburbs have now spilled out as far as this 142 metre crater, although the working of its medium-grained blue-grey stone has finally ceased as the better parts of the intrusion have been worked out. Its blocks also helped build the docks at Southampton, Portsmouth and Sheerness, to say nothing of the Bell Rock lighthouse. A slightly different mineral composition is found in the Don-side quarry at Kemnay, 21 kilometres away, whose light-grey granite has been utilized locally at the Marischal College and also for dock construction at Leith, Newcastle, Sunderland and Hull. Finally, at Corrennie, 30 kilometres west of Aberdeen, there is a coarser-grained granitic gneiss, with bright pink feldspars, which has been used mainly for decorative purposes, notably in Glasgow's municipal buildings.

Granite is only one, albeit the best known, of the rocks which make up the hills and plains of the north-eastern coastlands. A glance at a geological map will confirm that this corner of Scotland possesses one of the most complex mixtures of lithologies and structures in the whole country (Fraser, 1963) (Fig. 13.3), produced mainly during the Caledonian orogeny. More than 600 million years ago the ancient Archaean landmass, currently represented by the Lewisian gneisses

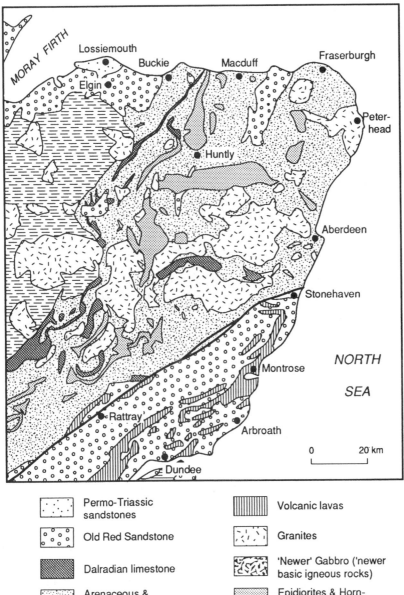

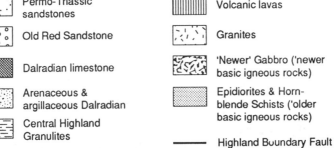

Permo-Triassic sandstones

Old Red Sandstone

Dalradian limestone

Arenaceous & argillaceous Dalradian

Central Highland Granulites

Volcanic lavas

Granites

'Newer' Gabbro ('newer basic igneous rocks)

Epidiorites & Horn-blende Schists ('older basic igneous rocks)

—— Highland Boundary Fault

Figure 13.3 The Geology of north-east Scotland (based on material prepared by the British Geological Survey).

and Torridonian Sandstones of the North-West, is known to have provided many of the sediments which rivers carried away south-eastwards to the linear oceanic basin which had developed in a zone stretching from Ireland to Scandinavia. As these various sediments were deposited in the basin, so their accumulated weight caused a crustal sag, creating what is known as a *geosyncline* – in this instance, the Caledonian Geosyncline. Two contrasting rock facies have been recognized within the geosynclinal sediments: first, the so-called Moinian Assemblage (the lower group), composed of fairly uniform deposits from the shallow waters of a slowly subsiding zone in the early phase of the geosyncline; and second, the so-called Dalradian Assemblage (the upper group), characterized by a greater diversity of sediments accumulated during the later, rapidly subsiding, phase of the geosyncline (Johnstone, 1966). Rocks of the younger part of the Moinian Assemblage are now thought to be the marine equivalent of the Torridonian terrestrial sandstones (Kennedy, 1951), which makes them of late Precambrian age, while the Dalradian rocks, though conformable on the Moinian, are thought to range in age from late Precambrian to Lower Cambrian (Johnson, 1991). In the present chapter only the Dalradian rocks will be studied (Read, 1960).

By referring to Fig. 13.3 it can be seen how varied are the rocks which comprise the complex Dalradian Assemblage. As if this complexity were not enough, these sediments were at the outset complicated by the addition of a succession of igneous rocks in the form both of lavas and of intrusive sills and plutons. Such vulcanicity merely heralded the onset of the Caledonian orogeny, during which the geosynclinal sediments were folded and uplifted into a gigantic mountain chain, comparable with the present Himalayas – a tectonic episode which continued intermittently until Old Red Sandstone times. As a result of the great lateral pressures exerted, the sedimentary rocks become totally metamorphosed and are now termed *metasediments*, while the igneous intrusives were frequently changed into such rocks as epidiorites and serpentines (the 'greenstones' of the earliest geological maps).

The differing degrees (or grades) of metamorphic change depended upon the fluctuating pressures, the varying temperatures of the thermal metamorphism (from the igneous activity) and the different chemical compositions of the original rocks. Where thermal metamorphism was limited or absent, for example, the rocks would have been affected by pressure alone, often resulting in the development of a slaty cleavage, as in much of Banffshire, where sporadic slate-quarrying was once carried on. Elsewhere, the combined effects of pressure and heat (dynamo-thermal metamorphism) caused recrystallization of the rocks, and platy metamorphic minerals, such as mica, to be developed with a markedly linear preferred orientation. Where there was a preponderance of platy minerals the rocks sometimes took on a schistosity, and this was particularly true of the fine-grained argillaceous rocks whose beds became pressed into minutely puckered folds. These mica-schists range in colour from black or grey (often with graphitic properties), like those found between Huntly and the Lower Spey, to a lustrous silvery hue, such as those around Garron Point between Cullen and Portsoy. The less easily deformed siliceous ribs of the coarser bands in the semi-argillaceous rocks, where the minerals were granular rather than platy, became stretched out into lenticles or 'eyes' within the schistose rocks. This was especially true in the so-called 'schistose grits' or 'quartzose schists' of the Upper Dalradian metasediments, which probably represent the former greywackes of the deep-sea floor.

Such rocks make up much of the Kincardineshire plateau and the undulating coastal platforms of Formartine to the north of Aberdeen.

The effect of the metamorphism on the quartz-rich sandstones of the geosynclinal sediments was to cause recrystallization into strongly lineated quartzites, while the pebbles of the coarser sandstones were elongated and squashed. In north-east Scotland the quartzites are both flaggy and massive and are particularly important in the coastal cliff scenery between Buckie and Cullen and in the low hills to the south of Fraserburgh. Since quartzite is a particularly resistant rock in most cases it forms a conspicuous eminence wherever it occurs in the succession.

The last of the more important metasediments in the Dalradian Assemblage are the metamorphosed limestones. Generally these occur only as thin ribs amongst the schists, but they can occasionally be found as thick beds of crystalline limestone or marble, although these are rarely of building or ornamental quality because of their dull-grey colour and irregular texture. Despite the fact that thick metamorphic limestones crop out on Deeside, near Aboyne, they are of such poor quality that they have little value except as a roadstone. In contrast, the county of Banffshire is well endowed with limestones of high quality for agricultural purposes, so they have been quarried on a considerable scale. It will be realized that in a mountainous environment where heavy rainfall, peat bogs and silica-rich rocks combine to produce extremely acid soils, the addition of lime in some form is essential for satisfactory crop growth. The best-known Dalradian limestones in this region are the so-called Sandend Group, named from their coastal outcrop near Portsoy (Sutton and Watson, 1955). From here they can be traced inland as a discontinuous band past Keith and Dufftown for a distance of 65 kilometres.

Because many basic intrusions and lavas had become interbedded with the sediments of the Caledonian geosyncline, they too became severely metamorphosed, resulting in the formation of hornblende schists and epidiorites (Johnson, 1962). The earliest granitic intrusions, such as those near Keith and Portsoy, were also subjected to great regional pressures. Some of these so-called 'Older Granites' were converted into gneisses by dynamo-thermal metamorphism, while a second phase of invading granitic material (either as magma or as hydrothermal solutions) diffused through all the existing metamorphic rocks to create what are known as 'migmatites', similar in character to the banded gneisses. The third and final phase of Caledonian igneous activity in this area coincided with the end of the main folding and metamorphic episodes, and the resulting rocks can be grouped into two main types – the gabbro intrusions and the 'Newer Granites'. Since the latter's evolution has been examined in Chapter 11 one need look only briefly at the gabbros of this area (see Fig. 11.3).

The newer gabbros occur as thick, sill-like masses which have been intruded into the Dalradian rocks of Buchan and Strathbogie (Stewart and Johnson, 1961). Their discontinuous outcrop runs in a semicircle from Portsoy, through Huntly and Insch (Read *et al.*, 1965), to Maud in central Buchan (see Fig. 11.3). Unlike many of the sills that have been described in earlier chapters, these gabbroid sills have been denuded more easily than the rocks into which they were injected, with the result that they almost invariably correspond with tracts of lower land. More importantly, since these gabbroid rocks are richer in such minerals as calcium, phosphorous and iron than the surrounding granites and slates, their overlying tills have weathered into extremely fertile soils. Studies have shown that in the Insch Valley, for example, the inhabitants as far back as Neolithic times made good use of this fertility, which was added to by the growth in post-glacial times of a broad-leaved deciduous woodland (Beavington, 1972). It is no surprise to discover, therefore, that in the district known as the Garioch a well-farmed lowland basin penetrates deeply past Insch into the Grampian foothills. Framed to the South by the granite of Bennachie (528 m) and the schists of the Correen Hills (487 m), and to the north by the slaty ridges of Foudland (466 m) and Tap o' Noth (564 m), this amphitheatre is now overlooked by the Clashindarroch Forest (Fig. 13.4). The westernmost end of the Insch embayment is formed from a narrow basin of Old Red Sandstone corresponding with a narrow lowland which runs southwards past Rhynie to the renowned Kildrummy Castle. This is one of several such depressions (for example, around Glenlivet and Cabrach) that have been created where structural basins of Old Red Sandstone have survived in patches above the Moinian and Dalradian rocks. The disposition of the larger Old Red basins around the Moray Firth leads one to ponder on the former extent of these 'cover-rocks' prior to their almost complete removal from the Grampian region. Their relics in this north-eastern corner of Scotland suggest that a blanket of old Red Sandstone may once have covered all the coastal

Figure 13.4 Clashindarroch Forest blankets the foothills of the slaty ridges of Foudland and the prominent summit of Tap o' Noth in the hinterland of Aberdeen.

plateaux. If this were true it would go a long way towards explaining the form and low elevation of the coastlands, because Buchan might simply be the exhumed surface of the pre-Devonian floor after the unconformable Old Red Sandstone 'veneer' had been stripped away.

To gain an impression of the Aberdeenshire countryside there is no better viewpoint than Brimmond Hill (265 m), to the west of Aberdeen itself. From its summit it is possible to look eastwards over the city, northwards across the Don to the rolling moors and farmlands of Formartine, westwards to the forested granites of Bennachie and Hill of Fare (471 m) and southwards to the famous braes of Deeside. Immediately below are the so-called 'freedom lands', once 'a dreary waste . . . a wilderness of marshy bog and stony crag, a rude primeval, undeveloped heath' (Coull, 1963). Today, however, these granite hillslopes support a patchwork of flourishing plantations and well-cultivated fields, all demarcated by gigantic walls of boulders cleared from the fields. The walls are known as the 'consumption dykes', and were constructed from the fourteenth century onwards as these farmlands were painfully reclaimed from the waste (Reed, 1983). Down on the riverbank is Peterculter, the only industrial community on Deeside, built on terraces of glacio-fluvial outwash. The mills are actually on a tributary, the Leuchar Burn, which has cut a rocky gorge as it enters the Dee, having lost its preglacial valley, which is now drift-plugged. In the Dee gorge nearby, the cataracts of Corbie Linn and the Thunder Hole add character to the sylvan scene.

Deeside is well known for its many imposing castles, such as Crathes, Aboyne, Balmoral and Braemar, set among thick pine forests and granite hills. At Aboyne, however, the hillsides retreat as the influence of a limestone outcrop makes its presence felt (see p. 313). Nevertheless, the haughlands of the valley hereabouts are underlain by very coarse boulder-strewn outwash from the Dinnet kame and kettle area. On the north bank the tiny Dess Burn has cut a gorge into the softer limestone where its acid waters leave the Cromar granite exposure, while the Falls of Dess at the head of the attractive gorge are caused by the tough granite margin. Also near to Dinnet is the spectacular Burn o' Vat, where a small tributary stream, known as the Vat Burn, follows a deep ravine to a gigantic circular pothole cut down 15 metres into the solid granite. The surrounding Dinnet kames and outwash terraces were created by glacial meltwaters from what was once termed the Dinnet ice limit (Clapperton and Sugden, 1972) and which were probably also responsible for the excavation of the Burn o' Vat channel. Not far to the north, where the Howe of Cromar lies cradled beneath the towering hills, the so-called Queen's View is another worthwhile vantage point. Far away to the south the sharp, isolated cone of Mount Keen (938 m) rivals the 'steep frowning glories of dark Lochnagar' (1,154 m) which once sported its own ice cap (Sissons and Grant, 1972). Both mountains owe their eminence to the resistance of the Newer Granites. The poet Byron, who lived for a time at Ballater, was equally impressed with 'Morven of the Snow', although no doubt blissfully unaware that its 873 metre summit was carved from epidiorites and hornblende schists, rather than from the more famous granite. Such a lithological contrast means that the base-rich soils of Morven give it a grassy rather than a heathery vegetation.

The contrasts in land use between the Dee and Don valleys have been highlighted in a local jingle: 'The River Dee for fish and tree, the River Don for horn and corn'. The difference can be accounted for by comparing the acid, bouldery outwash of Deeside with the more fertile and less acid clay soils of Donside.

Some of the clays may have been derived from the extensive glacio-lacustrine deposits that occur between Inverurie and Dyce, having been formed at a time when a number of ice-dammed lakes existed there in the late Devensian (Aitken, 1990). The well-fenced fields along the Don, with their sleek herds of Aberdeen Angus beef cattle, give way downstream to a ribbon of industrial development which has now linked Dyce with Aberdeen itself. Where the Don has entrenched itself into the coastal platforms, the numerous rapids between Cothall and Woodside have long been harnessed to provide power for linen, cotton and woollen mills. The abundance of water power and local linen were also responsible for the location of the well-known paper-making industry of Donside.

Once across the Don it soon becomes evident that the soils of the coastal plateaux are more fertile than those of south-west Aberdeenshire. The acid, bouldery granitic soils of Deeside gradually give away northwards to more freely draining loams associated with the schists and basic intrusions of the north-eastern corner. Reflecting the transition, the moorlands and forests of the thinner, poorer soils are gradually replaced by the well-ordered farmlands of Formartine and Buchan. In this prosperous triangle some 20 per cent of Scotland's arable farming is carried on, with root crops and oats being produced as winter feed for the pedigree beef cattle. Barley is also widely grown to meet the enormous demands of the Scottish distilleries, but this is too far north for wheat to be successful.

Buchan

Several geomorphologists have studied these north-eastern coastlands and have concluded that in general one can identify a staircase of coastal platforms between sea level and 300 metres. Although the highest of the platforms, at around 300 metres, is very extensive and easily recognized as a sort of plinth from which the high Grampians rise, it has been regarded by some as an uplifted and dissected peneplain and by others as being of marine origin, possibly created in Pliocene times. The lower rock platforms, such as the so-called Grampian Valley Benches (between 260 and 300 metres), are also a source of controversy, because as they are traced up the valleys of the Dee and Don they rise in elevation, with every appearance of having been formed sub-aerially by river action. On the other hand, the widespread 'Buchan platform' at around 105–120 metres and the 'coastal platform' of some 60 metres' elevation, have generally been regarded as uplifted wave-cut benches of Plio-Pleistocene age. There is a continuing reluctance on the part of many geologists to accept the implications of such high sea levels just prior to the Ice Age, although the alternative, of stepped sub-aerial peneplains (see p. 173), with the concomitant process of rapid scarp retreat, is also a difficult hypothesis to countenance. It is on the 'Buchan platform' that some puzzling superficial deposits of quartzite pebbles and Cretaceous flints have been discovered (Fig. 13.5). These gravels, which are overlain by the oldest till of the district, were once thought to be of Pliocene age and to represent a possible pre-glacial marine submergence in this area of at least 120 metres (Flett and Read, 1921; Merritt and McMillan, 1982).

Whatever their derivation, the platforms have been carved by erosional agents indiscriminately across the complex lithology, although the quartzites appear to have resisted the general levelling, and make a major impact on the coastal cliffs. Wherever this rock type occurs a bold hill has resulted, as at the Bin of Cullen

(320 m) and the Hill of Mormond (234 m) behind Fraserburgh. Not only is quartzite resistant to weathering but it is also deficient in soil-forming nutrients. Thus, its sporadic occurrence is marked by strongly leached infertile pockets of podzoilic soils which give patches of moorland among the rolling farmlands of the region. It would be wrong to suppose that the landscape of Buchan has always been one of prosperous husbandry, for some two centuries ago these rolling hills were nothing but a barren moorland. Near Hill of Fishrie (228 m), for example, is a newly created farming landscape, painstakingly reclaimed from a heathery waste of bogland. Its planned villages represent an attempt to resettle many of the Highland crofters who were evicted during the infamous 'Clearances' in the aftermath of Culloden. New Byth, Strichen, Mintlaw, New Deer, Cuminestown, New Pitsligo and the ambitiously named New Leeds, were all created during the so-called 'Miracle of Buchan' between 1763 and 1803 (Walton, 1963b).

The suggestion that the coalescing piedmont ice sheets from the Moray Firth, Strathmore and the Dee Valley failed to override central Buchan during the last glaciation has led to its title of 'moraineless Buchan'. Deeply rotted rocks may have survived from an interglacial, or even a pre-glacial, episode, although some modern authorities believe that the disintegrated granite represents nothing more than severe frost-shattering during a period of periglacial activity as Buchan became uncovered by the melting of the last ice sheets (Clapperton and Sugden, 1975). Nevertheless, the long smooth slopes of the hills of central Buchan carry few traces of ice-sheet erosion or glacial drift, while the survival of the Pliocene gravels suggests that glacial erosion must have been very selective during the Upper Pleistocene (Hall, 1984).

From the mouth of the Don to the mouth of the Ythan a 16 kilometre curve of sand dunes has grown up in front of the ancient cliffline of the post-glacial

Figure 13.5 The so-called 'Buchan Platform' which has been eroded indiscriminately across the complex rock structures and contrasting lithologies which make up the north-east coastland. The Grampian foothills may be seen in the distance.

raised beach. So unbroken is the visibility along this low coastline, where neither tree nor hill breaks the monotony of the sandy shore, that it was used by the Ordnance Survey as the base line in the original 1817 triangulation for the mapping of Scotland. The greatest development of dunes on this coastline is found at the well-known Sands of Forvie, where the Ythan breaks through this miniature Sahara to reach the sea. The Sands of Forvie have been investigated in great detail and a complex picture of ice advances, pro-glacial lakes, fluctuating sea levels and vegetation changes has been reconstructed. As the ice sheet waned, so late-glacial seas invaded the area to a height of 23 metres, leaving a series of raised beaches in the Ythan Valley between this elevation and 9 metres during the subsequent phase of falling sea level. A further rise of sea level saw the formation of the post-glacial raised beach on which some of the earliest traces of human habitation in Scotland have been found. This final marine transgression brought with it vast quantities of silt and sand which, together with the earlier glacio-fluvial outwash, were then fashioned by southerly winds into seven large east–west 'waves' of dune sand. Although the three southern 'waves' are immobile, the four northern sand masses are still moving northwards as parabolic dunes. Old ridge-and-furrow patterns are occasionally uncovered from beneath the sand, as are the ruins of Forvie church, which have been exposed for some years.

Northwards, past the old Castle of Slains, the schists recur as the main cliff-formers until the pink Peterhead granite begins to dominate. The master-jointing of this porphyritic, flesh-coloured granite (which is highly prized for its ornamental qualities) can be seen to run in a north–south direction, with the secondary joints at right angles. Marine erosion has carved these joint patterns into an intricate maze of stacks, caves and 'yawns', in addition to the natural arches at the Bow and Dunloss. A good deal of quarrying has disfigured the clifftop near Boddam, although the spectacular chasm of the Bullers of Buchan is not man-made. Although the granitic outcrop extends farther north, its last major influence can be seen at Peterhead itself, where gleaming red granite houses cluster around its harbour and rocky peninsula. Beyond this important oil service port the coastline returns to a series of long, curving dune-fringed strands all the way to Fraserburgh. Near Rattray longshore drift has succeeded in sealing off a former arm of the sea between the rocky outcrops at Rattray Head and Inzie Head. There is evidence that during late-glacial times a bay existed here, the old cliff-lines of which can be traced to the west of the Loch of Strathbeg. The erosion of an exposure of boulder clay at Inzie Head nourished the southward growth of a long shingle spit, fashioned by waves whose maximum 'fetch' was from the north-east. In time the spit reached almost to Rattray Head, thereby creating a harbour of some importance, trading regularly with the Low Countries. By the seventeenth century, however, the narrow outlet had become badly silted, and the entrance was finally sealed about 1720 by a major storm, to form the freshwater Loch of Strathbeg (Walton, 1956).

The Coastlands of the Moray Firth

Once round Kinnairds Head, where the well-known fishing port of Fraserburgh stands four-square against the uncompromising North Sea storms, the coast road quickly takes the traveller past the largely deserted fishing harbours of Sandhaven and Rosehearty. From this point westwards the landscape assumes an altogether different character, with the north-facing coastline's combination of magnificent cliff scenery, picturesque villages and the myriad of wild flowers in the roadside verges being reminiscent of the more famous northern coasts of Devon and Cornwall. The presence of the Old Red Sandstone between New Aberdour and Gardenstown extends this comparison, for the rich red soils which flank the moorlands of Windyheads Hill and the deeply incised valley of the Tore of Troup could quite easily be mistaken for Exmoor. Crouching on the tiny ledges beneath the towering 90 metre cliffs of Troup Head, where metamorphic grits and phyllites crop out, the tiny fishing harbours of Pennan, Crovie and Gardenstown are claimed by many to be the prettiest in Scotland. Each has to be approached by hairpin bends down fearsome gradients where the tough Old Red conglomerates have weathered into slabbed and pinnacled precipices. The long, narrow line of sandstone cottages at Pennan circles a picturesque harbour; at Crovie the dwellings turn their gable ends to the northern seascape; at Gardenstown the niches and ledges of the bright red cliff itself are crammed with a tumbling succession of brightly painted houses perched in improbable positions above the harbour. To the west of Gardenstown the wall-like form of the coastal cliffs changes as the Old Red Sandstone gives way to metamorphic rocks, their more intricate detail reflecting the less uniform lithology of the metamorphic succession (Sutton and Watson, 1955). Banffshire has been described by Scott-Moncrieff (1939) as 'a rugged bridge between the austerities of Buchan and the lovely Laich or Lowlands of Moray'.

The irregular character of the next 40 kilometres of coastline is due partly to the rapidly changing lithology and the tight folding of the Dalradian rocks and partly to the depositional history of the glacial and post-glacial sediments (Ogilvie, 1923). Structurally, this whole complex of Cambrian and Precambrian rocks is part of the recumbent fold of the so-called Iltay Nappe (see p. 327), the upper limb of which has itself been torn off from its 'roots' and transported bodily by large-scale Caledonian thrusting along a basal plane of sliding known as the Boyne Lag. Considering that the whole area has also been affected by faulting and igneous intrusions, it is little wonder that the stratigraphy is so confusing. But, thanks largely to the detailed work of Read (1936; 1955), it is now possible to identify the Dalradian rock groups with some confidence, since the coastline cuts discordantly across the strike of a virtually complete succession of the Upper and Lower Dalradian (see Fig. 13.3), making this a classic area for their study.

The complex folding of the Macduff group of metasediments clearly demonstrates the principles of differential coastal erosion. Between Gamrie Bay and the mouth of the river Deveron the precipitous coastal cliffs have coves excavated in the less resistant blue slates while the promontories coincide with the steeply dipping flagstones. Most of the larger headlands, however, are carved from the almost vertical beds of pebbly grit, especially at Knock Head near Banff itself. Along the foreshore of Boyndie Bay a prominent scatter of large glacial erratic blocks is called the Tumblers, those of black diorite being known locally as the Boyndie Heathens. The old town of Banff, with its many fine churches and public buildings, is built on three levels which represent river terraces of the Deveron. The pebbly grits, limestones and flags to the west of Whitehills produce a coastline of lower elevation, while Boyne Bay is carved in an even less resistant limestone which marks the base of the Upper Dalradian succession. Here is the line of discontinuity known as the Boyne Lag (see above), for the headland of

Cowhythe Hill has been carved from Lower Dalradian gneiss. This same rock also forms the craggy cliffs of East Head, overlooking the picturesque haven of Portsoy, whose trimly painted houses surround the old 'marble' factory on the shore. In reality this 'marble' is a narrow intrusion of serpentine, now worked only for small-scale ornamental purposes. Westwards again, the rapid alternation of the Durn Hill quartzite and the Sandend dark schists results in the crenellated coastline between Redhythe Point and Garron Point. The coast road now sweeps down to Cullen, the colourful 'gem' of the 'Banffshire Riviera', with its 'singing' white sands (whose spherical quartz grains emit a muffled squeak when trodden) and the prominent quartzite sea stacks of the Three Kings. These are products of the tough Cullen quartzite, which has been sharply folded into steep anticlines and synclines. This hard rock creates not only the isolated wooded hill of the Bin of Cullen but also the spectacular Bow Fiddle rock at Portknockie, whose harbour has been carved from a breached anticline (Fig. 13.6).

In Morayshire, the Dalradian rocks are replaced by those of the Old Red Sandstone, and once again this change is reflected in the topography. Except for the New Red Sandstone cliffs between Lossiemouth and Burghead, solid rock is not seen again at the coast until Inverness is reached. The low coastal

Figure 13.6 The sea stack of the Bow Fiddle, Portknockie, on the southern coast of the Moray Firth, has been carved from steeply dipping beds of Dalradian quartzite.

plateaux of Banffshire are replaced by the tree-girt, sandy bays of Spey, Burghead and Culbin, one of the finest areas in Britain for studying coastlines of deposition. The ever-shifting mouth of the Spey, Scotland's fastest-flowing river, displays good examples of channel-braiding (Lewin and Weir, 1977). The river has sufficient energy to carry enormous amounts of coarse material from the uplands but where the gradient slackens near sea level this load is dumped, to be variously worked by stream currents into numerous islands or by marine waves into shingle spits along the coast. Such beach ridges are common along the coasts of Moray and Nairn, frequently deflecting the river mouths to the west (for instance, at Lossiemouth and Findhorn). Superb examples of spit formation can be examined in Burghead Bay, although at Culbin the finest shingle ridges have been obliterated by the thick mantle of conifers which has been planted to stabilize the shifting dunes (Steers, 1937). The coastal marshes are swarming with birdlife, while sea-pinks (*Armeria maritima*), sea-asters (*Aster tripolium*) and sea-spurreys (*Spergularia salina*) give patches of brilliant colour among the grey-green salt pans. It appears that dominant waves are causing the Bar to migrate slowly westwards, at the rate of about 1.6 kilometres per century, leaving the ends of eighteen recurved spits terminating in the salt marshes. Such migration once deflected the River Findhorn westwards in a course now marked by the silted Buckie Loch; a major storm then breached the spit in 1702, forming a new river mouth and causing Findhorn to be rebuilt in its present location.

West of the Spey both late- and post-glacial beaches are very extensive, possibly because of the greater supply of glacial deposits and the greater efficiency of the rivers as agents of transport. The attractive town of Elgin, for example, is located on a delta fan built out by the Lossie into the late-glacial sea amid a decaying ice sheet. This sandy flat was subsequently uplifted to 30 metres above sea level. Raised beaches of similar origin are found near the mouths of all the major rivers along this coast, all uptilted to the west in the manner of the Forth and Tay beaches (see pp. 292 and 304). The post-glacial marine transgression is thought to have inundated the low-lying tract to the north of Elgin known as the Laich of Moray. The rocky islands created at Burghead and Branderburgh have now become tied to the mainland by reclamation of the intervening raised-beach marsh. The cave-dotted northern cliffs of these former islands have been formed from Permian and Triassic sandstones (Watson and Hickling, 1941), some of which have been quarried for building-stone at the well-known Hopeman quarries. It is noticeable how the land use reflects the changing soils and geology in this tract, the dark arable land of the Spynie flats (where Loch Spynie is the last remnant of the coastal marsh) contrasting with the rocky coastal ridge of sandy, heath-covered soils. On the foothills south of Elgin a buried podzolic soil at Teindland, dated at 28 000 years, is one of the first sites in Scotland at which a Devensian interstadial episode has been recognized (Fitzpatrick, 1965). A few kilometres west of Forres the Findhorn Valley runs close to the borders of Nairnshire. It was at this point that Johnson and Boswell noted that 'fertility and culture' were left behind, whilst they reckoned that at Nairn 'we may fix the verge of the Highlands', for here they first heard Gaelic spoken and encountered their first peat fires.

Bibliography

Aitken, J.F. (1990) Glacio-lacustrine deposits in Glen Nochty, Grampian Region, Scotland, UK. *Quaternary Newsletter*, **60**, 13–20.

Beavington, F. (1972) A brown forest soil at high altitudes in Aberdeenshire. *Scot. Geog. Mag.*, **88**, 134–40.

Bremner, A. (1942) The origin of the Scottish river system. *Scot. Geog. Mag.*, **58**, 15–20, 54–9, 99–103.

Browne, M.A.E. (1980) Late-Devensian marine limits and the pattern of deglaciation of the Strathearn area, Tayside. *Scot. J. Geol.*, **16**, 221–30.

Clapperton, C.M. and Sugden, D.E. (1972) The Aberdeen and Dinnet glacial limits reconsidered, in C.M. Clapperton (ed.), *North East Scotland Geographical Essays*. Aberdeen University Press. 5–11.

Clapperton, C.M. and Sugden, D.E. (1975) The glaciation of Buchan: a reappraisal, in A.M.D. Gemmell (ed.), *Quaternary Studies in North East Scotland*. Aberdeen University Press. 19–22.

Coull, J.R. (1963) The historical geography of Aberdeen. *Scot. Geog. Mag.*, **79**, 80–94.

Cullingford, R.A. and Smith, D.E. (1980) Late Devensian raised shorelines in Angus and Kincardineshire, Scotland. *Boreas*, **9**, 21–38.

Fitzpatrick, E.A. (1965) An interglacial soil at Teindland, Morayshire. *Nature*, **207**, 621–2.

Flett, J.S. and Read, H.H. (1921) Tertiary gravels of the Buchan district of Aberdeenshire. *Geol. Mag.*, **58**, 215–25.

Fraser, W.E. (1963) The geology and structure, in A.C. O'Dell and J. Mackintosh. *The North East of Scotland*. Central Press, Aberdeen. 3–15.

Geikie, A. (1901) *The Scenery of Scotland Viewed in Connection with its Physical Geology* (3rd edn). Macmillan. 481 pp.

Hall, A.M. (ed.) (1984) *Buchan*. Field Guide. Quat. Res. Assoc. 120 pp.

Harry, W.T. (1956) The Old Red Sandstone lavas of the western Sidlaw Hills, Perthshire. *Geol. Mag.*, **93**, 43–56.

Harry, W.T. (1958) The Old Red Sandstone lavas of the eastern Sidlaws. *Trans. Edinb. Geol. Soc.*, **17**, 105–12.

Johnson, M.R.W. (1962) Relations of movement and metamorphism in the Dalradians of Banffshire. *Trans. Edinb. Geol. Soc.*, **19**, 29–64.

Johnson, M.R.W. (1991) Dalradian, in G.Y. Craig (ed.) *Geology of Scotland* (3rd edn). The Geological Society, London. 125–60.

Johnstone, G.S. (1966) *The Grampian Highlands* (3rd edn). British Regional Geology. HMSO. 103 pp.

Jones, S.J. (ed.) (1968) *Dundee and District*, Winter & Son. 391 pp.

Kennedy, W.Q. (1951) Sedimentary differentiation as a factor in the Moine-Torridonian correlation. *Geol. Mag.*, **88**, 257–66.

Lenman, B. and Gauldie, E. (1968) The industrial history of the Dundee region from the 18th century to the early 20th century, in S.J. Jones (ed.), *Dundee and District*. Winter & Son. 162–73.

Lewin, J. and Weir, M.J.C. (1977) Morphology and recent history of the Lower Spey. *Scot. Geog. Mag.*, **93**, 45–51.

Linton, D.L. (1940) Some aspects of the evolution of the rivers Earn and Tay. *Scot. Geog. Mag.*, **56**, 1–11 and 69–79.

Linton, D.L. (1951a) Watershed breaching by ice in Scotland. *Trans. Inst. Br. Geog.*, **15**, 1–16.

Linton, D.L. (1951b) Problems of Scottish scenery. *Scot. Geog. Mag.*, **67**, 65–85.

Linton, D.L. (1962) Glacial erosion on soft-rock outcrops in central Scotland. *Biuletyn Peryglacjalny*, **11**, 247–57.

Macgregor, D.R. (1948) The Kincardineshire Plateau. *Scot. Geog. Mag.*, **64**, 81–9.

Mackinder, H.J. (1902) *Britain and the British Seas*. Heinemann.

Merritt, J.W. and McMillan, A.A. (1982) The 'Pliocene' gravels of Buchan: a reappraisal. *Scot. J. Geol.*, **18**, 329–32.

Morrison, J., Smith, D.E., Cullingford, R.A. and Jones, R.L. (1981) The culmination of the Main Postglacial Transgression in the Firth of Tay area, Scotland. *Proc. Geol. Assoc.*, **92**, 197–209.

O'Dell, A.C. and Mackintosh, J. (eds), (1963) *The North East of Scotland*. Central Press, Aberdeen. 256 pp.

Ogilvie, A.G. (1923) The physiography of the Moray Firth coast. *Trans. R. Soc. Edinb.*, **53**, 377–404.

Patterson, I.B. (1974) The supposed Perth Readvance in the Perth district. *Scot. J. Geol.*, **10**, 53–66.

Peach, B.N. and Horne, J. (1930) *Chapters on the Geology of Scotland*. Oxford University Press.

Read, H.H. (1936) The stratigraphical order of the Dalradian rocks of the Banffshire coast. *Geol. Mag.*, **73**, 468–75.

Read, H.H. (1955) The Banff Nappe: an interpretation of the structure of the Dalradian rocks of north-east Scotland. *Proc. Geol. Soc.*, **66**, 1–28.

Read, H.H. (1960) *North East Scotland: The Dalradian*. Guide no. 31. Geol. Assoc. 17 pp.

Read, H.H., Sadashivaiah, M.S. and Haq, B.T. (1965) The Hypersthene Gabbro of the Insch Complex, Aberdeenshire. *Proc. Geol. Assoc.*, **76**, 1–12.

Reed, M. (1983) *The Georgian Triumph: 1700–1830*. Paladin.

Rice, R.J. (1962) The morphology of the Angus coastal lowlands. *Scot. Geog. Mag.*, **78**, 5–14.

Scarth, A. (1968) Physiography, in S.J. Jones (ed.), *Dundee and District*. Winter & Son, 22–38.

Scott-Moncrieff, G. (1939) *The Lowlands of Scotland*. Batsford.

Simpson, J.B. (1933) The late-glacial readvance moraines of the Highland border west of the River Tay. *Trans. R. Soc. Edinb.*, **57**, 633–45.

Sissons, J.B. (1963–4) The Perth Readvance in central Scotland. *Scot. Geog. Mag.*, **79**, 151–63 and **80**, 28–36.

Sissons, J.B. (1966) *The Evolution of Scotland's Scenery*. Oliver & Boyd. 259 pp.

Sissons, J.B. and Grant, A.J.A. (1972) The last glaciers in the Lochnagar area, Aberdeenshire. *Scot. J. Geol.*, **8**, 85–93.

Smith, H.D., Hogg, A. and Hutcheson, D.M. (1976) Scotland and offshore oil: the developing impact. *Scot. Geog. Mag.*, **92**, 75–91.

Steers, J.A. (1937) The Culbin Sands and Burghead Bay. *Geog. J.*, **90**, 498–523.

Stewart, F.H. and Johnson, M.R.W. (1961) The structural problem of the younger gabbros in North East Scotland. *Trans. R. Soc. Edinb.*, **54**, 553–72.

Sutton, J. and Watson, J. (1955) The deposition of the Upper Dalradian rocks of the Banffshire coast. *Proc. Geol. Assoc.*, **66**, 295–332.

Turner, W.H.K. (1957) The textile industry of Perth and District. *Trans. Inst. Br. Geog.*, **23**, 123–40.

Turner, W.H.K. (1958) The significance of water power in industrial location: some Perth examples. *Scot. Geol. Mag.*, **74**, 98–115.

Turner, W.H.K. (1966) The concentration of jute and heavy linen manufacture in east central Scotland. *Scot. Geog. Mag.*, **82**, 29–45.

Walton, K. (1956) Rattray: a study in coastal evolution. *Scot. Geog. Mag.*, **72**, 85–96.

Walton, K. (1963a) Geomorphology, in A.C. O'Dell and J. Mackintosh (eds), *The North East of Scotland*. Central Press, Aberdeen. 16–32.

Walton, K. (1963b) Regional Settlement, in A.C. O'Dell and J. Mackintosh (eds), *The North East of Scotland*. Central Press, Aberdeen. 87–99.

Walton, K. (1963c) The site of Aberdeen. *Scot. Geog. Mag.*, **79**, 69–73.

Waterston, C.D. (1965). The Old Red Sandstone, in G.Y. Craig (ed.), *The Geology of Scotland*. (1st edn). Oliver & Boyd. 269–308.

Watson, D.M.S. and Hickling, G. (1914) On the Triassic and Permian rocks of Moray. *Geol. Mag.*, **6**, 339–402.

The Grampian Highlands and Argyll

14

The mountains and glens of the Scottish Highlands are among the greatest glories of British scenery and have been highlighted by poet, writer and artist (Thompson, 1974). The Grampians form the heartland of these well-known uplands, and their scenic detail has been described so precisely by Archibald Geikie (1901), the eminent nineteenth-century geologist, that his words are worth repeating here:

> The mingling of mouldering knolls with rough angular rocks, the vertical rifts [sic] that gape on the face of crag and cliff . . . the strange twisted crumpled lines of the stratification, the blending of white bands of quartz with dark streaks of hornblende that vary the prevailing grey or brown or pink hue of the stone, the silvery sheen of the mica and the glance of the felspar or the garnets, the crusts of grey and yellow lichen or of green velvet-like moss . . . these are features which we recognize at once as distinctively and characteristically highland.

All that remains is to explain some of the ways in which these important constituents of the Grampian landscape were created.

In the first place, the two main lithological divisions, the Moinian Assemblage and the Dalradian Assemblage (see p. 312), can be contrasted. The former, occurring in the northern and north-western Grampians, comprises well-stratified thicknesses of fairly uniform argillaceous and arenaceous metasediments. The Dalradian, on the other hand, is much more diverse in both lithology and thickness of strata (Johnson, 1965), so that differential erosion has caused a more rapid alternation of topographic detail in the Highland border tract which stretches south-westwards from Banffshire to the Clyde (Anderson, 1947). Generally speaking, therefore, it is the southern Grampians which exhibit the most diverse relief, while the Moinian areas farther north have yielded to denudation in a more uniform manner, producing somewhat featureless plateau lands such as the Monadhliath. It must be remembered, however, that wherever igneous rocks appear in the Grampians the apparently simple relationship between lithology and relief outlined above is certain to be affected. It will be shown, for example, that the granites of Cairngorm and Rannoch make significant impacts (albeit very contrasting ones) on the Grampian scene, as do the volcanics at Glencoe and Ben Nevis (see Chapter 15) (Mercy, 1965).

Because of the lack of fossils in the Moinian and Dalradian rocks, their structures have long defied analysis. Although it was soon realized that these rocks had been severely folded and faulted by the Caledonian mountain-building episode (Watson, 1963), for many years it was impossible to determine whether the succession was the right way up (Fig. 14.1a), was inverted by overfolding (Fig. 14.1b) or was reduplicated by numerous isoclinal folds (Fig. 14.1c). However, by the use of such criteria as the orientation of current-bedding and graded-bedding it ultimately became possible to decipher the complex structures and stratigraphy, although there is still controversy among geologists concerning some of the tectonics. Thanks largely to the work of Bailey (1922; 1923), it can

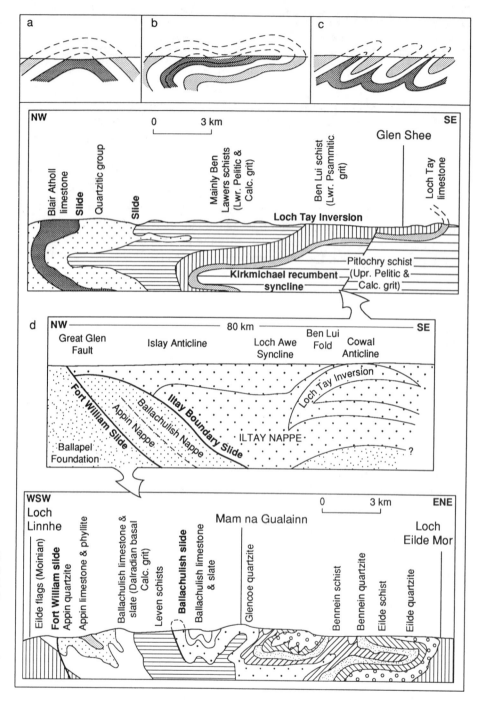

Figure 14.1 Geological structures of the Grampians (after J.G.C. Anderson and T.R. Owen). (a) The succession right way up. (b) The succession inverted. (c) The succession reduplicated by isoclinal folds. (d) Generalized sections of Iltay nappe (top) and Ballapel Foundation (bottom).

now be demonstrated that the Grampians have been carved from a number of enormous recumbent folds, similar to Alpine nappes (Harris *et al.*, 1976), often separated from each other by low-angle thrusts, known as 'slides', along which overlying folded strata have been transported bodily across the underlying rocks for considerable distances towards the north-west (Fig. 14.1d).

Initially it was believed that two major structural units could be identified (Read, 1948): in the south, the so-called 'Iltay Nappe' ('Iltay' meaning that it belongs to the geographical tract between Islay and Loch Tay), and, in the Lochaber district of the north, the 'Ballappel Foundation' (from Ballachulish, Appin and Loch Eilde), the two units being separated by the 'Iltay Boundary Slide' (Johnstone, 1966). It is now thought more appropriate to call the two structural units the 'Southern Grampians Nappe Complex' and the 'Northern Grampians Nappe Complex' respectively (see Fig. 14.4). The Grampian scenery will be examined in three parts: the northern area of Speyside and the Cairngorms; the complex Central Grampians where the two units meet; and the southern zone of the Highland border (Macnair, 1908). The landforms of all three sub-regions have been severely modified by Pleistocene ice-sheets (Sissons, 1977).

Speyside and the Cairngorms

One of the most famous river valleys of the Grampians, long renowned for its salmon and its pearls, Strathspey not only serves as a broad avenue of access to the interior but also exhibits a great variety of striking scenery. Like the neighbouring Nairn and Findhorn, the Spey has cut deeply into the schists and granites of the massif, assisted in part by the fact that their courses are closely adapted to the south-west to north-east (Caledonian) strike. Ice sheets have deepened and broadened the Spey Valley to such an extent that it is wide enough to be termed a 'strath', rather than a 'glen', and it now exhibits a series of broad glacio-fluvial terraces known as 'haughlands', which can be traced up the valley for many miles. Such factors have had an important influence on the soils and vegetation, which in turn have helped encourage a narrow tongue of settlement and improved land to penetrate deeply into the mountainous interior. Today Strathspey is one of the most densely populated areas of the Highlands, despite its long history of emigration and abandoned farming. A great deal of Speyside lies between 210 and 300 metres, and it is somewhat surprising to find that cultivation in some favourable areas continues to elevations as high as 370 metres. When compared with the cultivation limits of some 90 metres along the western coasts (see Chapters 15 and 16) this is a remarkable achievement, but it is largely because the east has lower rainfall and more sunshine and lacks the degree of dissection and preponderance of bare rock due to ice erosion which prevail farther west. Nevertheless, plots of oats and potatoes, intermingling with the infrequent hayfields, have been won from the rough grazings and forests of the valleyfloor only with difficulty.

Lower Strathspey is one of Scotland's most famous whisky-distilling areas. The east-bank tributaries of Glenlivet and Glenfiddich, for example, are renowned for their malt-whiskies, the quality of which is reputed to be greatly influenced by the local geology. Experts claim that water draining off granite through peat gives a superior whisky to that produced either near Elgin, where the water has drained through Old Red Sandstone, or near Keith, where a band of Dalradian limestone affects the quality (Storrie, 1962). Upstream towards the district of Badenoch, the stone walls and scattered farms give way to a zone of thick forests, where conifer trees flank the meandering river and carpet the neighbouring valleys and hill slopes. Among the pine forests, birches not only clothe the cleared forest land but also survive on the thinner, stonier soils of the bouldery hillsides (Gunson, 1975). In this zone the valleyfloor is no longer flat, for a stillstand of the Spey glacier has left a confusion of glacio-fluvial hummocks on which heather vies with whortleberry as a ground cover. Between the kame-like hummocks lie kettle holes and ill-drained flats, many of which contain lochs, especially in the tract from Boat of Garten to Kincraig. Loch an Eilein with its insular castle, Loch Pityoulish with its climbing woodlands, and the attractively embowered Loch Alvie are all tourist haunts, but none is so famous as the kettle hole of Loch Garten in Abernethy Forest (Birks and Matthews, 1978), which has a much-frequented osprey nesting site.

Above Loch Insh the valleyfloor changes once more into a broad, flat and almost treeless strath. Here the gradient of the Spey is extremely low, so that the river meanders for several kilometres across a marshy plain of permanently rush-choked pasture. The flatness of the valleyfloor hereabouts has been explained in terms of a former valley lake of which Loch Insh is the shrunken remnant. Originally delimited downstream by a rocky barrier which crossed the valley near to Alvie, this narrow, ice-overdeepened basin of upper Strathspey became a 13 kilometre post-glacial ribbon lake similar to the modern Windermere in the Lake District of England. Infilling by sedimentation from upstream, however, has obliterated all but the easternmost end of the former lake basin. Some authors believe that, prior to this, the upper valleys of the Findhorn and Spey held ice-dammed lakes during the retreat of the glaciers, although others disagree on the mode of recession, and favour downwasting of the glacier ice *in situ* (Young, 1978).

To the west of upper Strathspey are the rolling peat-covered uplands of the Monadhliath (Gaelic, meaning 'the grey mountains'). Carved largely from uniform layers of mica schists (Whitten, 1959), these flat-topped mountains are almost devoid of corries and are virtually featureless and trackless, a widespread wilderness of peat and moorland rising gently from around 750 metres to heights of some 900 metres, as part of the so-called Grampian Main Surface (see p. 331). The Monadhliath have always been a great barrier to communications – both road and rail routes to Inverness utilize the fortuitous glacial meltwater channel of the Slochd to climb out of Strathspey beyond Carrbridge – and their bulk still forms a physical and cultural boundary in the wilderness of Moinian and Dalradian rocks that stand between Badenoch and the lands of the Great Glen (Anderson, 1955).

In contrast to the Monadhliath, the Cairngorms are granite-cored and corrie-scarred, and form the most extensive area of land above 1000 metres anywhere in Britain. Despite their bulk, they have become one of Scotland's best-known tourist attractions, largely because of their magnificent scenery and ski-slopes. The Cairngorms are a National Nature Reserve which, at more than 26 000 hectares, is not only the largest in Britain but also one of the most extensive in Europe. Here a great variety of wildlife flourishes in the numerous habitats, but none is more exciting than the reindeer, reintroduced on to the Cairngorm summits, having become extinct in Scotland some 800 years ago. The 1200 metre plateaux, so similar in character to those of the Scandinavian mountains, produce sufficient growth of the lichen *Cladonia rangiferina* (reindeer moss) to support an extensive herd, but the summits are also the home of an interesting Arctic-

Alpine flora, relics of a vegetation which flourished elsewhere in Britain during the Ice Age. This includes the starry saxifrage (*Saxifraga stellaris*) and the bright pink flowers of the moss campion (*Silene acaulis*) which grow strongly on the bare, inhospitable granite.

The rose-coloured Cairngorm granite is part of a gigantic pluton whose outcrop, covering 410 square kilometres, is intruded into the surrounding Moinian metasediments. The red feldspars give the overall colouring to the bare rock exposures, but large quartz crystals and flecks of mica add to the glistening appearance of the coarse-grained granite. During the cooling phase of the granitic magma, cavities became filled with 'smoky' quartz inclusions, varying in colour from yellow to black, and these crystals now constitute the famous 'cairngorm' gemstones. Two types of jointing have developed in the granite exposures: a set of vertical joints, which have often been picked out by glacial erosion to form the precipices of the corrie headwalls; and a type of laminar pseudo-bedding which occurs as horizontal sheeting in the surface layers of the rock. It has been shown that in all instances the pseudo-bedding lies parallel with the rolling hilltops of the massif, but that it is clearly truncated by the cliffs of glacial erosion. Leading on from this observation, Sugden (1968) has demonstrated that a clear distinction may be made between the pre-glacial elements and the glacial elements of the Cairngorm scenery. He sees the subdued rolling summits, with their tors, stone stripes and their deep layers of regolith or rotted rock, as survivals from a pre-glacial landsurface in which the granite was exposed to deep chemical weathering under a warmer climate than that of today. Thus, such features as the smooth summit of Cairn Gorm (1245 m), the bouldery plateau of Ben Macdhui (1310 m) and the tors of Beinn Mheadhoin (1184 m) were created before the Pleistocene and were little modified by an ice sheet which subsequently moved across them in a north-easterly direction.

In contrast, the landforms of glacial erosion were selectively impressed upon this landsurface when the ice sheet's power to erode was greatly influenced by the configuration of the existing topography (Sugden, 1968). Glacial troughs, such as Glen Einich, Glen Geusachan and that which cradles Loch Avon, were excavated along those of the pre-glacial drainage lines that were suitably orientated to take the north-easterly discharge of the Grampian ice sheet. Where pre-glacial valleys stood at right angles to the ice movement, however, as in Glen Quoich, Glen Derry and even the north–south element of Glen Geusachan, the valleys managed to retain their original fluvial form. This is not to say that they remained unfilled by ice, for the great gash of the well-known Lairig Ghru, across the centre of the pre-glacial watershed, was bulldozed by glacial diffluence when ice filling Glen Dee could find no suitable outlet to the north (Fig. 14.2). Another good example of glacial breaching can be seen at the Saddle, to the east of Cairn Gorm. Here an ice sheet flowing down Glen Avon lowered the former divide at the head of Strath Nethy, thus sending an ice stream northwards as well as north-eastwards. Sugden (1969) claims that the Cairngorm corries show evidence of having been formed at different stages of the Ice Age, the older, larger corries having been overrun by the regional ice sheet subsequent to their excavation. These larger corries are usually grouped around north-east-facing pre-glacial valley heads, such as those which isolate Braeriach (1295 m) from Cairn Toul (1293 m). The younger corries, however, exhibit no such preferred orientation, being found on the flanks of the troughs and even within the larger corries

Figure 14.2 The Cairngorms, looking south from the forested Glenmore basin through the deep glacial breach of the Lairig Ghru, cut through the main pre-glacial watershed. Ben Macdhui is the highest summit shown in the centre of the photograph.

themselves, on west-, north-, and east-facing slopes. Two examples of such composite corries are those which carry the well-known lingering snow patches below the Cairn Gorm–Cairn Lochan summit ridge. Deeper and more precipitous than the ski-slopes of Coire Cas, these spectacular hollows of Coire an-t-Sneachda and Coire an Lochain carry tiny moraine-dammed lochans (small lochs) which are backed by great amphitheatres of bare granite slabs.

There has been a great deal of controversy about the late-glacial history of the Cairngorms and the neighbouring massif known as Gaick Forest during the phases of their deglaciation (Sissons, 1972; 1974; 1979). Some authors believe that the Cairngorm ice cap, like those of Gaick and the mountains south of Lochnagar, disappeared progressively in a single phase of downwasting, interrupted only by a slight reactivation during the late cold period associated with the Loch Lomond Readvance. Others believe that during the last interstadial, or break in the glacial conditions, the Cairngorms, together with the rest of Scotland, became totally ice-free before the rapid rebirth of a new ice cap (equivalent to the Loch Lomond Readvance) created widespread hummocky moraines, meltwater channels and outwash terraces. It seems probable that on the ice-free ground of the Highlands much periglacial activity would have taken place during the late-glacial, with frost-shattering freshening up the summit tors, cliffs and screes, while major solifluxion transformed the gentler slopes (Sugden, 1970). In modern times the climate of these high plateaux remains the severest in Britain, and it is no surprise to discover that large stone 'polygons' and 'stripes' have continued to form at intervals (King, 1971).

There is no better viewpoint than these high plateautops from which to ponder the concept of uplifted peneplains, because from here the roof of Scotland appears as a vast dissected tableland, with all the highest Grampian peaks rising as isolated residuals above an accordant 730–915 metre plateau of the 'Grampian Main Surface' – the 'High Plateau' of Peach and Horne (1930). Although there is no agreement so far as their genesis is concerned, most authors are agreed that the complex Caledonian fold structures have been planed right across, to create such a remarkable accordance of summits and spurs that it has been said of the eastern Grampians that they exhibit more flat ground on the hilltops than on the valleyfloors. From the high tops it is also possible to look down on the far-spreading forests which envelop the north-western flanks of the Cairngorms like a blue-green ocean (Dubois and Ferguson, 1985). In the basin of Glenmore, remnants of the old natural Scots pine forest have survived around Loch Morlich and in the Pass of Ryvoan, although newly planted stands include many hectares of spruce as well as pine. Research has shown that the natural tree-line of the Cairngorms reached an elevation of some 790 metres during the post-glacial climatic optimum, 4000–5000 years ago. Today, however, because the climate is cooler the forests extend only up to the 460 metre contour (Pears, 1967). Like the neighbouring Abernethy Forest, those of Glenmore and Rothiemurchus were once part of the great Wood of Caledon, which formerly extended from Glen Lyon and Rannoch to Strathspey and Strathglass and from Glencoe eastwards to the Dee. But the axes, fires and domestic livestock of mankind have depleted the Grampian pine forests as surely as the climatic deterioration (McVean, 1964).

The Central Grampians

To the south of Strathspey the road and railway climb steadily across the wastes of Badenoch to Drumochter Pass. Here, in the very centre of the Grampians, away from the forests and the spectacular Cairngorm cliffs, there is a chance to concentrate on the three elements which constitute so great a part of the Highland scene – the ubiquitous moorland, the mountain stream and the trackless bogland.

It will be remembered that in the Southern Uplands heather moor is uncommon, for, as in the Western Highlands, the grasses and sedges have ousted it from its dominant position. But in the Eastern Highlands heather dominates the acid soils on the sweeping slopes of moorland and peat bog alike up to heights of some 820 metres, above which only blaeberry and crowberry survive as darker patches in the tawny colour of the *Nardus* grasslands. Three species of heather abound – *Calluna vulgaris* and *Erica cinerea* on the drier sites, and *Erica tetralix* in the damper situations – and these have been perpetuated in the eastern Highlands by regular moor-burning. In the wetter Western Highlands, however, continued burning is tending to eliminate heather in favour of its grass and sedge competitors.

Today's systematic moor-burning to improve grazing value merely perpetuates the wanton forest and scrub destruction of earlier centuries which, more than anything, is responsible for the emergence of the Highlands as a landscape of moorlands rather than forests. Modern rotational moor-burning is practised as much for the benefit of the grouse as for the sheep, since the red grouse is very dependent on heather as its major food supply. Deforestation has extended the territory of the grouse partly at the expense of the red deer, which prefers the forested or scrubby habitats at certain seasons of the year. Since burning for grouse in the wetter west has merely reduced the amount of heather moor, the 'Glorious Twelfth' means more in the Grampians than it does in the Western Highlands (McVean and Lockie, 1969).

Turning now to look at the streams of the Central Grampians, it becomes clear that once away from Speyside the drainage pattern exhibits very little regard for the underlying Caledonian structures. Apart from the valley of Loch Laggan (which is virtually a south-west extension of the line of Strathspey) or the fault-guided trench of Loch Ericht, the majority of the river valleys run discordantly across the structure. Certain writers, notably Linton (1951) have concluded that the original drainage of the Grampians, and indeed of most of Scotland, was dominated by east-flowing rivers. Linton also showed how in the Central Highlands, the headwaters of the east-flowing Don have been captured by the Avon, and similarly those of the Geldie–Dee by the Feshie–Spey (see Fig. 13.2a). He believed that the initial streams once flowed eastwards on an unconformable cover of Chalk deposited on a marine-cut surface which trimmed the underlying Caledonian structures. He further believed that the highest Scottish peaks are remnants of such a surface that was tilted gently towards the east, thereby initiating the Scottish river system. After denudation had removed the Cretaceous cover, the drainage would have become superimposed on to the underlying rocks (thus explaining the present discordance), but would subsequently have been dismembered by streams such as the Spey which had already become adjusted to structure. Unfortunately for this interesting hypothesis, it is possible to show that while many discordant streams do flow eastwards, an equal number of equally discordant rivers flow in other directions, notably those flowing south-eastwards to Strathmore (see Fig. 13.2b). Other writers, such as George (1966), have attempted to explain the drainage anomalies by recourse to the idea of a major marine submergence of the Scottish massif in mid-Tertiary times. According to this hypothesis the various erosion surfaces, such as the Grampian Main Surface and the Valley Benches, were formed during pulsatory uplift. At the same time the rivers were initiated, flowing in a variety of directions across the newly emerged shore platforms towards the slowly evolving coastlines and being constantly rejuvenated into their sometimes discordant courses as the landmass was tectonically uplifted.

The third element in a typical Grampian landscape is the peat bog. Distinguishable from the raised bog and valley bog of lower altitudes, the extensive blanket bogs of the Scottish Highlands add to the desolation of the lonely upland plateaux and basins. There are numerous examples of raised bog in the Scottish lowlands (see Chapter 12), where the peaty carselands are known as 'mosses', but the type of peat bog which develops in any area depends on the plant association which has created it and this in turn depends on the mineral nutrients available in both the ground water and the rainfall. The raised bogs of the lowlands and the blanket bogs of the Grampians and the Northern Highlands differ not only in form but also in genesis and age, for they were created in different ways. The lowland raised bogs were formed after the ice sheets had retreated from the Midland Valley and many badly drained basins of boulder clay were left behind. In addition, the former coastal mud flats of calcareous clays in the Forth estuary were soon to be uplifted by post-glacial isostatic warping. Together, these waterlogged landscapes provided an ideal environment for the growth of fen-peat. The large tussocks of certain fen plants appear ultimately to have built up the surface of the fen above the level of the alkaline ground water, so that the natural acidity of the decaying vegetation was no longer neutralized. This allowed the bog moss known as *Sphagnum* and other plants, such as cotton grass (*Eriophorum vaginatum*), which thrive only in more acid water habitats, to gain a hold on the fen surface. In this way the peat grew upwards as a raised bog, the surface of which became typically convex and which now required sufficient atmospheric humidity if its upward growth was to be maintained. It must be emphasized, however, that raised bogs grew by vegetational increments as described above and that their epithet 'raised' is not related to the fact that some of them occupy raised shorelines, as on the carselands; many raised bogs are to be found in areas which have not been tectonically upwarped.

On turning to examine the blanket bogs, one finds that, unlike raised bogs, they have remained largely independent of ground-water supplies, while depending more on high rainfall and atmospheric humidity. Thus the Central Highlands and the western seaboard of Scotland exhibit ideal conditions for the growth of blanket bog, which has become a typical vegetation type, or 'climatic formation', in these heavy-rainfall areas. As it did not need to arise from local fen basins, the ubiquitous acid peat gradually blanketed much of the terrain (except on steeper slopes) during the cool, wet phases of the Flandrian. The featurelessness of many of the landscapes of Badenoch, Atholl and the Monadhliath is partly explained by their extensive blanket bogs; these areas also stand in an important transition zone in relation to the bog-vegetation character. To the west of this zone the main constituents of the blanket bogs are ling, bog myrtle, cotton grass, moor grass (*Molinia caerulea*) and deer's hair grass (*Scirpus caespitosus*), in addition to the *Sphagnum* mosses. In the lower-rainfall areas farther east, however, the blanket bogs possess much more ling, crowberry, blaeberry and cloudberry – especially on the plateau summits of the Cairngorms and Lochnagar – while bog myrtle is usually absent (Holden, 1952).

One of the best areas to view blanket bog is the Moor of Rannoch, acclaimed by many as one of the most desolate yet awesome landscapes to be found anywhere in Scotland (Walker and Lowe, 1979). Its dreary wastes of dun-coloured grasses are flecked with grey granite exposures, blotched with black peat-hags and dotted with pools of dark water. Rannoch Moor has been designated a National Nature Reserve, since its inner recesses are nearer to being a true wilderness than most other areas in Britain. On examining the geology of the area, it is somewhat surprising to discover that the great amphitheatre occupied by the Moor is floored by a medium-grained grey granite, whereas the surrounding mountains are composed mainly of schists and quartzites. An explanation seems to lie in the lithology of the rocks which surround the perimeter of the pluton: to the east and north are the Moinian quartzites, to the south the Dalradian quartzites and quartzose mica schists, to the west, beyond the pyramid of Buachaille Etive Mor (Fig. 14.3), the volcanic rocks of Glencoe (see Chapter 15). All of these peripheral rocks exhibit a resistance to denudation greater than that of the particular granite in question, so that once a shallow upland basin had been fashioned here, the ice sheets would have removed the thick accumulations of rotted rock as they overdeepened the relatively 'weak' granitic terrain (Lowe and Walker, 1976; Thorp, 1987).

There is a marked asymmetry in the west–east valley of Loch Tummel and Loch Rannoch. On the steep north-facing slopes the Scots pines of the Black Wood of Rannoch represent the largest remnant of the great Wood of Caledon to have survived south of Rothiemurchus. The south-facing slopes of the valley are not as steep as those opposing them across the loch; indeed, they are called in Gaelic *An Slios Min*, meaning 'the side of gentle slopes'. The contrast in gradient is partly reflected in the land use, for patches of improved land are common on the gentler (and also sunnier) south-facing slopes. The asymmetry is largely a result of the geological structure here, for, while the slopes to the north of Loch Rannoch are virtually dipslopes, lying almost parallel with the forty-degree south-easterly dip of the strata, those to the south of the loch oppose the angle of dip and are therefore modified escarpments. Here the shapely peak of Schiehallion (1083 m) dominates the southern skyline, its conical form resulting from the steeply dipping, tough Dalradian quartzite (Fig. 14.4) (Rast, 1958). Hereabouts is a linear outcrop of the Schiehallion Boulder Bed, a conglomerate which occurs low down in the Dalradian succession. Embedded within a layer of metamorphic

Figure 14.3 Rannoch Moor, Grampians. The blanket peat, with its ancient pine stumps, in the foreground, overlies the Rannoch Moor granite, while the peripheral peaks in the background are carved from harder metamorphic rocks of Moinian age and, in the case of Buachaille Etive Mor (centre) from Lower Old Red Sandstone lavas.

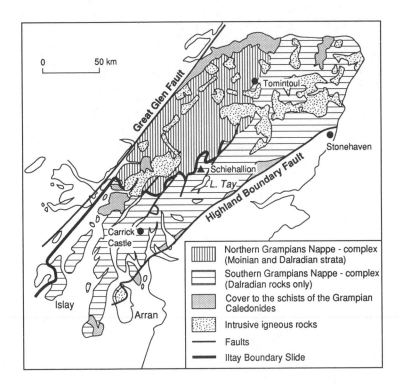

Figure 14.4 Structural divisions of the Grampians (based on material prepared by the British Geological Survey).

grit, numerous cobbles and boulders of 'erratic' lithology can be seen, all exotic to the rocks of the Central Highlands. In its general disposition the Boulder Bed is exactly like an indurated boulder clay, and it is now usually regarded as a metamorphosed till (or tillite) of the same Precambrian age as that at Portaskaig in Islay (see p. 350).

Near to Loch Tummel is the zone of the Iltay Boundary Slide (Fig. 14.4), where the Northern and Southern Nappe Complexes meet (see p. 327). Not only is the metamorphic succession complicated by overfolding and thrusting (Sturt and Harris, 1961), but it has also been severely sliced through by major north-north-east trending wrench or tear-faults (Fig. 14.4). Lateral movements of up to 8 kilometres took place – mainly in Hercynian times, for igneous dykes of Lower Old Red Sandstone age have been offset by the faulting. The latter has often resulted in the formation of belts of shattered rock, which in turn have been picked out by agents of denudation as zones of weakness. It is therefore no surprise to find that the alignment of Glen Tilt with the kink in Loch Tay, as well as the linear shapes of Loch Ericht and Loch Laidon (across Rannoch Moor), are all due to the presence of major faulting.

Loch Tummel and Loch Rannoch are not fault-guided and have often been used as an example of the discordant drainage pattern of the Central Highlands. The Rannoch valley was seen by Linton (1972) as one of fifteen major glacial troughs in the south-west Grampians which illustrate the concept of radiating valleys in glaciated lands (Figure 14.5). He was able to reconstruct the former limits of the most powerful centre of ice dispersal in Scotland by plotting the stream-lines of former ice movements, many of which followed the existing valleys carved along the strike of the Dalradian rocks. He noted that, if the existing valley

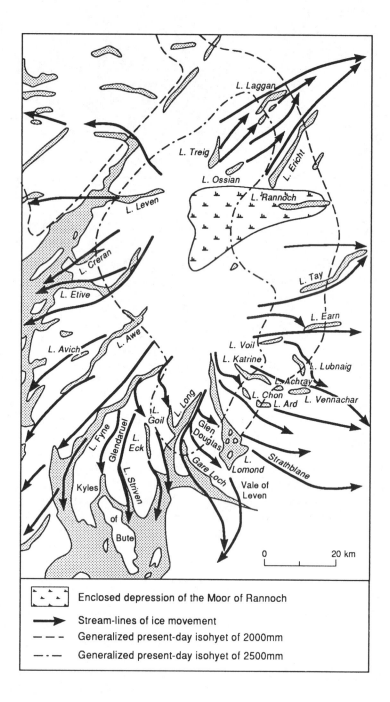

pattern did not allow radial ice dispersal, glacial breaching created new valleys
by overriding watersheds. Examples of this type of glacial breaching can be
seen in the main east–west Grampian watershed itself, now occupied by the
through-valleys of Loch Ericht and Loch Treig (Fig. 14.5).

The Highland Border Country

The topographic contrast between the high Grampians and the lower terrain of the Midland Valley is considerably simpler than the geology and structures which flank the Highland Boundary Fault itself (Ramsay, 1962), because, to the south of the Cairngorms, there is a rapid succession of contrasting strata in the Highland Border Country. To the south of the main Grampian watershed, now crossed at Drumochter Pass (452 m) by the highest railway in Britain, the River Garry flows discordantly across the regional strike south-eastwards towards Strathmore, joining first the Tummel and then the Tay near Pitlochry. In so doing it crosses from the Moinian schists on to the Dalradian rocks near Blair Atholl, where thick layers of grey and white limestones are interbedded with the slates and schists. The effect of these less resistant rocks on the scenery is quite striking, for, below the desolate moorlands around Drumochter, Glen Garry descends into the wide, fertile basin of Atholl. Although green-veined marble occurs sporadically in nearby Glen Tilt, the main Blair Atholl Limestone is quarried only for agricultural purposes and road construction. The effect of the calcareous rocks on the soils and vegetation, however, is manifest: the grassy slopes surrounding the beautiful parklands of Blair Castle seem a brighter green than usual amid the general picture of dark, rush-choked pastures on the acid Grampian soils. But it is the woodland which really takes the eye, for around Blair Atholl occur the oldest and finest larch plantations in Britain, a legacy of systematic planting in the eighteenth and nineteenth centuries by the Dukes of Atholl. Downstream the effect of the Schiehallion quartzite is seen to constrict the valley width as the Garry plunges into a thickly wooded gorge at the notorious Pass of Killiecrankie. The neighbouring Falls of Tummel were also created as a knick-point held at the edge of the tough quartzite exposure, but the falls have now, alas, been reduced in stature by the Tummel–Loch Faskally hydro-electric scheme. The peak of Ben Vrackie (841 m), carved from hard sills of epidiorite among the schists (Pantin, 1956), is an excellent viewpoint at the junction of the Garry and the Tummel; from its heathery slopes there are wide-spreading vistas of the Highland Border Country. To the east and north stretch the high Grampian tablelands, deeply scored by glacial troughs; to the west are the shining ribbon lakes of Tummel and Rannoch, with their 'Road to the Isles'; to the south, across the Ben Lui structural fold (Cummins and Shackleton, 1955; Roberts and Treagus, 1964) lies Strath Tay, whose forested flanks look down on the ancient grey cathedral of Dunkeld; to the south-west the burrowing waters of the upper Tay thread through its sinuous loch to the farmlands near Aberfeldy.

The tract of country from Breadalbane to Aberfeldy, dominated by Glen Lyon, Ben Lawers and Loch Tay, is thought to mark a transition zone between the more heavily glaciated Western Highlands and the less deeply scoured and eroded landscapes farther east. Modern writers see this as a contrast between the more deeply dissected 'weather side' of western Scotland, with its heavier precipitation both in the Pleistocene and at present, and the drier, less fragmented massifs of the Eastern Highlands. The contrast is emphasized by the fact that the last major ice advance (the Loch Lomond Readvance) reached no farther east than this transition zone. Thus the outwash from the last ice front has been carved into a number of broad, flat terraces, which in the Fortingall–Kenmore–Aberfeldy area have been an important factor in the land use of the region. Four major relief facets have been recognized in the landscape hereabouts which epitomize the broader straths of this Highland Border Country, where fingers of lowland farming and settlement infiltrate into the mountainland. The first of these is the 'haughland' of the alluvial floodplain and its associated river terraces, where the relatively fertile soils support crops of oats, turnips and hay – all fodder for the cattle and sheep of these virtually 'lowland' farms. The second facet, known as the 'braes', comprises the rocky benches and patches of hummocky glacial drift which flank the valleyfloor, where variable soils and slopes give generally poorer grazing land on which smaller marginal stock farms wage a battle against the encroaching bracken and scrub. Such rough grazing is even more characteristic of the glacially oversteepened slopes which constitute the third facet, but this land is now generally blanketed with Forestry Commission plantations. The final facet of these Highland border landscapes is made up of the open plateaux and summits above the tree-line, where peaty uplands with their acid soils and heather moor are diversified by the narrow outcrops of the Blair Atholl and Loch Tay Limestones that bring sweeter soils and bands of greener vegetation to the Highland scene (Gould and Robertson, 1985). The limestone exposures can often be picked out not only by the vegetation contrasts but also by abandoned limekilns and the sites of former 'shielings', which were the temporary summer dwellings of the crofters and their livestock during the once important but now defunct practice of transhumance.

Nowhere is the influence of calcareous soils on the mountain flora better seen than at Ben Lawers (1215 m), whose lofty summit towers above Loch Tay (Treagus, 1964). This Grampian giant is renowned for the richness of its Arctic-Alpine flora. In this case the vital factor is not so much the limestones themselves as the calcareous Ben Lawers Schists and their associated epidiorite sills, which have weathered into the basic minerals conducive to the growth of a *calcicole* (calcium-loving) flora.

Not far to the west are the Trossachs, often referred to as the 'Scottish Lake District'. Their rugged mountains, tree-clad slopes and the sparkling waters of Lochs Katrine, Achray and Vennacher are grouped in a similar pleasing combination of rock, wood and water. As the Lake District has its supporting poets, so the Trossachs have no less a bard than Sir Walter Scott, who immortalized the area in Rob Roy and the Lady of the Lake. The literal meaning of the name 'Trossachs' is 'the bristly place', and it was Archibald Geikie (1901) who was the first to see that the actual lithology was more important than absolute height in the creation of high-quality scenery. He noted how the quartzose rocks created a 'gnarled, craggy outline'. In fact the major relief has been carved from steeply dipping Dalradian schistose grits which here form part of the inverted limb of the so-called Iltay Nappe (Shackleton, 1958). The two most important members are the Ben Ledi Grits (Bowes and Convery, 1966) and the Leny Grits, which together help build the twin sentinels of the Trossachs – Ben Ledi (876 m) and Ben Venue (727 m). Much of the lower, wooded ground between the Loch Ard Forest and Loch Achray has resulted from the appearance of thick beds of red, purple and green slates within the Dalradian succession, since these are generally less resistant than the intervening grits. The slates have long been worked as a roofing material in the quarries near Aberfoyle, where their 60–70 degree dip on the skyline illustrates how weathering and erosion can produce a 'bristly' detail even in rocks which are reputedly of poor resistance to denudation. It is the steepness of the dip, allied with the rapid alternation of lithology, therefore, which helps give the region its rugged character, but Pleistocene ice has also played a significant part, for the water bodies of the Trossachs are part of the radiating pattern of glacial troughs recognized by Linton (see Fig. 14.5). Loch Chon and Loch Ard follow one radiating line, while Lochs Katrine, Achray and Venachar follow another. Glacial scouring has overdeepened the valleys at all these localities, but it is noteworthy that wherever the grits occur the valleys narrow (as at the Pass of Leny and at the Trossachs Hotel) where hard rock bars cross the valleyfloors. Like Lochs Ericht and Treig farther north, however, Loch Lubnaig, near Callander, occupies a depression cut right across a pre-glacial watershed by diffluent ice unable to find a suitable exit elsewhere.

Scotland's best-known stretch of water, Loch Lomond, is also part of the radiating pattern of glacial troughs created by the most powerful centre of ice dispersal in Britain. Its shape reflects this genesis in part, for the narrow, linear northern stretch of the loch is a repetition of all the water-filled troughs of the south-west Grampians, whether they are freshwater lochs or sea-lochs (like neighbouring Loch Long). But as Loch Lomond approaches the Highland Boundary Fault at Balmaha it changes from a narrow glacial trough 180 metres deep to a broader, shallower lowland lake a mere 23 metres in depth. The main change occurs at Luss, where a zone of slates crops out, and although the Leny Grits cross the loch at Strathcashell Point it is the Old Red Sandstone that fashions the scenery at the southern end of the loch. Here the wooded islands with their

Figure 14.6 The Highland Boundary Fault at Loch Lomond, showing the fault-line scarp of Conic Hill (background) and the linear islands in the loch. The tougher Dalradian rocks of the Grampians (left) rise above the relatively less resistant Upper Palaeozoic rocks of the Midland Valley (right).

backdrop of uplands are reminiscent of Derwentwater, although the geology is very different. The alignment of the landforms along the Boundary Fault is particularly noteworthy, the sharp ridge of Conic Hill (358 m) continuing south-eastwards through Balmaha and the islands of Inchailloch, Torrinch, Creinch and Inchmurrin to the western shores (Fig. 14.6). Away to the north, the Grampian hump of Ben Lomond (973 m) – the most southerly mountain over 900 metres in Scotland – blocks the northern skyline, but the low southern shores, with their prosperous farmlands and neat oak woods, mark the sudden transition from the Highlands to the lowlands. A study of the evolution of Loch Lomond during the Ice Age demonstrates how ice breached the former watersheds hereabouts, thereby cutting off the pre-glacial headwaters of Inveruglas from their former eastern outlet through Inversnaid to Loch Katrine. The original west–east valley now carries the artificial reservoir of Loch Arklet in a 'hanging valley' 150 metres above Loch Lomond's present trench (Fig. 14.7). It has been suggested that similar glacial interference also disrupted the former drainage pattern of the Douglas and the Luss streams farther south, which are thought originally to have flowed south-eastwards to the Endrick Water and Strathblane (Linton and Moisley, 1960). Their former courses have, however, been obliterated by the erosional capability of the major Loch Lomond Readvance glacier, which bulldozed southwards before fanning out as a piedmont lobe to the south of Luss about 10 300 years ago. An exact contemporary of the Menteith glacier (see p. 292), the Loch Lomond glacier left its mass of terminal moraines near the present lake outlet in the Leven Valley to the south of Balloch.

South Argyll

To the west of Loch Lomond one can sense the presence of the sea. The mountainous terrain of the Grampians becomes fragmented as the oceanic environment permeates the scene. Sinuous channels of sea water infiltrate the soaring peaks, while bony fingers of mountainland poke resolutely south-westwards into the Atlantic waves. Here is the ancient kingdom of Dalriada, which has given its name to the Dalradian rocks of the geological succession. Peopled by an ancient folk whose affinities lay, not surprisingly, with Ireland rather than Scotland, these peninsulas and islands of south Argyll were once a focal point in the seaways of the Celtic 'fringe', at a time during the Dark Ages when civilization had virtually disappeared elsewhere in Europe. The area now possesses such a vast number of archaeological treasures that it has been referred to as the historic cradle of Scotland, remaining the seat of Scottish power until Kenneth Macalpin conquered the Highland Picts and moved his capital to Perthshire in the ninth century AD. Today the islands, hills and glens of ancient Dalriada are scattered with old churches, Celtic crosses, megaliths, duns, vitrified forts and carved stones as a testimony to its former importance. But these same hills and glens are now virtually deserted; only the tiny coastal settlements survive amid the ubiquitous moorlands and scattered forests of this mountainous terrain. It is a land where the geology is as complicated as the remarkable coastline, a land of rocky knolls, hidden lochs, forested braes and tiny cultivated fields, where every turn in the road brings a fresh vista of seaweed-draped shorelines, rugged islands and lingering sunsets reflected in the restless ocean waters.

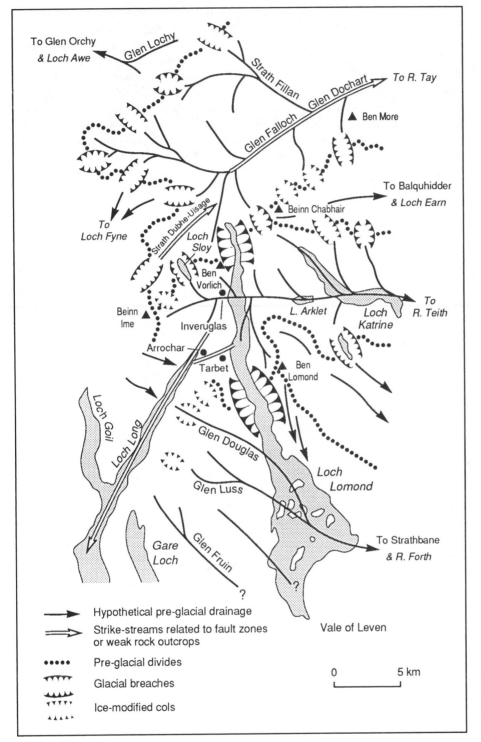

Figure 14.7 Hypothetical reconstruction of the evolution of Loch Lomond (after D.L. Linton and H.A. Moisley).

As in the Southern Grampians the structures are dominated by the gigantic recumbent overfold known as the Iltay Nappe (Roberts, 1974). In south Argyll the upside-down succession forms the so-called Cowal Arch or 'antiform' (Fig. 14.8), whose axis can be traced from the northern end of Loch Lomond, through Ben Vorlich (941 m) and Ben Ime (1012 m) in Arrochar, south-westwards through the hills of Cowal and across Loch Fyne into the peninsula of Kintyre. Thus, the hills, lochs and peninsulas of Kintyre and Cowal have the same south-west to north-east 'grain' of the Grampian Highlands. As if to counterbalance the upfold described above, the same folding has produced a complex downfold, or 'synform', farther north in Knapdale and Lorn. Here the so-called Loch Awe Syncline (Fig. 14.8) (Bailey, 1913) can be traced south-westwards from that loch and out into the Sound of Jura, where it separates the anticlinal forms of Islay and Jura from the mainland. The less resistant rocks of this complex northern

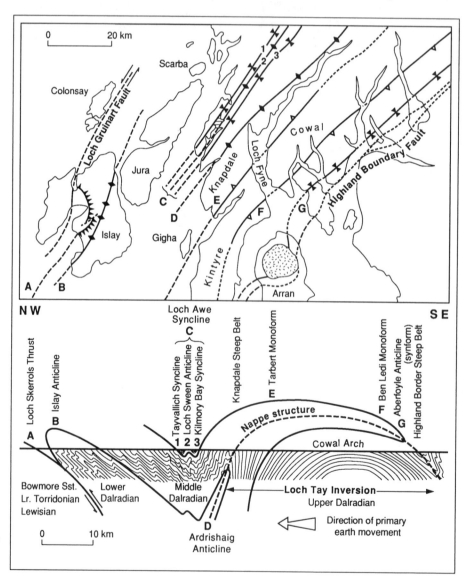

Figure 14.8 Structure of south Argyllshire (after J. L. Roberts).

downfold have been denuded into low hills and a plethora of ribby peninsulas *Cowal and Kintyre* 343
and islands in Knapdale and Nether Lorn although the harder rocks of Jura
and Islay form a final western expression of the Grampian mountains themselves.

Cowal and Kintyre

All who travel by land into Cowal must follow the twisting road from Tarbet
through Glen Croe. Above the skirts of forest the brooding Cobbler (881 m)
overlooks the lonely glens where Loch Goil and Loch Long bring the sea deeply
into the high peaks of Arrochar. The distinctive shapes of the mountains here
are due partly to the tough intrusive diorites among the quartzose mica schists,
while farther west the mountains overlooking the slender freshwater Loch Eck are
carved largely from the highly folded schistose grits of the Dalradian Assemblage
(King and Rast, 1956). The valleys are so heavily wooded with spruce and pine
that they appear gloomy and sombre after the scenic sparkle of the Trossachs
and Loch Lomond, although the natural oak woods of Strachur and Glen Branter
bring some relief. The tiny farms are few and far between in this region of
steep slopes, acid soils and heavy rainfall; except on the narrow raised beaches,
improved land is rarely found in the southern peninsulas of Cowal. Two exceptions occur, however, on the eastern and western perimeters. In the east, around
the tourist resort of Dunoon, a belt of more friable slaty soils has encouraged
the growth of market gardening and the presence of dairy herds on the pasturelands in response to the demands of tourism. Along the western shores, facing
Loch Fyne, the Loch Tay Limestone reappears and this, together with the iron-
and magnesium-rich rocks of the so-called Green Beds (whose colour is due largely
to the mineral chlorite), helps create a narrow belt of flourishing agriculture,
best seen between Otter Ferry and Ardlamont Point. On the whole, however,
Cowal will be remembered for its forests – the Argyll National Forest Park was
the first of its kind to be created in Britain.

When the broader stretches of Loch Fyne are reached, colour returns to the
landscape. In addition to the multi-coloured fodder crops and whitewashed farms
on the wider raised beaches, the shoreline contributes its red, brown and green
covering of seaweeds on the grey, knobbly rocks. The tiny fishing villages which
dot the coastline are a reminder of the former importance of Loch Fyne in the
history of the Scottish herring industry.

During the eighteenth century iron-smelting was commonplace on this forested
south-western seaboard. Following the establishment of ironworks at Bonawe
in 1711 and at Invergarry in 1730, that on Loch Fyne was set up in 1754, depending
largely, like its forerunners, on imported Cumberland ore. Although some local
haematite was used, from the valley of the River Leacainn, the location of the
industry was decided by the extensive natural woodlands of oak, ash, beech, birch
and holly, all excellent for producing charcoal. Although the deep sea-lochs
provided a cheap means of transport, the short-term exploitation meant that
thousands of acres of Scottish woodland were lost before the Carron works at
Falkirk began to utilize coal instead of charcoal and steam instead of the ordinary
water power of the burns (see p. 291).

Like its smaller eastern counterparts in Arrochar and Cowal, the great sea-loch
of Loch Fyne is an example of a fjord. In contrast to the broad estuaries of

Scotland's eastern coast, the mountainous western seaboard is deeply funnelled and scored by these sinuous water bodies (see Fig. 14.8). They represent the drowned seaward ends of a pre-glacial drainage system that has experienced severe overdeepening by ice sheets during the Pleistocene, the ice sheets having been centred much closer to the western than to the eastern coasts. Thus, the major fjords of Loch Fyne and Loch Long have been deeply eroded along the 'grain' of the Caledonian folding by ice from the important dispersion centre of the south-west Grampians. Loch Awe follows a similar orientation, although the post-glacial marine submergence has failed to inundate its deeply ice-scoured trough. Farther south the change in direction of Loch Fyne, together with the Kyles of Bute, Loch Striven and Loch Goil, has been taken as evidence of a former south-easterly-draining river network now drowned by the post-glacial transgression.

Where Loch Fyne reaches the open sea to the north of Arran, the long, narrow peninsula of Kintyre protrudes some 65 kilometres into the Atlantic to the south of the fjord of West Loch Tarbert, which almost cuts through the neck of the peninsula. Composed essentially of the same lithology and structures as Cowal, the backbone of the peninsula nevertheless fails to achieve the high relief of its Grampian neighbour across Loch Fyne. For this reason many would regard Kintyre as being outside the Highlands, despite its location to the north of the Highland Boundary Fault. Indeed, as if to demonstrate this transitional character, its southern limits include exposures of Old Red Sandstone and Carboniferous rocks. Furthermore, from a historical and sociological standpoint Kintyre has few affinities with the Highlands, as befits a region in the same latitude as Ayrshire. Since the Campbells of Argyll chose to settle the peninsula with successive plantations of Lowlanders, it is not surprising that the traditional Highland way of life is missing (Carmichael, 1974). Thus, crofting villages will not be found, since they have long been replaced by medium-sized farms and large fields. Kintyre's low-lying western coast, with its reduced rainfall and better soils, contrasts with the hilly eastern margins, many of which have been given over to forests. Agriculturally, the western and southern coastlands of Kintyre, together with the fertile island of Gigha, are the most favoured parts of Argyll, with arable land more extensive than elsewhere, although the main concern is with dairying, especially on the loamy soils of the extensive raised-beach terraces. The metamorphic limestones and mineral-rich Green Beds also crop out along the western margins, bringing more fertile soils wherever they occur. Finally, in the Laggan, the lowland around Campbeltown, Carboniferous Limestone adds to the richness of the soils, while Old Red Sandstone has a similar effect in the south-eastern corner around Southend. Only at the Mull of Kintyre itself do the wild moorlands and steep 430 metre hills foster a feeling of the Highlands. The survival of the Limestone Coal Group at Macrihanish in south Kintyre (McCallien and Anderson, 1930), surrounded on all sides by Dalradian rocks, appears to be the fortuitous result of downfaulting.

Knapdale and Nether Lorn

To the north of Loch Fyne and Loch Tarbert the regions of Knapdale and Nether Lorn lie north-west of the Iltay Nappe, so that, unlike the inverted strata of

Cowal and Kintyre, their lithological succession is the right way up. This is the zone known as the Loch Awe Syncline (see Fig. 14.8), although the minor folding within this structure is enough to warrant the term 'synclinorium' (Bailey, 1913). In Knapdale the detailed folding is so tight that a series of steep anticlines and synclines dominates the Caledonian structures. Denudation has picked out the latter to create a perfect example of the phenomenon known as *inversion of relief* where all the anticlinal arches, being most vulnerable to erosion because their joints are under tension, have ultimately been worn down to form lowlands or valleys. Conversely, the more resistant synclinal structures, their joints closed by compression, are frequently left upstanding to form tracts of higher land. So it is in Knapdale, where the invasion of the sea into the glacially overdeepened valleys has merely served to emphasize the influence of structure upon relief. Thus, Loch Sween and Loch Caolisport have been eroded along the anticlinal axes, while the rugged peninsulas of Tayvallich and Kilmory correspond with the synclinal arrangement of the tough Crinan Grits (see Fig. 14.8) (Allison, 1940).

Although narrow exposures of metamorphic limestone in the Tayvallich peninsula and near Loch Crinan help alleviate the general acidity of the soils, the widespread outcrop of the Crinan Grits in Knapdale militates against major land improvement. The scene is therefore one of poor-quality farming, and it is fortunate that the Forestry Commission has made great efforts to increase the land potential by planting the extensive forests of Knapdale and Kilmichael. These have augmented the natural oak woods of the rocky peninsulas around the head of Loch Sween to create a sylvan scene rarely encountered on the western coastlands, partly because Knapdale is sheltered from the searing Atlantic winds by the high mountains of Jura. The Caledonian trend is clearly reflected in the terrain and land use around Loch Awe, where the rough grazing and birch scrub often mark the linear outcrops of the quartzites and the countless epidiorite sills that protrude as rocky ridges above the forests and scattered strips of improved land, which in turn are restricted to the narrow parallel depressions that have been glacially etched out in the less resistant limestones. The contrast between the landscapes of Kintyre and Knapdale could not be more marked. The virtually treeless Kintyre, with its coastal cliffs and far-ranging seascapes, is replaced by the thickly wooded coastline farther north, characterized by its hidden bays, rocky ridges and restricted views. The better soils of the south, where the large prosperous farms have 50 to 60 per cent of their land under arable, contrast with the poorer acid soils and rush-choked pastures of the north, on whose tiny crofts and small farms the farmers succeed in ploughing only about one-third of their holdings because of the rocky terrain.

The old drover's route through Inverary, from the Hebrides to the lowland markets, has been travelled and described by Burns, Keats, Wordsworth, Johnson and Boswell, while Turner painted its bays, hills and woods with an artistic ecstasy that soared above all considerations of topographical detail. The reasons for such popularity are not far to seek, for in Lorn the high Grampian peaks are mirrored in the waters of Loch Linnhe, Loch Awe and Loch Etive, giving a forestaste of the spectacular scenery that makes western Scotland so renowned.

The tough granite of Ben Cruachan (1125 m) overlooks the ice-scoured and lake-dotted plateau of Nether Lorn, to the south-east of Oban. This plateau is made up largely of successive sheets of basaltic lavas, lying upon and intercalated with beds of purple grits, grey shales and red sandstones. Archibald Geikie (1882) noted that these sediments were of Old Red Sandstone age and suggested that, since their basal conglomerates were composed of volcanic and metamorphic boulders of local origin, this Old Red outlier was formed as a shallow lake deposit, now surviving only by virtue of its thick blanket of contemporary Oban lavas. The conglomerates extend into Upper Lorn, where they form much of the coastline from Ganavan Bay to Dunstaffnage Castle, as well as Maiden Island at the mouth of Oban harbour. Dunstaffnage looks acrosss Loch Etive to the Moss of Achnacree, a bog that accumulated on a bank of glacial outwash from the Loch Lomond Readvance. Here an ancient *palaeosol*, buried under a few metres of sub-Atlantic (Late Flandrian) peat, demonstrates a rare example of soil degradation due to primitive cultivation practices. (Soulsby, 1976). The ivy-smothered Dunollie Castle sits on a basalt-capped sandstone crag at Oban's harbour entrance, while the town itself has grown in tiers like an amphitheatre around the bay. The handsome terraces of the Victorian esplanade were built on a raised-beach platform, whose low rock cliff is pitted with sea caves now raised to a height of about 12 metres above the present shore. Such caves once provided shelter for some of Scotland's earliest inhabitants: numerous Mesolithic artefacts have been discovered there, testifying to the hunting and gathering lifestyle of the so-called Azilian culture some 8000 years ago.

The islands of south Argyll

The terraced island of Kerrera, which acts as a breakwater for Oban Bay, is composed of a combination of Old Red Sandstone, igneous basalts and metamorphic graphitic schists. Farther south are the islands of Seil, Luing, Easdale, Shuna and Torsa, known as the Slate Islands which, with the Ballachulish quarries on Loch Leven, once supplied most of the roofing material for western Scotland. On Seil the friable slates weather to reasonable soils which support good grazing land amid the low hillocks and ridges, but on Easdale, the desolate quarries around the harbour are now flooded and closed. When visited by Thomas Pennant in 1772, Easdale alone was exporting over 2 million slates to England and across the Atlantic each year, and less than a century later this annual output had passed the 7 million mark. All production has now ceased in the Slate Islands.

The hilltop behind Ellanbeich village on Easdale Sound is a wonderful viewpoint for the islands of south Argyll. Away to the south-west lies the angular outline of the Garvellach Isles, their cuesta-like form presenting vertical cliffs north-westwards to the Firth of Lorn. These holy 'Isles of the Sea', composed of Precambrian quartzose tillites and easily weathered limestones, contain some of the oldest Christian ecclesiastical buildings surviving in the British Isles. To the south the dark pyramid of Scarba raises its head high above the low-lying slaty isles of Lunga and Luing, for it is bolstered by the tough Islay Quartzite which also forms the backbone of Jura and Islay. On all these islands the poor thin soils of the quartzitic rocks support only moorland.

Except for a narrow band of slates, conglomerates and phyllites along its eastern margin, where the majority of the settlements are found, Jura is built entirely of this unyielding Middle Dalradian quartzite which dips fairly steeply south-westwards to the Sound of Jura (Fig. 14.9). Such a tough metamorphic rock is invariably associated with steep upland landforms, and this barren island is no

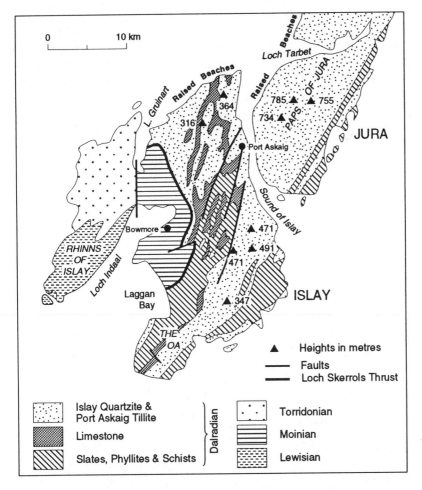

Figure 14.9 Geology of Islay
and southern Jura (based on
material prepared by the
British Geological Survey).

exception. Its mountainous spine culminates at the southern end in the three
shapely cones known as the Paps of Jura – Beinn an Oir (784 m); Beinn Siantaidh
(755 m); and Binn a'Chaolais (734 m). MacGregor (1953) believes that their
steep-sided elegance can be compared only with the famous Cuillins of Skye.
They rise abruptly from the narrow coastal plain, and their conical summits
are surrounded by shimmering aprons of angular screes which make any ascent
to their massive cairns an arduous business.

The name 'Jura' means 'deer island', and even today it carries an overwhelming
number of red deer (some twenty times the human population) and whose
numbers, according to Darling (1955), are too high for an ecological balance to
be preserved. The few bays and natural harbours along the eastern coast have
been carved from the less resistant slates and phyllites; where, as at Loch na Mile
and Lowlandman's Bay, off-shore reefs of epidiorite sills occur they act as
natural breakwaters (Fig. 14.9). It is on Jura's west coast, however, that its greatest
geological interest may be found, for here is a unique collection of raised-beach
phenomena (Fig. 14.10). First mapped in detail by McCann (1961), this staircase
of Late Pleistocene erosional and depositional shore forms reaches its zenith in
western Scotland. The highest strandline stands at an elevation of about 33 metres
in Jura, and its broad rock platform is backed by high wave-cut cliffs. Although

McCann believed this High Rock Platform in west Jura and north-east Islay to be of interglacial age, others suggest that it could have been produced by a combination of wave and frost action during both the Loch Lomond Readvance and the previous glacial (Sissons, 1982). Calculations show that a platform of this width could have taken some 28 000 years to be eroded (Dawson, 1982; 1983). At several places in west Jura beach-shingle ridges occur on the High Rock Platform, separated from it by a layer of till, suggesting that a glacial episode intervened between the fashioning of the platform and the deposition of the beach shingle. The raised-beach shingles are terminated seawards by the clifftop of a lower rock platform, termed the Main Rock Platform, which has been correlated with a similar feature in the Firth of Lorn and eastern Mull (Gray, 1974). First thought to be of interglacial age it is now believed to owe its origin to periglacial shore erosion in glacial times (Gray, 1978). The Main Rock Platform of Jura stands at 8 metres but declines in elevation as it is traced southwards from Jura to Islay (at more than 0.5 metres per kilometre gradient), while a similar feature on the mainland between Knapdale and Kintyre is also tilted by glacio-isostatic

Figure 14.10 Raised beaches on the Isle of Jura, also showing the quartzite peaks of the Paps of Jura beyond the inlet of Loch Tarbert. The late-glacial beach ridges (foreground) stand at 33 metres, above the conspicuous cliffline which overlooks two lower raised beaches, at 8 metres and 1–2 metres, respectively.

warping (0.12 metres per kilometre gradient). Finally, a very low shore platform (1–2 metres above OD) is found in Jura, Islay and Colonsay. Although washed by present tides it bears the marks of glacial erosion and must pre-date the region's last ice advance (Dawson, 1980). Since a widespread feature at a similar elevation throughout the Hebrides appears to be unwarped it must have been unaffected by glacio-isostatic uplift (Dawson, 1984).

Islay has a much more complicated geological structure than Jura (Allison, 1933), and this is reflected in its unusual shape and topography (Fig. 14.9). Nevertheless, certain lithological continuities between Jura and Islay can be recognized, since the Sound of Islay is very narrow, despite its glacial overdeepening. In the first place, the slates and phyllites of eastern Jura continue into south-east Islay, where they create a similar low-lying landscape of bare epidiorite ridges, slaty hollows of rough grazing and birch-oak scrub, all bounded by a broken coastline of linear bays and islands. A further scenic comparison is possible between the mountainous ridge of quartzite in Jura and its continuation south-westwards along the Caledonian 'grain' into the peaks of south-east Islay, although in this case the summits scarcely rise above the 490 metre contour. Nevertheless, as with the Paps of Jura, their corries and drift-dammed lochans suggest that small ice caps existed on both these islands during the Loch Lomond Readvance cold phase.

The steep south-easterly dip of the Islay Quartzite is similar to that in Jura, and together the structures of their highest hills may be taken as the south-eastern flank of the so-called Islay Anticline (Fig. 14.9) (Bailey, 1917). The opposing north-westerly-dipping flank can be seen in northern Islay, where the quartzite reappears to form the sharp hills which terminate at the magnificent raised beaches on the lonely headland of Rubha a'Mhail. The intervening crest of the anticline has been denuded so that the quartzites have been destroyed and the underlying slates, limestones and phyllites uncovered (Fig. 14.9). Since this complex succession of metamorphics (known collectively as the Mull of Oa Phyllites) has proved less resistant to erosion than the flanking quartzites, they now correspond to a lowland corridor between Port Askaig and Bowmore (Green, 1924). As these relatively softer rocks are traced south-westwards past Duich and Laggan Bay into the southern peninsula of the Oa itself, they form a broad coastal lowland. Despite its low elevation, however, quite extensive peat bogs and coastal dunes have restricted the land use, so that there is mainly rough grazing in between the few scattered arable plots around the cottages. A distinctive feature of this lowland is the series of gigantic peat stacks which line the road from Bowmore to Port Ellen. Much of this peat is still used commercially in the production of the well-known Islay malt whisky, although lowland coal is now imported for heating the distilleries, whilst island-grown barley is no longer used.

The other wide coastal lowlands which surround the sea inlets of Loch Gruinart and Loch Indaal are also thickly covered with superficial deposits of boulder clay, raised beach, peat bog and blown sand. Where the land is well drained, therefore, large stretches of arable and high-quality pastureland can be seen on the red loamy soils around Bowmore, Gruinart and Port Charlotte. In addition, there are the broad bands of Islay Limestone, which bring swathes of brighter green to the pastures of the central corridor and have been quarried at Ballygrant for use both as a crop fertilizer and as a source of lime-wash for the houses.

The redness of the soils around Bowmore is due to the fact that a major geological boundary has been crossed. Although it cannot easily be seen beneath the superficial deposits, an important line of thrust-faulting occurs between Laggan Bay and Loch Gruinart. This is the so-called Loch Skerrols Thrust, which marks the line where Dalradian rocks were forcibly pushed westwards onto the older Bowmore Sandstone along a steeply angled plane of faulting during the Caledonian deformation (see Figs 14.8 and 14.9). It has been suggested that the Loch Skerrols Thrust is in fact the Islay equivalent of the Moine Thrust (see Fig. 15.7). Furthermore, the Bowmore Sandstone is now thought to be Moinian in age, although the western peninsula of the Rhinns of Islay is composed of Torridonian and Lewisian rocks, the oldest so far encountered in Scotland and a further reminder that one is moving gradually towards the Archaean 'foreland' of the north-west. The Torridonian grits, slates and conglomerates occupy the northern end of the peninsula, where they have been worn down to a lake-studded, peat-covered coastal platform. Farther south, however, the true Rhinns of Islay are composed of acid and basic Lewisian gneisses, seamed with epidiorite intrusions. The knobbly, ice-polished, rocky surface, with its low rounded hills, rock pools and peat bogs, gives a preview of the landscapes of the Outer Hebrides. But, as with those islands, patches of blown sand, shelly beaches and raised-beach terraces bring welcome oases of pastoral green to these cliff-girt, storm-lashed western headlands. The curving western coastlines of both Loch Indaal and Loch Gruinart have been carved along a different type of fault – a tear- or wrench-fault, the Loch Gruinart Fault, which cuts off the Archaean rocks of the Rhinns from the Bowmore Sandstone in the east.

Before leaving the fascinating scenery of Islay, two other points of geological interest must be noted. The first of these concerns the presence of the so-called 'Boulder Bed' which is exposed between the Islay Quartzite and the underlying limestones near to Port Askaig (Kilburn *et al.*, 1965). This is another example of the Precambrian boulder clay or tillite already encountered on the slopes of Schiehallion in the Central Grampians (see p. 335). The second phenomenon is the suite of late-glacial raised beaches occurring around the coasts, but which is especially well developed along Islay's northern shores.

Farther north on Colonsay and Oronsay, similar late-glacial strandlines can be traced in between the low rocky hillocks from coast to coast. It is partly owing to these marine sands and gravels that the isles of Colonsay and Oronsay are among the most fertile of the Hebrides. In addition, however, the Lower Torridonian mudstones, flagstones and phyllites (Stewart, 1962) have a moderately good lime content, so that the light gravelly soils support extensive tracts of hayfield and arable land. Despite the lowness of its hills – Carnan Eoin reaches 143 metres – rare examples of natural woodland survive in the sheltered hollows, with birch and oak predominant among the scrubland of hazel, rowan, willow and aspen.

One of the most remarkable features on Colonsay is the northern vale of Kiloran, which Weir (1971) describes as 'slung like a yellow hammock between hills of purple heather'. Sheltered by its surrounding ridges from the Atlantic winds, this fertile flower-decked, loch-filled valley is one of the most delightful of the Hebridean landscapes. The tidal island of Oronsay, at the south end of Colonsay, is also a place of dazzling beaches, dunes and rocky skerries (MacGregor, 1953). It was here that St Columba first landed in Scotland in AD 563, but since he could still see Ireland from the highest hill he sailed on to Iona (see Chapter 16). Nevertheless, the ancient priory ruins survive on the site of his original foundation, although it is the much older Mesolithic remains among the dunes which have brought most fame to Oronsay. Here some of Scotland's earliest inhabitants lived some 8000 years ago by hunting and fishing along these hospitable shorelines. Known as strand-loopers, these Azilian folk (similar to those of the Oban caves, see p. 346) left sand-hill middens of mussel shells and bones, including those of the now extinct great auk (Wright and Peach, 1911).

Bibliography

Allison, A. (1933) The Dalradian succession in Islay and Jura. *Quart. J. Geol. Soc.*, **89**, 125–44.

Allison, A. (1940) Loch Awe succession and tectonics: Kilmartin–Tayvallich–Danna. *Quart. J. Geol. Soc.*, **96**, 423–45.

Anderson, J.G.C. (1947) The geology of the Highland border: Stonehaven to Arran. *Trans. R. Soc. Edinb.*, **61**, 479–515.

Anderson, J.G.C.(1955) The Moinian and Dalradian rocks between Glen Roy and the Monadliath Mountains. *Trans. R. Soc. Edinb.*, **63**, 15–36.

Bailey, E.B. (1913) The Loch Awe Syncline (Argyllshire). *Quart. J. Geol. Soc.*, **69**, 280–307.

Bailey, E.B. (1917) The Islay Anticline (Inner Hebrides). *Quart. J. Geol. Soc.*, **72**, 132–59.

Bailey, E.B. (1922) The structure of the South West Highlands of Scotland. *Quart. J. Geol. Soc.*, **78**, 82–127.

Bailey, E.B. (1923) The metamorphism of the South West Highlands. *Geol. Mag.*, **60**, 317–31.

Birks, H.J.B. and Matthews, R.W. (1978) Studies in the vegetational history of Scotland. 5: Late Devensian and early Flandrian pollen and macrofossil stratigraphy at Abernethy Forest, Inverneshire. *New Phytol.*, **80**, 455–84.

Bowes, D.R. and Convery, H.J.E. (1966) Ben Ledi Grits and albite schists. *Scot. J. Geol.*, **1**, 295–9.

Carmichael, A. (1974) *Kintyre*. David and Charles.

Cummins, W.A. and Shackleton, R.M. (1955) The Ben Lui Recumbent Syncline (S.W. Highlands). *Geol. Mag.*, **92**, 353–63.

Darling, F.F. (1955) *West Highland Survey: An Essay in Human Ecology*. Oxford University Press. 438 pp.

Dawson, A.G. (1980) The Low Rock Platform in western Scotland. *Proc. Geol. Assoc.*, **91**, 339–44.

Dawson, A.G. (1982) Lateglacial sea-level changes and ice-limits in Islay, Jura and Scarba, Scottish Inner Hebrides. *Scot. J. Geol.*, **18**, 253–65.

Dawson, A.G. (1983) *Islay and Jura, Scottish Hebrides*. Field Guide. Quat. Res. Assoc. 31 pp.

Dawson, A.G. (1984) Quaternary sea-level changes in western Scotland. *Quat. Sci. Rev.*, **3**, 311–43.

Dubois, A.D. and Ferguson, D.K. (1985) The climatic history of pine in the Cairngorms based on radiocarbon dates and stable isotope analysis, with an account leading up to its colonisation. *Rev. Palaeobot. Palynol.*, **46**, 55–80.

Geikie, A. (1882) *A Textbook of Geology*. Macmillan.

Geikie, A. (1901) *The Scenery of Scotland viewed in Connection with its Physical Geology* (3rd edn). Macmillan. 481 pp.

George, T.N. (1966) Geomorphic evolution in Hebridan Scotland. *Scot. J. Geol.*, **2**, 1–34.

Gould, J.H. and Robertson, J.H. (1985) Soils and their related plant communities on the Dalradian limestones of some sites in central Perthshire, Scotland. *J. Ecol.*, **73**, 91–112.

Gray, J.M. (1974) The Main Rock Platform of the Firth of Lorn, western Scotland. *Trans. Inst. Br. Geog.*, **61**, 81–99.

Gray, J. M. (1978) Low-level shore platforms in the south-west Scottish Highlands: altitude, age and correlation. *Trans. Inst. Brit. Geog.* (NS.), **3**, 151–64.

Green, J. F. N. (1924) The structure of the Bowmore–Portaskaig District of Islay. *Quart. J. Geol. Soc.*, **80**, 72–100.

Gunson, A. R. (1975) The vegetation history of north east Scotland, in A. M. D. Gemmell (ed.), *Quaternary Studies in NE Scotland*. Aberdeen University Press, 30–8.

Harris, A. L., Bradbury, H. J. and McGonigal, M. H. (1976) The evolution and transport of the Tay Nappe. *Scot. J. Geol.*, **12**, 103–13.

Holden, A. E. (1952) *Plant Life in the Scottish Highlands*. Oliver & Boyd. 319 pp.

Johnson, M. R. W. (1965) Dalradian, in G. Y. Craig (ed.), *The Geology of Scotland*. (1st edn). Oliver & Boyd. 115–60.

Johnstone, G. S. (1966) *The Grampian Highlands* (3rd edn). British Regional Geology HMSO. 103 pp.

Kilburn, C., Pitcher, W. S. and Shackleton, R. M. (1965) The stratigraphy and origin of the Portaskaig Boulder Bed series (Dalradian). *Geol. J.*, **4**, 343–60.

King, B. C. and Rast, N. (1956) The small-scale structures of south-eastern Cowal, Argyllshire. *Geol. Mag.*, **93**, 185–95.

King, R. B. (1971) Boulder polygons and stripes in the Cairngorm Mountains, Scotland. *J. Glaciol.*, **10**, 375–86.

Linton, D. L. (1951) Problems of Scottish scenery. *Scot. Geog. Mag.*, **67**, 65–85.

Linton, D. L. (1972) Radiating valleys in glaciated lands. In C. Embleton (ed.), *Glaciers and Glacial Erosion*. Geographical Readings. Macmillan. 130–48.

Linton, D. L. and Moisley, H. A. (1960) The origin of Loch Lomond. *Scot. Geog. Mag.*, **76**, 26–37.

Lowe, J. J. and Walker, M. J. C. (1976) Radiocarbon dates and deglaciation of Rannoch Moor, Scotland. *Nature*, **264**, 632–3.

MacGregor, A. A. (1953) *Skye and the Inner Hebrides*. Hale. 328 pp.

Macnair, P. (1908) *The Geology and Scenery of the Grampians*. Glasgow.

McCallien, W. J. and Anderson, R. N. (1930) The Carboniferous sediments of Kintyre. *Trans. R. Soc. Edinb.*, **56**, 599–625.

McCann, S. B. (1961) The raised beaches of North East Islay and western Jura, Argyll. *Trans. Inst. Brit. Geog.*, **35**, 1–16.

McVean, D. N. (1964) Ecology of Scots pine in the Scottish Highlands. *J. Ecol.*, **51**, 671–86.

McVean, D. N. and Lockie, J. D. (1969) *Ecology and Land Use in Upland Scotland*. Edinburgh University Press. 134 pp.

Mercy, E. L. P. (1965). Caledonian igneous activity, in G. Y. Craig (ed.), *The Geology of Scotland*. (1st edn). Oliver & Boyd. 229–67.

Pantin, H. M. (1956) The petrology of the Ben Vrackie epidiorites and their contact rocks. *Trans. Geol. Soc. Glasgow*, **22**, 48–79.

Peach, B. N. and Horne, J. (1930) *Chapters on the Geology of Scotland*. Oxford University Press.

Pears, N. V. (1967) Present tree-lines of the Cairngorm Mountains. *J. Ecol.*, **55**, 815–30.

Ramsay, D. M. (1962) The Highland Boundary Fault: reverse or wrench-fault? *Nature*, **195**, 1190.

Rast, N. (1958) The tectonics of the Schiehallion Complex. *Quart. J. Geol. Soc.*, **114**, 25–46.

Read, H. H. (1948) *The Grampian Highlands* (2nd edn). British Regional Geology. HMSO.

Roberts, J. L. (1974) The structure of the Dalradian rocks in the South West Highlands of Scotland. *J. Geol. Soc. Lond.*, **130**, 93–134.

Roberts, J. L. and Treagus, J. E. (1964) A re-interpretation of the Ben Lui Fold. *Geog. Mag.*, **101**, 512–16.

Shackleton, R. M. (1958) Downward-facing structures of the Highland border. *Quart. J. Geol. Soc.*, **113**, 361–92.

Sissons, J. B. (1972) The last glaciers in part of the south east Grampians. *Scot. Geog. Mag.*, **88**, 168–81.

Sissons, J. B. (1974) A late-glacial ice cap in the central Grampians, Scotland. *Trans. Inst. Br. Geog.*, **62**, 92–114.

Sissons, J. B. (1977) *The Scottish Highlands*. INQUA Guide. Geo Abstracts. 48 pp.

Sissons, J.B. (1979) The Loch Lomond Readvance in the Cairngorm Mountains. *Scot. Geog. Mag.*, **95**, 66–82.

Sissons, J.B. (1982) The so-called high 'interglacial' rock shoreline of western Scotland. *Trans. Inst. Br. Geog.* (NS), **7**, 205–16.

Soulsby, J.A. (1976) Palaeoenvironmental interpretation of a buried soil at Achnacree, Argyll. *Trans. Inst. Br. Geog.* (NS), **1**, 279–83.

Stewart, A.D. (1962) On the Torridonian sediments of Colonsay and their relationships to the main outcrop in north-west Scotland. *Liv. and Manch. Geol. J.*, **3**, 121–55.

Storrie, M.C. (1962) The Scotch whisky industry. *Trans. Inst. Br. Geog.*, **31**, 97–114.

Sturt, B.A. and Harris, A.L. (1961) The metamorphic history of the Loch Tummel area, central Perthshire. *Liv. and Manch. Geol. J.*, **2**, 689–711.

Sugden, D.E. (1968) The selectivity of glacial erosion in the Cairngorm Mountains, Scotland. *Trans. Inst. Br. Geog.*, **45**, 79–92.

Sugden, D.E. (1969) The age and form of corries in the Cairngorms. *Scot. Geog. Mag.*, **85**, 34–46.

Sugden, D.E. (1970) Landforms of deglaciation in the Cairngorm Mountains, Scotland. *Trans. Inst. Br. Geog.*, **51**, 201–19.

Sugden, D.E. (1973) Delimiting Zone III glaciers in the eastern Grampians. *Scot. Geog. Mag.*, **89**.

Thompson, F. (1974) *The Highlands and Islands*. Hale. 315 pp.

Thorp, P.W. (1987) Late Devensian ice sheet in the western Grampians, Scotland. *J. Quat. Sci.*, **2**, 103–12.

Treagus, J.E. (1964) Notes on the structure of the Ben Lawers Synform. *Geol. Mag.*, **101**, 260–700.

Walker, M.J.C. and Lowe, J.J. (1979) Post-glacial environmental history of Rannoch Moor, Scotland, 2. *J. Biogeog.*, **6**, 349–62.

Watson, J. (1963) Some problems concerning the evolution of the Caledonides of the Scottish Highlands. *Proc. Geol. Assoc.*, **74**, 213–58.

Weir, T. (1971) Rediscovering Colonsay. *Country Life*, **1026**.

Whitten, E.H.T. (1959) A study of two direction of folding: the structural geology of the Monadhlaith and mid-Strathspey. *J. Geol.*, **67**, 14–47.

Wright, W.B. and Peach, A.M. (1911) The Neolithic remains of Colonsay, etc. *Geol. Mag.*, **8**, 164–75.

Young, J.A.T. (1978) The landforms of Upper Strathspey. *Scot. Geog. Mag.*, **94**, 76–94.

Glen Mor and the Western Highlands

The Firth of Lorn, together with its continuation, Loch Linnhe, marks an important line of transition in the Scottish landscape, for northwards lie the remarkable landforms of the farthest Hebrides; furthermore, once across the Great Glen one has left the Grampians for the Western and Northern Highlands.

Nowhere else in Britain is a topographical boundary line so linear as that followed by the chain of lochs between Loch Linnhe and the Moray Firth. Here is the gigantic gash known as Glen Mor, or the Great Glen of Albyn, which has been carved along the line of one of Britain's major faults. This remarkable physical feature, where selective erosion by glaciers has transformed the shatter zone of the fault line into a steep-sided trough, runs across Scotland for a distance of almost 160 kilometres from the island of Lismore to beyond Inverness. This line of weakness in the mountainous Highlands has provided a ready-made means of communication from coast to coast, which is partly reflected in the Caledonian Canal, constructed between 1803 and 1822. Originally surveyed by James Watt but later built by Thomas Telford, this artificial channel linked together the existing lochs of Glen Mor, thus allowing small vessels to avoid the stormy northern passage of the Pentland Firth.

Loch Linnhe and its region

Where the enclosed waters of Loch Linnhe pass imperceptibly seawards into the Firth of Lorn, the estuary contains many islands, including Shuna, Lismore and its satellites. These islands, together with the wooded peninsulas of Barcaldine and south Appin, nowhere rise above the 150 metre contour, thus providing ribbons of coastal lowland, most with a reasonable agricultural potential in a region which is almost completely dominated by relatively unproductive mountainland. This favoured eastern shoreline of Loch Linnhe, midway between the thriving urban centres of Oban and Fort William, supports a rural way of life not dissimilar to that of other marginal hill country in south Argyll. A contrast is at once apparent, therefore, between these lands of Appin, Benderloch and Lorn and the more rugged, empty mountains and moorlands of Ardgour and Morvern that flank the western shores of Loch Linnhe and which will be examined later in this chapter.

Lismore, with its familiar lighthouse, is a long narrow island which dominates the watery crossroads where the Sound of Mull and the fjord of Loch Etive intersect the broader marine straits of Linnhe and Lorn. Like neighbouring Shuna, Lismore is composed of a Dalradian metamorphosed limestone which has weathered into a fertile *rendzina* soil. Since the limestone has also been extensively quarried and burned in the past for use as an agricultural fertilizer, it is not difficult to understand the derivation of the name 'Lismore', which means the 'great garden'. Some of the old lime kilns were constructed in caves and notches of the raised-beach Main Rock Platform which makes such a distinctive feature on these islands (Gray, 1974). This is the same platform which occurs around Oban, where the well-known Dog Stone is in fact an uplifted sea-stack, and also on Kerrera, whose 'raised' wave-cut arch below Gylen Castle is another local curiosity. This raised shoreline creates one further noteworthy landform, the so-called Shepherd's Hat on Eilean nan Gamhna, where the unconsumed rock knob of the central 'crown' stands above the wide 'brim' of the platform.

In this region the signs of glacial erosion are manifest everywhere, but are nowhere better illustrated than in the long, curving fjord of Loch Etive (Gray, 1975). Like its neighbouring fjords of Loch Creran and Loch Leven, Loch Etive was gouged out by glaciers along pre-existing lines of weakness, including a section of the Pass of Brander fault-line (Fig. 15.1). This same fracture, incidentally, was instrumental in downfaulting the Old Red Sandstone lavas of the Lorn Plateau relative to the massif of the Etive granitic complex (see below). The sea-bed profile of Loch Etive's overdeepened glacial trough, unlike a normal drowned river valley, or *ria*, does not deepen systematically as it is traced seawards, but is composed of a series of interconnected rock basins. These are a response to selective glacial erosion, whereby glaciers tend to overdeepen when the trough walls are constricted by hard rock zones (such as the Etive granites). Farther seaward, however, where glaciers pass into tracts of less resistant rocks and where the valley widens, they have room to expand laterally, thus reducing downcutting and leaving a rock barrier or threshold across the valley mouth.

Figure 15.1 Loch Etive, Grampians, looking north-east along this lengthy fjord. The granite peak of Ben Starav dominates the skyline to the right of the loch's upper reaches, while the distant peaks belong to the Glencoe volcanic complex (see also Fig. 15.2).

During the post-glacial rise of sea level, however, many of the coastal troughs became drowned to form fjords characterized by a shallow submerged threshold at the newly created sea-loch entrance. Such is the case at the mouth of Loch Etive, for beneath the Connel Bridge the submerged rock barrier has produced the well-known Falls of Lora. At ebb tide the waters of Loch Linnhe fall faster than those of Loch Etive because of the restricting threshold, thus creating a cataract several metres high. During flood tide the opposite situation prevails, so that sea water descends noisily into Loch Etive at the Falls of Lora.

Having crossed a curving fault line, whose weakness is picked out by the aligned valleys of the Pass of Brander and Glen Salach, the upper reaches of Loch Etive, above the Bonawe ferry, assume the deeply incised grandeur of a Norwegian fjord. The steep valley walls in places plunge well over 750 metres into the sea waters of the narrow loch, especially near Ben Starav (1052 m), where ice has gouged

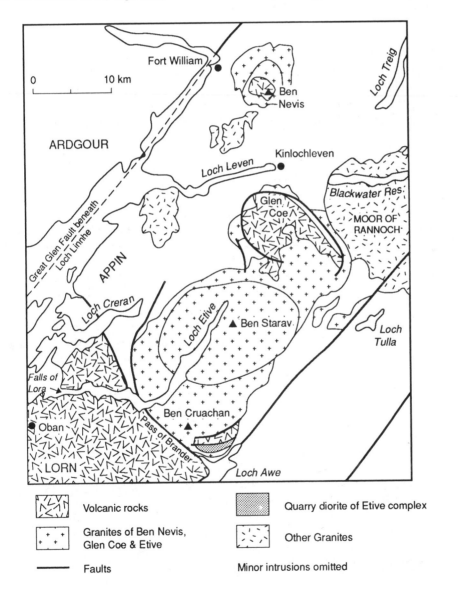

Figure 15.2 Volcanic rocks | Quarry diorite of Etive complex

Granites of Ben Nevis, Glen Coe & Etive | Other Granites

Faults | Minor intrusions omitted

Figure 15.2 The igneous rocks of the western Grampians (based on material prepared by the British Geological Survey).

a breach in the mountain chain more than 1200 metres in depth. The reason for this sudden change in scenic character is not far to seek, for the curving Pass of Brander fault line is related to part of the ring fracture of the Etive Complex, whose tough granites have resisted downwearing more successfully than the metamorphic and volcanic country rock' into which they were emplaced in Lower Old Red Sandstone times (Fig. 15.2).

The Etive Complex, through which Loch Etive and Glen Etive have been incised, comprises one of the largest granitic emplacements in Britain, since its outcrop covers some 360 square kilometres of mountainland. The mechanism of cauldron subsidence is described in Chapter 12, but the Etive subsidence differs from that in central Arran by virtue of the fact that the granite emplacement occurred entirely underground without the formation of a caldera. It will be seen that in this respect the cauldron subsidence of the Etive Complex also differs from those of neighbouring Glencoe and Ben Nevis (Fig. 15.3A). Thanks largely to the work of Bailey (1934) and J.G.C. Anderson (1937), it has now proved possible to recognize four or five successive granitic intrusions around Loch Etive, each having been formed by rising magmas of slightly different chemical composition related to successive phases of cauldron subsidence. It has been suggested that during each period of cauldron formation a cylindrical block of 'country rock' subsided within the ring fracture, thus allowing magma to ascend the fracture zone and occupy the space vacated by the subsiding block (Fig. 15.3). Erosion has now destroyed the enveloping 'country rock' and denuded the underlying granites to reveal their ring-dyke structures, which become progressively younger towards the centre. The peripheral grey Quarry Diorite, above Loch Awe railway station, is the oldest; the second oldest is the Cruachan Granite, which varies in colour from grey to pink; next are the extensive bare pink slabs of the Meall Odhar Granite which make up the summit cliffs of Ben Cruachan itself; the youngest granites are the pink Starav Granites of the centre, where a distinction can be made between the porphyritic outer zone and the non-porphyritic central mass which builds the bare slopes of Ben Starav.

It is only a short journey from the remote fastnesses of Glen Etive, past the towering portals of Buachaille Etive Mor (1020 m) (see Fig. 14.3), beloved by climbers, to the overwhelming spectacle of Glencoe. The sudden descent into Glencoe from the apparently endless wastes of Rannoch Moor must rank high among the most spectacular scenic experiences in Scotland. For sheer impact the cliffs of the 'Three Sisters' and the precipitous slopes of Aonach Eagach (966 m) at the Pass of Glencoe, when seen from the 'Study', create one of the most impressive views in the Highlands. The Three Sisters referred to are Beinn Fhada (951 m), Gearr Aonach (762 m) and Aonach Dubh (869 m), all shoulders of Bidean nam Bian (1148 m), which itself divides Glencoe from Glen Etive.

Some early writers claimed that Glencoe was initially fashioned by a major consequent river which, rising near Ardnamurchan, flowed eastwards via the valleys of Loch Sunart, Glen Tarbert and Glencoe, and thence by Rannoch Moor and the Tummel River to the North Sea. This was merely one of several hypothetical river courses that were once 'reconstructed' in an attempt to explain some of the puzzling drainage lines of Highland Scotland. Modern opinion, however, generally supports the suggestion that the gigantic 'through-valleys' which run from west to east across the primary watershed of Scotland were created not by rivers but ice sheets during several episodes of glacial breaching (see p. 335).

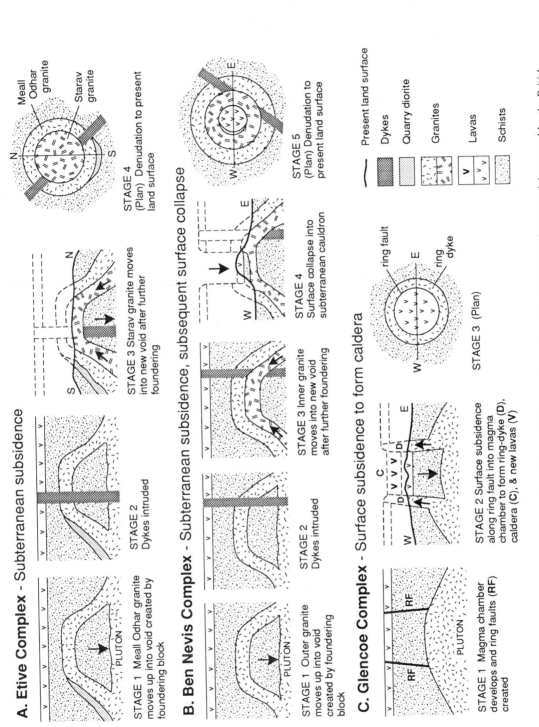

A. Etive Complex - Subterranean subsidence

Meall
Odhar
granite

Starav
granite

STAGE 4
(Plan) Denudation to present
land surface

STAGE 3 Starav granite moves
into new void after further
foundering

STAGE 2
Dykes intruded

STAGE 1 Meall Odhar granite
moves up into void created by
foundering block

PLUTON

B. Ben Nevis Complex - Subterranean subsidence, subsequent surface collapse

STAGE 5
(Plan) Denudation to
present land surface

STAGE 4
Surface collapse into
subterranean cauldron

STAGE 3 Inner granite
moves into new void
after further foundering

STAGE 2
Dykes intruded

STAGE 1 Outer granite
moves up into void
created by foundering
block

PLUTON

C. Glencoe Complex - Surface subsidence to form caldera

ring fault

ring
dyke

STAGE 3 (Plan)

STAGE 2 Surface subsidence
along ring fault into magma
chamber to form ring-dyke (D),
caldera (C), & new lavas (V)

STAGE 1 Magma chamber
develops and ring faults (RF)
created

R.F.

R.F.

PLUTON

Present land surface

Dykes

Quarry diorite

Granites

Lavas

Schists

Figure 15.3   An explanation of the mechanics of cauldron subsidence in the western Grampians (based on material prepared by the British Geological Survey).

In the case of Glencoe, the breach was initiated by the enormous reservoir of ice that accumulated over Rannoch Moor before finding escape routes via such west-flowing river valleys as Glen Etive and Glencoe (see Fig. 14.5). Thus the pre-glacial valley-head cols were destroyed, and the valley floors lowered considerably until they took on the typical U-shape of glacial erosion. Such down-wearing was facilitated in Glencoe by an isolated layer of phyllites from which the ice fashioned a basin later to be occupied by Loch Achtriochtan. Wherever harder rock bands appeared, however, they resisted glacial erosion to a greater degree. Examples are to be seen at the valley step beneath the Study and in the precipitous cliffs on the slopes of Aonach Dubh and Gearr Aonach, all of which are made up of rhyolite.

Many fine examples of glacial moulding and polishing can be seen around Glencoe, including roches moutonnées, glacial pavements and grooving, while morainic debris and perched blocks (including the remarkable Rannoch Moor Granite erratics on the ridge of Aonach Eagach) illustrate the type of load once carried by the ice. As one might expect, the major corries face north-eastwards, so that the crags of Aonach Dubh and Gearr Aonach are divided from each other by one of these armchair depressions, out of which a waterfall plunges over the lip of the glacially oversteepened walls of Glencoe. From a geological standpoint the most interesting corrie is Coire nam Beith, which lies between Aonach Dubh and the peak of An t-Sron, for here can be seen yet another example of cauldron subsidence (Bailey *et al.*, 1909) (Fig. 15.3C). The ring fracture itself has been picked out by erosion to form a prominent gully running up the slopes of An t-Sron to its summit (Fig. 15.4). This fault is in fact a boundary between the granite of An t-Sron (which welled up as a magma around the ring fracture) and the existing volcanic succession (of Old Red Sandstone age), which subsided more than 1200 metres into the cauldron and has thus survived subsequent denudation. The cliffs and crags of the Three Sisters have been carved from these rugged volcanics, as have the summits of Bidean nam Bian, which stands at the back of Coire nam Beith. The cliffs of Aonach Dubh, for example, were built by three massive flows of rhyolitic lava, each some 45 metres thick.

To the north of the notched ridge of Aonach Eagach, another long arm of the sea penetrates deeply into the mountains as Loch Leven. Rising from its shores, the prominent quartzite knob of the Pap of Glencoe (741 m) forms a distinctive feature among the gentler surrounding slopes of schist and metamorphosed limestone, with the latter contributing to the relatively fertile pastures at the lower end of Glencoe. At the head of Loch Leven the industrial town of Kinlochleven grew up, amid the rugged hills of Mamore Forest (Bailey, 1934), because of the availability of copious hydro-electric power, which is used for the production of aluminium at the Kinlochleven plant (Chilton, 1950). To achieve the high temperatures required to smelt the imported bauxite the British Aluminium Company received permission to create the lengthy Blackwater Reservoir by damming the headwaters of the west-flowing River Leven. Water is now led off from this upland valley and taken through enormous pipes to drive the turbines as it falls to the overdeepened fjord of Loch Leven. Later expansion of the aluminium company led to the development of a second smelter at Fort William, whose water power is derived from Loch Laggan and Loch Treig via a 24 kilometre tunnel beneath the northern foothills of Ben Nevis.

The waters of the Leven, like those of the neighbouring River Spean, may

Figure 15.4 Coire nam Beith, Glencoe, a glacial cirque occupying the site of an ancient ring fracture. The ring fracture is picked out by a prominent gully below the summit of An t-Sron (right) and separates the granite of An t-Sron (right of the gully) from the Old Red Sandstone volcanics let down by cauldron subsidence (left of the gully). (See also Fig. 15.3C).

not always have flowed westwards: there is good reason to believe that in the Ben Nevis area deep glacial breaching of Scotland's primary north–south watershed has caused a reversal of drainage in some of the pre-glacial river systems. Thus, Sissons (1966) states that the Leven's sudden 300 metre descent from the gently sloping floor of the Blackwater Valley down to Kinlochleven 'is clearly a relatively recent development in the history of the drainage and strongly suggests that formerly the Leven flowed eastwards to be continued by the Tummel'.

Glen Mor

North of Loch Leven is the region termed Lochaber, where the tides of Loch Linnhe creep far into the Great Glen until they reach almost to the foot of Britain's highest mountain, Ben Nevis (1343 m). Before examining its gigantic bulk, however, a short detour into Glen Nevis provides a preview of the monolithic scenery hereabouts – scenery which has been compared in stature with that of the Himalayas by the well-known mountaineer, W. H. Murray (1968). He sees in the Nevis gorge a peculiar combination of cliff, woodland and water unparalleled in Britain and reminiscent of the Nepalese valleys. The hayfields and the oak, birch and pine woods of the lower glen flourish on the more fertile soils derived from an outcrop of the Ballachulish Limestone. A bend in the valley ensures that the full impact of the dramatic Nevis gorge is withheld until the last moment. But then the character of the valley changes immediately, for the main river foams and tumbles through a narrow, twisting cleft, carved partly through a band of steeply dipping Glencoe Quartzite which crosses the valley at Steall. To the north a silvery cascade from a high corrie sweeps down the dark, heathery talus slopes which mantle the pink granite of Ben Nevis, which at this point creates the highest amplitude of relief in Britain: an almost continuous slope of more than 1200 metres descends from its summit to the valleyfloor. To the south a waterfall leaps some 100 metres from a perfect example of a hanging valley. This is Allt Coire a'Mhail, which drains the shapely peaks of the Mamore range, whose highest point is Binnein Mor (1128 m). Although rising from a base of Leven Schists, the graceful summits of, for example, Stob Ban and Sgurr a'Mhaim owe their form to a cap of white Glencoe Quartzite which is often mistaken for a snow cover.

When viewed from Glen Nevis, Britain's highest mountain is too foreshortened to appear attractive, and even from the western shores of Loch Linnhe it is impossible to appreciate its great height. When seen from the north-west, however, its majestic ice-quarried cliffs are revealed, their frost-riven 600 metre precipices unequalled in height even by those of the Cuillins (see Chapter 16). At their base extensive snow patches lie in the gullies and hollows, frequently surviving the summer in their sheltered north-east-facing corries and serving to demonstrate how easily corrie glaciers could regenerate in this marginal 'sub-Arctic' environment. Although the U-shaped hanging valley of Coire a'Mhuilinn, like the lower slopes and shoulders of Ben Nevis, has been carved from granite, the cliffs and uppermost parts of the mountain are made of volcanics of Lower Old Red Sandstone age (see Fig. 15.2). It may be seen in Fig. 15.3B that the granites of the pluton were subsequently affected by the collapsed roof of a sub-terranean cauldron (established during earlier subsidence), thus allowing the former cover of lavas and their underlying schists (which belong to a massive recumbent fold (Hickman, 1978)) to sink about 460 metres into the Inner Granite while it was still in liquid form. It is these bedded lavas and volcanic agglomerates which today form the summit dome of Ben Nevis.

Not far to the north lie the remarkable phenomena known as the Parallel Roads of Glen Roy, where, high up on the mountainside, three grassy terraces stand out in the darker masses of heather as if to mark contour lines along the slopes (Peacock and Cornish, 1989). So artificial do they look that local legends claim them as the 'King's Hunting Roads', constructed by ancient monarchs who

(a)

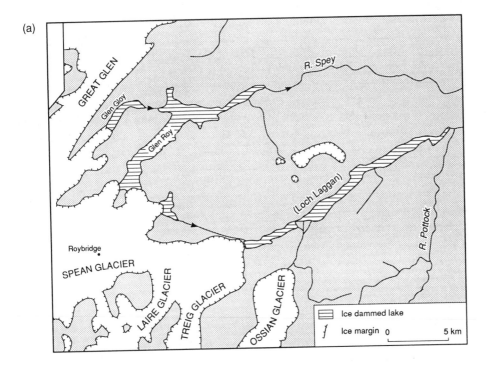

(b)

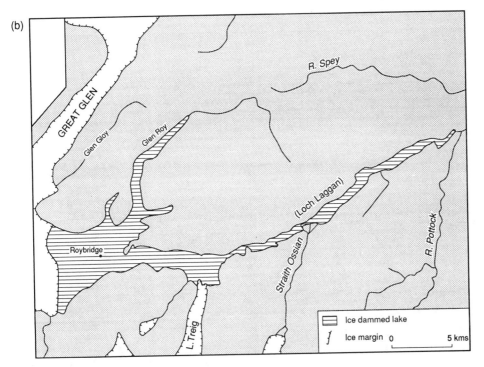

Figure 15.5 Reconstruction of the proglacial lakes of the Glen Roy area during the Loch Lomond Advance (after J. B. Sissons). (a) Lake at 350 metres (b) Lake at 260 metres.

dwelt at Inverlochy (Fort William). Despite the contention in 1840 by an eminent Swiss glaciologist, Louis Aggasiz, that these parallel terraces could relate to a slowly draining pro-glacial lake (ice-impounded), Charles Darwin thought that they were marine formations. He remained sceptical even when the ice-dammed lake overflow (relating to the middle 'road') was discovered in 1847. Darwin finally admitted that he was wrong in the 1860s, by which time the chronology of the former pro-glacial lake had been fully worked out. It is now known that a tongue of Loch Lomond Readvance ice blocked the drainage not only in Glen Roy but also in neighbouring Glen Gloy and Glen Spean, creating marginal lakes similar to the modern Marjelen See at the Aletsch glacier in Switzerland (Sissons, 1978; 1979). The Parallel Roads are in fact strandlines of a lake which, in Glen Roy, stood at a maximum height of about 350 metres. As the ice front retreated the lake was progressively lowered first to approximately 320 metres and then to 260 metres, as overflow cols were revealed from beneath the ice (Fig. 15.5). Apart from the 'roads' of Glen Gloy and Glen Spean, similar strandlines have been found elsewhere in Scotland only at Rannoch Moor, but here they are on a smaller scale.

In the Great Glen, between Loch Lochy and Loch Oich, the imperceptible watershed between west-flowing and east-flowing drainage has been displaced 24 kilometres to the north-east by glacial breaching and subsequent river capture, for the primary pre-glacial watershed lay near to Ben Nevis. Beyond Fort Augustus Loch Ness exhibits gigantic dimensions. At 230 metres maximum depth, it is Scotland's second deepest loch, but since its depth remains more than 200 metres for the greater part of its 37 kilometre length it holds the largest volume of water. Its capacity of 7443 million cubic metres is almost three times

Figure 15.6 Loch Ness, the largest of the narrow but deep lakes occupying the fault-guided and ice-deepened trough of Glen Mor.

that of Loch Lomond and more than three times that of the deepest loch, Loch Morar. Nothing illustrates the efficiency of glacial scouring along a fault shatter-belt better than this set of figures. When one pauses to consider that from the loch floor the valley walls rise abruptly some 650 metres, it is clear that Loch Ness occupies one of the greatest glacial troughs in the British Isles (Fig. 15.6). Its shores are so steep that aquatic vegetation is virtually absent, while its waters are so dark that it is little wonder that Loch Ness is associated with legends of living 'fossils' which may have survived from earlier geological periods. But no one has yet explained how such creatures survived the bulldozing effects of the glaciers!

On the eastern shores of Loch Ness, and reputed to be the first hydro-electric scheme in Britain, the power station at Foyers, like those at Kinlochleven and Fort William, was initially required for the smelting of bauxite. The aluminium works here was closed down in 1967 to be replaced by a pumped storage scheme, similar to that which operates between Ben Cruachan and Loch Awe. The idea is to utilize off-peak periods (when electricity demand is low) to pump water the 180 metres from Loch Ness up to Loch Mhor, thus allowing the water to descend again and generate 300 megawatts of electricity during periods of peak demand. The location of hydro-electric schemes in Scotland is often related, nor surprisingly, to the presence of the oversteepened walls of glacial troughs.

The lack of islands in the lochs and the steepness of the flanking slopes of the Great Glen highlight the efficiency of the ice in clearing out not only the fault breccia but also much of the less resistant faulted outlier of Old Red Sandstone which occupies part of the floor of the Great Glen. But ice has also scoured out much of the regolith, so that the valley flanks of these central glens are both too steep and too rocky for agricultural improvement. Instead they have been given over almost entirely to forestry, so that the majestic water vistas of Loch Ness are now framed by endless ranks of dark conifers marching along the valley sides. Some of Scotland's largest forestry plantations are to be found in this region, especially in the sheltered valleys of Glen Moriston, Glen Urquhart and neighbouring Glen Affric. Here, around the ice-scoured knolls, podzolic soils have formed on the glacial tills and outwash deposits. Magnificent remnants of the ancient Caledonian pine forests, such as that of Glen Affric, have survived in these sheltered eastern glens where the tree-line is considerably higher than on the exposed western coastlands and islands. Native forest once covered this region but has been largely destroyed by man and his grazing animals, which has often led to soil deterioration and the formation of thin iron pans. However, the growth rate of conifers in Scotland far exceeds that in Scandinavia and in central Europe, so that afforestation became the most important land use in these central glens and led to the location of a gigantic pulp mill at Corpach, near Fort William, to utilize the forest 'crop' (Turnock, 1966).

Before leaving the confines of Glen Mor at the town of Inverness, it is important to examine the mechanism of the faulting which created the line of weakness from which the corridor was eventually created. The mechanisms of normal faulting and thrust faulting have been explained in Chapters 12 and 14, respectively, while Fig. 15.7 also illustrates some of the major wrench- or tear-faults which affect the geology of the northern Grampians. The Great Glen Fault falls into the last category; indeed, it is the best example of a wrench-fault in the British Isles. Although following a 'Caledonoid' trend, the Great Glen Fault is known to be largely of Hercynian age, though lateral displacement took place at intervals up until post-Carboniferous times. Indeed, minor earth tremors, recorded on several occasions at Inverness since 1769, demonstrate that movement has not yet ceased.

In the knowledge that a sinistral movement had transported the Northern Highlands block bodily south-westwards in relation to the remainder of Scotland, Kennedy (1946) claimed that two of the Great Glen granites, those of Foyers (Mould, 1946) and Strontian, were once part of the same geological unit and that the Strontian part of this granite pluton has been moved 104 kilometres south-westwards to its present position opposite Lismore Island (Fig. 15.7). However, subsequent research has shown that the granites in question were never joined (Marston, 1971; Munro, 1965). Nevertheless, the sinistral displacement may have been as much as 160 kilometres (Mykura, 1975; Piasecki *et al.*, 1981). Later work suggested that in post-Jurassic times there was another major shift along the Great Glen Fault, but this time a dextral movement (in the opposite direction) of some 6–8 kilometres. New palaeomagnetic data now suggest a 600 kilometre late Caledonian sinistral movement and a 300 kilometre Hercynian dextral displacement (Storevedt, 1987). Finally, the impossibility of matching the

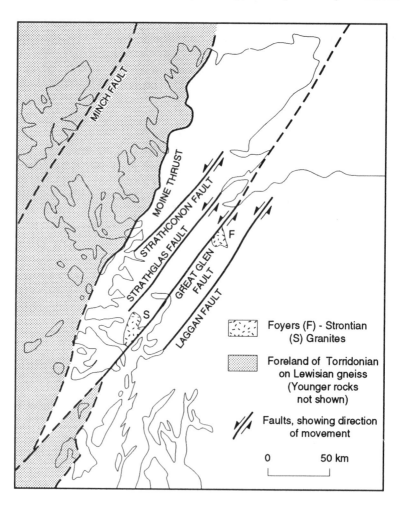

Figure 15.7 The major wrench-faults of northern Scotland and the Moine Thrust.

Foyers (F) - Strontian (S) Granites

Foreland of Torridonian on Lewisian gneiss (Younger rocks not shown)

Faults, showing direction of movement

0   50 km

alignment of the Tertiary dyke swarms of Morvern and Lismore with those to the south-east of the Great Glen has pointed to a possible post-Tertiary movement along this major line of faulting. Since the Great Glen Fault extends as a submarine fracture as far as the Shetlands (Flinn, 1961) it is not surprising that it is associated with basin formation (McQuillin and Donato, 1982) and oil accumulation in the North Sea oil field (Linsley *et al.*, 1980).

It is also not surprising that an important urban settlement grew up at the more sheltered north-eastern end of this great natural corridor, where the waters of Ness debouch into the Moray Firth. Inverness, the 'capital of the Highlands', commands this nodal position at a bridging-point of the river on the edge of its delta. Once the capital of the Pictish kingdom, the town has remained important throughout Scotland's chequered history, since it dominates the only viable north–south route across the Scottish Highlands at a point where it crosses both Glen Mor and the route to the eastern coastlands. East of Inverness a scenic transition occurs due in part to the appearance of the Old Red Sandstone with its rolling topography and more fertile soils, but due also to the fact that, during the Pleistocene, ice sheets utilized the basin of the Moray Firth as a dumping ground for the products of their mountainland erosion. Thus, by comparison with the hard rock landforms of the Great Glen proper, the topography around the inner recesses of the Moray Firth has been moulded (partly by the sea) very largely from relatively unconsolidated materials of Pleistocene and Recent age. These can be classified according to their origin as glacio-fluvial deposits, glacial deposits and marine deposits. Between Inverness and Nairn, the Quaternary landforms are as complex as those in the Firth of Forth (Auton *et al.*, 1990).

The area between Dochgarroch and Tomnahurich, just west of Inverness, has some excellent examples of the glacio-fluvial landforms known as eskers. Not as well developed as the magnificent Flemington esker complex around Croy (to the east of Inverness), those which flank the River Ness are nevertheless excellent illustrations of the principle of sub-glacial deposition. Where the modern river has truncated these narrow, sinuous ridges it is possible to see that they are composed of bedded layers of unconsolidated sand and gravel, orientated in the general direction of the former ice movement. Although it was once believed that eskers were remnants of the biblical Flood, it is now generally accepted that they were formed by glacial meltwaters in tunnels beneath the ice.

The ice sheets beneath which the eskers were formed also left a variety of glacial deposits around Inverness, including so-called 'boulder-trains', erratics and extensive till sheets. In addition, their periodic stillstands, during the deglaciation of this region, have left extensive late-glacial coastal landforms, none being more important than those at Alturlie and Ardersier. At each of these locations the smooth coast of the Moray Firth is broken by low headlands of complex glacio-fluvial and marine deposits. Previously explained as having been formed, respectively, around readvance and recessional moraines (Synge and Smith, 1980), the forelands of Ardersier and Alturlie are now regarded simply as marine-modified kame-kettle topography unrelated to any former ice margins (Auton *et al.*, 1990; Firth, 1989b). A much simpler mode of Devensian deglaciation of the Moray Firth has now been suggested (Firth, 1989a) based on an uninterrupted fall of Late-Glacial sea level as the ice receded. Ten raised shorelines exist, all tilted glacio-isostatically from 30 metres OD at Inverness and descending gently (at less than 1 metre per kilometre gradient) as they are traced north-eastwards into the Moray Firth. Below them, at an elevation of 3 metres OD at Beauly, and sloping at a similar gradient north-eastwards, is the shoreline associated with the Loch Lomond Readvance and equated by Sissons (1981) with the Main Late-glacial Shoreline of the Forth Valley. Finally, rising to elevations between 3 and 7 metres OD, fragments of four or five post-glacial raised beaches have been mapped to the west and east of Inverness (Firth and Haggart, 1989).

The Western Highlands

To the west of the Great Glen and to the south of Loch Duich (where the Moine Thrust leaves the Scottish mainland) there is a little-known mountain massif in which the 1000 metre peaks at the head of Glen Affric give way to a series of lower but equally attractive summits as they approach the greatly fragmented coastline of the Western Highlands. Here, in a remote region where the sea-lochs penetrate deeply into the heart of the Highlands, is a land which remained partly uncharted by the Geological Survey for over a century. Few roads traverse the area even today, so that the western peninsulas of Knoydart, Morar, Moidart, Ardnamurchan and Morvern are virtually cut off from the thoroughfare of Glen Mor by their mountain bastions, lochs and fjords (Turnock, 1967a).

From Loch Ness itself there is a choice of two routes to gain access to the western coast: the northern, via Glen Moriston to the delectable Glen Shiel, with its entourage of conical peaks known as the Five Sisters of Kintail; or a more central route past Loch Garry and Loch Quoich to the hidden sea waters of Loch Hourn. When one considers that the slopes of Glen Moriston and Glen Garry are now thickly clothed with mature plantations of fir, pine and spruce, it is instructive to read how the famous Dr Johnson witnessed a very different scene when passing this way two centuries ago. He sardonically remarked that the mountains to the west of Glen Mor represented 'matter incapable of form or usefulness, dismissed by nature from her care and disinherited of her favours, left in its original elemental state or quickened only with one sullen power of useless vegetation'. It is true that even today farming in Lochaber is difficult because of the leaching of soil nutrients due to the heavy rainfall (Turnock, 1967b), but the burning and destruction during the infamous Highland Clearances must only have exacerbated the desolation of the scene in this, the wettest area of the Highlands (with an annual precipitation of more than 3000 millimetres), and one where the Loch Lomond Readvance glaciers lingered longest.

The extremely complicated lithology and structure of the Western Highlands, due to considerable deformation and metamorphism, has made it difficult to elucidate the succession of the Moine rocks but a threefold division of the strata has been suggested (Johnstone and Mykura, 1989). First, the so called Morar Division appears to be the oldest grouping of Moinian metamorphics, made up of a mixture of basal Moine strata and exposures of the Lewisian 'basement' gneisses occurring within the Moinian metasediments. Although the underlying Lewisian gneiss, which crops out extensively in Glenelg (Barber and May, 1956) to the north of Loch Hourn, originally formed the cores of the earliest anticlines, later phases of folding and thrusting have deformed all these rocks of the western coastlands (Lambert and Poole, 1964). The Morar Division rocks make up the rugged scenery from Loch Hourn southwards (Ramsay and Spring, 1962) past

Lochs Nevis, Morar, Ailort (Powell, 1964) to Lower Loch Sunart in Morvern. Second, is the so called Glenfinnan Division in which the younger Moinian metasediments are separated from the older rocks of the Morar Division by the Sgurr Beag Slide and from which the central mountains, between Loch Quoich, Loch Shiel and Upper Loch Sunart, have been carved. Finally, the youngest group, the so called Loch Eil Division, is less deformed than the other two divisions and contains marbles in Ardgour of possible Dalradian age (Stoker, 1983). The change (at the so-called Loch Quoich Line) from the steeply inclined structures of the west to the more gently folded strata of Loch Eil and Ardgour has been taken as the easterly limit of severe Early Palaeozoic deformation (Roberts and Harris, 1983).

Subsequent denudation has worked not only upon a recumbent fold, termed the Knoydart Fold, but also upon later structures known as the Morar Antiform and the Ben Sgriol Synform (Kennedy, 1954). The resulting fold complex is, therefore, responsible for the generally north–south alignment of the individual rock types in these western peninsulas, an alignment later to be crossed obliquely by many of the Tertiary dykes belonging to the Skye 'swarm' (see Chapter 16 and Fig. 16.2). Not that this alignment has manifested itself in the scenery hereabouts, for one is much more conscious of the deep glens and fjords which trench the mountains in an east–west direction, at right angles to the regional strike. Furthermore, as if to demonstrate that geological relationships are not always as straightforward as one would suppose, the highest peaks of this area – for example, Ladhar Beinn (1019 m) and Meall Buidhe (946 m) – are more often than not built from the reputedly less resistant argillaceous metasediments (pelites) rather than the tougher metamorphosed arenaceous rocks (psammites) (Poole, 1966). This is probably to be explained by the fact that many of these high summits coincide with the axis of the Ben Sgriol Synform, so that their joints are tightly closed – yet another example of 'inversion of relief'.

Each of the westward-trending valleys between Glen Mor and the coast (most of which carry the only communications in the region) crosses Scotland's primary watershed by means of a deep glacial breach: that which carries both road and rail past Loch Eil to Mallaig is now a mere 18 metres above sea level. The elevation of the breached cols behind Lochs Hourn and Nevis is, however, considerably greater, thus adding to their inaccessibility. The high peaks and steep flanks of Loch Hourn make it the closest Scottish counterpart to a Norwegian fjord and, like neighbouring Loch Nevis, it exhibits the typical submerged threshold across its entrance. Farther south, however, the post-glacial marine submergence has failed to cross the rocky threshold at the western end of Loch Morar, so that this, the deepest of British lakes (about 310 m), has remained a freshwater loch. Today it drains seawards across a narrow isthmus, where its once picturesque waterfall has now been reduced to a trickle by a hydro-electric scheme. Although ice is undoubtedly responsible for the prodigious overdeepening of its rock basin, the scouring may have been faciliated by the presence of a submerged fault, similar to that along which the nearby linear valley of Loch Beoraid was excavated. Even though many of the glens and fjords of western Scotland have been carved along fault lines, there is no need to revert to the views of Gregory (1927) who argued for their tectonic origin. He suggested that all these western valleys were created almost exclusively by faulting or even rifting, with glacial processes being relegated to a minor role.

South of the River Morar the Mallaig coast road passes through some of the most magnificent coastal scenery in the whole of Scotland. The harsh bareness of the Knoydart moorlands gives way to the softer oak and birch woods of Arisaig, while the narrow outcrop of a micaceous psammite has weathered into the glittering silvery sands which adorn the multitude of tiny bays.

Ardnamurchan and Morvern

Were it not for a narrow isthmus near Salen, the long arm of Ardnamurchan would be insular, but instead it remains the westernmost point of mainland Britain. In most other ways, however, it is Hebridean, not least in its remarkable geology and scenery (Gribble, 1976). Like the flanking mountains of Moidart, Ardgour and Sunart, the hills at the base of the Ardnamurchan peninsula have been carved from Moinian metasediments similar to those described above, but the western end of Ardnamurchan presents a very different scene. Here, the landforms have been carved from a Tertiary igneous complex even more complicated than that of Arran (Emeleus, 1983; Richey, 1933) described in Chapter 12.

The central intrusion complex of Ardnamurchan clearly illustrates most of the major examples of Tertiary igneous activity, including ring-dykes, cone-sheets (Richey, 1932; E.M. Anderson, 1937), volcanic vents, sills, dykes and plateau basalts, most of whose formations have been described in Chapter 12. In contrast with the Central Ring Complex of Arran, however, Ardnamurchan had three centres of intrusion (Fig. 15.8), while another difference between the two areas becomes apparent when one examines their petrology. If the dykes and other minor intrusions (except cone-sheets) are excluded, virtually all the Ardnamurchan plutonic rocks are of basic composition (mainly gabbro and dolerite); Arran, on the other hand, is almost exclusively an island of granite and granophyre (that is, acid) composition, so far as its plutonic rocks are concerned.

Although plateau basalts occur on a limited scale in both Ardnamurchan and Morvern (see below), their influence on the landforms is not as marked as it is in Mull, so a full description of basaltic characteristics will be deferred until Chapter 16. In Ardnamurchan the most important igneous activity began with the formation of the first explosion vents, which were punched right through both the plateau lavas and their underlying Moine Schists and Mesozoic sedimentaries. By referring to Fig. 15.8 the reader will be able to follow the succeeding history of the igneous activity as the Ardnamurchan volcanic pile grew steadily in stature. The following time sequence has been recognized, as the centre of activity shifted its position: first, the volcanic vents of Centre 1, picked out by their agglomerates, were cut through by the massive cone-sheets and intrusions of the opening phase; second, as the activity shifted westwards, Centre 2 produced a further series of cone-sheets and a succession of massive ring-dykes now exposed in the western end of the peninsula; finally, the activity shifted back to an intermediate location and Centre 3 was responsible for an innermost set of magnificent ring-dykes which are both basic and acid in composition. Denudation has lowered the massive volcano to nothing more than a 'basal wreck', although the concentric pattern of the structure is still clearly discernible in the landforms.

Ardnamurchan's highest peak, Ben Hiant (527 m), has been carved from a complex of vent agglomerates emanating from Centre 1, bolstered by an intrusive

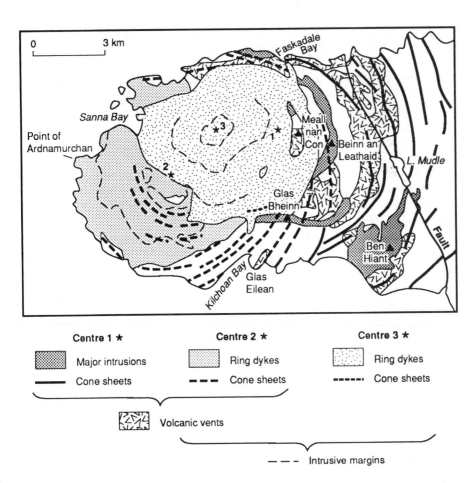

Figure 15.8 Igneous geology of Ardnamurchan (based on material prepared by the British Geological Survey) Unshaded areas include rocks of Moinian and Jurassic age.

mass of quartz-dolerite which forms the summit. To the west of Kilchoan Bay the ring-dykes and cone-sheets associated with Centre 2 have helped create a curving rampart of low hills surrounding a semi-circular valley, which in turn gives way to the tougher gabbroid ring-dyke eminence of Beinn na Seilg (342 m) (Wells, 1954). But it is the ring-complex of Centre 3 which is most noteworthy, for it is the best preserved example of ring-dyke formation extant in Britain. The most striking of the ring-dykes, as far as the scenery is concerned, is that of the very basic Great Eucrite whose hardness has been responsible for an almost unbroken circle of hills some 5 kilometres in diameter. Its inner margin coincides with a ring of steep slopes and crags which in turn give way to a nested series of circular valleys and ridges centred around the settlements of Glendrian and Achnaha. As these inner ring-dykes are traced inwards, their composition becomes progressively more acid, culminating in a tiny central exposure of quartz-monzonite. Marine erosion is currently battering away at the outer ramparts of the igneous complex, and at Sanna Bay has broken through as far as the Great Eucrite ridge. The coasts of western Ardnamurchan, therefore, are characterized by an alternation of dark, forbidding cliffs and headlands with delightful hidden bays backed by beaches of creamy shell sand.

The last of the peninsulas which make up the varied scenery of the Western

Highlands is that of Morvern, cut off from Ardnamurchan by the 30-kilometre incursion of Loch Sunart. This broad peninsula can be divided into three contrasting areas: first, the deserted eastern massif, which coincides with the outcrop of the Strontian granite; second, the central hills of Moine Schists, whose scenery is little different from that of neighbouring Moidart and Sunart and whose broken terrain has inspired the title of Taobh Garbh (Gaelic, meaning 'the rough side'); and, finally, the basaltic plateaux of the west, which flank the Sound of Mull and whose forested eastern escarpment overlooks the loch-filled glens of central Morvern.

The Strontian granite is composed of three main intrusions (Munro, 1965). These exhibit evidence of increasing acidity as they are traced inwards from the surrounding tonalite through a granodiorite to the inner core of biotite-granite, and they are thought to represent successive phases of emplacement. Only the biotite-granite exhibits a resistance to denudation comparable with that of the surrounding Moinian, so that the high granite peaks of Kingairloch are now separated from the Moinian summits of central Morvern by a depression floored with granodiorite and tonalite and followed by the waters of Allt Beitheach. Following the discovery in 1791 of 'strontianite', the element of strontium was isolated and named after the tiny village of Strontian at the head of Loch Sunart. This area remained an important lead-mining centre between 1722 and 1872, although production has now ceased. The galena is part of a zone of mineralization occurring in the Moinian rocks that surround the Strontian Granite, which itself is of Caledonian age. Although there appears to be some genetic connection between the granitic emplacement and the mineralization, isotopic datings show that the Strontian lead was formed in at least two phases between Permo-Triassic times and the Early Tertiary. It is possible that the structural doming caused by the granite pluton resulted in a crustal weakness which was later to act as a focus for rising geochemical solutions at different periods of geological time.

At Lochaline the coastal loch is overlooked by towering cliffs of Tertiary plateau basalts which, with their silvery waterfalls, give a foretaste of Mull. Entombed beneath the black lava cliffs there are thin layers of sedimentary sandstones, shales and limestones resting unconformably on the Moinian floor, the very pure, friable sandstones being quarried for glass sands (Humphries, 1961). Furthermore, the outlying basal hills of central Morvern – for instance, Beinn Iadain (571 m) – overlie narrow bands of similar rocks, including Liassic shales (MacLennan, 1953). It comes as something of a surprise to discover these layers of Triassic, Jurassic and Cretaceous rocks, because they are isolated by several hundred kilometres from their more extensive counterparts in England. In fact, such Mesozoic sedimentary rocks are not uncommon in the Hebrides, for the seas of Keuper, Jurassic and Upper Cretaceous times extended far to the north. The fact that so few remnants now survive, however, indicates the enormous amount of denudation that has subsequently taken place in Scotland. The majority of the Mesozoic rocks in northern Scotland owe their preservation to the Tertiary lavas which flooded over them and gave them a protective cover. There is little doubt that the Morvern lavas formerly extended farther east, judging by the outliers to the north of Loch Arienas; all of these were once part of the main lava plains of Mull and Morvern, but erosion has cut them off from the main basaltic exposure. The prominent east-facing scarp of Sithean na Raplaich

(551 m) does not therefore, represent the terminal limit of the lava flows, for this scarp was produced by subsequent uplift and denudation of the lava plains. With the gradual wearing back of the escarpment since the lavas were first extruded in Palaeocene times, small undestroyed outliers have remained to the east of its present cliffs, representing unconsumed relics of a former continuous basaltic cover.

Bibliography

Anderson, E.M. (1937) Cone-sheets and ring dykes: the dynamical explanation. *Bull. Volcan.*, **2**(1) 35–40.

Anderson, J.G.C. (1937) The Etive Granite Complex. *Quart. J. Geol. Soc.*, **93**, 487–533.

Auton, C.A., Firth, C.R. and Merritt, J.W. (1990) *Beauly to Nairn*. Field Guide. Quat. Res. Assoc. 149 pp.

Bailey, E.B. (1934) West Highland tectonics: Loch Leven to Glen Roy. *Quart. J. Geol. Soc.*, **90**, 462–523.

Bailey, E.B., Clough, C.T. and Maufe, H.B. (1909) The cauldron subsidence of Glencoe and the associated igneous phenomena. *Quart. J. Geol. Soc.*, **65**, 611–78.

Barber, A.J. and May, F. (1976) The history of the western Lewisian in the Glenelg Inlier, Lochalsh, Northern Highlands. *Scot. J. Geol.*, **12**, 35–50.

Chilton, L.V. (1950) The aluminium industry in Scotland. *Scot. Geog. Mag.*, **66**, 153–62.

Emeleus, C.H. (1983) Tertiary igneous activity, in G.Y. Craig (ed.), *Geology of Scotland* (2nd edn). Scottish Academic Pres. pp. 357–97.

Firth, C.R. (1989a) Late-Devensian raised shorelines and ice limits in the inner Moray Firth, northern Scotland. *Boreas*, **18**, 5–21.

Firth, C.R. (1989b) A reappraisal of the supposed Ardersier Readvance, inner Moray Firth. *Scot. J. Geol.*, **25**, 249–61.

Firth, C.R. and Haggart, B.A. (1989) Loch Lomond Stadial and Flandrian shorelines in the Inner Moray Firth area, Scotland. *J. Quat. Sci.*, **4**, 37–50.

Flinn, D. (1961) Continuation of the Great Glen Fault beyond the Moray Firth. *Nature*, **191**, 589–91.

Gray, J.M. (1974) The Main Rock Platform of the Firth of Lorn, western Scotland. *Trans. Inst. Br. Geog.*, **61**, 81–99.

Gray, J.M. (1975) The Loch Lomond Readvance and contemporaneous sea-levels in Loch Etive and neighbouring areas of western Scotland. *Proc. Geol. Assoc.*, **86**, 227–38.

Gregory, J.W. (1927) The fjords of the Hebrides. *Geog. J.*, **69**, 193–216.

Gribble, C.D. (1976) *Ardnamurchan: a guide to geological excursions*. Geol. Soc. Glasgow.

Hickman, A.H. (1978) Recumbent folds between Glen Roy and Lismore. *Scot. J. Geol.*, **14**, 191–212.

Humphries, D.W. (1961) The Upper Cretaceous White Sandstone of Loch Aline, Argyll, Scotland. *Proc. Yorks. Geol. Soc.*, **33**, 47–76.

Johnstone, G.S. and Mykura, W. (1989) *The Northern Highlands of Scotland* (4th edn). British Regional Geology HMSO. 219 pp.

Kennedy, W.Q. (1946) The Great Glen Fault. *Quart. J. Geol. Soc.*, **102**, 41–76.

Kennedy, W.Q. (1954) The tectonics of the Morar Anticline and the problem of the North-West Caledonian Front. *Quart. J. Geol. Soc.*, **110**, 357–90.

Lambert, R. St J. and Poole, A.B. (1964) *Guide to the Moine Schists and Lewisian Gneisses around Mallaig, Inverness-shire*. Guide no. 35. Geol. Assoc. 11 pp.

Linsley, P.N., Potter, H.C., McNab, G. and Racher, D. (1980) The Beatrice Field, Inner Moray Firth, UK North Sea, in M.T. Halbouty (ed.), *Giant Oil and Gasfields of the Decade 1968–78*. Amer. Assoc. Petroleum Geol. Memoir, **30**. 117–29.

MacLennan, R.M. (1953) The Liassic sequence in Morvern. *Trans. Geol. Soc. Glasgow*, **21**, 447–55.

Marston, R.J. (1971) The Foyers granitic complex, Inverness-shire, Scotland. *Quart. J. Geol. Soc.*, **126**, 331–68.

McQuillin, R. and Donato, J.A. (1982) Development of basins in the Inner Moray Firth and the North Sea by crustal extension and dextral displacement of the Great Glen Fault. *Earth Planet. Sci. Lett.*, **60**, 127–39.

Mould, D.D.C.P. (1946) The geology of the Foyers 'granite' and the surrounding country. *Geol. Mag.*, **83**, 249–65.

Munro, M. (1965) Some structural features of the Caledonian granitic complex at Strontian, Argyllshire. *Scot. J. Geol.*, **1**, 152–75.

Murray, W.H. (1968) *The Companion Guide to the West Highlands of Scotland.* Collins. 415 pp.

Mykura, W. (1975) Possible large-scale sinistral displacement along the Great Glen Fault of Scotland. *Geol. Mag.*, **112**, 91–4.

Peacock, J.D. and Cornish, R. (1989) *Glen Roy Area.* Field Guide. Quat. Res. Assoc. 69 pp.

Piasecki, M.A.J., Van Breemen, O. and Wright, A.E. (1981) Late Precambrian geology of Scotland, England and Wales, in J.W. Kerr and A.J. Fergusson (eds), *Geology of the North Atlantic Borderlands.* Mem. Can. Soc. Pet. Geol. 7, 57–94.

Poole, A.B. (1966) Stratigraphy and structure of north-east Morar. *Scot. J. Geol.*, **2**, 38–53.

Powell, D. (1964) The stratigraphical succession of the Moine Schists around Lochailort (Inverness-shire) and its regional significance. *Proc. Geol. Assoc.*, **75**, 223–46.

Ramsay, J.G. and Spring, J. (1962) Moine stratigraphy in the Western Highlands of Scotland. *Proc. Geol. Assoc.*, **73**, 295–326.

Richey, J.E. (1932) Tertiary ring structures in Britain. *Trans. Geol. Soc. Glasgow*, **19**, 42–140.

Richey, J.E. (1933) Summary of the geology of Ardnamurchan. *Proc. Geol. Assoc.*, **44**, 1–56.

Roberts, A.M. and Harris, A.L. (1983) The Loch Quoich Line – a limit of early Scotland. *J. Geol. Soc. Lond.*, **140**, 883–92.

Sissons, J.B. (1966) *The Evolution of Scotland's Scenery.* Oliver and Boyd, 259 pp.

Sissons, J.B. (1978) The parallel roads of Glen Roy and adjacent glens, Scotland. *Boreas*, **7**, 183–244.

Sissons, J.B. (1979) The later lakes and associated fluvial terraces of Glen Roy, Glen Spean and vicinity. *Trans. Inst. Br. Geog.* (NS), **4**, 12–29.

Sissons, J.B. (1981) Lateglacial marine erosion and a jokulhlaup deposit in Beauly Firth. *Scot. J. Geol.*, **17**, 7–19.

Stoker, M.S. (1983) The stratigraphy and structure of the Moine rocks of eastern Ardgour. *Scot. J. Geol.*, **19**, 369–85.

Storevedt, K.M. (1987) Major late Caledonian and Hercynian shear movements on the Great Glen Fault. *Tectonophysics*, **143**, 253–67.

Synge, F.M. and Smith, J.S. (1980) *Inverness.* Field Guide. Quat. Res. Assoc. 29 pp.

Turnock, D. (1966) Lochaber – West Highland growth point. *Scot. Geog. Mag.*, **82**, 17–28.

Turnock, D. (1967a) Glenelg, Glengarry and Locheil: an evolutionary study in land use. *Scot. Geog. Mag.*, **83**, 89–104.

Turnock, D. (1967b) Evolution of farming patterns in Lochaber. *Trans. Inst. Br. Geog.*, **41**, 145–58.

Wells, M.K. (1954) The structure and petrology of the hypersthene-gabbro intrusion, Ardnamurchan, Argyllshire. *Quart. J. Geol. Soc.*, **109**, 367–95.

The Hebrides

16

The Hebrides are unique in terms of British scenery. They not only contain large tracts of Britain's oldest rocks, the Lewisian gneisses, of which they are the type-locality, but also include spectacular uplands carved from igneous rocks created by prolonged periods of vulcanicity dating from Tertiary times. Add to these attributes their insularity, their isolation, lack of development and widespread areas of wilderness, then it will be realized that they exhibit landscapes quite different from those encountered so far (Murray, 1966; Richey et al., 1961). Moreover, aspects of their natural history are unique within the British Isles (Boyd and Boyd, 1990).

It was convenient to examine their southernmost islands of Islay, Jura and Colonsay in Chapter 14 because of their structural continuity and geological similarity with the nearby Scottish mainland. The remainder of the Inner Hebrides, Mull, Rhum and Skye, however, are primarily made up not only of ancient rocks (mainly Precambrian in age) but also of numerous Mesozoic sedimentaries almost buried by lava flows and injected by a variety of igneous intrusives all linked with gigantic volcanic centres that functioned some 40–50 million years ago (Donaldson, 1983) at a time when some of Britain's youngest sediments were being laid down as sands and clays in the London Basin. In complete contrast, it will be shown how the Outer Hebrides, beyond the Minch, have been fashioned from rocks older than any of the strata in England and Wales. Finally, the Hebrides exhibit excellent examples of Pleistocene ice action and in the Inner Hebrides there are to be found some of Britain's best-developed raised shorelines (Sissons, 1983).

Mull

When travelling along the indented coastlines of Ardnamurchan and Morvern it is impossible to ignore the gigantic presence of Mull, that island of contrasts (MacNab, 1970), seemingly only a stone's throw away. Moreover, its cloud-capped southern mountains have formed an impressive backdrop to the oceanic vistas for countless tourists in the mainland resort of Oban. To understand fully its scenic complexity, however, it is necessary to land on the island of Mull itself, and there is no better place to commence an excursion than Tobermory.

Few ports can claim so romantic a setting as Tobermory, with its curve of gaily painted quayside houses surmounted by a halo of sycamore woodland clinging to the steep lava cliffs. The luxuriance of these deciduous woodlands is deceptive, however, for not far inland it soon becomes apparent how Mull received its name, which may be interpreted as meaning in Gaelic 'high, wide tableland'. So far as the northern part of the island is concerned this is an apt description, for here is a formerly treeless plateau of deeply dissected Tertiary lavas, surpassed in extent only by the basaltic plateaux of Skye. Nevertheless, Mull has some compensation in that its 1800 metres of basalt far exceed the thicknesses found elsewhere in the British Isles, and there are few places in Scotland where a volcanic 'trap' landscape is so clearly exemplified. The term 'trap' is derived from the Swedish word *trappa*, meaning 'step', and is used internationally to describe the way in which differential erosion of successive lava flows gives a stepped character to the landscape. Where rivers and ice have combined to deepen the valleys and isolate the plateau remnants into tabular hills, the structural benches created by the lava flows can be traced for many miles along the hillslopes. Each of the 'treads', having weathered into a gently sloping terrace on the more friable upper surface of each lava flow, is generally covered with peat and a heathery vegetation. Separating the 'treads' of this volcanic staircase are the steeper, and sometimes precipitous, 'risers' which represent the more resistant lower layers of each lava flow.

The road westwards from Tobermory zigzags up and down the lava terraces, affording glimpses of the lonely Loch Frisa, whose newly planted forest hides the steep slopes of a glacially overdeepened valley. Beyond the conspicuous volcanic plug of S'Airde Beinn (292 m) stretch the bleak headlands of Mishnish, Quinish and Mornish, which complete the steep, cliff-girt coast of northern Mull. The suffix *nish* means 'a flat headland', for this is a coastline carved entirely from basaltic lavas. Dr Johnson spoke of these northern plateaux as a 'gloom of desolation' and suggested that they should be planted with trees to give them a 'more cheerful face'. Some two centuries later the Forestry Commission has obligingly clothed the moorlands with widespread conifer plantations, a policy which has created some controversy among farmers and conservationists alike. This is because the base-rich basalts weather into an excellent soil which, where adequately drained and maintained, produces 'the most fertile land in the Highlands and some equal to the best in the kingdom' (Darling, 1955). It is fair to comment, however, that long before the Forestry Commission turned its attention to Mull the rich cattle grazing lands had already been abandoned to the ubiquitous sheep. Their more selective grazing has meant the appearance of a profuse growth of bracken and hazel scrub in many of the hollows of northern Mull. Studies have demonstrated that during the earliest millennia of the postglacial the Flandrian vegetation of Mull comprised hazel, birch, and oak forest until the arrival of domestic livestock (Lowe and Walker, 1986).

Foremost among the glories of these northern headlands are the views which they afford northwards to the mountains of Ardnamurchan and Rhum, although the coastal walker will also find hidden coves whose dazzling white shell-sand beaches are often carpeted with sea-pinks and dotted with aquamarine pools. Beyond the pretty village of Dervaig the road reaches the west coast at Calgary, whose attractive wooded bay contains a typical Hebridean *machair* landscape, in which shelly sands and coastal dunes combine to support a carpet of flowery grassland (Jeremy and Crabbe, 1978) on the 'sweeter' soils, although the Calgary *machair* is only a tiny pocket in comparison with those of Tiree and the Outer Hebrides. From Calgary southwards the coast road runs along an intensively farmed shelf which stands more than 30 metres above the sea and is backed by the steep scarped edge of the basalt plateau. In many places this shelf is a structural bench, created by erosion of a lava flow, but as it is traced out into the headlands it becomes clear that it is also a raised-beach platform whose abandoned wave-cut notch stands some 40 metres above modern sea level. Since it can be seen that ice has moulded parts of the platform it is now regarded as part of the raised High Rock Platform (Late Devensian) already encountered in Islay and Jura (see Chapter 14). More positive proof of its antiquity has been found on the neighbouring island of Ulva where, not far from the summit of A'Chrannog, an ancient sea-cave, about 45 metres above present sea level, has glacial till surviving on its floor, pushed there by former glaciers. The island of Ulva, composed entirely of basaltic lavas, rises in regular tiers to its flat-topped summit (312 m) and is another excellent example of a trap landscape. But it has also been singled out by Darling (1955) as a warning to Hebridean landowners because of the way in which bad land management on the fertile basaltic soils has led to the profuse growth of bracken in place of the once flourishing natural grassland.

Beyond the narrow channel at Ulva Ferry, where a dolerite plug forms the conspicuous conical hill of Dun Mor, the lengthy sweep of Loch na Keal carries an arm of the sea eastwards to the narrow central isthmus of Mull. The name of this sea-loch means 'loch of the cliffs', and it is impossible to traverse its shores without being aware of the prodigious Gribun scree-skirted precipices which flank its southern coastline (Dawson *et al.*, 1987). At Gruline, where the waist of the island is less than 5 kilometres across, one enters a very different region, much larger than the northern tract, a great deal more mountainous and more geologically complex. Indeed, a glance at an official geology map supports the claim made by the officers of the Geological Survey of Scotland, who noted in 1924 that here was 'the most complicated igneous centre as yet accorded detailed examination anywhere in the world'. Although the apparently interminable sequence of basaltic rocks recurs in even greater thicknesses where these form the island's highest summit of Ben More (966 m), the topography of this mountainous area has been carved very largely from a complex sequence of igneous intrusions which break through the extrusive lava flows. Before coming to grips with the somewhat daunting complexity of southern Mull, however, one must turn to the western headland of Ardmeanach, for here are to be found not only some of the most remarkable landforms in Mull but also some geological phenomena unmatched elsewhere in Britain.

At Gribun cliffs the coast road is one of the most spectacular in Scotland, but also one of the most hazardous, owing to the constant rockfalls and occasional landslips. The instability of the 300 metre basaltic precipices is due to the underlying Mesozoic sedimentaries, which have been eroded by ice sheets moving parallel with the cliff face to cause local oversteepening. Such land-slipping, due to the so-called 'incompetent strata' beneath the lava flows, will be described in greater detail in Skye. The Gribun area serves to demonstrate not only the detailed stratigraphy of the Mesozoic sedimentary rocks where they are sandwiched between the Moinian gneiss and the Tertiary basalt in the sea-cliffs of Loch na Keal, but also the climates which prevailed in Scotland some 100–250 million years ago. At the base of the cliffs Triassic sandstones lie unconformably on the Precambrian, and in earlier centuries some of their beds, of the calcareous type known as *cornstone*, were quarried at Gribun for use as millstones. The neighbouring island of Inch Kenneth is also built from Triassic sandstones, and here the pale cornstones not only form the cliffs below the chapel ruins but also create the basis of the rich sandy soil which, in earlier times, provided a veritable granary for the monks of Iona. Today, cornstone is being formed only in tropical climates where there is a marked alternation between the dry and wet seasons. Alkali-charged ground water is evaporated during the dry season to create concretions of calcium carbonate in the sandy subsoil. The basal conglomerates of the Trias also reflect the palaeoclimate which prevailed in western Scotland some

250 million years ago, for the coarse pebbles appear to have been washed into desert basins by periodic flash-floods (Rast *et al.*, 1968). The torrential rivers of that time must have risen on a western landmass which has now virtually disappeared, since the grey pebbles of the conglomerate came from a Cambrian limestone and the bright red pebbles from the Torridonian.

Above the Trias are good exposures of the so-called 'Rhaetic beds' which mark a transition from Triassic into Jurassic times: the dark, sandy limestones of Gribun, crammed with lamellibranch fossils, constitute the best example of *in-situ* Rhaetic rocks in Scotland. Although traces of Lower Lias (Jurassic) are also present at Gribun, it is the overlying Cretaceous rocks which are of most interest. Except for some of the Morvern outcrops (for example, Beinn Iadain), nowhere else in Scotland displays such a complete succession of Upper Cretaceous sediments, for here the Greensand is overlain by a white quartzose sandstone and a layer of flint-banded chalk. The well-rounded 'millet seed' grains of the intermediate white sandstone are of particular importance, since it has been suggested that they were blown from a neighbouring desert into the Cretaceous sea. Moreover, the Gribun chalk has solution cavities infilled with wind-blown sand grains. In places these formed a thick Early Tertiary sandstone which, together with the underlying chalk, became silicified during tectonic uplift before the lavas were extruded. The final rewards of the Ardmeanach headland are reserved for the intrepid walker, since they can only be reached after several kilometres of scrambling along the shore to the foot of the basaltic cliffs which form the aptly named 'Wilderness'. The northern approach passes the gigantic Mackinnon's Cave, formed perhaps by the higher late glacial sea level which carved the Main Rock Platform of western Scotland (Gray, 1974). Fingal's Cave on Staffa (p. 384) may be of similar age. At the farthest extremity of the headland, below the gigantic basaltic cliffs and screes of the Wilderness are the remains of MacCulloch's Tree. This remarkable geological phenomenon was discovered in 1810, but owing to 'erosion' by fossil-hunters it is now only a 12 metre cast of the original fossil tree which had been buried by the basaltic lavas. Only the lowest part of the trunk can now be seen, a partially silicified cylinder of fossil wood glistening with quartz crystals and surrounded by a sheath of soft, black, charred wood. The 'tree', which stands vertically in the lava cliffs above highwater mark, is rooted in a carbonaceous mud with a film of coal, overlying a bed of red volcanic ash. It is one of only three examples recorded in the Ardmeanach promontory and is clearly related to the organic beds discovered at Ardtun, on the opposite shore of Loch Scridain (see p. 383). However, before examining these deposits, which give evidence of the vegetation prevailing during the volcanic episode, attention must be given to the mountains of southern Mull, for these have been carved from a vast central intrusion complex which in its early history probably acted as a feeder for the extensive plateau basalts.

During the nineteenth century there were two schools of thought relating to the formation of the basaltic lavas of this igneous province. On the one hand Professor J.W. Judd (1889) believed that the basalts were associated with the gigantic central vent volcanoes of Skye, Ardnamurchan and Mull, of which only the 'basal wrecks' remain. Archibald Geikie, on the other hand, supported the contention that the lavas were extruded from linear fissure eruptions fed from dyke-swarms, by analogy with the modern lava plains of Idaho in North America.

In Mull, however, there is evidence to support Judd's hypothesis, since the dykes were created far too late in the Tertiary igneous record for them to have acted as feeders for all the lavas (Tilley and Muir, 1962). Furthermore, there is some indication that a massive caldera, or basaltic crater, existed in central Mull during part of the basaltic period (Fig. 16.1a), although almost all traces of it have been obliterated by the subsequent intrusion of the plutonic rocks.

After the eruption of the extrusive lavas, updoming occurred as volcanic activity increased in intensity, thus building an enormous central vent volcano from which acid volcanics were ejected with explosive force (Fig. 16.1b). This second phase of activity was also marked by the intrusion of the granophyres along the concentric margin of the early basaltic caldera (Fig. 16.1b), and these hard rocks

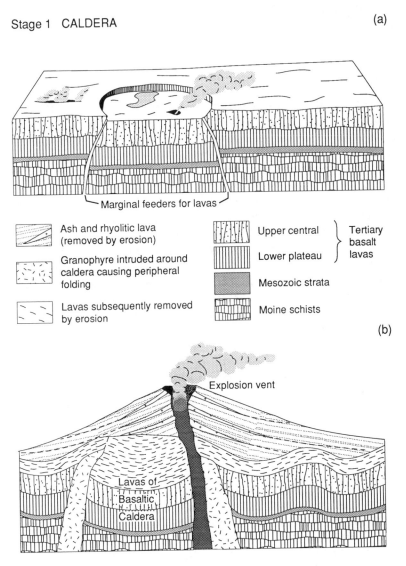

Stage 1   CALDERA   (a)

Marginal feeders for lavas

Ash and rhyolitic lava (removed by erosion)

Granophyre intruded around caldera causing peripheral folding

Lavas subsequently removed by erosion

Upper central · Tertiary basalt lavas
Lower plateau

Mesozoic strata

Moine schists

(b)

Explosion vent

Lavas of Basaltic Caldera

Stage 2   CONE VOLCANO DEVELOPED FROM CALDERA
(Stage 1 above)

Figure 16.1 Hypothetical reconstruction of (a) the caldera and (b) the cone volcano of southern Mull (based on material prepared by the British Geological Survey).

now form the eminence of Glas Bheinn (491 m) overlooking Loch Spelve. In addition, this early intrusion of granophyre gave rise to peripheral folding of the existing rocks, including those of the Loch Don anticline in the south-east (see p. 381). Slightly later the acid magma was replaced by one of basic composition as olivine-rich gabbro was intruded along the early caldera margin. The gabbro now forms the conical mountain of Ben Buie (718 m), behind Loch Buie, and the lesser ridge of Bein Bheag farther north-east, near Glen Forsa. During this early phase of alternating acid/basic magmatic activity large numbers of cone-sheets were injected, themselves reflecting the differences in mineral composition.

As in the case of Ardnamurchan, one finds that there was a progressive shift of igneous activity away from the initial centre (Skelhorn *et al.*, 1969). So far as Mull is concerned, this meant a two-stage shift towards the north-west, Centre 1 being at Beinn Chaisgidle and Centre 2 at Loch Bà. Since the mechanism of ring-dyke formation has already been described in some detail (see pp. 358–9), it will suffice to comment on some of the more prominent landforms which now pick out several of the igneous phenomena. The curving shape of Glen More, for example, that lonely valley of hurrying mists and sweeping rain, has been carved, partly by ice sheets, along the outermost quartz-gabbro ring-dyke (Koomans and Kuenen, 1938) of the Beinn Chaisgidle centre. It is also apparent that the circle of mountains which surrounds Glen Cannel, and whose drainage runs radially inwards towards Loch Bà, reflects the concentric pattern of ring-dykes around this first centre. The Glen Cannel granophyre, however, which marks the opening phase of igneous activity around Loch Bà, appears to have been less resistant to the forces of erosion than have the surrounding lavas and ring-dykes, for its topographic expression corresponds largely with the glacially overdeepened trough of Glen Cannel and Loch Bà. The felsite ring-dyke of Loch Bà is virtually unbroken and marks the boundary of the final caldera formation (Lewis, 1968). The block of country which it encloses is known to have subsided, relative to the surrounding rocks, a vertical distance of more than 900 metres.

A final note is necessary concerning the dyke-swarms of Mull, many of which cut through the Centre 2 ring-dykes, with which they should not be confused. Each of the central intrusion complexes of western Scotland had its own radiating dyke-swarm. Although these were created throughout the entire period of volcanic activity, there seems to be a greater concentration of dyke formation towards the closing phases of the Tertiary volcanic period, perhaps at a time when the igneous activity had insufficient energy to reach the surface. Western Scotland is seamed with thousands of such narrow linear igneous outcrops, which cut indiscriminately through the country rocks, be they igneous, sedimentary or metamorphic. Dykes, which occur as thin vertical sheets along lengthy fissures, or cracks in the crust, are characterized by a finely crystalline structure, suggesting that the lava cooled rapidly as it was forced vertically upwards from the magma chamber through thousands of metres of overlying crust. The dyke-swarms can be traced to the Outer Hebrides in one direction and as far as northern England in the other (Fig. 16.2), having everywhere baked the rocks through which they were injected, this baking being known as *contact metamorphism* (Richey, 1939). Occasionally the metamorphosed rock may be so tough that it has resisted denudation more effectively than the dyke itself, so that a linear trench marks the topographic expression of the intrusion. More often, however, the dyke itself is harder than the surrounding rocks and stands up from the landscape like an

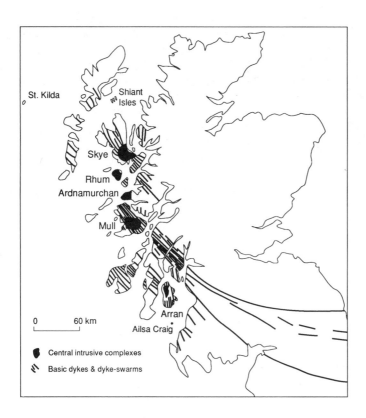

Figure 16.2 Tertiary dyke-swarms and central intrusive complexes of north-west Scotland (based on material prepared by the British Geological Survey).

artificial wall (or 'dyke'). Dykes are particularly visible on the seashore all along the south-eastern coast of Mull.

The curving shorelines of this south-eastern coast, together with the parallel arcuate trend of Loch Uisag and Loch Spelve, reflect the concentric structures of the island's central intrusion complex. The concentric folds around the perimeter of this igneous complex can best be studied in the Loch Don area. Here a sharply folded anticline, possibly of Tertiary age (Bailey, 1962), has been denuded sufficiently to uncover the Dalradian schists of its central core, where the overlying Palaeozoic lavas, Mesozoic sedimentaries and Tertiary basalts have been stripped away. The present landforms reflect the cigar-shaped inlier (or *window*) of older rocks where these emerge from beneath the ubiquitous cover of basaltic lavas. The tiny Loch a Ghleannain marks the central outcrop of the Dalradian Schists; the steep surrounding ramparts, such as the forested ridge of Druim Mor Aird, have been carved from the tougher lavas of Old Red Sandstone age; the narrow perimeter vales of Glen Rainich (to the west) and Glen Ardnadrochet (to the east) show the less resistant qualities of the slender outcrop of the Lower Jurassic shales and Inferior Oolite.

From a structural point of view, the occurrence of a blue-grey Dalradian limestone at the centre of the Loch Don anticline is of more than academic interest. That the limestone can be correlated with that of Lismore Island, at the mouth of Loch Linnhe (see p. 355), suggests that the Great Glen Fault crosses into Mull to the west of Loch Don and that it was probably bent southwards by the Tertiary folding described above. Furthermore, late movements along this major fault can be shown to have affected both the Mesozoic strata and the Tertiary basalts of Duart Bay, where the well-known thirteenth-century castle stands majestically on its black lava cliffs (Duart is from *Dubh Ard*, meaning 'black point'). The neighbouring bay at Craignure has also been carved from an anticlinal structure, with Triassic as well as Lower Jurassic rocks revealed along the shoreline. These include the greenish Lower Lias shales (equivalent to the Pabba Shales of Skye), which can be traced intermittently south-westwards around the coast, where they project from beneath the lava cliffs to form a conspicuous coastal shelf between the mouths of Loch Spelve and Loch Buie. Between Port Donain and Port nam Marbh the shales are accompanied by a thick, white, cliff-forming sandstone (Middle Lias – the Scalpa Sandstone of Skye), together with the Upper Liassic shales and the Inferior Oolite. The mountain-girt recesses of Loch Spelve and Loch Buie are also of great interest, for the Triassic sandstones are well represented and the extremely fertile soils of this area have caused it to be called the 'Garden of Mull'.

Glaciers have clearly been responsible for the overdeepening of Loch Spelve (36 m), whose waters now spill seawards over a shallow submarine threshold. The ice was probably generated from the neighbouring mountains of southern Mull, for it is known that Mull had its own ice cap during the Main Devensian and again in the Loch Lomond Stadial when the Ben More glaciers crossed the present coastline near Salen, and at Loch Spelve, Loch Buie and Loch na Keal (Gray and Brooks, 1972). The marine shells of the Kinlochspelve moraine have been dated by radiocarbon techniques which indicate an age of some 11 000 years, suggesting that the local glaciers scooped up marine deposits which had been laid down during the preceding interstadial period of the Late Pleistocene, when sea waters must have flooded into the arcuate corridor. Further research has finally established that the Loch Spelve moraines are of Loch Lomond Readvance age. Other terminal moraines of this age may be seen at the western ends of Glen More and Loch Bà, while Glen Forsa exhibits hummocky lateral moraines and an outwash fan at its northern end (Walker *et al.*, 1985). Whether or not it was this late piedmont phase which caused the major glacial breach now followed by the Lussa River, where it breaks out of the eastern end of Glen More, is a matter for conjecture.

Also on the south coast of Mull, at Carsaig, there is an interesting succession of Mesozoic rocks. The richness of the soils in this tiny pocket of calcarous rocks introduces an unusual oasis of prosperous farmland and watercress beds into the deserted moorlands of the basaltic trap landscape. Below the grey basaltic beach sands, Carsaig Bay is floored by flat slabs of dark grey shales (Pabba Shales) crammed with fossil ammonites, each glinting with pyrite minerals. The overlying Scalpa Sandstones, of Middle Lias age, form the cliffs to the west of the bay, where, near the so-called Nun's Pass, they were once quarried for use in the doorways, pillars and windows of the renowned abbey on Iona. This massive creamy sandstone, much in demand as a freestone in earlier centuries, is unusual in possessing large, sandy, calcarous inclusions known as 'doggers', which are generally darker and harder than the main sandstone, in which they were formed as lime-rich concretions. The overlying Cretaceous greensand and thin Tertiary sandstone are only of academic importance, although the Tertiary lignitic coals and the Nun's Cave sapphires have been of more widespread interest. The latter occur as tiny impure crystals of corundum associated with the thermal metamorphism created by the doleritic sills, while the carbonaceous deposits represent ancient weathered land surfaces which existed during the Tertiary volcanic episode in Mull. Similar carbonaceous deposits are more clearly exhibited at Ardtun, several kilometres farther west, where the trap landscape of Brolass is terminated abruptly by the line of the Bunessan fault. Like the lignite bands, the famous 'leaf-beds' of Ardtun Head substantiate the belief that the Tertiary volcanoes of the Inner Hebrides were not continuously in eruption. During dormant periods soils and vegetation became established on the basaltic lava plains, only to be buried by later eruptions. The leaf remains demonstrate that the trees growing in the warmer climate of Early Tertiary times had Far Eastern affinities and were not related to modern British varieties. Of these the maidenhair tree (*Ginkgo*) of China, the *Cryptomeria* of Japan and the beautiful *Magnolia* appear to have been the most exotic, although species of oak, hazel and plane were also present. The leaf-beds were deposited in temporary lakes on the lava surface which also acted as receptacles for the gravels and sands that now mark the interbasaltic horizon (Cooper, 1979).

To the west of Bunessan the undulating terrain of the Moinian mica schists soon gives way to the rolling, peat-covered moorlands and bare hills of the Caledonian granite of the Ross of Mull. Varying in colour from pale to deep red, this coarse biotite granite has been extensively quarried as a building stone. The quarries near Fionnphort, at the western tip of the peninsula, demonstrate how the widely spaced jointing and the proximity of natural harbours facilitated the export of the gigantic blocks to all parts of Britain. Thus, the Mull granite was utilized in such London structures as Blackfriars Bridge, Holborn Viaduct and the Albert Memorial. Its earliest recorded use, however, was in the seventh-century Abbey of Iona itself, where rounded glacial erratics and other surface blocks were used in the rubble walling.

Iona and Staffa

From the low hill of Dun on Iona it is possible to view some of the scenic elements that make up Iona's incomparable landscape. To the north, the misty hills of Rhum are framed by the headlands of Mull and Coll; nearer at hand the basaltic specks of Staffa and the Treshnish Isles are outliers of Mull's northern tablelands; below is the green *machair* whose white shell-sands continue off shore along Iona's northern coast, turning the encircling sea into pools of brilliant turquoise and hyacinth. Westwards the low hills of Tiree are barely visible in the pearly Atlantic haze, but southwards the surf breaks uneasily on the treacherous granite fangs of the Torran Rocks. Far away beyond them the Paps of Jura announce their unmistakable presence, while to the east the deep blues and soft purples of the cloud-capped mountains of southern Mull contrast with the shining red granite of the Ross and the sparkling waters of the Sound of Iona itself. The overall effect is completed by the pale shell-like iridescence of the Atlantic light, diffused by the moisture-laden air.

The ancient Lewisian and Torridonian rocks of Iona are so different from the Mull succession that it has been suggested that the Moine Thrust is submerged beneath the Sound of Iona (see Fig. 15.7). Few of these rocks have, however, been utilized in the ecclesiastical buildings themselves. The nunnery and Cathedral walls, for example, are constructed largely from pink Ross granite, local black schists and the creamy Carsaig freestone. Some of the older roofing and flooring is made of flaggy Moinian schists, quarried on a small scale on the Ross of Mull, but much of the newer restoration has been carried out with imported materials. In addition to the Carsaig freestone used in the mouldings, the interior of the Cathedral has some ornamentation created from the Iona Marble, whose attractive green and white rock – a white metamorphosed limestone streaked by a green variety of serpentine – occurs in narrow veins among the Precambrian rocks of the seashore at the south end of the island, especially at Port na Churaich, named after St Columba's historic landfall in AD 563.

When one considers its minute size (smaller than Ailsa Craig), it is surprising to find that Staffa is one of the best-known islands in Britain (MacCulloch, 1957). Although its geological wonders must have been known to the inhabitants of Mull, Ulva and Iona, it was not until the visit of Sir Joseph Banks in 1772 that this basaltic masterpiece became more generally known. The aesthetic appeal of the island is based entirely on its geological character; the basalts of its sea cliffs are not only excellent examples of columnar structures, but also have the advantage of remarkable caves. At Fingal's Cave the structural differences within a single lava flow, reflecting the contrasting rates of cooling after its intrusion, are clearly shown (Fig. 16.3). The slaggy crust cooled rapidly from above to produce an almost structureless capping (now forming the roof of Fingal's Cave); the middle part of the flow also cooled from above, but at a slower and more uniform rate, the loss of water and regularity of contraction leading to the formation of narrow polygonal columns; the lowest part of the flow cooled from below, with an even more uniform rate of contraction, to produce the massive, regularly spaced columns which now form the 'causeway' leading into the cave. The columns are always arranged at right angles to the cooling surface,

Figure 16.3 The Isle of Staffa, the sea-caves of which, including Fingal's Cave (right), have been carved in the lower columnar horizons of a basaltic lava flow. The slaggy crust of the flow forms the cave roofs.

and most of them are vertical because in the majority of cases this isothermal surface was horizontal. If, however, the lava spilled into an existing hollow or valley, as at the Buchaille Rock and Clamshell Cave, then in some sections the columns will be curved or tilted obliquely.

The neighbouring Treshnish Isles are, like Staffa, parts of the same lava sheets which form the western headlands of northern Mull and the isles of Ulva and Gometra. Their tabular form is most pronounced, especially on the island of Bac Mor (The Great Hump), popularly known as the Dutchman's Cap, where the 'brim' is a marine-eroded platform and the 'crown' a remnant of several over-lying lava flows. The wave-cut platform stands at an elevation of some 30 metres and appears to be part of the High Rock Platform raised shoreline of the Western Isles. Today the Treshnish Isles are given over to grazing sheep because of their high-quality grasslands.

Tiree and Coll

Most visitors to these isles will probably note that their geology and scenery are more reminiscent of the Outer Hebrides than of Mull, an impression which the widespread presence of the lime-rich *machair* confirms. It is more convenient to examine them at this point, however, because of their geographical proximity to Mull. The contrast in relief between the latter and these off-shore satellites is most marked, for, while Mull is characterized by the vertical planes of high mountains and precipitous sea-cliffs, Tiree and Coll exhibit a remarkable horizontality, neither of them rising above 135 metres.

Despite its low hills of Lewisian gneiss (Westbrook, 1972), Tiree gives a persistent impression of flatness. This is because of its widespread deposits of blown shell-sand (*machair*) and its suite of late-glacial and post-glacial raised beaches. The resulting fertile pasturelands have been described thus by Scott-Moncrieff (1951): 'a brilliant green flatness contained beneath a great domed bowl of sky . . . [giving] a rare and exhilarating quality to the sense of space and light . . . light pouring from the sky and bouncing back from the sea, enveloping everything'. The low elevation of the island has meant that although clouds do not persist (making it one of the sunniest spots in Britain) the wind is almost constant, inhibiting virtually all tree growth. Wind has also affected the architectural style: the older buildings are squat stone cottages with walls almost 3 metres thick. The reason for such thickness is that these buildings (known as 'black-houses') were usually double-walled, the space between being filled with sand into which rainwater ran from the thatched or tarred roof. Because of the shortage of local timber the roof-beams were made of driftwood and thus mostly short, making the roofs incongruously low and narrow but less wind-resistant. Today the mortared jointing of the rubble-walled houses has sometimes been picked out in white paint with the centres of the stone left bare, giving a bizarre giraffe-like patterning to the domestic architecture.

Because of its exceptional physical endowment, Tiree supports one of the most successful crofting communities in the Hebrides, one in which the crofter does not have to rely on supplementary incomes from forestry or fishing (Coull, 1962). The underlying Lewisian gneiss creates only a handful of low, rocky hills in Tiree, and it seems clear that these must have become insular skerries during the higher sea levels of raised-beach times. The ancient tripartite division of land use reflects the three different types of terrain on the island. First, there is the lime-rich *machair* of the coasts and the central lowland (known as the Reef), which is given over entirely to the grazing of cattle and sheep (Vose *et al.*, 1959). Second, there are the slightly heavier soils of the raised beaches, where blown shell-sand has alleviated some of the acidity due to impedance of drainage. This land is devoted to arable farming and is termed *achadh*. Finally, there are the hill masses of acid peat and bare rock, together with some of the bogs on the raised beaches, which will support only rough grazing, locally known as *sliabh*. Although the majority of the land-holders have equal shares in these lands of contrasting quality – *machair*, *achadh* and *sliabh* – overstocking on the *machair* is tending to break up the sward, generating 'blow-outs' and the encroachment of dune-sand.

Although of approximately equal size to Tiree, the neighbouring island of Coll exhibits a very different landscape because the acid Lewisian gneiss is exposed over three-quarters of its surface area (Drury, 1972). The virtual absence of glacial drift (as found in Lewis) or rich basaltic soils (as found in Mull) means that thin moorland and peat bog occur directly on the stony surface. Nevertheless, about one-sixth of Coll is covered by shell-sand, so that *machair* is found along the windward fringes of the western and southern coasts. The very small area of land suitable for cultivation has meant that crofting has virtually disappeared on the island, except on the raised beaches of Sorisdale at the northern tip. The more fertile swards of the southern end have been devoted to cattle-grazing ever since the crofters were 'cleared' in the nineteenth century and replaced by Kintyre dairy farmers with their Ayrshire cows.

The Small Isles

Lying between the rugged Ardnamurchan peninsula and the mountain fastnesses of southern Skye is a cluster of islands whose geographical grouping has led to them being dubbed the 'Small Isles of Inverness-shire' as an administrative convenience. Nevertheless, these delightfully named islands of Muck, Eigg, Canna and Rhum each have a distinctive character, different from that of their neighbours.

The smallest island, Muck, is also one of the most fertile of the Hebrides because of its deeply weathered basaltic rocks, its glacial-drift cover and its veneer of calcareous beach sands which have been blown inland. The fertility of the island's soils is reflected in the richness of its pasturelands, which in early summer are carpeted with masses of purple vetches, dazzling blue cornflowers and golden marigolds. Because of the low elevation and relatively low rainfall, peat has never accumulated to any extent, so the few remaining islanders use imported coal now that they have stopped visiting the copious Ardnamurchan bogs for their peat supplies. Basaltic lavas form the land surface, although shales and limestones of Middle Jurassic age are exposed as tidal reefs along the south-west coast. The lavas are virtually horizontal and generally give rise to low moor-covered plateaus, except in the south-west, where the isolated hill of Beinn Airein (137 m) exhibits a terraced form because of its intrusive sills of dolerite. Among the most distinctive features of Muck are its shore platforms, since these are seamed by a multitude of intrusive igneous dykes. Running into the sea with remarkable regularity, these wall-like doleritic dykes rise 6 to 9 metres above the wave-cut platforms, having resisted erosion more successfully than the basaltic lavas into which they were injected.

When compared with Muck, the island of Eigg presents a very different scene, despite the similarity of their trap landscapes. For a start it is about four times as large; it also has a much greater exposure of Mesozoic rocks and its basalts build considerably higher hills; but above all, it is the overwhelming presence of the famous Sgurr which makes Eigg significantly different. The thick lava succession rises from a plinth of Mesozoic rocks to form two flat-topped plateaux in the western and eastern halves of the island, separated by a fault-guided valley along which most of the island's settlement is located. As elsewhere in the Hebrides, the trap landscape is bounded by precipitous cliffs, which are especially marked in the north-eastern corner of the island. This is due partly to the fact that the basalts lie directly on a series of so-called 'incompetent strata' (which they have helped preserve), including thin Cretaceous sandstones and thick sedimentaries of middle Jurassic age. The latter are made up of alternating limestones and shales whose erosion has facilitated landslipping (and therefore constant 'freshening' of the overlying lava cliffs), together with some 60 metres of calcareous sandstones which have weathered to produce fertile soils wherever they are exposed.

Some of the best soils are found at the small crofting village of Cleadale, which nestles peacefully on the grassy, south-facing slopes beneath the black basaltic cliffs at the northern tip of the island. Here too are the well-known 'singing sands' of Camas Sgiotaig ('the bay of the musical sand') derived from the weathering of the calcareous Jurassic sandstone, and which emit a curious squeaking note when walked upon. Another interesting feature, in the eastern part of Eigg, is the so-called Reptile-bed among the Upper Jurassic shales which crop out on the foreshore to the north of Kildonan village (Turner, 1966). Discovered by the eminent geologist, Hugh Miller (see p. 430), during his Hebridean cruises in the famous *Betsey*, this Jurassic stratum contains some of the earliest described remnants of fossil reptile bones and teeth, together with pterodactyl and dinosaur remains.

All of these phenomena pale into insignificance, however, by comparison with Eigg's most notable landform, the great volcanic skyscraper of An Sgurr (Bailey, 1914). Rising in smooth precipitous cliffs of columnar pitchstone and associated felsite sheets to a height of 394 metres, the remarkable Sgurr of Eigg is unique in the British Isles. Towering above the landing pier at Galmisdale the pitchstone ridge presents a profile matched only by that of Suilven in Sutherland. Its genesis has been interpreted in several ways, none more intriguing than that of Geikie (1888), who saw it as the remains of a sinuous lava flow which infilled a former valley carved in the surrounding basalts. The glassy pitchstone lava is seen to overlie 'a bed of compacted shingle, in which there is an abundance of coniferous wood, in chips and broken branches', thought by Geikie to mark a former river-course developed after the plateau basalts had solidified. It has been suggested that when the pitchstone lava-flow had overrun the Tertiary vegetation of this valley and itself solidified, its resistance to erosion proved greater than that of the surrounding basalts. By now the latter have been denuded sufficiently to leave the long ridge of the Sgurr rising abruptly above the south-western corner of the island.

Unlike the other members of the Small Isles group, Canna has no Mesozoic rocks exposed from beneath the plateau basalts. Indeed its structure is extremely simple, for the virtually horizontal Tertiary lavas make up most of the geological succession apart from the interbedded agglomerates and tuffs, while doleritic sills merely emphasize the terraced appearance of the hill slopes in this trap landscape. This step-like succession of the various volcanic strata can best be studied in the precipitous sea cliffs of Compass Hill (137 m) at the north-eastern end of the island. The singular name of this coastal eminence is derived from the fact that the iron content of its lavas is sufficiently high to deflect the magnetic compasses of ships sailing through the sound. Canna's narrow island, like neighbouring Sanday (to which it is linked at low water), exhibits the soil fertility which one has come to associate with deeply weathered basalts. The grazing supports a high density of sheep and cattle, although the area near to the village of A'Chill is given over to arable farming on the even richer soils derived from the volcanic tuffs. This sheltered, south-facing slope of eastern Canna, protected by the island of Sanday, can produce the earliest potato crops anywhere in north-west Scotland because of its favoured soils and aspect (Campbell, 1984). Although only a few trees grow there today, fossil pollen-grains within the peat bogs show that pine, hazel, willow, birch, oak and alder flourished on Canna and Sanday during different periods of post-glacial time.

The bright green grasslands of Muck, Eigg and Canna are not repeated on the larger isle of Rhum. The mountainous nature of the island is partly responsible for this, but in addition the widespread occurrences of granitic and felsitic igneous rocks, and an extensive outcrop of Torridon Sandstone, have combined to produce much more acid soils. When one adds to these factors the widespread blanket bogs and the intensive leaching of mineral salts from many of Rhum's soils, owing to its excessive rainfall, it can be seen why the island has a vegetation cover and land use very different from those of its smaller neighbours.

Since the Nature Conservancy Council took over the management of the island, visitors are normally granted permission to land only at Loch Scresort, where the tiny settlement is fringed by the only woodland and farmland on the entire island. From this eastern inlet the glen penetrates deeply into the deserted heart of the island, where it opens out into a curious 'crossroads' of radiating valleys. To the north lies Kilmory Glen, which is incised deeply into a flat-topped boggy plateau of Torridon Sandstone (Black and Welsh, 1961); southwards, the valley which encloses the ribbon-lake of Loch Long leads into the hidden corries of Rhum's southern mountains. The linearity of these north–south valleys in central Rhum can be explained by the presence of a major fault which slices through all the island's rocks and along whose line of weakness erosion is obviously facilitated. The 'crossroads' is completed by the west-trending Glen Shellesder, which crosses to an anomalous Triassic exposure and the remote cliffs and waterfalls of the north-western coast. The valleyfloors and the Torridonian plateau surfaces of northern Rhum carry a thick cover of blanket bog, while the intervening valley-slopes and the better-drained surfaces are more conducive to the growth of *Calluna* moorland, which flourishes on the acid soils and supports large herds of Red Deer.

A contrast in scenery occurs in the more rugged southern sector of the island. Here the surface of the Torridonian strata gives way suddenly to the dark, rocky crags of Tertiary plutonic rocks, whose summits rise dramatically from the boggy sandstone tableland to heights of more than 750 metres. Their cliff-faces, jagged sawtooth ridges, pinnacled summits and vast aprons of screes are analogous with those of the more famous Cuillins in Skye, and it is no surprise to discover that the geology of the two massifs is extremely similar. This is yet another example of the remarkable scenery created from the igneous rocks of a central intrusion complex of Tertiary age (Black, 1952). Many of the lithological and structural phenomena of Arran, Ardnamurchan and Mull are repeated here: the bounding ring-fault, the cone-sheets, the radial dykes, and the central plutonic complex from which the highest peaks have been carved.

The major differences between Rhum and the other central intrusion complexes are, first, the paucity of its plateau basalts (hence the absence of a trap landscape), and second, the fact that its plutonic rocks include a greater development of ultrabasic rocks than anywhere else in Britain. In addition to the basic gabbro and eucrite, such rocks as, for example, peridotite, harrisite and allivalite help create the rugged crags, the two latter taking their names from their British type-sites of Glen Harris and the peak of Allival (or Hallival), respectively (Dunham and Emeleus, 1967).

The bare rock summits of Allival (721 m) and Askival (811 m) have a markedly stepped pyramidal form, due to the differential weathering of the alternating bands of allivalite and peridotite (Brown, 1956): the small escarpments (or risers) have been carved from the tougher bands of allivalite and the more gentle intervening slopes (or treads) from the peridotite. Since the eucrites and gabbros were later intruded as sheets both beneath and into the ultrabasic rocks noted above, they now form a pronounced plinth from which the high summits rise (Tomkieff, 1945). One noteworthy feature of these lower slopes is the way in which the stony screes give way downhill to a relatively herb-rich heathland, where the soils have been enriched by such minerals as calcium and magnesium from the underlying basic rocks. Not all the southern peaks have been carved from basic rocks, however, for Sgurr nan Gillean (763 m) has a summit-capping of quartz-felsite, as does the attractively conical peak of Beinn nan Stac (Hughes, 1960). Over on the west coast a substantial Tertiary granitic intrusion is largely responsible for the more gently domed mountain group of western Rhum. Here the central microgranite has been attacked by Atlantic waves to produce the spectacular sea cliffs of Schooner Point and Wreck Bay (McCann and Richards, 1969). A basaltic lava capping helps create the scarped summit plateau on the granite peak of Orval (570 m), but the neighbouring summit of Ard Nev has been carved from an anomalous exposure of Lewisian gneiss. This, like similar outcrops near Loch Long and on the slopes of Sgurr nan Gillean, has been interpreted as a slice of the ancient basement brought to the surface along steeply inclined fractures during the Tertiary igneous episode.

A final word is necessary concerning the Pleistocene history of Rhum, for much of its distinctive scenery must have been created by glaciers. The scattered patches of glacial drift at all elevations suggest that the island, like the remainder of the Inner Hebrides, was completely overridden by early ice advances from the mainland. The glacial striations demonstrate, however, that at some subsequent stage Rhum carried its own distinct ice cap, and at that time the island's central glens became greatly overdeepened as the valley glaciers moved radially outwards. Although much of the glacial smoothing and quarrying relates to these earlier advances, the final etching appears to have been the work of the local equivalent of the Loch Lomond Readvance (Ballantyne and Wain-Hobson, 1980). The corries of the southern peaks contain moraine-dammed lakes, and it seems probable that Glen Dibidil and upper Glen Harris carried small glaciers, judging by their morainic accumulations. Meanwhile the bare rock peaks were sharpened by frost-shattering, thus adding to the cliff-foot screes which abound in Rhum (Ryder and McCann, 1971). It also seems likely that during this last glacial phase there was a second tiny ice cap in the granitic terrain of the north-west, for the northern slopes of Orval have long stretches of glacially plucked cliffs.

Skye

Skye is an island of superlatives: measuring 80 by 32 kilometres, it is the largest of the Hebrides; it has the grandest mountain group in the British Isles; it boasts the largest expanse of basaltic plateaux in Britain (Bell and Harris, 1986). Few would dispute that it is an island of great diversity and a place of changing mood – from the wind-lashed and cloud-mantled melancholy of winter to the overwhelming beauty of a sunny spring or summer day, when the mountains are sharply etched against the sky (Sillar and Meyer, 1973). Skye is a land of bold peninsulas, which dominate its shape to such an extent that there are those who claim that its name is derived from *sgiath*, the Gaelic word for 'wing' – hence its oft-used sobriquet, the Winged Isle. One senses a recurring presence of the ocean, with the sea-lochs biting deeply into the interior to create a majestic picture of high mountains mirrored in restless tidal waters, none more so than where Loch Coruisk and Loch Scavaig are cradled beneath the towering Cuillins rhapsodized by Scott, recaptured by Turner's paintings and claimed by some writers to be the finest mountains in the British Isles.

At the island's southern end, where only the narrows of Kyle Akin and Kyle Rhea detach Skye from the mainland, the ribby peninsula of Sleat bears a closer resemblance to the mainland than the remainder of Skye. Although the Torridon Sandstone rises to about 600 metres in the twin sentinels of Sgurr na Coinnich and Beinn Aslak, which overlook Kyle Rhea, these barren sandstones and shales more often coincide with the lower boggy hills which form the backbone of the peninsula. Few crofts can be found in this peat-covered landscape of northern Sleat, but south of Loch na Dal there is a surprising change of scene, not all of it capable of explanation merely in terms of the geology. Southern Sleat was considerably involved in the Caledonian nappe formation and thrust movements with both Lewisian gneisses and Moinian metasediments (Bailey, 1955) being carried westwards along three thrust planes including that of the Moine Thrust; the Torridonian itself has also been thrust bodily across the younger Cambrian near to Loch Eishort (Cheeney and Matthews, 1965) (Fig. 16.4). Traditionally, Lewisian gneiss is associated with barren landscapes in which thin soils, rocky outcrops and peat bogs combine to produce a wilderness unconducive to agricultural improvement. Along the Sound of Sleat, however, the Archaean gneisses belie this reputation, so that between Isle Ornsay and Armadale the farming has an air of prosperity missing from the Torridonian country farther north. It is difficult to account for this apparent anomaly, although the presence of basic

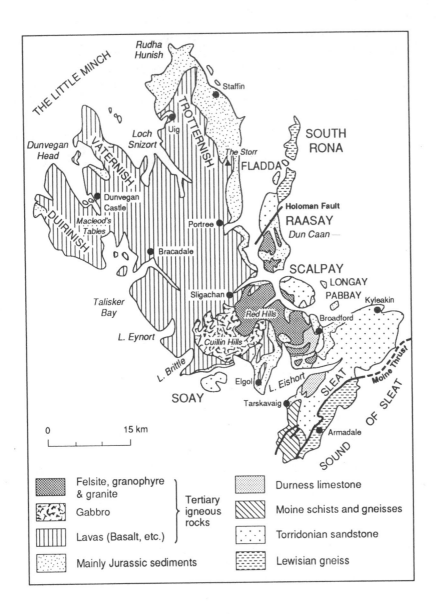

Figure 16.4 Geology of Skye (based on material prepared by the British Geological Survey).

intrusions and the lighter soils of the raised-beach terraces may have some bearing on the answer.

On the western side of the Sleat peninsula, the prosperous crofts near Ord can be picked out by their lush hayfields, flourishing crops and extensive woodlands, a landscape so different from the remainder of the island that it has been dubbed the 'Garden of Skye'. It is a great deal easier to explain this oasis of fertility, however, because the well-drained soils hereabouts are derived in part from a patch of Cambrian limestones, the southernmost example of the Durness Limestone which stretches as a linear outcrop from here to Cape Wrath. Its limited exposure in Sleat is marked not only by a richer limestone flora but also by a few caves and hollows (known as swallow-holes) where the drainage has disappeared below ground owing to the porous nature of the limestone. In addition, a sparkling white Cambrian quartzite helps form a line of hills behind Ord, with the same beds extending into Loch Eishort to form a number of islands. A natural ash wood which flourishes on the limestone at Tarskavaig is so unusual in 'treeless Skye' that it has been designated a site of special scientific interest. Although not found on the limestone, a mixed oak and birch woodland survives on the Cambrian quartzites near Ord.

The isthmus between Loch Eishort and Broadford Bay is something of a surprise, for its peat-covered lowland is floored by one of the largest exposures of Mesozoic rocks in the Hebrides (Fig. 16.4). From Loch Slapin around to the Scalpay narrows in the north, the curving lowland corresponds largely with an outcrop, 3 kilometres wide, of Triassic and Liassic rocks. Although thin limestones occur in the Lower Liassic succession – known as the Broadford Beds (Hallam, 1959) – the predominant rocks are the gently dipping Pabba Shales, whose type-site is the remarkably flat island of Pabbay, lying off Broadford Bay. In contrast, the tiny island of Longay even farther off shore is made up of Torridonian rocks, as is the larger, hump-backed island of Scalpay, which hugs Skye's eastern shores, except for a limited downfaulted outcrop of Scalpa Sandstone of Middle Lias age, near Scalpay House (Howarth, 1956). Despite the apparent fertility of the Liassic soils on Scalpay and Pabbay, the prosperous farmlands of England's Liassic Vale of Evesham are not repeated in Skye, because the rainfall is too heavy, the drainage too poor and the felsite intrusions too numerous both in Strath and the peninsula of Strathaird which is reached via the curving Strath Suardal, around the footslopes of Beinn na Caillich's granite peak (733 m). Because of its thick infilling of glacial drift, there are few pointers to the change of lithology in Strath Suardal apart from the increased woodland in the lake-filled valley. The strath, with its richer vegetation, has in fact been carved along the junction of the Tertiary igneous rocks with the less resistant Cambrian limestones, already encountered in Sleat. Here, however, the anticlinal limestone outcrop is more extensive, sweeping around the base of the granite mountains in a wide crescent from coast to coast. It is interesting to note that the eastern margin of the Cambrian limestone is terminated by the line of a major thrust-fault marking the western limit of the Kishorn Nappe, where the Torridonian strata can be seen to overlie the Cambrian (Bailey, 1954). Glen Suardal and Loch Lanachan have been etched out along this line of weakness as the thrust-fault curves round to follow the strike of the Cambrian anticlinal axis. Although the Tertiary granite of Beinn an Dubhaich (Raybould, 1973) has invaded the limestone upfold, there are excellent exposures of the limestones, with grike development exhibited where they form the low ridge of Ben Suardal. But, as with the neighbouring Liassic limestones, their agricultural potential has not been realized, owing to the drift cover and the igneous intrusions. Nevertheless, in an environment where acid soils predominate, the Torrin quarry on Loch Slapin now exports great quantities of stone both for agricultural and for building and decorative purposes. It is locally known as 'Skye marble', for where the limestone comes into contact with the igneous intrusions of Beinn na Caillich and Beinn an Dubhaich it has been converted into a hard marble by thermal metemorphism. Like their counterparts at Ord, the majority of the Strath Suardaig limestones are of a dolomitic variety – that is, the normal calcium carbonate ($CaCO_3$) has been bolstered by the addition of magnesium to form a dolomite.

The promontory of Strathaird, which divides Loch Slapin from Loch Scavaig, offers a splendid viewpoint at Elgol: westwards to the flat Torridon Sandstone island of Soay, southwards to Rhum and Eigg and, especially, north-westwards to the Cuillins. The peninsula itself has a foundation of Middle to upper Jurassic rocks, ranging from the Inferior Oolite through the Great Estuarine Series (Hudson, 1962) to the Oxford Clay. In the west, however, these Mesozoic sandstones, shales and limestones are capped by thick plateau basalts and dolerite sills; the Elgol road serves to divide the igneous hills, such as Ben Meabost (343 m), from the till- and peat-covered sedimentary platform of the south-eastern shores, where numerous sea-caves have been carved into the well-jointed calcareous sandstones.

Compared with the complexities of Mull and Ardnamurchan, the Tertiary plutonic masses of Skye have a relatively simple arrangement of their component parts, partly because of the contrasting topography of the granite and the gabbro hills (Brown *et al.*, 1969). Moreover, the magnificent plateau-lava country of northern Skye adds another type of remarkable scenery. A distinction has always been made between the Red Hills and the Black Cuillins; this reflects not only the differences in colour between the granite and the gabbro but also the contrasts in texture, form and elevation. The highland massif of central Skye can in fact be subdivided into four mountain groups, each corresponding to a separate plutonic centre: first, the gabbro hills of the Black Cuillins (Fig. 16.5); second,

Figure 16.5 The Black Cuillins of Skye. The ridge of Sgurr nan Gillean has been sharpened by glacial and periglacial processes, fashioning the obdurate dark gabbro into frost-splintered pinnacles.

a complex group comprising the isolated peak of Blaven and the granite of Meall Dearg and Ruadh Stac; third, the granitic Western Red Hills (sometimes called Lord Macdonald's Forest) (Fig. 16.6); fourth, the granitic Eastern Red Hills including Beinn na Caillich (see Fig. 16.4). These represent, in age, a generally eastward shift of activity of the intrusive complexes (Bell, 1976).

In essence, the Cuillins are an arcuate mass of ultrabasic peridotite which has subsequently been invaded by a large number of olivine-rich gabbro sheets. The whole plutonic complex has been intruded into the earlier basaltic lava plains which underlie the drift mounds and peat bogs around Sligachan. To the south of Sligachan the spire of Sgurr nan Gillean (966 m) soars into the sky, its pinnacled northern ridge running out like a gigantic flying buttress (Fig. 16.5). Here the corrie of Am Bhasteir holds a tiny lochan, backed by the savage cliffs of Am Bhasteir and the pinnacle of the Bhasteir Tooth, all carved from frost-shattered gabbro.

The ravines and vertical gullies which seam the bare rock-faces of the Cuillins have been eroded into basic dykes, part of the major dyke-swarm running north-west to south-east. Where these intersect the ridges and ice-steepened arêtes they often form notches in the skyline (as in the Waterpipe Gully of Sgurr an Fheadain), which accounts in part for the serrated appearance of the peaks themselves. On the Red Hills, however, the basic dykes are not as numerous and are generally more resistant to erosion than the surrounding granite, so that they tend to stand out in relief. This is occasionally true of the Cuillin dykes also, the most famous example being the so-called Inaccessible Pinnacle, which stands up as a narrow wall on the summit of Sgurr Dearg (977 m).

Figure 16.6 The Western Red Hills of Skye, whose pinkish rocks and screes contrast in colour with those of the Black Cuillins (Fig. 16.5). The granite mountain of Beinn Dearg (left) and the sharper peak of Marsco (right) are both formed of granite, though the latter contains complex intrusions of a different rock, termed marscoite. Note the hummocky moraine of the Loch Lomond Readvance around the Sligachan Hotel.

The crest of the main Cuillin ridge is a sawtooth arête curving away southwards until it plunges directly into the sea at Loch Scavaig. No fewer than twenty of its summits attain heights of over 900 metres, the highest being the peak of Sgurr Alisdair (1009 m), which, like the southernmost peak, Gars-Bheinn, has a cap of basaltic lava surviving on its summit. According to Harker (1941), who mapped the Tertiary igneous rocks of Skye, these isolated lava cappings on the high summits represent remnants of the 'roof' of the plutonic intrusion, dating from the time when the plateau basalts were updomed by the ultrabasic and basic magma injections. It was Harker, too, who noted the very marked inclination of the rock structures of the gabbro ridges. These structures take on the form of a pseudo-stratification, although it must be remembered that these are igneous, not sedimentary, rocks. At Sgurr nan Gillean, at the ridge's northern end, the steep dip is towards the south; along the main Cuillin ridge it is towards the east; at Sgurr na Stri (near Loch Coruisk) it is towards the north (Weedon, 1961), while on Blaven it is towards the west. Thus all the structures dip inwards to a central point beneath Glen Sligachan, because they are made up partly of the inward dip of the gabbro banding and partly of the steeply inclined cone-sheets. These last, which form the most classic example in Britain of this type of structure, are restricted to the gabbro and do not invade the granites of the Red Hills farther east.

Needless to say, the final form of the Cuillins owes much to the work of ice and frost. The erosive action of former glaciers is everywhere manifest (Harker, 1901); the detailed chiselling of the numerous corrie walls and narrow arêtes and the polishing of the massive 'boiler-plate' slabs of Coire a Ghrunnda are small-scale examples of this process; the oversteepening of the valley shoulders, the truncating of the major spurs and the wholesale excavation of the magnificent trough of Coruisk represent the more grandiose aspects of glacial erosion, much of it dating from the Loch Lomond Readvance ice cap (Ballantyne *et al.*, 1991). The ultimate veneer has resulted from frost-shattering on the oversteepened cliffs and pinnacles, so that the main ridge is everywhere draped around with scree slopes. The most spectacular of these is the Great Stone Shoot, which plummets for over 450 metres from Alisdair's summit to the tiny corrie lake of Coire Lagan.

The Western Red Hills are separated from the Black Cuillins by the long funnel of Glen Sligachan, and were it not for the gabbroid pinnacles of the Cuillins their graceful domes would take pride of place in Skye's scenic inventory. As it is, their granites have weathered to a paler colour and a smoother, more rounded form than the neighbouring gabbro into which they were intruded at a slightly later date. Their well-known conical summits are crowned with layers of pinkish, frost-shattered detritus which can be traced as runnels of scree down their sweeping, uninterrupted slopes. The Western Red Hills are composed of a number of granitic injections which were intruded concentrically as major ring structures in a cauldron complex similar to those of Arran and Mull (Bell, 1966). The granitic complex caused a local updoming of the basaltic lavas, as demonstrated by the steeply tilted lava capping that has survived on the summit and eastern slopes of Glamaig's stately cone, which towers 773 metres above Loch Sligachan. Elsewhere the basaltic cover has been almost entirely stripped off by denudation. Similar basaltic remnants can also be seen on the slopes of the Eastern Red Hills, which have been carved from granites emplaced by similar mechanisms but from a separate intrusion centre. Although the splendid summits of Beinn na Caillich, Beinn Dearg Mhor, Beinn na Cro and Glas Beinn Mhor are built solely from granite, their lower slopes are complicated both by faulting and by a mosaic of gabbros, volcanic lavas, vent agglomerates and tuffs which, together with a 'skin' of Mesozoic sedimentary rocks, once formed the 'country rock' into which the granites were injected from below. The attractive peak of Marsco (736 m) in the Western Red Hills (Thompson, 1969) (see Fig. 16.6) is composed partly of basic magma that has been acidified by the inclusion of granitic material to form a hybrid rock known as 'marscoite' (Wager *et al.*, 1965). This can be distinguished as narrow strips separating the different Marsco granites from each other and from the included gabbro.

The three great northern peninsulas of Duirinish, Vaternish and Trotternish repeat the trap landscapes of northern Mull, where basaltic lavas of Palaeogene age buried an Early Tertiary low-relief surface that had been carved across a variety of Mesozoic and earlier rocks (George, 1966). Like those of Mull, the Skye basalts are now thought to be related to a number of separate intrusion centres, rather than having been intruded from lengthy fissures, as was formerly suggested. The massive lava pile which has resulted from these basaltic out-pourings now forms a series of remarkable scarps and coastal headlands. It has been pointed out that many of the north Skye sea cliffs cannot be explained merely by marine erosion, because the work of ice sheets and the mechanism of land-slipping may have been of greater importance in the fashioning of the coastline (Richards, 1969). Moreover, many of the present basaltic cliffs are ostensibly fault-line scarps or even fault-scarps, especially those in Trotternish. Although Steers (1973) states that the linear north-westerly trend of the sea-lochs of northern Skye (for instance, Loch Harport) owes a great deal to fault control, he is at pains to emphasize that this is not to say their origin lies entirely in faulting.

In the westernmost peninsula of Duirinish, the plateau basalts have been sculptured into a magnificent example of trap landscape, with the two flat-topped peaks of MacLeod's Tables (Healaval Mhor and Healaval Bheag) epitomizing the characteristically tabular landforms of eroded lava plateaux. To the north of Dunvegan the sea-loch coastline has tiny coves with dazzling white beaches which, at first sight, remind one of Arisaig or Tiree. Closer examination, however, reveals a third type of white beach. In Arisaig the beach sands are products of the breakdown of the local Moinian micaceous quartzites; in Tiree, as in all the *machair* lands of the Hebrides, the creamy beaches are formed largely of broken marine shells; but here, near Claigan in northern Skye, the strands are composed of broken coral. Tiny pieces of this attractive, pinkish material have apparently been broken off the main growths which flourish just off shore in a few fathoms of water. The Hebridean coral (like that at Tanera Beg in the Summer Isles) is the product not of a tropical coral polyps but of a seaweed called *Lithothamnion calcareum*, which abstracts carbonate of lime from sea water (Haldane, 1939).

Trotternish, the northernmost peninsula, is the most imposing of the three northern 'wings', from both geological and scenic points of view. Although the basaltic lavas are again dominant in the landforms, the underlying Mesozoic rocks have also played an important, if indirect, part in the make-up of the present landscape. Unlike the plateau-lavas farther west the Trotternish basalts are steeply tilted, so that they now form an excellent example of a cuesta, with

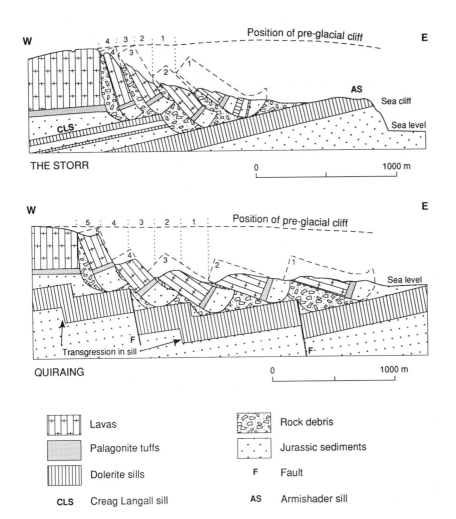

Figure 16.7 Diagrammatic section of the Storr (top) and the Quiraing (bottom), Skye, illustrating the mechanics of landslipping.

the gentler dip-slope descending westwards to Loch Snizort and the escarpment cliffs facing eastwards to the Sound of Raasay. This line of fearsome precipices, standing some distance back from the coast, runs for almost 32 kilometres between Portree and Staffin. At both the Storr and the Quiraing there are examples of the largest and most spectacular landslipping in Britain (Ballantyne, 1987) (Fig. 16.7). In front of the escarpment peak of the Storr (720 m) a confusion of screes, boulders and rock pinnacles marks the undercliff zone of slipping, including the 50 metre pinnacle of the Old Man of Storr which projects above the jumbled mass (Fig. 16.8). The latter was created when the 'incompetent' underlying Jurassic clays and limestones became incapable of bearing the weight of the overlying lavas, having previously been oversteepened by ice sheets moving northwards along the scarp face. Similar landslips are to be found in eastern Raasay (Fig. 16.9) (see p. 400). Farther north, at the Quiraing, almost identical landforms have been created by the same process of rotational slipping, although in this case major step-faults have also played a part, in addition to the typically curving glide-planes (Fig. 16.7). A contrast is also apparent between the Storr landslip, which fails to reach the sea and is now relatively stable, and the Quiraing landslip, which is currently unstable as the ocean waves erode the 'toe' of the slip in Staffin Bay. Here the slip has buried wide outcrops of Kimmeridge clay and Corallian Limestone of Upper Jurassic age (Wright, 1973).

The slipping on this eastern face probably started as the mainland ice sheet began to retreat in late Pleistocene times, withdrawing the stabilizing support of the ice mass itself from the potentially unstable precipices. This Late Devensian ice sheet was never thick enough to override the highest points of the Trotternish scarp judging by the periglacial debris and tors above the so-called 'trimline' at about 500 metres around the Storr and its neighbouring summits (Ballantyne, 1990). During the Loch Lomond Readvance of late-glacial times only two small glaciers are thought to have been regenerated on the eastern face of the Trotternish ridge, but a much larger ice cap was re-established in the Cuillins, with steep-sided kame-and-kettle drift being deposited over an area of 155 square kilometres of south-central Skye (Ballantyne, 1989). This hummocky morainic terrain can be seen on the roadside near to Sligachan (see Fig. 16.6), though it is currently being planted by the Forestry Commission to offset the legendary treelessness of Skye. The island has not always been treeless, however, for pollen analysis has shown that the southern parts had extensive birch, hazel and alder woods until they were destroyed by cattle grazing about 300 years ago. By contrast, the more fertile soils of northern Skye appear to have lost their woodlands from 5000 years ago to slowly be replaced by cereal crops associated with the numerous Iron Age duns and brochs (Birks and Williams, 1983). Similar research has indicated that after the ice sheets had melted Skye first became clothed with grassland and dwarf shrub heath (Walker *et al.*, 1988). It was on these northern pastures that cattle were once grazed and where the old custom of transhumance lasted longest (MacSween, 1959). Some of the old shielings can still be found in the uplands.

Figure 16.8 The Storr, Isle of Skye. The basaltic plateau of Trotternish is terminated by an escarpment moulded by ice sheets and frost action into cliffs, buttresses and pinnacles, including the isolated Old Man of Storr. Owing to the incompetence of the underlying Jurassic sedimentaries the scarp has collapsed into a jumble of landslips (see also Fig. 16.7).

In some of Skye's morainic hollows, but more especially in the depressions of the landslip topography, small freshwater lakes appear to have accumulated in post-glacial times. Some of these have survived, but many have subsequently been infilled by a whitish deposit known as *diatomite*. Composed of the siliceous skeletons of millions of tiny diatoms which formerly lived in the lakes, the *diatomite* is now quarried for industrial use (it has absorbent and filtering properties) at Loch Cuither in northern Trotternish. Much more widespread are the peat deposits which mantle most of the flatter land.

Below the lava precipices of Trotternish, the glacial drifts, landslips and peat deposits have buried the wide shelf of underlying Mesozoic rocks to such an extent that these are rarely exposed at the surface, except in the vertical sea cliffs between Portree and Staffin. Thus the thick Jurassic limestones play little direct part in the inland topography and have had only a localized effect on soils and land use. The sedimentary rocks have here been invaded by numerous 'leaves' of a thick sill of dolerite, which have helped produce some of the spectacular scenery of this northeastern coast. There is Kilt Rock, for example, which derives its name from the alternate light and dark banding of the interleaved sedimentary and igneous rocks, and nearby, where the cliff-edge Loch Mealt drains directly into the sea, there is a 52 metre vertical waterfall.

Figure 16.9 The eastern cliffs of the Isle of Raasay. The Jurassic shales and calcareous sandstones of the escarpment have slumped and slipped to form a landslide-impounded lake, because of the incompetence of the underlying Liassic shales (cf. Fig. 16.8).

Raasay and South Rona

Seen from the sheltered natural harbour of Portree, Skye's capital, which is hidden between flanking basaltic headlands, the neighbouring island of Raasay presents only a featureless shoulder of heath-covered Torridonian rocks. However, such a viewpoint gives a misleading impression, for, in proportion to its size, Raasay is one of the most geologically diverse of the Hebrides (see Fig. 16.4). This diversity is reflected not only in its undulating topography but also in the remarkable contrasts in land use between the northern and southern parts of the island.

A visitor arriving by sea at the main village of Inverarish will be astonished to find that the southern end of Raasay is characterized by yellow hayfields, deciduous woodlands and emerald pastures dotted with dairy cattle. Such fertility in southern Raasay results from the extensive exposure of Mesozoic rocks which range in age from Triassic sandstones (Bruck *et al.*, 1967), through the Liassic shales and limestones, up into the Inferior Oolite, the Great Estuarine Series and even the Cornbrash (Bradshaw and Fenton 1982) (all of Jurassic age). Many of these rocks also occur in Skye, but the crucial difference is that in Raasay the Mesozoics are virtually drift-free, so that there is a fair amount of high-quality soil waiting to be farmed. Darling (1955) goes so far as to say that Raasay is 'almost unique in the Highlands and one of the few places where deep ploughing and direct re-seeding of hill land could be applied'. This soil fertility is due largely to the high calcium content, of course, but also of great importance is the fact that the narrow north–south ridge of Raasay lay parallel with the direction of movement of the mainland ice sheets, so that pockets of deep soil have managed to survive the general glacial scouring. Nevertheless, the bulldozing effect of the former ice sheets is illustrated by the remarkable depths of the sea-channels which flank the islands of Raasay and South Rona. In fact the Inner Sound, between Raasay and the mainland, has the deepest submarine hollows in the British sector of the continental shelf (Robinson, 1949; Cheshner *et al.*, 1983). The presence of major faults on Raasay suggests that the entire chain of islands may be fault-controlled. The Holoman Fault of post-Cretaceous age, running off shore north-eastwards past the ruined castle of Brochel, has clearly played a part in the fashioning of the linear eastern coastlines of both north Raasay and South Rona (see Fig. 16.4). Some of their eastern shores may have been carved from fault-line scarps, and the neighbouring ocean deeps excavated along the relatively softer rocks of the downfaulted sedimentary basins.

The highest point of Raasay is the conical Tertiary basalt cap of Dun Caan (444 m), which serves as a splendid viewpoint for the entire island (Davidson, 1935). Immediately to the east is a unique geological phenomenon, so far as Scotland is concerned, for here is a 300 metre scarp consisting entirely of Jurassic sediments, just as if a section of the Cotswolds had been bodily transferred to the Hebrides. As in northern Skye, the unstable Jurassic clays and shales (in this case those of Liassic age) have collapsed, creating gigantic landslips, because the scarp, mainly of Mid-Jurassic sandstones (Morton, 1965), had earlier been oversteepened by ice sheets (see Fig. 16.9).

In the south of Raasay are the ruins of an ironstone mine in the thickly wooded valley of the Inverarish Burn, for beneath the Inferior Oolite a 2.4 metre band of Liassic ironstone occurs, similar in character to the well-known Cleveland Ironstone of northern England. Although the Raasay Ironstone has a 30 per cent iron content, its high percentage of lime makes it generally uneconomic to work. Mining ceased after the First World War, despite the 10 million tonnes of estimated reserves. The final surprise of this Jurassic country in southern Raasay is the occurrence of a bed of oil shale at the base of the Great Estuarine Series, but unlike the iron ore this mineral deposit has not yet been worked. The Holoman Fault acts as a major scenic boundary for it serves to cut off the fertile landscape of the southern Mesozoics from the moorlands and peat bogs of northern Raasay (Fig. 16.4). At Loch Arnish the Torridonian sandstones give way to the knobbly Lewisian gneiss which forms the remainder of the island, as well as the whole of South Rona and the tiny isle of Eilean Tigh. Only the boggy, green pasturelands of Eilean Fladda diversify the northern wilderness of bare, pink, ice-polished slabs and patchy heather, for this remarkably flat island (the Gaelic word *fladday* means 'flat isle') is made of gently dipping basal Torridonian rocks (Selley, 1965). South Rona is now uninhabited, largely because of its unyielding Lewisian gneiss, mineral-deficient soils, treelessness and inaccessibility.

A final word is necessary on the raised shorelines of Skye and Raasay, for both High Rock Platforms (20–30 m), and lower rock platforms (2–7 m) have been recognized, with the former essentially found only in northern Skye and Raasay while the latter occurs around much of the coast of central and southern Skye, especially around Sleat and Strathaird. It has been suggested that the lower rock platform is equivalent to the Main Rock Platform of the southern Hebrides (Gray, 1974), formed during the Loch Lomond Readvance, particularly since it is missing from the heads of Lochs Sligachan, Ainort and Slapin, all of which carried glaciers during the Loch Lomond stadial (Benn, 1991).

The Outer Hebrides

West of Skye, across the turbulent waters of the Minch, lie the Outer Hebrides, or Western Isles (MacGregor, 1952) which, because of their remoteness and dream-like silhouette against the setting sun, have been described in romantic terms by countless writers nurtured on the myths of the 'Celtic fringe'. For the most part, however, this 208 kilometre chain of islands, lashed by Atlantic gales and often swathed in low clouds, has a treeless, austere aspect. In general the rural way of life remains spartan in a land of peat bogs, bare rocks and waterlogged soils. Nevertheless, it cannot be denied that on days of bright sunshine, when the ethereal, rain-washed atmosphere amplifies the colours in the landscape, there are few places in Scotland which can emulate the splendours of this island scenery.

Here is a special kind of Hebridean scenery, for one is no longer concerned with the intricate and often spectacular landforms of the Tertiary igneous rocks, nor with the curious if limited impact made by isolated outliers of Mesozoic sedimentary rocks, as in Mull and Skye; missing also are the bizarre pyramids of the Torridon Sandstone and the Cambrian quartzite. All these Precambrian, Palaeozoic and Mesozoic sedimentary rocks, having been deposited in basins sharply limited in the west by the Minch Fault (Dearnley, 1962) and its much older predecessor, may, apart from the Stornoway Formation, never have been laid down in the Outer Hebrides. Instead, the landforms of the Western Isles are governed almost entirely by the intractable Lewisian gneiss: apart from the anomalous Stornoway Beds of possible Permo-Triassic age, the ancient igneous intrusions (Myers, 1971) and a limited exposure of schists in Harris, it is the gneisses that dominate the scene, as they should in the type-locality of these most ancient of British rocks (Watson, 1965). The Western Isles comprise a fault-bounded horst that has stood above sea level for a billion years, the bastion upon which the remainder of the British rock formations have slowly accumulated throughout the rest of geological time (Watson, 1977).

The complex basement of crystalline rocks which is collectively known as the 'Lewisian gneiss' in all geological literature is not a geological formation in the ordinary sense of the word, since it includes a wide variety of metamorphic rocks of considerably different ages. Although they were formed during early Precambrian times, the rocks were metamorphosed and deformed during two periods of mountain-building activity associated with pre-Caledonian orogeneses (Davies *et al.*, 1975). The older deformation known as the Scourian (from Scourie in Sutherland), dates from 2400 to 2800 million years ago, while the younger orogenesis, termed the Laxfordian (from Loch Laxford in Sutherland), has been dated as about 1800 million years old. Not only are these among the oldest known rocks in the world, but the interval of time which elapsed between the formation of the oldest and youngest gneisses is a great deal longer than that spanning the period from the Cambrian to the Holocene. Although many of the former Precambrian rocks have been so altered by heat and pressure that it can be difficult to determine their previous character, two broad classifications of the Lewisian gneiss have been made. Where former sedimentary rocks have been converted into metasediments, such as marbles or mica schists, they are known as *paragneisses*; where former igneous rocks have been modified they are termed *orthogneisses*.

In the Western Isles orthogneiss is more common in the landscape, and a visitor will soon become familiar with the mica-spangled foliation of alternating white and grey or pink granitic material which forms the typical banded gneiss. Richly garnetiferous dark green to black hornblende-gneiss also occurs in pillow-like masses among the banded rocks, many of which are laced with white quartz intrusions. Their complex folding can be seen everywhere, ranging in magnitude from gigantic recumbent folds and crumples to minute puckering, so that the individual rocks exhibit much of interest even to the layman. In south-west Harris the paragneisses become more dominant; marbles, quartzites, quartz schists and graphite schists build the rugged country between Toe Head and Renish Point (Davidson, 1943; Dearnley, 1963). Here, too, is a massive intrusion of unaltered gabbro-diorite which reminds one that the Lewisian complex was subsequently invaded by plutonic granites (Bowes *et al.*, 1971) and numerous intrusive sill sheets and dykes of all ages, including the Tertiary.

To complete the apparent confusion of the Lewisian Complex there is a great belt of crushed rocks, known as mylonites and crush breccias formed in association with a major thrust-fault which extends along the entire eastern coastline of the Outer Hebrides. The thrusting, from an easterly direction, has caused intensive shearing of the gneisses in a zone several kilometres wide, while pressure-melting has converted some of the gneisses into a blue-black splintery rock, known as 'flinty crush' because of its similarity to the better-known Cretaceous flints of considerably younger age.

Minor differences in the mineral constituents of the gneiss mean that the various lenticles, bands and inclusions exhibit differing resistance to erosion, so that one of the most characteristic features of the Lewisian country is the knobbliness of the hard rock landforms. The topographic complexity has been exaggerated by a complicated fault mosaic criss-crossing the islands which has been picked out by differential erosion, especially by ice, to form a bewildering pattern of hill and valley. A glance at a map of North Uist or Lewis (Fig. 16.10) will reveal the maze of watery depressions, some filled by fresh water and others by the sea.

As on the mainland of Scotland, most of the present-day scenery owes much to the effects of the Pleistocene glaciation. The Western Isles were crossed by mainland ice sheets which not only scoured the gneisses into a wilderness of bare, rocky knolls but also left boulder clay in the depressions to induce post-glacial waterlogging. The highest mountains of South Uist and northern Harris escaped the invading ice but appear to have nourished their own glaciers. Of the outlying islands (see p. 410), only Rockall and St Kilda were unaffected by the Scottish ice sheets at their maximum extent. The corries of Lewis, Harris and South Uist appear to have carried small glaciers during the Loch Lomond Read-vance), judging by the moraines and fresh striations which cross the older ones at discordant angles.

The final touches in the make-up of the physical landscape came in post-glacial times, which saw the slow development of three distinct phenomena that were to have very important effects on the life of the succeeding inhabitants. The first of these was the formation of peat bogs in the numerous ice-scoured basins and on the badly drained plateaux. Although these acid blanket bogs have resisted virtually all attempts at land improvement over wide expanses of the islands,

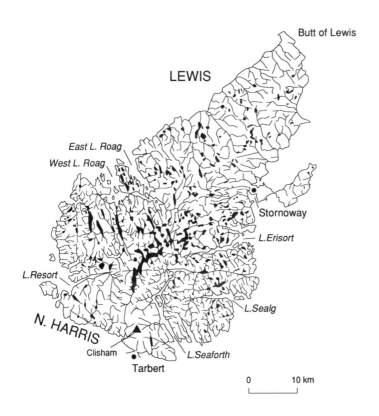

Figure 16.10 Drainage patterns in Harris and Lewis, Outer Hebrides.

they have provided a constant fuel supply in a region lacking both coal and timber. The second phenomenon was the gradual accumulation of calcareous sands along the western coastal margins to form the well-known *machair*, which has made some of the formerly barren tracts capable of extensive land improvement. The third post-glacial episode has been a gradual inundation of the landmasses by the inexorably rising ocean.

This positive eustatic movement has, of course, affected the entire British Isles, but it must be remembered that near the centres of the former ice sheets an uplift of land has partly offset the sea-level rise. This uplift was an isostatic recoil from the original crustal downwarping caused by the weight of the ice mass. The Western Isles, however, were on the perimeter of the ice sheets and thus suffered little crustal downwarp and therefore no significant post-glacial uplift. This accounts for the lack of raised beaches in the Outer Hebrides, in contrast with the mainland, and also for the gradual drowning of their coastlines since Pleistocene times. Thus, what was formerly one elongated island (still often referred to as the 'Long Island') has now been split into scores of individual islands and skerries by the gradual marine transgression rising at the rate of about 1 metre per century (Ritchie, 1966). As a measure of this drowning, Neolithic chambered cairns in North and South Uist are now partly submerged at high tide, while numerous examples of submerged peats (containing tree roots in growth position) are known from all the islands' coasts.

Darling (1955) has highlighted the way in which the uneven distribution of the fertile *machair* between the northern and southern halves of the Outer Hebrides has created a disparity in the agricultural scene. Thus, while Lewis and Harris have a land area three times that of the southern islands, they possess less than 47 per cent of the improved land. Since the *machair* is limited almost entirely to the windward coasts, most of the agricultural settlement of the Outer Hebrides consists of scattered villages along the Atlantic shores. Because these low coastlines have few inlets or safe anchorages (with the major exception of Loch Roag, Lewis), fishing fleets and their associated harbours are absent. The opposite is the case with the eastern shores. These are generally steeper and rockier than those of the west, so that here agriculture is at a premium. It is, however, this eastern coastline that has the deep-water bays and fjords which provide sheltered harbours, so here are to be found the fishing fleets and all the major urban settlements.

The Southern Isles

The rocky and cliff-fringed islands which surround Barra and Vatersay are now deserted, save for their numerous colonies of sea-birds, but in the nineteenth century seven of these isles carried a total population of over 400 souls. The finely shaped mountain of Heaval (384 m) dominates the Barra scene, for it stands in the middle of this compact little island. The cottages, amid their clustered fields of hay and potatoes, are arranged around its footslopes just above the fringe of *machair* and shell-sand beaches (Fig. 16.11) which are such a feature of the island's coastline (Thompson, 1974). Shell-sand is taken from the beach as a basis for the preparation used in the 'harling' (lime-washing) of house walls in such settlements as Castlebay, nestling around the sheltered haven in which the picturesque Kiesimul Castle stands on an islet of flinty-crush rock (Jehu and Craig, 1923).

Beyond the island of Eriskay (Jehu and Craig, 1925), the much larger islands of South Uist, Benbecula (Jehu and Craig, 1926) and North Uist present some 80 kilometres of virtually unbroken sandy shorelines to the Atlantic waves. Although it can boast a group of steep rocky hills along its eastern side, culminating in the rounded summits of Beinn Mhor (620 m) and Hecla (606 m), both carved from tough gneisses of the Lewisian basement (Coward, 1972; 1973), South Uist is best remembered for its widespread exposure of *machair*. Research suggests that its sand content was derived largely from the glacial drifts on the shallow off-shore platform and that it represents a symptom of coastal adjustment to excess sand supply immediately after glaciation. The calcareous component was added from the numerous marine organisms and the final landform produced by erosion and reworking, mainly by the wind. Since there is currently little movement of sand from the modern beaches to the *machair*, the depositional phase is now thought to be over, the major period of building having taken place between 5700 and 2000 years ago, according to Ritchie (1979). The datings are based on radiocarbon readings from buried organic horizons and on first-century archaeological remains. Ninth-century Viking settlements were similarly buried by drifting sand. Today, after many hundreds of years of agricultural activity, the *machair* is a stable, mature surface whose flatness is related to the water-table, which in turn acts as a base-level for wind erosion. Vast areas are

Figure 16.11 The west coast of Barra, Outer Hebrides, showing a bare hill of Lewisian gneiss and the wide expanse of *machair* behind the coastal sand dunes.

flooded in the winter, thus providing wet receptacles for blown sand and its associated plants (MacLeod, 1948).

Ecological studies by Darling and Boyd (1969) have demonstrated that the *machair* formation is primarily dependent on the 'fixing' of the coastal dunes by marram grass and associated species such as sea-sedge (*Carex arenaria*). A later stage sees the establishment of a dune pasture based on red fescue (*Festuca rubra*), meadow grass (*Poa pratensis*) and several species of clover and plantain, together with surviving clumps of marram. As the nitrogen-fixing plants increase, so the rich calcareous soil becomes more stable and the marram gradually disappears, to be replaced by a wide variety of colourful wild flowers. These, together with the profusion of blue butterflies, make the *machair*, according to Darling and Boyd, 'a brilliant place in July, offset by the blue of sky and sea, the white edge of surf and the cream expanse of shell-sand beaches.' A final note of warning must be sounded, for historical records show that the delicate turf has been both overgrazed and overcultivated on several occasions, and once the sward is broken the fierce Atlantic winds cause severe 'blow-outs' and drifting (Moss and Dickinson, 1979).

Three major soil belts may be recognized as one proceeds inland from the Atlantic coasts of the Outer Hebrides: first, the highly calcareous *machair* (the 'white' land); second, an intermediate zone of darker, alkaline soil where shell-sand has blown on to the peaty margins; third, the acid soils of the waterlogged peatlands with their rocky outcrops (the second and third categories being known as 'black' land). The village settlements, termed 'townships', were arranged in strips, at right angles to the coast, to include a share of each of the three contrasting soil belts. The true *machair* was particularly valued for its ease of ploughing, despite its lower crop yields and need for regular fallowing, but the intermediate zone of 'black' land was more productive, even though cultivation was more difficult. Before the advent of machinery this intermediate zone, with its long, narrow, unfenced fields, was traditionally dug by the spade or the *caschrom* (a crooked spade, or 'foot-plough') and formed into 'lazy beds' separated by open drains. To complete this communal agricultural pattern, known as the 'run-rig' system, the townships were each allotted a proportion of common grazing land on the poorer acid soils of the bounding hills from which the peat supplies also came.

The apparently simple patterns of land-use zoning in the Western Isles are complicated by the remarkably high incidence of water bodies, for the maze of sinuous lakes and sea-lochs in Harris and Lewis is repeated in both North and South Uist and in Benbecula. These low-lying tracts of lake-dotted terrain include water bodies of different origins (Nicol, 1936): some occupy ice-scoured rock basins, some hollows in the glacial drift; some are coastal lagoons of depositional origin and some are marine-eroded inlets in solid rocks or in unconsolidated superficial deposits; some of the smaller ones are merely pools among the peat-hags.

Harris and Lewis

Although often referred to as separate islands (Caird, 1951), Harris and Lewis are in fact a single body of land with the boundary lying almost (but not quite) along the borders of the Harris mountains and the Lewis plateaux (Thompson, 1973). Compared with the remainder of the Western Isles, Harris boasts a much greater proportion of mountainland, culminating in Clisham (779 m) (Fig. 16.12), but it has only a small extent of valuable *machair*. Indeed, in Harris a mere 1 per cent of the land is cultivated and 96 per cent remains as peaty moorland or ice-scoured rock. Thus, the soils of Harris are acid, waterlogged and mineral-deficient, and the absence of raised beaches, with their lighter soils, does not help. It is therefore astonishing to discover that on the tiny pockets of improved land in the so-called Bays area of eastern Harris there was once a population density of over 500 per square mile, the result of early nineteenth-century evictions from the few *machair* lands of the western coast. Resettlement has subsequently taken place along what is known as the West Side, but the lazy beds, or *feannagan*, remain along the hostile eastern shores, where the lack of level ground and the rockiness of the soils exclude virtually all mechanization from eastern Harris.

On days of good visibility the high hills of north Harris make splendid view-points, not only for the lake-studded boglands of Lewis but also for the remainder of the Western Isles, including the renowned islands of St Kilda, 72 kilometres away to the west. Signs of glacial action are to be seen everywhere in these barren mountains and, although there are few corries, the U-shaped valleys can be studied here to great advantage (Sissons, 1980). Indeed, the lonely valley of Ulladale boasts what can be described as the most unusual truncated spur in the British Isles. Here the notorious Strone rock-face has been so undercut by glacial erosion

Figure 16.12 The Hills of Harris, Outer Hebrides, looking from Ardhasig, near Tarbert, across the ice-scoured Lewisian gneiss to Clisham (right), the highest peak of the Outer Hebrides.

that its upper-most 230 metres form a considerable overhang.

Like the sea-lochs, the glacially deepened valleys have often been picked out along three predominant alignments, all of which reflect structures within the underlying gneisses. The north-west to south-east regional strike of the foliation has the greatest influence on the topography of south Harris, whereas in southern Lewis an east–west grain becomes more dominant; the third element is a subordinate south-west to north-east alignment. Loch Seaforth, the magnificent fjord of the Park district of Lewis, exhibits all three alignments in its 24 kilometre length (Fig. 16.13; see also Fig. 16.10). This mountainous tract of Park, slashed with radiating fjords, must be one of the largest trackless and uninhabited wilderness areas in the entire United Kingdom.

In northern Lewis the rolling, loch-studded moorlands show the Lewisian gneiss in all its uncompromising bleakness and austerity. As elsewhere in the Western Isles, the settlements and improved lands are almost entirely peripheral, so that the interior remains a treeless waste of peat-hag, moorland and ice-scraped rocks (Hulme and Blyth, 1984). Nevertheless, there is widespread evidence to show that at various periods of post-glacial time the Outer Hebrides were more hospitable than they are today. Although it has been claimed that much of Lewis, like Caithness, Orkney, and Shetland, has been a natural tundra type of moorland for long spells of the Flandrian (Birks and Madsen, 1979), nevertheless, beneath the blanket bogs which flourished in the cooler, wetter conditions which returned just before the Christian era (the so-called Sub-Atlantic period), there are many tree-stumps, remnants of the Sub-Boreal forest which clothed all but the highest

Figure 16.13 Loch Seaforth, Outer Hebrides, one of the longest fjords in the outer isles.

Scottish summits around 6000 to 2500 years ago (Wilkins, 1984). During this drier climatic period Bronze Age man arrived in the Hebrides, erecting the remarkable Callanish Stones, second only to Stonehenge in archaeological importance, on the shores of East Loch Roag (western Lewis) some 3000 years ago. When this circle of standing stones was first excavated in 1857, some 1.5 metres of Sub-Atlantic peat had first to be removed, thus providing a valuable yardstick for the reconstruction of the vegetational history of Lewis. Not far to the north, Dun Carloway, also on the sea shore, is the best-preserved Hebridean example of the massive Scottish drystone circular buildings called 'brochs', whose age and purpose are open to debate (Mackie, 1965).

Before concluding this brief summary of the archaeological heritage of Lewis, mention must be made of the traditional Lewis dwelling known as the 'black house'. This thick-walled, single-room cottage, similar to those on Tiree (see p. 385), was thatched with a motley collection of bracken, turf or bent-grass from the dunes, held down by weighted ropes of straw, and was usually without chimney or windows. The only source of light was from the single door, used by family and livestock alike, the cattle dung being removed once a year. The rough stone corners were characteristically rounded, leaving nothing on the outer face to catch the wind. Not surprisingly, few of these primitive dwellings have survived as habitations, although several are currently in use as byres or barns. The rough stones from which the older houses were constructed were often collected from the boulder clay, laid bare by countless centuries of peat-cutting. Such ground is termed 'the *gearraidh*', meaning 'the skinned land', and it now provides a poor-quality grazing which is nevertheless better than that of the peat-bogs themselves.

Apart from the west-coast *machair* lands in the district of Uig, the only areas in Lewis where the soils are of reasonable fertility are Ness, near the Butt of Lewis, and the Eye Peninsula. In both cases the general acidity of the ground has been alleviated by the marine-shell content of the glacial drifts, for it must be remembered that, far removed from the Harris uplands, these northern peninsulas received the unrestricted passage of the mainland ice sheets, which had in transit dredged up the former sea-floor deposits of the Minch (Flinn, 1978). In one small area of north Lewis, however, an ice-free area may have survived the passage of the Devensian ice sheets and here an interglacial deposit has been preserved (Sutherland and Walker, 1984).

In the Stornoway area the calcareous drifts of the Eye Peninsula (in fact a former island now tied to Lewis by a 'tombolo' of superficial material) have become mixed with the sandy soils derived from the underlying Stornoway Beds. Long thought of as a Torridon Sandstone, these coarse, reddish-brown conglomerates and finer cornstones, into which Broad Bay is carved, are now reputed to be yet another example of the Hebridean Permo-Triassic rocks (Steel and Wilson, 1975; Storevedt and Steel, 1977). It has been suggested that they were formed as alluvial fans in association with a subsiding basin of sedimentation, itself closely related to tectonic movements within the Minch Fault zone (see Fig. 15.7). The red sandstone houses of Stornoway, backed by the thick woodlands of the Castle grounds, single out this urban settlement as an atypical feature in the landscape of the Western Isles, although the grid-iron plan of the town merely follows the layout of the old fields and ditches (Geddes, 1947), while the fishing fleet reminds one of the long-standing dependence of the islanders on the surrounding seas.

Within these seas lie isolated but well-known islands, such as St Kilda, which merit a brief summary to complete the survey of the Western Isles. The most remote is Rockall, about 320 kilometres to the west of North Uist, which is no more than a 21 metre pinnacle of Tertiary granite rising from a submarine platform of volcanics of similar age to those of the Inner Hebrides (Fisher, 1956).

St Kilda, because of its spectacular coastal scenery and its fascinating cultural history, is better chronicled than many of the less remote Scottish islands (Williamson and Boyd, 1960). Not only does this group possess the highest sea-stack in the British Isles (Stac an Armin, 191 m), it also has sea cliffs 300 metres in height. The rugged nature of the islands is due to their having been carved from a Tertiary igneous complex (Harding *et al.* 1984), the gabbroid rocks of which are comparable with those already encountered in Rhum and Skye (Cockburn, 1935). Because of the basic mineralogy of its gabbro, the manuring of sea-birds and the lack of acidic mainland glacial drift, St Kilda possesses an alkaline peat (similar to the Fenland peats of England) possibly unique in Scotland. It has been suggested, furthermore, in view of St Kilda's isolation from the mainland ice sheets, that its flora may have survived from pre-glacial times, despite the fact that it once possessed its own small glacier (Sutherland *et al.*, 1984).

Closer at hand, the Flannan Isles, Sula Sgeir, North Rona, Sule Skerry, and Sule Stack, are all fragments of gneiss, presumably of Lewisian age (MacGregor, 1969). The Shiant Isles, however, are composed of a Tertiary igneous sill (Gibb and Henderson, 1984) overlying Liassic rocks, with the northern cliffs of Eilean Mor exhibiting the tallest examples of columnar basalt anywhere in the British Isles (Walker, 1930). Although the Shiants lie in the Minch, only a few kilometres from the shores of Park, their fabric is clearly related to the Tertiary rocks of Skye, and is cut off from Harris by the Minch Fault (see Fig. 16.2).

Bibliography

Bailey, E. B. (1914) The Sgurr of Eigg. *Geol. Mag.*, **1**, 296–305.

Bailey, E. B. (1954) Relations of Torridonian to Durness Limestone in the Broadford–Strollamus district of Skye. *Geol. Mag.*, **91**, 73–8.

Bailey, E. B. (1955) Moine tectonics and metamorphism in Skye. *Trans. Edinb. Geol. Soc.*, **16**, 93–166.

Bailey, E. B. (1962) Early Tertiary fold movements in Mull. *Geol. Mag.*, **99**, 478–79.

Ballantyne, C. K. (1987) Landslides and slope failure in Scotland: a review. *Scot. Geog. Mag.*, **102**, 134–50.

Ballantyne, C. K. (1989) The Loch Lomond Readvance on the Isle of Skye, Scotland: glacier reconstruction and palaeoclimatic implications. *J. Quat. Sci.*, **4**, 95–108.

Ballantyne, C. K. (1990) The Late-Quaternary glacial history of the Trotternish Escarpment, Isle of Skye, Scotland and its implications for ice-sheet reconstruction. *Proc. Geol. Assoc.*, **101**, 171–86.

Ballantyne, C. K. and Wain-Hobson, T. (1980) The Loch Lomond Advance on the Island of Rhum. *Scot. J. Geol.*, **16**, 1–10.

Ballantyne, C. K., Benn, D. I., Lowe, J. J. and Walker, M. J. C. (1991) *The Quaternary of the Isle of Skye*. Field Guide. Quat. Res. Assoc. 172 pp.

Bell, J. D. (1966) Granites and associated rocks of the eastern part of the Western Red-Hills Complex, Isle of Skye. *Trans. R. Soc. Edinb.*, **66**, 307–43.

Bell, J. D. (1976) The Tertiary intrusive complex on the Isle of Skye. *Proc. Geol. Assoc.*, **87**, 247–71.

Bell, J. D. and Harris, J. W (1986) *An Excursion Guide to the Geology of the Isle of Skye.* Geol. Soc. Glasgow.

Benn, D. I. (1991) Raised shorelines in Skye, in C. K. Ballantyne, D. I. Benn, J. J. Lowe, and M. J. C. Walker, *The Quaternary of the Isle of Skye.* Field Guide. Quat. Res. Assoc. 90–7.

Birks, H. J. B. and Madsen, B. J. (1979) Flandrian vegetational history of Little Loch Roag, Isle of Lewis, Scotland. *J. Ecol.*, **67**, 825–42.

Birks, H. J. B. and Williams, W. (1983) Late Quaternary vegetational history of the Inner Hebrides. *Proc. R. Soc. Edinb. B*, **83**, 269–92.

Black, G. P. (1952) The Tertiary volcanic succession of the Isle of Rhum, Inverness-shire. *Trans. Geol. Soc. Edinb.*, **19**, 208–15.

Black, G. P. and Welsh, W. (1961) The Torridonian succession of the Isle of Rhum. *Geol. Mag.*, **98**, 265–76.

Bowes, D. R., Hopgood, A. M. and Taft, M. B. (1971) Granitic injection complex of Harris, Outer Hebrides. *Scot. J. Geol.*, **7**, 289–91.

Boyd, J. M. and Boyd, I. L. (1990) *The Hebrides.* Collins. 416 pp.

Bradshaw, M. J. and Fenton, J. P. G. (1982) The Bajocian 'Cornbrash' of Raasay, Inner Hebrides: palynology, facies analysis and a revised geological map. *Scot. J. Geol.*, **18**, 131–45.

Brown, G. M. (1956) The layered ultrabasic rocks of Rhum, Inner Hebrides. *Phil. Trans. R. Soc. A.*, **240**, 1–53.

Brown, G. M., Drever, H. I., Dunham, K. C. *et al.* (1969) *The Tertiary Igneous Geology of the Isle of Skye.* Guide no. 13. Geol. Assoc. 37 pp.

Bruck, P. M., Dedman, R. E. and Wilson, R. C. L. (1967) The New Red Sandstone of Raasay and Scalpay, Inner Hebrides. *Scot. J. Geol.*, **3**, 168–80.

Caird, J. B. (1951) The Isle of Harris. *Scot. Geog. Mag.*, **67**, 85–100.

Campbell, J. L. (1984) *Canna: The Story of a Hebridean Island.* Oxford University Press. 340 pp.

Cheeney, R. F. and Matthews, D. V. (1965) The structural evolution of the Tarskavaig and Moine nappes in Skye. *Scot. J. Geol.*, **1**, 256–81.

Cheshner, J. A., Smythe, D. K. and Bishop, P. (1983) The geology of the Minches, Inner Sound and Raasay. *Inst. Geol. Sci. Reports*, 83–6. 29 pp.

Cockburn, A. M. (1935) The geology of St Kilda. *Trans. R. Soc. Edinb.*, **58**, 511–47.

Cooper, J. (1979) Lower Tertiary freshwater mollusca from Mull, Argyllshire. *Tertiary Research*, **2**, 69–74.

Coull, J. R. (1962) The Island of Tiree. *Scot. Geog. Mag.*, **78**, 17–32.

Coward, M. P. (1972) The eastern gneisses of South Uist. *Scot. J. Geol.*, **8**, 1–12.

Coward, M. P. (1973) The role of heterogeneous deformation in the development of the Laxfordian complex of South Uist, Outer Hebrides. *J. Geol. Soc. Lond.*, **129**, 139–60.

Darling, F. F. (1955) *West Highland Survey: An Essay in Human Ecology.* Oxford University Press. 438 pp.

Darling, F. F. and Boyd, J. M. (1969) *Natural History in the Highlands and Islands.* Collins. 405 pp.

Davidson, C. F. (1935) The Tertiary geology of Raasay, Inner Hebrides. *Trans. R. Soc. Edinb.*, **58**, 375–407.

Davidson, J. F. (1943) The Archaean rocks of the Rodil district, South Harris. *Trans. R. Soc. Edinb.*, **61**, 71–112.

Davies, F. B., Lisle, R. J. and Watson, J. V. (1975) The tectonic evolution of the Lewisian complex in Northern Lewis, Outer Hebrides. *Proc. Geol. Assoc.*, **86**, 45–62.

Dawson, A. G., Lowe, J. J. and Walker, M. J. C. (1987) The nature and age of the debris accumulation at Gribun, western Mull, Inner Hebrides. *Scot. J. Geol.*, **23**, 45–8.

Dearnley, R. (1962) An outline of the Lewisian complex of the Outer Hebrides in relation to that of the Scottish mainland. *Quart. J. Geol. Soc.*, **118**, 143–76.

Dearnley, R. (1963) The Lewisian complex of South Harris with some observations on the metamorphosed basic intrusions of the Outer Hebrides, Scotland. *Quart. J. Geol. Soc.*, **119**, 243–307.

Donaldson, C. H. (1983) Tertiary igneous activity in the Inner Hebrides. *Proc. R. Soc. Edinb.*, **83**, 65–81.

Dunham, A. C. and Emeleus, C. H. (1967) The Tertiary geology of Rhum, Inner Hebrides. *Proc. Geol. Assoc.*, **78**, 391–418.

Drury, S. A. (1972) The tectonic evolution of a Lewisian complex on Coll, Inner Hebrides. *Scot. J. Geol.*, **8**, 30–33.

Fisher, J. (1956) *Rockall*. Geoffrey Bles. 200 pp.

Flinn, D. (1978) The glaciation of the Outer Hebrides. *Geol. J.*, **13**, 195–9.

Geddes, A. (1947) The development of Stornoway. *Scot. Geog. Mag.*, **63**, 57–63.

Geikie, A. (1888) A report on the recent work of the Geological Survey in the north-west Highlands of Scotland. *Quart. J. Geol. Soc.*, **44**, 378–441.

George, T. N. (1966) Geomorphic evolution in Hebridean Scotland. *Scot. J. Geol.*, **2**, 1–34.

Gibb, F. G. F. and Henderson, C. M. B. (1984) The structure of the Shian Isles sill complex, Outer Hebrides. *Scot. J. Geol.*, **20**, 21–29.

Gray, J. M. (1974) The Main Rock Platform of the Firth of Lorn, western Scotland. *Trans. Inst. Br. Geog.*, **61**, 81–99.

Gray, J. M. and Brooks, C. L. (1972) The Loch Lomond Readvance moraines of Mull and Menteith. *Scot. J. Geol.*, **8**, 95–103.

Haldane, D. (1939) Note on the Nullipore or Corallian Sand of Dunvegan, Skye. *Trans. Geol. Soc. Edinb.*, **13**, 442–4.

Hallam, A. (1959) Stratigraphy of the Broadford Beds of Skye, Raasay and Applecross. *Proc. Yorks. Geol. Soc.*, **32**, 165–184.

Harding, R. R., Merriman, R. J. and Nancarrow, P. H. A. (1984) *St. Kilda: an Illustrated Account of the Geology*. Report of the British Geological Survey, **16**, HMSO.

Harker, A. (1901) Ice erosion in the Cuillin Hills, Skye. *Trans. R. Soc. Edinb.*, **40**, 221–52.

Harker, A. (1941) *The West Highlands and the Hebrides*. Cambridge University Press.

Howarth, M. K. (1956) The Scalpa Sandstone of the Isle of Raasay, Inner Hebrides. *Proc. Yorks. Geol. Soc.*, **30**, 353–70.

Hudson, J. D. (1962) The stratigraphy of the Great Estuarine Series (Mid. Jurassic) of the Inner Hebrides. *Trans. Geol. Soc. Edinb.*, **19**, 139–65.

Hughes, C. J. (1960) The Southern Mountains Igneous Complex, Isle of Rhum. *Quart. J. Geol. Soc.*, **116**, 111–131.

Hulme, P. D. and Blyth, A. W. (1984) A classification of the peatland vegetation of the Isle of Lewis and Harris, Scotland. *Proc. 7th Int. Peat Congress, Dublin*, **1**, 188–264.

Jehu, J. T. and Craig, R. M. (1923) The geology of the Outer Hebrides, Pt. I. The Barra Isles. *Trans. R. Soc. Edinb.*, **53**, 419–41.

Jehu, J. T. and Craig, R. M. (1925) The geology of the Outer Hebrides, Pt. II. South Uist and Eriskay. *Trans. R. Soc. Edinb.*, **53**, 615–41.

Jehu, J. T. and Craig, R. M. (1926) The geology of the Outer Hebrides, Part III. North Uist and Benbecula. *Trans. R. Soc. Edinb.*, **54**, 467–89.

Jermy, A. C. and Crabbe, J. A. (eds) (1978) *The Island of Mull: A Survey of its Flora and Environment*. British Museum.

Judd, J. W. (1889) The Tertiary volcanoes of the Western Isles of Scotland. *Quart. J. Geol. Soc.*, **45**, 187–219.

Koomans, C. and Kuenen, P. H. (1938) On the differentiation of the Glen More ring-dyke, Mull. *Geol. Mag.*, **75**, 145–60.

Lewis, J. D. (1968) The form and structure of the Loch Ba Ring Dyke, Isle of Mull, Scotland. *Proc. Geol. Assoc.*, **79**, 59–60.

Lowe, J. J. and Walker, M. J. C. (1986) Lateglacial and early Flandrian history of the Isle of Mull, Inner Hebrides, Scotland. *Trans. R. Soc. Edinb.*, **77**, 1–20.

MacCulloch, D. B. (1957) *The Wondrous Isle of Staffa*. Oliver & Boyd, 205 pp.

MacGregor, A. A. (1952) *The Western Isles*. Hale. 365 pp.

MacGregor, A. A. (1969) *The Farthest Hebrides*. Michael Joseph. 204 pp.

Mackie. E. W. (1965) Brochs and the Hebridean Iron Age. *Antiquity*, **39**, 266–78.

MacLeod, A. M. (1948) Some aspects of the plant ecology of the Island of Barra. *Trans. Bot. Soc. Edinb.*, **35**, 67–81.

MacNab, P. A. (1970) *The Isle of Mull*. David and Charles.

MacSween, M. D. (1959) Transhumance in North Skye. *Scot. Geog. Mag.*, **75**, 75–87.

McCann, S. B. and Richards, A. (1969) The coastal features of the Island of Rhum in the Inner Hebrides. *Scot. J. Geol.*, **5**, 15–25.

Morton, N. (1965) The stratigraphy of the Bearreraig Sandstone Series of Skye and Raasay. *Scot. J. Geol.*, 189–216.

Moss, M. R. and Dickinson, G. (1979) Evolution of the dune and *machair* grassland surface of South Uist, Outer Hebrides, Scotland. *Environmental Conservation*, 6, 287–92.

Murray, W. H. (1966) *The Hebrides*. Heinemann.

Myers, J. S. (1971) The Late-Laxfordian granite-mignatite complex of western Harris, Outer Hebrides. *Scot. J. Geol.*, 7, 254–84.

Nicol, E. A. T. (1936) The brackish-water lochs of North Uist. *Proc. R. Soc. Edinb.*, 56, 169–95.

Rast, N. Diggens, J. N. and Rast, D. E. (1968) Triassic rocks of the Isle of Mull; their sedimentation, facies, structure and relationship to the Great Glen Fault and the Mull caldera. *Proc. Geol. Soc. Lond.*, 1645, 299–304.

Raybould, J. G. (1973) The form of the Beinn an Dubhaich granite, Skye, Scotland. *Geol. Mag.*, 110, 341–50.

Richards, A. (1969) Some aspects of the evolution of the coastline of north east Skye. *Scot. Geog. Mag.*, 85, 122–31.

Richey, J. E. (1939) The dykes of Scotland. *Trans. Geol. Soc. Edinb.*, 13, 393–435.

Richey, J. E., MacGregor, A. G. and Anderson, F. W. (1961) *Scotland: The Tertiary Volcanic Districts* (3rd edn). British Regional Geology. HMSO. 120 pp.

Ritchie, W. (1966) The post-glacial rise in sea-level and coastal changes in the Uists. *Trans. Inst. Br. Geog.*, 39, 79–86.

Ritchie, W. (1979) Machair development and chronology in the Uists and adjacent islands. *Proc. R. Soc. Edinb. B*, 77, 107–22.

Robinson, A. H. W. (1949) Some clefts in the Inner Sound of Raasay. *Scot. Geog. Mag.*, 65, 20–25.

Ryder, R. H. and McCann, S. B. (1971) Periglacial phenomena on the island of Rhum in the Inner Hebrides. *Scot. J. Geol.*, 7, 293–303.

Scott-Moncrieff, G. (1951) *The Scottish Islands*. Batsford.

Selley, R. C. (1965) The Torridonian Succession on the Islands of Fladday, Raasay and Scalpay, Inverness-shire. *Geol. Mag.*, 102, 361–9.

Sillar, F. C. and Meyer, R. (1973) *Skye*. David and Charles.

Sissons, J. B. (1980) The glaciation of the Outer Hebrides. *Scot. J. Geol.*, 16, 81–4.

Sissons, J. B. (1983) The Quaternary geomorphology of the Inner Hebrides: a review and reassessment. *Proc. Geol. Assoc.*, 94, 165–75.

Skelhorn, R. R., MacDougall, J. D. S. and Longland, P. J. N. (1969) *The Tertiary Igneous Geology of the Isle of Mull*. Guide no. 20. Geol. Assoc. 35 pp.

Steel, R. J. and Wilson, A. C. (1975) Sedimentation and tectonism (Permo-Triassic?) on the margin of the North Minch basin, Lewis. *J. Geol. Soc. Lond.*, 131, 183–202.

Storevedt, K. M. and Steel, R. J. (1977) Palaeomagnetic evidence for the age of the Stornoway Formation. *Scot. J. Geol.*, 13, 263–9.

Sutherland, D. G. and Walker, M. J. C. (1984) A Late-Devensian ice-free area and possible interglacial site on the Island of Lewis, Outer Hebrides. *Nature*, 309, 701–3.

Sutherland, D. G., Ballantyne, C. K. and Walker, M. J. C. (1984) Late Quaternary glaciation and environmental change on St Kilda, Scotland and their palaeoenvironmental significance. *Boreas*, 13, 261–72.

Thompson, F. (1973) *Harris and Lewis*. David and Charles.

Thompson, F. (1974) *The Uists and Barra*. David and Charles.

Thompson, R. N. (1969) Tertiary granites and associated rocks of the Marsco area, Isle of Skye. *Quart. J. Geol. Soc.*, 124, 349–85.

Tilley, C. E. and Muir, I. D. (1962) The Hebridean Plateau Magma type. *Trans. Geol. Soc. Edinb.*, 19, 208–15.

Tomkieff, S. I. (1945) On the petrology of the ultrabasic and basic rocks of the Isle of Rhum. *Mineralog. Mag.*, 27, 127–36.

Turner, J. A. (1966) The Oxford Clay of Skye, Scalpay and Eigg. *Scot. J. Geol.*, 6, 371–8.

Vose, P. B, Powell, H. G. and Spence, J. B. (1959) The machair grazings of Tiree, Inner Hebrides. *Trans. Proc. Soc. Bot. Edinb.*, 37, 89–110.

Wager, L. R., Vincent, E. A., Brown, G. M. and Bell, J. D. (1965) Marscoite and related rocks of the Western Complex, Isle of Skye. *Phil. Trans. R. Soc. A*, 257, 273–307.

Walker, F. (1930) The geology of the Shiant Isles (Hebrides). *Quart. J. Geol. Soc.*, **86**, 355–96.

Walker, M.J.C., Gray, J.M. and Lowe, J.J. (eds) (1985) *Island of Mull*. Field Guide. Quat. Res. Assoc. 89 pp.

Walker, M.J.C. *et al.* (1988) A reinterpretation of the late glacial environmental history of the Isle of Skye, Inner Hebrides, Scotland. *J. Quat. Sci.*, **4**, 95–108.

Watson, J. (1965) Lewisian, in G.Y. Craig (ed.) *The Geology of Scotland*. (1st edn). Oliver & Boyd. pp. 49–77.

Watson, J. (1977) The Outer Hebrides: a geological perspective. *Proc. Geol. Assoc.*, **88**, 1–14.

Weedon, D.S. (1961) Basic igneous rocks of the Southern Cuillin, Isle of Skye. *Trans. Geol. Soc. Glasgow*, **24**, 190–212.

Westbrook, G.K. (1972) Structure and metamorphism of the Lewisian of east Tiree, Inner Hebrides. *Scot. J. Geol.*, **8**, 13–30.

Wilkins, D.A. (1984) The Flandrian woods of Lewis, (Scotland). *J. Ecol.*, **72**, 251–8.

Williamson, K. and Boyd, J.M. (1960) *St Kilda Summer*. Hutchinson. 224 pp.

Wright, J.K. (1973) The Middle and Upper Oxfordian and Kimmeridgian Staffin Shales of Staffin, Island of Skye. *Proc. Geol. Assoc.*, **84**, 447–58.

The Northern Highlands

17

As in other regions of Scotland, there are remarkable contrasts in both geology and scenery between the western and eastern halves of the northernmost tract of the Scottish mainland. The west is a region of ancient rocks, clothed with a natural vegetation of birch, oak and pine forest, heather moor and blanket bog, less inhabited now than a century ago and with single-track roads which discourage all but the most avid naturalist or those who seek solitude off the beaten track (Thompson, 1974). In contrast, the eastern coastlands of Ross and Cromarty, Sutherland and Caithness exhibit the veneer of the twentieth century, for there are railways, main roads and towns amid extensive areas of improved agricultural land (O'Dell and Walton, 1962). There, too, is a zone which looks eastwards to the off-shore oil fields of the North Sea, so that it has recently succumbed to the type of major industrial development which was previously confined to the coalfields of the Midland Valley.

The dichotomy between west and east is further emphasized by contrasts in the topography which reflect both the geological and the geomorphological history of the region. As with the remainder of western Scotland, the west coast is characteristically both rugged and ragged because of its rock types and its deeply penetrating sea-lochs, but, unlike those in the southern sector of the western seaboard, the fjords of the north-west take on a markedly north-west to south-east orientation. This is primarily because to the north of Loch Carron the so-called 'Caledonian grain' (north-east to south-west), which dominates so many of the Scottish structures and landforms, fails to reach the western coast. Instead, the much older Scourian and Laxfordian orogenic trend of the Lewisian gneissic structures, orientated north-west to south-east (Bott *et al.*, 1972; Bowes, 1969), and already encountered in the Western Isles (Chapter 16), has an important influence on the shape of the coastline, which runs discordantly across the regional strike. On the east coast, however, the 'Caledonian' trend still prevails and the coastline itself is broken by fewer sea-lochs. But it must not be assumed that these morphological differences between west and east are to be explained simply in terms of tectonic structures, for much of the contrast also stems from lithological disparities. In the west, for example, a great diversity of Precambrian and Cambrian rock types has been picked out by erosion to form a deeply dissected mountainous terrain with many associated linear water bodies. The eastern coastlands, however, have been carved very largely from rocks of uniform lithology, for the Old Red Sandstone extends from the Moray Firth to Caithness and Orkney. In general, the eastern shorelines are accordant with the 'grain', the relief is more uniform and the lochs less numerous in a landscape of smooth, rolling hills and open valleys. Moreover, corries, glacial troughs and ice-moulded surfaces are far more common in the western tracts than they are in the east, for, as today, the western mountains were the zones of highest precipitation during the Pleistocene. t follows that the ice caps lay nearer to the western than to the eastern coast and explains why many of the western sea-lochs have been converted into fjords by periods of intensive glacial overdeepening which most of the eastern sea-lochs failed to experience. Thus, while western coasts are often ice-scrubbed and barren (albeit picturesque), eastern coasts sometimes take the form of constructional shorelines in which marine waves have fashioned the enormous volume of glacial outwash into long, sandy beaches backed by prosperous farmland.

The North-West Highlands

North-west Scotland is one of the classic areas in the annals of British geology, and its Geological Survey memoir (summarized by Peach and Horne, 1930) is often claimed to be the most important ever produced. One reason for this is that some of the major principles of structural geology were established in this region, following the discovery of the Moine Thrust in 1883 (McIntyre, 1954). This event led Archibald Geikie to conclude: 'the correct explanation of this structure introduced to geologists a new type of displacement in the earth's crust'. Indeed, this was the first place in the world where the normal order of stratigraphic superposition was found to be reversed because of thrusting. Once the relationships between the Precambrian rocks and those of Lower Palaeozoic age had been worked out, analysis of the entire rock succession of Britain was set upon a firm foundation.

Reference to Fig. 17.1 will show that the line of the Moine Thrust separates two contrasting areas of rocks: to the west, with structures and lithologies matching those of the Outer Hebrides, is the ancient 'foreland' of Lewisian gneisses and Torridon Sandstones, where Moinian schists are virtually unknown; to the east is the main Caledonian fold-belt, where the widespread Moinian rocks are extremely deformed (Sutton and Watson, 1954), Torridon Sandstone is unknown and Lewisian gneiss can be seen only as inliers beneath the contorted schists. It is important to remember that a thrust will occur if rock deformation is driven beyond the limits that can be accommodated by folding during a period of mountain-building. Thrusts are, therefore, often developed along the margins of mountain belts, where the mobile nappes of the orogenic belt (composed of rocks from within the geosyncline) meet a flanking zone of more stable rocks, termed a *foreland*. Thus the waves (nappes) of Caledonian folding broke against the stable foreland of north-west Scotland, made up largely of the Lewisian and Torridonian. So fierce was the tectonic pressure from the east-south-east, however, that parts of the foreland surface itself were sheared off and carried bodily forwards along these planes of low-angled dislocation. The marginal belt of Caledonian thrusting can be traced for some 320 kilometres north-north-eastwards from Islay to Loch Eriboll near Cape Wrath (see Fig. 15.7). The belt is in fact composed of a few large thrusts and numerous small thrusts; it was the latter which first caused the newly created sedimentary nappes to be driven on to the front of the crystalline western foreland, at the outset producing what is known as an *imbricate* structure, analagous with overlapping tiles on a roof (Fig. 17.1d) (Bailey, 1934). Further compression seems to have caused a gradual pile-up of these minor structures, and as resistance increased, so the whole pile was ultimately driven many kilometres across the foreland, carried forward along several major thrust-planes. The basal thrust is termed the *sole* of the slide; it is succeeded upwards by the Glencoul Thrust, the Ben More Thrust and finally the Moine Thrust itself, which is the most easterly of these planes of dislocation (Fig. 17.1c).

The spectacular character of the mountains in the former counties of Sutherland

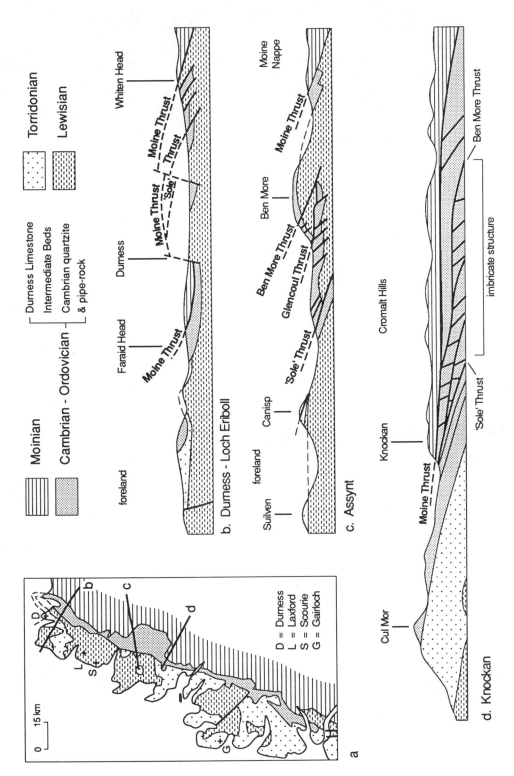

Figure 17.1 Structural geology of north-west Scotland (based on material prepared by the British Geological Survey and T. N. George).
(a) Location map. (b) Section near Durness. (c) Section at Ben More Assynt. (d) Section at Knockan.

and Wester Ross is largely the result of the differential erosion of contrasting rocks of Lewisian and Torridonian age. Before looking in detail at the scenery of these western coastlands, however, it is important to understand the general history of sedimentation which led to the formation of the Torridonian succession, since many of Scotland's most remarkable mountains have been carved from these tough arenaceous rocks.

Research has established that there are three different types of Torridonian rock (Fig. 17.2). The oldest are the greywackes, but they are restricted only to Islay and Colonsay. Above these are great thicknesses of interbedded sandstones, and shales, termed the Diabaig Group and found mainly in Skye and its satellite islands. The uppermost facies are composed of feldspar-rich sandstones (known as the Applecross and Aultbea Groups), and it is these which build the extraordinary mountains of Torridon and Assynt (Stewart, 1975). The feldspathic sandstones are commonly regarded as having been produced by erosion under desert conditions, but the underlying sandstones and shales are indicative of shallow-water marine or even fluvial environments. In general, the upward sequence of facies is characteristic of the gradual infilling of a geosyncline which must have stood south-east of the Lewisian foreland 750–1000 million years ago (Moorbath, 1969). As the sediments succeeded in filling this vast basin, so they became tectonically uplifted above sea level to create the desert landscape so admirably preserved in the detailed structures of the Applecross and Aultbea Groups. For example, rain-pitted shales and sun-cracks have been recognized, while the exposed hills of Lewisian gneiss appear to have introduced screes and hillwash into the arid valleys of that time. Ephemeral water bodies must also have been present, since it has been shown that streams brought tourmaline-quartz pebbles into the Torridon rocks from sources far beyond the surviving Lewisian of the Outer Hebrides. The mountainous foreland must then have extended much farther west (before the opening of the Atlantic) and from this landmass major rivers flowed south-eastwards, depositing thick alluvial fans as they debouched from the mountain front in Wester Ross and Sutherland (Williams, 1969). Farther east, beyond these primeval estuaries, deltas and land-locked basins, lay the open waters of the geosyncline in which the younger Moinian sedimentary rocks were being laid down, so that the younger Moines are probably

Figure 17.2 Section to illustrate the relationship between the Lewisian, Torridonian and Cambro-Ordovician rocks of north-west Scotland (after T. N. George).

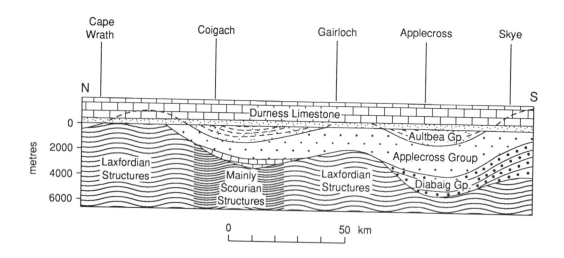

altered sediments of Torridonian age (Kennedy, 1951). The oldest Moinian rocks, however, are older than the Torridonian rocks. Thus the Torridonian and Moinian were deposited under different sedimentary environments in widely separated areas, but were subsequently brought together by the thrusting of Caledonian times described above (Johnson, 1965).

As the Torridonian sediments accumulated, so they buried an old land surface that had already been sculptured from the Lewisian gneisses of the foreland. This 'fossil' land surface had its own hills and valleys, showing a relative relief of some 400 metres (Stewart, 1972), which are now becoming slowly exposed as the overlying Torridonian is weathered away (Fig. 17.2). The best example of this buried relief may be seen on the slopes of Slioch (981 m) above Loch Maree, not far from the site where the unconformity between the Lewisian and the Torridonian was first remarked upon by John Macculloch as early as 1819. But before looking at the detailed scenery of this fascinating landscape, one must commence the journey farther south at Loch Alsh, where the Moine Thrust Belt runs out to sea before reappearing in Skye (See Fig. 15.7).

The coast road between Kyle of Lochalsh and Balmacara not only provides provocative views of Skye but also enables one to see wonderful sections of the Applecross and Diabaig Groups of the Torridonian in the cliffs which overlook it. The eastward-dipping beds are in fact part of the inverted limb of a gigantic recumbent fold known as the Kishorn Nappe. As the rocks are traced eastwards they become more deformed and crushed until near Balmacara they become mylonites, while at nearby Ard Point the equally pulverized Lewisian gneiss can be seen overlying the younger Torridonian, driven there by the tangential movements of this thrust-belt (Barber, 1965).

Once across Loch Carron and Loch Kishorn, most travellers will continue north to the delightful village of Shieldaig on Loch Torridon. Some, however, may venture up and over the fearsome glacial breach of Bealach-na-Bà (which means 'pass of the cattle', and is arguably the worst road in Scotland) (Fig. 17.3) to reach the wooded Triassic–Liassic basin of Applecross, set like an oasis amid the dull, featureless moorland which clothes this stubby peninsula of Torridonian rocks. Few scenic contrasts in north-west Scotland are greater than that which differentiates the northern and southern shores of Loch Torridon. To the south lies the relatively unremarkable coastal scenery of Applecross, with the pine-clad isles of Loch Shieldaig being a notable exception; to the north are the gigantic towering peaks of the Torridon Highlands themselves (Macrow, 1953). Torridon village is sited among moraines of Loch Lomond Readvance age (Hodgson, 1985) (regarded as one of the finest areas of hummocky moraines in Britain), and crouches at the foot of a large debris-cone built of material carried down the gullies which seam the precipitous southern face of Liathach (1054 m). This mountain's name means 'the grey one', which may refer either to its swirling mists or to the apron of screes below its beetling cliffs. Four of its seven summits, from which much of the frost-shattered debris is derived, are composed of rocks younger than the Torridon Sandstones of the slopes. In fact, although the Torridon mountains are built mainly of reddish-brown sandstones (of the Applecross Group), some of the high peaks are capped by a layer of white Cambrian quartzite which can be seen dipping gently eastwards across the Torridonian rocks until it disappears beneath the Moine Thrust near Kinlochewe.

Of the Torridon mountains, the graceful peak of Beinn Alligin (985 m) is composed only of Torridonian rocks, but part of the 11 kilometre summit ridge of Beinn Eighe has its tiers of red sandstone adorned with a shimmering crown of snowy quartzite. In order fully to appreciate the grandeur of Beinn Eighe, however, one should really ascend Glen Grudie from Loch Maree, for this 8 kilometre walk commands a magnificent vista of the stark precipices in the northern face, termed Coire Mhic Fhearchair (Fig. 17.4). In the imposing ice-carved amphitheatre, the vertical cliffs of red sandstone and white quartzite soar 400 metres from the lonely corrie lake to the summit (1009 m). The Torridon Highlands, An Teallach and the Fannich Mountains were ice centres not only during the Loch Lomond stadial but also during the so-called Wester Ross Readvance between 13 500 and 13 000 years ago, a readvance so-far unrecognized elsewhere in Scotland. At this time glaciers reached far down Loch Torridon, Loch Gairloch and Loch Ewe (Ballantyne and Sutherland, 1987; Robinson and Ballantyne, 1979).

The eastern half of Beinn Eighe is now a nature reserve, the first to be purchased by the Nature Conservancy Council after its creation in 1949. Apart from rare fauna, such as wild cat, pine marten, golden eagle and ptarmigan, the reserve is best known for its wonderful stand of Scots pine along the southern shores of Loch Maree – a genuine remnant of the historic Wood of Caledon which once clothed most of the Highlands but has since been devastated by fire and axe (Durno and McVean, 1959). The Council's aim is to rehabilitate the native pine forest by fencing against deer and sheep, thus allowing the young pines to

Figure 17.3 Bealach-na-Bà near Applecross, Wester Ross. The zig-zag road climbs steeply from Loch Kishorn through the deep glacial breach, cut into thick layers of Torridon Sandstone.

Figure 17.4 The summit ridge of Beinn Eighe, Torridon, Wester Ross. Horizontal layers of Torridon Sandstone are capped by a layer of white Cambrian quartzite, both of which have been deeply incised by a suite of north-facing cirques (right). The farthest cirque, occupied by a loch, is the gigantic amphitheatre of Coire Mhic Fhearchair.

regenerate successfully. Mention should also be made of the oak woods at neighbouring Letterewe, for at Loch Maree the native oak reaches its northern limit on the west coast. On south-west-facing slopes of rich brown soils, derived from basic sills of epidiorite within the acid Lewisian, the fresh green canopies of mature oak woods are reflected in the waters of Loch Maree. It is fortunate that they have survived, for during the seventeenth century, along with other Scottish woodlands (Dickson and Innes, 1959), the Wester Ross oak woods were extensively felled to supply charcoal for the local iron-smelting industry. The iron ore was shipped from Cumberland to Poolewe, and thence to the furnace at Letterewe. After the timber supplies had been virtually exhausted, the introduction of coking coal for smelting caused the transfer of the iron industry to the Midland Valley, where it has remained.

The modern road leaves the fault-guided valley of Loch Maree (Fig. 17.5) and winds its way circuitously to the beach-fringed coastline of Gairloch (Park, 1964) before returning to the Loch Maree fault line at Poolewe. Here a prominent fault-line scarp of Lewisian gneiss runs north-westwards for 20 kilometres and overlooks the marine inlet of Loch Ewe. Although this loch is carved essentially from Torridonian rocks, the brighter green fields at the southern end of its island, together with the col leading across to Gruinard Bay, suggest the presence of a different lithology. Sure enough, a narrow outcrop of Triassic and Liassic rocks lies unconformably on the Precambrian hereabouts, but the well-known 'sub-tropical' gardens of Inverewe owe nothing to these more fertile soils: paradoxically, this 'Oasis of the North' was created entirely on the less tractable soils of the Torridonian. Numerous viewpoints along the coast road of Loch Ewe provide opportunities to view the eastern skyline of striking Precambrian mountains. The castellated tops of An Teallach (1062 m) are of Torridon Sandstone,

Figure 17.5 Loch Maree, Northern Highlands, looking south-eastwards along the fault-line scarp and the Loch Maree Fault. Lewisian gneiss occupies the foreground but the cloud-capped summit of Slioch (left) is carved from the overlying unconformable Torridon Sandstone. The sunlit south-west facing slopes (left) are clothed with native oak woodland, surviving on the fertile soils derived from basic sills within the gneiss.

although the Lewisian gneiss of the Fisherfield Forest creates many high peaks, with A'Mhaighdean ('the maiden'), above Fionn Loch, taking pride of place.

The longest sea-loch of the Northern Highlands, Loch Broom, penetrates almost 32 kilometres into the mountains from the archipelago of the Summer Isles which clusters across its entrance. To the south of Ullapool is one of Scotland's finest waterfalls, at the head of the Corrieshalloch Gorge. The river Droma flows down the U-shaped valley of a large glacial breach in the main Highland watershed (see p. 429) until suddenly, at the Falls of Measach, its waters plummet 60 metres into a narrow forested cleft. Since the gorge is incised into the floor of a glacial trough, it has often been taken to indicate the degree of post-glacial river entrenchment. It seems more likely, however, that the incision took place very largely during the Upper Pleistocene, when enormous quantities of glacial meltwaters were coursing around the glacier fronts and cutting similar meltwater channels. The thriving fishing port and resort of Ullapool has lines of white houses that seem to float in Loch Broom when viewed from afar. Raised strand-lines can be seen almost everywhere around the sea-loch, pointers to the varying amounts of isostatic uplift which have taken place in Wester Ross during post-glacial times. There is no better place for their study than Ullapool itself, for there a late-glacial river delta, created at the mouth of Glen Achall, has been affected by wave action at various times during its pulsatory uplift. The northern part of the town is located on the highest part of the uplifted delta terrace, but the bulk of the settlement is perched at an elevation of 12 metres on a flat terrace, also of

late-glacial age. Ullapool's waterfront settlement is packed tightly into the notch behind the post-glacial raised beach (Kirk *et al.*, 1966).

To the north are the striking peaks of Coigach and Assynt, whose soaring buttresses and pyramids are unmatched in verticality anywhere in Britain. It is not merely that their corrie head-walls are precipitous; most of their summits are almost completely ringed by walls of virtually unscaleable cliffs. Some, such as Ben More Coigach (743 m) and Quinag (809 m) are relatively flat-topped eminences, but others, like Cul Beag (769 m), Canisp (847 m) and Cul Mor (849 m), are stately pyramids. It is, however, the monolith of Suilven (731 m) which always catches the eye, for it stands alone as a sort of Torridonian lighthouse above an alien sea of Lewisian gneiss (MacGregor and Phemister, 1958). Like the peaks of the Torridon Highlands, these remarkable hills were carved from thick layers of Torridon Sandstone which must once have completely obliterated the Lewisian basement. But erosion has now laid this bare, so that the surviving mountain residuals rise abruptly from the lake-dotted and ice-scoured terrain of gneissic-rocks. The major scouring must have resulted from main Devensian and earlier ice sheets, because the Loch Lomond Readvance glaciers were limited in extent in Assynt (Lawson, 1986). The sandstone peaks of Quinag and Cul Mor have isolated layers of white Cambrian quartzite remaining on their summits, while from Canisp's peak the quartzite capping declines eastwards in the form of a far-spreading dipslope until it passes beneath the Moine Thrust Complex to the south of Inchnadamph (see Fig. 17.1d). Elsewhere however,

Figure 17.6 Stac Pollaidh (Stac Polly) (left) and Cul Beag (right). These mountains of Torridon Sandstone rise steeply above the blanket bogs in the Assynt district of the Northern Highlands.

there is merely a scatter of white quartzite boulders surviving on the summit of Suilven while the peak of Stac Polly (*Stac Pollaidh*), farther south-west, has long since lost its tough Cambrian cap-stone, so that its summit ridge (612 m) is now a splintered cockscomb of red sandstone, rising from plains of blanket peat (Fig. 17.6).

In the area of complex geology around Ben More Assynt (998 m) depicted in Fig. 17.1c the distance between the Moine Thrust and the sole of the thrust complex at Loch Assynt is no less than 13 kilometres. At Knockan, however, the Moine schists have been transported such a distance westwards along the Moine Thrust that they have completely overridden the slightly older planes of thrusting (Fig. 17.1d); some have claimed that the total Late Caledonian thrustal displacement was as much as 120 kilometres (Johnstone and Mykura, 1989), a remarkable amount of crustal shortening. The final result can be viewed with comparative ease at Knockan Cliff, where the undisturbed Cambrian basal quartzite and its overlying Lower Palaeozoic sedimentary rocks are capped by the *older* Moine schists of the Cromalt Hills (Fig. 17.1d). The junction between the greyish-white Durness Limestone and the darker overlying Moinian psammite is the Moine Thrust itself (point 11 on the Nature Trail here), although both rocks have been crushed into mylonites by the thrust movements (Christie, 1960) (Fig. 17.7).

The effect of a limestone outcrop on the generally acid vegetation of the Scottish Highlands has been highlighted on several occasions. None is more remarkable

Figure 17.7 Knockan Cliff, near Elphin, Northern Highlands. The undisturbed Cambrian quartzite and the overlying Cambrian–Ordovician sedimentaries are overlain by tilted strata of Durness Limestone and older Moinian schists, carried westwards along the Sole Thrust (below) and Moine Thrust (above). (See also Fig. 17.1d.)

than that which results from the appearance of a narrow exposure of Durness Limestone among the acid gneisses, sandstones and quartzites of Assynt. Unlike that occurring in Skye (see p. 392), this calcareous Cambro-Ordovician rock is largely drift-free. Thus, near Elphin and Inchnadamph significant tracts of limestone are exposed, bringing swathes of brighter green into the dark-coloured moorlands. Such plants as holly fern, bladder fern and stone bramble thrive on the more fertile soils, while mountain avens (*Dryas octopetala*) and other rare Arctic/Alpine species are everywhere abundant.

To the north of Inchnadamph, near the picturesque ruins of Ardvreck Castle on the shores of Loch Assynt, the dipslope of Cambrian quartzite can be seen rising westwards to the summit of Quinag. Along this mountain's northern face the irregular nature of the unconformity between the knobbly Lewisian and the horizontally bedded Torridonian is clearly visible, although the base of the Cambrian everywhere forms an even plane (Fig. 17.1d).

Once across the Kylesku ferry one has entered that corner of Sutherland where the Scourian and Laxfordian gneisses create a Lewisian wilderness of lumpy crags and tiny lochans (Evans and Lambert, 1974), comparable with the naked landscapes of South Rona, central Lewis and the Inverpolly Nature Reserve in Western Assynt. This is the region where Lewisian stratigraphy was finally resolved (Sutton and Watson, 1951). Tiny lochans, bestrewn with water lilies and water lobelias, seem a bizarre extravagance in this treeless expanse of ice-scraped rock, where a classic 'knock and lochan' terrain is exemplified. Bare rock surfaces abound because heather does not flourish on gneiss; its place is usually taken by coarse grass, bog myrtle and deer's hair sedge. The mountains of Cambrian quartzite stand some kilometres back from the coast, so that there are few viewpoints on the twisting narrow road across this undulating gneissic platform. The hinterland is uninhabited; the few tiny settlements here hug the rock-bound coast. Like their Viking forerunners the crofters look to the sea both for their livelihood and their means of communication in a land which offers little inducement to agricultural improvement. Along the fretted Atlantic coastline of Sutherland the gneissic sea-cliffs are nowhere impressive until one reaches the remote fastnesses of Cape Wrath, where they rise to 135 metres. Moreover, the occasional patches of Torridonian also make an impact on the cliff scenery, especially along the northern coast (Fig. 17.8) and at the island of Handa, near Scourie. Here the horizontal stratification of the sandstone in the 120 metre cliffs provides countless nesting sites in one of Britain's most important bird sanctuaries.

Cliffs of a different origin can be seen farther inland: the peaks which lie to the east of Laxford Bridge and Rhiconich are deeply notched by a dozen corries. Although Ben Stack (721 m) is a shapely cone of Lewisian gneiss, the neighbouring summits of Arkle (787 m), Foinaven (909 m) and Cranstackie (802 m) stand resplendent in their white caps of Cambrian quartzite. One interesting difference between these statuesque hills and their Assynt counterparts is that here the quartzite rests directly on the gneiss, the Torridonian having been destroyed in a period of erosion prior to the formation of the Cambrian cover rocks (see Fig. 17.2). The juxtaposition of the gneiss and the quartzite has had an important effect on corrie morphology: where glacial erosion has scooped out a corrie in gneissic rocks only, the depression is generally shallow and dish-shaped with no steep walls; when a corrie is located in the quartzite, however, the cliffs are

Figure 17.8 The coastal scenery looking eastwards from Cape Wrath. The nearer headlands are composed of Lewisian gneiss but the further promontories have been carved from Torridonian sedimentaries.

steeper because this material has better jointing properties. Usually the corries are composite, each possessing a semicircular quartzite wall and a heavily polished gneissic floor, as in the immense northern amphitheatre of Arkle, where Loch an Easain Uaine is constantly supplied by the waterfalls from four hanging corries. Because the quartzite is a well-jointed, brittle rock it yielded to frost-shattering throughout the Pleistocene, so that today the summit ridges of Arkle and Foinaven (*Foinne Bheinn* means 'white mountain') are a confusion of broken rocks, while their scree slopes are so unstable that they have been likened to glittering spoil-heaps rising from a platform of gneiss (Fig. 17.9). Mass movement of the mountain-top detritus evidently continued into the post-glacial period, for a buried soil profile on Arkle shows that a vegetation layer flourished there more then 5000 years ago before being inundated by solifluxion (Mottershead, 1978). Today, however, these almost sub-Arctic mountains are bare, and their litter of boulders provides ideal breeding grounds for the rarely seen snow bunting and pine marten.

Separating Foinaven and Cranstackie is the River Dionard, which meanders northwards down a broad strath before emptying into the tidal waters of the Kyle of Durness. Here the landscape becomes less rugged, but the greyish-white rock is not the barren Cambrian quartzite but the more yielding Durness Limestone of Cambro-Ordovician age (Walton, 1965). Since the rugged and obdurate Lewisian gneiss is not so prevalent on this northern section of the Scottish coastline, the barren, rock-bound fjords of the west coast are now superseded by the smoother curves of sand-dunes and yellow sand-banks along the shallow estuary of the Kyle of Durness. The 'softer' outlines of the topography are matched by a change in the colour of the landscape: the dark, peaty moorlands disappear as if by magic, to be replaced by the emerald pastures characteristic of calcareous soils. The featureless boglands give way to a mosaic of stone-walled fields enclosing flocks of Cheviot sheep, while the few bare limestone 'pavements' are reminiscent of the northern Pennines, albeit on a more restricted scale. Although the windswept coastal location precludes any significant tree growth, a rich ground flora exists, including an unusual *Dryas* heathland at Borralie, near the tiny farming centre of Durness (Hobson, 1947).

Figure 17.9 The quartzite peak of Arkle, Northern Highlands, rising above the glacially scoured platform of Lewisian gneiss near Kinlochbervie.

Of greatest scenic interest, however, are the sinkholes, caves and underground water-courses of this well-jointed limestone terrain. Because of the porous nature of the limestone, the surface streams disappear at sinkholes once they cross from the surrounding impervious rocks, their underground courses often being marked by lines of hollows or actual shafts where the roof has collapsed. For example, the waters of the Allt Smoo plunge 24 metres vertically down a shaft before reappearing at sea level from the mouth of Smoo Cave (from the Norse *smuga*, meaning 'cleft'), whose cliff-face aperture is 37 metres wide (Fig. 17.10). It has been created partly by the underground river and partly by marine erosion. In the Durness Limestone at Traligill farther south near Inchnadamph, a cave some 213 metres long has been explored, while at Knockan Cliff the caves include a vertical pothole 40 metres deep. Excavations in some of the Inchnadamph caves have revealed that during the Pleistocene they gave shelter to animals, such as lynx and bear, no longer native to Scotland.

Figure 17.10 Smoo Cave, Durness, Northern Highlands. This wide cave, eroded in Durness Limestone, opens on to the beach but was fashioned largely by a subterranean river which enters the back of the cave as a waterfall.

Although patches of Durness Limestone flank the shores of Loch Eriboll, tough gneisses and quartzites bolster its surrounding hills and its imposing portal of Whiten Head (see Fig. 17.1b). This is the northern limit of the Moine Thrust Belt (Soper and Wilkinson, 1975); westwards lies the isolated headland of Cape Wrath, carved from Lewisian gneiss capped with Torridonian; eastwards lie the seemingly endless hills and plateaux of Moinian metamorphic rocks, named after the nearby district of A Mhoine. It is time, therefore, to return southwards to examine the little-known mountainlands of central Sutherland before exploring

the long eastern and northern seaboard of northern Scotland. Any of three routes can be followed south-eastwards to Bonar Bridge on the Dornoch Firth: one goes by the Kyle of Tongue, with its conglomerates of possible Old Red Sandstone age (O'Reilly, 1983) and past the bold mountains of the Ben Loyal (763 m) igneous complex (King, 1942); another follows Loch More and the almost endless Loch Shin; the southernmost, via Strath Oykel, retraces the Moine Thrust country around Ben More Assynt (see Fig. 17.1c).

One has already encountered in earlier chapters the capacity of ice sheets for overriding pre-glacial watersheds, thereby creating deep glacial valleys where none existed before. The primary watershed of the Northern Highlands is no exception: in its 160 kilometre extent between Ben Fhada (Kintail) and Foinaven it displays no less than 14 major breaches (Dury, 1953). The road to Loch Shin follows one, that to Strath Oykel follows another, and so do all the main roads between Inverness and the west-coast towns; one of the lowest breaches, at Achnasheen, is also followed by the railway to Kyle of Lochalsh. Achnasheen also exhibits large delta terraces and shorelines, marking the site of a former ice-dammed lake, created when four valley glaciers converged but failed to meet each other (Sissons, 1982) in the Late Devensian. At the beginning of this century Peach and Horne (1930) observed that during the Pleistocene 'what may conveniently be described as ice-cauldrons were set up in Central Sutherlandshire'. These were later termed 'basins of impeded outflow' by Linton (1951). Thus in areas of heaviest snowfall (in such localities as the present-day Loch Naver, Loch Shin and Strath Bran) ice caps accumulated, and it was these which were responsible for the glacial 'transfluence' or breaching described above. In one of these glacial breaches, at Loch Droma, not far from the Corrieshalloch Gorge (see p. 422), a buried organic deposit of late-glacial age has thrown fresh light on the history of deglaciation in the Northern Highlands (Kirk and Godwin, 1963). Investigation of this important site has indicated that the ice sheet which left such conspicuous frontal deposits on both western and eastern coasts (in Wester Ross and Cromarty Firth) had practically disappeared by 12 800 years ago, just prior to the reappearance of small ice caps during the Loch Lomond Stadial. In Wester Ross these final tiny glaciers succeeded in crossing the line of the present coast only at Loch Torridon and Loch Kishorn (Hodgson, 1985).

Today the glens of the Northern Highlands are occupied by a river pattern which can be divided into three distinct categories: first, the west-flowing streams, which are short, fast-flowing and in part structurally adjusted to the rocks of the foreland; second, the much longer east-flowing streams, which cut discordantly across all the major structures of the Moinian Series; finally, the short streams of the north coast, which, being adjusted to the regional strike, have succeeded in capturing some of the headwaters of the eastern rivers. George (1966) suggested that the drainage of Scotland was created upon a primary upland surface of late-Tertiary age into which 'present-day valleys have become deeply incised by a rejuvenation partly brought about in adjustment to emergence on the one hand, supplemented by an erosively contracting coastline on the other'. In northern Scotland such dissection by rivers (and also by ice) has succeeded in isolating the high residuals of Ben Hope (927 m), Ben Klibreck (962 m) and Ben Wyvis (1047 m) from the main massif of the Northern Highlands.

The north-eastern seaboard

The summit of Ben Wyvis is as good a place as any to get a panoramic view of the indented coastline of Easter Ross. Because of the general linearity of Scotland's eastern coasts, the complex interfingering of land and sea represented by the firths of Beauly, Cromarty and Dornoch is something quite exceptional, since in part they are discordant to the structure, as demonstrated by the way the mouth of the Cromarty Firth breaks through a line of hard Precambrian rocks. But as most of the incision of these sea-lochs took place into the relatively uniform lithology of the Old Red Sandstone, especially during the phase of glacial overdeepening, these eastern firths exhibit nothing of the rugged irregularities of the western sea-lochs whose geology is so complex. Instead, here are landscapes of low, sandy shorelines with extensive raised-beach remnants cut into the thick mantle of glacio-fluvial deposits and reddish-brown boulder clay. Interbedded within the Pleistocene deposits (at heights rising northward) from 4 metres OD at Montrose to 19 metres OD at Sullom Voe in Shetland), there is a thin but uniform marine layer, now thought to indicate an inundation caused by a sudden tsunami, or ocean surge, generated by a massive submarine slip off the Norwegian coast, known as the Storegga Slide. The gigantic ocean wave has been dated to 7000 years ago and is known to have overwhelmed a Mesolithic settlement (Dawson *et al.*, 1988; Long *et al.*, 1989).

In general, these sandy east-coast drifts provide good loamy soils although some of the glacio-fluvial outwash fans yield such light soils that they are given over to patches of lowland heath, as at Muir of Ord. Nevertheless, the general prosperity of the farming scene and the large areas of arable are reminiscent of the fertile landscapes to the south of the Moray Firth. The contrast with the subsistence crofting of the rocky western coast is only too apparent, for the low rainfall and prolonged sunshine of this sheltered eastern seaboard encourage not only a wide variety of root crops but also excellent yields of barley and wheat. Consequently the farms here are large, with trim hedgerows, shelter-belts and well-maintained buildings, in keeping with the better-quality soils and the low, flat terrain. As soon as one crosses the western limits of the Old Red Sandstone basin, however, the relief becomes higher and more rugged, the vegetation changes to heather moor and peat-bog and the farms get smaller and more sporadic – in fact, the scenery becomes more typically Highland (Small and Smith, 1971).

The oddly named peninsula of the Black Isle has a fringe of farmlands (Cruickshank, 1961) around its thickly forested central ridge, which attains an elevation of 256 metres before descending north-eastwards to the small town of Cromarty. The ridge is formed from the red and yellow layers of the Millbuie Sandstone, whose pebbles of andesite and porphyritic basalt are probably derived from erosion of Middle Old Red Sandstone lavas no longer exposed. The peninsula is aligned along a broad synclinal structure in the Old Red Sandstone, the axis of which runs south-west to north-east along the Millbuie ridge. It was the presence of the fossil-fish-bearing beds at the base of the Millbuie Sandstone which gave early inspiration to Hugh Miller, the Cromarty stonemason who became one of the most famous in a long line of eminent Scottish geologists. Coincidentally, another leading geologist, R.I. Murchison, made his home at Tarradale House, at the western end of the Black Isle.

The linearity of the Cromarty Firth suggests that its upper reaches may be structurally controlled. It is, therefore, no surprise to discover that it is aligned along an anticline parallel to the Millbuie Syncline. Although it has been suggested that the pre-glacial drainage flowed generally north-eastwards along the regional 'grain', with the 'Cromarty River' debouching somewhere near to present-day Tain, there is evidence to show that ice sheets not only overdeepened the Cromarty Valley near Invergordon but also succeeded in breaking through the rim of the Cromarty Basin at the Sutors of Cromarty. These prominent hills, which flank the present entrance to the firth, are composed of a narrow outcrop of Moinian rocks so resistant to glacial erosion that they caused a constriction of the valley glacier and a consequent overdeepening of the narrow entrance near Cromarty. Subsequent drowning of the Cromarty Basin by the post-glacial marine trans-gression led to the ultimate use of this land-locked deep-water firth as a naval base, centred on Invergordon. In the 1970s the same combination of a deep channel and a flat coastal shelf saw the development of a major oil-rig-platform construction yard at the Bay of Nigg. Neighbouring Alness, with its aluminium smelter, also helped place the stamp of industry firmly on the pastoral landscape of the Cromarty Firth.

The remarkable straightness of the coastline between Tarbat Ness and Fortrose (on the Black Isle) is clearly related to the submarine extension of the Great Glen Fault. The enormous lateral movement of the fault (see p. 366) has caused a great displacement of the Mesozoic rocks which fringe the basin of the Moray Firth. Fragments of Jurassic sediments can be seen along this shore, both north and south of the Sutors of Cromarty. The shallow waters of the Dornoch Firth are flanked by an interesting suite of coastal spits and forelands, some of which were initially fashioned during the higher sea levels of the post-glacial transgres-sion, when tidal waters temporarily linked Dornoch Firth with Nigg Bay. Since then the sandy foreland of Morrich Mhor, near Tain, has grown outwards into the firth as the sea level has slowly fallen. This has happened through the succes-sive addition of sandy barriers thrown up by wave action on Whiteness Sands, the end result of which has been the silting-up of Tain harbour and the end of its function as a port.

The final marine inlet on this eastern coastline is Loch Fleet, which causes a deviation of the coast road between Dornoch, with its squat sandstone cathedral, and Golspie, the county town of Sutherland. Originally an open bay at the seaward end of the deeply incised Strath Fleet, the loch has been almost cut off from the North Sea by the gradual growth of spits from both the northern and southern shores. Like most of the other constructional coastal landforms around the Moray Firth, these beach ridges appear to have been fashioned partly by waves of post-glacial raised-beach age. Steers (1973) has compared the Loch Fleet opposing spits with similar phenomena at Poole Harbour in England and at the western end of the Menai Straits in North Wales, although the explanations of their genesis may be different – the complex configuration of the Dornoch Firth coastline would certainly have affected the angles of wave approach in the case of Loch Fleet. Today its pine woods, shingle ridges and sheltered waters constitute an important nature reserve.

To the north of the trim town of Golspie and its fairy-tale castle of Dunrobin, seat of the Duke of Sutherland, the breccias and conglomerates of Old Red Sandstone age form a west-facing scarp at Ben Horn (520 m), but their fault-guided eastern slopes are even more steeply marked where the coastal plain widens around Brora. In this coastal strip, however, in place of the ubiquitous chocolate sandstones of the Old Red, a downfaulted strip of Mesozoic sediments fringes the upland massif. Their effect on the topography is innocuous enough – the prosperous farming scene owes as much to the superficial deposits as it does to the underlying Triassic and Jurassic limestones, clays and sandstones. But it is the now defunct Brora colliery and its associated brick pits which seem out of place in the Highlands, a long way from any Carboniferous rocks. The same carbonaceous deposits which gave Raasay its Jurassic oil shales (see p. 401) have given Brora a metre-thick seam of good-quality coal within the Estuarine Series (of Lower Oolite age) which are well represented here. In the associated clays, petrified wood and plant impressions have also been discovered, although it is the overlying blue-grey shaly clays of Lower Oxfordian age which have been extensively exploited for brick-making.

Near the tiny port of Helmsdale, nestling in its deeply incised river gorge, the coastal plain peters out where the bounding fault of the Mesozoic sedimentary basin runs out to sea. Granite hills now hug the shore and cliffs replace the sandy beaches of the Brora lowland, while the coast road zigzags into the numerous re-entrants carved in the steep coastal slope by the short, torrential streams. So precipitous is this tract of coastline between Helmsdale and Berriedale that the nineteenth-century engineers took their railway line inland on a remarkably circuitous route before regaining the Caithness coast at Thomas Telford's planned town of Wick. The railway surveyors utilized the Strath of Kildonan, where the Helmsdale River breaks out of the mountainous desolation of central Sutherland on its way to the North Sea. The Strath of Kildonan received considerable publicity a century ago, when the discovery of alluvial gold in tributaries of the Helmsdale led to a two-year gold rush. The mineralization was probably associated with the thermal metamorphism induced by the emplacement of a granite pluton, but the veins were subsequently eroded, so that all the discoveries to date have been in stream beds, not in the solid rock. Examination of a map of the Helmsdale suggests that its natural headwaters should be sought in the River Mudale, far to the west of Loch Naver. The deeply embowered waters of Loch Coire, beneath the heights of Ben Klibreck, must also have contributed to the pre-glacial catchment of the Helmsdale. However, the piratical, north-flowing River Naver has beheaded the Helmsdale, taking all the former headwaters away down the structurally adjusted valley of Strath Naver. One suspects that glacial interference may also have had some part to play in this change of direction. Few of the Scottish glens exhibit such a melancholy air as that of Strath Naver, for here is a zone whose population was utterly decimated by the Highland Clearances. Where once the black cattle of the crofters grazed on the broad valleyfloor and crofting villages dotted the hillside, nothing remains but the grass-grown ruins, the transient sheep and the interminable ranks of Forestry Commission conifers consisting mainly of Scots pine and lodgepole pine (Mather, 1971).

During the melting phase of the Pleistocene ice sheets, Strath Naver carried a great volume of meltwater, judging by the terraces of glacio-fluvial material on the valleysides. The outwash deposits have undoubtedly been responsible for the great expanse of intertidal sandbanks in Torrisdale Bay, and these in turn have contributed to the extensive dune formation of these parts. Strong northerly winds have blown the beach sands high on to the rocky ridges of Moinian metasediments to create a hummocky terrain unusually rich in flora. The Bettyhill

Nature Reserve has been established to preserve some of the rare mountain flowers which here descend to sea level. Raven and Walters (1956) describe how one small hillock exhibits 'a veritable carpet of mountain avens interspersed with other such calcicoles as globe-flower, yellow mountain saxifrage, purple saxifrage and dark red helleborine'. In addition, one may also find the Scottish bird's-eye primrose (*Primula scotica*) and the purple oxytropis (*Oxytropis halleri*), which is widely regarded as one of Britain's loveliest plants.

It is not only the vegetation which makes this lonely northern coast attractive, but also the landforms. Part of its beauty springs from the fact that the great variety of Moinian rocks which make up the Northern Highlands are here stripped of their peat cover and are seen in all their intricate detail, for the coastline cuts discordantly across the regional strike. Since the narrow bands of Moinian metamorphic rocks and their igneous intrusions exhibit varying degrees of resistance to erosion, the coast is broken up into a series of rocky headlands and picturesque bays. Faults, dykes and jointing patterns have been etched out by erosion to create a detailed mosaic of stacks, arches, caves and geos, to say nothing of the constructional features created by the relentless waves along this exposed Sutherland coastline.

Few counties exhibit such a geological uniformity as Caithness: its western hills are of granite and its bordering mountains of quartzite and basal conglomerate but its rolling plains are all floored by an enormous thickness of Old Red Sandstone. This is part of the structural basin known as the Orcadian Basin, which extends northwards into the Orkneys and contains some 5000 metres of Middle and Upper Old Red Sandstone (Donovan *et al.*, 1974) Since, however, volcanic rocks are virtually absent, steep crags and high relief, such as are to be found in the Sidlaws and Ochils, are not a feature of the Caithness scene, whose drama lies mainly in its coastline. Only there can the horizontally bedded yellow and red sandstones and the grey flagstones be appreciated in full, for elsewhere the pre-glacial topography is buried beneath the glacial drifts and post-glacial peat of the so-called Flow Country. Here, one of Europe's greatest wetlands has recently been subjected to extensive draining and afforestation (Lines and Neustein, 1966), to the consternation of many leading environmentalists (Ratcliffe and Oswald, 1988). Yet, by the end of the eighteenth century many boglands in eastern Caithness had been reclaimed for agriculture, so that nearer the coast the present landscape is one of prosperous dairy farms. Along some of the older field boundaries slivers of Caithness flagstone have been used as a means of field enclosure. Set on end, these slabs of grey stone form excellent 'fences', and they crisscross the treeless and hedgeless pastures like interminable rows of gravestones. The flagstones have also been used locally for both wall construction and roofing purposes in the older buildings, but production at the Thurso quarries has now ceased. When the quarries were fully operative the 'Caithness flags' were sent to all parts of the United Kingdom, where, being highly durable, they have withstood the tramping of countless millions of pedestrians in British towns and cities. The flagstones belong to the Middle Old Red Sandstone and are part of a series of alternating sandstones, mudstones and limestones which together comprise a further example of a cyclothem (see p. 213). It has been suggested that these different sediments represent the contrasting environmental conditions which operated when vast, ephemeral desert lakes (known as *playas*) were being infilled and subjected to intense evaporation in the slowly subsiding Orcadian Basin, some 370 million years ago.

Although most of Caithness is a flat, monotonous plateau, it is rimmed by a girdle of magnificent coastal scenery carved from the horizontal Caithness flags (Fig. 17.11). It is here that James Hutton, the founder of modern geology, noted that the affinities of the strata in Caithness and Orkney pointed to a former land connection between the two. He was led to this conclusion by viewing the 'perpendicular cliff of sandstone, lying in a horizontal position', and by observing that 'there are small islands, pillars and peninsulas of the same strata, corresponding perfectly with that which forms the greater mass'. Of the pillars, the gigantic sea-stacks near Duncansby Head (64 metres) are the most spectacular, although a fault-controlled outcrop of scarlet and gold Upper Old Red Sandstone creates even higher cliffs at Dunnet Head (91 m), the northernmost point of mainland Britain. Between these two imposing headlands lies the renowned settlement of John o' Groats, a disappointment scenically and because it is in fact neither the northernmost nor even the north-easternmost point of the mainland. But John o' Groats is the end of the road and the former location of the Orkney ferry.

Figure 17.11 The horizontally bedded Caithness Flags in the sea cliffs near Duncansby Head, northern Scotland.

Bibliography

Bailey, E. B. (1934) The Glencoul Nappe and the Assynt culmination. *Geol. Mag.*, **72**, 115–65.

Ballantyne, C. K. and Sutherland, D. G. (eds) (1987) *Wester Ross*. Field Guide. Quat. Res. Assoc. 184 pp.

Barber, A. J. (1965) The history of the Moine Thrust Zone, Lochcarron and Lochalsh, Scotland. *Proc. Geol. Assoc.*, **76**, 215–42.

Bott, M. H. P. *et al.* (1972) Geophysical evidence concerning the structure of the Lewisian of Sutherland, north west Scotland. *J. Geol. Soc. Lond.*, **128**, 589–612.

Bowes, D. R. (1969) The Lewisian of Northwest Highlands of Scotland. In M. Kay (ed.), *North Atlantic Geology and Continental Drift: A Symposium*. Mem. Am. Assoc. Pet. Geol. 12. 575–94.

Christie, J. M. (1960) Mylonitic rocks of the Moine Thrust-zone in the Assynt region, north west Scotland. *Trans. Edinb. Geol. Soc.*, **18**, 79–93.

Cruickshank, J. B. (1961) The Black Isle, Ross-shire: a land use study. *Scot. Geog. Mag.*, **77**, 3–14.

Dawson, A. G., Long, D. and Smith, D. E. (1988) The Storegga Slides: evidence from eastern Scotland for a possible tsunami. *Marine Geol.*, **82**, 271–6.

Dickson, J. A. and Innes, R. A. (1959) Forestry in north Scotland. *Forestry*, **32**, 65–109.

Donovan, R. N., Foster, R. J. and Westoll, T. S. (1974) A stratigraphical revision of the Old Red Sandstone of north-eastern Caithness. *Trans. R. Soc. Edinb.*, **69**, 167–201.

Durno, S. E. and McVean, D. N. (1959) Forest history of the Beinn Eighe Nature Reserve. *New Phytol.*, **58**, 228–36.

Dury, G. H. (1953) A glacial breach in the North Western Highlands. *Scot. Geog. Mag.*, **69**, 106–17.

Evans, C. R. and Lambert, R. S. J. (1974) The Lewisian of Lochinver, the type area for the Inverian metamorphism. *J. Geol. Soc. Lond.*, **130**, 125–50.

George, T. N. (1966) Geomorphic evolution in Hebridean Scotland. *Scot. J. Geol.*, **2**, 1–34.

Hobson, P. M. (1947) Durness Parish. *Scot. Geog. Mag.*, 63–83.

Hodgson, D. M. (1985) A study of fluted moraines in the Torridon area, north west Scotland. *J. Quat. Sci.*, **1**, 109–18.

Johnson, M. R. W. (1965) Torridonian and Moinian, in G. Y. Craig (ed.), *The Geology of Scotland*. (1st edn). Oliver and Boyd, pp. 79–114.

Johnstone, G. S. and Mykura, W. (1989) *The Northern Highlands of Scotland* (4th. edn). British Regional Geology. HMSO. 219 pp.

Kennedy, W. Q. (1951) Sedimentary differentiation as a factor in the Moine–Torridonian correlation. *Geol. Mag.*, **88**, 257–66.

King, B. C. (1942) The Cnoc nan Cuilean area of the Ben Loyal igneous complex. *Quart. J. Geol. Soc.*, **98**, 147–85.

Kirk, W. and Godwin, H. (1963) A late-glacial site at Loch Droma, Ross and Cromarty. *Trans. Roy. Soc. Edinb.*, **65**, 225–49.

Kirk, W., Rice, R. J. and Synge, F. M. (1966) Deglaciation and vertical displacement of shorelines in Wester and Easter Ross. *Trans. Inst. Br. Geog.*, **39**, 65–78.

Lawson, T. J. (1986) Loch Lomond Advance glaciers in Assynt, Sutherland, and their palaeoclimatic implications. *Scot. J. Geol.*, **22**, 289–98.

Lines, R. and Neustein, S. A. (1966) Afforestation techniques for difficult sites – wetlands. *Scot. For.*, **20**, 261–77.

Linton, D. L. (1951) Watershed breaching by ice in Scotland. *Trans. Inst. Br. Geog.*, **15**, 1–16.

Long, D., Smith, D. E. and Dawson, A. G. (1989) A Holocene tsunami deposit in eastern Scotland. *J. Quat. Sci.*, **4**, 61–6.

MacGregor, M. and Phemister, J. (1958) *Geological Excursion Guide to the Assynt District of Sutherland*. Geol. Soc. Edinb.

Macrow, B. G. (1953) *Torridon Highlands*. Hale. 212 pp.

Mather, A. S. (1971) Problems of afforestation in north Scotland. *Trans. Inst. Br. Geog.*, **54**, 19–32.

McIntyre, D. B. (1954) The Moine Thrust. Its discovery, age and tectonic significance. *Proc. Geol. Assoc.*, **65**, 203–19.

Moorbath, S. (1969) Evidence for the age of deposition of the Torridonian sediments of north-west Scotland. *Scot. J. Geol.*, **5**, 154–70.

Mottershead, D. N. (1978) High altitude solifluxion and post-glacial vegetation, Arkle, Sutherland. *Trans. Bot. Soc. Edinb.*, **43**, 17–24.

O'Dell, A.C. and Walton, K. (1962) *The Highlands and Islands of Scotland.* Nelson.

O'Reilly, K.J. (1983) Composition and age of the conglomerate outliers around the Kyle of Tongue, north Sutherland, Scotland. *Proc. Geol. Assoc.*, **94**, 53–64.

Park, R.G. (1964) The structual history of the Lewisian rocks of Gairloch, Wester Ross, Scotland. *Quart. J. Geol. Soc.*, **120**, 397–433.

Peach, B.N. and Horne, J. (1930) *Chapters in the Geology of Scotland.* Oxford University Press.

Ratcliffe, D.A. and Oswald, P.H. (eds) (1988) *The Flow Country: the Peatlands of Caithness and Sutherland.* Nature Conservancy Council.

Raven, J. and Walters, M. (1956) *Mountain Flowers*, Collins. 240 pp.

Robinson, M. and Ballantyne, C.K. (1979) Evidence for a glacial readvance pre-dating the Loch Lomond Advance in Wester Ross. *Scot. J. Geol.*, **15**, 271–7.

Sissons, J.B. (1982) A former ice-dammed lake and associated glacial limits in the Achnasheen area, central Ross-shire. *Trans. Inst. Br. Geog.* (NS), **7**, 98–116.

Small, A. and Smith, J.S. (1971) *The Strathpeffer and Inverness Area.* British Landscapes through Maps no. 13. Geog. Assoc. 25 pp.

Soper, N.J. and Wilkinson, P. (1975) The Moine Thrust and Moine Nappe at Loch Eriboll, Sutherland. *Scot. J. Geol.*, **11**, 339–59.

Steers, J.A. (1973) *The Coastline of Scotland.* Cambridge University Press, Cambridge, pp. 205–6.

Stewart, A.D. (1972) Pre-Cambrian landscapes in north west Scotland. *Geol. J.*, **8**, 111–24.

Stewart, A.D. (1975) Torridonian rocks of western Scotland in A.L. Harris *et al* (eds), *Pre-Cambrian Special Report*, no. 6. Geol. Soc. Lond. 43–51.

Sutton, J. and Watson, J. (1951) The pre-Torridonian metamorphic history of the Loch Torridon and Scourie areas in the North-West Highlands and its bearing on the chronological classification of the Lewisian. *Quart. J. Geol. Soc.*, **106**, 241–307.

Sutton, J. and Watson, J. (1954) The structure and stratigraphical succession of the Moines of Fannich Forest and Strathbran, Ross-Shire. *Quart. J. Geol. Soc.*, **110**, 21–53.

Thompson, F. (1974) *The Highlands and Islands.* Hale. 315 pp.

Walton, E.K. (1965) Lower Palaeozoic Rocks – stratigraphy, palaeogeography and structure, in G.Y. Craig (ed.) *The Geology of Scotland.* (1st edn). Oliver and Boyd, pp. 161–227.

Williams, G.E. (1969) Characteristics of a Precambrian pediment. *J. Geol.*, **77**, 183–207.

The northern archipelagos of Orkney and Shetland, isolated in the restless Atlantic, convey a variety of moods to the people who know their landscapes. To some their scenery is hauntingly beautiful, a jewel-like mosaic of rocks and skerries dominated by the immensity of the sky, the shifting dapple of sun and cloud shadow and the ever-present fringe of creamy surf on cliff-girt shores. Others view the islands more prosaically: for them the wind-seared, treeless hills are merely stark and gaunt, ravaged by Atlantic waves and Arctic storms in a land where farmer and fisherman alike wage constant war against the elemental forces of Nature (Marwick, 1951; Wainright, 1962; Fenton, 1978). Remarkably, their geology and scenery are quite different from each other (Mykura, 1976; Wilson and Knox, 1936).

Orkney

To appreciate fully the character of the Orkney environment, one should aim to arrive by sea from the Caithness port of Scrabster. Only then can the immensity of the western cliffs be properly grasped, as the Orkney ferry crosses the troubled waters of the Pentland Firth and creeps past the overwhelming precipices of Hoy. Here the Old Man of Hoy raises its renowned pinnacle of sandstone from a sea-washed base of contemporaneous lavas (Halliday *et al.*, 1977) to create one of the most memorable of Scottish scenes (Fig. 18.1). The neighbouring cliffs of St John's Head are even more imposing in some ways, for their red and yellow

Figure 18.1 The Old Man of Hoy, Orkney. The renowned sea-stack of Hoy Sandstone (Old Red Sandstone) rises from a ledge of contemporaneous lavas which form the shore platform beneath the 300 metre cliffs. Ward Hill can be seen in the distance (right).

sandstones rise vertically tier upon tier to a height of 348 metres, making this one of the highest vertical sea cliffs in the British Isles. Like the high cliffs of Dunnet Head in Caithness, the mural precipices of Hoy are carved from thick layers of Upper Old Red Sandstone, known as the Hoy Sandstones (Fig. 18.2). These tough, pebbly sandstones, which often stand on a pedestal of dark basalt (Kellock, 1969), are found nowhere else in Orkney and give Hoy a distinctive form and elevation missing from the other islands. North of Hoy Sound, however, there is a different, more typical, Orkney landscape of low whale-backed hills and burrowing silver waters, where the Orkney flagstones and the less resistant sandstones of Middle Old Red age have produced a more subdued landscape of gentle slopes and favourable soils. Here the land-locked waters and low coastlines have attracted seafarers throughout history, their sheltered firths and sounds offering havens from the stormy ocean. In the course of time the seamen settled on the islands, having discovered that the Old Red Sandstone soils could be tilled with comparative ease and that their pastures could support large numbers of livestock. A contrast is immediately apparent, therefore, between prosperous

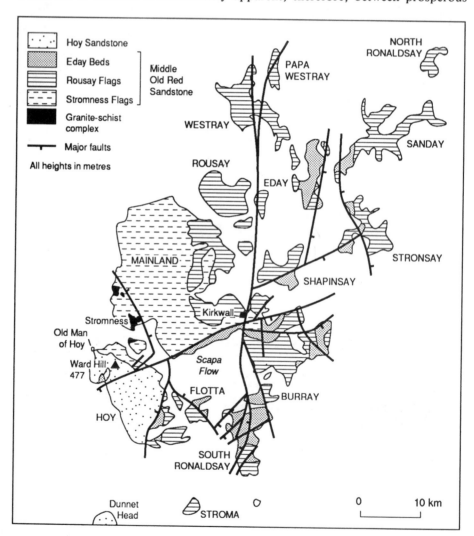

Figure 18.2 Geology of the Orkneys (based on material prepared by the British Geological Survey).

Orkney and the poorer agricultural economies encountered in the equally remote regions of Harris, Lewis and Sutherland, where the intractable gneiss holds sway.

The modest hill of Brinkies Brae, which rises steeply behind the fascinating port of Stromness, is an excellent viewpoint. At first glance the character of the hilltop is reminiscent of the Scottish mainland, for this is the only Orcadian locality where Precambrian granites and schists of the 'basement' are exposed at the surface. Not only do they give a knobbly aspect to the landforms, but their rounded boulders have been cleared from the fields and used in local boundary-wall construction. Such walling is unique here, for elsewhere in Orkney the ubiquitous Orcadian flagstones – including the Eday Beds, Rousay Beds and Stromness Beds (see Fig. 18.2) – have been built into splendid drystone walls (Miller, 1976). These well-jointed and laminated flags have also been extensively used for domestic building stone, as a glance at the Stromness houses will verify. The ochre-coloured walls of the older dwellings have been constructed from the Stromness Flags, whose thinner beds were successfully utilized as roofing materials in much the same manner as the Caithness Flags, which they resemble in both age and character. Their most widespread use, however, has been as paving-stones in the narrow alleyways which serve as streets in both Stromness and the older parts of Kirkwall. The so-called streetline of the linear settlement of Stromness is completely haphazard, because the gable-ends of the houses face the deep water of the harbour so that each may have its own pier or boatslip. The farther one moves from the Scottish mainland the easier it is to see the Scandinavian influence on the cultural landscape. This is reflected in the urban plan of Stromness (formerly Hamnavoe), although, owing to the treelessness of Orkney, Scottish stone replaces the ubiquitous timber houses of a Norwegian port.

As one travels between Stromness and Kirkwall, the remainder of the Orcadian scene slowy unfolds. The outer islands emerge late into view – low hills with standing stones and primeval earthworks, ocean waters penetrating every embayment and tiny creek, foam-ringed skerries with warning lights, scattered farms and houses set among regular field patterns, but no villages to speak of. The archipelago has manifestly been created by the drowning of a once continuous sandstone plateau that had been gently folded and faulted along predominantly north–south lines. A secondary set of faults runs from south-west to north-east, and the resulting fault mosaic has helped create a structural depression now occupied by the inland sea of Scapa Flow (Fig. 18.2). Indeed, differential erosion of contrasting lithologies within the Old Red Sandstone series that were brought together by faulting probably goes a long way towards explaining the configuration of the complex Orkney coastlines.

The land-locked basin of Scapa Flow (Fig. 18.3), known to generations of sailors as the finest natural anchorage in Britain, is connected to the open ocean by a series of narrow but deep channels thought to represent pre-glacial valleys drowned by the post-glacial transgression. That the entire archipelago is still continuing to be inundated is demonstrated by the occurrence of submerged peats and tree stumps along the island strands and by the absence of raised beaches. It is clear that Orkney, like Shetland, must have been far enough removed from the centres of the main Scottish ice sheets to have been virtually unaffected by glacial 'loading'; thus, isostatic 'recoil' seems to have played little part in the post-glacial tectonic history of either group.

The northern island of Sanday and the tiny island of Flotta at the southern entrance to Scapa Flow have erratic boulders of Scandinavian origin in their glacial drifts, which supports the hypothesis that the earliest ice sheets crossed Orkney from east to west, though the Devensian ice is thought to have been of entirely Scottish derivation. The numerous broken shells and Mesozoic erratics which have been glacially bulldozed from the North Sea floor, help create the calcareous boulder clays that have contributed greatly to the soil fertility of some of the eastern islands; this is in contrast to those of the west whose poorer, acid soils are reflected in a greater proportion of unimproved land.

The most widespread tract of moorland and rough grazing is to be found in the mountainous terrain of Hoy (Prentice and Prentice, 1975) (Norse, meaning 'high island'), the only island of sufficient elevation to nurture local glaciers during the Ice Age. Both Ward Hill (477 m) and Cuilags (433 m) have been glacially modified by corries, the most spectacular being that near the Kame of Hoy, which is spanned by a conspicuous moraine and located above the northern sea cliffs. A few valley moraines and glacio-fluvial deposits are strewn in the ice-deepened valleys to the north of the picturesque, deserted settlement of Rackwick. However, a very different type of geomorphological phenomenon can be found high up on the slopes of Ward Hill, for here are widespread examples of periglacial 'patterned ground'. Freeze-thaw processes appear to have been active here in relatively recent times, as if to demonstrate that this is still a marginally sub-Arctic environment. Like Ronas Hill in Shetland (see p. 445), it is one of the southern outliers of the Icelandic/Scandinavian terrain known

Figure 18.3 Scapa Flow, Orkney. The intermingling of land and water, so typical of Orkney, creates the large natural harbour of Scapa Flow. Note the higher hills of Hoy in the distance.

as 'fell-field'. Three major categories of patterned ground occur on Ward Hill: turf-banked terraces; wind stripes; and hill dunes. Most of the terrace surfaces are devoid of vegetation, while the plant growth along the terrace fronts is gradually being overwhelmed by currently mobile soil and rock waste (solifluxion material) which has been loosened by frost and transported downslope by the action of frost-heaving and rain-wash. The wind stripes and hill dunes owe their origins to the interaction of frost and wind after breaching of the turf cover (by natural or artificial means) had created an exposure of bare earth. Frost action has broken up the exposed mineral soil and allowed the fierce Atlantic winds to blow out the loose material, thereby undercutting the turf. The stripe pattern is thought to be a result of differential erosion caused by the action of wind eddies in alternate wind-break and exposure situations. Such a process of wind erosion, known as *deflation*, has resulted in the almost complete destruction of the turf cover on parts of Ward Hill (Goodier and Ball, 1975), resulting in a tundra-like scene.

It is a striking fact that as one journeys northwards in Scotland the altitudinal zoning of vegetation decreases in absolute elevation. Thus, the montane flora seen only on mountaintops in the Southern Uplands is found in Orkney and Shetland at much lower levels because of the more severe climatic restrictions (Bullard and Goode, 1975). Wind exposure is undoubtedly the most important factor in determining the upper limits of agricultural improvement, and on the exposed windward coasts of Hoy and Mainland the montane moorland extends virtually down to sea level. This is also true of certain parts of the northern isles, such as Rousay and Westray, although in some cases (for instance, Eday) it is the impervious character of the till-covered bedrock which has led to water-logging and the subsequent growth of peat (Goodier, 1975). Yet half the total land area of the archipelago is farmed and in these parts the sheltered valleys and slopes are devoted to intensive agriculture up to heights of about 90 metres. Because of the incessant wind Orcadian woodlands are rare; a well-screened deciduous stand near Finstown and a couple of forlorn, wind-trained conifer plantations in Hoy and Eday are exceptional. 'One usually thinks of trees shelter-ing houses; in Orkney houses shelter trees and the largest trees on the islands are to be found in central Kirkwall' (Bailey, 1971). Apart from the famous tree in the centre of Kirkwall's flagstoned main street, the majority of its trees are found around the splendid sandstone ruins of the Earl's and Bishop's Palaces. But overshadowing these is the redoubtable St Magnus's Cathedral, whose imposing Norman architecture brings to these remote northern isles something of the majesty of Durham. Constructed from blocks of red Eday Sandstones from the neighbouring coastal quarry at Head of Holland, the edifice recalls the days when Orkney came under Scandinavian rule.

Despite its windiness Orkney exhibits no extensive dune system comparable with, for example, those of the Moray Firth, although there are wide stretches of *machair*, especially on the northern group of islands (Berry, 1985). A great deal of the improved land of North Ronaldsay, Sanday, Stronsay and Westray is related to the calcareous soils of the fixed dunes and *machair*; the shell-sands of Westray are so thick that they were once exported to the less well-endowed islands for agricultural purposes (Coull, 1966). Smaller patches of blown sand occur on Mainland at Deerness and Birsay, although the most celebrated example is that at the Bay of Skaill. Here, on the exposed Atlantic shoreline, one of the most remarkable of British prehistoric sites has been laid bare of its blanket of coastal dunes. The cluster of flagstone-built huts at Skara Brae is now known to have been built some 4000 years ago by Stone Age inhabitants (Childe, 1931). Long before these earliest Orcadians had discovered the use of metal, they were capable of erecting quite sophisticated domestic dwellings of the drystone construction favoured in an environment containing plentiful flagstones.

It was these same Neolithic folk, gathering shellfish on the Orkney strands and pasturing their flocks and herds on the fertile grasslands, who were responsible for the erection of the renowned stone-built chambered tombs sited generally near the shoreline (Davidson *et al.*, 1976). Although the gigantic mound of Maeshowe (Childe, 1954), near the Stromness–Kirkwall road, is the best known, other important 'cairns', as they are called, occur on Wideford Hill and at Unston, near the Loch of Stenness. The funeral pottery recovered from the latter tomb has a great affinity with that from Windmill Hill, near Avebury in Southern England, and makes Orkney one of the most important Neolithic sites in Britain (Renfrew, 1985). When one adds to these the Bronze Age standing stones and stone circles, the Iron Age fortified towers or 'brochs' (the largest drystone structures in Britain), Celtic structures, such as the Broch of Birsay, and the later churches of Eynhallow and Egilsay, to say nothing of the Viking heritage, it is easy to understand why some regard Orkney as one of the archaeological treasures of the British Isles (Laing, 1974).

Shetland

Mid-way between Orkney and Shetland is the isolated but populated speck of Fair Isle (Waterston, 1946). This outlier of Old Red Sandstone (Mykura, 1972) has many more sheep than people and their wool is the basis of a famous knitware industry (Willis, 1967).

There is a well-known Scottish dictum that the Orcadian is a farmer with a boat, while the Shetlander is a fisherman with a croft (Cluness, 1951). Nothing highlights the contrasting environments of the two groups of islands better than these different cultural responses. Indeed, a closer examination of their land use demonstrates that despite Shetland's greater land area it has only about one quarter of the arable and grassland acreage of Orkney. Tracts of peat bog and moorland occupy about two-thirds of the Shetland landscape, while its scattered plots of arable include few of the golden fields of oats and barley which do so much to diversify the prevalent Orkney greensward. The Shetland scene is a tapestry of more muted colours: against a background of dun-coloured grasslands, the russet browns and olive greens of its moorlands are slashed with black peat-cuttings, stitched about and fringed with bare grey and red rocks and threaded with steely blue waters (Nicolson, 1972). Nowhere in this tattered archipelago of Shetland is more than 5 kilometres from the sea.

The geology of Shetland is quite different from that of Orkney and is as bewildering as the complexity of its coastline. Besides a great variety of severely folded and faulted Dalradian metasediments and acid igneous intrusives, the Mainland exhibits a restricted unconformable cover of Old Red Sandstone and its associated volcanics (Mykura, 1970) along both its western and eastern fringes, while its north-western limits (in North Roe) have been carved from a complex of granite, schists and Lewisian gneiss (Pringle, 1970). Yell, Fetlar and Unst, however, while possessing many of the Mainland's schistose rocks, lack the numerous bands of Dalradian limestone which characterize the central Mainland area from Tingwall to Delting (Fig. 18.4) Unst and Fetlar have, instead wide expanses of ultrabasic gabbro and serpentine (Read, 1934) which have contributed to the relative fertility of the Fetlar soils and caused this island to be known as the 'Garden of Shetland'. However, although part of an archipelago where sheltered harbours abound, Fetlar is not well endowed in this respect and is thereby suffering a decline in population. Yell, on the other hand, has an abundance of sheltered anchorages along its eastern coast, but owing to its waterlogged

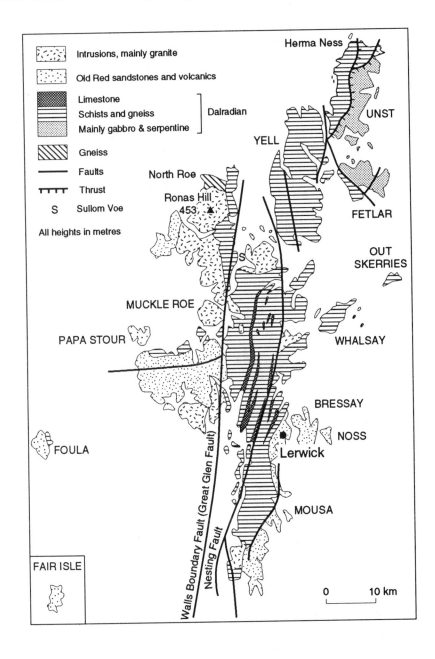

Figure 18.4 Geology of the Shetlands (based on material prepared by the British Geological Survey).

soils is the least fertile of the Shetlands; in fact, some two-thirds of Yell is covered with blanket bog (Berry and Johnston, 1980).

Turning once more to the Mainland, one finds that its variety of rocks is reminiscent of the Grampians of central Scotland, although its topography fails to achieve the mountainous grandeur of those parts. Shetland's highest eminence, Ronas Hill, attains the modest height of 453 metres, which places it more on a par with the subdued relief of the Outer Hebrides than with Ben Nevis, for example. And yet, somewhat surprisingly, in its geological succession Shetland has greater affinities with the lands around Glen Mor than it has with Orkney, Caithness or Sutherland, its nearest neighbours. While Orkney is an off-shore portion of Caithness, Shetland is really a far-removed section of the Dalradian Assemblage of the Grampians (see p. 312). It has been suggested that an extension of the Great Glen Fault bisects the Shetlands as the Walls Boundary Fault (Fig. 18.4), in which case the greater part of Shetland must be structurally continuous with the Grampians themselves (Flinn, 1961).

In fact, Shetland forms a geological stepping-stone between the intensely folded Caledonian belt of central Scotland and the equally contorted Dalradian rocks of Norway, which lies only 300 kilometres away. Thus the central 'backbone' of Shetland, from Fitful Head in south Mainland to Gloup Ness in north Yell, is composed of a tightly folded complex of green schists, schistose conglomerates, quartzites and blue-grey crystalline limestones, all of which had been invaded by acid and basic gneisses before the phase of high-grade metamorphism. The structural alignment of this central 'backbone' is generally north to south, the direction followed by the major Shetland faults (Fig. 18.4), so that the rock succession appears as numerous parallel bands of varying hardness (Flinn *et al.*, 1972). Given the varying resistance of the rocks to erosion, it is not surprising to find that this central block of Shetland shows a marked relationship between the geological 'grain' and the landforms. The most obvious manifestation of the geological 'grain' is to be found in central Mainland, where the alternating bands of schists and limestones have produced remarkably linear ridges and vales (Flinn, 1967). The long ridges of West Kame, Mid Kame and East Kame are separated by north–south limestone valleys whose greenness reflects the agricultural value of calcareous rocks among the acid moorland soils (Goodier, 1974). The narrow limestone outcrops can also be picked out by the lines of ruined lime kilns, in use until a century ago for the manufacture of agricultural lime, whose burning was facilitated by the abundance of local peat (Knox, 1985). Today, however, the limestone is quarried only for road metal, and Shetland's major extractive industries are now confined to Unst, although copper and iron were once mined here (Dron, 1908). On Unst the broad exposure of serpentine around Balta Sound also contains important deposits of chromite and soapstone; the former is no longer being exploited, but the soapstone is the basis of a small-scale talc industry.

There seems little doubt that the general configuration of the coastline reflects the geological structure of Shetland, and this is especially true of the location and alignment of many of the lengthy marine inlets (or rias) known here as 'voes'. Although Steers (1973) has claimed that the correspondence between the voes and the bands of less resistant rock may be more apparent than real, it is difficult to refute the exact alignments of Whiteness Voe, Weisdale Voe, Dales Voe and Colla Firth (all in central Mainland) with bands of Dalradian limestone, while the deep and narrow channel of Clift Sound, between the islands of East Burra and Mainland, must owe its form to erosion of a limestone band to the south of Scalloway. Yet the voes of Unst, Yell and Northmavine exhibit no corresponding relationship with the Dalradian rock structures. Again, in the Old Red Sandstone terrain of Walls (Finlay, 1930; Flinn *et al.*, 1968) the relationship is no longer apparent, with Gruting Voe and Bixter Voe cutting indiscriminately through sandstone and granite alike.

As in Orkney, the ever-present glint of sea water infiltrating deeply into the heart of the Shetlands is the outcome of a lengthy period of marine submergence. The gradual drowning of the Shetland hills to form the island cluster, with the inundation of the valleys creating the voes themselves, is the overriding theme in any study of landscape evolution in these northern islands. Studies by Flinn (1964) demonstrate that, like the faraway Scilly Isles, the Shetlands are merely the summits of hills rising from the flat plains of the ocean floor, which is here situated some 120 metres below sea level. Isostatic depression due to ice-sheet loading must have been minimal hereabouts, so that post-glacial tectonic uplift has been insignificant. Raised beaches are therefore absent, and the current marine transgression has succeeded in drowning a post-glacial peat which accumulated on a land surface more than 5500 years ago.

During an earlier glacial phase of the Pleistocene, Shetland seems to have been overridden by Scandinavian ice sheets, although its later glacial history was governed largely by a local ice cap which probably deflected the encroaching Scandinavian ice sheet around it (Mykura, 1976). Such an interpretation is based not only on the numerous glacial striae but also on the presence of some Scandinavian erratics, such as 2000 kilogram boulder at Dalsetter in southern Mainland. Pollen analysis suggests that a till-covered peat at Fugla Ness may represent the Hoxnian Interglacial (Birks and Ransom, 1969), while radiocarbon dating of other organic deposits has further suggested that the local ice cap disappeared around 12 000 years ago (Hoppe, 1974).

Although the major Shetland valleys were probably created in pre-glacial times by sub-aerial agencies working along fault shatter-belts and bands of less resistant rocks, there seems little doubt that glacier ice deepened the valleys by clearing out debris, if nothing more. Despite the steepness of the terrain, however, Shetland is not characterized by U-shaped troughs, properly developed corries or fjords. Only in the Old Red Sandstone on isolated Foula is there a semblance of glacially excavated corries on the Old Red Sandstone hill of the Sneug (419 m); the granite dome of Ronas Hill (see p. 444) exhibits no such phenomena. Instead Shetland's highest summit has, despite its modest elevation, a wealth of 'patterned ground' features which, according to Ball and Goodier (1974), are 'seen more clearly here than on any other British site'. Just as frost and wind are both important agents of erosion at Ward Hill, Orkney, so also are they on this exposed, gale-torn summit in Shetland. Turf-banked terraces, wind stripes and hill dunes are all present on this granite blockfield, while farther north, on Unst, the gentle slopes of serpentine gravel on the Keen of Hamar (60 m) constitute the lowest post-glacial frost-patterned ground recorded in Britain, at a latitude of almost 61°N.

Because of its periglacial features and its Arctic–Alpine flora, Ronas Hill has been designated a Site of Special Scientific Interest. So, too, has the Keen of Hamar, for this belt of serpentine rock also has particular interest to botanists,

Figure 18.5 Herma Ness, Isle
of Unst, Shetland. The near-
vertical cliff, close to
Scotland's northernmost
point, comprises steeply
dipping beds of Precambrian
gneisses and schists with
intervening sills of epidiorite.
Note the white staining of
guano from the countless
seabirds and the stacks of
Muckle Flugga beyond.

as does the neighbouring islet of Haaf Grunay ('green island in the deep sea'), which became a National Nature Reserve in 1959. Shetland's other Nature Reserves, however, have been created to preserve two of the most prolific cliff-breeding colonies of sea-birds in Britain. The largest of these is at Herma Ness and includes Britain's northernmost islands of Muckle Flugga and Out Stack. The high, almost vertical cliffs of Herma Ness, facing out to the Atlantic storms, are stained white with the guano of thousands of guillemots, gannets and kittiwakes (Fig. 18.5). The other colony is on the Isle of Noss, whose flat bedded rocks are in complete contrast to the dark Dalradian gneissic rocks of Herma Ness. Here, off the south-eastern coast, the Noup of Noss cliffs are built from bright red sandstone of Old Red age (Plate 18.6). As with the Torridon Sandstone of Handa (see p. 425) and the Old Red Sandstone of Foula (Donovan *et al.*, 1978) and Fair Isle, the gently dipping strata provide countless nesting ledges for the vast numbers of sea-birds.

The Old Red Sandstone has also been used for building; as in Orkney, the thinly bedded series provides roofing materials and paving stones. The flagstones which once paved the streets of Lerwick came from the tiny, grassy island of Mousa, although the most renowned use of these flags was in the construction of the famous broch of Mousa. The even bedding of the Mousa flagstones aided the meticulous creation of the drystone structure in this, the best preserved of the Scottish brochs. On the larger island of Bressay the Old Red Sandstone was once quarried as a domestic building stone from the now abandoned quarries

Figure 18.6 The Noup of Noss, Shetland. The vertical cliffs of Middle Old Red Sandstone on the island of Noss, have many ledges on the bedding planes of the flagstone rocks, now utilized by an enormous colony of seabirds.

at Bard Head and Ord Head (Finlay, 1926). Most of the older buildings in Lerwick were constructed from this bright red sandstone, but, as a result of the great expansion of harbour facilities to accommodate the North Sea oil bonanza, most buildings in Shetland are now constructed from imported materials.

Oil is, perhaps, an appropriate note on which to end a survey of Scottish geology and scenery, for nothing has made such an impact on specific parts of the Scottish landscape since the Highland Clearances and the Coming of the Sheep. The lonely Sullom Voe, carved in primeval granites and schists in Shetland's northern Mainland, is Britain's newest oil port, meeting, like Flotta in Orkney, all the oilmen's site requirements. It has a sheltered, deep-water anchorage; it is close to the oilfields of the east Shetland basin, such as Brent, Thistle, Ninian, Dunlin, and Hutton (the last named in tribute to the great geologist); it is also an under-developed and unpopulated area.

Bibliography

Bailey, P. (1971) *Orkney*. David and Charles.

Ball, D.F. and Goodier, R. (1974) Ronas Hill, Shetland: a preliminary account of its ground pattern features resulting from the action of frost and wind, in R. Goodier (ed.) *The Natural Environment of Shetland*. Nature Conservancy Council. 89–106.

Berry, R.J. (1985) *The Natural History of Orkney*. Collins. 304 pp.

Berry, R.J. and Johnston, J.L. (1980) *The Natural History of Shetland*. Collins.

Birks, H.J.B. and Ransom, M.E. (1969) An interglacial peat at Fugla Ness, Shetland. *New Phytol.*, **68**, 777–96.

Bullard, E.R. and Goode, D.A. (1975) The vegetation of Orkney. In R. Goodier (ed.), *The Natural Environment of Orkney*. Nature Conservancy Council. pp. 31–46.

Childe, V.G. (1931) *Skara Brae, A Pictish village in Orkney*. Kegan Paul.

Childe, V.G. (1954) Maes Howe. *Proc. Soc. Antiq. Scotl.*, **81**, 16–42.

Cluness, A.T. (1951) *The Shetland Isles*. Hale.

Coull, J.R. (1966) The economic development of the island of Westray, Orkney. *Scot. Geog. Mag.*, **82**, 154–68.

Davidson, D.A., Jones, R.L. and Renfrew, C. (1976) Palaeoenvironmental reconstruction and evaluation: a case study from Orkney. *Trans. Inst. Br. Geog.* (NS), **1**, 346–61.

Donovan, R.N., Collins, A., Rowlands, M.A. and Archer, R. (1978) The age of sediments on Foula, Shetland. *Scot. J. Geol.*, **14**, 87–8.

Dron, R.W. (1908) Iron and copper smelting in Shetland. *Trans. Geol. Soc. Glasgow*, **13**, 165–9.

Fenton, A. (1978) *The Northern Isles, Orkney and Shetland*. John Donald. 721 pp.

Finlay, T.M. (1926) The Old Red Sandstone of Shetland. Part I. South-eastern area. *Trans. R. Soc. Edinb.*, **54**, 553–72.

Finlay, T.M. (1930) The Old Red Sandstone of Shetland. Part II. North-western area. *Trans. R. Soc. Edinb.*, **56**, 671–94.

Flinn, D. (1961) Extension of the Great Glen Fault beyond the Moray Firth. *Nature.*, **191**, 589–91.

Flinn, D. (1964) Coastal and submarine features around the Shetland Islands. *Proc. Geol. Assoc.*, **75**, 321–39.

Flinn, D. (1967) The metamorphic rocks of the southern part of the Mainland of Shetland. *Geol. J.*, **5**, 251–90.

Flinn, D., Miller, J.A., Evans, A.L. and Pringle, I.R. (1968) On the age of the sediments and contemporaneous volcanic rocks of western Shetland. *Scot. J. Geol.*, **4**, 10–19.

Flinn, D., May, F., Roberts, J.L., and Treagus, J.E. (1972) A revision of the stratigraphic succession of the East Mainland of Shetland. *Scot. J. Geol.*, **8**, 335–343.

Goodier, R. (ed.) (1974) *The Natural Environment of Shetland*. Nature Conservancy Council.

Goodier, R. (ed.) (1975) *The Natural Environment of Orkney.* Nature Conservancy Council. 164 pp.

Goodier, R. and Ball, D. F. (1975) Ward Hill, Hoy, Orkney: patterned features and their origin, in R. Goodier (ed.), *The Natural Environment of Orkney.* Nature Conservancy Council. 47–56.

Halliday, A. N., McAlpine, A. and Mitchell, J. G. (1977) The age of the Hoy Lavas, Orkney. *Scot. J. Geol.*, **13**, 43–52.

Hoppe, G. (1974) The glacial history of the Shetland Islands. *Trans. Inst. Br. Geog.*, Special Pub. no. 7. 197–210.

Kellock, E. (1969) Alkaline basic igneous rocks in the Orkneys. *Scot. J. Geol.*, **5**, 140–53.

Knox, S. A. (1985) *The Making of the Shetland Landscape.* John Donald. 266 pp.

Laing, L. (1974) *Orkney and Shetland. An Archaeological Guide.* David and Charles.

Marwick, H. (1951) *Orkney.* Hale.

Miller, R. (1976) *Orkney.* Batsford.

Mykura, W. (1970) Late- or post-Devonian vulcanicity in the Shetland Islands. *Proc. Geol. Soc. Lond.*, **1663**, 173–5.

Mykura, W. (1972) The Old Red Sandstone sediments of Fair Isle, Shetland Islands. *Bull. Geol. Survey Gt. Br.*, **41**, 33–53.

Mykura, W. (ed.) (1976) *Orkney and Shetland.* British Regional Geology. HMSO. 149 pp.

Nicolson, J. (1972) *Shetland.* David and Charles. 246 pp.

Prentice, H. C. and Prentice, I. C. (1975) The hill vegetation of North Hoy, Orkney. *New Phytol.*, **75**, 313–67.

Pringle, I. R. (1970) The structural geology of the North Roe area of Shetland. *Geol. J.*, **7**, 147–70.

Read, H. H. (1934) The metamorphic geology of Unst in the Shetland Islands. *Quart. J. Geol. Soc.*, **90**, 637–88.

Renfrew, C. (ed.) (1985) *The Prehistory of Orkney.* Edinburgh University Press. 314 pp.

Steers, J. A. (1973) *The Coastline of Scotland.* Cambridge University Press, 335 pp.

Wainwright, F. T. (ed.) (1962) *The Northern Isles.* Nelson.

Waterston, G. (1946) Fair Isle. *Scot. Geog. Mag.*, **62**. 111–16.

Willis, D. P. (1967) Population and economy of Fair Isle. *Scot. Geog. Mag.*, **83**, 113–17.

Wilson, G. V. and Knox, J. (1936) Geology of the Orkney and Shetland Islands. *Proc. Geol. Assoc.*, **47**, 270–82.

Index of place names

Figures in *italics* indicate that there is a map, figure or illustration on that page.

461

Index of terms

Figures in *italics* indicate that there is a map, figure or illustration on that page.